THE REAL ESTATE CHALLENGE

▼

CAPITALIZING ON CHANGE

WILLIAM J. POORVU
HARVARD GRADUATE SCHOOL OF BUSINESS ADMINISTRATION

Prentice Hall
Upper Saddle River, NJ 07458

Library of Congress Cataloging-in-Publication Data

Poorvu, William J.,   1935–
    The real estate challenge : capitalizing on change / William J.
  Poorvu.
       p.   cm.
   ISBN 0-13-452137-4
   1.   Real estate business—United States.   2.   Real estate
  investment—United States.   I. Title.
  HD255.P66   1996
  333.33'068—dc20   95–26522
                                          CIP

Acquisitions Editor: *Catherine Rossbach*
Production Editor: *Denise Brown*
Director of Manufacturing & Production: *Bruce Johnson*
Manufacturing Buyer: *Ed O'Dougherty*
Editorial Assistant: *Jennifer Collins*
Cover: *Miguel Ortiz*
Formatting/page make-up: *Peter Amirault/Type A*

© 1996 by Prentice Hall, Inc.
Upper Saddle River, NJ 07458

Printed in the United States of America

10 9 8 7 6 5 4

ISBN 0-13-452137-4

Prentice-Hall International (UK) Limited, *London*
Prentice-Hall of Australia Pty. Limited, *Sydney*
Prentice-Hall of Canada, Inc., *Toronto*
Prentice-Hall Hispanoamericana, S. A., *Mexico*
Prentice-Hall of India Private Limited, *New Delhi*
Prentice-Hall of Japan, Inc., *Tokyo*
Pearson Education Asia Pte. Ltd., *Singapore*
Editora Prentice-Hall do Brasil, Ltda., *Rio de Janeiro*

CONTENTS

def. leverage

ACKNOWL

PART I Basics

1   The
    V
    S

ng real estate in the United
this fragmented, cyclical, yet
s-on approach to understand-
an awareness of the broader

2   Current Trends and Chan...
Specific examples of changes in demograp... echnology, capital markets and
the regulatory environment highlight some of the key challenges facing those who
will be involved in the real estate industry over the coming decade.

3   Anderson Street   27
Although inexperienced in real estate, Charlie Leonard hopes in June 1987 that
youthful enthusiasm and a $25,000 inheritance will help him enter the real estate
business. His experience chronicles the process of finding, evaluating, and acquiring a four-unit brownstone in need of renovation in the Beacon Hill area of
Boston. The case also identifies the various players in the process.

4   The Millegan Creek Apartments   42

In March 1994, Tom Hayden, a Vice President in Commercial Real Estate at Fleet Bank is about to make a brief presentation about a proposed $15,715,000 loan for a 390 unit garden apartment project in Austin, Texas. Because it is a new market, a new developer and a large loan without a takeout, he has to show whether all elements are in place to make this project work.

5   Fan Pier   71

In April 1989, plans for the development of Fan Pier, an ambitious mega-project on Boston's waterfront, have come to a halt as the result of: (1) a major fallout between the property owner and his development partners that in 1987 resulted in litigation and (2) a shift in the political climate that affected the approval process. Both the partners and the city officials have to decide what to do next. The case also presents the successful experience of a similar project, Battery Park City on Manhattan's waterfront, to highlight the overall public and private sector issues relating to large scale urban waterfront development.

6   SouthPark IV   91

In January 1990, George Laflin, a local investor, has raised $450,000 to invest in commercial and industrial properties in Houston, Texas. Laflin is interested in purchasing the 80,000 square foot SouthPark IV office/warehouse facility from a local savings and loan institution. The case takes the student through the mechanics of project valuation using a back of the envelope analysis.

7   Angus Cartwright, Jr.   103

In April 1995, John and Judy DeRight, looking to diversify their investment portfolios, have retained Angus Cartwright, Jr. to identify prospective real estate acquisitions. Mr. Cartwright has been offered four potential properties which merit an in-depth analysis. The case provides an opportunity to examine the various components of real estate return—cash flow, tax benefits, and futures—and measure the profitability of a proposed investment through the calculation of net present value, internal rate of return, and capitalization rate. The class session permits discussion not only about techniques of financial analysis, and their usefulness, but adaptation of those methods to the needs of a particular investor.

PART II Financing of Real Estate

8   Graybar Syndications   118

In March 1958, the Graybar Building, a one million square foot office structure in midtown Manhattan, is facing competition from a new generation of buildings. Its proposed acquisition by a syndicate is predicated on a tiered structure of financing and returns to a complex array of participants. The challenge is to wade through the legal documentation of the offering, decipher the priority and breakdown of the cash flow from the property, and decide who gets what return and when. The case deals with many of the issues relating to financial deal structuring.

9   Twinbrook Metro   134

In August 1990, Ben Jacobs, a managing partner of The JBG Companies was trying to determine a proposed price and terms to offer for the Twinbrook Metro portfolio in Montgomery County, MD being sold by Equitable Life. The Portfolio consists of 29.2 acres of land which has been built out with 19 buildings containing 554,054 square feet of office and R&D space. His concerns were whether after a major downturn in the real estate industry, the local rental market had stabilized and how he could attract limited partners to provide the equity needed to make the acquisition.

10   The Bourland Companies   151

In February 1995, Michael Bourland faced a dilemma as to what type of permanent financing would be best for two recent acquisitions made during the recent downturn in real estate. The Bank of Boston was offering a new commercial mortgage securitization program, which the bank felt was competitive with options from traditional lenders. Being a family business, he also had to consider his decision in the light of family dynamics.

11   The McArthur/Glen Realty Corp.   172

The market for real estate investment trusts (REITs) is currently booming with over $7 billion of new equity offerings during the first ten months of 1993. With the stock market at an all time high and bonds offering returns under 5%, Jonathan Potter is considering diversifying into real estate by purchasing shares in a new offering of the McArthur/Glen Realty Corp., a leading developer of off-price specialty retail centers in the U.S.

12 The JKJ Pension Fund 207

In September 1994 Sarah Griffin, portfolio manager for real estate of the $3.5 billion JKJ Pension Fund, must assess the individual values for the 11 properties held by the fund and propose an overall portfolio strategy. After several years of a holding pattern of activity, the Trustees had indicated a willingness to increase the fund's investments in real estate from slightly over 5% to 10% of the total portfolio.

13 JKJ/Gelco 229

In July 1995, Sarah Griffin, the Portfolio Manager for Real Estate Investments for JKJ Pension Trust is considering an investment in a new fund developed by Gelco, a major New York investment bank. Gelco already active in real estate is trying to enter the pension fund market with a product that combines direct property investments and listed securities and is intended to be liquidated in approximately five years.

Part III Development of Real Estate

14 503 Cricket Road 248

In 1995, Mason Sexton, a young, inexperienced developer, was making plans to replace a rooming house he had inherited next to the University of Virginia campus in Charlottesville with a new 14 unit, 5 story apartment house. His attempts to assemble the information, approvals and resources necessary to go ahead point out the steps and risks inherent in the development process. Using the example of a small scale residential project, the case illustrates development lessons that are often applicable to projects of any scale.

15 Concord Center 263

In the spring of 1993, Jennifer White, a junior partner with Morgan Sachs, faces a complex problem in trying to put together the financing for a $133 million three story super-regional shopping center at the confluence of three major highways in Concord County, 45 minutes from Metropolis. The joint venture partners, the Sturgess Group and Galatic Insurance Company had spent ten years and $28 million getting to this point. At issue is whether the retail market will support a project of this size and cost.

16 Grosvenor Park 282

In September 1988, Dick Dubin is attempting to gain final approval for a 189 unit single family home subdivision in Bethesda, Maryland targeted to young, upwardly mobile professionals working in the Washington, D.C. area. The case spans the project life cycle from predevelopment to sellout, and addresses issues ranging from land acquisition, construction phasing, finance, design, and marketing to managing a critical relationship with a powerful local planning board.

17   Peterborough Court   299

In May 1988, Sheridan Schechner was scheduled to appear before the Management Committee with an update on the development of Goldman Sachs' proposed corporate headquarters in London. The decision to construct a new London facility would represent the largest single commitment of capital the firm had ever made. Both his career and the profitability of the firm would be dramatically affected by the success or failure of this project. In the context of the development practice in the U.K., he had to recommend whether Goldman should be pro-active in managing the details of the process.

18   The Domik Project   321

In May 1994, Cameron Sawyer, after working in real estate in Moscow for several years, wants to build there a 1,200 square meter office building costing $2.3 million. He has found a site, prepared plans and pro formas, and negotiated a joint venture agreement with the land owner. He is searching for U.S. equity financing of $800,000. The case discusses the process as well as the risks and rewards of developing Russian real estate.

PART IV Repositioning of Real Estate

19   The Textile Corporation Building   341

In March 1987, Martin Donwill hopes to submit the winning offer in a sealed bid auction for a 350,000 square foot Boston office complex. Although he feels his skills in management and rehabilitation, as demonstrated specifically in the case, give him an economic advantage over his competitors, he has to quantify the ways in which he can create value, and profitably outbid his competitors. The art of bidding, can be discussed within the greater context of theories of negotiation.

20   Lakeside Center   356

In November 1989, Maria Sanchez, the leasing agent for a 95,000 s.f. class A office building in Boca Raton, Florida, has to prepare and negotiate lease proposals with three prospective tenants. The once hot Boca Raton market has cooled considerably. This case is designed to expose students to the strategy and tactics of lease negotiations in a deteriorating market, and the impact of such an environment on financial and partnership structures.

21   Tysons Corner   374

In July 1989, the partnership owning the once highly successful Tysons Corner Marriott in Virginia is facing a cash flow deficit. The opening of a number of new hotels in the area, and the increased trend to product segmentation have resulted in lower occupancy rates and reduced cash flow. This case provides an overview of the hotel industry, the history of this particular hotel, and the dilemma of the general partners as they deal with changes in the market environment.

22   The Schneider Building   394

In May 1995, Jonathan Schneider, the President of the Schneider Company needs to find a new facility that can accommodate his expanding business and to decide whether to lease or purchase this new facility. He also needs to decide what to do about the existing facility which he leases from his father.

PART V Technical Notes

23   Management of the Real Estate Process   411

This one page compendium lays out a conceptual framework for looking at issues affecting The Projects, The Players, The Panorama, and The Process. For each of these categories sub-issues are identified that should be considered in analyzing the cases in this book.

24   Financial Analysis of Real Property Investments   412

This note examines the methods by which real property investments are analyzed, offers suggestions about those analytical techniques, and provides sources of useful information. The note examines the three components of real estate returns—cash flow, tax effects, and future benefits—and looks at the impact of financial structuring on returns. This note is helpful in providing a financial framework for analysis of cases throughout the course.

25   Note on Taxation   439

This note provides a broad overview of the income tax factors most relevant to real estate ownership and operation. Every real estate transaction is affected substantially by the tax consequences which result from its form and substance. This note is not a definitive guide to the area of taxation, but is intended to help the student better understand basic tax factors and their interrelationships.

26   Note on Forms of Real Estate Ownership   461

This note looks at the advantages and disadvantages of the various legal forms of organization used in owning and operating real estate properties. It examines these structures both from a general management point of view, and from a tax perspective.

ACKNOWLEDGEMENTS

The development of a real estate case study is a complex endeavor. It starts with an actual project or situation. But, to make the case an effective teaching device, it must be more than just a history of the events that took place. The challenge is to enrich the situation by incorporating the interpersonal and political dynamics with the dates and numbers. The readers should be left with problems to solve and decisions to make in a complex setting reflective of what the participants faced. The information should give them adequate grounds for making a recommendation, without making the answer obvious. Since the external events that eventually determine the success or failure of a project are not always apparent at the time, a certain amount of poetic license in structuring the case or adjusting the numbers can enhance the learning experience. There rarely is one right answer.

While each case study, as well as each property, is unique, it is hoped that the study of a number of cases using the analytic framework we have developed will result in an understanding of industry-wide themes and practices. Equally important, the cases help illustrate the issues of process, implementation and negotiation that are such an important part of this business. There is an art to successful case development.

Once a case is written, we are fortunate to be able to take advantage of one of the best test sites available for our product, the classroom. To watch 30 to 100 students explore the issues that are raised in the case, sometimes to find inconsistencies in what we have laboriously crafted, and to see new insights which we have not thought about, is both humbling and rewarding for the teacher. The many settings in which these cases are taught provide feedback from participants with vastly different backgrounds and experiences in real estate and other fields. Based on this feedback, cases are often rewritten. In other words, these cases are a collaboration of practitioners, case writers, teachers and students all of whom have had input into both the content of this book and our approach to looking at the field of real estate.

Wanda Ferragamo, the CEO of an Italian-based apparel firm, was asked how she would describe the customers who purchased her shoes. She responded that they were wonderful. Well, all of those who over many years have helped and stimulated me in my work are also wonderful. But, I would like to thank a few of those who have been especially wonderful in putting together this particular book.

John Vogel, who has taught sections of our course at Harvard Business School and who teaches a similar course at the Amos Tuck School of Business Administration at Dartmouth, has been a major collaborator with me both in writing many of the cases and teaching notes, as well as in conceptualizing the framework for this book. His input has been essential to its completion.

Donald Brown and Elizabeth McLoughlin have enthusiastically and constructively contributed cases, notes, practical advice and editing suggestions. Several cases and notes written by Richard Crum and Katherine Sweetman a few years ago are still timeless in their lessons and had to be included. Catherine Rossbach at Prentice Hall has researched the market for this book and suggested many ways to make it more useful. She has also served as an intermediary with the many departments that make up a publishing company.

My business associates Seth Klarman, Sam Plimpton and son Jonathan Poorvu have made suggestions both about the book and about my need for continuing education. On both accounts they were generally right. John Achatz has always been available to make sure that legal issues described in several of our real estate cases have some basis in the law. Former students and colleagues who have chosen real estate as a career share their war stories, often providing the material and contacts that are the basis for our cases. In particular I am indebted to Denise Delaney, Ben Jacobs, Jonathan Isaacson, Charles Lavin, Peter Malkin, Michael Miles, Sheridan Schechner, and Joseph Thompson for their assistance in providing case materials for this particular book.

What keeps all of this together is my long-time assistant at the School, Linda Kelly-Hayes. Her patience, good humor and technical and management skills are needed and most appreciated.

Being at Harvard Business School has been crucial to my ability to produce this book. The collegial advice and resources for course development I have received from the School have been extraordinary. Although real estate is not a core subject at the School, my colleagues, especially Howard Stevenson, have given me the perspective to see real estate in new ways and to understand the excitement and insights that can be generated through effective teaching by the case method. John McArthur, who has recently retired as Dean of the School, has always encouraged me to set high standards for myself and to commit myself to trying to achieve them, asking only how he could help.

We all are products of our continuous upbringing. My mother May Poorvu, my wife Lia and my daughter Alison Jaffe have never failed to remind me through their thoughtful questions that clear and logical thinking does not come automatically, even for a Harvard professor.

PART I   BASICS OF REAL ESTATE

1

THE FIELD OF REAL ESTATE

Why would anyone want to invest in income producing real estate in the United States? The industry is fragmented, the economics are cyclical, the payoff is back-end loaded and the markets are inefficient. The old saying is that location, location, location are the three keys to success in real estate. The real-world problem is that locations often do not hold their value. Changes in work, shopping, living and recreational patterns continue to transform our physical and investment landscape. With few barriers to entry, it is an unusually competitive field. Yet these very uncertainties are what continue to create outstanding opportunities for the astute investor or provider of services to this $4 trillion market.

Real estate should always be considered one asset at a time. Although a company or individual may own multiple properties, each property normally stands alone legally to minimize cross-liability and is separately financed based upon its own cash-generating capabilities. Real estate is a transaction-oriented business complicated and made more costly and illiquid by the legal requirements associated with transfer and financing.

Investing in real estate requires a more hands-on approach with more concern for details than most other asset classes. One must begin by understanding what distinguishes the business of real estate, a field that involves multi-functional, multi-disciplinary and multi-faceted approaches. The diagram below is a starting point and indicates four primary forces that affect a property's value.

The four forces that impact a property can have local, national and global origins. For example, local supply and demand are affected by the strength of the national economy, the demographics of household formation, income levels, employment patterns, immigration and migration. Technology affects jobs, work environments and building obsolescence.

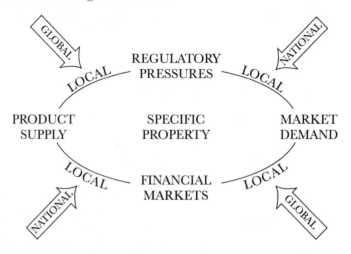

In the center of this matrix is a specific property, a long-lived asset in a fixed location. It is impacted by forces over which the owner often has little control but which profoundly affect its value. Starting with the *product supply*, one confronts the fact that each property is unique: the building's design and construction, its setting and land use, its physical condition and applicability for current and future uses. Supply often gets out of sync with demand, as owners build and lenders finance based upon the assumption that their individual building will be the only one constructed to meet a market need. The experience is that once a "hot market" is identified many players will build and oversupply that market.

To analyze *market demand* is not an easy task. Not only is each property unique but at the neighborhood and local level, users generally have many options as to where they will locate. Changing neighborhoods, technologies, wage rates, tax policies, transportation patterns and shopping options encourage relocation. As office and industrial lease terms generally range from three to ten years, tenants are not restricted from moving periodically. Moreover, the switch from an industrial or manufacturing-based to an information-based economy using computers, gives more flexibility to tenants since their space needs become more generic. The days when many employees walk to work are gone. With the workforce now domiciled throughout the region and with ownership less likely to be local, few companies have long term ties to a specific site or community. The downsizing of many corporations and the trend to purchasing services from a number of outside suppliers impacts the occupancy requirements of the firm. Landlords must be more pro-active and knowledgeable to serve their changing markets.

While the tenant has greater flexibility, the property owner's ability to use a site is constrained by *regulatory pressures* and governmental actions. At the local level, there are many controls exercised by a panoply of regulatory bodies covering such areas as zoning, building codes and property tax assessments. How these regulations are enforced or interpreted often reflects the mood of communities toward growth or change. Their actions not only affect a property directly but indirectly through expanding or limiting competition from others. Also, many properties serve markets beyond their most immediate community and are affected by actions taken there. As an illustration, changes in regional transportation patterns may alter the desirability of a particular location.

At the national level the federal government impacts the real estate business more than most other types of businesses. The rate of taxation is important to all, but there are many separate tax issues for real estate that relate to depreciation allowances, tax credits and subsidies especially those designed to assist lower income families find housing and to encourage historic rehabilitation. The government as a purchaser of defense products and research creates a demand for space. Environmental laws alter the use and value of properties. Subsidies for roads, airports and public transport influence where people live and work. International trade agreements and patterns lead to job movement. In other words, one can be impacted from many directions that cannot be easily identified from the narrow perspective of Main Street.

As a capital intensive industry, real estate is heavily impacted by the condition of the *financial markets*, by the availability and cost of financing, which often accounts for as much as 80% of the capital structure of a property and consumes 50-70% of the cash flow. Traditionally financing was obtained locally. However, the development of larger scale projects and the need to provide capital to new areas without adequate sources necessitated the involvement of regional and national lenders, who nevertheless make use of local market knowledge and contacts. But, when a local economy becomes troubled, both local and national sources of financing dry up.

A broad view of financial markets is essential for property owners. Much of the cyclicality in real estate comes from significant changes in lending patterns. As an example, the federal legislation permitting mutual savings banks to convert to stock ownership led to dramatic increases in real estate lending by the thrift industry. The subsequent overbuilding was costly both to the shareholders of these institutions and to the federal government which had to bail out the depositors of the many thrifts that became insolvent.

Another traditional source of financing to the real estate industry has come from locally based commercial banks. As these banks have been permitted to consolidate and become nation-wide banks, their ability to serve local markets becomes less certain. What capital is made available and what authority and guidelines are given to lending offices at the local level will have a major impact on the real estate industry.

A further concern is the impact of inflation on real estate. Inflation and short term interest rates are usually positively correlated. During the 1970s when inflation spiraled up, interest rates rose above 15%. The inflationary pressures did not immediately lead to higher rents, however, since the economy weakened, partially as a result of these higher rates. Over a long period of time inflation seems to enhance property values as new construction becomes more expensive. Over the short term, it can deflate values and make new projects or those under construction unfeasible.

The interplay of these forces yields a complex and changing environment for real estate investment. The challenge is to make intelligent decisions and to implement them amidst such an environment where it is necessary to think locally and globally simultaneously. For both active and passive investors in real estate, number crunching can at best contribute only part of the answer. Dynamic problem solving must be a large part of the solution. That is why this book does not provide mechanical formulas for decision-making, but instead offers a template that will enable and encourage the reader to ask the right questions and develop solutions appropriate both to the project and the investor.

The ability to perform quantitative analysis in real estate is not particularly complicated and can be easily taught. A command of first year algebra is generally sufficient. What is crucial, however, is to focus on the assumptions behind the numbers, often using a "back of the envelope" format to highlight the key issues. The ability to perform discounted cash flow analysis is useful, but it is essential to recognize that the numbers are not the reality but merely a tool for estimating the implications of a specific set of assumptions at a point in time. What is difficult is to combine quantitative with qualitative thinking. It is important to understand the quantitative implications of a qualitative commitment or the converse before the decision is set in stone. There is also the need to think visually, training that is rarely provided in our educational system at any level.

One area of concern that has rightfully received increasing attention from the players in the field is the definition of appropriate ethical behavior. Because real estate is project oriented, there can be the temptation to cut corners, to rationalize questionable behavior to complete a deal. Any area that is heavily regulated comes under suspicion. In most circumstances, appropriate behavior is obvious, but there are gray areas. Although all would claim to have high standards, ethical dilemmas often put one's own short term self interest against those of one's partners, tenants, lenders, suppliers or community.

Expectations of acceptable behavior vary from one locale or country to another. One guideline is to ask yourself whether you would be comfortable to have a story describing your actions published in your own local newspaper. The desire to complete a particular project may tempt one to take short cuts, especially if all one's assets are committed to it through direct investment or personal guarantees. But, if one wants a successful, long-term career in real estate and to be included in the next venture, one's word and reputation are paramount. There is no corporate veil to hide behind in a field where the owner has to be involved in most decisions.

Many fortunes have been made in real estate; a number have been made and then lost. The numbers of individuals in the Forbes Magazine's annual list of 400 wealthiest Americans who made their fortunes primarily in real estate rose from 71 in 1984 to 87 in 1988, and then plunged to 26 in 1994. A key factor exacerbating these swings is the amount of financial leverage utilized in most real estate deals. When a property is subject to a mortgage of 75% of its value, a swing of just 25% in the overall property value could either wipe out or double the equity of the investor.

Value in real estate is usually created over a long period of time and the ability to survive downturns is crucial. The development period itself takes several years, and a decade or more may pass before the operating income stream is maximized. Unexpected inflation or other external events may wreck havoc with one's projections. Real estate investments require capital commitments to a fixed asset in a fixed location. Although neighborhoods and regions can undergo tremendous change, and supply and demand can ebb and flow, it is not possible to move one's inventory to another location or inexpensively redesign the product to meet changing market needs.

Hundreds of thousands of properties are bought and sold over time in a fragmented marketplace. The unique nature of each property, the fact that each individual property is infrequently traded and the illiquidity of the market in general leads to a system of non-standard pricing. Not only is the price of the product variable, but the unique aspects of each property transaction make it hard to determine the "real" price.

Although these challenges appear daunting to the average investor, there are ways to tilt the risk/reward balance in one's favor. Information and analysis make it easier to identify and deal with market, construction, financial, regulatory and people risks. In recent years, a new set of consultants have emerged who can provide sophisticated market studies that are useful to the property owner and not just paperwork for the banker's file. Commercial brokerage companies have upgraded their research areas to help investors track economic, demographic, financial market, and business trends. Many lawyers are helpful in structuring transactions and partnership agreements and in dealing with environmental, contract and regulatory areas. Limiting personal guarantees by owning each project in a separate legal entity allows the investor to avoid having problems in one project affect his or her interest in others.

But, in the last analysis whether one is to be an active practitioner or a relatively passive investor, a service provider, a regulator or a user, this business requires more hands-on investigation and involvement than most. It requires multi-disciplinary, multi-functional skills. For example, a typical day in the life of a real estate practitioner might involve an early morning meeting with a contractor, a showing to a **prospective** tenant, a visit to the bank, a negotiation with lawyers over a lease, a look at a property up for sale and end with a public meeting in the evening with a planning board.

Opportunities exist in this entrepreneurial field not only to make money but to have a positive effect on our physical environment and to help to create viable, interactive communities. Whether one is part of a large corporation, a small investor or a practitioner, the field of real estate is so broad that one can find an appropriate niche defined by location, size, property type and/or price. Although financial markets are consolidating and debt capital is not as easy to obtain, real estate is still a field of comparatively easy entry which is one of the reasons why for centuries people have looked to real estate as one of the major ways to accumulate personal wealth.

To succeed in this field requires vision and perseverance, as well as analytical, quantitative and negotiating skills. Successful practitioners utilize local knowledge, salesmanship, management capabilities, luck and being in the right place at the right time. Despite trends toward securitization, public companies and institutional ownership, the uniqueness of each property will always make real estate a hands-on industry. The fragmentation and inefficiency of such markets will always allow the entrepreneur the opportunity to exploit the anomalies of a particular local situation.

CONCEPTUAL FRAMEWORK AND THE CASE STUDY APPROACH

This book presents a series of case studies that we have developed for use at the Harvard Business School. In these cases, we examine a breadth of issues facing owners and providers of services in this field, a field characterized by primarily small local firms, although a trend to consolidation is occurring in regard to ownership of larger properties. Our goal is to emphasize the unique aspects of dealing with each property while showing that there are patterns of inquiry that cut across the field.

The case studies have as their focal point the property rather than a company. This reflects the reality that each property is generally owned by a separate partnership. Partners are often ad hoc groups, some of whom may provide management skills, others local knowledge or contacts, services, land and/or capital. Most functions are provided by outside suppliers. The case studies highlight the interpersonal dynamics that become especially complicated under such circumstances. These dynamics become even more complicated when some of the parties are members of the same family. At another level, as institutions become larger holders of investment properties, their need to combine overall portfolio asset management with property-specific decisionmaking has created the need for new types of relationships.

The importance of negotiation both with outsiders as well as with one's own partners is not often dealt with in real estate textbooks. Yet, as any real estate practitioner knows, even though careful analysis is important, implementation requires the cooperation of a multitude of players whose interests are not always aligned with one's own. The careful drafting of a partnership agreement permits the financial rewards of a specific project to be allocated in a way that aligns the interests of the participants and recognizes the special contribution of each. But, over time the needs, attitudes and resources of the players change. Dealing with the various players in a non-hierarchial structure can be instructive, challenging and exciting, but also frustrating.

To facilitate analysis of the case studies in this book we have constructed a one-page conceptual framework, *The Management of the Real Estate Process*, which is shown at the back of this book in the section titled: Technical Notes. The conceptual framework focuses on four areas: the Project, the Players, the Panorama and the Process. Within each of these four are listed a number of sub-areas which should be considered. The diagram looks like an exhaustive and exhausting list of points to consider. However, unless one questions the applicability of each to the success of the project, one runs the risk of missing a key element that must be dealt with. The interactive and managerial nature of real estate must be understood to achieve success. Finding projects that score positively in each of these four areas as well as in combination with one another is the goal.

The Project

The starting point for analysis is the project itself. Properties come in many sizes and types, with varying physical and market conditions, diverse locations and timeframes for development. The matching of a particular property to a market niche is not an easy task. Legal constraints restrict what can be built. Inaccurate assessments of how long it will take to change these constraints has resulted in the demise of many partnerships. There is the need to be attuned to change in the local political climate. Most properties generate rents that will cover operating costs. The cash flow that remains impacts the amount of debt which can be placed on a property. Lenders have two main tests they apply in deciding how much money they will lend on a particular project: a loan to value ratio and a coverage ratio of operating income to debt service. Proper financial structuring can enhance value on the equity side. The split of the benefits and obligations for a particular project can be adapted to the needs of the principals through their partnership agreement. The problem is there may not be a true alignment of interest between the promoter or developer and the providers of capital over a long time period, especially since it is difficult to judge how much capital will eventually be needed to complete the project.

Trying to encapsulate into one paragraph all the elements of a project that must be investigated oversimplifies the problem. An in-depth analysis of all the factors that must be considered will be conducted more fully in studying the case studies that follow.

The Players

Each property must be treated as a separate business, pulling together product, market, financial and legal considerations. But, as with many businesses, it must fit the skill, experience, contacts and resources of the actual players involved. It is exciting for a group to get together to launch a new venture. The initial project idea might come from a local land owner, an attorney, a broker, an architect, or from a local or out of town developer, investment advisor or potential investor. The potential use or plan for the particular property is the focal point for assembling the team. As such, the participants may not have previously worked together. But, when the project takes longer, requires more capital or involves a change of concept, different skills and resources may be required. Often, real estate professionals try to take on projects beyond their capabilities. There is the tendency to assume that real estate is one business where it is possible to handle many types and sizes of real estate projects and to operate in many cities. In fact, each sub-area or locale requires particular skills and experience. Real estate is a niche business. The amalgamation of ownership of many properties within a single entity must be handled with care.

Players in this industry must have a strong ego and be able to withstand public criticism. What is created is very visible. How a building fits contextually with its neighborhood should be a high order of priority. The opportunity to change and improve the physical environment can provide a great source of pride to the participants. A personal identification with one's product is not as easily accomplished in other businesses since one rarely is involved with so many aspects of its creation. Since relationships in real estate are less hierarchical, there is also more opportunity to influence the decision-makers even without being the boss. For better or worse, one can make his or her mark.

The Panorama

Matching the players to the project is complicated enough. But, the panorama of what is happening at national and/or international levels also affects the outcome. Our initial diagram that shows a property surrounded by four forces: product supply, market demand, regulatory pressures and financial markets could be drawn with a series of concentric circles around each of them. Each outer circle takes a broader view as to how each of these forces can impact a particular property. It is doubtful that any of us can qualify as simultaneous experts in history, sociology, politics and technology. But, an awareness of what is going on in our community, country and world is important. NAFTA, the Internet, global warming, economic growth in China, balanced budget amendments and immigration policies are just some of the various happenings which can at some point impact the value of a particular property or location. How we apply these factors to our own activities depends on a whole host of other variables, but the perceived remoteness of these issues should not lead us to ignore them. Real estate is part of a bigger picture.

In that regard, this book includes two cases that are set in other countries: England and Russia. One of the purposes of these cases is to demonstrate that the variables delineated in our conceptual framework are applicable as a basis for analysis in other countries even though the ways of doing business and the importance of each variable may differ from country to country. The same caveats that apply to doing business without local knowledge and contacts in one area of the U.S. versus another are more dramatically seen in studying areas where our own backgrounds make us less sensitive to local nuances and practices. Also, the need to understand the panorama of interrelationships in a world where what goes on in one country affects another is becoming more apparent. As companies become global in both their activities and in their use of outside suppliers, the demand for space is affected. Media coverage normally highlights only the loss of jobs, not the success stories. There are many U.S. companies whose ability to export U.S.-made products or services represents a substantial portion of their business.

The Process

It is always essential in looking at a field to understand not just how things should work, but how they actually do work in the real world. The process of acquiring, developing and repositioning property is interactive. It is multifunctional and dynamic. Real estate is an extremely capital intensive business with high fixed costs and few, if any, economies of scale. Decisions as to when and how to decide to commit time and capital cannot be made with much certainty. The question is how to understand the process and to manage risk at each stage in the life cycle of a project. Experience with the local market helps enormously at the conceptual stage. A site visit, some phone calls, a couple of meetings and a few back of the envelope calculations cost little, but can be sufficient to make a preliminary decision to investigate further or to abandon a deal. Then looking at market information, optioning a site, pre-leasing space and recruitment of the appropriate financial partners reduces risk. If the plans are well drawn, builders will commit to fixed construction costs. The terms of a lease to a tenant can offer protection from future cost increases. There is much that can be done, but at each subsequent stage of involvement, the upfront costs can increase substantially.

Moreover, the system does not lend itself to solving problems sequentially. As an example, the local approval process rarely proceeds as planned. What is built is of concern to abutters, competitors, local officials and environmental groups, each of whom can challenge a decision in court. But, until developers know what they can build, they do not want to spend much money to buy a property. Yet, until the property is under agreement the developer is reticent to go public with plans for fear of alerting competitors or raising the price.

It is also not easy to get potential tenants to make commitments when the owner has not made the commitment to buy the site or does not have the necessary approvals or financing. Without approvals, developers cannot give tenants a firm timetable of when the building might be available for occupancy. There is also the issue of how much the project will cost since contractors cannot give actual bids without detailed drawings and specifications which are expensive to produce. Without final regulatory approvals, the design cannot be set. There is also the danger of making so many compromises in a plan in order to obtain approval of all the participants that sight is lost of the original vision. The ability to juggle is certainly part of the developer's job description.

The project dynamics require an analysis of the impact of each functional area and how they all interrelate at each stage of the process from conceptual through preliminary and detailed feasibility to construction, marketing, management, repositioning and harvesting.

Each project must be looked at in terms of its physical condition and design, market, legal status, and financial and ownership structure. As the process goes on, each subsequent stage requires more capital. In recent years, more developers are becoming providers of fee services to landowners, tenants or financial institutions. Being a service provider is a way to limit risk reflecting the increased cost and uncertainty of doing business as well as the developer's desire to limit personal financial exposure. Risk is often highest for a new development project, but even in buying an existing building or repositioning one that is already owned requires total management of a multi-functional approach. Each property should be looked at as being in transition.

ORGANIZATION OF BOOK

How all the variables interact in a project can best be seen through use of case studies. Case studies show the richness of the situation without attempting to dictate a single solution to the problem. Moreover, what may turn out to be the best solution at a given time for one project, may not be the same for another project in another location at another time. But, we can learn from a study of the process as we see it unfold in several situations with a wide variety of participants. Many of the cases in this book involve younger, less experienced professionals with whom the reader might identify. Their experiences can be helpful in seeing ways to participate in and learn about the field.

For pedagogical purposes, this book is divided into five parts.

Part I: The Basics of Real Estate
Part II: The Financing of Real Estate
Part III: The Development of Real Estate
Part IV: The Repositioning of Real Estate
Part V: Technical Notes

The case studies in *Part I: The Basics of Real Estate* present situations which provide an opportunity to learn the analytical process for evaluating real estate and to use the conceptual framework to recognize issues fundamental to all real estate decisions. Although the first three case studies in this section range from a small rehabilitation property to a 390-unit multi-family development to an urban mega-project development, the methodology for analysis is remarkably similar.

The final two cases in this section deal with the basics of financial analysis. The exercises in these cases illustrate "back of the envelope" as well as discounted cash flow analysis. Issues of how to decide on an appropriate capitalization rate, calculate after tax returns and how to assess the implications of leverage are presented in a way that show not only how these techniques work but when and for what purpose to use them. By learning most of the quantitative techniques early on, the reader of each subsequent case has the tools to decide how much quantitative analysis would be useful to deal with the problems presented.

Part II: The Financing of Real Estate describes options for financing, structuring, and owning real estate and how use of these options can add value in this capital intensive industry. The cases involve private syndications, different types of mortgages, public real estate investment trusts and pension funds. With major changes occurring in the roles of various financial institutions, new types of relationships are explored between providers and users of capital. Service firms are taking on new roles. How to share the legal and financial benefits of a property's value point up the importance of deal making and deal structuring. But, in all situations it is important to realize that it is the underlying property which must provide the cash flow.

Part III: The Development of Real Estate focuses on making decisions in a multifunctional context at each stage of the property development process, as well as using and integrating both qualitative and quantitative analysis. The impact of time and timing on the end result is emphasized. The interaction of a project with its community, how it fits in a diversified social and physical environment is shown to be essential to responsible and successful development. Seeing the interplay of design decisions on marketing strategy, financial structure on development flexibility and regulatory constraints on construction management are all part of understanding the process of changing the use of a site or building. Small and larger scale residential, office and retail projects in many parts of the U.S. and other countries are used to illustrate the variety of situations one can face.

There are so many parts to assembling the puzzle we call a building, with so many conflicting players, that good negotiation strategy and execution become a necessity. Not just what you should do in a particular situation, but how you would do it given the specific people involved, is what is important. Carrying out a plan of action involves working with many players who have their own agendas. To convince others requires a willingness to listen and to respond effectively, to think on one's feet and to be able to present compromises. The ability to negotiate is especially valuable to the real estate investor because of the inefficiency of the markets which permit one to capitalize on differing perceptions of value.

Part IV: The Repositioning of Real Estate focuses on what can happen to properties and locations over time, and what can be done to maintain and enhance value. Complacency on the part of a landlord can be disastrous. The entrepreneur who creates value through acquisition and development often loses interest once the deal is done, moving on to new ventures. The ability to foresee changes in the macro-environment or in particular neighborhoods, to anticipate real estate cycles and to conceive of ways properties can be reused provides major opportunities at times when there is little incentive to new construction. The tendency in real estate is to hold rather than sell a property. The use of depreciation allowances to reduce taxable income only defers and builds up taxes due on sale, while refinancing is a non-taxable event and is often the preferred way to take out capital. Investors rarely spend the time analyzing when to sell a property that they do when they buy it. Moreover, the sale of real estate is far more complicated than the sale of a stock or bond. Real estate is a far less liquid asset.

In many ways the skills needed to reposition property are similar to that of developing new property. The same management, marketing, construction, and financial capabilities are needed. Constraints of existing leases, physical conditions, financial or partnership arrangements may reduce one's options. But, the failure to act or to pay close attention can be foolhardy if one owns property. Conversely, if one sees a new use for a property, one often can purchase it at a price that leads to a competitive advantage. As an example we are seeing today that many urban office buildings are being converted to residential, hotel or retail uses as a way of combatting the high current vacancy rates. Creative re-use can have a substantial payoff.

Part V: The Section on Technical Notes starts with the conceptual framework, The Management of The Real Estate Process, followed by: Note on Financial Analysis, Note on Taxation and Forms of Real Estate Ownership. The notes are based on practices, laws and regulations existing in 1995, but they also attempt to give some history as to what changes have occurred over time, since over the course of a career or ownership of a particular investment, the ground rules will most assuredly be altered.

Much of the information in these notes will be useful in analyzing and understanding individual cases. For this purpose, it might be useful to skim the notes as a supplement to reading the first part of the book on The Basics. Then, when applicable, the notes can be referred to in some depth to facilitate analysis of a particular situation or case.

SUMMARY

What a person learns from this book will vary depending upon the goals and background of the reader. It is designed for a wide range of people interested in: owning, developing, providing services to or investing in this huge, dynamic industry. The cases can be looked at from many points of view and at many levels. Experience in the field is useful but not expected. Few will have had the breadth of experiences that make them experts in all the types of real estate covered. The ability to negotiate is a key skill and can be enhanced through role playing in discussing the cases.

Few investors are accustomed to taking into account all elements of the *project, the players, the panorama and the process*. The focus of most participants in the real estate industry is short run. They perform a specific function for which they expect to receive their commission or fee. Yet it is the overall perspective, that leads not only to the recognition of opportunities, but to the judgment as to whether one can personally implement that opportunity. Our goal is to narrow the gap between being an observer or analyst and a player.

The following ten qualities might help to describe the challenges of this most exciting field. They do not presume to achieve ten commandment status or expect that any individual will embody all these characteristics. But, as with the ten commandments, they provide us with goals that we can hope to attain.

1. The ability to understand, coordinate, and motivate people in a multitude of ad hoc relationships;
2. The creativity and good taste to shape and reshape a vision that will be fixed in concrete in a changing environment;
3. An analytical mind-set that integrates qualitative and quantitative thinking;
4. An attention to detail where the parts are interdependent;
5. The skill to manage risk and establish operating controls in a capital intensive environment where commitments must be made upfront;
6. An understanding of how to create value through financial structuring;
7. The willingness to assume individual responsibility as a manager, as a leader, and as a constructive and ethical member of a community;
8. An awareness of and responsiveness to local and national needs;
9. A flair for marketing;
10. The good fortune to be in the right place at the right time with the right people.

While many of the lessons learned throughout these cases are specific to real estate, there are other fundamental lessons which are transferrable across a range of disciplines—issues of ethics, accountability, or even prudent business management. Today's real estate professional must be increasingly well-informed, with an understanding and acceptance of social and environmental issues as well as project economics. Changes in financial markets, fundamental shifts in demographics and in emerging technologies, can most probably be exploited by sophisticated practitioners. Yet, investors or intermediaries with common sense, analytical skills, and an ability to interact with others, may be in the best position to create entrepreneurial opportunities.

Future opportunities for creating real estate value may be significantly different than they have been in the past. Increasing institutional and global investment in the industry is making for a more level playing field, wider access to project capital, and less fragmentation of markets. Alternatively, the demographics for development are more constraining, and the need for equity capital higher. Ultimately, however, the creation of value will in all cases rest on project specific criteria: the project as it stands in relation to its own market, its own management, and its own rewards. Real estate will continue to be a hands-on, local industry, with broad, exciting, and potentially rewarding ramifications. The cases that follow are intended to provide exposure to just a few of the dramatic examples that can be found in every community. We hope you will see in them relevance to your own opportunities over the coming decades.

2

CURRENT TRENDS
AND CHALLENGES

The first chapter provides a picture of the industry as a whole. This chapter will focus on the specific trends and challenges in demographics, technology, capital markets and regulation which have become increasingly important, and will affect the players in this field in important ways over the next decade. How should participants in a cyclical industry like real estate deal with a significant slowdown in both household growth and in the number of new entrants to the workplace? How should one assess the value of a property when both the rate of locational and technological obsolescence and the cost of complying with regulations are rising? How can one anticipate capital flows and their impact on the balance of supply and demand? How can one budget with confidence when tenants want custom layouts at lower rents and when cyclical oversupply gives tenants the upper hand? Depreciation is often a real cost, not just a mechanism for reducing tax liabilities. Obtaining funds at acceptable terms is an increasing problem in an environment where many financial institutions are undergoing restructuring and consolidation.

MARKET DEMAND/PRODUCT SUPPLY

Let us consider each of these challenges in turn. By examining readily available demographic information we can learn a good deal about the total historic demand for space, especially residential. The U.S. population grew 18.5% in the 1950s, (when the baby boom generation was born), and then the rate of increase declined for the next 30 years to 13.4% in the 1960s, to 11.4% in the 1970s and to 10.3% in the 1980s. It is now projected to grow gradually by 10.5% in the 1990s and 10.9% in the first decade of the next century.

For housing developers knowing the rate of household growth is even more crucial than knowing total population growth. The growth rate for households was 21.3% in the 1950s, 21.1% in the 1960s, 27.4% in the 1970s and 15.5% in the 1980s. This growth rate was substantially in excess of the rate of population growth, providing major opportunities for residential developers. A further breakdown shows that 45% of the increase in households came from non-family households, a category that went from 10.8% of the total number of households in 1950 to 29.2% in 1990. It is no wonder that so many rental apartments and condominiums were built over that span.

The age distribution of the population is an issue. In the 1980s there was a high percentage of young people in the 25-44 year age bracket, which is the age when most new households are created. But over the next fifteen years, the major growth will occur in the 45-64 year age bracket, which should go from 19.8% of the total population in 1995 to 26.2% in 2010. Already in the period 1990 to 1993 the growth in households had dropped to 3.3%. From this data, one might postulate that there will be less need for new residential construction, but rather an increasing market for renovation to meet needs of homeowners upgrading their current residence rather than moving.

Another question of interest to the potential investor is where people will live. Where will new units be needed? We see from the chart below that most of the population growth from 1970 to 2010 has been or is projected to occur in the South and West.

POPULATION BY REGION (MILLIONS)

	1950	1960	1970	1980	1990	2000	2010
Total Population	151.3	179.3	203.3	226.5	249.9	267.7	282.0
Region							
Northeast	39.5	45.7	49.0	49.1	50.9	52.4	53.8
Midwest	44.5	51.6	56.6	58.9	60.3	60.5	59.7
South	47.2	55.0	62.8	75.4	86.6	95.6	103.5
West	20.2	28.0	34.8	43.1	52.2	59.2	65.0

By the year 2010 there should be almost as many people in the South as in the entire Northeast and Midwest. The implications for future development are obvious. Additional statistics could be cited as to which sub-areas have greatest potential. The growth in jobs and population is expected to continue to occur primarily in the suburbs and exurbs rather than in major cities. The growth curve of new business expansion is decidedly in favor of the suburbs, especially for the small cap firms many claim have been the engines of growth in the U.S. economy.

Another important issue is the size of the national workplace and its distribution by industry. This has significant implications for the types and locations of buildings that are needed, and the likelihood of obsolescence in existing facilities. Total U.S. employment grew from 89.7 million in 1970 to 112.3 million in 1980 and 137.2 million in 1990, a dramatic growth in jobs as the result of a generally robust economy. But the changes in employment by industry are notable.

EMPLOYMENT BY INDUSTRY (FULL AND PART-TIME)
(Millions People)

	1970		1980		1990	
	Total	%	Total	%	Total	%
Manufacturing	19.6	21.9	20.8	18.5	19.8	14.4
Trade: Wholesale	4.5	4.6	5.7	5.1	6.6	4.8
Retail	13.6	15.2	17.9	15.9	22.8	16.6
Finance, Insurance, Real Estate	4.9	5.5	7.5	6.7	10.1	7.4
Services	16.6	18.5	14.4	21.7	37.6	27.4
Construction	4.4	4.9	5.6	5.0	7.3	5.3
Government and Government Enterprises	16.3	18.2	18.8	16.7	21.1	15.4
Other 10.1	11.2	11.6	10.4	11.9	8.7	
Total Employment	89.7	100.0	112.3	100.0	137.2	100.0
% Increase Over Prior Decade			25.2%		22.2%	

Several conclusions can be drawn. Our economy has created a substantial number of new jobs both in absolute and percentage terms since 1970. The new jobs were filled by both a large number of young, new entrants to the workforce and an increase in the number of women. In industry terms, the number employed in manufacturing has remained relatively constant even though we are producing substantially more goods. In percentage terms, virtually all of the new jobs have been created in the areas of retail trade, finance, insurance, real estate and services.

Demographic trends suggest a limited future for office job growth. There will be fewer new entrants into the workforce. Also, the same pressures to raise productivity by downsizing employment that occurred in the manufacturing sector are taking hold in service industries. The number of firms delivering health care and financial services is declining due to industry consolidation. Computers continue to replace clerical employees and middle managers. Government employment at the federal level has recently been stable and should not grow further while recent growth in employment by state and local governments may reverse itself. Higher, as well as lower skilled jobs, are being moved to countries with lower wage scales. The portability of technology may lead to more work being done at home. It is possible that there will be fewer private offices. Some experts predict that the average space per worker may drop from 225 square feet to 150 square feet, which would over time create a 33% increase in office vacancy from current inventory alone.

The resultant lowering of demand for space comes at a time when most of our office markets still have relatively high vacancy rates in the 15% range with most downtown rates slightly higher than suburban rates. Industrial vacancies are less than 10% across the board. For a variety of reasons, especially the availability of cheap financing, new construction occurred at an unsustainable rate in the 1980s. The total amount of office space grew by almost 1.4 billion square feet, representing 27% of all U.S. office space existing in the U.S. Warehouse space grew by 34%, hotels by 59%, and retail by 18%. The total square footage of single family units grew by 16% and of multi-family units by 25%. The large increase in multi-family units reflects key demographic trends of the 1980s, the growth in households occupied by younger families starting out, plus older people living longer and moving from their homes to apartments.

The result of overbuilding in the 1980s has been a rapid curtailment of new construction as falling occupancy rates made new projects uneconomic. There were approximately 620,000 new apartment starts in 1986 but only 220,000 in 1993. Office completions totalled approximately 140 million square feet in 1986 and just 75 million square feet in 1993. Obviously it would tax one's ingenuity and contingency planning skills to create a long term strategic plan for a company in an industry with such cyclicality. Flexibility and staying power are certainly critical to long term success.

Yet real estate is an industry where flexibility is hardly the norm. Not only is it counterproductive to stop a project once under construction, but there is often a strong incentive for a project to get started once it has been permitted and designed even in a weakening market. The upfront money for such costs has often been advanced by the developer. That money will be returned by the financial partner or lender only after construction commences. In addition, permits which often take years to obtain may expire if work does not commence.

In spite of all the statistical and demographic information available, the industry tends to be guided by anecdotal and project specific experience. A successful project spawns many imitators and overbuilding often occurs. The barriers to entry are not great, especially since the financial markets are also fragmented and rarely exercise systemic controls. Within each metropolitan area, there are so many permitting jurisdictions that regional planning controls rarely work. In other words, the system puts the burden on property owners to protect themselves through systematic research of market opportunities, pre-leasing, and conservative financial structures. Sound development practices can help property owners cope with the inevitable cycles.

PRODUCT OBSOLESCENCE

Real estate is traditionally valued on the basis of its cash flow from operations or cash flow after debt service over time. Depreciation of real estate is deducted for the purpose of determining any income tax payable, but since historically most investors have presumed that their property will be worth more in the future, depreciation is rarely considered as a real cost in calculating the value of a property. Reserves for tenant improvements may be correlated with the current lease expiration dates, assumptions as to the percentage of tenants renewing their leases and the downtime and re-leasing costs for space assumed to be vacated. But, it has been historically assumed that rents will rise more than enough to cover replacement reserves. Capitalization rates used to determine value may have to be raised if this assumption is rejected.

In recent years, many properties have declined in value or even become obsolete. What used to be the 100% location in a community has often become an albatross. For example, competition in the retail area has resulted in downtown stores moving to larger suburban malls, the new "downtowns". Big box retailers such as Wal-Mart have made major inroads. A variety of new specialty stores have taken business from established department stores, although department stores are changing their product lines to attempt to reverse this trend. **Looking at the retail industry from a long-range perspective, future competition** may derive from computer, television or telephone shopping. Since the U.S. has the highest proportion of retail space to population of any country, there is the need to be highly selective in choosing retail location and product mix.

There are many similar examples of how changes in other areas affect real estate values. As corporations downsize and use more outside suppliers, there is a need for easily subdividable buildings that cater to small tenants. However, betting on smaller tenants is often like committing higher risk venture capital money. Manufacturers have come to expect "just in time" delivery, reducing inventory requirements and the need for storage space. The optimum height for warehouses varies with changes in moving equipment and the types of products being moved, outmoding existing warehouses. Telecommunication requirements may dictate office location.

LEASING

The amount of rent landlords charge their tenants has always been an item of negotiation. For companies experiencing reasonable growth, rent has generally been a relatively minor expense. Paying the going rent was considered less important than increasing sales and building the business. But today, many companies are downsizing their operations and reducing their product costs each year. Every expense, including rent, is being scrutinized. Tepid demand and greater attention to costs have combined with the glut of available office space to put downward pressure on rents in the 1990s. Although some areas of the country are exceptions, there will be little new office construction in the U.S. in the near future. Existing office buildings continue to trade well below replacement cost.

Increased cost consciousness has not tempered corporate demands for higher quality space finishes. Most companies realize that attractive, efficient space with modern conveniences results in better productivity. It is just that they do not want to pay extra for it. The landlord is expected to custom-design the layout and reconfigure the space to meet a tenant's particular needs as part of the building standard, and as part of the base rent. Likewise, the installation of new air conditioning systems and energy-efficient windows and lighting fixtures has become a routine request. The amount of the reserve needed for future tenant improvements and upgrades is difficult to calculate in advance and will depend on future market conditions. However, this is one area where landlords have lately found that they have not fully anticipated their costs.

THE CONSTRUCTION PROCESS

The fragmented nature of the construction industry makes costs difficult to predict or control. Although architects use their own and others' experience in their work, few architects would ever design a building identical to one that has been built before. With the exception of franchised food and a few other retail chains and some low-end residential products, each property is, to some extent, custom designed. One valid explanation is that lot sizes, topography, shapes and surroundings vary, but the net result is greater uncertainties and higher costs. The design profession itself is not integrated. Each building requires numerous consultants and engineers, together producing a design that cannot be priced until each firm has finished its drawings and specifications.

The actual construction of a building can become a nightmare. Hundreds of independent subcontractors and suppliers must work together and coordinate their time schedules. For such contractors, most of whom are small and local, the challenge of staffing a number of jobs, many of which tend to be behind schedule, is great. Changes in design often require going back to not only the architect but to the various engineers, plus a number of subcontractors who all must rebid portions of the work. Keeping costs under control under such circumstances is a challenge. Renovation is even more difficult to price because of uncertain field conditions and smaller, thinly capitalized contractors and subcontractors. Prices often vary ±10% depending upon the competitive situations.

REGULATORY PRESSURES

The public also has raised its sights as to what it expects from the private property owner. Pressures by voters to reduce their residential property taxes leads to higher fees or linkage payments on new construction and higher property taxes on non-residential properties. Since many homeowners see growth in their own neighborhoods as adversely impacting their quality of life, with ensuing traffic congestion, pollution, and visual disarray, there is much more oversight and concern over what is built. From a public standpoint this may be good, and from the standpoint of the private developer it may well result in a better product over the longer term. However, regulatory compliance adds a measurable cost. The problem is to balance community needs with those of the developer. New construction is generally more costly and requires higher rents than buildings in the market are currently charging. The developer's fears are that the premium is not obtainable right away, and, if costs are out of line, the project will not be able to meet its short term financing costs and will have to be returned to the lender who is not anxious to have to cope with the problems of ownership.

On the federal level, but with similar impact, public pressure for lower taxes has led to eliminating benefits for those investing in real estate. This shift has been accomplished by lengthening depreciation schedules four times since 1986. This lengthening lowers depreciation allowances and raises taxable income. Investors who do not spend most of their time practicing in the real estate field have been prohibited, since 1986, from deducting losses from real estate against other income, a reaction to an earlier period when buildings were constructed not for economic use but for their ability to generate tax losses. Given pressures to cope with budget deficits, it is unlikely that investors in real estate will get special tax benefits. Moreover, income tax rates for wealthier taxpayers have gone up substantially. On the positive side, the widening spread between ordinary income tax rates and capital gains rates may ultimately benefit long-term investors in real estate. Institutional investors who do not have a tax burden have a competitive advantage which should encourage them to invest more in real estate.

For many years, federal policy was to increase the availability and affordability of housing for families with lower incomes through subsidies. Without such subsidies many properties, especially in inner cities, will be negatively impacted. Eliminating deductibility for mortgage interest would affect all homeowners.

Public concerns have also led to two major national legislative initiatives which, while laudatory in purpose, have had a negative effect on real estate values. The first is the Americans Disability Act which mandated that owners of most properties provide wheelchair access to virtually all areas of their buildings. The cost of handicapped accessible bathrooms, ramps, mechanized lifts and elevators is a major burden especially to investors who want to rehabilitate small, multi-level buildings. It also accelerates the movement from cities to the suburbs where newer, one story structures are more common. These rules are less of a problem for new construction where these specifications can be incorporated from the start. For existing buildings facing pressures to maintain rental levels, it is often difficult to absorb these added costs.

The second national initiative is the passage of environmental protection acts designed to eliminate pollutants from our land, buildings, air, and water. Who could be against such a goal? The burden is on the current property owner to bring the property into compliance whether or not the damage was inflicted by the tenant or the landlord and whether or not it was done during the current owner's period of ownership. This was the only way for the government to accomplish its purposes without involving itself in endless litigation to prove fault. Since the people setting the standards tend to be scientifically or politically oriented and rarely consider the costs as primary, the standards tend to be stringent and conservative. The process for achieving compliance is often uncertain and public agencies are rarely willing to give a property owner a clean bill of health. The usual document an owner can expect is a letter that says that based on what the particular agency knows now, and the current standards, the property will not be cited at this time as being in non-compliance. Lenders are loathe to put themselves in a potential ownership position if there is environmental uncertainty since, if the borrower defaults and there is an environmental problem, the "deep-pocketed" lender may become institutionally responsible if it becomes the legal owner.

From the landlord's perspective, if there is an environmental problem, it can be time consuming and costly to determine and prove which of many tenants in a long stream of occupants actually did the damage. And even if one locates the culprit, that company may no longer exist or be financially solvent. The pollution may well have come from a neighboring site. Older, urban sites, used in the past for industry, are most at risk. It is no wonder that a very high percentage of the money that is spent goes to lawyers and engineers, not to the cleanup itself. Recently, many general partners have transferred their ownership interests to a corporate general partner or limited liability company which they in turn own to minimize their personal liabilities. By now most landlords insert clauses in their leases protecting themselves from current tenant environmental infractions. Tenants themselves are more familiar with the regulations and are much more apt to run their operations accordingly. The problem is: who should pay for past activities? And, what is the appropriate level of remediation?

Another potential liability for real estate owners is the historical use of asbestos in insulation, the harmful effects of which have only become apparent in recent years. For decades asbestos was a preferred method of insulation, and vinyl asbestos flooring and asbestos ceiling tiles were considered desirable. Costs of removal today can be high and sometimes involve vacating entire buildings. Encapsulation of the asbestos is usually permissible, but only defers the problem since eventually removal will be necessary. The valid public policy issues aside, the reality is that the costs will fall on today's property owner. As a corollary the situation with asbestos leads today's property owner to wonder which of the materials now legally being used will be deemed hazardous in the future.

The adverse financial impact of public regulation on real estate is compounded by the ease of litigation in our society. It is not costly to file a law suit which is, at best, time consuming and, at worst, financially disastrous. The side with greater financial resources may cause the other to spend enormous sums to defend its position. The ease of filing appeals and a history of erratic court decisions adds further uncertainty. There is a trend toward alternative dispute resolution but unless agreed on by the parties as an enforceable remedy well before the dispute arises, it is rarely adopted.

The bottom line is that it is imperative for a property owner to be aware of the myriad levels of regulations and the process for enforcing them and be attuned to the attitudes of the surrounding communities. Many types of changes will occur that affect the value of a property. It is not a simple matter to alter the physical structure or use of a building to accommodate these changes.

FINANCIAL MARKETS

Another challenge is dealing with a financial industry which is in the midst of substantial change. The chart below shows what has been happening to the mortgage markets serving the real estate industry over the period 1978 to 1993.

OWNERSHIP OF COMMERCIAL AND MULTI-FAMILY MORTGAGES
($ Billions)

	1978	1983	1988	1993
Life Companies	82	125	218	220
Government Agencies	26	48	74	93
Thrifts	124	156	264	131
Commercial Banks	76	140	340	368
Other	37	34	72	101
Pension Funds	2	7	25	31
TOTAL	**347**	**510**	**983**	**944**

Several observations flow from this data. First, the virtual doubling of mortgage financing in the 1983 to 1988 period was a major factor in bringing forth the oversupply which severely damaged property markets in the late 1980s and early 1990s. Second, the prime casualty was the thrift industry which expanded into areas of real estate where it had little or no expertise. The damage was so extensive that the federal government had to take over and liquidate the assets of hundreds of thrifts at enormous cost to the taxpayers. Third, the largest supplier of funds was the commercial banking industry which purchased market share and increased its loans by $200 billion in the 1983 to 1988 period. It took several years of profitable business in other areas of their operations for banks to restore their capital base from the losses that ensued. Now with healthier balance sheets, commercial banks are again making construction loans. The most serious question is who will provide take-out financing in today's environment for these short term loans?

There is some hope that purchase of commercial mortgage backed securities by pension funds and private investors will take up some of the slack and that insurance companies will expand their lending. However, many insurance companies are reluctant to increase their exposure to real estate and, in fact, are looking to reduce their exposure because of new regulations that force them to carry higher capital reserves for such loans. Because of past losses, senior managers of most financial institutions have become more conservative, reducing their permissible loan to value ratios and being more selective in deciding to whom they will loan.

Another challenge facing financial institutions is the need for more sophisticated lending officers. In making a new loan or dealing with one in default, lenders need to think and act like owners to understand the market forces that affect property values. Institutional investors also found that they cannot rely solely on outside advisers. Appraisals, for example, tend to project the future based on the immediate past which is rarely an accurate predictor. Adoption of projections of automatic growth in rental rates has proved to be a Pandora's box. Yet, it is rare that institutions adequately train or compensate their real estate employees to underwrite based on an in-depth understanding of the forces affecting the individual property. Too many lenders focus primarily on individual net worth or the sponsor's background or the strength of the company's balance sheet as is common in most forms of commercial lending. Too often, either a project must meet specific quantitative parameters or it is turned down. Because of past problems, and perhaps because of undertrained and underpaid personnel, lenders are reluctant to give much authority to those on the firing line. The tendency for owners of a portfolio of properties is to demand a panoply of detailed reports from the property or asset managers. Portfolio techniques permit analyzing portfolios in many ways and look at the interdependency of locations, tenancy types and lease expenditures. More reports may make senior officers feel better. The question is whether the information facilitates profitable investing and informed oversight.

One overriding concern is the effect of the massive restructuring taking place in the lending industry. Financial institutions are shedding many of their traditional businesses where they do not see adequate profit margins. Nobody knows who is going to be in what businesses. Recent merger mania in the banking industry will likely lead to the elimination of at least half of the 10,000 banks in the U.S. The new national banks will probably emphasize providing loans to larger borrowers, with aggregate net staff reductions. What will happen to smaller, local borrowers who require more than plain vanilla financing? Yet, debt financing is crucial to the typical investors in small properties. They represent the vast majority of U.S. property owners in number if not in size. For every Class A building in a market, there are many more smaller, Class B and C structures. In many cases, our neighborhoods are dependent upon these older buildings for stability. If capital is constrained they will deteriorate or not be able to convert to other uses.

The outlook is not entirely negative. Given the stable economic environment, moderate inflation and relatively low interest rates that have categorized the mid-1990s, there has been some return to the lending market by some institutions, especially insurance companies. It is hoped that pension funds, which by international standards have a low exposure to real estate, will double their investment in this area, providing another $120 to $150 billion in funds. It is difficult, though, to sell the real estate story in a rapidly rising equity stock market. While foreign investment in U.S. real estate has fallen off from the high levels of the mid-1980s, because of losses from investments made during that period plus a weakening dollar, the U.S. is still one of the few developed countries that attracts and welcomes foreign investment.

The rash of new share issuance in real estate investment trusts (REITs) is another optimistic sign. The REITs of today are generally better structured than those offered in the 1970s and 1980s, since property owners are usually exchanging their assets for shares in the new funds, and the cash being raised is used to repay debt on the properties, not to pay out the sellers. Many pension fund advisers, investment bankers, and mutual fund managers are encouraging the formation of larger pools of properties and capital for the benefit of the industry and themselves. The number of providers of commercial mortgage backed securities has increased and their rates are becoming more competitive. But, for the average property owner, it is apparent that securitized mortgages will not be a big factor. Who will provide the funds, for what type properties, for how long, on what terms, and in what amounts? Access to the financial market has and will continue to change. The need for increased professionalism in order to participate is a given.

CONCLUSION

The challenges of reduced market demand, more rapid obsolescence of properties and chaotic financial markets have been looked at as national problems. But their impact is felt at the local level in different ways. The manufacturing employment cutbacks in the midwest, the oil crisis in the southwest, the computer industry consolidations in Massachusetts and the defense industry reductions in California did not occur at the same time. There is not just one national cycle; the regions have their own cyclicality.

Surprisingly, the best opportunities frequently occur by acting counter-cyclically in areas where there are downturns. The disposition of real estate portfolios by financial institutions at prices well below replacement costs have permitted their buyers to compete at rental levels below that of comparable properties. Even though vacancy rates of 15% are high, 85% of the space is still occupied. There are tenants searching for space. Moreover, with little new construction on the horizon, vacancy rates will decrease and rental rates will stabilize and move up in many markets. There are always specific locations within each market that will do better than others.

In other words, there are many mixed messages. The impact on individual properties differs depending upon the local factors and the property's unique characteristics. A bottom up approach to analyzing each property is the starting point. The problem is that one never knows exactly how much the macro trends will affect value. But, by understanding the individual property and market in such a context, one can dramatically increase one's chances for success in a highly fragmented marketplace. That is the thrust and purpose of the case studies in this book, which we hope will better prepare you to recognize and capitalize on change.

3

ANDERSON STREET

Although inexperienced in real estate, Charlie Leonard hopes in June 1987 that youthful enthusiasm and a $25,000 inheritance will help him enter the real estate business. His experience chronicles the process of finding, evaluating, and acquiring a four-unit brownstone in need of renovation in the Beacon Hill area of Boston. The case also identifies the various players in the process.

Discussion Questions:

1. How did Leonard go about searching for and evaluating this property?
2. What people helped Leonard in the process and what functions did they perform?
3. What are the problems relating to the rehabilitation work proposed?
4. Should Leonard make this investment?

In June of 1987, Charlie Leonard began searching for a small income-producing apartment building in which to invest. Leonard had just graduated from Harvard College, and he was working for a manufacturing firm in Newton, Massachusetts. He had grown up in Boston and was attracted to the investment potential of the Back Bay–Beacon Hill area, which he considered the best residential section of downtown Boston. Many of his contemporaries were renting apartments or had purchased homes there, and he and his wife had attended many of their parties. He considered paying rent to someone else a waste of a capital building opportunity, since he was building up someone else's equity.

Leonard wanted to gain experience in the real estate field, and build an equity base for future real estate investments. He hoped to increase his return by managing and operating his property on weekends and after normal working hours. Leonard had recently received an inheritance from a great aunt of $25,000, and he wanted to achieve maximum leverage for this equity. Although he had no real estate experience, he had a working knowledge of carpentry from three years of designing and building sets for Harvard's Hasty Pudding Show.

BEACON HILL PROPERTIES

Leonard began to spend all his free evenings and weekends becoming familiar with the area. He obtained a copy of the U.S. Census Tract, Boston Standard Metropolitan Statistical Area (SMSA) to check the demographic data on age breakdowns, education, employment, marital status, income, length of stay, and ethnic background of present Beacon Hill residents. Most were transient, and either single or newly married. He checked maps for distances to the city's office, shopping, cultural, and entertainment centers, and found that Beacon Hill was close to all of these urban amenities.

He studied the real estate sections of newspapers for brokers' names and to get an idea of the types of offerings and range of prices available. He found that the Sunday papers had by far the largest real estate advertising sections. He answered some advertisements in order to meet real estate brokers, and learn about the available properties. He specifically attempted to visit those offices that did the most advertising (or that appeared to do the most business in the area).

Adjunct Professor William J. Poorvu prepared this case as the basis for class discussion rather than to illustrate either effective or ineffective handling of an administrative situation.

Many were located around Charles Street, the major commercial street of Beacon Hill. Normally, the brokers wanted to know the type of property in which he was interested, the amount of cash he had to invest, and whether he would live in the building.

Leonard was quite disappointed in the offerings that were shown to him. Although the income and expense statements of one building on Myrtle Street had made it seem quite attractive, the situation was very different when he actually visited the building. It was in a rundown state, and the apartments, occupied by groups of students, were in deplorable condition. The income statement of another property on Myrtle Street showed a 20% return on the cash investment; however, this made no allowance for repairs, vacancies, or management expenses. When considered, these costs reduced the return to 3%. Rentals in another building seemed too high. When Leonard spoke with one of the tenants, he found that the landlord had asked a rental of $810 per month for the apartment, but, when offered $675 per month, accepted on the condition that there be a one-year lease with no rent the first two months and then $810 rent per month for the remainder of the term. This arrangement would enable the landlord to show a higher monthly income after the initial two months.

Most properties sold for $270,000 and higher, and required an investment of more than $25,000. Leonard expected to obtain a bank loan for part of the purchase price through a mortgage (a legal instrument by which property is hypothecated to secure the payment of a debt or obligation). But institutional lenders were reluctant to lend more than 60–80% of the capitalized value of the property. Additional money might be raised by placing a second or junior mortgage on the property, but interest rates on this type of secondary financing were higher, and the personal credit of the borrower was often required as additional collateral. However, sellers were often willing to take a purchase money mortgage to facilitate the sale of the property. Nevertheless, having only $25,000 equity proved a major factor in limiting the building Leonard might purchase.

Leonard became discouraged. Although the real estate brokers were friendly, they never seemed to show him what he considered desirable properties. There rarely appeared to be an opportunity to create value by increasing rents or reducing expenses; if there were, the seller had already taken it into consideration in establishing his price. Leonard soon learned that many of the brokers owned buildings themselves, and were thus, in a sense, competitors of their own customers. Few properties in the area were sold by the owners themselves. Usually they were listed with several brokers who competed to receive a 5% sales commission by selling the property to one of their customers. Since there was considerable investor interest in the area, and listings were rarely exclusive with one broker, the brokers had to act quickly on the desirable properties to make their commissions. Therefore, most of the brokers had a few favored customers to whom they gave first chance. These customers usually had the necessary resources to act quickly to acquire the most desirable situations.

FACTORS AFFECTING VALUE

The same factors which caused Leonard to want to purchase on Beacon Hill had attracted many doctors, engineers, and businessmen also anxious to own real estate. As a result, the market values of many buildings on the Hill had tripled in the past ten years.

The area's location had considerable natural advantages. To the west was the Charles River; to the south was the Boston Public Gardens which led to Newbury Street, Boston's best shopping area; and to the east was the State House and Boston's financial district. The West End slums and the undesirable commercial activity of adjacent Scollay Square to the north had restrained values in the 1940s and 1950s. This had been especially true of the northern slope of the Hill, which had become known as the "back slope" because of its many lower-rent rooming houses. Under Boston's urban redevelopment program, however, in the 1960s and 1970s, the West End slums were torn down and were replaced by Charles River Park, a luxury apartment house development. Scollay Square was replaced by a new Government Center.

As a result of this redevelopment, values all over Beacon Hill had increased, but most drastically on the back or north slope. Rentals and condominium values there had increased as real estate operators began to buy and improve the property. Rents now ranged from $675–$800 for one-bedroom apartments and $900–$1100 for two-bedroom apartments. In spite of this, because most purchasers in this section were real estate speculators who expected a high return on their investment, Leonard felt there would be further growth as investors who were accustomed to lower returns from properties on the lower section of the Hill began to buy buildings on the north slope from these real estate speculators. The recent conversion of rental units to condominiums also caused values to increase.

The Massachusetts State Legislature had established the entire Beacon Hill area as an historic district, and set up a commission to preserve the character of the area. The approval of the commission had to be obtained for any changes to the exterior of a structure before the building department would issue a building permit. The commission would not permit the erection of any new buildings in the area. While this protected and enhanced the values of existing buildings, it provided a ceiling on land values, since land could not be reused for a different, more valuable purpose.

Leonard knew that this activity and interest in the area, which had driven prices up and was proving a disadvantage in his attempts to buy a property, would turn into an advantage once he owned a building. Many investors in Beacon Hill appeared to be satisfied with an 8% return on cash, which meant that for every $1,000 of cash flow, which remained after deducting all charges or costs from gross income, he could expect a buyer to pay $12,500. In some areas an investor might look for a 12.5% return, in which case $1,000 of cash flow would be worth only $8,000.

All of these factors led Leonard to believe that there was considerable safety in an investment in the area. There was little chance of depreciation for functional or economic causes. To obtain maximum capital appreciation, however, he would probably have to narrow his investment search to the back slope of Beacon Hill, where values were still not as high as on the "lower slope." He also realized that he would have to purchase a building that would require considerable renovation. Otherwise, once the income had become established the owner would ask a high selling price that would preclude much short-term growth in value. He had learned that he would have to act quickly if he did find an attractive opportunity. He would also have to check all figures given him carefully since few small buildings had audited financial statements and he could not rely solely on statements made by real estate brokers. Lastly, he knew that his $25,000 equity would limit him to acquiring a relatively small building.

ANDERSON STREET

In August of 1987, Leonard learned of a 4-unit apartment house on Beacon Hill that was for sale. A local broker with whom he was friendly had called to tell him that a building on Anderson Street had just come on the market, and that if he acted quickly, he might be able to outbid several real estate brokers who were interested in the property. Leonard knew that brokers always attempted to convey a sense of urgency, but since he was aware that desirable properties did sell quickly, he decided to investigate the property at once.

The property was located on the "back slope of the Hill" in an improving neighborhood. There had already been some increases in property values, and Leonard expected still greater increases as little new housing was being built in Boston. The property was located in the middle of the block, and was set back 100 feet from the road, which would afford an opportunity for creating an attractive entrance way and garden. The property had been built in the mid-1800s, probably as a middle-income town house. After being used as a rooming house for 20 years it had been gutted by a fire in 1986. Only the structural shell remained. An architect had purchased the shell for $120,000, but after spending $45,000 of what looked to be a $100,000 renovation job, he decided the total cost was beyond his cash availablity and placed the property on the market. Leonard felt that the architect's plans for renovation were in good taste and that thus far the work had been done well. Each of the first three floors was to have one two-bedroom apartment while the fourth floor would have a large one-bedroom apartment. For the first time, Leonard felt that he had seen a property that met his investment criteria. The property had profit potential; it was aesthetically desirable, in the area he wanted, and, with an asking price of $168,000, was within his price range.

Leonard was told that the $168,000 price was firm because considerable interest had already been shown in the property. A contractor to whom Leonard was referred confirmed that it would cost approximately $55,000 to complete the architect's plans.

Leonard prepared an income and expense statement to see whether the net income of the property would justify its price (see **Exhibit 1**). He figured that each of the three two-bedroom apartments could be rented at $990 per month, and the top floor one-bedroom apartment at $880 per month. Rentals would total $46,200 annually. From this figure, he subtracted a 5% vacancy allowance, which would represent two apartments sitting vacant for slightly more than a month. There was the additional possibility that if he did not rent the apartments himself, he would have to pay a broker's commission of 5% of the annual apartment rental. The broker, licensed by the state, received this commission for showing the property to prospective tenants, from bringing the tenants and landlord together, and helping to negotiate the contract between them.

Leonard estimated real estate taxes at 9.5% of the rental income or $4,200. This represented an assessed value of $250,000, which was approximately full market value, and $75,000 above the present $175,000 assessment. He obtained a quotation of a $1,000 annual premium from his real estate broker's firm for a package insurance policy providing protection against fire, extended coverage perils, public liability, loss of rents, and boiler explosion. The tenants would pay the electric bills for their own apartments, but the landlord would pay the bill for the public areas. A janitor would keep the public halls clean, change the light bulbs, and take out the trash. There were several services around Beacon Hill that performed this function for an annual fee of $1,200. Leonard had expected to do some of the repair work and all of the management work himself to increase his cash return, but his broker told him that since potential mortgage lenders or future purchasers would include these costs in their "setups," Leonard would have to do so, too. Also, if he should leave the area, he would have to hire outside firms to perform these services. Therefore, he included an allowance of 5% for repairs and a similar amount for management. His projections showed a cash flow before financing of $30,800, without any allowance for the work he would do himself. (See **Exhibit 1**.)

Leonard was very pleased. He told his wife that he had found a building that would be just right. With its skylights, beamed ceiling, and natural brick walls, the top floor apartment was just what they wanted to live in. They could live "rent free," while making money by doing their own managing and renting. They could take out the trash and clean the halls themselves. Although outside management would be more experienced, he would be more attentive and efficient. Rent from the other apartments would pay the other expenses, and he would gain real estate experience.

His wife said that while the apartment seemed very nice, she was not sure she liked the idea of living in a building they owned. They would get tenants' complaints at home. Also, she thought there might be a problem in doing business with their neighbors if they got friendly with them. She doubted that they would be able to charge maximum rents or raise rents.

The real estate broker questioned his decision to act as his own general contractor because of his lack of experience and time. He said that it was difficult, particularly on a part-time basis, to coordinate several subcontractors who never showed up when they said they would. The work might take longer than Leonard anticipated. Also, the Boston Building Department had a maze of rules and many inspectors; his renovation could be quite costly if he were forced to comply exactly with every regulation. Experienced contractors usually found ways of getting around these requirements. He would have to be careful however, to minimize changes and avoid extras once the job had been started, since most subcontractors would charge a premium for extras, because it would be too late to get competitive quotes on small amounts of work.

Leonard replied that any remodeling job would involve changes in adapting to field conditions. One of the reasons he wanted to do the work himself was to avoid the extra charges by subcontractors. Any outside contractor would carry a heavy contingency allowance in bidding the job. Certainly the contractor who gave him the $55,000 estimate to complete the renovation must have carried at least $5,000 for profit. Leonard reasoned that he had at least that $5,000 to spend before his lesson in remodeling began to cost him money.

MORTGAGE FINANCING

Leonard then went to see Jerry Smith, the mortgage officer of the savings bank who had recently given a $180,000 loan on the building for a 20 year period at a 10% interest rate. Smith told him that the existing mortgage was on a constant payment basis of 11.6% or $20,900 per year, which meant that the payments, including amortization and interest, remained the same throughout the entire term of the loan, but that the portion applicable to interest became less as the balance of the mortgage loan decreased. Correspondingly, the portion applicable to amortization increased. The mortgage payment plus a payment of one-twelfth of the estimated real estate taxes were made to the bank monthly. The bank also kept two months' real estate taxes in escrow as additional security. The banker explained that the loan could be paid off at any time, but that it would charge a prepayment penalty of 2% of the unpaid balance.

Leonard explained his plans for finishing the work and gave Smith his projected income and expense statements for the property. Smith noticed that Leonard's rental figures were $5,600 higher than those originally submitted by the present owner. At that time the bank had valued the property at $225,000 and given an 80% mortgage, the maximum permitted by bank policy. He asked whether Leonard knew his total costs. Leonard told him of the contractor's $55,000 bid. Smith told him that he should also consider carrying costs while the renovation work was going on. The bank might waive principal payments on the mortgage for six months during construction, but interest of $9,000 on the $180,000 must be paid, as well as real estate taxes of $1,400 assuming the $175,000 assessment would remain in effect until the renovation was complete. In addition, he still had to pay for six months' insurance at $500 and heat and electricity at $1,100. These costs totalled $12,000. There was also the two-month real estate tax escrow of $1,000, which was a cash outlay even though it would eventually be returned to him. Leonard could but did not need to assume the architect's existing mortgage, thus eliminating the need for new documents and a new title search by the bank's lawyer. (Assumption of a mortgage occurs when, in purchasing a property, the buyer assumes liability for payment of an existing note secured by a mortgage on the property.)

He asked whether the bank would increase its mortgage to $210,000. He explained that he might live in the building, manage it, and do some of the work himself, which would create more cash flow to serve the debt. The banker replied that he could not take this extra income into account in making his decision, since the bank always had to consider a loan in light of the costs the bank would incur if it had to foreclose and run the property itself. (A foreclosure sale occurs when property pledged as security for a loan is sold to pay the debt in the event of a default in payment or terms.)

Smith doubted that the bank would be interested in increasing its loan at this time since it was not certain that Leonard could get the increased rentals. However, Smith added that if the income level was increased when the building became rented and seasoned, the bank might reexamine his request.

Leonard next visited Sarah Harris, the mortgage loan officer at another local savings bank, to find out whether her bank would be interested in a $210,000 mortgage. Leonard showed her the income and expense projections, told her his costs, and explained his plans. Harris said that because of the 80% policy restriction, her bank would have to appraise the property at $262,500 to justify a $210,000 loan. Appraisals, she told Leonard, could be made on the basis of replacement cost, income, or market value based on recent comparable sales. She said that her bank preferred the income approach as the most realistic. Taking a capitalization rate of 11.6% on the $30,800 projected cash flow, she arrived at an appraised value of $265,500. Harris considered it likely that based on this appraisal she could justify a $210,000 mortgage at 10% interest for 20 years. She believed that the $30,800 annual cash flow from operations would be adequate to carry the $24,300 financing charge. She added that she was familiar with the area and considered Leonard's projected figures realistic, although she would have to see the property to be certain of her judgment.

She questioned Leonard about his current personal income. Leonard told her that his present salary was $26,000 per year. Harris said she would require credit references and certain other information about Leonard since he would be signing the note personally as additional protection to the bank against loss. Leonard asked why he would have to become personally liable since there was ample value in the property. He knew that his friends who had bought brownstones in New York had not assumed any personal liability. Harris said that this was the policy of virtually all savings banks in the Boston area for smaller buildings, especially when the loan to value ratio was as high as 80%. If Leonard had confidence in the building, he should not worry. Each year his liability declined as a portion of the mortgage loan was amortized.

Leonard asked whether there were other costs in closing the mortgage. Harris replied that Leonard would be responsible for legal and title expenses at closing, amounting to about $1,000, which would cover the cost of the bank's lawyer. The bank's lawyer is responsible for certifying to the bank that the owner has a valid fee simple ownership in the property, which means that the owner has the right to dispose of it, pledge it, or pass it on to his heirs as he sees fit. Also, the lawyer ascertains that there are no liens on the property senior to the bank's interest. Unless the document's conditions specify otherwise, the seniority of a lien depends on the date it was recorded in the County Registry of Deeds Office. When a lien is paid off a discharge is put on record. There are some liens that are a matter of record that a bank will accept as senior to its position. These include zoning or use regulations, building codes, party wall agreements (where two buildings share the same wall) or certain easements where one party has specific rights or privileges on the land of the other. The certification of title is often done through the issuance of an insurance policy written by a title insurance company at a one-time cost paid by the borrower or purchaser. Harris also told him he should not rely on the bank's attorney to represent him. He should budget about $900 for his own attorney and other miscellaneous costs. Lastly, there would be a 1% loan origination fee of $2,100 payable to the bank upon closing.

LEGAL ADVICE

Leonard then consulted Josh Guberman, his family's attorney, about the whole transaction. Leonard was very disturbed about the bank's requirement that he sign the mortgage note personally. His attorney told him that he did not want to understate the risk, but that this was a customary bank practice in making small mortgage loans in Massachusetts, where banks were often more conservative than in other areas of the country.

Leonard inquired about alternate methods for raising the extra $30,000 besides accepting the new mortgage. Guberman believed that secondary financing could be obtained, but at an interest rate of 15% and only with a personal endorsement. The seller might take back a purchase money second mortgage, but again Leonard would probably have to sign the note personally and repay the entire loan over a 3- to 5-year period. In addition, if the demand for the property were as strong as Leonard indicated an all-cash offer might have a better chance of winning the property than one contingent upon a purchase money second mortgage.

Leonard asked whether he would not be taking a big risk in making an offer for the property without having his financing secured. Guberman explained that while he would have to submit a written offer for the property, together with a deposit to be held by the real estate broker, he could make his offer contingent upon his being permitted to assume the seller's mortgage. This would give him some safety, while still permitting him to attempt to find a higher mortgage.

If Leonard's offer were accepted, a purchase and sales contract would be signed, based on a standard Boston Real Estate Board form (see **Exhibit 2**). Guberman said that in case of forfeiture as a result of the buyer's failure to perform, the sales deposit, normally 5%–10% of the purchase price, would be kept by the seller as liquidated damages. Therefore, Leonard's risk would be limited to $8,400 if the seller would accept a 5% deposit. Also, if the seller could not deliver a quit-claim deed, relinquishing any interest he held in the property and giving a clear title to the buyer, the buyer would be entitled to a refund of his deposit.

Guberman then asked Leonard whether he had adequate funds to complete the project even with a $210,000 mortgage. The asking price for the property was $168,000; the remodeling cost $55,000; carrying costs during construction were now $13,500 because of the higher mortgage; closing costs $4,000; and escrow funds $1,000. These costs totalled $241,500. The $210,000 mortgage or mortgages and his $25,000 equity would still leave him $6,500 short. Leonard replied that he planned to save money by acting as his own general contractor, and he hoped to remodel and rent the property in four months rather than six months. A $210,000 first mortgage with an annual carrying charge of $24,300, although requiring a personal guarantee, would give him leverage, making the pretax return on his $25,000 cash investment 27.0% versus 13.1% on a free and clear or all-cash basis. In addition, he would be amortizing a mortgage. The return would be even greater if he lived in the building and managed it himself.

Guberman asked why Leonard was not selling the units as condominiums. He should be able to get about $80,000 per unit, which could net him $60,000 for all four units after sales costs. Moreover, at a later time a conversion might run into problems given the difficulties of evicting existing tenants. Leonard responded by saying that he wanted to maximize the long-term opportunity of what he considered an excellent market in an excellent area. He was not in it for a short term gain. Rents should increase over time. Although the 1986 tax law reduced the advantages of being able to depreciate real property, he expected that about $8,000 of his income from the property would be sheltered from taxes.

The lawyer said that Leonard's analysis seemed reasonable, but his estimates did not put a dollar value on Leonard's time. He wondered whether this should be considered. Also, he wanted Leonard to realize the seriousness of this time commitment since his full-time job was still his prime responsibility. Finally, he asked him to consider carefully the amount of the offer he was submitting and the risks involved.

Exhibit 1

Income

1st floor		$990/month
2nd floor		990/month
3rd floor		990/month
4th floor		880/month
		$3,850 × 12 = $46,200
Allowance for vacancies		2,310
		$43,890

Operating Expenses

Real estate taxes	$4,200	
Heat	1,490	
Electricity	400	
Water	400	
Insurance	1,000	
Janitor	1,200	
Repairs @ 5%	2,200	
Management @ 5%	2,200	
		$13,090

Cash flow from operations[1] $30,800

[1]Sometimes referred to as free and clear cash flow or net operating income.

Exhibit 2   Standard Form Purchase and Sale Agreement

From the Office of:

**STANDARD FORM
PURCHASE AND SALE AGREEMENT**

1. PARTIES
(fill in)

This _____ day of _____ 19 ____

hereinafter called the SELLER, agrees to SELL and

hereinafter called the BUYER or PURCHASER, agrees to BUY, upon the terms hereinafter set forth, the following described premises:

2. DESCRIPTION
(fill in and include title reference)

3. BUILDINGS, STRUCTURES, IMPROVEMENTS, FIXTURES

(fill in or delete)

Included in the sale as a part of said premises are the buildings, structures, and improvements now thereon, and the fixtures belonging to the SELLER and used in connection therewith including, if any, all wall-to-wall carpeting, drapery rods, automatic garage door openers, venetian blinds, window shades, screens, screen doors, storm windows and doors, awnings, shutters, furnaces, heaters, heating equipment, stoves, ranges, oil and gas burners and fixtures appurtenant thereto, hot water heaters, plumbing and bathroom fixtures, garbage disposers, electric and other lighting fixtures, mantels, outside television antennas, fences, gates, trees, shrubs, plants, and, ONLY IF BUILT IN, refrigerators, air conditioning equipment, ventilators, dishwashers, washing machines and dryers; and

but excluding

4. TITLE DEED
(fill in)
Include here by specific reference any restrictions, easements, rights and obligations in party walls not included in (b), leases, municipal and other liens, other encumbrances, and make provision to protect SELLER against BUYER'S breach of SELLER's covenants in leases, where necessary.

Said premises are to be conveyed by a good and sufficient quitclaim deed running to the BUYER, or to the nominee designated by the BUYER by written notice to the SELLER at least seven   days before the deed is to be delivered as herein provided, and said deed shall convey a good and clear record and marketable title thereto, free from encumbrances, except
(a) Provisions of existing building and zoning laws;
(b) Existing rights and obligations in party walls which are not the subject of written agreement;
(c) Such taxes for the then current year as are not due and payable on the date of the delivery of such deed;
(d) Any liens for municipal betterments assessed after the date of this agreement;
(e) Easements, restrictions and reservations of record, if any, so long as the same do not prohibit or materially interfere with the current use of said premises;
* (f)

5. PLANS

If said deed refers to a plan necessary to be recorded therewith the SELLER shall deliver such plan with the deed in form adequate for recording or registration.

6. REGISTERED TITLE

In addition to the foregoing, if the title to said premises is registered, said deed shall be in form sufficient to entitle the BUYER to a Certificate of Title of said premises, and the SELLER shall deliver with said deed all instruments, if any, necessary to enable the BUYER to obtain such Certificate of Title.

7. PURCHASE PRICE
(fill in); space is allowed to write out the amounts if desired

The agreed purchase price for said premises is

dollars, of which

$ _____ have been paid as a deposit this day and
$ _____
$ _____ are to be paid at the time of delivery of the deed in cash, or by certified, cashier's, treasurer's or bank check.

$ _____
$ _____   TOTAL

Exhibit 2   (continued)

8. TIME FOR PERFORMANCE; DELIVERY OF DEED *(fill in)*

Such deed is to be delivered at   o'clock   M. on the   day of
19   , at the

Registry of Deeds, unless otherwise agreed upon in writing. It is agreed that time is of the essence of this agreement.

9. POSSESSION and CONDITIONS of PREMISES. *(attach a list of exceptions, if any)*

Full possession of said premises free of all tenants and occupants, except as herein provided, is to be delivered at the time of the delivery of the deed, said premises to be then (a) in the same condition as they now are reasonable use and wear thereof excepted, and (b) not in violation of said building and zoning laws, and (c) in compliance with provisions of any instrument referred to in clause 4 hereof. The BUYER shall be entitled to an inspection of said premises prior to the delivery of the deed in order to determine whether the condition thereof complies with the terms of this clause.

10. EXTENSION TO PERFECT TITLE OR MAKE PREMISES CONFORM *(Change period of time if desired).*

If the SELLER shall be unable to give title or to make conveyance, or to deliver possession of the premises, all as herein stipulated, or if at the time of delivery of the deed the premises do not conform with the provisions hereof, then any payments made under this agreement shall be forthwith refunded and all other obligations of the parties hereto shall cease and this agreement shall be void without recourse to the parties hereto, unless the SELLER elects to use reasonable efforts to remove any defects in title, or to deliver possession as provided herein, or to make the said premises conform to the provisions hereof, as the case may be, in which event the SELLER shall give written notice thereof to the BUYER at or before the time for performance hereunder, and thereupon the time for performance hereof shall be extended for a period of thirty   days.

11. FAILURE TO PERFECT TITLE OR MAKE PREMISES CONFORM, etc.

If at the expiration of the extended time the SELLER shall have failed so to remove any defects in title, deliver possession, or make the premises conform, as the case may be, all as herein agreed, or if at any time during the period of this agreement or any extension thereof, the holder of a mortgage on said premises shall refuse to permit the insurance proceeds, if any, to be used for such purposes, then any payments made under this agreement shall be forthwith refunded and all other obligations of the parties hereto shall cease and this agreement shall be void without recourse to the parties hereto.

12. BUYER'S ELECTION TO ACCEPT TITLE

The BUYER shall have the election, at either the original or any extended time for performance, to accept such title as the SELLER can deliver to the said premises in their then condition and to pay therefor the purchase price without deduction, in which case the SELLER shall convey such title, except that in the event of such conveyance in accord with the provisions of this clause, if the said premises shall have been damaged by fire or casualty insured against, then the SELLER shall, unless the SELLER has previously restored the premises to their former condition, either

(a) pay over or assign to the BUYER, on delivery of the deed, all amounts recovered or recoverable on account of such insurance, less any amounts reasonably expended by the SELLER for any partial restoration, or

(b) if a holder of a mortgage on said premises shall not permit the insurance proceeds or a part thereof to be used to restore the said premises to their former condition or to be so paid over or assigned, give to the BUYER a credit against the purchase price, on delivery of the deed, equal to said amounts so recovered or recoverable and retained by the holder of the said mortgage less any amounts reasonably expended by the SELLER for any partial restoration.

13. ACCEPTANCE OF DEED

The acceptance of a deed by the BUYER or his nominee as the case may be, shall be deemed to be a full performance and discharge of every agreement and obligation herein contained or expressed, except such as are, by the terms hereof, to be performed after the delivery of said deed.

14. USE OF MONEY TO CLEAR TITLE

To enable the SELLER to make conveyance as herein provided, the SELLER may, at the time of delivery of the deed, use the purchase money or any portion thereof to clear the title of any or all encumbrances or interests, provided that all instruments so procured are recorded simultaneously with the delivery of said deed.

15. INSURANCE *Insert amount (list additional types of insurance and amounts as agreed)*

Until the delivery of the deed, the SELLER shall maintain insurance on said premises as follows:

Type of Insurance	*Amount of Coverage*
(a) Fire	$
(b) Extended Coverage	
(c)	

16. ADJUSTMENTS *(list operating expenses, if any, or attach schedule)*

Collected rents, mortgage interest, water and sewer use charges, operating expenses (if any) according to the schedule attached hereto or set forth below, and taxes for the then current year, shall be apportioned and fuel value shall be adjusted, as of the day of performance of this agreement and the net amount thereof shall be added to or deducted from, as the case may be, the purchase price payable by the BUYER at the time of delivery of the deed. Uncollected rents for the current rental period shall be apportioned if and when collected by either party.

Exhibit 2   (continued)

17. **ADJUSTMENT OF UNASSESSED AND ABATED TAXES**

If the amount of said taxes is not known at the time of the delivery of the deed, they shall be apportioned on the basis of the taxes assessed for the preceding year, with a reapportionment as soon as the new tax rate and valuation can be ascertained; and, if the taxes which are to be apportioned shall thereafter be reduced by abatement, the amount of such abatement, less the reasonable cost of obtaining the same, shall be apportioned between the parties, provided that neither party shall be obligated to institute or prosecute proceedings for an abatement unless herein otherwise agreed.

18. **BROKER'S FEE** *(fill in fee with dollar amount or percentage; also name of Broker(s))*

A broker's fee for professional service of
is due from the SELLER to

the Broker(s) herein, but if the SELLER pursuant to the terms of clause 21 hereof retains the deposits made hereunder by the BUYER, said Broker(s) shall be entitled to receive from the SELLER an amount equal to one-half the amount so retained or an amount equal to the Broker's fee for professional services according to this contract, whichever is the lesser.

19. **BROKER(S) WARRANTY** *(fill in name)*

The Broker(s) named herein
warrant(s) that the Broker(s) is(are) duly licensed as such by the Commonwealth of Massachusetts.

20. **DEPOSIT** *(fill in, or delete reference to broker(s) if SELLER holds deposit)*

All deposits made hereunder shall be held in escrow by the Broker(s) subject to the terms of this agreement and shall be duly accounted for at the time for performance of this agreement, provided however that in the event of any disagreement the Broker(s) may retain said deposits pending instructions mutually given by the SELLER and the BUYER.

21. **BUYER'S DEFAULT; DAMAGES**

If the BUYER shall fail to fulfill the BUYER'S agreements herein, all deposits made hereunder by the BUYER shall be retained by the SELLER as liquidated damages unless within thirty days after the time for performance of this agreement or any extension hereof, the SELLER otherwise notifies the BUYER in writing.

22. **RELEASE BY HUSBAND OR WIFE**

The SELLER'S spouse hereby agrees to join in said deed and to release and convey all statutory and other rights and interests in said premises.

23. **BROKER AS PARTY**

The Broker(s) named herein join(s) in this agreement and become(s) a party hereto, insofar as any provisions of this agreement expressly apply to the Broker(s), and to any amendments or modifications of such provisions to which the Broker(s) agree(s) in writing.

24. **LIABILITY OF TRUSTEE, SHAREHOLDER, BENEFICIARY, etc.**

If the SELLER or BUYER executes this agreement in a representative or fiduciary capacity, only the principal or the estate represented shall be bound, and neither the SELLER or BUYER so executing, nor any shareholder or beneficiary of any trust, shall be personally liable for any obligation, express or implied, hereunder.

25. **WARRANTIES AND REPRE-SENTATIONS** *(fill in); if none, state "none"; if any listed, indicate by whom each warranty or representation was made*

The BUYER acknowledges that the BUYER has not been influenced to enter into this transaction nor has he relied upon any warranties or representations not set forth or incorporated in this agreement or previously made in writing, except for the following additional warranties and representations, if any, made by either the SELLER or the Broker(s):

26. **MORTGAGE CONTINGENCY CLAUSE**

In order to help finance the acquisition of said premises, the BUYER shall apply for a conventional bank or other institutional mortgage loan of $_____, payable in no less than _____ years at an interest rate not to exceed _____ If despite the BUYER's diligent efforts a commitment for such loan cannot be obtained on or before_____ , 19_____ the BUYER may terminate this agreement by written notice to the SELLER(S) and/or the Broker(s), as agent for the SELLER, prior to the expiration of such time, whereupon any payments made under this agreement shall be forthwith refunded and all other obligations of the parties hereto shall cease and this agreement shall be void without recourse to the parties hereto. In no event will the BUYER be deemed to have used diligent efforts to obtain such commitment unless the BUYER submits a complete mortgage loan application conforming to the foregoing provisions on or before _____,19_____.

Exhibit 2   (continued)

27. **CONSTRUCTION OF AGREEMENT**
This instrument, executed in multiple counterparts, is to be construed as a Massachusetts contract, is to take effect as a sealed instrument, sets forth the entire contract between the parties, is binding upon and enures to the benefit of the parties hereto and their respective heirs, devisees, executors, administrators, successors and assigns, and may be cancelled, modified or amended only by a written instrument executed by both the SELLER and the BUYER. If two or more persons are named herein as BUYER their obligations hereunder shall be joint and several. The captions and marginal notes are used only as a matter of convenience and are not to be considered a part of this agreement or to be used in determining the intent of the parties to it.

28. **LEAD PAINT LAW**
The parties acknowledge that, under Massachusetts law, whenever a child or children under six years of age resides in any residential premises in which any paint, plaster or other accessible material contains dangerous levels of lead, the owner of said premises must remove or cover said paint, plaster or other material so as to make it inaccessible to children under six years of age.

29. **SMOKE DETECTORS**
The SELLER shall, at the time of the delivery of the deed, deliver a certificate from the fire department of the city or town in which said premises are located stating that said premises have been equipped with approved smoke detectors in conformity with applicable law.

30. **ADDITIONAL PROVISIONS**
The initialed riders, if any, attached hereto, are incorporated herein by reference.

NOTICE: This is a legal document that creates binding obligations. If not understood, consult an attorney.

_____   _____
SELLER (or spouse)   *SELLER*

_____   _____
BUYER   *BUYER*

_____
Broker(s)

EXTENSION

Date_____
The time for the performance of the foregoing agreement is extended until_____o'clock_____ _____M. on the_____day of_____19_____, time still being of the essence of this agreement as extended. In all other respects, this agreement is hereby ratified and confirmed.
This extension, executed in multiple counterparts, is intended to take effect as a sealed instrument.

_____   _____
SELLER (or spouse)   SELLER

_____   _____
BUYER   BUYER

_____
BROKER(S)

This form has been made available by courtesy of the Greater Boston Real Estate Board and is protected by the copyright laws.

4

THE MILLEGAN CREEK APARTMENTS

For Tom Hayden, a Vice President in Commercial Real Estate at Fleet Bank, Tuesday, March 1, 1994 would be a very important date for his Millegan Creek Apartment loan. He was to make a brief presentation about his proposed $15,715,000 loan for a 390 unit garden apartment project in Austin, Texas. Because it was a new market, a new developer and a large loan without a take-out, he had to show whether all elements were in place to make this project work.

Discussion Questions:

1. Would you recommend that Fleet Bank make this loan on the terms negotiated?
2. Is this project likely to be successful? What do you think of the location, the project, and the pricing? How does it stack up against the competition?
3. With all the new projects coming on line, do you think there is sufficient demand for a project this size? Of the market information provided, what is most useful?
4. How much profit can the developer expect to receive from this project? What are JPI's biggest risks?

Joanne McClatchy, the senior credit officer in commercial real estate at both Fleet Financial Group and its key subsidiary (Fleet Bank), had asked Tom to prepare a brief presentation and answer a few questions about his proposed $15,715,000 loan for a 390 unit apartment project in Austin, Texas. Joanne indicated that because it was a new market, a new developer and a large loan, she wanted to get additional information before Tom wrote up the project for credit committee approval.

Tom knew that it was Joanne's job to ask the tough questions. He knew that she was concerned about the market, and particularly the amount of new construction. He also expected that she would ask him about the sponsors, including their financial capacity and development expertise. Most importantly, Tom thought that Joanne would question him about the lack of a commitment for permanent financing. A takeout or permanent loan from an institution like an insurance company is the way that most construction loans are repaid. Over the last five years, Fleet and other commercial banks had lost billions of dollars because when their construction loan came due, the economics of the project had deteriorated and no one was willing to make a permanent mortgage loan that was sufficient to repay their loan.

FLEET'S ENTRY INTO TEXAS

After six years working for another bank, Tom Hayden joined Fleet Bank in 1989 and spent the next three years dealing with troubled loans in the bank's "work-out" division. Although Fleet was one of the few commercial banks to continue to make commercial real estate loans after the market crashed in the late 1980s and early 1990s, it was not until November, 1992 that Tom was reassigned to originate new loans. Tom's assignment was to seek financing opportunities in real estate in the State of Texas and help Fleet diversify its loan portfolio out of the Northeast.

As a first step, Tom did some research to learn who the best developers were. He met with mortgage bankers, attended forums and conferences, and read all the articles he could find. One name that came up repeatedly as an active developer who had survived the Texas real estate crash and was building a large number of apartments was JPI Multifamily Inc. (JPI).

Lecturer John H. Vogel Jr. prepared this case under the supervision of Adjunct Professor William J. Poorvu as the basis for class discussion rather than to illustrate either effective or ineffective handling of an administrative situation.

Tom was introduced to the principals at JPI by a well known mortgage banker, Holliday, Fenoglio, Dockerty and Gibson (Holliday Fenoglio). Mortgage bankers help developers to obtain financing by collecting information and preparing the kind of feasibility analysis that lenders require. Mortgage bankers usually work with a variety of lenders, though they sometimes have a special correspondent relationship with a particular financial institution. Fleet preferred to work directly with developers, but was willing to work with mortgage bankers as long as it was clear from the outset that the developer would cover the full cost of the mortgage banker's fee, which usually came to about 1% of the loan, and that Fleet would continue to have direct access to the developer.

In early 1993, Holliday Fenoglio began sending Tom preliminary deal packages, to see if Fleet was interested in financing one of JPI's apartment projects. Tom reviewed several proposals that looked interesting, especially a couple of apartment projects that had takeout commitments from General Electric Credit Corporation. Because of the strength of these takeouts, however, JPI wanted Fleet to finance 100% of the cost of these projects, which was contrary to Fleet's credit policy of requiring that developers invest equity equal to 10–20% of the total project cost.

Tom also saw a very interesting package on a JPI apartment project in Dallas. When he visited the site, however, he discovered that it was in one of those eclectic neighborhoods where it was hard to tell in which direction the neighborhood was headed. After giving it some careful consideration, he decided it was just too hard a location for an out of town lender to underwrite.

Finally, in November 1993, Holliday Fenoglio sent him a package about a 21.5 acre site just outside of the City of Austin. In his travels to Texas, Tom had been impressed with the Austin market. So after nearly a year of reviewing financing opportunities, he felt this might be just the right opportunity for Fleet to get into the Texas apartment market with a first class developer.

JPI MULTIFAMILY INC.

JPI was founded in 1989 by John Carpenter and Frank Miller who had worked together at Southland Financial. At Southland, they had done several large scale developments in Las Colinas, Texas, including several thousand apartment units. When the real estate crash hit Texas, JPI found that their apartment projects held up better than any of their other real estate properties, so when they set up their own company they decided to focus exclusively on the development and management of luxury apartments.

In the real estate industry, JPI is known as a "merchant builder" meaning that they develop properties with the intention of selling rather than owning them. JPI tries to achieve at least a 150 basis point spread between the initial yield and current market capitalization rates. "To illustrate," JPI writes in their statement about their investment strategy, "the cap rates for institutional grade, apartment product ranges between 8% and 9% in today's top marketplaces. Accordingly, JPI is seeking development opportunities which provide a going-in cap-rate (or cash on cash return) of at least 10% on total project cost."

Since JPI was formed in 1989, they have developed approximately 2,800 apartment units and sold 1,640 apartments. This track record is in line with their investment strategy of targeting a "holding period for development projects of two to three years." They currently have eight projects with 2,700 units under construction, four of which are under agreement to be sold upon completion.

Nationsbank, Guaranty Federal Savings Bank (in Dallas), BankOne and General Electric Credit Corporation have provided most of the construction financing. Because of the volume of deals they are doing, JPI is currently looking for additional lenders because some of their existing lenders have reached the limit of the exposure they want with any one borrower.

FLEET BANK

Fleet Bank is the largest bank in New England with over $45 billion in assets and about 10% market share (measured by deposits). Initially Rhode Island based, it has grown rapidly through acquisitions, the two biggest being the merger with Norstar Bank in 1987 and the acquisition from the FDIC of the Bank of New England in 1991.

When Tom Freeman joined Fleet in 1991 to head up its commercial real estate department, he inherited a real estate portfolio in which 75% of the loans were under $500,000. While Tom acknowledged the importance of serving local credit needs, he knew that small loans were very expensive to originate and manage, and that they had a higher delinquency rate during an economic downturn than the rest of the portfolio.

Because Fleet's capital base was stronger than many of its competitors, Tom was able to convince top management to continue making real estate loans even in the early 1990s when the market crashed in New England. As a result, Fleet had the opportunity to develop relationships with some of the top developers in the country.

For 1994, Tom set the following goals for the commercial real estate division:

- Originate and close $1.5 billion of new loans (which would essentially replace loans that were being paid off) and maintain an overall commercial real estate portfolio of about $4.3 billion.
- Reduce concentration in the franchise geographic area (i.e., New England and New York) from 75% to 60% over the next four years.
- Improve credit quality through focused calling on well capitalized, experienced developers and by financing leased properties to credit worthy tenants like K-Mart and Rite-Aid.
- Increase average loan size in the portfolio.
- Be a preeminent national provider of real estate financial services.
- Meet or exceed corporate financial targets (Return on Assets, Return on Equity).

THE MILLEGAN CREEK PROJECT

The Millegan Creek site is located in Williamston County, adjacent to the city limits of Austin and approximately 11 miles northwest of the central business district (see **Exhibit 1**). The site is an irregular, rectangular shape consisting of about 21.5 acres, with 904 feet of frontage along McNeil Road (see **Exhibit 2**). The site is level with no significant subsurface rock, which would create construction problems. A fifty foot utility easement divides the site, but can be paved over and used for parking. All utilities including electric, gas, water, sewer, telephone and cable are available to the site.

For JPI this site would be their third apartment development in Austin. According to David Ward, a former employee of Southland Financial and JPI's Austin Partner, JPI had begun to seriously investigate the Austin apartment market in 1991. At that time the market showed excellent potential in terms of population and job growth, but the rents were too low to justify new construction. Over the next year, however, JPI did an extensive survey of the whole city for sites that could accommodate at least 200–300 units at a density of about 17–18 units per acre.

They purchased their first site in early 1992, which was a "trophy property" on a hilltop in the Southwest part town with great views of downtown Austin. It took a major effort to get the site rezoned and permitted, but by February 1993, they were able to start construction on this 210 unit project. According to David Ward, lease-up of the first units in this development was currently underway and going very well.

The second property JPI purchased in Austin was located in the North Central area. It was acquired shortly after the start of construction on the first project. Construction on this second 342 unit property started in September 1993 with leasing scheduled to begin in May 1994.

In April 1993, JPI began to look for a site in Northwest Austin because of the employment growth taking place in the area. They also noted that the apartment complexes on Jollyville Road in this section of Austin had performed better than most of the other apartments in Austin during the downturn in the mid-1980s. JPI found, however, that there were only three good sites left on Jollyville Road and that those sites were very expensive.

Rather than go to an established multifamily location, David Ward and JPI began to consider the area to the North of Jollyville Road and outside of the Austin City limits. Parmer Lane had recently been expanded from a two lane to a six lane road and provided excellent north–south access. McNeil Road brought about 15,000 cars in an east west direction past the site each day and had recently been upgraded from a two lane to a five lane road. McNeil Road was currently being extended three miles to connect to Wells Branch Parkway.

In the summer of 1993, when JPI began to investigate this site on the corner of McNeil Road and Los Indios trail, they contacted Texas Commerce Bank (TCB), which had foreclosed on it in the late 1980s. Because it was outside the City of Austin, JPI knew that the property taxes would be lower and zoning approval would be easier. After some intense negotiations, JPI offered TCB $1,425,000 which equated to $3,654 per unit for the 390 units they planned to build. As part of the purchase and sales agreement, TCB agreed to provide $805,000 of financing for two years. Based on this land price and the lower real estate taxes, JPI believed they would be able to charge $75 per unit, per month less than any comparable, new development on Jollyville Road.

JPI also felt this site would work well because it was close to many of Austin's high tech companies. Texas Instruments has a big campus located across the street. Others in the area included: Abbott Laboratories, Tandem Computers, 3 M, and State Farm Insurance. Apple Computer had also announced plans to build a new, $28 million, 300,000 square foot facility, to house its U.S. Customer Support Center three quarters of a mile east of the site on Parmer Lane.

THE AUSTIN ECONOMY

In describing the City of Austin people tend to use superlatives. Despite its relatively small size of about a half million people and an SMSA of about 880,000, Austin often ranks near the top of the list of the most desirable cities in which to locate businesses. For example:

- In November 1993, Fortune ranked Austin 5th on its list of the 10 best cities for Knowledge workers.
- In November 1993, Austin ranked No. 1 in the U.S. for economic growth over the last three years with a 12.2% growth rate.
- In October 1993, Entrepreneur magazine ranked Austin among the top twenty cities in which to locate a business.
- In October 1993, Ernst and Young ranked Austin 6th in the nation as a preferred location for a new manufacturing facility.

The foundation of the Austin economy has always been universities and government. There are four colleges located within the Austin City limits with a population of over 100,000 students. About half the students are enrolled at the University of Texas which consistently ranks second to Harvard in the number of National Merit Scholars admitted. As the State Capital, Austin has a government workforce of over 110,000 including State, county and city employees. Between 1992 and 1993, the government sector added another 3,000 jobs.

In recent years, Austin has developed a strong base of high technology companies. Companies are attracted to Austin by the presence of university based research and its very desirable climate (an average temperature of 68 degrees and mild winters that average 60 degrees). In 1988 Sematech, a consortium comprised of 14 major high tech companies, chose Austin over 134 competing cities and now employs 725 workers. Similarly, in the Spring of 1992, Apple Computer, IBM and Motorola leased 68,000 feet to begin their joint venture to create a compatible personal computer system. Advanced Micro Devices and Motorola had also announced that each one was going to build a new plant that could manufacture $1 billion worth of chips each year. A partial listing of the largest, private sector employers in Austin includes: Motorola Inc. (8,000 employees), IBM (7,100 employees), Dell Computer (Headquarters and 3,878 employees), Advanced Micro Devices (2,500 employees) and Texas Instruments (1,850 employees).

Another important feature of the Austin economy is its very active community of environmentalists. In May, 1990, partly due to their efforts, the U.S. Fish and Wildlife Service declared a number of species of birds, insects and plants as endangered species including the Toothed Cave Beetle, the Pseudoscorpion, the "golden cheeked" warbler and the "black capped" vireo. In 1992, the voters in the City of Austin approved a $22 million bond offering to purchase 11,725 acres as a nature preserve.

Many developers have had their project held up by environmental concerns. For example, each site must be carefully inspected to see if a rare species of flower, the Bracted Twist Flower, is located on their site. This inspection is difficult because the Bracted Twist Flower only blooms in April. Another major expense was dealing with the rules related to the treatment of rainwater and rules about replacing the trees that are cut down during development with similar, caliber inches of new trees. On the Millegan Creek site, there are some cracks in the ground known as Karst Caves, and as a result, two acres must remain as wooded, undeveloped land.

THE APARTMENT MARKET

As can be seen on the chart below, the Austin Apartment market has gone through significant ups and downs over the last twelve years. Between 1986 and 1987, the market bottomed out with a drop in occupancy and rents. Since 1989, the market has improved rapidly, and the last three years have been very strong.

Table A   The Austin Apartment Market

YEAR	OCCUPANCY/%	RENTS/SF/MO	# OF UNITS CONSTRUCTED	APT. AS % OF TOTAL RES. STARTS
1982	95.9	$0.54	2,228	N/A
1983	93.9	0.56	6,058	N/A
1984	92.2	0.57	15,100	64
1985	90.0	0.59	9,094	62
1986	83.1	0.56	8,637	63
1987	86.3	0.48	2,088	47
1988	91.6	0.48	512	20
1989	94.4	0.49	0	0
1990	95.0	0.55	0	0
1991	97.2	0.59	0	0
1992	99.1	0.64	148	3
1993	98.8	0.71	1,651	21

Source: Austin Insight Report, Dec. 1993.

According to the City of Austin, as of December 31, 1993, there were 2,064 apartments under construction, 1,037 units approved for construction and 5,643 units waiting for construction approval. For his worst case analysis, Tom assumed that over the next three years all of these units (8,744) would get built.

Tom also assumed that single family home building would continue to boom and that multifamily properties would be able to capture no more than the 28% of the market that it captured the last ten years. This 28% figure was also in line with the overall housing mix in Austin. In 1993, Austin had approximately 353,524 housing units, of which 97,450 were apartments.

Of the units under construction, 1,400 were in the Northwest part of the City where Millegan Creek is located. Part of the attraction of building in Northwest Austin is that in apartment complexes of over fifty units, the average rents are currently 10% higher than in the rest of Austin.

Another way to look at the apartment market is in terms of the demand for rental units. Even though no new units were being built in the early 1990s, people continued to move into Austin and rent apartments. The following information from Grubb and Ellis shows the absorption of apartment units between 1989 and 1993.

Table B   Austin Apartment Absorption

YEAR	ABSORPTION (APPROX. # OF UNITS)
1989	2,833
1990	2,235
1991	1,151
1992	1,256
1993 (estimated)	1,700

In order to predict the demand for new apartments, Tom Hayden also wanted to carefully analyze recent population growth in Austin. Since 1989, Austin had experienced significant population growth and local economists expected these trends to continue. To convert these raw, population numbers into a more useful form, Tom assumed the average family size would continue to be about 2.43 people per household.

YEAR	POPULATION
1987	745,901
1988	748,397
1989	756,895
1990	781,575
1991	805,801
1992	830,779
1993*	856,532
1994*	883,087
1995*	913,998

*Estimates and Projections

Source: U.S. Census Bureau and Austin Insight Report.

Finally, Tom felt that the strength of the apartment market would be heavily dependent upon continued growth in the local job market. As of September 1993, Austin's employment totalled 425,800 and its unemployment rate was at about 4.5%. Over the last two years Austin had added almost 30,000 jobs (15,500 in 1992 and 13,300 in 1993). The Texas Comptroller of Public Accounts projected job growth for the next two years to continue in the 3% to 3.2% range. (See **Exhibit 3** for additional statistical information about the apartment market and employment characteristics.)

THE PRODUCT

In addition to developing apartments, JPI Multifamily currently manages about 10,000 apartment units. Based on their experience and periodic surveys of their residents, JPI tries to continually refine and improve their buildings and amenity packages.

Jefferson at Millegan Creek Apartments (Millegan Creek) would be a typical, JPI, luxury apartment complex. According to David Ward, the apartments would target renters with high discretionary incomes who could probably afford a single family home, but had made a lifestyle choice to live in rental apartments. That lifestyle choice might be because: the renter had just moved to Austin, was recently divorced, was single, wanted to save for a downpayment, or liked the freedom and amenities of apartment living.

Site amenities included two swimming pools, a clubhouse, fitness center with sauna and steam rooms, and laundry facilities (see **Exhibit 4**). Over time, JPI found that they were better off building a small club room and "jazzing it up with nice art work, a big fireplace and a large TV." They had also found that it was a good idea to create a big exercise room, because 50–60% of the renters they surveyed considered this amenity "very important." David Ward noted, parenthetically, that only 10% of the renters actually used the exercise room on a regular basis.

Standard features in each apartment included nine foot ceilings which gave a sense of spaciousness that "could not be matched by adding an extra foot of width to each room." Also, standard with each apartment was: a security system, crown molding and upgraded white on white appliances (**Exhibit 5** shows three typical apartment layouts).

JPI found that they could get a premium on optional amenities if they limited their availability. Thus, they created 160 detached and in-line garages so that only 40% of the renters could have them. They planned to charge an extra $70 per month for each garage. Similarly, they charged a premium for the one third of the units that had fireplaces and the one third that had vaulted ceilings.

THE NEGOTIATIONS

When Tom Hayden received the preliminary package on Millegan Creek, he realized that he would have to act quickly. JPI's standard practice was to go to at least three banks with each deal and see which one offered the most favorable financing. Knowing the general characteristics of the apartment market in Austin, having a general sense of the location, and being aware of JPI's reputation for quality, gave Tom confidence that this might be a good project. Using the preliminary package and his knowledge of the market, he plugged numbers into his computer using a sophisticated real estate modeling program called ARGUS which generates a discounted cash flow projection and an internal valuation. A quick analysis of these numbers showed that if all the assumptions checked out, Tom would have a project that fit Fleet's underwriting parameters.

Tom then arranged to meet with the borrower and the mortgage banker. In this meeting with JPI, Tom made it clear that they should work out the business terms directly before bringing in the lawyers. As David Ward, of JPI recalled, he had expected Fleet to hire a "hardball lawyer" who would draft an agreement with "about 5,000 things" that everyone knew would have to be taken out. So he was pleased by Tom's approach of "let's cut out the B.S. and the giant legal fees."

Following their meeting, on November 30, 1993, Tom put together a six page letter outlining the "Terms and Conditions" on which Fleet would make this loan. Tom made clear several times in the letter that, "This Summary of Terms and Conditions is not a commitment to lend, either express or implied." But the letter did set forth a framework, enabling JPI to evaluate whether they were interested in pursuing the loan.

To move the process forward, Fleet required that JPI sign the "Terms and Conditions" letter and send a $20,000 deposit which would be refundable (less Fleet's costs and expenses) if Fleet did not "approve the loan substantially under the terms of the letter." Upon receiving the deposit, Fleet promised to order an appraisal and "commence our full due diligence."

As Tom expected, David Ward responded to this letter with a number of comments aimed at reducing JPI's costs and/or improving its flexibility. David requested that Fleet: drop its interest rate by half a percent (0.5%), reduce the commitment fee by a quarter of a percent (0.25%), extend the loan from 24 months to 36 months, raise the loan to value ratio from 75% to 80% and reduce the debt coverage ratio from 1.25 to 1.1. These were all points that Tom expected to negotiate.

One thing that surprised Tom, however, was that JPI wanted Fleet to reduce the amount of its loan commitment from $16,250,000 to $15,715,000. In the past, a developer would never ask for less money. In this case, however, JPI was required to provide equity equal to approximately 20% of the total development cost, and all but $750,000 of that equity had to be cash which had to be invested in the project before Fleet would fund any of its loan. Thus, as JPI grew confident that construction costs could be kept in line, they recalculated their development budget and reduced their loan request.

On December 16, Tom sent a follow-up letter responding to JPI's comments. In some cases, Fleet agreed to JPI's requests such as reducing the amount of the loan and the amount of the commitment fee. In other cases, they offered a compromise by, for example, increasing the term of the loan from twenty four months to thirty months, rather than thirty six months requested. In some cases, Fleet held firm, such as the requirements that there be a 75% loan to value ratio, and 1.25 debt coverage ratio.[1]

Clearly, the two sides were getting close, but the negotiations continued through the holiday season. JPI was concerned about the amount of control Fleet would exercise and wanted more flexibility to shift line items in the budget and to make change orders without Fleet's permission (so long as the overall budget stayed in balance). JPI also wanted a lower interest rate. Finally, at the end of December, the two sides reached a middle ground. Fleet would allow changes in the construction budget of up to $50,000 individually and $150,000 cumulatively "without its prior written consent." Fleet also agreed to drop its loan rate by one quarter of a percent (0.25%). On January 14, JPI sent back a signed copy of the revised "Terms and Conditions" letter and a $20,000 "application fee."

---

[1]Although Fleet's loan would be made at a floating rate based on **LIBOR** or Prime, to calculate the debt coverage ratio, Tom assumed that in 30 months the property would be 95% rented and a permanent fixed-rate loan with a 10-year term, a 25-year amortization schedule and an 8% interest rate would be available. These rates and terms were currently available from a number of major insurance companies.

DUE DILIGENCE

For the rest of January and February, Tom filled his due diligence notebook with 200 pages of material, documenting his assumptions about the sponsor, the location and the market. Working with JPI, the appraiser, and the mortgage banker, Tom came up with a list of comparable properties (see **Exhibit 6**) that he thought provided justification for the level of rents that JPI was projecting. He also tore apart the deal and put it back together and requested that JPI revise their numbers until he had a project budget (see **Exhibit 7**) and a pro-forma income statement (see **Exhibit 8**) that he felt comfortable presenting to the credit committee.

Because this loan did not have a takeout, Tom also investigated who was buying apartment properties. The most active players were the large, institutional investors like Metropolitan Life, Prudential, General Electric Pension Trust and the big California Pension funds. His investigations confirmed that these institutional buyers were currently paying cap rates in the 8–9% range. REITs were also active in the apartment market, but they tended to buy apartments that were older and provided a higher yield (9–10%). Tom also looked at the mortgage market for take-out and permanent loans. He found that a number of major insurance companies were actively making permanent loans on multifamily, residential properties once the properties were completed and leased.

During this time, JPI continued its development work: securing permits, negotiating construction contracts and pushing the architects to complete the plans. They also continued to work with a series of consultants who helped them identify and address issues related to: environmental concerns, traffic access, fire control access, utilities, groundwater, drainage, plantings and geotechnical issues. They kept in regular communication with Tom to make sure everything was moving along at his end.

THE MEETING

As Tom prepared for his meeting with Joanne McClatchy, he tried to anticipate her concerns. With a new borrower, Tom knew that Joanne would be particularly interested in their track record and character. Although the borrower would technically be a single purpose, limited partnership, Tom had secured guarantees from the three principals of JPI (see **Exhibit 9**). Joanne would also want to know about JPI's financial capability, its contingent liabilities and other financial risks of the sponsor.

Tom also thought he should be prepared to address the construction risk. Because it was a flat site and an experienced developer Tom did not see any unusual issues. The bank would, however, require full engineering and environmental reports prior to closing to confirm that the site was clean and had no unusual impediments to building. Second, he had begun negotiations with a well regarded construction consultant from Dallas who, if the loan was approved, would review the plans and then inspect the site on a monthly basis to be sure that all construction work was satisfactorily completed before Fleet paid each requisition. Thirdly, Tom would also insist that the construction contractor be fully bonded, so that if it got in trouble, the bonding company would provide the money to complete the project.

A third concern Tom was sure that Joanne would raise was: How well is the bank protected against increases in interest rates? What would happen if interest rates rose 1% or 2% during the next thirty months while the project was in development? Was there a reasonable interest reserve built in to the project budget?

Finally, Tom anticipated a sharply focused discussion about the real estate. Joanne had a unique position in that she reported to both the head of commercial real estate (Tom Freeman) and the head of credit for Fleet Financial Corporation. This position allowed her to be more objective, and less concerned about achieving the real estate department's volume goals. Thus, Joanne would expect Tom to provide a detailed analysis of the property and the market. Especially with no takeout commitment, Fleet's chances of getting repaid rested in large measure on how the property and market performed. And if Fleet bank made the loan, it would be based on Tom's judgment that this property would perform well.

Exhibit 1

N ↓

Exhibit 2 Carports

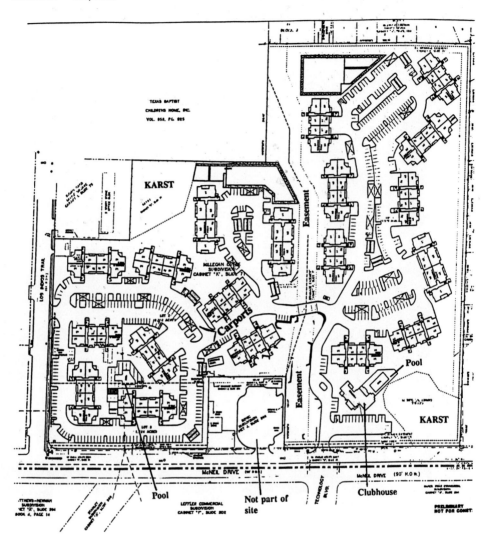

Exhibit 3   Pop-Facts: Full Data Report by National Decision Systems
Prepared for Holliday, Fenoglio, Dockerty and Gibson based on 1990 Census Data
Site: McNeil Road and Technology Blvd., Austin, Texas

DESCRIPTION	1.0 MILE RADIUS	3.0 MILE RADIUS	5.0 MILE RADIUS
Occupied Units	3905	21132	41690
Owner Occupied	47.72%	52.83%	52.22%
Renter Occupied	52.28%	47.17%	47.78%
1990 Persons Per Household	2.34	2.50	2.45
1994 Estimated Households by Income	4666	24567	47966
$150,000 +	1.96%	1.57%	1.74%
$100,000 to $149,999	3.30%	5.59%	5.59%
$ 75,000 to $ 99,999	9.22%	11.24%	10.18%
$ 50,000 to $ 74,999	25.00%	23.79%	22.70%
$ 35,000 to $ 49,000	18.02%	19.79%	20.17%
$ 25,000 to $ 34,999	14.58%	14.02%	14.64%
$ 15,000 to $ 24,999	15.01%	12.80%	13.33%
$ 5,000 to $ 14,999	9.83%	9.14%	9.55%
Under $5,000	3.07%	2.05%	2.10%
1993 Estimated Average HH Income	$48,329	$51,371	$50,634
1993 Estimated Median HH Income	$41,619	$45,428	$44,332
1993 Estimated Per Capita Income	$21,749	$21,182	$21,256
Marital Status	7010	40647	79339
Single Male	12.85%	13.02%	14.03%
Single Female	12.48%	11.28%	11.78%
Married	58.24%	60.75%	59.01%
Previously Married Male	5.80%	5.10%	5.25%
Previously Married Female	10.64%	9.85%	9.93%
Median Age	30.08	31.79	32.04
Average Age	29.71	30.84	31.04
Population 16+ by Occupation	5507	30844	60433
Executive and Managerial	20.58%	21.63%	20.76%
Professional Specialty	19.62%	20.94%	20.90%
Technical Support	10.02%	8.15%	7.65%
Sales	14.68%	15.02%	13.84%
Administrative Support	16.78%	17.25%	17.42%
Other	8.75%	7.29%	7.61%
Precision Production & Craft	4.85%	5.22%	6.09%
Machine Operator	2.40%	2.05%	2.74%
Transportation & Material Moving	0.88%	1.07%	1.44%
Laborers	1.44%	1.39%	1.56%

Exhibit 3   (continued)

DESCRIPTION	1.0 MILE RADIUS	3.0 MILE RADIUS	5.0 MILE RADIUS
Families by Number of Workers	2391	14226	27312
No Workers	3.10%	4.17%	4.08%
One Worker	26.87%	25.53%	25.42%
Two Workers	58.93%	58.66%	59.09%
Three + Workers	11.10%	11.64%	11.41%
Population by Transportation to Work	5435	30534	59981
Drive Alone	85.67%	84.61%	84.46%
Car Pool	9.13%	9.71%	10.07%
Public Transportation	1.21%	0.95%	0.98%
Motorcycle	0.08%	0.19%	0.28%
Walked only	1.59%	1.23%	1.09%
Other Means	0.41%	0.45%	0.52%
Worked at Home	1.90%	2.85%	2.60%
Population by Travel Time to Work	5435	30534	59981
Under 10 minutes	12.06%	14.12%	14.54%
10 to 29 minutes	56.84%	56.07%	59.14%
30 to 59 minutes	28.30%	27.26%	23.99%
60 to 89 minutes	1.08%	1.26%	1.15%
90+ Minutes	1.73%	1.29%	1.18%
Average Travel Time in Minutes	22.31	21.45	20.62
Median Property Value	$87,502	$98,947	$97,647
Total Rental Units	2004	9783	19558
Median Rent	$413	$420	$417
Persons in Unit	3905	21132	41690
1 Person	32.49%	26.49%	28.11%
2 Persons	29.99%	30.93%	31.46%
3 Persons	17.47%	18.62%	17.76%
4 Persons	13.65%	16.44%	15.36%
5+ Persons	6.40%	7.52%	7.30%
Housing Units by Year Built	3939	21306	41768
Built 1989 to March 1990	2.85%	2.05%	1.74%
Built 1985 to 1988	56.27%	27.10%	28.02%
Built 1980 to 1984	23.83%	38.66%	37.73%
Built 1970 to 1979	15.63%	29.53%	28.31%
Built 1960 to 1969	1.41%	2.16%	3.68%
Built 1950 to 1959	0.00%	0.15%	0.27%
Built 1940 to 1949	0.00%	0.20%	0.12%
Built 1939 or Earlier	0.00%	0.15%	0.13%

Exhibit 4   The Improvements

The Millegan Creek Apartment project includes 390 apartment units housed in two- and three-story walk-up, garden style apartment buildings. Other improvements to the site include: an office/clubhouse facility with fitness center; laundry facilities; two swimming pools; detached and in-line garages accommodating 160 vehicles; carports for 80 vehicles; open concrete parking for 450 vehicles; and concrete driveways and walkways. The total site contains 21.497 acres of land which results in a project density of 18.14 units per acre. The following is a summary of the physical characteristics of the subject property.

General:

Gross Building Area:	340,046 SF
Net Rentable Area:	336,094 SF
Average Unit Size:	862 square feet (Net Rentable Area)

Structure:

Foundation:	Steel reinforced concrete slab on compacted fill and concrete footings
Frame:	Wood frame
Floors:	Lightweight concrete second level decking and balconies
Exterior Walls:	Stucco
Roofing:	Pitched with composition shingles
Doors:	Metal hollow core exterior doors, wood hollow core interior doors
Windows:	Tinted, single-hung aluminum
HVAC:	All electric individual heating and cooling units
Hot Water:	Individual water heaters—Assumed to be gas

Interior:

Flooring:	Carpet and padding in living areas and bedrooms, vinyl tile in kitchen and bath areas; ceramic tile entry
Walls:	Standard drywall, textured and painted, with some wallpaper; Crown molding in the living and dining areas
Ceilings:	Nine foot ceilings with vaulted ceilings on the third floor
Other Features:	Special features of the units include typical kitchen package with microwave ovens, frost-free refrigerators with ice-makers, mini-blinds, ceiling fans, wired for master antenna T.V., wired for intrusion alarms, and washer/dryer connections. Some units have fireplaces.

Exhibit 5

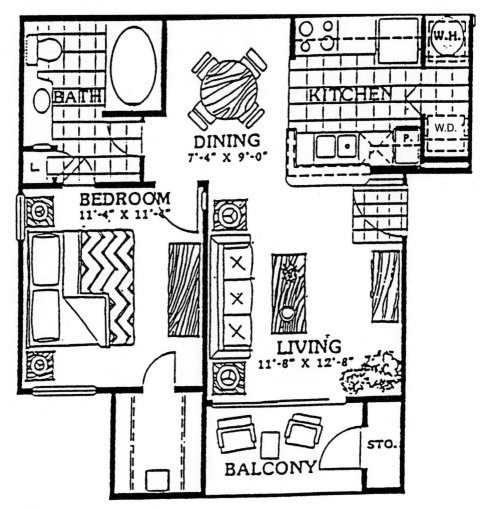

DINING
7'-4" X 9'-0"

KITCHEN

W.H.

W.D.

P.

BEDROOM
11'-4" X 11'-8"

LIVING
11'-8" X 12'-8"

BALCONY

STO.

ONE BEDROOM/ONE BATH 602 S.F.

*W.H. = Water Heater; W.D. = Washer/Dryer

Exhibit 5   (continued)

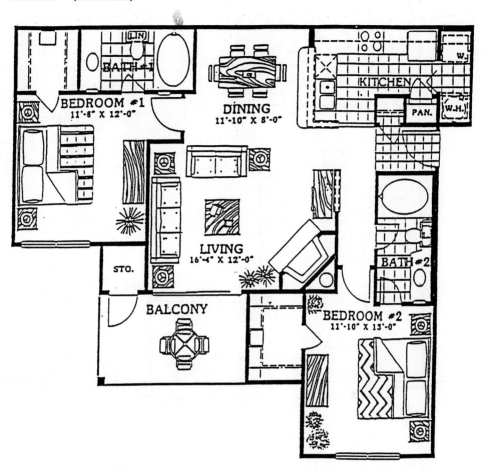

Exhibit 5   (continued)

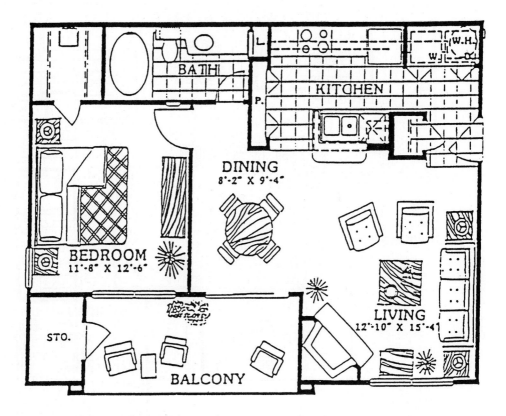

Exhibit 6

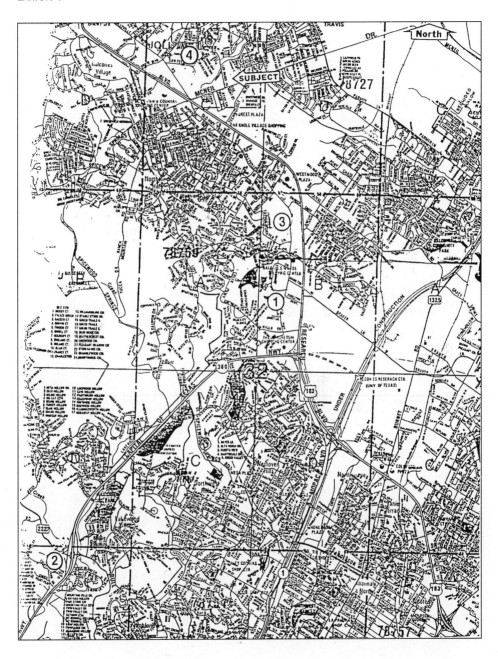

Exhibit 6   (continued)

COMPARABLE RENTAL NO. 1

Project Name:	Hard Rock Canyon
Location:	10100 Jollyville Road
Number of Units:	246
Year of Construction:	1993
Net Rentable Area:	236,406 square feet
Average Unit Size:	961 square feet
Reported Occupancy:	96%
Average Rent/SF/Month:	$0.860
Project Amenities:	An office/clubhouse, swimming and volleyball pools, controlled access gates, exercise room, enclosed garages, and covered parking.
Unit Features:	Full kitchen appliance package including frost-free refrigerators with icemakers, gas ranges, microwave ovens, fireplaces, nine foot ceilings, crown molding, mini-blinds, ceiling fans, washer/dryer connections, tile entry, patio/balcony, alarm systems.
Lease Term:	6 months – 1 year
Concessions:	None known

Unit Mix & Rents:

NO. UNITS	PLAN TYPE	SIZE (SF)	NO. RENT	NO. RENT/SF
N/A	1 Bed/1 Ba	744	$650	$0.87
N/A	1 Bed/1 Ba	763	$675	$0.88
N/A	1 Bed/1 Ba	854	$750	$0.88
N/A	1 Bed/2 Ba	999	$860	$0.86
N/A	2 Bed/2 Ba	1071	$895	$0.84
N/A	2 Bed/2 Ba	1081	$900	$0.83
N/A	2 Bed/2 Ba	1170	$935	$0.80
N/A	2 Bed/2 Ba	1483	$1,350	$0.91

Comments: This property is the same property as Improved Comparable No. 1. It is very similar in terms of age, quality, and location. The apartment manager would not disclose the unit mix. The appraisers have assumed based upon the average unit size that the units with 999 square feet are the most numerous with the number of particular types decreasing as the NRA's move away from average unit size. Consequently, an overall rental rate of $0.86 per square foot per month

Exhibit 6   (continued)

COMPARABLE RENTAL NO. 2

Project Name:	Monte Vista Apartments
Location:	6000 Shepherd Mountain Cove
Number of Units:	348
Year of Construction:	1992
Net Rentable Area:	299,690 square feet
Average Unit Size:	861 Square feet
Reported Occupancy:	94%
Average Rent/SF/Month:	$0.905
Project Amenities:	Two swimming pools w/Jacuzzi, exercise room, clubhouse with business equipment, volleyball court, enclosed garages and open carports, and laundry facilities.
Unit Features:	Full kitchen appliance package including frost-free refrigerators w/icemakers, microwave ovens, mini-blinds, ceiling fans, washer/dryer connections, cable television, and a patio/balcony.
Lease Term:	6 months – 1 year
Concessions:	None

Unit Mix & Rents:

NO. UNITS	PLAN TYPE	SIZE (SF)	NO. RENT	NO. RENT/SF
88	1 Bed/1 Ba	650	$615	$0.95
94	1 Bed/1 Ba	752	$695	$0.92
36	1 Bed/1 Ba	868	$800	$0.92
48	1 Bed/2 Ba	985	$850	$0.86
46	2 Bed/2 Ba	1069	$945	$0.88
36	2 Bed/2 Ba	1075	$1,095	$0.89

Comments: This apartment community is located south of the subject, but still in the northwest submarket. This project is situated on a hillside with a view overlooking western Austin which is considered to enhance its market appeal. The property was considered to be in good condition and is regarded as a Class A apartment property. Rental rates depicted above are typical base amounts, however, additional amenities (i.e., washer/dryer units, etc.) are also available for an added monthly charge.

Exhibit 6   (continued)

COMPARABLE RENTAL NO. 3

Project Name:	La Mirage
Location:	11400 Jollyville Road
Number of Units:	348 total; 152 complete
Year of Construction:	1994
Net Rentable Area:	295,232 square feet total
	128,951 square feet completed
Average Unit Size:	848 Square feet
Reported Occupancy:	34% based upon total units, completed and proposed;
	69% based upon completed and leasable units
Average Rent/SF/Month:	$0.813
Project Amenities:	Swimming pool, office/clubhouse, controlled access entry, laundry facilities, garages and carports.
Unit Features:	Full kitchen appliance package including frost-free refrigerators w/ice-makers, microwave ovens, mini-blinds, woodburning fireplaces, walk-in closets, ceiling fans, washer/dryer connections, tile entry, patio/balcony, alarm systems.
Lease Term:	6 months – 1 year
Concessions:	None
Unit Mix & Rents:	

NO. UNITS	PLAN TYPE	SIZE (SF)	MO. RENT	NO. RENT/SF
128	1 Bed/1 Ba	706	$585	$0.83
188	2 Bed/2 Ba	904	$725	$0.80
32	3 Bed/2 Ba	1091	$900	$0.82

Comments: This project is located along the west line of Jollyville Road approximately 2 miles southwest of the subject property. This is a Class A apartment community and which is still under construction and has been leasing since the last week in November. It is considered to be in very similar to the subject in terms of quality and location.

Exhibit 6   (continued)

COMPARABLE RENTAL NO. 4

Project Name:	Martha's Vineyard
Location:	7920 San Felipe, Austin
Number of Units:	360
Year of Construction:	1986
Net Rentable Area:	253,012 square feet
Average Unit Size:	703 Square feet
Reported Occupancy:	97%
Average Rent/SF/Month:	$0.838
Project Amenities:	Swimming pool, Jacuzzi, tennis court, office/clubhouse, gym, tanning beds, free aerobics, dry sauna, and laundry facilities.
Unit Features:	Full kitchen appliance package including frost-free refrigerators w/icemakers, walk-in closets, mini-blinds, ceiling fans, washer/dryer connections, basic cable television, patio/balcony.
Lease Term:	6 months – 1 year
Concessions:	None
Unit Mix & Rents:	

NO. UNITS	PLAN TYPE	SIZE (SF)	NO. RENT	NO. RENT/SF
40	1 Bed/1 Ba	432	$430	$1.00
72	1 Bed/1 Ba	533	$480	$0.90
48	1 Bed/1 Ba	646	$540	$0.84
32	1 Bed/1 Ba	736	$590	$0.80
24	1 Bed/1 Ba	740	$600	$0.81
28	1 Bed/1 Ba	827	$630	$0.76
32	1 Bed/1 Ba/Den	798	$660	$0.83
32	1 Bed/1 Ba/Den	885	$705	$0.80
28	2 Bed/2 Ba	1014	$775	$0.76
24	2 Bed/2 Ba	1125	$825	$0.73

Comments: This complex is located only approximately 1/4 mile from the subject. It is older than the subject but is similar in that it provides numerous interior and exterior amenities.

Exhibit 7   Jefferson at Millegan Creek Development Budget

DEVELOPMENT ITEM	TOTAL	EQUITY	DEBT
Land Cost	$ 1,425,000	$ 1,425,000	
Site Work	2,238,750	1,756,000	482,750
Construction	12,717,250		12,717,250
Contingency	598,000		598,000
Ad Valorem Taxes	36,000		36,000
Architect/Engineering	261,000		261,000
Financing	157,150		157,150
Legal Expenses	183,850		183,850
Furniture & Fixtures	135,000		135,000
Interest Reserve*	420,000		420,000
Marketing	75,000		75,000
Operating Deficit	502,000		502,000
Overhead/Administrative	748,000	748,000	
Pre-Development	50,000		50,000
Title & Other	97,000		97,000
TOTAL	$19,644,000	$3,929,000	$15,715,000

*Assumes an interest rate during construction and lease-up of 8.5%.

Exhibit 8   Pro-Forma Income Statement

Rental Income (336,094 sf @ $.83/psf per month)*	$3,344,697
Other Income	
Garages (160 @ $75/month)	144,000
Carports (98 @ $20/month)	23,520
Other ($9/unit/month)	<u>42,336</u>
Total Potential Gross Revenue	$3,554,553
General Vacancy (7%)	<u>$(248,819)</u>
Effective Gross Revenue	$3,305,734

Operating Expenses		
Administrative	$.08/sf	$26,888
Repairs/Maintenance	.40/sf	134,438
Marketing	.13/sf	40,331
Salaries	.76/sf	255,431
Utilities	.32/sf	107,550
Taxes	1.42/sf	477,253
Insurance	.10/sf	33,609
Management	4%	<u>134,438</u>
Total Operating Expenses		$1,209,938
Net Operating Income		$2,095,796
Leasing & Capital Costs		
Structural Reserve	.10/sf	$ 33,609
Replacement Reserve	$200/unit	<u>78,000</u>
Total Expenses		<u>$1,321,547</u>
Cash Flow Before Debt Service		$1,984,187

Loan Amount	**Int. Rate**	**Amortization**	**Debt Service**
$15,715,000	9%	25 years	$1,582,557
$15,715,000	8%	25 years	$1,455,491

*

DESCRIPTION	# OF UNITS	BASE/SF	BASE RENT/MO.	RENT/SF/MO.
1 Bed/1 Ba	90	602	$535	$0.89
1 Bed/1 Ba	70	704	$601	$0.85
1 Bed/1 Ba	50	838	$705	$0.84
2 Bed/1 Ba	48	912	$745	$0.82
2 Bed/2 Ba	84	1,028	$830	$0.81
2 Bed/2 Ba	30	1,209	$951	$0.79
3 Bed/2 Ba	<u>18</u>	<u>1,352</u>	<u>$1,050</u>	<u>$0.78</u>
TOTAL	390	862	$714	$0.83

Exhibit 9   Excerpts from JPI Financial Information*
($ in millions, 9/30/93)

	ASSETS	NET WORTH	LIQ. ASSETS	NET CASH FLOW[4][5]	CONTINGENT LIABILITIES
JPI Investment Co.	54[1]	19	4.0	2.0	0
Partners[2]	12	8	1.0	0.2	100[3]
Total	$66	$27	$5.0	$2.2	$100

(1) The corporate assets consist almost exclusively of rental real estate ($23 million) and construction in progress ($18 million). The real estate is exclusively multi-family.

(2) Combined personal financial statements of the three guarantors who are the principals of JPI excluding their interest in JPI Investment Co.

(3) Of these Contingent Liabilities $64.5 million are covered by non-recourse permanent takeouts with General Electric Capital Corporation to be taken down upon issuance of certificate of occupancy. The value of the underlying real estate totals $114 million (cost basis).

(4) JPI anticipates that during the third quarter of 1994 it will receive profits from the sale of two of its properties (currently under Purchase and Sale Agreement) of $4 million. Should these multifamily sales fall through, the properties will generate a 1.22x debt coverage ratio if the construction loan is refinanced at current, long term, interest rates.

(5) After excluding gains on sales of rental real estate, losses in 1992 were reported at $3 million. Gains from sales were $3.6 million, resulting in positive cash flow of $.6 million.

*Numbers disguised for case purposes.

5

FAN PIER

In April 1989, plans for the development of Fan Pier, an ambitious mega-project on Boston's waterfront, have come to a halt as the result of: (1) a major fallout between the property owner and his development partners that in 1987 resulted in litigation and (2) a shift in the political climate that affected the approval process. Both the partners and the city officials have to decide what to do next. The case also presents the successful experience of a similar project, Battery Park City on Manhattan's waterfront, to highlight the overall public and private sector issues relating to large scale urban waterfront development.

Discussion Questions:

1. What were the goals of each of the players in forming this partnership? How would you evaluate the relationship of Athanas and HBC over the years?
2. Assess the approval process governing this megaproject.
3. What would you recommend be built on the site at this point in time? What might be the recommendation of a South Boston community leader, or the Director of the Boston Redevelopment Authority?
4. Compare the story of Fan Pier to that of Battery Park City. What lessons can be learned?

The Superior Court of the State of Massachusetts handed down its decision in the case of HBC v. Athanas on April 18, 1989. The decision did not decide the fate of the Fan Pier site on Boston Harbor in South Boston, but did deliver a strong opinion as to why the partnership collapsed, why the development stalled and where the fault lay. Judge Abrams ruled that the owner of the land comprising **Fan Pier**, Anthony Athanas, had unlawfully obstructed the efforts of his development partner, HBC Associates, headed by Richard Friedman, in obtaining the approvals necessary to build the $800 million mixed use project they had planned together. The extent of the damages would be determined by the trial starting in the fall of 1989 unless the feuding partners found another solution outside the courts.

The spectrum of potential outcomes from the trial was broad: the court could order that Athanas pay HBC amounts ranging from the $13 million HBC declared it had invested to date up to an amount equal to the net present value of the profits HBC had been denied through Athanas' actions, plus damages. Some guessed this number to be over $100 million. The court could also rule for "specific performance," requiring that HBC be permitted to develop the project as planned. Of course, Athanas could appeal any of these outcomes and delay satisfying any court-ordered reparations for years. Meanwhile, the site would continue to sit as vacant land.

Any new solution for the development of the site would have to take into account important changes which occurred in the development environment during the two-year litigation between the partners. First, both the first class office and residential condominium markets had softened significantly between 1987 and 1989. First class office vacancies had risen from 6 percent in 1987 to 10 percent in 1989 and were predicted to rise to 13 percent by 1991. The luxury condominium market stagnated after rapid rises in the early 1980s and was considered to be overbuilt. Secondly, the area in which Fan Pier was located fell under the guidelines of the Boston Redevelopment Authority's new master plan. It reduced the buildable square footage of the area by 30 percent and significantly downsized allowable heights. The master plan also included a lengthy community review and approval process for any development in the area.

Anthony Athanas was a 77 year old restaurateur who was badly disappointed by the stumble of the megaproject for which he had begun assembling parcels in the early 1960s. Richard Friedman, although happy to be vindicated by the

Research Assistant Katherine Sweetman prepared this case under the supervision of Adjunct Professor William J. Poorvu as the basis for class discussion rather than to illustrate either effective or ineffective handling of an administrative situation.

court ruling, was still frustrated by the uncertainty surrounding the ultimate outcome of the project. Each of the parties tried to consider what went wrong and what would be an appropriate strategy for the future. They were aware that another major development, Battery Park City, a megaproject on New York City's waterfront was reputed to be a great success (see **Exhibit 1**). Did it provide any lessons for Fan Pier?

FAN PIER DEVELOPMENT

Fan Pier is the collective name for Piers 1, 2 and 3 on the Boston Harbor in the Fort Point channel section of South Boston next to downtown Boston (see **Exhibits 2 and 3**). Fan Pier is comprised of 18.5 acres, of which 2.6 are underwater and therefore unbuildable. Fan Pier had once served an important maritime function, benefitting from New England's shipping and fishing industry and its own location near Boston's downtown. By the early 1960s, however, Boston's piers lay abandoned and in disrepair due to declines in the regional maritime economy. Boston itself was going through an economic slump with little office growth and considerable social unrest. Few, if any, other than Athanas saw much value in those piers in South Boston.

The history of the attempted development of the Fan Pier can be divided into three stages: 1) the land assemblage, the initial joint venture agreement, and the early plans under Mayor White's administration, 2) the reexamination of the plan under Mayor Flynn's administration, and 3) the breakdown of the joint venture agreement and the subsequent lawsuit.

THE INITIAL STAGES

In 1963, on the 16.4 acre Pier Four site, Anthony Athanas built Anthony's Pier Four, a large seafood restaurant. The site was so removed from the dinner circuit that Athanas inaugurated the restaurant by inviting all area taxi drivers to a gala opening. The restaurant was an immediate success and enjoyed many cabdriver referrals for years. He later assembled at favorable prices the various adjoining parcels that now comprise Fan Pier.

Although the land was purchased in the 1960s, it was not until the late 1970s that growth in downtown Boston was sufficient to justify development on the Fan Pier parcel. Initially, Athanas envisioned a large convention hotel which would spark a revitalization of the entire area and encourage a steady source of patrons for his restaurant business. In 1979, local Boston broker/developer Richard Friedman, head of Carpenter & Co., brought together his client, Hyatt Corporation, and Athanas. Athanas agreed to lease the Fan Pier site and grant certain development rights to a Hyatt and Carpenter joint venture partnership named HBC.

The January 1981 agreement defined the roles. HBC would act as developer, hiring the master planning/architectural team and lawyers who would help the project through the approvals process. Athanas would retain rights of review on Fan Pier and the future development rights to the undeveloped portion of Pier Four.

The early plans were being made during the administration of Mayor Kevin White and reflected the optimism of an innovative development proposed to a pro-growth mayor. Most of the rest of the Boston waterfront had been redeveloped during White's tenure, and he helped to make the Fan Pier site economically feasible by more than doubling the permissible floor area ratio (FAR) from 2.0 to 4.2.

HBC proposed to develop the site in two parts over a ten year period (see **Exhibit 4**). The first would be a commercial development including at least one hotel of not less than 1,000 rooms. The commercial development would comprise at least 8 acres and be located on Northern Avenue frontage. The residential component would be at least 6 acres and would be developed slightly later. The 1981 Agreement set rent for the commercial ground lease at $90,000 per acre per year. The residential land would be sold to HBC for $1 million per acre.

In 1983, at Athanas' suggestion, HBC modified the original agreement and arranged to pay the restaurateur ten percent of HBC's share of net sales and net rental profits in addition to the land sale and ground lease amounts agreed upon in 1981. The Outside Closing Dates for construction to begin on the various phases were extended to June 30, 1988 and December 31, 1988.

The next step was to go through the approval process—city zoning, city planning, state environmental review and a buzzing confusion of other agencies who control the permits necessary for construction. The State of Massachusetts requested that both the Fan Pier and Pier Four projects be viewed together since the projects both involved Athanas and were closely linked physically and politically. After all, the surrounding neighborhood viewed the projects essentially as one. This requirement forced Athanas to hire an architect to prepare his own plan for Pier Four.

Despite strong community concerns, the project proceeded apace. In the fall of 1983, Cesar Pelli & Associates of New Haven was selected by HBC to design the hotel. Pelli's firm became master planner of the entire project in fall of 1984. Pelli had a large vision for Fan Pier which reflected his experience as the primary architect for the commercial portion of the Battery Park City development in Manhattan which was soon to open.

THE FLYNN YEARS

While Pelli busily sketched his plans, Boston elected a new mayor, Raymond Flynn, in 1984. Where White had been distinctly pro-development, Flynn had run on a political ticket promising to decentralize Boston, to give more power back to the individual neighborhoods, to listen to and empower people like those in South Boston. Most significantly, South Boston was Mayor Flynn's home base and greatest source of support.

Surrounding South Boston was a homogeneous, primarily Irish–American community with a strong tradition of extended families living within blocks of each other. Household incomes in South Boston were more modest than the average household income throughout the region as a whole. Even though South Boston had suffered during the recession of the 1970s, losing 16 percent of its workforce, the residents retained a strong loyalty to their homes. They feared that pier development would raise property values to the point where the neighborhood would become unaffordable to their own children.

Residents were also concerned about transportation issues. The influx of cars, buses and trucks would require complicated rerouting of transportation, construction of new roads, repairs to the Northern Avenue Bridge, perhaps an additional stop on the subway's Red Line. Nearby, at the edge of downtown, construction of a $4 billion underground roadway and new tunnel to the airport were expected to cause major congestion for the next 12 years regardless of what happened at Fan Pier.

Flynn and Stephen Coyle, the director of the Boston Redevelopment Authority, encouraged the formation of the Citizens Advisory Committee (CAC) to solicit input from the residents of abutting neighborhoods regarding development on Fan Pier. The agenda which emerged from the CAC included developer contributions toward affordable housing, guaranteed jobs for local residents, rent protection for members of the arts community currently located in the Fort Point Channel area, mandatory inclusion of harbor uses, and careful attention to transportation issues. Such requirements are known as "linkage payments" because they are public benefits directly linked to the approval of private development.

It was apparent that it was no longer Athanas and the BRA alone who would review HBC's project.

In April of 1985, Pelli unveiled his $800 million master plan (see **Exhibits 5 and 6**). The project encompassed a public waterfront park and a vast mixed use complex with an average FAR of 4.63:

LAND USE	GROSS SQ. FT.
Residential	834,000
Hotel (850 rooms)	854,000
Office	1,400,000
Retail	150,000
TOTAL	3,238,000

Pelli's ambitious concept featured a waterfront "island" to be formed by dredging a 90 foot wide "canal" strip inland. The island would house the hotel complex and three apartment buildings, each exceeding twenty stories. Two bridges from the island would extend to the office segment fronting on Northern Avenue. The hotel was especially controversial, a tall thin spire which some critics feared would permanently damage the Boston Harbor skyline. However, by connecting the project by bridges to the surrounding community, the architect tried to blunt criticism of the earlier master plan which was more focused internally.

One objection to the project was that its style, scope, density and height made Fan Pier an extension of the downtown highrises which had punctuated the Boston's modest skyline in recent years. The Pelli plan was considered by some insensitive to the low scale and low density of the existing South Boston neighborhoods. Pelli felt that the site plan and proposed buildings were an exciting use of urban space, where the public would be encouraged to use the waterfront and its walks.

In addition, Athanas' architects announced plans for his Pier Four site: a 300 room hotel, 750 apartments, a 55,000 square foot restaurant, 13,500 square feet of retail and a 1,500 car garage.

Between the two projects, the office space planned for Fan Pier and Pier Four was sufficient to absorb more than 40 percent of the new space needs predicted for downtown Boston in the near future. Negative press reinforced the neighborhood's fears about transportation issues. Owners of large neighboring parcels complained that the scale of Fan Pier would limit the potential development of their sites.

In December 1986, a Joint Draft Environmental Impact Statement for Fan Pier and Pier 4 was submitted by the developers to the State of Massachusetts. In January 1987, the South Boston community again voiced rising concern over the threat of traffic in its neighborhood. In February, the community became more organized and strident. Environmental, housing and civic groups urged rejection of the Fan Pier project by both city and state officials, primarily on the basis of height and density. Mayor Flynn made it clear that it would be the developer's job not only to satisfy the surrounding community, but also to pay the costs associated with meeting their linkage demands.

In February and March of 1987, the two projects were reviewed jointly by the BRA and the Boston Zoning Commission with Athanas' support. Both received the necessary first round approvals. In March, HBC offered $8 million in public benefits including off-site affordable housing to the community. To provide more variety, a number of well-known architects had been selected to design the individual buildings.

In April, HBC received BRA approval of the development plan with some reductions in size. But at the State level, after considerable political pressure, the environmental agency ruled that it needed more information, a declaration which essentially put the project on hold for six to nine months, until the end of 1987.

THE BREAKDOWN

Athanas was beginning to chafe under the constraints, and question the adequacy of his return from the project. A booming Boston economy pushed downtown real estate values higher every year in the mid 1980's, and Athanas felt that even the deal he had renegotiated in 1983 was insufficient. The vacancy rate for first class office space in Downtown Boston in 1987 was only 6 percent and rental rates seemed to increase daily. The residential condominium market was hot: the newest waterfront condominiums across the harbor next to downtown Boston sold in the million dollar range, about $500 per square foot.

From February through May of 1987, Athanas requested a new agreement from HBC in exchange for his continued cooperation during the approvals process. When HBC replied that the 1983 deal was firm, Athanas forcefully criticized the project on the eve of a critical public hearing and officially withdrew all support. He claimed that HBC had dragged its heels since 1981 and that it would not be able to meet the December 1988 deadline for start of construction. The restaurateur argued that he had been grievously harmed financially by the downscaling and delays.

Athanas' action compounded HBC's problems in meeting its obligatory Closing Date. Also as a consequence, two major downtown Boston law firms who had announced their intention to move to the project began to look elsewhere. The financial commitment from the Japanese bank which had agreed to participate in the project was put on hold at least temporarily. The result was litigation between HBC and Athanas for almost two years.

BRA'S NEW PLAN

The Boston Redevelopment Authority and the community groups of South Boston seized the opportunity granted by the court battle and pushed forward their own plans while the sparring partners poked and jabbed.

In March 1989, the BRA announced plans for the 900 acre area it called the Fort Point District. Geographically, Fan Pier represented only a small part of the plan in terms of size, but its ambitious plans, as well as its location near the downtown and transportation made it an important site (see **Exhibit 6**). Of all the BRA's new goals for the area, the one most affecting the Fan Pier was the declared intent to manage growth through zoning and community controls. Overall FAR was reduced to 3.0, a dramatic decrease from the Pelli plan.

New height and use restrictions would define what could be built, while "Capacity Based Planning" would temper growth to match the capacity of the transportation and utility infrastructure. For example, guidelines stated that for every two square feet of new office space, one square foot of new housing must be built. A proper mix of service (office), manufacturing, industrial and water-dependent uses in the district would be encouraged to even out cycles in the economy.

The BRA and the community also shared a social agenda which mandated that private developers use some of their profits from commercial development to finance up to 2,500 units of market-rate and affordable rate housing.

In terms of design, the district would avoid any superblock proportions; instead a well-scaled street grid reflecting the surrounding neighborhood would be required. This would also help to maintain and improve existing water views and help create new ones.

PROJECT ECONOMICS

Clearly, the potential returns to the project and to the partners were dependent on the market and the allowable build-out. An outside viewer had calculated the following table in an effort to evaluate what the project might have been worth to all the partners when completed. Since the area was new, comparables were at best an estimate. Real estate rents and values had been weakening.

In any case, the numbers below would have to be considered optimistic. The real return would have to be discounted to reflect the risk involved, the long time frame before receipt of profits and the portion of the returns that would have to be allocated to financial partners who might furnish debt and equity capital.

Total Project Costs and Expected Profit

	SQ. FT. (000)	COST PER SQ. FT.	TOTAL COST (000)[a]	NET OPERATING INCOME	VALUE (000)	PROFIT (000)
Residential	834	$250	$208,500	N/A	$250,200[b]	$ 41,700
Office	1,400	200	280,000	$35,000[c]	350,000	70,000
Retail	150	160	24,000	3,300[d]	33,000	9,000
	2,384	$610	$512,500	$38,300	$633,200	$120,700
Hotel	850	$180,000	$153,000	$18,830	$188,300	$35,300
Total	N/A	N/A	$665,500	$ 57,130	$821,500	$156,000[e]

[a]including infrastructure and soft costs; excluding land value
[b]value of $300 per square foot as condominiums
[c]net operating income of $25 per square foot per year
[d]net operating income of $20 per square foot per year
[e]before payments to Athanas

CONCLUSION

Some observers felt that an out-of-court settlement would be the best way to conclude the dispute and allow both Athanas and Friedman to get on with their lives. The legal system did not lend itself to quick or inexpensive settlement. Each had to evaluate not only where he wanted to end up but how to get there. Given the past history, each knew it would not be easy. The development process in the United States was certainly fragmented, but in megaprojects such as this one, the problems seemed to be compounded. On the other hand, neither party wanted to give up a dream that had been so long a major part of their lives.

Exhibit 1   Battery Park City Development

Battery Park City is on a 92 acre site created from landfill during the 1960s and 1970s located in Lower Manhattan along the Hudson River (see **Exhibit 1A**). The project was first proposed in the mid 1960s and underwent many political, economic and architectural changes. Four stages can be identified in the 20 years of planning and development of Battery Park City. The first stage marks the beginnings: 1963–1967, when early notions of a high-rise, futuristic megaproject were promoted. During the second stage, between 1968 and 1972, negotiations between the City of New York and the State of New York established control over the site. Construction of the infrastructure and the marketing of the site was started. From 1972 to 1979, the project was stalemated by a variety of factors and threatened with bankruptcy. Finally, in the 1980s, a reworking of the plan and its control systems (with the good fortune of a renewed economy) enabled Battery Park City to be developed in its present form. In the end, the project has been a tremendous commercial success.

Stage 1: 1963–1967

In the 1950s, the combination of new transportation technologies, shifting economies and competitive pressures depressed the maritime industry of Lower Manhattan. As maritime activity slowed and the piers gradually rotted with neglect, certain areas of the waterfront in lower Manhattan were filled in. State and civic leaders, notably New York State Governor Nelson Rockefeller and New York City Mayor John Lindsay took strong interest in the site on the Hudson River.

The plan Rockefeller announced in early 1966 included housing for 14,000 families, including 6,000 middle income and 1,500 low income families in sixteen 31 story buildings and several townhouses. The plan also included a hotel of 2,200 rooms, two office buildings of 67 stories each, plus space for manufacturing below a covered deck. There would be recreation and shopping facilities, indoor parking and parks. This plan was modified three months later, eliminating the manufacturing component but retaining the scale. The governor announced that he would seek legislation to create a public benefit corporation which would oversee the development (see **Exhibit 1B**).

Stage 2: 1968–1972

But at the start of Stage 2, from roughly 1968 to 1972, the Mayor of the City of New York John Lindsay had his own plans for the site. With a mayoral election coming up in 1969, Lindsay was anxious to retain control over this important property. He felt pressure to promote a socially progressive political agenda which would appeal to voters who were feeling the pain of increasing housing prices. The governor and the mayor negotiated, arriving at a compromise plan which increased the ratio of lower and middle class units to two-thirds of the residential component. The City would receive a rent set at 6 percent of fair market value of the land, certain payments in lieu of taxes, and ground rents, as well as any surplus revenue earned by the Authority. The Master Lease required that the project be completed in ten years, that is, by mid-1978. The Battery Park City Authority would have to comply with a Master Development Plan and be subject to City review bodies. In 1969, the City of New York created the Special Battery Park City District to expedite the development of the landfill.

Architect Phillip Johnson was commissioned to design the Master Plan. In keeping with the large spirit of Rockefeller's idea, Johnson envisioned an integrated complex connected by a spine. The infrastructure would be financed by project bonds issued with the moral backing of the State of New York. While the State would not be legally bound to back these bonds, it was expected that the State would take care of any default.

Exhibit 1 (continued)

Stage 3: 1973–1979

During Stage 3 there were problems. By 1973, a recession had fouled Manhattan's expectations for growth and Manhattan office space was glutted. Six million square feet of office space lay vacant in 1973; an additional seven million square feet was coming to market when the World Trade Center across the street from Battery Park was completed. Annual absorption rates led experts to predict that the excess space would be absorbed by 1976 at best.

Second, the plan for Battery Park City had been adjusted to help New York alleviate its chronic housing crisis. Only one-third of the 14,100 residential units would reflect conventional (market rate) rents or sales. The remaining two-thirds would be subsidized by the State and would house middle, moderate and low income families. But by the mid 1970s, it was no longer easy to find the subsidy dollars required.

Third, the City of New York suffered severe and well-publicized financial difficulties at this time which interfered with the financing of the residential component. The Authority had originally planned to borrow $80 million from investors, but the default by the State Urban Development Corporation on other bond issues made these bonds unsaleable.

Stage 4: 1979–1989

Thus in 1979 began the final stage. Decision makers at both the City and State level realized that changes had to be made quickly. A major reworking of the City/State agreement was imperative.

The work-out of Battery Park City included five elements: 1) takeover of the Authority by the State Urban Development Authority under the control of newly-elected Governor Hugh Carey; 2) the removal from the commercial portion of onerous review specifications imposed by the City of New York; 3) the substitution of a simpler, less expensive design; 4) the guarantee that the State would honor its moral obligation on the debt payment; and 5) a mandate to develop the entire project at market rates without the subsidized housing. In addition, the City gave up its claim to ground rents and tax equivalency payments. The City even agreed to provide a tax abatement for the first of the office buildings. In return, the City would own the site after the retirement of the bonds and the repayment of any state advance.

The newly streamlined Authority was encouraged by the recovering real estate market of 1979. Absorption rates were increasing and the World Trade Center was leasing quickly. A new, much simplified Master Plan by Alexander Cooper of the firm Cooper/Eckstut was commissioned. This plan organized the site as an extension of Lower Manhattan, with traditional streets and blocks, public access to the waterfront, and large amounts of open space. The "superblock" motif was abandoned in favor of a contextual solution which would provide the residential segment the variety of building types and design which make distinctive older New York neighborhoods (see **Exhibit 1C and 1D**).

The total cost of the development was re-estimated to be $4 billion, including the privately financed $1.5 billion commercial portion. When fully developed, the working population of Battery Park City was estimated to be 40,000 and the residential population estimated to be 25,000.

Exhibit 1   (continued)

A major factor in the success of the commercial component was the selection of Canadian developer Olympia & York in November of 1980. O&Y proposed to help take care of the Authority's existing debt problem by paying it $2 million per year starting immediately. This ground rent would rise modestly thereafter, and the Authority would receive a participation in the net income from the office space after 10 years. In exchange, O&Y wanted the 6 million square feet of office space to be built at one time in only four interconnected buildings called the World Financial Center. O&Y felt that larger-sized floors would better meet the needs of major financial institutions who were fast outgrowing the smaller spaces available in the Wall Street area.

O&Y was right. The four buildings with floorsizes averaging 40,000 square feet were soon taken by Merrill Lynch, American Express, Oppenheimer and Dow Jones. A fifth financial tower is now planned to the north.

The residential segment, which eventually will have 14,000 units, also benefited from the economics propelling the expansion of those same financial institutions. The Authority established strict zoning and building regulations and then selected a number of firms to develop their own individual buildings within these restrictions. The market rate rentals and condos were quickly filled by well-educated young professionals, or "Yuppies," working in the financial district who needed convenient places to stay and who could afford to pay. Rental rates quickly approached top of the market, and many of the condos developed in recent years ranged in prices from $300,000 to $500,000. The two components together were such an economic success that excess Authority revenues have been committed to pay the debt service for $400 million of bonds that will support low and middle income housing in *other* parts of New York City.

The project characteristics changed greatly over the decades. A number of people tried to draw conclusions from what had happened. While the location was always desirable and there was no surrounding residential community to raise objections, many external factors came into play. The perception of planning in the sixties with respect to Battery Park City was seen as being visionary. The focus was on dramatic design and idealistic social goals with less regard for economic realities and the scale of day to day living. Large scale federal and state subsidies were expected to absorb the costs. The seventies were considered a time of upheaval, when profound readjustments in the economics and politics of the city paralyzed new development including Battery Park. The eighties, however, saw a strong pragmatism on the parts of the politicians, the planners and the developers in regard to this site. A single authority with a clear mission controlled both land and the approvals process, funded the infrastructure, reacted quickly to an improved economy and with the help of strong private developers capitalized on growth segments in both the commercial and residential sectors.

Exhibit 1A   Map of Lower Manhattan

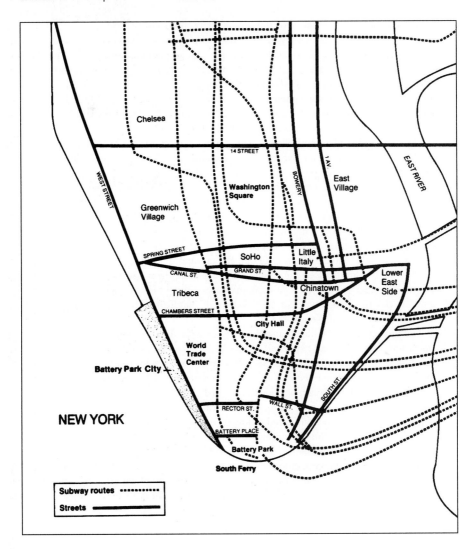

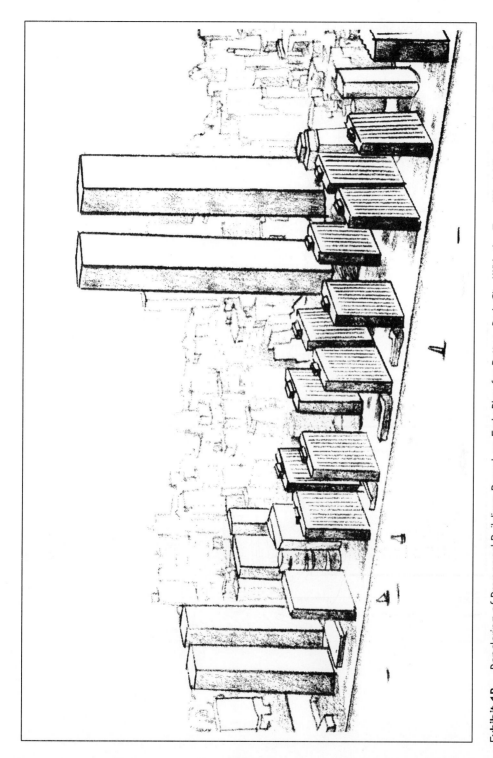

Exhibit 1B   Rendering of Proposed Buildings Based on Early Plan for Battery Park City With the Two World Trade Center Towers in Background

Exhibit 1C   New Site Plan for Battery Park City

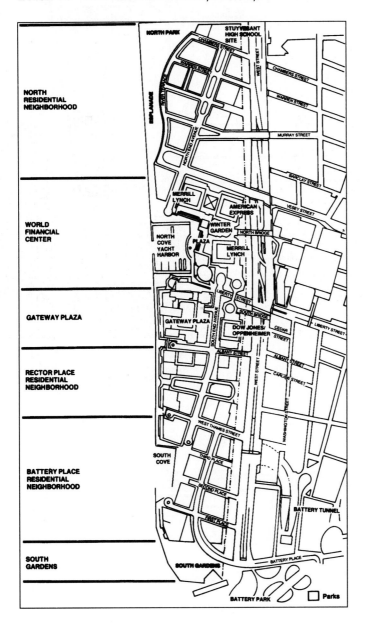

Exhibit 1D   Rendering of Proposed Buildings in Battery Park City

Exhibit 2   Plan of Downtown Boston and Fan Pier Area

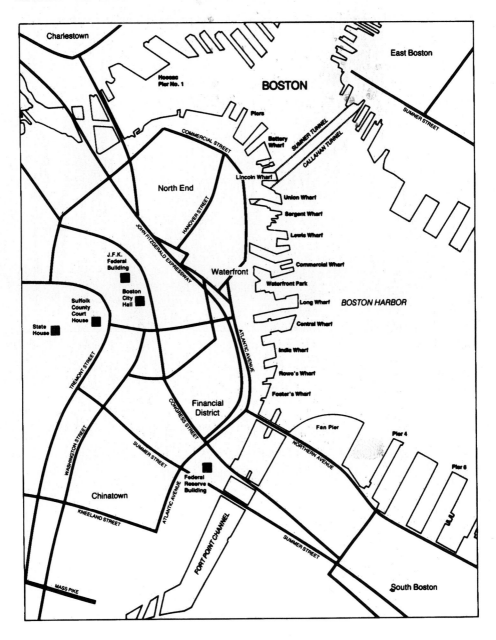

Exhibit 3   Plan of Piers on Fort Point Channel

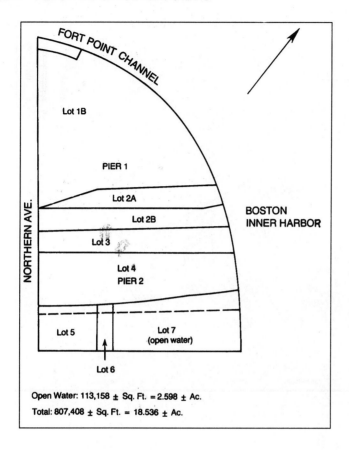

FORT POINT CHANNEL

Lot 1B

PIER 1

Lot 2A

Lot 2B

Lot 3

Lot 4
PIER 2

Lot 5

Lot 7
(open water)

Lot 6

NORTHERN AVE.

BOSTON
INNER HARBOR

Open Water: 113,158 ± Sq. Ft. = 2.598 ± Ac.

Total: 807,408 ± Sq. Ft. = 18.536 ± Ac.

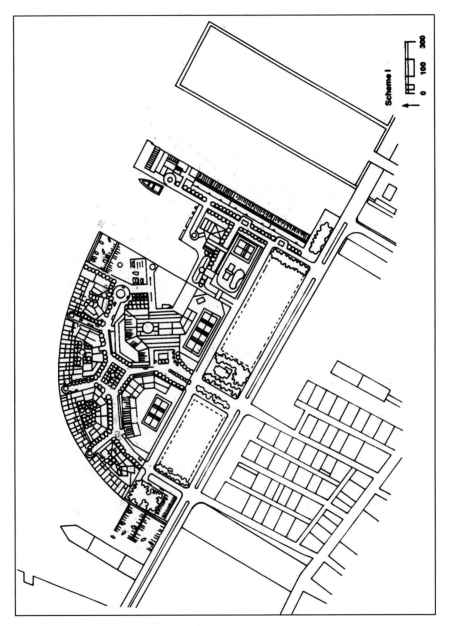

Exhibit 4 1981 Master Plan for Fan Pier

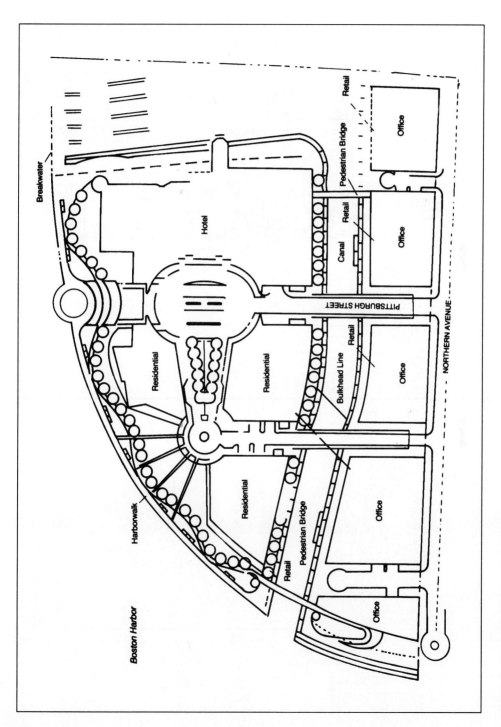

Exhibit 5   Revised Fan Pier Master Plan

Exhibit 6   Rendering of Proposed Buildings for Fan Pier

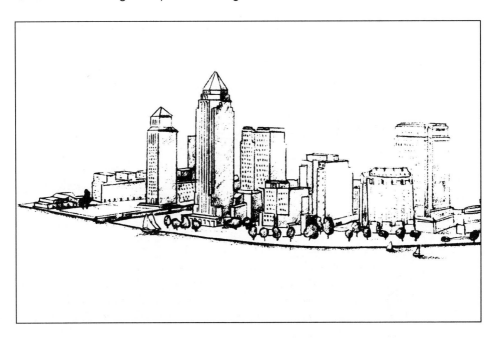

6

SOUTHPARK IV

In January 1990, George Laflin, a local investor, has raised $450,000 to invest in commercial and industrial properties in Houston, Texas. Laflin is interested in purchasing the 80,000 square foot SouthPark IV office/warehouse facility from a local savings and loan institution. Before he proceeds any further, Laflin wants to determine what the potential returns are from the project and calculate a realistic offer. The case takes the student through the mechanics of project valuation using a back of the envelope analysis.

Discussion Questions:

1. Is this a good property for Laflin to acquire?
2. What assumptions has Laflin made in creating his setup for SouthPark IV? What changes, if any, would you make to his setup? What is your projected return for SouthPark IV?
3. What price should Laflin offer for SouthPark IV? What conditions should he attach to his offer? How might Lonestar try to justify a higher price? What might SouthPark IV be worth in five years?
4. Why are there wide variations in the valuation of real property assets?

George Laflin was intrigued by the packet of papers that lay in front of him. The papers comprised a brochure that Lonestar Savings & Loan had put together in an effort to sell the SouthPark IV Distribution Center in Houston, Texas. SouthPark IV was an 80,000 square foot Office/Warehouse facility located on the south side of Houston. Lonestar was asking $1.5 million for the property.

It was January of 1990 and the Houston real estate market was beginning to show a few signs of recovery from a decade long slump. Laflin had recently raised $450,000 to invest in troubled properties and he wondered whether SouthPark IV would make a good investment.

GEORGE LAFLIN

Laflin had been born and raised in Houston. After graduating from Rice University with a degree in electrical engineering, he had accepted a job with a large computer manufacturer in Houston. During the past ten years, he had seen both explosive growth and rapid declines in real estate values. Now, at the age of 32, he wanted to invest in real estate and hopefully build equity through appreciation.

He had convinced eight friends to join him in committing $50,000 each to buy one or two troubled properties within the greater Houston area. Laflin had decided to initially focus on office/warehouse properties due to their relatively small size and their strong historical performance.

During his initial discussions with his friends, Laflin had expressed his hope that the properties would achieve both a reasonable current return and substantial appreciation. Laflin would take 10% of the deal for putting it together and acting as an asset manager. He would hire a professional property management firm to manage any properties that were purchased.

SOUTHPARK IV

Built in 1980, the SouthPark IV Distribution Center was located in the 100 acre SouthPark Industrial Center. The building had 185 foot bay depths and 22 foot clear ceilings. Approximately 15% of the space was finished as office space (see

Research Assistant Richard E. Crum prepared this case under the supervision of Adjunct Professor William J. Poorvu as the basis for class discussion rather than to illustrate either effective or ineffective handling of an administrative situation.

Exhibit 1 for a floor plan). The exterior walls were simple concrete panels. Loading docks were located in the front of the building and access to rail service was available from the back of the building. There was parking for 80 cars.

In general, the building was considered to be in excellent condition. The one exception was the roof which needed to be repaired. Lonestar had recently received an estimate of $50,000 to repair the roof.

As part of the sales book, Lonestar had provided a summary of SouthPark IV's operating results as of October 1989. Lonestar's numbers projected that SouthPark IV would have $252,000 in total income, $52,000 in total expenses, and $200,000 in cash flow from operations for 1989.

The building was fully leased to four tenants. The leases ranged in size from 12,000 square feet to 30,000 square feet. All four leases were due to expire on June 30, 1990 (see **Exhibit 2** for a summary of the lease terms). The leases were net of common expenses, taxes, and insurance. Lonestar paid these expenses and then was reimbursed by each tenant on a per square foot basis. These payments were shown on the income statement as expense reimbursement.

All four tenants had indicated to Lonestar that they would be willing to extend their leases for five years but only at the current market base rental rate of $2.00 per square foot. If Laflin purchased the property and extended the leases, he would incur no additional costs. If he brought in new tenants, however, he would most likely incur a tenant improvement expense of $2.50 per square foot and a leasing expense, on a five year lease, of 15% of the first year's rent. The tenant improvement expense represented a negotiated amount that an owner often gave to a new tenant to customize the tenant's space.

The land under SouthPark IV had recently been appraised at $300,000 and the building at $1,200,000. In arriving at his result, the appraiser had used three methods to calculate the property value: cost, income, and market data. Under the cost approach, the appraiser had applied current construction costs to the appropriate square footages within the building (see **Exhibit 3**). For the income approach, he had set up a ten year discounted cash flow (see **Exhibit 4**). Finally, the market data approach used recent comparable sales to arrive at a value (see **Exhibit 5**).

Lonestar had foreclosed on the property when the original developer had been forced into bankruptcy by the failure of another project. When no one else had bid at the foreclosure auction, Lonestar had bid in at its mortgage amount in order to protect its position. Federal regulators were pushing the bank to dispose of its real estate holdings. Lonestar had responded by aggressively marketing its properties and by offering attractive financing terms.

FINANCING

Lonestar was offering a $1,200,000 loan secured by a purchase money first mortgage on the property with a 10 year term, 30 year amortization period and an 8%

interest rate. (See **Exhibit 6** for the interest and principal payments associated with this loan.) The mortgage payment constant for this loan was 8.9%. Both the promissory note and the mortgage had an exculpatory clause which meant that the bank had no recourse to the personal assets of the borrower. The property being pledged was the sole security for repayment.

A purchase money mortgage is a mortgage from the seller to the buyer. It may or may not be similar in its terms to a "market rate" mortgage. In this case, Lonestar had sweetened the deal by offering a below market interest rate and a long amortization period. The current market terms for this type of loan were 11% interest with a 20 year amortization period and a 10 year term. The resulting constant was 12.4%.

ANALYSIS

Laflin had looked at a lot of brochures over the past six months. Before he spent any more time or money on market research, he wanted to do a rough, back of the envelope valuation of the property. If the returns to his investors didn't make sense, he knew that there would be no reason to waste his time on detailed financial analysis.

As a starting point, Laflin decided to create a "setup" for the project using the financial information that Lonestar had supplied. A setup was a real estate term for a simplified cash flow statement for a project. From the Lonestar numbers, Laflin deducted a 5% vacancy allowance, a 4% management fee, and a $15,000 structural reserve allowance.

SouthPark IV Setup ($000s)

	ORIGINAL	REVISED
Base rent (80,000 s.f.)	$200	$200
Expense reimbursement	52	52
Gross Income	252	252
Vacancy (5%)	—	−13
Net income	252	239
General expenses	−12	−12
Real estate taxes	−30	−30
Insurance	−10	−10
Management fee (4%)		−10
Structural reserve	—	−15
Total expenses	−52	−77
Cash flow from operations	200	162

The $1.5 million asking price reflected a capitalization rate of 13.3% on the original projection of $200,000 in cash flow from operations. With a cash flow from operations of $162,000, the capitalization rate was 10.8%. As an investor, Laflin was more interested in the cash flow after financing (CFAF) and the cash flow after taxes (CFAT). To determine these two numbers, he had to calculate the interest and principal payments on the Lonestar loan and the taxable income or loss that the property would incur.

SouthPark IV Setup (Including Financing and Taxes) ($000s)

Cash flow from operations	162
Interest	−96
Principal	−10
Cash flow after financing	56
+ Principal	10
+ Structural Reserve	15
− Depreciation	−31
Taxable Income	50
Income Tax (39.6%)	−20
Cash flow after taxes	36

The interest and principal payments had been fairly straightforward to calculate. The loan had constant monthly payments of $8,882. As the outstanding mortgage balance was reduced by each principal payment, the amount of interest in each payment would decrease and the amount of principal would increase. Since the term of the loan was 10 years, the outstanding mortgage balance would come due as a lump sum payment at either the end of the 10th year or upon the sale of the building.

To calculate taxable income, Laflin had added back the principal and the structural reserve allowance, since neither was tax deductible, and then subtracted depreciation. He had calculated the depreciation figure by taking the $1,200,000 appraised value of the building and dividing by its depreciable life of 39 years.[1] Laflin then multiplied the taxable income by the current tax rate of 39.6% to arrive at the income tax. In this case, there was no state or county tax to consider.

The $36,000 in cash flow after taxes represented a 12% current return on a $300,000 equity investment. If he could achieve this level of return, he knew that his investors would be quite happy. If his numbers were accurate, he knew that he didn't need to spend much time or effort calculating the benefits of future rental increases or sale proceeds. But how accurate were his numbers, especially given the problems in the rental market?

[1]In 1990 the depreciation or cost-recovery period for commercial real estate was actually 31.5 years, which would have meant a depreciation deduction of $38,095. In 1993 the depreciation period was increased to 39 years, so we are using the 39-year period for these calculations in order to comply with current tax policy rather than be historically accurate. We have also used the current 39.6% federal income tax rate.

THE HOUSTON MARKET

By 1990, the Houston economy was slowly recovering from the collapse of the oil industry in the early eighties. Both employment and population levels had crept to roughly at or past 1985 levels (See **Tables 1 and 2** for population and employment data.) Oil prices, which had been as high as $35 per barrel in 1982 and as low as $14 per barrel in 1986, had recently risen to $16 per barrel.

Table 1   Houston Area Population (1985–1988)

	1985	1986	1987	1988
Houston CMSA	3,663,700	3,545,900	3,553,100	3,580,800
Harris County	2,755,000	2,714,400	2,718,900	2,742,900

Note: The City of Houston is located within the Houston–Galveston–Brazoria Consolidated Metropolitan Statistical Area (CMSA) and it is the county seat of Harris County.

Table 2   Houston Employment (1980–1989)

YEAR	SERVICES	CONSTRUCTION	MANUFACTURING	OTHER	TOTAL
1980	281,800	134,900	428,500	606,900	1,452,100
1981	307,800	142,800	481,200	643,700	1,575,500
1982	301,500	134,500	405,300	642,200	1,483,500
1983	310,700	118,700	369,600	649,600	1,448,600
1984	339,200	111,000	371,000	679,300	1,500,500
1985	341,100	102,800	353,700	681,600	1,479,200
1986	342,000	86,200	305,200	655,900	1,389,300
1987	361,900	81,400	310,100	647,900	1,401,300
1988	386,900	87,900	324,900	666,200	1,465,900
1989	395,600	88,900	324,300	660,900	1,469,700

Source: Texas Employment Commission

The outlook for the real estate industry in Houston was not clear. Economic growth would generate fresh demand for space, although almost every category of real estate had a tremendous supply of vacant space. There was also a concern that the collapse of the Savings & Loan industry in Texas might further depress prices and rents by flooding the market with deeply discounted properties.

Houston, with almost 210 million square feet of industrial space, was the 9th largest industrial market in the U.S. Between 1981 and 1985 approximately 35,000,000 square feet of industrial space was added. From 1986 to 1989, there had been no speculative construction in the area. A limited amount of build-to-suit construction had taken place during this period (See **Table 3** for Houston industrial occupancy data).

Table 3   Houston Industrial Occupancy Data (000s)

YEAR	TOTAL	OCCUPIED	NEW SUPPLY	ABSORPTION	VACANCY
1981	175,580	154,738	9,800	9,600	11.9%
1982	185,380	164,338	7,400	2,200	11.4%
1983	192,780	166,538	8,000	1,900	13.6%
1984	200,780	168,438	5,900	500	16.1%
1985	206,680	168,938	3,300	1,400	18.3%
1986	209,980	170,338	0	600	18.9%
1987	209,980	170,938	0	5,500	18.6%
1988	209,980	176,438	0	6,238	16.0%
1989	209,980	182,676	0	7,434	13.0%

Within the submarket in which SouthPark IV was located, there were nine buildings that were considered to be competitive to SouthPark IV. Occupancy and rental rate information, based on their current tenants, are shown below in **Table 4**.

Table 4   Competitor Occupancy & Rental Rates, October, 1989

BUILDING	TOTAL AREA	% OCCUPIED	AVG. BASE RENT
1.	95,600	100%	$2.40
2.	287,350	35%	$2.30
3.	546,717	97%	$2.50
4.	342,510	98%	$2.20
5.	228,900	98%	$2.15
6.	117,692	100%	$2.60
7.	198,944	80%	$2.40
8.	113,420	78%	$2.00
9.	102,840	53%	$2.30
Total	2,033,973	84%	$2.34

Most of these leases, however, were written many years ago at higher rents. At the current market rental rate of $2.00 per square foot, Laflin realized that he would not obtain Lonestar's projected rents. Obviously, the returns would be lower.

But Laflin had been following the local real estate market closely. He felt that the local economy was gaining strength and that a resurgence in economic activity would cause a rise in rental rates and real estate values. He also felt that the near collapse of the Savings & Loan industry in Texas presented a unique opportunity to invest in troubled real estate properties at a substantial discount.

Somehow he would have to incorporate both current market rates and potential future rates in his analysis. If he didn't, he felt that someone else would outbid him for the property.

If the partnership invested in SouthPark IV, Laflin assumed that the partnership would hold the property for five years. Over this period, he believed that both income and expenses for office/warehouse properties in Houston would grow at a 3% annual rate. He also believed that he would be able to sell the property at a 10% cap rate.

To complete his analysis, Laflin had to calculate the net cash flow from a sale. To do this, he would take the net selling price and subtract the net book value in order to get the gain on sale. He would then calculate the tax liability by multiplying the gain on sale by the 28% tax rate. This would allow him to calculate the net cash from sale by taking the net selling price and subtracting the mortgage balance and the tax liability. Net book value was defined as the purchase price plus capital improvements minus accumulated depreciation. He assumed that the cost of selling the project would be 5% of the gross sales price.

Laflin wondered if the asking price itself was too high. Even with future rental increases and future sale proceeds included, it was difficult to make the numbers work. The fixed mortgage payments could lead to either positive or negative leverage depending on the actual rental rate that he achieved. If he could negotiate a lower sales price with Lonestar, he might be able to improve the returns to his investors. Of course, he also knew that Lonestar would not lend the partnership more than 80% of the purchase price.

It was time for Laflin to do some calculations: a revised income statement, a five year projection, and, using the back of the envelope approach, an analysis of the impact of a lower purchase price. Only then could he see if SouthPark IV was the right investment for his group. There were opportunities in Houston but he also had to consider the risks. After all, the numbers were at best projections.

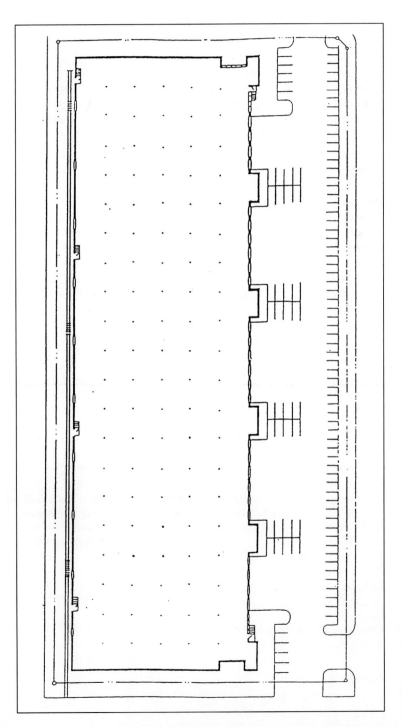

Exhibit 1   Floor Plan

Exhibit 2   Rent Roll—October 1989

TENANT	S.F.	RATE (PSF)	ANNUAL RENT	EXPIRATION
Tower Distribution	30,000	$2.70	$81,000	30–June–90
Bayview Nissan	22,000	$2.50	$55,000	30–June–90
Ace Products	16,000	$2.35	$37,600	30–June–90
Boyertown Gaskets	12,000	$2.20	$26,400	30–June–90
Totals/Averages	80,000	$2.50	$200,000	30–June–90

Exhibit 3   Cost Valuation

Direct Costs

Site Preparation:	Preparation	109,497 sf × $.12 psf	$13,140
	Fill for Floors	185,055 sf × $.17 psf	31,459
Concrete Foundation:	Non-Bearing Walls	80,000 sf × $ 1.18 psf	94,400
Frame:	Steel	80,000 sf × $ 4.07 psf	325,600
Floor Structure:	Concrete on Ground	80,000 sf × $ 2.03 psf	162,400
Floor Cover:	Vinyl Tile	5,759 sf × $ 1.03 psf	5,932
	Carpet/Pad	7,755 sf × $ 1.75 psf	13,571
Ceiling:	Suspended Fiber, Insulation	13,514 sf × $ 1.55 psf	20,947
Frame, Interior Partitions:	Tenant Space	13,514 sf × $ 8.06 psf	108,923
	Demising Walls, Block	12,210 sf × $ 2.28 psf	27,839
	Demising Walls, Gypsum	8,140 sf × $ 2.36 psf	19,210
Plumbing:		80,000 sf × $ 1.29 psf	103,200
Fire Sprinklers:		80,000 sf × $ 1.05 psf	84,000
HVAC:	Heat	80,000 sf × $ 0.73 psf	58,400
	AC	2,100 sf × $ 4.30 psf	9,030
	Ventilation	12@ $1,125 ea.	13,500
	Office Heat/AC	13,514 sf × $ 3.20 psf	43,245
Electrical:		80,000 sf × $ 0.94 psf	75,200
Exterior Wall:	Concrete Tilt Wall	24,968 sf × $ 8.55 psf	213,476
	Glass/Concrete	3,320 sf × $15.75 psf	52,290
	Overhead Doors	25 @ $1,000 ea.	25,000
Roof Structure:	Steel Joists, Deck Concrete	80,000 sf × $ 4.22 psf	337,600
Roof Cover:		80,000 sf × $ 0.43 psf	34,400
Total Direct Costs			$1,872,762

Indirect Costs

Architect's Fees	$90,000
Finance Fees	40,000
Other Fees, Closing Costs	35,000
Total Indirect Costs	$165,000

Reproduction Cost New	$2,037,762

Exhibit 4

	7/90	7/91	7/92	7/93	7/94	7/95	7/96	7/97	7/98	7/99
Tenant Rental Income										
Base Rents	200,000	206,000	212,180	218,545	225,102	231,855	238,810	245,975	253,354	260,955
Expense reimburs.	52,000	53,560	55,167	56,822	58,526	60,282	62,091	63,953	65,872	67,848
Vacancy	(13,000)	(13,390)	(13,792)	(14,205)	(14,632)	(15,071)	(15,523)	(15,988)	(16,468)	(16,962)
Total gross income	239,000	246,170	253,555	261,162	268,997	277,067	285,378	293,940	302,758	311,841
Operating expenses										
General expenses	12,000	12,360	12,731	13,113	13,506	13,911	14,329	14,758	15,201	15,657
Real estate taxes	30,000	30,900	31,827	32,782	33,765	34,778	35,822	36,896	38,003	39,143
Insurance	10,000	10,300	10,609	10,927	11,255	11,593	11,941	12,299	12,668	13,048
Total expenses	52,000	53,560	55,167	56,822	58,526	60,282	62,091	63,953	65,872	67,848
Net operating income	187,000	192,610	198,388	204,340	210,470	216,784	223,288	229,986	236,886	243,993
Releasing/Fixed Costs										
Tenant Finish	80,000				80,000					80,000
Leasing commissions	9,600				9,600					9,600
Deferred maintenance	50,000				50,000					50,000
Total Rlsg/Fixed Costs	139,600				139,600					139,600
Cash flow before debt	47,400	192,610	198,388	204,340	70,870	216,748	223,288	229,986	236,886	104,393

Cash flow from sale	2,439,926
NPV of cash flow before debt	851,111
NPV of cash flow from sale	658,155
NPV for all cash flows	1,509,266

Assumptions: 14% discount rate

3% annual increase in revenues and expenses

5 year lease with 60% probability of renewal

10% capitalization rate assumed in year 10

Tax factors are not included

Exhibit 5   Sales Summary Chart

SALES NO.	SALES PRICE	LEASABLE AREA (SF)	PRICE PER SF	SALE DATE	OFFICE AREA %	YEAR BUILT	CEILING HEIGHT	SPRINKLER	RAIL SERVED
1	$963,865	50,998	$18.90	5/89	15%	1980	18 ft.	No	No
2	1,233,200	82,159	15.01	9/88	8%	1971	22 ft.	Yes	Yes
3	2,181,448	142,207	15.34	9/88	10%	1975	22 ft.	Yes	Yes
4	5,912,620	295,631	20.00	5/89	6%	1979	22 ft.	Yes	Yes
5	12,025,321	586,601	20.50	12/89	12%	1981	22 ft.	Yes	Yes
6	6,518,961	314,318	20.74	12/89	4%	1982	22 ft.	Yes	Yes
7	3,026,759	160,401	18.87	7/84	10%	1982	20 ft.	No	No
8	2,185,014	107,795	20.27	3/83	16%	1980	22 ft.	No	Yes
9	1,812,658	97,717	18.55	10/88	8%	1979	20 ft.	Yes	Yes
10	2,466,650	136,808	18.03	6/88	11%	1981	22 ft.	Yes	Yes

Exhibit 6   Mortgage Payments

	1990	1991	1992	1993	1994	1995	1999
Interest	$ 96,000	$ 95,152	$ 94,237	$ 93,249	$ 92,181	$91,028	$ 85,417
Principal	10,592	11,440	12,355	13,344	14,411	15,564	21,175
Mortgage balance	1,189,408	1,177,968	1,165,613	1,152,269	1,137,858	1,122,294	1,101,119

7

ANGUS CARTWRIGHT, JR.

In April 1995, John and Judy DeRight, looking to diversify their investment portfolios, have retained Angus Cartwright, Jr. to identify prospective real estate acquisitions. Mr. Cartwright has four potential properties which merit an indepth analysis. The case provides an opportunity to examine the various components of real estate return—cash flow, tax benefits, and futures—and measure the profitability of a proposed investment through the calculation of net present value, internal rate of return, and capitalization rate. The class session permits discussion not only about techniques of financial analysis, and their usefulness, but adaptation of those methods to the needs of a particular investor.

DiscussionQuestions:

1. Using the method for financial analysis employed by Cartwright for the Alison Green property, and assuming the figures given in the case, what are the financial returns for the other three properties? Fill out the exhibits in the case with backup analysis for Exhibits 5 and 8.
2. Consider under what circumstances it would be valuable for you to make the calculations in the various exhibits and what they tell you?
3. Which potential investment, if any, would you suggest for each of the investors?

PEOPLE

Angus Cartwright, Jr., an investment advisor, was based in Arlington, Virginia, the home of many members of the DeRight family. In April 1995 his attention focused on the needs of two cousins at different stages of their lives. John DeRight had recently sold his business to a medium-sized public company in exchange for $6 million of the company's stock. He then retired and expected to live comfortably on the $200,000 in dividends paid on the stock plus retirement and other income he had of an equal amount. He felt the need to diversify his investments, however, and planned to sell up to half of his stock even though his basis was negligible and reinvest the money from the sale after paying the capital gains tax in real estate and other investments.

Judy DeRight was President and sole stockholder of a small sized chemical company that had earned in excess of $800,000 before taxes and $550,000 after taxes in each of the previous five years. She had received many offers to sell her company in exchange for the stock of a public company; but she enjoyed the independence of running her own business. She had determined that her chemical business could best grow through internal expansion rather than by acquisition. On the other hand, she did feel it was wise for her to diversify her own investments. Over time, she personally had accumulated over $3,500,000 now invested in short term securities which she considered unnecessary for her present operations and thus available for outside investment.

Both felt that real estate would give them the benefits of diversity, protection from inflation and some tax advantages. Each DeRight wanted to purchase a property large enough to attract the interest of a professional real estate management company to relieve them of the burden of day-to-day management, and they wanted a minimum return on their investments of 12% after tax.

PROPERTIES

Angus Cartwright, Jr., like his father, had dealt with the DeRight family for many years and had located four properties which he felt might be suitable investments for his two clients. He had brokers show the properties to the two DeRights and

This case was prepared as the basis for class discussion rather than to illustrate either effective or ineffective handling of an administrative situation. It was substantially revised in 1995.

Copyright © 1975 by the President and Fellows of Harvard College. To order copies, call (617) 495-6117 or write the Publishing Division, Harvard Business School, Boston, MA 02163. No part of this publication may be reproduced, stored in a retrieval system, used in a spreadsheet, or transmitted in any form or by any means—electronic, mechanical, photocopying, recording, or otherwise—without the permission of Harvard Business School.

the DeRights were enthusiastic about them. One property was Alison Green, a 100-unit garden apartment project located in Montgomery County, Maryland. This property had been completed in 1990 and had been operating at a 97% occupancy level since the initial rentup. There was a building moratorium in parts of the county because of inadequate public facilities, preventing much short term competition. The asking price for Alison Green was $4.6 million, but the broker had received indications that a price of $4.4 million would probably be acceptable. The gross rental income from the property was $840,000 with cash flow before financing and reserves for capital expenditure of $476,000.[4] Real estate taxes in Montgomery County were generally about 14% of the gross rent roll. A new $3.2 million mortgage at a 9.5% interest rate had recently been arranged. The term was 10 years, but the amortization period was over 30 years. The land value of the property, for purposes of depreciation, was estimated at $500,000 and the depreciation period (cost recovery period) for the building would be 27.5 years. The method of depreciation since the enactment of the 1986 Tax Act would have to be straight line rather than an accelerated method.

Close by was the second property, a five-story, 40,000 square foot office building, 900 Stony Walk, with 33,500 square feet of rentable space. 900 Stony Walk was rented to lawyers, accountants and small service companies each of which rented between 2,000 and 5,000 square feet. 900 Stony Walk was completed in 1988 and had been operating at a 97% occupancy level since its initial rentup. The asking price was $3.9 million, but the broker believed a price of $3.75 million would be accepted. The gross rentals for 900 Stony Walk were $603,000 with cash flow before financing and reserves of $410,000. A new $2.9 million mortgage at a 10% interest rate had been arranged. The term was 10 years with amortization over 20 years. The land value for purposes of depreciation was estimated at $400,000. 900 Stony Walk, being a non-residential building, would have to be depreciated on a straight line basis over 39 years. Like Alison Green, real estate taxes would be at a rate of 14% of gross rent.

The third property was Ivy Terrace, an 80-unit garden apartment project under construction near Arlington, Virginia. The property was for sale for $3.7 million, but the broker was certain it could be purchased for $3.6 million. A 10-year, $2.3 million mortgage at a 9.5% interest rate with a 30-year amortization period had been arranged. The land was leased for 99 years with annual payments of $20,000. The buyer would take title upon completion of the construction. For depreciation purposes, the owner would be able to depreciate the full $3.6 million purchase price using a straight line method over 27.5 years. The gross rentals for the property were estimated at $768,000. The projected cash flow from operations after a vacancy allowance of 5% but before financing, reserves and leasehold payments would be $437,400. Cartwright knew that property taxes in Arlington were about 12% of the gross rent roll. Living nearby,

---

[4]Cash flow before financing = cash flow from operations, or net operating income. It is also referred to as free and clear cash flow.

Cartwright and the DeRights had checked the area closely and concluded that the rental and expense projections were reasonable.

Also under construction in Arlington was The Fowler Building, a two-story, 45,000 square foot office building with 38,000 square feet of rentable space. Leasing for the building had already begun with 80% of the space rented, mostly to small computer and consulting companies at what appeared to be below market rents. The Fowler Building was for sale for $4.9 million, but the broker was sure it could be purchased for $4.7 million. A 10-year, $3.3 million mortgage had been arranged at a 10% interest rate, amortized over 25 years. The land was leased for 99 years with annual payments of $55,000. As with 900 Stony Walk, the person who purchased The Fowler Building would depreciate it using straight-line depreciation over 39 years. The gross rentals for The Fowler Building were estimated at $722,000 and the cash flow before financing, reserves and leasehold payments was projected at $512,000 once the building reached 95% occupancy. These figures also seemed reasonable, but because a number of new properties were coming on the market in the Arlington area, Cartwright was able to negotiate a guaranteed return based on his pro-formas on both Ivy Terrace and The Fowler Building during the first three years until rentals reached the projected 95% occupancy levels.

Although Cartwright expected income from these properties to keep up with inflation, he made what he thought was a conservative assumption that the cash flow from operations would only increase at a rate of 3% per year except for the Fowler Building which he projected to grow at 5% per year. After talking with the DeRights, Cartwright also felt that it was logical to assume, for calculation purposes, that they would hold their investments for a ten year period. He therefore assumed a sale at the end of year ten and projected a sales price for all four properties based on projected cash flows and trends in the suburban Washington, D.C. apartment and office markets. For Alison Green he projected a sales price, net to the seller at the end of year ten, of $6,200,000. For 900 Stony Walk he projected a sales price of $5,900,000. Ivy Terrace he estimated would sell for $5,200,000, and The Fowler Building would sell for $7,800,000. He predicted the highest appreciation rate on that building since he felt that the present leases had been written at below market rent to facilitate lease-up.

In addition to the basic operating expenses, Cartwright felt it was important to include a capital reserve, a line item that was rarely included by people selling a property. For the apartments, he assumed that he would set aside in cash $250 per apartment per year. This reserve would build up so that sufficient funds were available when it came time to: replace the roof, repave the parking lot, replace carpeting and appliances every five to seven years, and periodically refurnish the clubhouse. If he actually decided to purchase one of the apartment properties he would hire a construction consultant to do a more detailed capital needs study, but for now, the $250 reserve, inflated at 3% per year, would be adequate.

For the office buildings, Cartwright found that he needed to set aside a reserve for capital expenditures which included tenant improvements and lease commissions. To be accurate, one needed to look at each lease and make an assumption about which tenants would leave and require him to do an extensive renovation for a new tenant as well as pay a brokerage commission. For this first cut, he decided to make the assumption that he would set aside $1 per rentable square foot per year (inflated at 3%or 5% for Fowler), to cover tenant improvements, lease commissions plus items such as roof replacement. Again, this was an assumption that would need to be carefully tested and could be reduced if he got tenants to sign leases longer than five years.

Finally, Cartwright needed to consider the tax implications of these reserves. As non-cash expenses, they were non-deductible for income tax purposes. In later years, when the reserves were spent they generally got added to the basis of the property and depreciated over the life of the property (27.5 years for residential and 39 years for commercial). In this case, for simplicity, he assumed that the entire reserves would be spent at the end of year 10 to prepare the property for sale. Keeping careful records of these expenses and consulting an accountant is important since certain of these expenses, such as lease commissions, can be deducted over the length of the lease. Still others could be deducted faster if the tenant moved out and the improvements had to be ripped out. For the purpose of this analysis, however, Cartwright felt the simplest solution was the conservative one of not taking into account depreciation and amortization of these items during the operating period but at the time of sale of the property increasing his book value by the total amount of the reserve since it was assumed to be spent at that time.

PRELIMINARY ANALYSIS

Time was valuable to Cartwright but he had always found a preliminary analysis worthwhile. It enabled him to identify quickly those properties where detailed financial analysis and a more careful physical inspection and examination of day-to-day operations were warranted. He knew from experience that he would then have to spend considerable time studying comparable projects if he were to validate the reasonableness of the purchase prices, operating expenses, rent levels and the amenities provided in the properties he felt were worth purchasing.

Cartwright first noted the assumptions underlying his analysis. He assumed that:
1. There would be an annual increase in the net operating income and reserves of 3% for Alison, Ivy, and Stony Walk and 5% for Fowler until the time of sale. The projected resale price was as shown earlier;
2. His clients would supply the necessary equity investment;
3. In spite of uncertainties as to future changes in income tax laws, for purposes of initial calculations an ordinary tax rate of 39.6% and a capital gain tax rate of 28% would apply (State income taxes would not be taken into account at this time although in some states the effective combined rate might be 45%);

4.   His clients could fully use any tax losses as they occurred against other income[2] and tax laws would not change again during the holding period.

Then, being methodical, he developed a list of the salient facts he would need in his analysis (see **Exhibit 1**).

Exhibit 1

	ALISON GREEN	900 STONY WALK	IVY TERRACE	THE FOWLER BUILDING
Number of units/or square feet of rentable space	100	33,500	_____	_____
A) Gross Purchase Price	$4,400,000	_____	_____	_____
B) Depreciable Base	$3,900,000	_____	_____	_____
C) Depreciable Life (Capital Recovery Period)	27.5	_____	_____	_____
D) Estimated Sales Price	$6,200,000	_____	_____	_____
E) Expected Year of Sale	10	_____	_____	_____
F) Net Operating Income	$ 476,000	410,000	437400	_____
G) Annual Increase in Operating Income	3%	_____	_____	_____
H) Leasehold Payments	$0	_____	_____	_____
I) Equity Investment	$1,200,000	_____	_____	_____
J) Amount of 1st Mortgage	$3,200,000	_____	_____	_____
1) Interest Rate	9.5%	_____	_____	_____
2) Term	10 years	_____	_____	_____
3) Amortization Period	30 years	_____	_____	_____
4) Constant Loan Payments[3]	10.17%	11.75%	10.17%	11.02%

Cartwright's next step was to develop the property set ups for each property. Once again he returned to the original brochures given to him by the brokers for each property. In general, the data was not in the form he found most useful. The setup Mr. Cartwright developed for Alison Green follows (**Exhibit 2**).

[2]For investors not primarily in the real estate business, the federal regulations permit the deduction of losses from real estate which is considered a passive investment only from other investments generating passive income. Although the DeRights in this case do not have other passive income, for the purpose of learning the mechanics, it is assumed that they can utilize any losses. In practice, investors now attempt to balance their real estate portfolio to take advantage of any losses.

[3]For simplicity of calculation on a calculator, this model assumes annual payments of rent, expenses, and debt service. In reality, monthly payments are the norm. Monthly payments would reduce the constant slightly, since the principal would be repaid more rapidly.

Exhibit 2   First Year Project Setups (000)

	ALISON GREEN	900 STONY WALK	IVY TERRACE	THE FOWLER BUILDING
Gross Rents	$840.00	603,000	708,000	722,000
– Vacancies	25.20	X.03%	X.05	X.15
Net Rents	814.80			
– Real Estate Taxes	117.60	X.14 (gross rent)	√12% gross rev	
– Other Operating Expenses	221.20			
Net Operating Income ("Free and Clear")	476.00			
– Capital Reserves	25.00			
– Finance Payments	325.38			
– Lease Payments	0			
BEFORE TAX CASH FLOW	125.62			

Cartwright then calculated the major comparable statistics for each property (**Exhibit 3**).

Exhibit 3   Purchase and Operating Comparables

Price/Unit or Price/Rentable Square Foot	$ 44,000	$111.94		
Real Estate Taxes/Gross Revenue	14%			
Other Operating Expenses/ Unit or Operating Exp./ Rentable Square Foot	$2,212	$2.70		
Other Operating Exp./ Gross Revenue	26.33%			
Average Monthly Rents for the apartments or yearly dollars per rentable sq. ft. of office space	$700	$18.00		
Actual or Projected Occupancy	97%			

Fowler

To validate the reasonableness of the asking price Cartwright would have to compare the capitalization rates and per unit costs of recent sales elsewhere in Arlington and Montgomery County. He would also attempt to establish the replacement costs of each project. Unit cost and operating expenses were usually related items.

Operating expenses for similar properties in the same general areas should be close to average, Cartwright believed. Good management could move them down a little, but very deviant expenses were typically signals of trouble and deserved detailed inquiries. Rents were affected by competition, both present and near-term future. What would have to be done to raise rents? What could be done to cut expenses? Basically, how could he increase the cash flow from operations while maintaining or enhancing future value? What would the owners' operating policies be? He felt the DeRights would want to keep their properties well-maintained rather than run them down, but this was a decision each would have to make. Then there were property taxes to consider.

Real estate taxes are an important expense of property ownership. Cartwright believed it was worth examining current property taxes and local tax practices, because, over time, tax increases could materially affect Net Operating Income. Property taxes varied widely throughout the country.

RISK ANALYSIS

Cartwright had noted that the use of financial leverage in each situation differed (see **Exhibit 1**). For example, the acquisition of Alison Green would be financed with a higher percentage of debt than the acquisition of Ivy Terrace. This leverage was expressed as a loan to value ratio which in the case of Alison Green was 72.73% (see **Exhibit 4**). Cartwright felt the loan to value ratio on Ivy Terrace might be affected by the fact that the property was still under construction.

His next step was to assess the nature of the operating risks attached to each property. Cartwright realized his later financial analysis would rest on the assumption that his clients could maintain the occupancy levels now prevailing. The ratio that is currently used by lenders to describe the operating risk is called the debt coverage ratio. This ratio expresses the relationship between net operating income and financial payments. In the case of Alison Green the debt coverage ratio is 1.46 which is above the 1.2 ratio many lenders currently use for properties of this type.

Using the set-ups he developed in **Exhibit 2**, Cartwright also thought he should assess the risk of an increase in vacancy through a rough first year break-even analysis (after financing) for each property. It was apparent to him, for example, that every 1% increase in occupancy added $8,400 to the before tax cash flow (BTCF) of Alison Green. This meant that a 14.95% decrease in occupancy in addition to the 3% already allocated for vacancy would wipe out the BTCF of the property (see **Exhibit 4**). Therefore, the break-even occupancy is 82.05%.

Exhibit 4   Break-Even Analysis

	ALISON GREEN	900 STONY WALK	IVY TERRACE	THE FOWLER BUILDING
Current or Projected Occupancy	97.00%			
Added Margin	14.95%			
Break-even Occupancy	82.05%			
Loan to Value	72.73%			
Debt Coverage Ratio	1.46			

Cartwright could envision problems which might necessitate additional cash investments in the Alison property. The break-even analysis suggested that risk might be related to reward in the set of properties he was examining.

FINANCIAL ANALYSIS

Since each of his clients was anxious to invest in real estate and because he felt that the four properties were potentially attractive investments, Cartwright decided to expand his analysis. Two simple measures of return are widely used in the real estate industry using the first year stabilized net operating income. The first is the free and clear capitalization rate or return on total assets or total project cost. The capitalization rate is determined by dividing the net operating income by the purchase price. Cartwright calculated that Alison Green had a capitalization rate of 10.82%. In practice, the capitalization rate on the free and clear income actually used by a potential buyer would be adjusted for his or her perception of the capital expenditures required. In a way this is similar to the approach investors take in assigning a price/earnings ratio to a stock's net income, before capital expenditures.

The second measure of return is called the cash-on-cash return which is derived by dividing the cash flow after financing and capital reserves but before income taxes by the equity investment. Some sellers and investors do not deduct the capital reserve for this ratio on the grounds that it is not a constant or predictable number. In this case an average reserve is used which gives more validity to the calculation than if nothing were included. Alison Green's cash-on-cash return was 10.47%. Cartwright felt, however, that these simple measures of return did not take into account any income tax payable or considerations for changes in future value. Additional steps were necessary.

Cartwright had been given a method for analyzing income producing real estate that he considered appropriate for the type of comparative analysis he wanted to make in this case (See **Appendix A**.) For the purpose of the calculations, he decided (as already noted) even though there were uncertainties as to future income tax laws, to assume a 39.6% tax rate for ordinary income, and a 28% capital gains tax rate.

Exhibit 5 Alison Green Projected Cash Flow ($000s)

	0	1	2	3	4	5	6	7	8	9	10
Net Operating Income		476.00	490.28	504.99	520.14	535.74	551.81	568.37	585.42	602.98	621.07
– Reserve		(25.00)	(25.75)	(26.52)	(27.32)	(28.14)	(28.98)	(29.85)	(30.75)	(31.67)	(32.62)
– Lease Payments		0.00	0.00	0.00	0.00	0.00	0.00	0.00	0.00	0.00	0.00
– Financing		(325.38)	(325.38)	(325.38)	(325.38)	(325.38)	(325.38)	(325.38)	(325.38)	(325.38)	(325.38)
Before Tax Cash Flow		125.62	139.15	153.09	167.44	182.22	197.45	213.14	229.29	245.93	263.07
+ Amortization	3,200.00	21.38	23.41	25.63	28.07	30.73	33.65	36.85	40.35	44.19	48.38
+ Reserve		25.00	25.75	26.52	27.32	28.14	28.98	29.85	30.75	31.67	32.62
– Depreciation		(141.82)	(141.82)	(141.82)	(141.82)	(141.82)	(141.82)	(141.82)	(141.82)	(141.82)	(141.82)
Taxable Income		30.18	46.49	63.42	81.01	99.27	118.27	138.02	158.57	179.97	202.25
Tax Payable @ 39.6%		(11.95)	(18.41)	(25.11)	(32.08)	(39.31)	(46.83)	(54.66)	(62.79)	(71.27)	(80.09)
After Tax Cash Flow		113.67	120.74	127.97	135.36	142.91	150.62	158.48	166.50	174.66	182.98
– Equity in	(1,200.00)										
+ Net Cash from Sale											2,511.80
Total Return	(1,200.00)	113.67	120.74	127.97	135.36	142.91	150.62	158.48	166.50	174.66	2,694.78

Purchase Price	$4,400.00		Sales Price	$6,200.00		Sales Price	$6,200.00
+Capital Exp.	$ 286.60		Net Book Value	(3,268.42)		–Income Tax	(820.84)
–Depreciation	($1,418.18)		Gain On Sale	$2,931.58		–Mortgage Balance	(2,867.36)
Net Book Value	$3,268.42		Tax Liability at 28%	(820.84)		Net Cash from Sale	$2,511.80

NET PRESENT VALUE AT 12%: $401.82

INTERNAL RATE OF RETURN: 16.51%

Because he had already assembled the critical facts about Alison Green .
Exhibit 1, it was easy for him to determine the Before Tax Cash Flow, the Ta.
Payable and the After Tax Cash Flow associated with the project over his projected ten year ownership period. The steps are outlined in **Appendix A**. Having
determined the potential cash flow after taxes, including the computation of net
cash from sale (see **Exhibit 5** on next page), Cartwright calculated the Internal
Rate of Return and the Net Present Value of the Project (NPV) at 12%. He felt
this last figure could be useful in setting a maximum purchase price for any subsequent negotiations. His calculations are summarized in **Exhibit 6**.

Exhibit 6   Financial Analysis

	ALISON GREEN	900 STONY WALK	IVY TERRACE	THE FOWLER BUILDING
Equity Required	$1,200,000	_____	_____	_____
Simple Return Measures				
Capitalization Rate—Purchase	10.82%	_____	_____	_____
Capitalization Rate—Sale	10.02%	_____	_____	_____
Cash-on-Cash Return (year 1)	10.47%	_____	_____	_____
Increase in Capital Value	40.91%	_____	_____	_____
$\left(\dfrac{Sales\ Price-Purchase\ Price}{Purchase\ Price}\right)$				
Discounted Return Measures				
Internal Rate of Return	16.51%	_____	_____	_____
Net Present Value @ 12%	401.82	_____	_____	_____
Profitability Index (Net Present Value)	33.49%	_____	_____	_____
$\left(\dfrac{Net\ Present\ Value}{Initial\ Equity}\right)$				

It was obvious that Alison Green more than met the DeRights' minimum return
requirements of 12% but Cartwright was intrigued. He wondered how the other
projects would measure up to Alison Green in **Exhibit 6**. Cartwright wanted to
determine the rank of each project on each measure in **Exhibit 7**.

Exhibit 7   Investment Ranking[1]

	ALISON GREEN	900 STONY WALK	IVY TERRACE	THE FOWLER BUILDING
Simple Return Measures				
Capitalization Rate—Purchase	_____	_____	_____	_____
Capitalization Rate—Sale	_____	_____	_____	_____
Cash-on-Cash Return	_____	_____	_____	_____
Discounted Return Measures				
Internal Rate of Return	_____	_____	_____	_____
Net Present Value	_____	_____	_____	_____
Profitability Index[1]	_____	_____	_____	_____

[1]All investment rankings reflect the perspective of the DeRights as prospective purchasers in year 1 and sellers in year 10 with 1 being the most favorable and 4 being the least. A higher capitalization rate projection in purchasing the property is more favorable. In case of sale the reverse is true.

Next, Cartwright wanted to examine the cash flows from the Alison Green project to see whether the source of return suggested an appropriate match of people to property. There are three sources of cash from a real property investment:
- *Before Tax Cash Flow*
- *Tax Effects*
- *Future Value.*

He separately listed the annual cash flows from each source for Alison Green and discounted them at the project's internal rate of return of 16.51%. This allowed him to look at the present values of each cash stream and compare the separate streams to one another and the initial investment. Since the internal rate of return can be found by discounting the cash flows at a rate which makes the net present value of the project zero, i.e., discounted costs equal discounted benefits, each separate discounted income stream could be compared with the total initial investment to identify the proportionate sources of benefits. **Exhibit 8** illustrates his analysis for Alison Green. The results are summarized in **Exhibit 9**.

Income tax consequences are important. In the early 1980s, with the shorter 15 year depreciation schedules properties often generated losses that could be used against other income. Today, albeit at lower levels, depreciation still helps to minimize taxes and make after tax returns more favorable than an investment in, for example, taxable bonds. Investors are especially concerned that the depreciation deduction exceed the mortgage amortization which is non-deductible for tax purposes. In the case of Alison Green, the income tax payable as a percentage of after tax cash flow rises from 10.5% in year 1 to 44% in year 10.

Mr. Cartwright then examined the breakdown of Alison Green's "Futures" into components on a simple proportionate basis, **Exhibit 10**. It was apparent that the increase in sales price over time was an important part of the total "future" cash flows, but capital gains taxes substantially reduced the net cash flow to the seller.

Exhibit 8   Breakdown of 16.51% Internal Rate of Return ($000s)

YEAR	CASH FLOW BEFORE TAX ACTUAL	CASH FLOW BEFORE TAX DISCOUNTED	INCOME TAX CONSEQUENCES ACTUAL	INCOME TAX CONSEQUENCES DISCOUNTED	FUTURES ACTUAL	FUTURES DISCOUNTED	TOTAL ACTUAL	TOTAL DISCOUNTED
1	$125.62	107.82	(11.95)	(10.26)	0	0	113.67	97.56
2	139.15	102.51	(18.41)	(13.56)	0	0	120.74	88.95
3	153.09	96.80	(25.11)	(15.88)	0	0	127.97	85.92
4	167.44	90.87	(32.08)	(17.41)	0	0	135.36	73.46
5	182.22	84.88	(39.31)	(18.31)	0	0	142.91	66.57
6	197.45	78.95	(46.83)	(18.72)	0	0	150.62	60.23
7	213.14	73.14	(54.66)	(18.76)	0	0	158.48	54.64
8	229.29	67.54	(62.79)	(18.50)	0	0	166.50	49.52
9	245.93	62.17	(71.27)	(18.02)	0	0	174.66	44.79
10	263.07	57.08	(80.09)	(17.38)	2,511.80	545.03	2,694.78	584.73
Total	1,916.41	821.77	(442.52)	(166.80)	2,511.80	545.03	3,985.69	1,200.00
Percent		68.48%		(13.90%)		45.42%		100.00%

Exhibit 9   Percent of Total Benefits (At Internal Rate of Return)

	ALISON GREEN	900 STONY WALK	IVY TERRACE	THE FOWLER BUILDING
Before Tax Cash Flow	68.48%	_____	_____	_____
Tax Benefits	(13.90%)	_____	_____	_____
Future Value	45.42%	_____	_____	_____

Exhibit 10   Angus Cartwright Breakdown of Futures

	ALISON GREEN ACTUAL $	900 STONY WALK ACTUAL $	IVY TERRACE ACTUAL $	THE FOWLER BUILDING ACTUAL $
Return of Initial Cash	1,200,000	_____	_____	_____
Recapture Mtg. Amortization	332,640	_____	_____	_____
Increase in Sales Price	1,800,000	_____	_____	_____
Capital Gains Tax on Depreciation	(397,090)	_____	_____	_____
Capital Gains Tax on Increased Sales Price[1]	(423,750)	_____	_____	_____
Total[2]	2,511,800	_____	_____	_____

[1]Gain reduced by increase in Net Book Value as a result of Capital Expenditures taken.
[2]Total $ return of futures as taken from Exhibit 8.

Cartwright felt that the "Breakdown of Futures" gave him information which would be useful in advising his clients. The breakdown suggested the need for careful planning of the eventual sale. It highlighted the impact of the growth in projected sales price, the rate and amount of mortgage amortization, and the rate and amount of taxation. He believed that by forcefully bringing the impact of these variables to his clients' attention he could help them understand better the assumptions underlying their actions.

Angus Cartwright had some additional analysis and some hard thinking to do. He decided to repeat his analysis for 900 Stony Walk, Ivy Terrace, and The Fowler Building. He wanted to match the needs of his clients with the characteristics of the properties and the returns they offered. He felt this was the best way to select an investment for each of the DeRights. Cartwright wished to test his intuitive perceptions of the properties against the ranking of each project, although he knew that differences in rankings could be due to differences in the implicit assumptions underlying each measure and the size of the original investment in each project.

Cartwright was not about to make a purchase without additional field work and analysis. However, his analysis would allow him to establish sensible priorities upon which he could efficiently allocate his time.

APPENDIX A   METHOD FOR FINANCIAL ANALYSIS OF INCOME PRODUCING REAL ESTATE

1. Establish the following variables:
    A. *Gross Purchase Price* or construction cost.
    B. *Depreciable base* which is gross purchase price less land value. (Land value is either actual value of land or is proportionate to the amount of real estate tax attributable to land.)
    C. *Depreciable life* of building (capital cost recovery period).
    D. Method of *Depreciation.*
    E. Estimated *Sales Price.*
    F. Estimated *Year of Sale.*
    G. *Net Operating Income* (Free & Clear) for each year of ownership. (Gross—Vacancies, Operating Expenses and Real Estate Taxes).
    H. Annual Increase or Decrease in Operating Income (% or $).
    I. Capital Reserves (if any).
    J. *Leasehold Payments* (if any).
    K. *Equity Investment* Required.
    L. Amount of *Mortgage* or *Mortgages.*
    M. *Interest Rate, Term, Amortization Period* and *Annual Carrying Cost of Mortgage or Mortgages.*
    N. *Income Tax Bracket* of Owner (if unknown, use 39.6% rate.)
2. Determine *Cash Flow Before Income Taxes* by deducting capital reserves, leasehold expenses and financing charges (interest and principal) from cash flow from operations. The ratio of cash flow before income taxes to cash investment gives simple return on investment, sometimes known as the cash on cash return. The ratio of cash flow from operations to total cost of investment is the free and clear return or the capitalization rate.
3. Determine *Taxable Income* by deducting leasehold expenses (if any), interest charges, and depreciation from cash flow from operations for each year. Annual depreciation is calculated by dividing the depreciable base by the total economic life if the straight line method is used. Prior to the 1986 Tax Act, accelerated depreciation methods were permitted for certain types of properties. For example, if a double declining balance method was used, the approach would be to multiply for each year the portion of the base still undepreciated by a percentage found by the product of 1/economic life times 200%.
4. Determine *Income Tax Payable* by multiplying taxable income by the income tax bracket of the owner.
5. Determine Cash Flow After Income Taxes by deducting income tax payable from either cash flow before income taxes or from taxable income plus depreciation less amortization and capital reserves.
6. Determine Gain on Sale from the future sale of property by deducting from net sales price, the book value of the property (original purchase price plus capital improvements less depreciation taken).
7. Determine the Capital Gains Tax payable on sale by applying the appropriate capital gains tax to the capital gain. If an installment sale, the tax paid each year is generally based on the ratio that the cash received bears to the total consideration for the equity of the property.
8. Determine Net Cash Flow from Sale by subtracting from the net sales price any mortgage balances and any taxes payable.
9. Determine Internal Rate of Return by applying the appropriate discount rate from the present value tables to the net after tax cash flow for each year, until the sum of these figures approximates the initial cash investment.
10. If the internal rate of return is known, the relative importance of each of the component cash flow streams can be ascertained by discounting the net after tax cash flows of each stream at the internal rate of return.

PART II Financing of Real Estate

8

GRAYBAR SYNDICATIONS

In March 1958, the Graybar Building, a one million square foot office structure in midtown Manhattan, is facing competition from a new generation of buildings. Its proposed acquisition by a syndicate is predicated on a tiered structure of financing and returns to a complex array of participants. The challenge is to wade through the legal documentation of the offering, decipher the priority and breakdown of the cash flow from the property, and decide who gets what return and when. The case deals with many of the issues relating to financial deal structuring.

Discussion Questions:

1. What are the key factors to consider when analyzing the rental income from this property? How would you evaluate operations?
2. What is the value of the property both in 1958 and 1977 to the various participants?
3. What are the potential advantages and disadvantages of investing in a real estate syndication? What has determined the form of ownership chosen for the Graybar Building?

In March 1958, Mr. Harold Morse was trying to decide whether to recommend an investment in a real estate syndication, "Graybar Building Associates." (See **Exhibit 1**.) At the time the Graybar Building was built in 1927, it was one of the largest office structures ever completed. In 1953, the controlling ownership of Graybar was sold in a package that included the acquisition of the 77-story Chrysler Building, the second tallest building in the world, and its 32-story annex, the Chrysler Building East. This $52 million deal, the largest real estate transaction in the city's history, followed by two years the landmark purchase of the Empire State Building, the world's tallest skyscraper, for $51 million.

Mr. Morse was a Long Island attorney whose many clients looked to him for financial advice. Most of these clients lived comfortably and were in tax brackets of about 50%. One of these clients, Dr. Planter, had sent Mr. Morse the Graybar prospectus. He had received it from friends who were planning to invest. Dr. Planter asked Mr. Morse to read it and advise him as to what he should do. The total capital being raised was $4.2 million, which was subject to an $18 million leasehold position simultaneously being acquired by Metropolitan Life and to a ground lease held by New York Central.

Mr. Morse reviewed the advantages of investing in real estate. He knew that real estate prices were rising sharply. He had read of the "big killings" many had made. The field was supposed to be an excellent hedge against inflation while providing a high annual cash return substantially above the 3.2% return currently obtained from dividends of stocks listed on the S&P 500 index. Depreciation allowances also permitted much of the income to be tax sheltered. Further equity was being built up through mortgage amortization. The New York area, where the property being syndicated was located, was supposed to be especially desirable. Since most of his clients' funds were invested in their own businesses, and in the stock market, real estate appeared to be a sound means of diversification.

Mr. Morse had heard a number of favorable reports recommending syndications as the correct vehicle for owning and investing in real estate. Before large-scale real estate syndication developed, investment in high-priced real estate was confined almost exclusively to the large real estate firms and to wealthy individuals. During the 1950s, however, there was a rapidly growing tendency for some properties to be owned by small investors, who pooled their cash in real estate syndicates. The idea of high guaranteed returns paid out in monthly checks was

Adjunct Professor William J. Poorvu prepared this case as the basis for class discussion rather than to illustrate either effective or ineffective handling of an administrative situation.

appealing. An investor not only could diversify holdings into another field, but diversify within the field by buying units in several properties of various types. Small investors would also benefit from experienced property management.

Syndications appeared to cure the prime drawback to real estate for the small investor, the lack of liquidity. The syndicators were sometimes providing markets for the resale of the units they had sold, often at higher than original prices. They appeared to be attempting to institutionalize their operations in the same manner as stock brokerage firms had. People said that the field was taking on a more professional character. He knew that during the depression many real estate syndications failed, but at this time in 1957 Mr. Morse felt that the economy was basically sound.

The decision then revolved around the soundness of this particular offering. Mr. Morse tried to list the questions he would want answered after he had completed his analysis. He first wanted to examine both the projected cash and after-tax returns offered to the investors, and the opportunities for higher returns through mortgage refinancing, appreciation in value, increase in rentals and income. How secure were these returns? How was leverage used in each case, and what bearing did it have upon the risks involved? How did the uses to which the properties were being put affect the risk factor?

He was interested in the role of the promoters. What risks were they taking, and what were they getting in return? Was there an equitable relationship between the two? Based upon the merchandising techniques used by the promoters in their prospectus, what type of investors should be attracted? Do the promoters appear reputable from their background, and the way they are presenting the investments? What protection is there from mismanagement by the promoters? Is there any government protection, and if not, should there be?

The Graybar offering was set up as a joint venture, with each of two partners acting as agent for one half of the investors (a one half interest). This created potential liability for each investor, as the participants would share proportionately in all profits and losses realized by the senior venturer from whom they purchased their partnerships. Any one participant could be liable to a person outside the venture for the full amount of any obligation to which the senior venturer might be subject by reason of his ownership in the property.

As a protection, tenant leases and debt financing agreements would have specific clauses exculpating the joint venturers from personal liability. General liability insurance would cover many property-related risks. Still, he wondered if there were any other areas uncovered that he should worry about. As an alternative he inquired about the limited partnership format, but was told that it created a danger of double taxation since in 1958 the IRS had certain provisions under which some partnerships were liable to be taxed as corporations.

Lastly, he was concerned about the adequacy and reliability of the information presented. What other information would he want? Can any real estate offering be evaluated solely from the figures?

Exhibit 1   Prospectus

PROSPECTUS

Graybar Building
420 Lexington Avenue
New York City

$4,180,000 of Participations in Partnership Interests in
GRAYBAR BUILDING ASSOCIATES

PRICE PER PARTICIPATION: $10,000 MINIMUM

THESE SECURITIES HAVE NOT BEEN APPROVED OR DISAPPROVED BY THE SECUR-
ITIES AND EXCHANGE COMMISSION NOR HAS THE COMMISSION PASSED UPON THE
ACCURACY OR ADEQUACY OF THIS PROSPECTUS. ANY REPRESENTATION TO THE
CONTRARY IS A CRIMINAL OFFENSE.

	Price to Public	Underwriting Commissions*	Proceeds to Issuer
Total	$4,180,000	None	$4,180,000
Per unit	10,000	None	10,000

*As to the remuneration and interest of the members of Associates in the
transactions described herein, see page 12.

The date of this Prospectus is March 10, 1958

Exhibit 1   (continued)

GRAYBAR BUILDING, NEW YORK, N. Y.
SUMMARY OF OPERATIONS

	December 31, 1953	December 31, 1954	December 31, 1955	December 31, 1956	December 31, 1957
INCOME FROM PROPERTY OPERATIONS:					
Rental Income (Including Percentage Rents)	$3,326,820.36	$3,479,537.07	$3,725,469.52	$4,087,447.83	$4,403,434.34
Other Charges to Tenants and Other Income (Note B)	438,427.09	471,452.85	407,816.25	775,400.19	1,012,526.39
Total income	$3,765,247.45	$3,950,989.92	$4,133,285.77	$4,862,848.02	$5,415,960.73
DEDUCT:					
Operating Expenses Exclusive of Items Below (Note C)	$1,673,346.87	$1,638,861.55	$1,550,019.88	$1,988,192.70	$2,319,425.79
Payroll Taxes	26,885.66	25,718.21	25,845.12	26,766.62	39,415.07
Maintenance and Repairs (Note D)	—	—	—	—	—
Real Estate Taxes	420,323.69	477,603.98	476,591.86	498,124.88	508,438.22
Total	$2,120,556.22	$2,142,183.74	$2,052,456.86	$2,513,084.20	$2,867,279.08
Operating Income Before Mortgage Interest, Depreciation and Amortization, Federal Income and State Franchise Taxes, Corporate Expenses and Rental under Basic Ground Lease or Leases Effective December 30, 1957	$1,644,691.23	$1,808,806.18	$2,080,828.91	$2,349,763.82	$2,548,681.65

NOTES:

A. The above statement has been prepared from income statements of the present and prior lessees for the applicable periods which have been restated to reflect a net refund of real estate taxes of $12,122.70 applicable to the year 1954 which was received in 1955.

B. Other Charges To Tenants And Other Income include gross billings for electricity, supplies and work orders chargeable to tenants and also commissions on towel service, telephone booths, etc. The fluctuations in "Other Charges To Tenants And Other Income" reflected in the above summary are due primarily to billings on tenant work orders. Prior to 1954 no separate record of such billings or the costs pertaining thereto were maintained, nor are they readily determinable. Gross billings on tenants' work orders amounted to $182,206 in 1954, $74,966 in 1955, $357,350 in 1956 and $597,399 in 1957.

The costs applicable to such tenants' work orders were in large measure responsible for the fluctuations in "Operating Expenses" shown in the summary. These costs were $106,940 in 1954, $240,975 in 1955, $38,087 in 1956 and $453,733 in 1957. The only other major variation was in salaries and wages which increased $139,104 in 1956 when compared with 1955.

C. Operations for the period from January 1, 1953 to October 9, 1953 include a fee based on collections which covered both management and renting services. Operations after October 9, 1953 include management fees and leasing commissions, computed at standard New York City Real Estate Board rates for commercial properties. The leasing commissions are charged into operations on a pro-rata basis over the term of the individual tenants' leases.

D. Maintenance and repairs are reflected in wages and other building expenses and are not separately classified as such in the accounts or readily determinable.

Exhibit 1 (continued)

No person has been authorized to give any information or to make any representations other than those contained in this Prospectus, and, if given or made, such information and representations must not be relied upon as having been authorized by Graybar Building Associates or by any of the members thereof.

CONTENTS

		Page
I.	General Nature of the Offering	3
II.	Terms of the Offering	3
III.	The Graybar Building	4
	1. Description	4
	2. Rental Statistics as of January 1, 1958	4
	3. Summary of Operations	5
IV.	Proposed Acquisition of the Leasehold by Associates	5
V.	Description of the Leasehold	6
	1. General	6
	2. Important Provisions	6
VI.	Operation of the Graybar Building Under the Sublease	7
	1. Provisions of the Sublease	7
	2. The Sublessees	8
	3. Physical Inspections	8
VII.	Formation of Associates	8
VIII.	Status of Purchasers of Participations	9
	1. Participating Agreements	9
	2. Tax Status of Associates and Joint Ventures	10
	3. Tax Treatment of Cash Distributions to Participants	10
IX.	Information as to Partners in Associates	11
	1. Biographical	11
	2. Remuneration and Interest in Transactions described herein	12
X.	Legal Opinions	12
XI.	Financial Statements	13

A Registration Statement has been filed with the Securities and Exchange Commission, Washington, D. C., by Graybar Building Associates and the individual partners therein, as Co-Registrants, for the Participations offered hereunder.

This Prospectus does not contain all of the information set forth in the Registration Statement, certain items of which are omitted or included in condensed form as permitted by the Rules and Regulations of the Commission. Statements contained herein as to the contents of any contract or other document are not necessarily complete, and in each instance reference is hereby made to the copy of such contract or other document filed as an Exhibit to the Registration Statement, each such statement being qualified in all respects by such reference.

Copies of the Registration Statement may be obtained from the Commission on payment of the prescribed charges.

Exhibit 1   (continued)

I.

GENERAL NATURE OF THE OFFERING

1. GRAYBAR BUILDING ASSOCIATES ("Associates") is a partnership consisting of Lawrence A. Wien and William F. Purcell. It has contracted to purchase a net lease of the Graybar Building, 420 Lexington Avenue, New York City, for $4,000,000 in cash.

The net lease to be purchased by Associates is referred to as the "Leasehold" in this Prospectus.

2. The Metropolitan Life Insurance Company is the Lessor under the Leasehold, and Associates will be its Lessee. The Metropolitan recently paid $18,000,000 for its position as Lessor.

3. The term of the Leasehold extends to May 30, 1976, but Associates has renewal options to the year 2030. Renewal of the Leasehold is automatic upon the giving of appropriate notice by Associates and does not require the payment of any additional consideration. The Leasehold requires the payment of certain rents, which are described at page 6.

4. Associates will not operate the property. It will purchase the Leasehold subject to an existing Sublease under which Webb & Knapp, Inc., and its wholly-owned subsidiary, Graysler Corporation, operate the premises.

5. The Sublease has a term and renewal options similar to the Leasehold. It provides for the payment by the Sublessees to Associates of an annual net rent in an amount sufficient to enable Associates

  (a) to pay all rents called for in the Leasehold;

  (b) to defray administrative costs; and

  (c) to make a monthly cash distribution to each participant equal to $1200 per year on each $10,000 Participation during the initial term of the Sublease.

  In the event of renewal of the Sublease at the end of the initial term in 1976, the rent payable by the Sublessees is rearranged so that thereafter the cash distribution to participants will be increased to $1900 per year.

An analysis of such cash distribution and a discussion of the assumptions on which it is calculated appear at pages 10 and 11.

6. The Sublessees pay all expenses connected with the operation of the Graybar Building. The rent payable to Associates will be a net rental, subject only to the expenses listed above. The Sublessees, however, may assign the Sublease under certain conditions, as set forth on page 8, and may then be relieved of further liability. The investment offered hereby should therefore be judged primarily on the basis of the income-producing capacity of the property itself. A summary of operations for the property appears at pages 9 and 10.

7. Each of the two partners in Associates will himself contribute $10,000 to the partnership capital, and is offering Participations of $2,090,000 in his partnership interest through this Prospectus. The total partnership capital will thus be $4,200,000, which will be used to purchase the Leasehold ($4,000,000), to defray costs incident to the acquisition ($175,000), and to pay the expenses of this offering ($25,000). Purchasers of Participations will share proportionately in the ownership of the partnership interests in Associates, under Participating Agreements with the partners (see page 9).

II.

TERMS OF THE OFFERING

1. The offering is being made by the partners in Associates.

2. Offers to purchase Participations will be accepted only from individuals of full age.

Exhibit 1   (continued)

3. Each offer to purchase shall be for a minimum of $10,000 or a multiple thereof.

4. A deposit of up to 25 per cent of the price may be required for any Participation. All deposits will be held in Special Account by counsel for Associates, Wien, Lane, Klein & Purcell, 60 East 42d Street, New York, New York.

5. The title closing is scheduled for April 30, 1958, with rights of adjournment to May 31 or June 30, 1958. If offers totaling $4,180,000 have not been accepted by June 30, 1958, all deposits will be repaid without interest. This amount, together with the $20,000 contribution of the two partners, is the sum required to make the payment under the purchase contract and defray the costs and expenses noted above.

6. The balance of each Participation will be payable at the office of Wien, Lane, Klein & Purcell, upon demand, at any time after the required amount of offers has been accepted.

III.

THE GRAYBAR BUILDING

1. Description. The Graybar Building is one of the largest and best known office buildings in New York City. It occupies the entire city block on the westerly side of Lexington Avenue between 43rd and 44th Streets, in the heart of New York's business center.

The building forms the eastern entrance to the Grand Central Station and provides a broad concourse leading directly to the Main Hall (upper level) of the terminal. It also affords connections to various subway lines and other transit facilities.

Completed in 1927, the Graybar Building is of fireproof, concrete and steel construction and contains 30 stories and penthouse, with ground floor stores and interior shops. It covers a ground area of some 68,400 square feet, has a volume of approximately 16 million cubic feet and a gross floor area of about 1,250,000 square feet. The net rentable area is approximately 971,163 square feet, including store space.

The building is serviced by 32 Otis, signal control, micro-leveling passenger elevators and 2 Otis freight elevators. About 74 per cent of the tenant areas in the building are air-conditioned through 2060 tons of water-cooled and air-cooled units, of which $315\frac{1}{4}$ tons are landlord owned. All units utilize permanent electric and water facilities installed by the landlord. Construction of a water cooling system sufficient for the entire building is planned. All requisite piping from the roof down to the second floor has been installed, and one 750 ton cell of the cooling tower has been erected on the roof.

The 406 tenants of the building are of widely diversified types, and include the Great Atlantic and Pacific Tea Company (executive offices), Conde Nast Publications, Inc., the J. Walter Thompson Advertising agency, the Chase Manhattan Bank, the Dictaphone Corporation, American Gas Company and Sun Oil Company.

2. Rental Statistics as of January 1, 1958. Associates is advised that on this date, the building was 99.86 per cent occupied. For the past ten years occupancy percentages were as follows:

1957 — 99.8%; 1956 — 99.7%; 1955 — 99.6%; 1954 — 99.9%;
1953 — 99.4%; 1952 — 99.8%; 1951 — 99.4%; 1950 — 98.9%;
1949 — 98.9%; 1948 — 98.9%.

On January 1, 1958, the average rate per square foot for the building was $4.61. The total annual rent roll was $4,474,160, exclusive of percentage rentals and tax escalator increases. In addition, leases already executed provide for annual increases amounting to $18,254 beginning in 1958, $5,910 in 1959, and $150,407 in 1960, or a total of $174,571.

Exhibit 1 (continued)

On January 1, 1958, the following lease expiration schedule applied:

Year	Square Ft. Area	% of Gross Rental Value
1958	102,446	11.06
1959	93,907	11.24
1960	250,447	22.13
1961	153,680	17.88
1962	67,386	6.79
1963	3,539	.41
1964	8,382	1.17
1965	100,535	11.35
1966	44,174	4.06
1967	29,019	3.66
1970	1,620	.21
1976	51,082	5.01
Statutory	62,594	4.96
Monthly	1,016	.07
TOTAL	969,827	100%
VACANT	1,336	
	971,163	

The Graybar Building competes with office structures in the Grand Central area and other sections of New York City. In the past five years, new construction has accounted for some 5,800,500 square feet of rentable space in the Grand Central area, which comprises the district between 38th and 50th Street, and Sixth and Second Avenues. Associates is advised that virtually all of this new space is rented, and for the most part is occupied by large tenants under long term leases. At present, other new buildings under construction are expected to result in approximately 3,500,000 square feet of additional space in this area. The greater portion of this space also is reported to be rented at this time.

3. Summary of Operations. A summary, showing the results of operations of the Graybar Building for the five year period ended December 31, 1957, is set forth at Page 15 of this Prospectus.

The total rent payable by the Sublessees to Associates under the Sublease will be $2,540,000 per year during the initial term. As shown in the summary of operations, the net operating revenue from the building in the year 1957 was sufficient to cover this rent, although the net operating revenues for the years prior to 1957 were not. However, neither the 1957 net operating revenues nor those for the previous years are indicative of the present net operating revenue.

For example, the rent roll as of January 1, 1958 was $70,726 more than the total rent collections shown for the year 1957, which in turn were substantially higher than those shown in the summary for prior years. In addition, based upon previous experience, it is expected that approximately $20,000 will be received during the current year for percentage rents and under tax escalator clauses. Also, as indicated above, future rent increases contained in leases already executed, will add approximately $174,571 annually to the rent roll over the next three years.

The present net operating revenues from the building are more than sufficient to cover the rent provided for in the Sublease. Of course, no representation can be made that such net operating revenues necessarily will continue without change in the future since that will depend upon competition and the general state of the economy.

IV.
PROPOSED ACQUISITION OF THE LEASEHOLD BY ASSOCIATES

(1) On December 30, 1957, Lawrence A. Wien purchased the Leasehold on the Graybar Building, subject to the Sublease. The purchase was made from Webb & Knapp, Inc., and Graysler Corporation.

Exhibit 1   (continued)

(2) The purchase price was $4,000,000, of which Mr. Wien paid $400,000 in cash and the balance by a 6 per cent Mortgage on the Leasehold, maturing July 1, 1958 and prepayable at any time.

(3) On January 22, 1958, Mr. Wien contracted to sell the Leasehold to Associates for $4,000,000 in cash. In addition to the purchase price, Associates will incur expenses of $200,000 in connection with the transactions described in this Prospectus. Thus, its total cost for the Leasehold will be $4,200,000.

(4) The $3,600,000 Leasehold Mortgage will be prepaid and discharged by Mr. Wien on the closing date of the sale to Associates.

(5) The sale is scheduled to close on April 30, 1958, but Associates has the right to adjourn the closing to May 31, 1958, or June 30, 1958.

(6) Until such closing, Mr. Wien will receive on his own behalf the rents paid under the Sublease and will discharge the obligations of the Leasehold and the Leasehold Mortgage. The net return on Mr. Wien's $400,000 investment during the period of his ownership will be $4,167 a month.

V.

DESCRIPTION OF THE LEASEHOLD

1. General. (a) The land under the Graybar Building is owned by the New York Central Railroad. Acting through a subsidiary real estate corporation, the railroad created a Ground Lease on the property to May 31, 1976, with renewal options to the year 2030. The original tenant under the Ground Lease built the Graybar Building in 1927.

(b) On December 30, 1957, the then tenant under the Ground Lease created the Leasehold as a net lease of the entire premises for the same term and renewal periods as it had under the Ground Lease, less one day.

(c) Immediately thereafter, Metropolitan Life Insurance Company purchased the position of tenant under the Ground Lease for $18,000,000, and Lawrence A. Wien purchased the position of Lessee of the Leasehold for $4,000,000.

(d) The Leasehold was purchased by Mr. Wien subject to a Sublease, also created on December 30, 1957, under which Webb & Knapp and its wholly-owned subsidiary, Graysler Corporation now operate the Graybar Building as Mr. Wien's Sublessees.

(e) When Associates acquires Mr. Wien's position it will become entitled to receive the rent payable by the Sublessees; the Metropolitan Life Insurance Company will receive the rent called for in the Leasehold; and the New York Central Railroad subsidiary will receive the annual Ground Rent.

2. Important Provisions. The important provisions of the Leasehold are:

(a) The initial term runs to May 30, 1976. By giving written notice, Associates may renew the Leasehold for three additional terms extending to the year 2030.

(b) Upon such notice, renewal of the Leasehold term is automatic. Renewal of the Leasehold also results in a like renewal of the Ground Lease.

(c) The Leasehold Rent payable by Associates to Metropolitan Life Insurance Company is $1,620,000 during the initial term. During all renewal periods the Leasehold Rent is $540,000 annually, or a reduction of $1,080,000.

(d) Associates, as Lessee, also will be required to pay the Ground Rent to the New York Central Railroad subsidiary. The Ground Rent is $390,000 per year during the initial term of the Leasehold and

Exhibit 1   (continued)

for each renewal year until 1988. During renewal years from 1988 to 2009, the Ground Rent will be a sum agreed upon by the parties to the Ground Lease or, failing agreement, a sum equal to 5 per cent of the value of the land (considered vacant and unimproved), but not less than $390,000. For the remaining period from 2009 to 2030, the Ground Rent shall be determined by the same formula, but shall not be less than that paid in the prior period.

(e)   Upon renewal of the Leasehold at the end of the initial term, the total rent payable by Associates (i.e., Leasehold Rent and Ground Rent) will be $930,000 per year.

(f)   Associates, as Lessee, will be obligated to pay all operating and maintenance expenses, including real estate taxes, make all necessary repairs, maintain insurance coverage of various types and rebuild or replace the building in the event of fire or other casualty.

(g)   The Lessee also is required to perform all obligations contained in the Ground Lease. Such obligations are the same in all material respects as those contained in the Leasehold itself. The Sublease described below, under which the premises are being operated, imposes upon the Sublessees obligations which are equivalent in all respects to those of Associates under the Leasehold and Ground Lease. The rent payable by the Sublessees includes the funds necessary to meet the Leasehold and Ground Lease rents. The Sublessees also pay all of the operating and maintenance expenses.

(h)   Associates may assign the Leasehold at any time, without consent of its Lessor, Metropolitan Life Insurance Company, provided the assignment is to a corporation the stock of which is owned equally by its two partners. Consent of the Metropolitan is required for any other type of assignment. In all cases, upon assumption by the assignee of the Leasehold, Associates will be relieved of any further obligation thereunder.

VI.

OPERATION OF THE GRAYBAR BUILDING UNDER THE SUBLEASE

1.   Provisions of the Sublease.

(a)   The Sublease is for the same initial term as the Leasehold, less one day and, therefore, extends to May 29, 1976. It has co-extensive renewal privileges.

(b)   The total annual rent payable to Associates by the Sublessees is $2,540,000 per year to December 31, 1972; $2,530,000 thereafter per year to May 29, 1976; and $1,774,000 per year in the event of renewal at the end of the initial term. This annual rent consists of three parts:

  i.   a sum sufficient to pay the Leasehold Rent to the Metropolitan Life Insurance Company;

  ii. a sum sufficient to pay the Ground Rent to the New York Central subsidiary; and

  iii. a basic rent which Associates will use to defray administrative costs and make its cash distributions to participants. This portion of the annual rent payable by the Sublessees will be $530,000 per year to December 31, 1972, $520,000 per year to May 29, 1976, and $844,000 annually during any renewal periods.

(c)   As previously stated, the annual Leasehold Rent payable to the Metropolitan Life Insurance Company reduces by $1,080,000 at the end of the initial term on May 30, 1976. In the event of a renewal of the Sublease at that time, both Associates and the Sublessees will share in the benefit resulting from this reduction as follows:

Upon any such renewal, the Sublessees will pay an additional $324,000 annually to Associates as basic rent under the Sublease, thus increasing Associates' portion of the total rent from $520,000 to $844,000.

Exhibit 1 (continued)

The Sublessees will have the benefit of the remaining $756,000 reduction in the annual Leasehold Rent. Thus, their overall rent obligation, upon a renewal at the end of the initial term, will be reduced from $2,530,000 to $1,774,000.

(d) As additional rent, the Sublessees shall pay to Associates one-third of the amount by which the Sublessees' net income derived from the operation of the premises, after payment of operating and maintenance expenses, real estate taxes and all rents, but before amortization of the cost of the Sublease and before income taxes, exceeds $600,000 in any year up to May 31, 1976 and $1,356,000 in any year thereafter.

(e) The Sublessees are obligated to pay all operating and maintenance costs and real estate taxes, keep the property in good repair, maintain full insurance coverage, rebuild in case of fire or other casualty, and satisfy all other obligations of Associates under the Leasehold.

(f) Consent of the Metropolitan Life Insurance Company is required for any assignment of the Sublease, except where the assignment is to a corporation or corporations each stockholder of which owns the same proportionate amount of stock in the Sublessees. Upon compliance with these provisions and the assumption by the assignee of the obligations of the Sublease, the present Sublessees would be relieved of any further obligation thereunder.

2. The Sublessees. In addition to the Graybar Building, Webb & Knapp, Inc., and/or its subsidiary, Graysler Corporation, operate such large New York City office structures, having the following net rentable areas, as: The Equitable Building at 120 Broadway (40 stories—1,215,270 sq. ft.); the Chrysler Building (75 stories—827,724 sq. ft.); Chrysler Building East (32 stories—401,620 sq. ft.); and 1407 Broadway (42 stories—982,000 sq. ft.).

3. Physical Inspections. Helmsley-Spear, Inc., one of New York City's leading real estate management firms, will be retained by Associates to make periodic physical inspections of the building and its equipment, to render reports thereon, and to act as consultant to Associates with respect to any matters arising out of the ownership of the Leasehold. Helmsley-Spear, Inc., will receive $10,000 annually for these services for the period ending December 31, 1972, and $4,000 per annum during the remainder of the initial term and during any renewals of the Leasehold.

VII.

FORMATION OF ASSOCIATES

1. Associates was formed in New York, by a written agreement dated January 20, 1958, to purchase the Leasehold on the Graybar Building, subject to the Sublease.

2. Under the partnership agreement, the partners will share equally in all profits and losses of the partnership.

3. The partnership will continue until it shall have disposed of all of its assets. The partnership is not to be interrupted by any other cause, including the death of a partner or assignment of his interest. Provision is made for succession to the interest of a deceased partner by a designee.

4. The consent of both partners is required for any sale, or other transfer of the Leasehold, the modification or renewal of the Leasehold, the making or modification of any mortgage thereon, the making or revision of any lease of the property by the partnership, or the disposal of any partnership asset.

5. Wien, Lane, Klein & Purcell will supervise the operation of the partnership agreement, and will maintain the requisite books and records for the partnership.

Exhibit 1 (continued)

VIII.

STATUS OF PURCHASERS OF PARTICIPATIONS

1. Participating Agreements. Each of the two partners in Associates will enter into a Participating Agreement with investors contributing $2,090,000 toward the $4,200,000 total required to acquire the property. Each partner also will contribute $10,000 toward the partnership capital.

Each Participating Agreement will create a joint venture among the parties thereto, who will own the particular partner's one-half interest in Associates in proportion to their respective contributions to its total cost. The Agreements will contain the following provisions:

(a) The partner will act as "Agent" for the participants in his one-half partnership interest.

(b) The participants will share proportionately in all profits or losses realized by the Agent as a partner in Associates. Under New York law, one participant may be liable to a person outside the venture for the full amount of any obligation of the Agent as a partner in Associates or any liability of the partnership. However, in such event he would be entitled to demand and receive pro-rata contributions from his co-participants. As stated previously at page 7, Associates may assign the Leasehold and thereafter be relieved of any further liability thereunder.

(c) The Agent may not agree to sell, or transfer the partnership interest or the Leasehold, to make or modify any mortgage thereon, to modify or renew the Leasehold, to make or modify any sublease of the premises, or to dispose of any partnership asset, without the consent of all his participants. However, if participants owning 80 per cent of the Agent's interest consent to any such action, the Agent or his designee shall have the right to purchase the interest of any non-consenting participant at its original cost, less any capital repaid thereon.

(d) The Agent will incur no personal liability for any action taken by him, except for wilful misconduct, gross negligence or any liabilities under the Securities Act of 1933.

(e) Except as above limited, the Agent may bind his participants, and the participants will agree to indemnify him proportionately against any liability arising by reason of his acting as Agent.

(f) The Agent may resign upon accounting to his successor for all funds he has received. He may be removed by the written direction of participants owning at least three-fourths of the Agent's interest.

(g) If the Agent dies, is removed, resigns or is unable to act, he will be succeeded by one of five persons named as successors in each agreement. If no such designee qualifies, the owners of at least three-fourths of the interest shall select the new Agent.

(h) Each joint venture shall continue until it shall have disposed of the entire interest which it owns in Associates. It will not be interrupted by any other cause, including the death of a participant or any transfer of his Participation.

(i) A participant may transfer his Participation in the joint venture to any individual of full age. Any transfer must be of the full Participation owned, unless such Participation exceeds $10,000. In the latter case, the transfer must be in multiples of $5,000, with a minimum transfer of a $10,000 Participation. The transferee must accept the transfer in writing, and duplicate originals of the transfer instruments must be filed with the Agent, before the transfer shall be effective.

(j) Upon the death of a participant, any individual of full age, designated in the decedent's will or by his executor or administrator, may succeed to his Participation. If no such individual

Exhibit 1   (continued)

qualifies within eight months after date of death, the surviving parties to the joint venture may purchase proportionately the Participation of the decedent, at its original cost, less any capital repaid thereon.

(k) The Agent shall receive no compensation for acting in that capacity.

2. Tax Status of Associates and the Joint Ventures. The status for Federal income tax purposes of Associates and the joint ventures described in this Prospectus has been passed upon by Roswell Magill, Esq., of Cravath, Swaine & Moore, 15 Broad Street, New York City, and by the firm of Stevenson, Paul, Rifkind, Wharton & Garrison, 1614 Eye Street, N.W., Washington, D.C., tax counsel.

Both such counsel have furnished Associates with separate opinions that the members of Associates and of the joint ventures to be formed under the Participating Agreements will qualify as partners for Federal income tax purposes. Therefore, each individual member of Associates and each participant will be taxed on his distributive share of the net income, but the net incomes of Associates and the joint ventures will not be taxable as such.

Both opinions note that the Treasury Regulations contain provisions under which partnerships or joint ventures may be taxed on their net income in the same manner as corporations and the members thereof may be taxed as shareholders. Each opinion, however, concludes that Associates and the joint ventures involved herein do not fall within the said provisions, and therefore should not be taxable as corporations.

3. Tax Treatment of Cash Distributions to Participants.

The following table, which assumes that Associates and the joint ventures will be taxable as partnerships, estimates the aggregate cash income to Associates in each year during the initial term of the Leasehold on the Graybar Building. It also shows the portion of such income distributable to participants under the Participating Agreements.

The rent income shown is based upon the minimum annual net rent provided for in the Sublease to Webb & Knapp, Inc., and Graysler Corporation. The table and the accompanying text below assume that the Sublease will continue in accordance with its terms over all of the years discussed. There is no assurance that the foregoing assumptions necessarily will hold true, but if such rent is paid and Associates and the joint ventures are taxable as partnerships, the following information is applicable:

Rent Income		$2,540,000.00
Expenses:		
Rent Expense (consisting of $1,620,000 Leasehold Rent and $390,000 Ground Rent)	$2,010,000.00	
Legal, accounting and consultant's fees	26,000.00	
		$2,036,000.00
Net Receipts, Before Leasehold Amortization		$ 504,000.00
Leasehold Amortization, write-off over 18 years and one month, 5.53% of $4,200,000		$ 232,258.00
Net Receipts allocable to Participants for Federal income tax purposes		$ 271,742.00

CASH AVAILABLE FOR DISTRIBUTION

Total (Net Receipts, before Leasehold Amortization, as above)		$ 504,000.00
Per $10,000 Participation		1,200.00

Exhibit 1   (continued)

The cash available for distribution, shown immediately above, will represent both income, and to the extent of annual Leasehold amortization, a return of capital. That portion which represents a return of capital will not be reportable as income for Federal income tax purposes. On this basis, each $1200 cash distribution will consist of $647 which constitutes reportable income, and $553 representing a non-taxable return of capital. Although each such return of capital constitutes a partial reduction of the cost of the investment, it does not in any way change the proportionate interest of each participant in Associates.

Deducting the return of capital from the original cost, the rate of income on the remaining invested capital increases each year. The average invested capital over the initial term of the Sublease is $2,100,000, or $5,000 per minimum Participation. The rate of income on the average invested capital over the initial term is 12.94%. Of course, these calculations are based on the assumption that the Sublease will continue and that the rent provided for will be paid throughout the initial term of 18 years and one month.

At the end of the initial term on May 30, 1976, the cost of the Leasehold will have been fully amortized and, thereafter, the entire amount of cash distributed annually in the event of any renewal of the Leasehold will be reportable as income. It should be noted that renewal of the Leasehold by Associates is automatic upon the giving of appropriate notice and does not require the payment of additional consideration.

As heretofore stated, the rent requirements of both the Leasehold and Sublease will change in the event of their renewal at the end of the initial term. In such case, Associates' Rent Income will be $1,774,000 and its Rent Expense will be $930,000. Legal, accounting and consultants' fees will be $46,000 per year during any renewal terms. Thus, upon any such renewal, the cash available for annual distribution to each $10,000 participant will be increased to $1900, all of which will constitute income.

In the above discussion, amortization has been calculated in accordance with present tax law. On January 20, 1958, the House of Representatives passed a bill which would change the law and could require that the cost of a renewable lease be amortized over both the original and renewal terms. This bill has not yet been enacted into law, but is pending before a Senate Committee for its consideration. If enacted, the bill would in no way change the amount of the yearly cash distributions described above. The only effect of the bill could be to decrease the amounts treated as nontaxable return of capital and increase the amounts treated as taxable income during the initial term. However, if this occurred, a portion of the cash distributions received during renewal periods would be treated as a return of capital, which is not the case under the amortization schedule which Associates presently plan to use. Thus, the total amount treated as a return of capital would not be affected by the proposed legislation. At this time, no prediction can be made as to whether or when the bill may become law.

IX.
INFORMATION AS TO PARTNERS IN ASSOCIATES

1. Biographical.

Lawrence A. Wien, Newtown Turnpike, Weston, Connecticut, is a graduate of Columbia College and Columbia Law School, and has been practicing law in New York City since 1928. He is the senior partner in the firm of Wien, Lane, Klein & Purcell. He has specialized in the field of real estate law for over twenty-six years and has been particularly active in creating investments in real property. Such investments include the Hotel Taft at Seventh Avenue and 50th Street, the Equitable Building at 120 Broadway, the Lincoln Building at 60 East 42nd Street, the Garment Center Capitol Buildings at 498, 500 and 512 Seventh Avenue, the Fisk Building at 250 West 57th Street, and the Broad-Exchange Building at 25 Broad Street, all in New York City, and the Warwick Hotel in Philadelphia.

William F. Purcell, 930 Fifth Avenue, New York City, is a graduate of Manhattan College and Fordham Law School, has been a member of the Bar of the State of New York since 1935 and is a partner in the firm of Wien, Lane, Klein & Purcell.

Exhibit 1   (continued)

---

2. Remuneration and Interest in Transactions Described Herein.

Wien, Lane, Klein & Purcell, as counsel for Associates, will be paid an annual fee to supervise the operation of the partnership agreement, from which sum they must defray all regular accounting costs and disbursements. Such fee will be $16,000 per year until December 31, 1972, $12,000 per year from January 1, 1973 to May 31, 1976, and $42,000 per year during all renewal periods.

Of the $200,000 to be used by Associates to defray expenses in connection with the transactions described herein, the firm will receive a legal fee now estimated at approximately $125,000.

As more fully set forth at page 6, Associates will purchase the Leasehold from Mr. Wien.

X.

LEGAL OPINIONS

The legality of the Participations, and other matters of New York State law relating to this offering, have been passed upon by Wien, Lane, Klein & Purcell, 60 East 42nd Street, New York, New York. Legal matters in connection with the Securities Act of 1933 have been passed upon by Milton P. Kroll, Esq., Cafritz Building, Washington, D. C. Questions relating to the status for federal income tax purposes of Associates and the joint ventures created under the Participating Agreements have been passed upon by Roswell Magill, Esq., of Cravath, Swaine & Moore, New York, New York, and by the firm of Stevenson, Paul, Rifkind, Wharton & Garrison, Washington, D. C.

CERTIFICATE OF INDEPENDENT PUBLIC ACCOUNTANTS

We have examined the summary of operations of the Graybar Building, New York, New York, for the five years ended December 31, 1957, during which years the property was leased by Eastern Offices, Inc. for the period from January 1, 1953 to October 9, 1953 and thereafter to the extent of an undivided 75% interest by Webb & Knapp, Inc., or its wholly-owned subsidiary, 65039 Corporation, and to the extent of an undivided 25% interest by Graysler Corporation. Our examinations were made in accordance with generally accepted auditing standards, and accordingly included such tests of the acounting records and such other auditing procedures as we considered necessary in the circumstances.

In our opinion, the summary of operations presents fairly the income from property operations of the Graybar Building, New York, New York, for the five years ended December 31, 1957, before deducting mortgage interest, depreciation and amortization, Federal income and State franchise taxes and other expenses, as noted thereon, in conformity with generally accepted accounting principles applied on a consistent basis.

HARRIS, KERR, FORSTER & COMPANY

New York, New York
March 6, 1958

9

TWINBROOK METRO

In August 1990, Ben Jacobs, a managing partner of The JBG Companies, was trying to determine a proposed price and terms to offer for the Twinbrook Metro portfolio in Montgomery County, MD being sold by Equitable Life. The Portfolio consists of 29.2 acres of land which has been built out with 19 buildings containing 554,054 square feet of office and R&D space. His concerns were whether after a major downturn in the real estate industry, the local rental market had stabilized and how he could attract limited partners to provide the equity capital he needed to make the acquisition.

Discussion Questions:

1. What would you offer for Twinbrook Metro? Complete Exhibit 2. What are the major risks?
2. How would you structure the deal financially? What are the anticipated returns to the parties? What are the advantages to a private limited partnership?
3. What is your negotiating strategy? What further due diligence is required?

In August 1990, Ben Jacobs, one of the founding partners of The JBG Companies (JBG) together with several of his colleagues were trying to determine a proposed price and terms to offer for the Twinbrook Metro portfolio being sold by the Equitable Life Assurance Society (Equitable). The portfolio consists of 29.2 acres of land which has been built out with 19 buildings containing 554,054 square feet of office and R&D space.

JBG was founded in 1962 and has been an owner, developer, manager and adviser in a broad spectrum of real estate projects, primarily in the greater Washington, D.C. area. JBG has completed development of more than 5.4 million square feet of office and retail space, more than 1,300 hotel rooms, approximately 10,000 rental apartment units, 1,400 units of for-sale housing, and 280,000 square feet of for-sale condominiums. A significant portion of these assets were done in joint ventures with individual and institutional investors.

In recent years, anticipating the overbuilding in the real estate market, JBG sold many properties, drastically curtailed its development activities, and emphasized build-to-suit projects, the acquisition of income producing properties and providing fee services for corporate and institutional accounts. As a result, the firm felt itself to be in better financial shape than many of its competitors.

THE OPPORTUNITY

The real estate crash in the late 1980s created a new set of opportunities for investors to make bulk purchases rather than buy individual properties. The Resolution Trust Corporation (which inherited the assets of failed savings and loans) and the Federal Deposit Insurance corporation found that it was more efficient to package a portfolio of properties and sell them competitively through a competitive bid process or an auction. Groups of wealthy individuals and a number of investment banks became active participants in this market. Some did very well.

As banks and insurance companies came under pressure to deal with their real estate problems, a number of them began to consider the advantages of creating packages including loans and foreclosed properties, which they could sell in bulk. Even though these portfolios sold at substantial discounts, the sales price was often higher than the marked down value at which the institution was carrying them on their books. Many banks and insurance companies found that after

Adjunct Professor William J. Poorvu prepared this case as the basis for class discussion rather than to illustrate either effective or ineffective handling of an administrative situation.

these portfolio sales, their stock price rose and they were rid of difficult to manage or otherwise troublesome assets. In strategizing about how to take advantage of this market opportunity, JBG felt they would do better concentrating on portfolios of properties in the Washington, D.C. area rather than large, geographically dispersed portfolios. Thus, in late June, when a commercial broker from Baruetta Associates presented Jacobs with the offering brochure describing Twinbrook Metro, it appeared like exactly the type of opportunity that JBG had anticipated (see **Exhibit 1** for excerpts from the brochure).

The brochure described the asking price, the properties and the market. It also provided 10 year financial projections prepared by the seller and the broker. The estimated cash flow before financing was $4.2 million and the asking price was $40 million all cash. On the surface, there were a number of pluses to the deal:

1. The seller was motivated. Equitable had complex financial issues with which it was dealing and was under considerable pressure to reduce its real estate holdings.
2. The Twinbrook Metro portfolio was part of a larger portfolio acquired by Equitable years prior. There might be some flexibility in allocating values to this portfolio that might minimize any writedown the company might have to take upon the sale of Twinbrook.
3. The nature of the portfolio with 19 buildings and many tenants made it management intensive, a factor that would discourage most potential institutional or out of the area buyers but would provide a special opportunity for a hands-on local operator such as JBG to add value.
4. Many of JBG's historical competitors were too wrapped up in solving their own problems to bid on this project.
5. Although the overall market was depressed, this particular property was 95% leased.

DUE DILIGENCE

Jacobs' next step was to arrange for a visit to the site. He liked the fact that the location was in Montgomery County where restrictive zoning regulations limited new construction and thereby minimized competition. The specific site was at a Metro stop and not far from a light rail station. He felt that any future development permitted in the area would be first allocated to areas such as this one. He verified that if JBG acquired the project it would be able to participate in the master planning process currently underway for the area. Although the large number of essentially low rise structures complicated property management, it permitted selective redevelopment of the 29.2 acres without requiring the owner to demolish all existing buildings; thus giving up all the existing income.

The nature of the tenancy was another positive to the project. Demand for space in the area is anchored by the immediately adjacent 1.3 million square foot Health & Human Services (HHS) facility and the significant life science constituency in Montgomery County. As a result, at Twinbrook Metro several federal agencies occupied 63% of the space, the state of Maryland 9% and a variety of commercial tenants 28%. Much of the work was paid for by the tenants who had a sizable portion of their space fitted out with expensive laboratories for life sciences or biomedical research. Jacobs felt that even though government related contracts were always uncertain, there was a much better future for this type of work than the defense-related contracts that accounted for much of the demand for space in northern Virginia.

When Jacobs returned from visiting the site he put together a project team headed by two of his associates, Rob Stewart and Sue Gschwendtner, to do further study. He asked them:

- To assess the market more closely, breaking down the statistics provided by Baruetta to see the vacancy rates and competition for the specific R&D type buildings in this portfolio. A consultant familiar with the GSA should be retained to analyze the federal contracts upon which the property's tenants depended to see if they were mainstream in the federal budget or experimental and likely to be cut.
- To examine the physical condition of the buildings to evaluate the need for capital improvements, to test Baruetta's estimates for operating repairs and maintenance, to assess any costs to make the buildings compliant with American Disability Act, and to identify any blatant code compliance issues. Eventually measurements of each building's gross and rentable space would have to be verified.
- To make a preliminary review of the site for environmental problems, such as the gas station he saw on the site. Eventually he would have to order consultants to do a Phase 1 assessment which involved a study of historical documents including public records and photographs as well as a non-invasive tour of the site and the insides of the buildings looking for such items as oil spills, asbestos, or uses of the properties that involved potential contaminants. If Phase 1 turned up any red flags, more intensive and expensive Phase 2 testing involving invasive testing and cost determination of quantities, type of contamination, and cost of removal would have to be done.
- To analyze the financial projections provided by Baruetta. On first glance, the assumed rate of growth for market rents and expenses of 4% per year seemed reasonable. Tenant work allowances of $10 per square foot for the rental of the 50% of the leases assumed not to be renewed seemed low. He thought $15 for new tenants and $5 for existing rollovers was more logical. However, overall he felt that Baruetta's projections were adequate for his analysis.

The broker also told him that Equitable's predecessor in title contractually claimed a commission on renewal of all existing tenants, which was alleged to include any U.S. government tenant, not just those specific government tenants in occupancy at the time of sale to Equitable. If the prior owner's claim was upheld, the cost could be up to $150,000 per year and had not been included in Baruetta's projections. The broker thought a settlement for $500,000 could be negotiated.

FINANCING

The financing of the potential purchase was a big unknown. Few lenders were in the market at all, let alone lenders for management intensive, multi-tenanted, Grade B office and R&D buildings. Even if available, the market interest rate would probably be about $9\frac{1}{2}\%$ with a term of 10 years and an amortization schedule of 20 years at a maximum loan to value ratio of 70%.

Although the offering did not say so, Jacobs felt that if Equitable wanted to sell quickly, the company would have to take back a purchase money mortgage of at least 80% of the price. Jacobs felt that he might be able to secure a mortgage at 8.5% because Equitable would be especially anxious to keep the stated price as high as possible to minimize any book capital loss. Jacobs also thought it was important to keep the terms of the mortgage flexible so that, for example, if he wanted to tear down and rebuild one of the buildings, he would be able to finance this redevelopment with a first mortgage rather than a second mortgage.

The availability of equity financing was also at issue. Investors in real estate had been badly burned in recent years. There did appear, though, to be some recognition that the market may have bottomed and bargains might be available. Moreover, JBG's investors had done better than most with the sale of several deals in the mid-1980s as well as the firm having undertaken no new syndications with individual investors during that period.

Since Jacobs did not see this as an institutional deal and since JBG itself did not want to commit more than a minor portion of its own capital, he knew he would have to offer an especially attractive deal to investors. He thought the following structure might work:

1. Ownership would be split 75% to the investors, 25% to JBG;
2. Investors receive a cumulative 10% preference on cash flow distributions from operations based upon their investment balance at the time of distribution (in effect, distributions under this clause would be reduced each year by 10% of any payments under 4 below);
3. JBG receives the next amount distributed from operations equalling 33% of (2) above, or the next $3\frac{1}{3}\%$;
4. Investors receive any remaining distributions from operations as well as any distributions from refinancing or sale of individual parcels until all equity capital has been returned;
5. All subsequent operating and capital distributions are split 75%/25% in accordance with ownership (see **Exhibit 2**);
6. JBG would have its out of pocket due diligence costs repaid at initial closing as well as a minor acquisition fee of $\frac{1}{2}\%$ of the purchase price plus on an ongoing basis a standard asset/property management fee of expenses plus 4% of gross revenues.

For tax purposes, the partnership would take the net operating income and subtract interest and depreciation to get the taxable income. Each party would then be allocated any distributions from 2 or 3 above. The balance would be split

75%/25%. Distributions to investors in 4 above are treated as return of capital and do not affect the allocation of taxable incomes.

He wanted the investors to perceive this deal as being fair, conservative and readily distinguishable from many of the deals of the 1980s where returns were more in the form of tax benefits rather than cash and the promoter received fees unrelated to the success of the project.

STRATEGY FOR ACQUISITION

Jacobs knew that the property would be shown to several of his competitors. He considered how he should approach the negotiations. He anticipated that it would take about a month for most of the parties to gather the information for a serious offer. The initial bid would take the form of a signed letter of intent with a returnable deposit which would then lead to a signed purchase and sales contract 30 to 60 days later with a larger deposit returnable only under certain conditions. The formal closing would take place 60 to 120 days later. Much of the legal investigation of title, tenant leases and contracts would be done during the last stage. He estimated that his total out of pocket costs would be $50,000 to the time of signing the purchase and sales contract and as much as $300,000 exclusive of any deposit, by the time of final closing, depending upon the amount of environmental testing that had to be done.

Jacobs wanted to tie up the property, but at the same time did not want to pass up the opportunity to take advantage of what might be a bargain opportunity by bidding too high. Most likely Equitable would call for bids in the next few weeks from a limited number of pre-qualified firms who had shown substantial interest in the portfolio. He prepared a sheet to fill out to discuss with his partners that he felt would take into account most of the issues he would have to deal with in making his offer (See **Exhibit 3**). He knew that price would not be the only criteria. The terms of the deal and the process that would lead to closing were also important.

Once he decided on his offer using the 10 year projections in **Exhibit 1** and assuming an 80% mortgage with interest only at $8\frac{1}{2}\%$, he would divide the returns between the limited and general partners based on the proposed deal structure between them. He could then determine the IRR or net present value at 15% for each party.

Equitable might accept his first offer but on the other hand might call for a second round of bidding. Based upon the facts known to date, the market and his intuition, Jacob's felt this was the project with which JBG should get back in the game. He was, at the same time, acutely aware of the number of others in the industry who were still struggling to recover from their wounds in the last round.

Exhibit 1

Exhibit 1 (continued)

The Twinbrook Metro Portfolio Offering Summary

Purchase Price:	$40,000,000
Total Rentable Area:	554,054 square feet
Land Area:	29.2 acres
Undeveloped FAR*:	Approximately 574,000 square feet
Net Operating Income:	$4,209,000
Percent Leased:	95%
Terms of Sale:	The buildings are being offered as a portfolio. All cash.

*The current zoning allowed approximately 0.9 square feet of building for each square foot of land, or a floor to area ratio (FAR) of point nine. Since there were 1,272,260 square feet of land it was possible under current zoning to build another 574,000 square feet of additional building area.

Total allowable development	(1,272,260 S.F. × .9) = 1,145,034 S.F. allowed
Currently built	(554,054 rentable) <u>571,034</u> gross S.F.
Undeveloped	574,000 square feet

Exhibit 1 (continued)

Executive Summary

The nineteen properties presented here for sale in the Twinbrook Metro Portfolio offer an extraordinary opportunity for the purchase of existing income properties with residual land value in Montgomery County, Maryland. The 1991 N.O.I. in the 95% leased properties is $4,209,000. This allows an owner to hold and schedule redevelopment as markets tighten, and the County's plans for the area are complete.

Montgomery County, Maryland has one of the highest per capita income levels in the U.S., and the area attracts industry which requires its educated labor pool. The National Institute of Health is located in Bethesda and has been a stimulus to an active bio-tech office market developing off Rockville Pike, where Twinbrook is located.

The Portfolio: There are nineteen properties in the Twinbrook Metro Portfolio with 554,054 rentable square feet located on 29.2 acres of land. The property mix includes: fifteen low-rise office and office/laboratory buildings; a warehouse; a gas station; a sub-shop; a 7–Eleven; and a parking lot. The portfolio is 95% leased with rents ranging from $6.00 per square foot, triple net to $15.50 per square foot, full service. The office/laboratory buildings, built between 1960 and 1972, have been gradually improved as needed for releasing.

The properties are tightly-concentrated around the Twinbrook Metro and fall into five groupings based on adjacencies. This presentation organizes the properties around adjacencies and legal descriptions as follows: Block B (11 properties); Block C (3 properties); Block D (2 properties); Block E (2 properties) and Parcel 8/9 (1 property).

Location: The properties are situated 20 minutes north of downtown Washington, D.C. in Twinbrook, a submarket of Rockville, Maryland. Located just off Rockville Pike, north of White Flint Mall; they are easily accessed by car or metro. Five minutes north is the downtown section of the City of Rockville and ten minutes south is the National Institute of Health (NIH).

Redevelopment Potential: The buildings are situated on 1,272,260 square feet of land in the Twinbrook Sector, comprising 34% of the Sector. The land is now zoned I–1, Light Industrial. Montgomery County is currently up-dating the 1978 North Bethesda Sector Plan which includes the Twinbrook Sector and a new plan for Twinbrook is expected in the fall of 1990. The county in its planning stage is flexible in considering a concept for the area.

Flexibility: The densities discussed in the 1978 plan range from .9 to 1.5 FAR depending upon parking, building height, and other regulation. At a density of .9 FAR there is an additional 574,534 square feet which could be built. At the present time, there is an opportunity for an owner to participate in the planning process with the county. A great deal of flexibility exists in this initial phase. An owner controlling a portfolio this size in the immediate Twinbrook area will be able to have an impact on the long range plan by working with governmental and citizen planing groups to develop a total concept for Twinbrook.

Many of the leases run five years, providing flexibility also in timing for redevelopment. The location of properties also gives flexibility to phasing, making it possible to develop block by block.

Tenancy: The 95% occupancy achieved in the portfolio buildings is outstanding in a suburban market where vacancies in some areas are as high as 19%. The high occupancy level is attributable to (1) the metro location, (2) available parking, (3) contiguity to agencies and other services related to bio-technology, and (4) competitive rents.

Tenants attracted to the Twinbrook Metro area have been primarily bio-technical, General Services Administration (GSA) agencies and private tenants that benefit from being near the 1.3 million square foot Health and Human Services facility on Fishers Lane which also houses the Public Health Service. There are also a significant number of private tenants, unrelated to the bio-technical market, moving into the area because of the Metro and attractive rents.

GSA tenancy comprises 54% of the Twinbrook Metro Portfolio, private tenants lease 28% of the space, 9% is leased by NIH and 9% to the State of Maryland.

Special Consideration: Four properties are on a single lot with two of the tenants, the gas station (Chevron) and the 7–11 holding a *thirty-day right of first refusal* on their demised premises. These are in Block B, 12729 and 12733 Twinbrook Parkway.

The portfolio is also subject to the terms of a Commission Agreement which requires the monthly commission be paid for certain tenants occupying space in the building. These commissions will be discussed with a purchaser during the period of due diligence.

Exhibit 1   (continued)

The Twinbrook Metro Office Market

Summary

The properties in the Twinbrook Metro Portfolio have their own special niche. This fact is attributable to their extraordinary accessibility and convenience to public and private transportation, their abundance of parking and their proximity to major GSA facilities such as HHS. Due to the Federal Government's emphasis on using public transportation, it can be anticipated that this will be a favored area for GSA and related bio-technical facilities.

Montgomery County Planners are also utilizing the strategy of encouraging redevelopment in older industrial pockets such as the Twinbrook Metro Sector to a higher and better use.

The county is currently in the process of updating the master plan with a redirected Twinbrook Sector Plan. The planing board has expressed a strong interest in maximizing densities at the Metro site to limit vehicular traffic within the county and encourage utilization of public transportation.

The Twinbrook Metro Sector is one that has been specifically noted for its lack of first class development and for an eclectic collection of existing structures. There will be county and planing pressure to attractively redevelop the property included in this portfolio. The zoning issues are discussed in detail in the zoning appendices.

Overview

The Twinbrook Metro office market in Montgomery County, Maryland is a unique submarket within the Washington, D.C. Metropolitan market. It can be characterized by five major factors:
- It is a specialized, well-defined market that is mainly focused on the bio-tech industry.
- Historically, it has had low vacancies, with a current vacancy of only 5.4%
- Its center is the Twinbrook Metro Station and it extends to those properties that are within walking distance of the Metro Station.
- It is comprised of a variety of older buildings which underutilize their sites.
- It is currently the subject of a revised sector plan by the Montgomery County Planning Commission with the goal of creating a more attractive market which makes better use of its subway location.

The land in this portfolio make up 33% of the Twinbrook Metro Sector. The following market section will describe both the micro market of Twinbrook and its context in the macro Washington, D.C. Metropolitan office market and that of Montgomery County.

As Part of the Greater Washington, D.C. Market

The Twinbrook Metro portfolio is located in Montgomery County, Maryland, and is part of the Washington, D.C. Metropolitan office market containing over 225 million square feet of office space, second in size only to New York City. The overall market includes the District of Columbia, Northern Virginia, and Suburban Maryland.

The Washington Metropolitan market remains one of the strongest in the United States. Continued office space absorption is fueled by job growth due to a highly educated work pool, the stimulation by the U.S. government and the desirability of the area for associations, corporations, and high-tech companies.

The market is further strengthened by its diversity. Private business now exceeds that of the Federal Government. While much of the private business is related to the U.S. government, increasingly international companies such as IBM, the Marriott Corporation, Mobil Oil and subsidiaries of large firms have a major presence in the area. Rapid growth of the past ad the indications of continued growth in the future has created a dynamic market. The amount of office space is a measure of this growth; and speculation in this "hot" market has resulted in over building in particular submarkets creating vacancy rates in some locations of 19%.

Exhibit 1   (continued)

Yet, the Washington, D.C. downtown office market has one of the lowest overall vacancies in the US. at 9%. The subject portfolio of properties is located in Twinbrook,, a suburban submarket with overall vacancy rates only slightly in excess of the actual 5.4% vacancy in the subject property.

The Micro Market

The Twinbrook Metro market is a specialized submarket located just off Rockville Pike, between Bethesda and the city of Rockville, in Montgomery County, Maryland.

The immediate Twinbrook Metro market is delineated as being in the North Bethesda Twinbrook Sector (see section on zoning) and contains approximately 2 million square feet of rentable space. Of the Twinbrook Metro market space, approximately 28% or 554,054 square feet is included in the subject portfolio of properties offered for sale.

The Twinbrook Metro market has a very different profile from the larger macro market in which it is located. The uniqueness of the Twinbrook Metro market is attributable to historical development, market segmentation, and proximity to the Twinbrook metro site.

Dominating the area is a highrise facility of 1.35 million square feet, occupied by the Department of Health & Human Services (HHS). This concentration of government services has stimulated the bio-tech market which is strong in Montgomery County and has attracted other businesses who contract with the government. It has also attracted to the area other government agencies related to HHS: the National Institutes of Health (NIH); Health and Human Services (HHS); the Food and Drug Administration (FDA); and the Nuclear Regulatory Commission (NRC). This has created the need for office as well as laboratory space, and most of the buildings in the area have combined office/laboratory space.

This market has also appealed to a diverse group of private tenants unrelated to the bio-tech market. Most of these tenants service the surrounding residential base. Types of tenants include financial institutions, service firms and computer and telecommunication related firms.

Almost all of the buildings included in the market area were constructed before 1969. While the original users of some of these buildings were light industrial, the majority of the buildings have had related GSA tenancy since the 1970s, following HHS's move to the area. Even before Metro, the proximity to HHS and the ample parking around the low-rise buildings attracted tenants.

Now Metro strengthens the desirability of the area. Many employers, and GSA in specific, place a premium on properties located within walking distance of Metro stations. In addition, most planning commissions have sought to concentrate higher densities immediately around Metro stations to take advantage of the pubic transportation system and relieve traffic congestion in the surrounding streets. This will be one of the objectives of the revised Sector Plan now under consideration for the area.

The most recent addition to the area, immediately adjacent to the subject properties, is an approximate 68,600-square foot building of outstanding quality with underground parking built by the U.S. Pharmacopoeia. The building demonstrates a user's belief in the long-term future of the area as one which will grow and be related to the bio-technical market.

Existing Land Uses in the Twinbrook Metro Market

The existing land uses in the Sector can be generalized as office and light industrial with some neighborhood services such as fast food and gas stations.

The Sector is dominated by the Parklawn Building, headquarters of the Public Health Service of the U.S. and the Department of Health and Human Services (HHS). It is a 14-story office building situated between Fishers Lane and Parklawn Drive, east of Twinbrook Parkway. It is alternatively called the Parklawn Building and the HHS Building. The Building itself is approximately 1.65 million gross square feet which includes approximately 300,000 square feet of structured parking; and 1.35 million square feet of office space for 6,000 employees.

Exhibit 1   (continued)

The North Bethesda Sector Plan, including this building, encompasses 1.85 million square feet of office space, 300,000 square feet of industrial area, and 60,000 square feet of general retail area.[1] The HHS building dominates the land use and also influences and attracts the type tenancy which surrounds it and which is characteristic of the tenants in the Twinbrook Metro Portfolio being offered.

Information on market rents in adjacent submarkets can be found in the appendices of this presentation.

In the Context of the Larger Rockville Pike and Rockville Market

Of the two major markets in suburban Maryland, Prince George's County and Montgomery County, the latter is the largest and most mature. From a current leasable base of approximately 36 million square feet, 6.3 million square feet is currently available resulting in the overall vacancy rate of 17.5%.

The Montgomery County market has benefited greatly from the county plan development policies and continues to implement a planned policy of growth which involves a billion dollar road improvement program to its major north/south artery, I–270. This corridor runs to the south and west of Rockville Pike and into the Capitol Beltway which connects Virginia and downtown Washington, D.C. to the County. Historically, the Montgomery County office market developed outward from the District of Columbia on this I–270 corridor in response to employers who were both price sensitive and desired new high-tech designed office space.

Such large employers as IBM, the Marriott Corporation, the Bureau of Standards and Nuclear Regulatory Commission strengthened this I–270 market. Office growth has now extended well beyond Rockville to Gaithersburg, Germantown, and is now moving toward Frederick.

The growth along I–270 was paralleled by increased growth along the Rockville Pike with the opening of the Metro stations. The area is anchored to the south by the White Flint Mall area and to the north by the city of Rockville. Rockville Pike has now become a concentrated mixed-use center for business with retail, restaurants, multi-family and office buildings. All of this development enhances the Twinbrook location as a service and employment area.

The City of Rockville, Maryland

As Montgomery County developed into a vital business center in its own right, the city of Rockville has emerged as the heart of Montgomery County. The Rockville area is serviced by three Metro stops, White Flint, Twinbrook, and Rockville. These have contributed to making the Rockville Pike corridor the home of the NRC, the FDA, and the HHS as well as the center of the Montgomery County government.

With an office base of approximately 14.5 million square feet, and available office space of 1.8 million, Rockville and Rockville Pike continues to have a steady growth with a vacancy rate of 12.4% compared to the 17.4% of the County as a whole.

The variety of enterprises based in Rockville has resulted in many different uses of office space, in a relatively concentrated area. newer highrise office buildings have rental rates ranging from $17.00 to $26.00 per square foot, full service. There coexists an active, newer office market side-by-side with older R&D and warehouse type buildings in some parts of the area.

---

[1]Based on the original 1978 report, however, very little new space has been added in the immediate study area. See Market Section.

Exhibit 1 (continued)

1990 Market-Rate Rent Schedule

ADDRESS	RENTAL RATE P.S.F.	TYPE OF SPACE	S.F.
Block B			
5615 Fishers Lane	$14.00 Full Service	Office	
	$9.25 NNN	Office/warehouse	32,985
5625 Fishers Lane	$8.00 NNN	Warehouse	39,281
5635 Fishers Lane	$15.00 Full Service	Office	
	$12.00 Full Service	Lower level	15,240
12701 Twinbrook Parkway	$15.00 Full Service	Office	14,984
12709 Twinbrook Parkway	$11.50 Plus Utilities	Office/lab	25,196
12721 Twinbrook Parkway	$11.50 Plus Utilities	Office/lab	15,378
12725 Twinbrook Parkway	$ 7.00 NNN	Warehouse	60,000
12729 Twinbrook Parkway (land)	$ 4.25 NNN (land rent)	Gas station	25,500
12733 Twinbrook Parkway (land)	$ 4.25 NNN (land rent)	7-Eleven	15,000
12739 Twinbrook Parkway	$25.00 NNN	Carry out	774
Halpine Lot	$60 per month per space	Parking	
Block C:			
5630 Fishers Lane	$15.00 Full Service	Office	48,165
5640 Fishers Lane	$15.00 Full Service	Office	23,674
12411 Parklawn	$11.50 Plus Utilities	Office/lab	49,685
Block D:			
12420 Parklawn	$11.00 Plus Utilities	Office/lab/storage	99,396
12501 Washington	$10.00 Plus Utilities	Office/lab	26,974
Block E:			
12720 Twinbrook Parkway	$10.50 Plus Utilities	Office/lab	50,235
12750 Twinbrook Parkway	$15.00 Full Service	Office	13,635
Block 8/9:			
1901 Chapman	$12.00 Plus Utilities	Office/lab	45,035

Twinbrook Metro Portfolio
10-Year Cash Flow Projection Assumptions

Rental Income:	Existing leases per Lease Schedule.
Parking Income:	1990 actuals.
Market Rents:	Per Market Rental Rate Schedule.
Vacant Space:	Assumed to lease as of October 1990 with 6 months free rent and $15 PSF tenant work at rents shown in Lease Schedule.
Operating Expenses:	1990 projected expenses based on stabilized 1989.
Real Estate Taxes:	1990 projected taxes based on 1989 actuals.

Exhibit 1   (continued)

Growth Rates:	CPI—4%. Market Rents—4%. Operating Expenses—4%. Real Estate Taxes—4%.
Management Fees:	2.5% of Gross Rental Income.
Operating Expense Passthroughs:	Private tenants—all actual increases over first year occupancy. General Services Administration—CPI increases over base year established by GSA.
Real Estate Passthroughs:	All increases over first year occupancy.
Rental Escalations:	Existing lease per Lease Schedule. Rollovers of private tenants standardized at 3% fixed annual increase.
Renewals:	Tenants with options assumed to renew. Tenants without options assumed 50% to renew and 50% to vacate. GSA is assumed to renew.
Vacancy:	Three months for new tenants.
Free Rent:	Three months for new tenants.
Tenant Work:	$10.00/P.S.F. in 1990 escalated 4% annually for all lease rollovers.
Leasing Commissions:	2% for renewals 4% for new tenants

Exhibit 1 (continued)

Consolidated Ten Year Cash Flow Projection

	CY1991	CY1992	CY1993	CY1994	CY1995	CY1996	CY1997	CY1998	CY1999	CY2000	CY2001
Total Minimum Rent	$6,118,077	$6,321,836	$6,646,390	$6,987,680	$7,125,725	$7,468,375	$7,690,719	$8,268,382	$8,574,201	$8,671,624	$8,773,899
Total Free Rent	(225,402)	(18,387)	(12,798)	0	(77,803)	(169,777)	(260,053)	(15,571)	(68,987)	(179,006)	(264,912)
Net Minimum Rent	$5,892,653	$6,303,469	$6,633,592	$6,987,680	$7,047,922	$7,298,598	$7,430,666	$8,252,011	$8,505,214	$8,492,618	$8,508,987
Total Recoveries	373,195	421,593	469,690	493,776	497,432	544,317	463,542	528,974	535,515	577,994	603,599
Overage Rents	9,980	10,639	11,417	12,225	13,068	13,944	14,885	13,238	11,680	12,685	13,751
Gross Rental Income	$6,275,738	$6,373,701	$7,114,699	$7,493,681	$7,556,422	$7,858,859	$7,909,063	$8,795,023	$9,052,389	$9,083,297	$9,124,337
Miscellaneous Income	143,895	149,650	155,656	161,861	198,850	206,804	215,076	223,680	232,626	241,932	251,809
Vacancy Allowance	(62,308)	(66,907)	(70,353)	(73,813)	(74,441)	(77,426)	(77,906)	(86,676)	(89,159)	(89,444)	(89,848)
Total Income	$6,357,325	$6,820,444	$7,199,982	$7,581,729	$7,682,631	$7,988,237	$8,046,233	$8,932,027	$9,195,856	$9,213,765	$9,288,098
Total Expenses	2,148,333	2,238,631	2,330,053	2,424,954	2,522,120	2,619,611	2,717,550	2,840,096	2,947,280	3,061,176	3,146,794
Net Operating Income	4,208,972	4,581,813	4,569,929	5,156,775	5,160,711	5,368,626	5,328,683	6,091,931	6,248,576	6,174,609	6,139,304
Commissions	187,198	257,602	116,109	175,944	181,294	106,009	369,348	75,658	219,325	194,055	210,658
Capital Improvements	9,950	7,348	2,444	2,517	0	0	0	0	0	0	0
Alterations	500,918	1,585,053	169,112	1,386,903	1,206,591	478,633	2,589,121	205,750	1,866,558	1,427,976	1,153,190
Cash Flow	$3,510,908	$2,731,810	$4,182,264	$3,591,411	$3,772,826	$4,783,984	$2,370,214	$5,810,523	$4,142,693	$4,552,578	$4,775,456

Exhibit 2

JBG Internal Offer Sheet

Price:
Seller Financing: Amount/Terms (if any):
Deposit: Amount/Conditions:
Closing Date:
Special Conditions:
Estimated After Tax Return:
Investors (IRR)
JBG (NPV @ 15%)

Exhibit 3   Hypothetical Scenario to Illustrate Cash Flow/Income Tax Allocations Under Proposed Partnership Structure For First Year, Assuming Sale at Beginning Second Year

Purchase Price:	$1,000,000
Financing: (9% int. only)	700,000
Equity:	300,000

Allocation of Cash Flows:
75% Limited Partners (LPs)
25% General Partners (GPs)
1. 10% Preference of Net Invested Capital to LPs
2. $\frac{1}{3}$ of LPs Preference to GPs
3. Return of Capital to LPs, then GPs
4. 75%/25% Split of Remainder

Stage 1: Acquisition

Land	$200,000	Loan Payable	$700,000
Building	800,000	Limited Partners (99%)	297,000
		General Partners (1%)	3,000
		Total Capital	300,000
Total Assets	$1,000,000	Total Liabilities, Capital	$1,000,000

Stage 2: Operations: Cash Flow

Net Operating Income	170,000
Capital Expenditures	20,000
Financing Costs (interest only)	63,000
Cash Flow After Financing and Capital Expenditures	87,000
LP (10% Preference)	29,700
GP ($\frac{1}{3}$ of LPs Preference)	9,900
LP Return Capital	47,400
Net Cash Flow	0

Exhibit 3   (continued)

Stage 3: Operations: Income Tax Consequences

Net Operating Income	170,000
Interest	63,000
Depreciation (39 years)	<u>20,500</u>
Net Income before Taxes	88,500
LPs (10% Preference)	29,700
GPs (⅓ of LPs Preference)	9,900
LPs (75% remainder)	35,175
GPs (25% remainder)	11,725
Summary: LPs Taxable Income	64,875
GPs Taxable Income	21,625

Stage 4: Sale: Cash Flow

Sales Price	1,400,000
Sales Commission/Expenses @ 5%	<u>70,000</u>
Net Sales Price	1,330,000
Mortgage Repayment	<u>700,000</u>
Proceeds Available for Distribution	630,000
LPs Capital Repayment ($297,000–47,400)	249,600
GPs Capital Repayment	<u>3,000</u>
Available for Further Distribution	377,400
LPs Share of Proceeds (75%)	283,050
GPs Share of Proceeds (25%)	94,350

Stage 5: Sale: Income Tax Consequences

Net Sales Price	1,330,000
Less: Purchase Price	1,000,000
– Depreciation	(20,500)
+ Capital Improvements	<u>20,000</u>
Net Book Value[2]	<u>3,999,500</u>
Taxable Gain	330,500
LPs Share (75%)	247,875
GPs Share (25%)	82,625

[2]In actuality, each year new capital improvements would be capitalized and put on an annual depreciation schedule. For purpose of simplicity it is assumed that the basis of the property is increased accordingly but depreciation is not taken.

10

THE BOURLAND COMPANIES

In February 1995, Michael Bourland faced a dilemma as to what type of permanent financing would be best for two recent acquisitions. The Bank of Boston was offering a new commercial mortgage securitization program. The bank was competitive with those of traditional lenders who had been hurt by the recent downturn in real estate. Being a family business, he also had to consider his decision in the light of family dynamics.

Discussion Questions:

1. Be prepared to discuss how the commercial securitization program might work, its strengths and weaknesses, its applicability to Bourland.
2. Filling out the forms on Exhibit 5, which financing approach would you recommend for each of your properties and why?
3. Given that the Bourland Companies is a family business, what related issues are raised in the case and how would you deal with them?

On February 1, 1995 with interest rates continuing to climb, Michael Bourland, President of the Bourland Companies, thought it was time to make a decision and move forward aggressively with the refinancing of two of his properties. Unlike many regional developers, the Bourland Companies had come through the recession in the early 1990s without losing any of its properties, and had been able to acquire some new properties in distressed sales. In 1992, the Bourland Companies purchased the Southshore Retail Center and the Bedrock Office Buildings at very attractive prices, but due to the credit crunch, had only been able to secure three year "miniperm" loans from the Bank of Boston to finance these acquisitions. Now with both properties performing well and renewed lender interest in real estate loans, Michael hoped to refinance them and pull out some equity.

Until yesterday, his refinancing options seemed fairly simple. He could go back to the Bank of Boston and negotiate a new three year miniperm loan, or he could follow up on his conversations with Goliath Insurance Company and try to negotiate a fifteen year mortgage. Yesterday, however, a letter had arrived in the mail from Denise Delaney, Division Executive, and Rusty Aertsen, Group Executive from the Bank of Boston announcing "a major new financing program that we believe will be of significant benefit to our customers who own and operate multi-family and commercial property" (see **Exhibit 1**). The new product was described as "long term, non-recourse, fixed rate financing" and was part of a "mortgage securitization program" in conjunction with Goldman Sachs. With its letter, Bank of Boston also included an invitation to a seminar for developers to learn more about the program.

In accepting the invitation to the seminar, Michael was able to arrange a private meeting after the seminar with Denise Delaney. Although he looked forward to learning the details of the program, Michael felt that he probably could learn enough in advance so that he could figure out how the securitization option measured up against his other two choices. He could then use the face to face meeting with Denise to begin negotiating either a miniperm or a securitized loan using an insurance company option as a starting point.

Lecturer John H. Vogel, Jr. prepared this case under the supervision of William J. Poorvu as the basis for class discussion rather than to illustrate either effective or ineffective handling of an administrative situation.

THE DEVELOPER

In 1991 at the age of 32, after four years working for his father, Michael Bourland took over his family's real estate business. During the mid-eighties, the Bourland Companies had grown rapidly. The company diversified out of apartments and began developing office and retail space in the Route 495 corridor around Boston and in Southern New Hampshire.

The Bourland Companies have always been conservatively managed and never took on the level of debt that other developers were able to secure. Also, because Michael's father Glen planned to retire to Florida, the company stopped doing new development in 1989 and was able to make some very profitable sales while the market was still strong.

In 1990 and 1991, like most New England real estate companies, the Bourland Companies hunkered down and tried to weather the recession. Although Glen had turned over operating control of the company in 1991 to Michael, he grew increasingly anxious as he watched the value of his investments continue to decline. He began making frequent trips to Boston and eventually took back his office with the new title of chairman, but none of the day to day responsibilities.

At first, Michael was uncomfortable with having his father back at the firm, but when good purchase opportunities appeared in the market in 1992, he was grateful to have access to some of his father's capital. Just as he was getting used to having his father around again, Michael got a second surprise. At Christmas, his sister, Ann, who was three years older, announced that she was tired of being a consultant, and planned to move back to Boston in the spring and join the family business. Michael was still unsure of the implications of his sister's decision and did not know how he should respond. His father seemed delighted with the idea.

Glen had always stressed the importance of relationships as a critical component for success in the real estate business. Although the Bourland Companies had relationships with a number of financial institutions, the Bank of Boston had always been their primary lender. In addition to lines of credit and construction loans, the Bank of Boston provided Glen Bourland with checking accounts, savings accounts, security boxes and trust services. At the present time, Glen had over $2 million in trust and depository accounts with the Bank of Boston, and, as he pointed out to his son, those accounts had been very helpful in securing loans during the credit crunch, in working out troubled properties and in negotiating more favorable terms on their real estate loans. Glen could never understand why other developers would jump from one institution to the next to gain a 25 basis point advantage.

THE SOUTHSHORE MALL

In May 1992, the Bourland Company purchased the 61,677 square foot South-shore Mall for $5,000,000 or about $81 per square foot. They obtained a $3,900,000 three year, 10% interest only loan ("bullet loan") from the Bank of Boston, and invested $1.1 million of their own cash. Glen had loaned his son 20% of the equity so that he would have a direct interest.

What the Bourlands found attractive about this property was its location just off a major 495 exit, which insured that 67,000 cars passed the site each day. The local retail demographics were also excellent and the eight and a half acre site had room for additional parking over the 300 cars already there and could easily accommodate a 50,000 square foot expansion.

When they purchased the property, it was 20% vacant and had several weak, local tenants. It did have a strong anchor, however, in T. J. Maxx which had a lease that ran through the year 2006 with three additional five year options. Over the next two years, the Bourland Companies leased a vacant 8,450 square foot space to Kinko's and replaced one of the weaker tenants with Boston Chicken. To-day the center is 92% leased and generating significant cash flow (see **Exhibit 2**).

THE BEDROCK OFFICE PARK

In September 1992, the Bourland Companies completed the purchase of three, three story office buildings in Granite, New Hampshire from the FDIC. The three buildings are situated on nineteen acres of land in a campus like setting with plenty of parking and enough land to develop an additional 40,000 square foot office building. The buildings are of steel construction with a brick front and solar bronze tinted windows.

The first 54,148 square foot building was completed in 1980. The second containing 52,938 was completed in 1984 and the third building containing 53,343 was completed in 1986. All three buildings were leased to a variety of tenants ranging in size from 1,280 square feet to 18,754. Among the tenants were: Prudential Insurance Company, GMAC, Hartford Fire Insurance Co., Coca Cola Bottling Company, Chrysler Credit Corp. and Federal Express.

When the Bourland Companies purchased the property in 1992 it was over 90% leased and has remained so during the last three years. (See **Exhibit 3** which contains a rent roll, cash flow projections and market analysis.) Michael Bourland purchased the land and buildings at auction for $7,000,000. He obtained a three year, 10.5% bullet loan for $5,000,000 and his father invested $2 million of equity interest. Again, Glen had loaned Michael 20% of the equity and, on both this loan and the one on the shopping center, Glen had guaranteed the loan personally.

MORTGAGE SECURITIZATION

The growing interplay between the real estate mortgage markets and the capital markets has been one of the most important and profound financial developments in the last twenty years. The real estate mortgage market is huge with over four trillion dollars of outstanding mortgages in 1994 and dwarfs the conventional bond market. Securitization, or the conversion of mortgages (which tend to be illiquid and customized) into investment grade securities (which are liquid and standardized) has long been one of the great challenges for Wall Street.

The single family mortgage market has been the first one to achieve a high level of securitization. The involvement of government guarantors like the Federal Housing Administration (FHA) and the Veteran's Administration (VA) and the involvement of quasi-government entities like the Federal Home Loan Mortgage Corporation (Freddie Mac) and the Federal National Mortgage Association (Fannie Mae) has led to the creation of standardized mortgage documents and underwriting criteria. In a typical transaction, an entity like Fannie Mae or Freddie Mac buys a pool of mortgages from an originator, like a bank, and issues securities against them. The investor does not have to analyze the individual loans, but can look to the credit worthiness of Fannie Mae which has a triple A credit rating. The growth and acceptance of this system can be seen in the fact that the percentage of securitized mortgages on 1 to 4 family houses has grown from 13% in 1980 to 49% in 1994. In the United States there are approximately $3.146 trillion of outstanding 1–4 family mortgages which mean that there are over $1.5 trillion of securitized mortgages that trade in the capital markets.

The multifamily residential market is more difficult to securitize because the product is less standard and the government has less incentive to guarantee the loans of multifamily developers than they do for individual home owners. Nevertheless, Freddie Mac developed a securitization program in 1984, Fannie Mae developed one in 1987 and the FHA has had some involvement in multifamily housing since the 1930s. As a result, of the $292 billion of outstanding multi-family mortgage debt in 1994, 11% has been securitized and both Fannie Mae and Freddie Mac are becoming increasingly active in this market.

Conventional commercial mortgages are the most resistant to securitization because of their size, customized nature and the lack of a guarantor to underwrite the risk. Nevertheless with $770 billion of outstanding commercial mortgages in 1993 (down from $815 billion in 1992) investment bankers have been challenged to come up with a way to securitize these mortgages. Thus far they have tried to deal with the lack of uniformity and other investor concerns by: (1) using only seasoned properties that are leased and have a positive operating history, (2) pooling the mortgages for diversification, (3) splitting the individual mortgages into different tranches (a triple A piece, a double A piece, a triple B piece, etc.) and (4) using the rating agencies like Standard and Poors and Moody's to rate the mortgage pools based on the type of property and the debt coverage ratios. As a result, the growth of the commercial mortgage securitization market has been sensational, going from less than $10 billion in 1991 to over $60 billion at the end of 1994. The potential is even greater with $100 to $200 billion of properties like the Granite Office Park and the Southshore Mall needing to be refinanced each year between 1994–96, and only 10% of these refinancings currently being securitized.

BANK OF BOSTON

Bank of Boston is a super-regional bank with assets of $44.6 billion. In 1994 Bank of Boston made construction and other real estate loans totaling $1.8 billion making it one of the five largest commercial real estate lenders in the United States. As of Dec. 31, 1993 Bank of Boston had a portfolio of real estate loans totaling $3.74 billion (down from $7.05 billion in 1989). In addition to traditional construction and miniperm loans on individual properties, Bank of Boston has established a major presence as a lender to large, national single family homebuilders and as a source of lines of credit and other forms of debt to real estate investment trusts (REITs).

In 1994 Bank of Boston established a Real Estate Capital Markets group under the direction of Denise Delaney. The first priority of the department was to develop a process whereby the Bank of Boston will originate, underwrite and warehouse pools of commercial mortgages and then sell the pools to Goldman Sachs (see **Exhibit 4**). Goldman Sachs will get the pools rated by an agency and then convert them into rated bonds which will be sold to investors. For Bank of Boston this product will provide fee income[3] and the ability to write mortgages that do not end up on their books with the associated capital requirements and portfolio implications. It will also enable Bank of Boston to underwrite longer term, fixed rate, non-recourse mortgages for its customer, a product it would otherwise not be able to offer because of Bank of Boston's need to match short term assets with its short term liabilities.

THE REFINANCING DECISION

After looking over the materials from the Bank of Boston, Michael Bourland decided to develop a worksheet to see how big a loan he could obtain for each property under each of the three options (see **Exhibit 5**). He knew that he would have to make some assumptions about the value of the property to see if it fit the

[3]In addition to the origination fee, Bank of Boston will also earn a fee from servicing these loans (collecting payments, monitoring the covenants, etc.). Bank of Boston's Treasury Department has created a hedging strategy (a collar) so that while the Bank is warehousing the loans, it has no interest rate risk if interest rates rise. Denise Delaney believes that the Bank will achieve some spread between the interest payments it is collecting at, say, 10% on the long-term mortgages and the short-term money that the Bank uses to fund the loan while it is being warehoused.

loan to value criteria, but he was comfortable applying a cap rate to the stabilized cash flow to get a reasonable estimate. He also knew that the interest rates on these loans were changing on a daily basis, but for his first cut he decided to use the following assumptions:

1. **The miniperm loan**: This loan would be a three year, variable rate, recourse loan priced at 1% over prime (currently 9%). For a fee of 2.2% of the loan, the Bank of Boston would guarantee that the rate would never exceed 11%. Although the term of the loan would be three years, the amortization period could be up to 20 years. The loan to value, debt coverage and other requirements are detailed on the underwriting guidelines in **Exhibit 1** in the column titled "Current BKB." As the Bank of Boston already held the loan there would be only 1/4% fee to renew the miniperm and the legal bills would be about $5,000. For this kind of loan, the Bank of Boston would allow pre-payment of the principal at any time without a penalty.

2. **The insurance company loan**: Goliath Insurance had indicated that it might be willing to make up to a fifteen year, non-recourse loan with a fifteen year amortization schedule. For the Southshore property they quoted a rate of 175 basis points over 15 year treasuries (currently about 7.85%) and a 1% upfront fee. For office properties the terms were generally the same except that they would be looking for 200 basis points over 15 year treasuries. For both properties Goliath expected a 1.25 debt coverage ratio and a 75% loan to value ratio. Since the Bourland Companies had worked through one of Goliath's mortgage banking correspondents, they would have to pay the correspondent 1.5% as an upfront fee. Goliath also required no prepayment for the first three years and then a 5% prepayment penalty in year four declining by 0.5% each year thereafter.

3. **The securitization option**: Michael assumed that he could obtain a 5, 7 or 10 year loan with up to a 25 year amortization period. As a first cut he assumed he would want a 10 year loan which would be priced at 240 basis points over 10 year treasuries (currently 7.72%) for retail properties and 300 basis points over 10 year treasuries for the office property. Bank of Boston would also charge an upfront fee of two points (2%). Once the Bourland Companies locked in a rate, it would become a fixed rate, non-recourse loan. (The rest of the terms and assumptions are spelled out in the guidelines in **Exhibit 1**.)

THE DECISION

Michael had learned over time that when he reduced real estate to a purely numerical exercise he usually got into trouble. He wondered if there were any qualitative factors that he should consider in choosing a refinancing option. Were both properties, for example, equally good prospects for securitization? Would he enhance his relationship with the Bank of Boston by participating in their new product initiative? Would his father be willing to reinvest the proceeds from this refinancing in new projects or would this be his chance to take money out of the company and move back to Florida, as Glen's wife had been urging?

Michael had met Denise Delaney before and thought that she was a very professional lender. He knew that her presentation would be interesting and informative. His job was to do enough homework so that he could come to her presentation with good questions and a reasonable sense of which direction he should go. Then he could begin negotiations in his face to face meeting, knowing that Denise would be looking for holes in his projections and his proposal.

How much should he request for a loan? What kind of restrictions might be put on his ability to operate the properties, what control on lease negotiations? Would these properties meet her lending criteria not only on a purely technical level but on the property level? She too remembers the 1980s.

Exhibit 1

Bank of Boston Long-Term Commercial Mortgage Program

Benefit:	By adding a long-term commercial mortgage product, Bank of Boston now becomes a single source of Real Estate Financing; from acquisition to construction to mini-perm to long-term financing.
Objective:	To provide long-term, non-recourse financing for developers, owners and operators of industrial, retail multi-family and certain selected office properties.
Use:	Refinance or Acquisition
Loan Amount:	$750,000 to $10,000,000
Loan Type:	5-, 7-, 10-year maturities (up to 20 years for multi-family)
Eligible Properties:	Economically stable industrial, retail, multi-family, and selected office properties in good condition.
Price:	Fixed rate, based on spread above comparable Treasury bond interest rate.
Assumability:	Permitted, subject to review and approval of the new owner by Bank of Boston and payment of an assumption fee.
Prepayment:	Permitted after year two, subject to a prepayment penalty determined by Bank of Boston.
Recourse:	Non-recourse. Must comply with all statutes, codes.
Third-Party Expenses:	Bank of Boston has lowered the cost of third-party expenses for the appraisal, environmental and structural assessments and legal fees by contracting with a single provider for each service.
Special:	Must comply with all statutes, codes including handicapped access. Must have clean environmental Phase I indication or escrow 150% cost of remediation.

Exhibit 1   (continued)

The Bourland Companies

BANK OF BOSTON

Dear Bank of Boston Customer:

We are pleased to announce a major new financing program that we believe will be of significant benefit to our customers who own and operate multi-family and commercial property.

Bank of Boston, in partnership with the investment banking firm of Goldman, Sachs & Co., can now provide you with access to long-term, non-recourse, fixed rate financing through our mortgage securitization program which converts commercial real estate mortgages into publicly traded securities. This program enhances our ability to meet the full life cycle needs of real estate property owners as it compliments our traditional acquisition, construction and mini-perm financing products with long-term, non-recourse, fixed rate financing.

Your relationship manager would welcome the opportunity to explain this program to you in more detail, or, you may call one of the toll free numbers listed below for further information.

Sincerely,

Guilliaem Aertsen
Group Executive

Sincerely,

Denise Delaney
Division Executive

The First National Bank of Boston - Real Estate Capital Markets Division
1-800-292-5955 Massachusetts, Maine, New Hampshire, Vermont, Rhode Island
1-800-355-9056 Connecticut & New York

Exhibit 1   (continued)

THESE ARE GUIDELINES ONLY. UNDER CERTAIN CIRCUMSTANCES, EXCEPTIONS CAN BE PERMITTED.

	Unsecured Retail	PRESENT BKB	Anchored Retail	PRESENT BKB	Office	PRESENT BKB	Multi-Family Garden	PRESENT BKB	Industrial/ Warehouse	PRESENT BKB	Hotel / Motel	PRESENT BKB
Loan Size	750,000-10,000,000		750,000-10,000,000		750,000-10,000,000		750,000-10,000,000		750,000-10,000,000		750,000-10,000,000	
Loan to Value	70%	75%	75%	75%	65%	75%	75%	75%	70%	75%	65%	65%
Debt Service Coverage	1.35	1.25	1.25	1.25	1.40	1.20	1.25	1.20	1.30	1.20	1.40	1.30
Term (years)	5,7,10	5	5,7,10	5	5,7,10	5	7,10,15,20	5	5,7,10	5	5,7,10	5
Amortization (years)	20	20	25	20	20	20	30	20	25	20	20	20
Occupancy (minimum)	90%	n/a	85%	80%	90%	80%	85%	90%	90%	80%	n/a	n/a
Property Age (maximum)	20	n/a	20	n/a	15	n/a	30	n/a	20	n/a	25	n/a
Origination Fees (basis points) [a]	200	varies	200	varies	225	varies	200	varies	200	varies	225	varies
Pricing Spreads (basis points)	100+	varies	240+	varies	300-375	varies	225+	varies	275-325	varies	400-450	varies
Application Fees [b] $750,000 to $2,500,000 $2,500,000 to $6,000,000 $6,000,000 +	12,000 15,000 19,000	none	12,000 15,000 19,000	none	12,000 15,000 19,000	none	12,000 15,000 19,000	none	12,000 15,000 19,000	none	12,000 15,000 19,000	none
Capex Escrow Reserve [c]	125% of A&E	none	125% of A&E	none	150% of A&E	none	125% of A&E	none	125% of A&E	none	150% of A&E	none
Replacement Reserve Escrow	20 psf	none	20 psf	none	20 psf	none	$150/unit	none	.15 psf	none	4% - 5% of total revs.	none
Environmental Escrow	150% of Problem	none	150% of Problem	none	150% of Problem	none	150% of Problem	none	150% of Problem	none	150% of Problem	none
Required Other Escrows	1/12th r/e taxes/mo 1/12th Insurance/mo	none	1/12th r/e taxes/mo 1/12th Insurance/mo	none	1/12th r/e taxes/mo 1/12th Insurance/mo	none	1/12th r/e taxes/mo 1/12th Insurance/mo	none	1/12th r/e taxes/mo 1/12th Insurance/mo	none	1/12th r/e taxes/mo 1/12th Insurance/mo	none
Property Size	Minimum 20,000 s.f.	none	Minimum 20,000 s.f.	none	Minimum 20,000 s.f.	none	Minimum 20 units	none	Minimum 25,000 s.f.	none	Minimum 50 units	N/A
Minimum Lease Term	3 years - small 10 years - anchor	none	3 years - small 10 years - anchor	none	3 years	none	Minimum 6 months	none	5 years	none	N/A	
Permitted other uses	Maximum 20% non-retail	none	Maximum 20% non-retail	none	Lenders discretion	none	Max. 20% non-resi.	none	Max. 20% non industrial	none	Max. 20% non-hotel	
Leases in place	50% of gross rents should exceed loan term	none	50% of gross rents should exceed loan term	none	50% of gross rents should exceed loan term [d]	none	N/A	none	50% of gross rents should exceed loan term	none	N/A	

[a] These spreads are subject to significant fluctuation. Over the last twelve months, they have trended downward.

[b] A&E refers to the architect and engineers report that is done on each property to determine if there are any capital projects or deferred maintenance that requires attention. Thus, if $10,000 of windows need to be replaced $12,500 would have to be escrowed at closing.

[c] Capex = Capital Expenditures

[d] The term of the existing leases should exceed the term of the loan. Thus, on a seven year loan, leases representing 50% of the gross revenue should have at least eight years remaining

Exhibit 2 Southshore Retail: 10 Year Financial Projection

	SQ. FT.	1995	1996	1997	1998	1999	2000	2001	2002	2003	2004
Income:											
TJ Maxx	29,615										
Rate		$11.63	$11.63	$11.63	$11.63	$11.63	$12.63	$12.63	$12.63	#12.63	$12.63
Income		344,422	344,422	344,422	344,422	344,422	374,037	374,037	374,037	374,037	374,037
Papa Gino's	3,600										
Rate		12.94	14.25	14.25	14.75	14.75	15.25	15.50	15.50	16.00	16.25
Income		46,584	51,300	51,300	53,100	53,100	54,900	27,900	56,700	57,600	58,500
Boston Chicken	4,200										
Rate		16.00	16.50	17.00	17.50	18.00	18.50	19.00	19.50	20.00	20.50
Income		67,200	69,300	71,400	73,500	75,600	77,700	79,800	81,900	84,000	86,100
Kinko's Copying	8,450										
Rate		16.00	16.50	17.00	17.50	18.00	18.50	19.00	15.50	16.00	16.50
Income		135,200	139,425	143,650	147,875	152,100	156,325	160,550	65,488	135,200	139,425
The Big Party	10,713										
Rate		15.00	15.00	15.50	16.00	16.00	17.50	18.00	18.50	19.00	19.50
Income		160,695	160,695	166,052	171,408	171,408	187,478	192,834	198,191	203,547	208,904
Vacant Space	5,099										
Rate		14.00	14.25	14.50	14.75	15.00	15.25	15.50	15.75	16.00	16.25
Income		17,846	72,661	73,936	75,210	76,485	77,760	79,035	80,309	81,584	82,849
Total Rental Income	61,677	$771,947	$837,803	$850,759	$865,516	$873,115	$928,200	$914,156	$856,625	$935,968	$949,825
Gross Income		$771,947	$837,803	$850,759	$865,516	$873,115	$928,200	$914,156	$856,625	$935,968	$949,825
Vacancy Allowance	5%	(38,597)	(41,890)	(42,538)	(43,276)	(43,656)	(46,410)	(45,708)	(42,831)	(46,798)	(47,491)
TOTAL INCOME		733,350	795,913	808,221	822,240	829,460	881,790	868,448	813,794	889,170	902,333
Expenses:											
CAM/RE Tax on Vacant Space	$2.50	(10,186)	(7,624)	(7,624)	(7,624)	(7,624)	(7,624)	(7,624)	(7,624)	(7,624)	(7,624)
Management Fee	5%	(36,668)	(39,796)	(40,411)	(41,112)	(41,473)	(44,089)	(43,422)	(40,690)	(44,459)	(45,117)
Structural Reserve	$0.20	(12,199)	(12,199)	(12,199)	(12,199)	(12,199)	(12,199)	(12,199)	(12,199)	(12,199)	(12,199)
TOTAL EXPENSES		$59,052	$59,619	$60,234	$60,935	$61,296	$63,913	$63,245	$60,513	$64,282	$64,940
NET OPERATING INCOME		$674,298	$736,294	$747,987	$761,305	$768,164	$817,877	$805,203	$753,281	$824,888	$837,394

Assumptions:
(1) TJ MAXX lease expires 2006, Kinko's lease expires 2001, Big Party expires 2001. Six month releasing time assumed when all leases expire.
(2) Vacant space leased 9/95.

Exhibit 3

Exhibit 3 (continued)

Bedrock Office Park Rent Roll, August 1994

TENANT	RENTABLE SQ. FT.	LEASE TERM (YRS)	LEASE COMMENCE	LEASE EXPIRATION	RENT/ SQ. FT.		OPERATING BASE	TAX BASE	OPTIONS
Building I									
Prudential Insurance	9,306	5.5	1/1/92	7/31/97	$13.08 $13.75	to 12/31/94	$5.48	$1.53	2 5-yr FMV*
Bedford Recruiters	1,280	3	6/1/92	5/31/95	$13.25		$4.80	$1.55	none
NMB	2,111	3	1/1/92	12/31/94	$14.25		$4.80	$1.55	none
GMAC	13,118	3.67	7/1/93	1/18/97	$14.00		$5.51	$1.53	1 3-yr FMV
GMAC Mortgage	5,495	3	1/20/93	12/31/95	$14.00		$5.48	$1.53	none
Coca Cola Bottling	18,754	5	6/1/94	5/31/99	$7.25	to 9/30/94	$5.51	$1.55	1 3-yr FMV
					$11.82	to 5/31/96			
					$12.07	to 5/31/97			
					$12.32				
Vacant	1,241								
Vacant	2,843								
Subtotal	54,148								
Building II									
Hartford Insurance	17,976	7	5/23/94	5/31/01	$14.50		CY 1994	FY 1994	1 5-yr FMV
NCR	4,909	5	4/1/93	3/31/98	$12.00		$4.84	$1.47	1 3-yr FMV
Connecticut Mutual Is.	6,435	5	5/1/94	4/30/99	$13.75		CY 1994	FY 1994	1 5-yr FMV
							(5% cap on increases)		
Credit Bureau Services	8,144	5	8/10/92	7/31/97	$13.25	to 7/31/94	$4.19	$1.47	none
					$13.50	to 7/31/95			
					$14.00				
Chrysler Credit	3,558	5	4/1/94	3/31/99	$14.00		CY 1994	FY 1994	2 3-yr FMV
Keane, Inc.	4,337	3.41	11/1/94	3/31/97	$13.50		$4.00	$0.83	none
Vacant	1,784								
Vacant	1,485								
Vacant	4,310								
Subtotal	52,938								

Exhibit 3 (continued)

Bedrock Office Park Rent Roll, August 1994, continued

TENANT	RENTABLE SQ. FT.	LEASE TERM (YRS)	LEASE COMMENCE	LEASE EXPIRATION	RENT/ SQ. FT.	OPERATING BASE	TAX BASE	OPTIONS
Building III								
Bio Development	5,343	3	7/1/94	6/30/97	$13.50	$4.74	$1.41	none
Progressive Insurance	3,496	3	9/1/93	8/31/96	$12.30	$5.20	$1.56	none
Friendly Ice Cream	1,375	5	3/1/93	2/18/98	$14.50	$4.84	$1.52	none
Universal Underwriters	5,056	5	4/1/93	3/31/98	$14.50	$3.77	$1.52	1 5-yr FMV
Honeywell Bull	3,689		Tenant at Will**		$16.75	$4.74	$1.41	none
Kellogg's	3,362	5	10/1/92	9/30/97	$12.50	$4.51	$1.52	1 5-yr FMV
				to 9/31/94	$14.50			
Greentree Financial	3,052	3	6/1/94	5/31/97	$14.25	CY 1994	FY 1994	1 1-yr FMV
HMM Associates	2,748	5	1/1/89	12/31/94	$14.50	$4.51	$1.50	none
Federal Express	12,225	5	6/1/90	5/31/95	$18.00	$4.74	$1.41	1 5-yr FMV
NH Society of CPA's	2,144	5	7/1/94	6/30/99	$13.85	CY 1994	FY 1994	none
Core Source	4,594	3.5	7/1/94	12/31/97	$14.00	CY 1994	$1.59	none
Northwest Mortgage	2,813	3	6/1/92	5/31/95	$13.75	$4.84	$1.52	1 3-yr FMV
Cafe	1,320							
Vacant	2,126							
Subtotal	53,343							

*Fair Market Value **Lease can be terminated by either party upon 30 days written notice.

Exhibit 3   (continued)

Bedrock Office Park, Granite, New Hampshire
Schedule of Prospective Cash Flow

	YEAR 1 DEC 1995	YEAR 2 DEC 1996	YEAR 3 DEC 1997	YEAR 4 DEC 1998	YEAR 5 DEC 1999	YEAR 6 DEC 2000	YEAR 7 DEC 2001	YEAR 8 DEC 2002	YEAR 9 DEC 2003	YEAR 10 DEC 2004
GROSS REVENUE										
Potential Rental Revenue	2,215,360	2,202,572	2,254,590	2,362,788	2,457,013	2,510,631	2,655,280	2,819,365	3,029,661	3,126,268
Absorption & Turnover Vacancy	(146,479)	(40,223)	(150,623)	(79,209)	(99,174)	(18,201)	(150,947)	(169,772)	(85,031)	(156,701)
Scheduled Base Rental Revenue	2,068,881	2,162,349	2,103,967	2,283,569	2,357,839	2,492,430	2,504,333	2,649,593	2,944,630	2,969,567
Expense Reimbursement Revenue	69,921	101,135	105,579	86,601	104,907	137,182	139,748	130,582	109,556	134,037
Miscellaneous Revenue	10,000	7,973	43,146	6,749	7,019	6,022	5,314	5,527	5,748	5,978
TOTAL GROSS REVENUE	2,148,802	2,271,457	2,252,692	2,283,569	2,357,839	2,683,200	2,646,849	2,785,702	3,059,934	3,109,582
General Vacancy	(73,749)	(121,036)	(17,345)	(92,247)	(80,161)	(167,326)	(46,354)	(40,175)	(134,714)	(87,464)
EFFECTIVE GROSS REVENUE	2,075,053	2,150,421	2,235,347	2,284,672	2,389,604	2,470,874	2,600,475	2,745,527	2,925,220	3,022,118
OPERATING EXPENSES										
Reimbursable Expenses	1,163,622	1,217,741	1,259,176	1,312,735	1,365,082	1,424,320	1,474,288	1,153,822	1,605,185	1,664,839
Non-reimbursable Expenses	60,375	62,714	65,211	67,418	70,254	72,918	76,141	79,600	83,479	86,620
TOTAL OPERATING EXPENSES	1,223,997	1,280,455	1,324,387	1,380,153	1,435,336	1,497,238	1,550,429	1,614,422	1,688,664	1,751,459
NET OPERATING INCOME	851,056	869,966	910,960	904,519	954,268	973,636	1,050,046	1,131,105	1,236,556	1,270,659

Key Assumptions:
1. Current market rent is $14.00 per rentable square foot, gross for large tenants (over 3,000 S.F) and $14.25 per rentable square foot for small tenants.
2. The annual growth rate for market rent is 4% for year 2, 6% for year 3, and 5% for years 4–10.
3. The annual inflation rate used for operating expenses is 4%.
4. The turnover vacancy period is 6 months.
5. The General vacancy plus the absorption and turnover vacancy total at least 7%.

Exhibit 3 (continued)

Bedrock Office Park, Granite, New Hampshire
Income Statement

BUDGET	1992	1993	BUDGET 1994	ACTUAL YTD THRU 9/94
Income				
Rent	$1,994,779	$1,847,903	$1,885,746	$1,344,370
Expense Reimbursement	86,506	88,306	74,252	71,184
Other	17,862	23,285	59,120	56,565
	$2,099,147	$1,959,494	2,019,118	1,472,119
Expenses				
Maintenance & Repair	57,937	57,867	75,920	47,344
Custodial	184,117	178,646	206,730	115,331
Utilities	390,856	406,514	414,906	346,201
Landscaping/Snow Removal	47,943	74,719	70,914	64,230
Taxes	243,268	243,557	253,257	190,578
Administrative*	180,576	170,003	183,211	134,286
Owner Maint. & Repair	21,221	22,435	26,750	15,136
	$1,125,918	$1,153,741	$1,231,688	$ 913,106
Net Operating Income	$973,229	$805,753	$787,430	$559,013
***Breakdown of Administrative Expenses**				
Legal	$ 9,441	$ 6,875	$ 15,125	$ 8,888
Accounting	9,300	11,200	8,700	6,525
Property Management Fee	104,958	97,975	98,220	73,607
Asset Management Fee	20,993	19,595	19,644	14,722
Advertising/Promotion	1,712	6,975	7,500	5,367
Consulting	7,592	3,148	6,000	2,092
Insurance	21,036	21,4909	22,572	16,929
Office/Miscellaneous	5,543	2,745	5,450	6,157
Total	$180,576	$170,003	$183,211	$134,287

Exhibit 3 (continued)

Market Overview (Excerpts)

Economic

During the 1980s companies seeking to expand into or within the northern New England market found New Hampshire to offer considerable advantages over other states: relatively low home prices and cost of living, no state sales or income taxes, positive business environment, available skilled and semi-skilled labor force, and proximity to high tech centers within Massachusetts. Granite shared these general qualities in addition to being located on a major highway between two of New Hampshire's largest cities, and having land available for development.

The distribution of employment in Granite in 1990 was heavily weighted towards manufacturing, accounting for 49.6% of employment. Other major sectors and their percent of employment are: wholesale and retail trade 21.6%; services 17.9%; construction 5%; finance, insurance, and real estate 3.4%; and transportation 2.5%. Granite's largest employers include Digital Equipment Corporation, Sanders Associates Inc., Kollsman Instrument Company, Nashua Corporation, Anheuser–Busch, Inc., and M/Acom Omni Spectra.

Market Analysis

The Southern New Hampshire economy expanded rapidly during the 1980's, fueled by growth in the computer, defense and real estate industries. However, as the national economy began to decline in the late 1980s, the Southern New Hampshire economy incurred significant declines. Cutbacks in the defense and computer industries resulted in increases in unemployment, foreclosures and bankruptcies. The speculative overbuilding of commercial and industrial properties resulted in declining prices and increasing vacancy rates, forcing many property owners to reduce rents to maintain control of their properties.

These problems ultimately led to a reduction in lending activities, as many banks attempted to work-out problem loans. The virtual elimination of available credit from banks only served to exacerbate the problems in the marketplace, and as restructuring or refinancing became impossible, many property owners lost their property to foreclosure. Ultimately, the weight of these problems led to five of the State's largest banks being shut down and consolidated by the FDIC.

The inventory of first class office buildings in the Southern New Hampshire market totals 4,481,000 square feet. The Granite area submarket comprises 956,000 square feet, or 21% of this market. Currently, this submarket has a vacancy rate of 23.2%, or 221,701 square feet; however, 75% of this vacancy is concentrated within only three of the twenty-four office buildings.

Bedrock Office Park is among the top tier of quality product in the market. The Park's direct competition is Farms Office Park located one half mile north of the property. Farms comprises six office buildings totaling approximately 315,000 square feet of space with a current vacancy rate of 38%. This large vacancy reflects difficulties arising from ownership changes and the lack of uniform management. Springs, a 60,000 square foot office building two miles west of the property, also competes but is currently 100% occupied.

Exhibit 4

Reprinted from

AMERICAN BANKER.

The Daily Financial Services Newspaper

Tuesday, August 9, 1994

Bank of Boston Exec Bullish On Commercial Realty Pools

By ANDREW REINBACH

By creating a pool of commercial mortgages that will be converted to bonds, Denise Delaney, division executive of the Bank of Boston's new Real Estate Capital Markets group, is keeping both her bank and herself on the cutting edge of real estate finance.

"This is going to be a very big business, and if we don't stay in front, we'll lose our customer base," said Ms. Delaney, a former Bankers Trust New York Corp. official who joined Bank of Boston in 1989.

Next year, Ms. Delaney, a division executive since 1991, expects to originate, underwrite, and sell to Goldman, Sachs & Co. about 100 mortgages, totalling $250 million, at par. Each mortgage will be in the $750,000-to-$10 million range. Ms. Delaney's group will service the mortgages, which will be made on multifamily, retail, and industrial properties.

Goldman, for its part, expects to market about $500 million in such bonds in 1995 as part of a new business line. It says it expects to eventually have three other banks supplying mortgages to its program.

Barnett Banks Inc. and NationsBank Corp. are among the commercial banks forming conduits similar to Bank of Boston's. Further competition is expected from insurance and securities companies.

Commercial mortgage conduits are similar to the more familiar residential mortgage-backed securities programs of the Federal National Mortgage Association, the Government National Mortgage Association and the Federal Home Loan Mortgage Corp.

A Refinancing Dilemma

Bankers hope such conduits will be the answer to a problem pondered in real estate circles since 1990: How to refinance the $300-to-$500 billion in commercial mortgages that are maturing between 1994 and 1996.

Eventually, most long-term commercial mortgages are expected to wind up in securities. For the Bank of Boston, moving from traditional, asset-holding mortgage business into this new arena will not mean major changes in its portfolio, said Ms. Delaney.

"I would say that assuming the bank stays the same size, our originations will roughly double over the next five years," she says. "Our real estate business won't change as a percentage of total assets, though the percentage of originations to held assets will." Ms. Delaney declined to be specific about the proportion of originated to held assets. Bank of Boston's 1993 mortgage underwritings were $1.8 billion, $1.2 billion of which were new originations, she said.

Strategically, the conduit busi-

Bullish In Boston

DENISE DELANEY of Bank of Boston is pioneering a new way to finance commercial real estate. As head of the bank's new conduit program, she expects to pool $250 million of loans and sell them to investors. "This is going to be a very big business," she says.

Exhibit 4 (continued)

Stella Johnson

DIVISION EXECUTIVE Denise Delaney says securitization "is going to be a very big business."

rowers will be given standardized mortgage forms to sign that are not subject to negotiation. These mortgages are destined for the $125 million in warehoused mortgages that the Bank will sell the Goldman twice a year. If the borrower insists on a customized mortgage, on the other hand, it will have to accept a recourse loan with a 3-to-5 year term. The alternative? Go elsewhere.

The new business is likely to change how commercial loans are processed and how the depart-

> ### The bank expects to originate, underwrite, and sell to Goldman, Sachs & Co. about 100 mortgages, totalling $250 million.

ment is organized, Ms. Delaney said. "In general I expect the commercial mortgage business to become more like the single-family mortgage industry, with segmented processing replacing one loan officer seeing the deal through to closing," she said.

The arrangement with Goldman will allow the Bank of Boston to return to a traditional construction lending business, Ms. Delaney said. "One element in the plan is to do construction loans, and then roll them into the conduit" as long-term permanent mortgages, she said. "But we may also do 3-to-5 year mini-perms, which is what we do now."

Six Tranches

The securities themselves will be sold in as many as six tranches,

including an interest-only and principle-only strip, Ms. Delaney said. Spreads over treasuries for the loans will be 225-to-250 basis points for retail and industrial property issues.

Yields at point-of-sale, of course, will vary, says Sheridan

> ### Bank of Boston says moving into this new arena will not mean major changes in its portfolio.

Scheckner, a vice president at Goldman Sachs

The bond market has been pricing similarly-rated mortgage bonds at about 100 basis points over treasuries for a Aaa piece, to 15 percent per year for unrated issues, he says.

Trimming Holdings

The Bank of Boston has worked hard to trim its real estate problems in the past five years, reducing its outstanding mortgage portfolio by $3.3 billion — from $7.05 billion in 1989 to $3.74 in 1993 — while writing down $1.09 billion loans and taking back $928 million in OREO in the same period, according to bank records.

The bank accomplished this, Ms. Delaney said, by selling many mortgages, and asking some customers to refinance elsewhere when their mortgages came due. "We recognized that there were some real holes in our portfolio, and there was a concerted effort to address our problems."

Mr. Reinbach is a freelance writer based in Lee, Mass.

ness will allow Bank of Boston to match its maturities by limiting originations for its own account to 3-to-5 year terms, and securitizing long-term debt, while reducing its outstanding portfolio of loans.

An added plus: Fewer mortgages on the books means lower required risk-based capital. "What we want to do is make our money in fees and from warehousing the

loans, and also by selling them through our Treasury department," says Ms. Delaney.

Choices, Choices, Choices

As mortgages come due, says Ms. Delaney, borrowers will be offered a choice of long-term, nonrecourse loans or short-term loans with recourse she says. If they choose the former, the bor-

Exhibit 5 Worksheet

Bedrock Office Park

	Miniperm	Insurance Co.	Securitization
Projected Rate	10%	9.85%	10.72%
Loan Term	3	15	10
Amortization	20	15	25
Debt Constant (principal and interest)	11.75%	13.04%	11.63%
Stabilized NOI*	851,056	851,056	851,056
Required Debt Coverage Service	1.25	1.25	1.4
Maximum Annual Constant Debt Service			
Maximum Loan Using Debt Coverage Test			
Capitalization Rate for Office Properties	9½%	9½%	9½%
Value Based on Cap Rate			
Required Loan to Value Coverage	75%	75%	65%
Maximum Loan Using Loan to Value Test			
Upfront Fees			
Recourse or Non-Recourse			
Prepayment Penalty			
Other Considerations			

*NOI is before lease commissions and tenant improvements. The assumption is that with a 1.25 debt coverage ratio there will be adequate cash flow to fund these capital expenditures.

Exhibit 5   Worksheet (continued)

Southshore Retail

	Miniperm	Insurance Co.	Securitization
Projected Rate	10%	9.6%	10.12%
Loan Term	3	15	10
Amortization	20	15	25
Debt Constant (principal and interest)	11.75	12.84	11.12
Stabilized NOI	674,298	674,298	674,298
Required Debt Coverage	1.25	1.25	1.25
Maximum Annual Constant Debt Service			
Maximum Loan Using Debt Coverage Test			
Capitalization Rate for Retail Properties	9%	9%	9%
Value Based on Cap Rate			
Required Loan to Value Coverage	75%	75%	75%
Maximum Loan Using Loan to Value Test			
Upfront Fees			
Recourse or Non-Recourse			
Prepayment Penalty			
Other Considerations			

11

THE MCARTHUR/GLEN REALTY CORP.

The market for real estate investment trusts (REITs) is currently booming with over $7 billion of new equity offerings during the first ten months of 1993. With the stock market at an all time high and bonds offering returns under 5%, Jonathan Potter is considering diversifying into real estate by purchasing shares in a new offering of the McArthur/Glen Realty Corp., a leading developer of off-price specialty retail centers.

Discussion Questions:

1. Is this a good investment for Potter? What is he betting on? What are his risks?
2. From the standpoint of McArthur/Glen, is setting up this REIT a good idea? Would other alternatives be better?
3. How would you evaluate the advantages–disadvantages of investing in real estate by purchasing shares in a real estate investment trust (REIT)?

In October 1993, Jonathan Potter, an independent telecommunications consultant based in Seattle, needed to make a decision about whether to invest in the newly formed McArthur/Glen Realty Corp. Potter had built an investment portfolio that now totaled slightly over $1 million. His primary investment objective was to build for his retirement, which was still 15 years away, but he also liked the security of current income in case he experienced a downturn in his consulting business. Over the years, Potter had followed an investment strategy of putting 45% of his assets in stocks, 45% in medium term, investment grade bonds, and 10% in cash. But with bonds yielding under 5% and the stock market at an all time high, his investment adviser, Angus Cartwright, suggested that he consider diversifying into real estate.

Unlike the stock market and the bond market, Cartwright explained, the real estate crisis of the 1990s had driven down real estate values in most markets by 30 to 35%. Office buildings, for example, were selling at prices that were 50% of what it would cost to replace them. These "bargain basement" prices would not last forever, Cartwright cautioned. Now was the time to get in.

Sensing Potter's resistance to investment in an industry that he knew little about, Cartwright suggested that Potter consider taking a "low risk" approach and invest in a real estate investment trust (REIT). "You can get a current yield that is higher than the yield on your bonds," Cartwright explained, "and still share in the upside when the real estate market recovers."

In particular, Cartwright urged Potter to consider the McArthur/Glen REIT. As Cartwright saw it, McArthur/Glen offered Potter a chance to buy into a portfolio of properties that was geographically diversified, as well as the opportunity to invest in a company with the expertise to acquire, develop, manage, and maximize the value of these properties. McArthur/Glen was scheduled to come to market in early October 1993 and Cartwright suggested that Potter get in on the initial public offering.

REAL ESTATE INVESTMENT TRUSTS

Real estate investment trusts (REITs) grew out of the Real Estate Investment Trust Act of 1960 and were designed to be a "mutual fund" for real estate, allowing

---

Lecturer John H. Vogel, Jr. and Adjunct Professor William J. Poorvu prepared this case as the basis for class discussion rather than to illustrate either effective or ineffective handling of an administrative situation.

small investors to own a piece of a large, diversified portfolio of properties. One key attraction of REITs is that although they are corporations and shield the investor from liability, they do not pay corporate taxes and thus avoid the problem of "double taxation." Another attractive feature is that, like any corporation, they can sell shares and get listed on a stock exchange and thereby provide significant liquidity.

To qualify as a REIT, a corporation must meet a series of tests which are described in the prospectus. Essentially there are four key requirements a corporation, business trust or association must meet to be treated as a REIT:

1. **Widely Held:** The REIT must have at least 100 shareholders of record. No more than 50% of the shares may be held directly or indirectly by five or fewer individuals.
2. **Invests Primarily in Real Estate:** At least 75% of the value of the company's total assets must be represented by real estate assets and "temporary" investments in cash, cash items, and government securities. Similarly, at least 75% of the REIT's gross income must consist of income derived from investments relating to real property or mortgages or temporary investments.
3. **Distributes Its Income Annually:** The REIT must distribute 95% of its taxable income to shareholders (excluding capital gains).
4. **Operates Like a Public Corporation:** The REIT must be managed by a board of trustees or directors, the majority of whom must be unaffiliated with the company's management. The REITs shares must also be freely transferable.

In the 1990s, a new form of REITs emerged—the Umbrella Partnership REIT, commonly called an UPREIT. One advantage of an UPREIT is that it helps to solve the tax problem faced by people like Cheryl McArthur and Alan Glen when they take their company public. In a traditional REIT, McArthur and Glen would sell their interest in the property for shares of stock in the REIT and then have to pay a large capital gains tax.

In an UPREIT, the investors in all the individual partnerships (which actually own the properties), have the option to exchange their limited partnership interests for units in an umbrella partnership. Investors can choose not to make this exchange in which case the umbrella partnership might end up owning only 80% or 90% of the underlying partnerships. The umbrella partnership then sells shares in a REIT to the public which in turn owns most of the umbrella partnership. Investors with units in the umbrella REIT can exchange their units for shares during the initial offering or anytime afterwards. These investors thus have the best of both worlds in that they can convert their interests to shares and obtain liquidity, or they can hold on to their units and avoid paying taxes until it is advantageous or necessary to do so.

The big drawback to the UPREIT structure is that it adds another layer of accounting and legal complexity, and makes the REIT prospectus even more difficult to understand. In the McArthur/Glen REIT, for example, Cheryl McArthur and Alan Glen received units that can be converted to 7,971,435 shares, but the book value of their interest as shown on the balance sheet and based on historical accounting (including depreciation) is negative. The difference in tax basis from the investors creates a potential conflict upon decisions as to whether or not to sell either individual properties or the entire company.

HISTORICAL PERFORMANCE

The REIT industry has had a checkered history. Begun in 1960, the REIT industry experienced its first growth spurt at the end of that decade. Between 1968 and 1972, REIT industry assets jumped from $1 billion to $14 billion. Most of this money was invested in short term construction loans, and to a lesser extent in land development loans. This type of short term lending was geared to take advantage of high short term interest rates. Many REIT sponsors found they could further enhance their returns through leveraging their investments and capturing the spread between their cost of funds and what they could charge their borrowers.

Unfortunately, the flood of money available to REITs in the late 1960s and early 1970s led to some poor underwriting. Many of the construction and land loans went into default, and the REITs ended up owning the properties. The REIT problems were further exacerbated in the mid-seventies by: (1) increasing inflation which drove up the price of the money the REIT's had borrowed, (2) an economic downturn which reduced demand for space, and (3) severely overbuilt markets which eroded rental rates. As a result, between 1972 and 1974 the average share price of a REIT fell 66% and the average price of mortgage REITs dropped 75%.

Devastated by this experience, it took a long time before investors were willing to consider whether the problem of the 1970s lay in the structure of the REIT or the quality of the REIT's investment. Gradually, however, shares in some of the REITs began to recover and by the early 1980s new REIT offerings began to appear. This trend was accelerated by the 1986 Tax Reform Act which took away many of the tax advantages of real estate, and therefore improved the attractiveness of REITs versus private limited partnerships.

Exhibit 1 traces the growth, decline and new growth of real estate assets controlled by REITs from 1961 to 1993. **Exhibit 2** contrasts the REIT investments of the 1970s with their emphasis on construction loans with the investment strategy of the 1990s with its emphasis on equity investments and long term mortgages. **Exhibit 3** provides a list of new REIT offerings from November 1991 to October 1993. It is noteworthy that during the first ten months of 1993, $7 billion of equity was issued by REITs versus $1.4 billion in all of 1992.

THE MCARTHUR/GLEN REALTY CORP.

Like a lot of the recently issued REITs, the McArthur/Glen offering allowed investors to buy into a particular type of real estate: in this case, manufacturer outlet shopping centers. These outlet centers offered high quality, brand name merchandise from manufacturers like Liz Claiborne, Anne Klein, Bass Shoes, Samsonite, Royal Dalton, and Nike. Customers were attracted primarily by the discount prices that these manufacturers offered. Customers also liked the fact that they could find each manufacturer's full line of offerings and liked the convenience of having a number of different manufacturer's outlets at one center. McArthur/Glen's research showed that the typical customer was: 39.9 years old, female (75%), married (62%), college educated (76%), affluent ($59,000), visited 4.6 times per year and drove 69 miles to the center. The reason people needed to drive so far was because of the clout of department stores which insisted that these centers be located away from major population centers so as not to compete with the retail stores who sold the same goods.

Cartwright said that the prospectus was particularly helpful in understanding the concept behind these centers. He was impressed by the statistic showing 99% occupancy at the 15 centers that McArthur/Glen had developed and that the new REIT would own. He was also interested in the fact that manufacturer outlet shopping centers were among the fastest growing segments of the retailing industry, with the number of such centers increasing at a compound annual growth rate of 20% the last five years.

McArthur/Glen had in operation 2.3 million square feet of space. By the end of 1993 another 440,000 square feet was expected to be completed. Plans for 1994 called for another million square feet and 1995 and 1996 another 2 million square feet. Of the $137 million required to finish the 1993 and 1994 expansions, $31 million was already spent and the company expected the remainder to be raised through additional debt. After all, if the company could build these centers at an average of $90 per square foot and lease them at a net operating income of $13 ($14.54 from prospectus less vacancies and non-reimbursable expenses), the future looked quite rosy.

THE DECISION

Potter visited the Pacific Edge Outlet Center in Burlington, Washington and was impressed by what he saw. As he looked at the McArthur/Glen Realty Corp. Prospectus—all 135 pages of fine print and legalese—he wondered why people spent so much time and money creating a document that was so hard to read and understand. The concept of full disclosure had turned into a shield for the sellers not the buyers. Still, he thought that if he spent an hour and a half looking at certain pages that his advisor, Angus Cartwright, had pointed out to him were especially important, he could boil it all down to a "back of the envelope" analysis of what an investor was receiving, and what the investor was paying for his share of the properties (see **Exhibit 4**). He remembered a course that he had taken at business school where the professor had made a fetish of such an approach.

In order to do this "back of the envelope approach," he needed to choose a specific date and create a new income statement. He thought that December 31, 1993 was probably the best date because by then the 445,000 square feet currently under construction would be completed and he would not have to try to value half built properties.

Basically, Potter hoped to answer two fundamental questions that would help him decide if the McArthur/Glen REIT was a good investment:

1. Why was McArthur/Glen creating this REIT? What were their other options?
2. For the investment to be successful, what was he betting on? What was he buying? Was it worth $21.50 per share?

Potter then opened the Prospectus determined to make a decision.

Exhibit 1

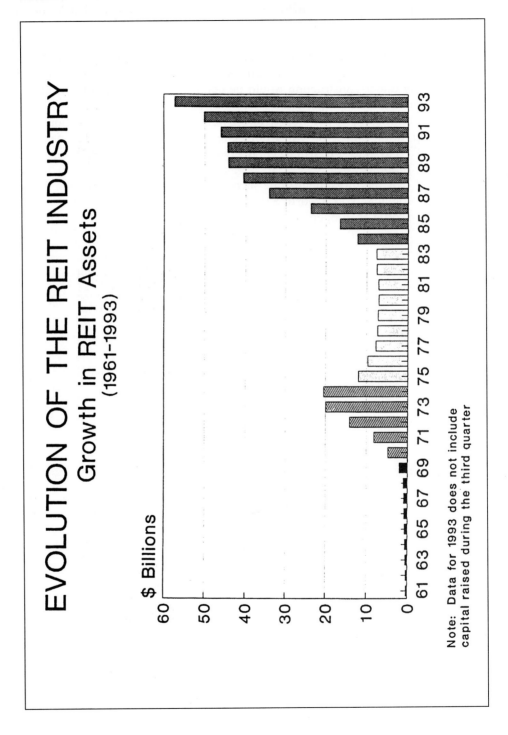

EVOLUTION OF THE REIT INDUSTRY
Growth in REIT Assets
(1961–1993)

Note: Data for 1993 does not include capital raised during the third quarter

Exhibit 2

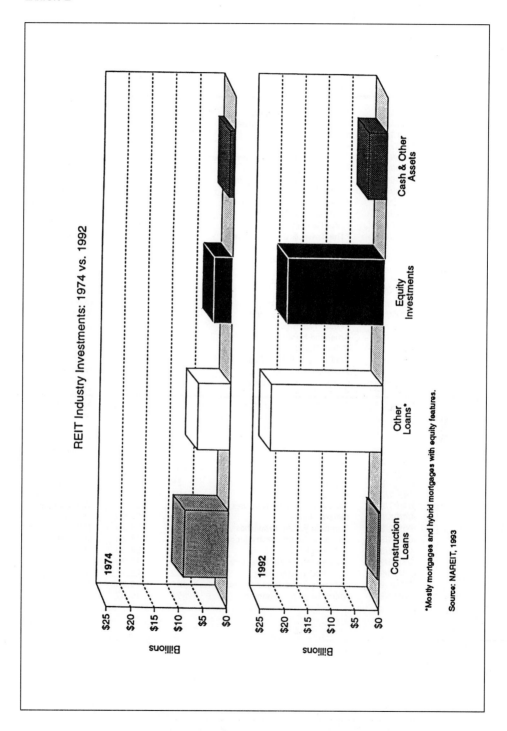

REIT Industry Investments: 1974 vs. 1992

*Mostly mortgages and hybrid mortgages with equity features.

Source: NAREIT, 1993

Exhibit 3 Domestic Common Stock Offerings by REITs

11/22/91-10/14/93

Offer Date	Issuer(a)	Global Dollar Amount (b)	Offer Price	Lead Manager
10/14/93	*MacArthur/Glen Realty	217	21.50	J.P. Morgan
10/13/93	Developers Diversified Realty	105	29.88	Dean Witter
10/13/93	Health Care REIT	63	25.13	Alex. Brown
10/07/93	Kranzco Realty Trust	53	24.00	Smith Barney Shearson
10/06/93	Manufactured Home Communities	139	44.75	Merrill Lynch
10/06/93	*Urban Shopping Centers	261	23.50	Merrill Lynch
10/05/93	*Tucker Properties Corporation	193	18.00	Kidder Peabody
09/28/93	*Duke Realty Investors	272	23.75	Merrill Lynch
09/22/93	*Colonial Properties Trust	195	23.00	Lehman Brothers
08/18/93	*ROC Communities	110	20.00	Kidder Peabody
08/18/93	*Saul Centers	228	20.00	Smith Barney Shearson
08/16/93	*The Town & Country Trust	323	22.00	Goldman Sachs
08/11/93	*Equity Residential	299	26.00	Merrill Lynch
08/11/93	*National Golf Properties	198	20.38	Morgan Stanley
08/10/93	*Crown American	423	17.25	Kidder Peabody
08/06/93	*RFS Hotel Investors	35	10.00	Morgan-Keegan
08/05/93	Price REIT	140	32.50	Merrill Lynch
08/04/93	*Excel Realty Trust	119	19.75	Merrill Lynch
07/22/93	*Camden Property Trust	163	22.00	Kidder Peabody
07/15/93	*Post Properties	235	25.50	Merrill Lynch
07/14/93	American Health Properties	75	24.88	Goldman Sachs
07/08/93	United Dominiun	72	13.50	Merrill Lynch
06/30/93	Bradley Real Estate Trust	47	8.50	Kidder Peabody
06/24/93	Wellsford	63	25.00	Merrill Lynch
06/23/93	Merry Land & Investment	100	25.00	Alex. Brown
06/11/93	*Holly Residential	153	23.00	Oppenheimer
06/02/93	*Factory Stores of America	122	23.00	Smith Barney
05/27/93	*Tanger Factory Outlet Centers	92	22.50	Merrill Lynch
05/26/93	Southwestern Property Trust	122	13.50	NatWest Security
05/26/93	*Mark Centers Trust	151	19.50	Merrill Lynch
05/26/93	*TriNet Corporate Realty	125	24.25	Merrill Lynch
05/26/93	*Healthcare Realty Trust	117	19.50	Donaldson Lufkin Jenrette
05/06/93	Vomado Realty Trust	178	35.50	Merrill Lynch
04/29/93	MGI Properties	28	13.88	Oppenheimer
04/07/93	Kimco Realty	102	34.25	Merrill Lynch
04/07/93	*General Growth Properties	417	22.00	Goldman Sachs
04/05/93	Federal Realty	70	28.00	Merrill Lynch
03/31/93	Burnham Pacific Properties	68	19.75	NatWest Security
03/26/93	Universal Health Realty Income	31	18.25	Smith Barney
03/22/93	BRE Properties	58	39.00	Dean Witter
03/10/93	Weingarten Realty Investors	105	42.00	Merrill Lynch
03/10/93	New Plan Realty Trust	62	25.12	Merrill Lynch
02/24/93	*Manufactured Home Communities	130	25.75	Merrill Lynch
02/12/93	Merry Land & Investment	75	16.87	Alex. Brown

Exhibit 3   (continued)

Offer Date	Issuer(a)	Global Dollar Amount (b)	Offer Price	Lead Manager
02/09/93	Property Trust of America	96	16.87	Goldman Sachs
02/08/93	*Carr Realty	172	22.00	Merrill Lynch
02/02/93	*Developers Diversified Realty	176	22.00	Dean Witter
01/28/93	Meditrust	87	30.62	County NatWest Securities
01/21/93	Health & Rehabilitation	131	12.75	Merrill Lynch
12/16/92	Bradley Real Estate Trust	50	7.37	Kidder Peabody
11/20/92	*Taubman Centers	335	11.00	Morgan Stanley
11/19/92	*Wellsford Residential Property	100	21.75	Merrill Lynch
11/12/92	*Kranzco Realty Trust	135	20.00	Smith Barney
10/22/92	IRT Property	63	11.00	Kidder Peabody
10/08/92	Cousins Property	55	14.00	Lazard Frères
08/11/92	Weingarten Realty Investors	67	33.62	Merrill Lynch
08/07/92	*Omega Healthcare Investors	128	21.00	Bear Stearns
08/05/92	Merry Land & Investment	28	10.12	Alex. Brown
07/30/92	Kimco Realty	53	25.37	Merrill Lynch
06/23/92	Washington Real Estate Inv. Tr.	40	17.00	Alex. Brown
06/02/92	Federal Realty Invest. Trust	70	20.50	Merrill Lynch
04/20/92	Health Equity Properties Inc.	25	8.50	County NatWest Securities
04/15/92	Property Trust of America	51	10.37	Merrill Lynch
03/12/92	New Plan Realty Trust	70	21.12	Merrill Lynch
02/25/92	Health Care Property Investors	70	44.00	Merrill Lynch
01/22/92	United Dominium Realty Trust (c)	82	20.50	Merrill Lynch
11/27/91	Federal Realty Invest. Trust	49	18.00	Alex. Brown
11/22/91	*Kimco Realty	128	20.00	Merrill Lynch

*   Indicates IPO's
(a)   Does not include mortgage REITs.
(b)   Dollars in millions. Includes over allotment where appropriate.
(c)   Reflects a 2 for 1 stock split in early May.
Source: Securities Data Company.

Exhibit 4 Selected Pages from Offering Prospectus

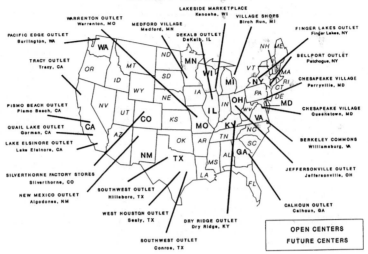

THE ATTORNEY GENERAL OF THE STATE OF NEW YORK HAS NOT PASSED ON OR ENDORSED THE MERITS OF THIS OFFERING. ANY REPRESENTATION TO THE CONTRARY IS UNLAWFUL.

IN CONNECTION WITH THIS OFFERING, THE UNDERWRITERS MAY OVER-ALLOT OR EFFECT TRANSACTIONS WHICH STABILIZE OR MAINTAIN THE MARKET PRICE OF THE COMMON STOCK AT A LEVEL ABOVE THAT WHICH MIGH OTHERWISE PREVAIL IN THE OPEN MARKET. SUCH TRANSACTIONS MAY BE EFFECTED ON THE NEW YORK STOCK EXCHANGE, IN THE OVER-THE-COUNTER MARKET OR OTHERWISE. SUCH STABILIZING, IF COMMENCED, MAY BE DISCONTINUED AT ANY TIME.

Exhibit 4   Selected Pages from Offering Prospectus   (continued)

Prospectus

10,100,000 Shares

McArthur/Glen Realty Corp.

Common Stock

(par value $.01 per share)

McArthur/Glen Realty Corp. (the "Company") will operate as a self-administered and self-managed real estate investment trust ("REIT") that will continue and intends to significantly expand the manufacturer outlet shopping center business developed by the McArthur/Glen Group. The Company will succeed to ownership interests in 15 centers currently in operation in 13 states and containing a total of approximately 2.4 million square feet of gross leasable area ("GLA"). The Company is currently constructing two new centers and expanding two existing centers which are all scheduled to open during 1993, increasing its total GLA to approximately 2.9 million square feet. The Company intends to pay regular quarterly dividends to its stockholders. The Company will be the sole general partner of, and will conduct all of its operations through, McG Outlet Centers Limited Partnership (the "Operating Partnership"). Consummation of the Offering is conditioned upon the closing of a $50 million loan (the "Debt Financing") to be made to the Operating Partnership pursuant to a commitment made by Morgan Guaranty Trust Company of New York.

All of the Common Stock, par value $.01 per share, of the Company (the "Common Stock") offered hereby is being sold by the Company (the "Offering"). Upon consummation of the Offering, management of the Company will own Common Stock and partnership interests which under certain circumstances will be exchangeable for Common Stock representing, in the aggregate, approximately 35.2% of all Common Stock on a fully diluted basis. The Common Stock has been approved for listing on the New York Stock Exchange, subject to official notice of issuance. Prior to the Offering, there has been no public market for the Common Stock. For factors considered in determining the initial public offering price, see "Underwriting."

See "Risk Factors" for certain factors relevant to an investment in the Common Stock including:

- Risk that the relatively short history of the manufacturer outlet shopping center industry may not be indicative of future performance;
- Substantial influence of certain stockholders, directors and executive officers of the Company on the affairs of the Company;
- Conflicts of interest, including those relating to partial ownership of certain properties;
- No third party appraisals were obtained and the value of the Company may not represent the fair market value of the properties and other assets of the Company;
- Risk that the Operating Partnership may be unable either to repay or refinance the Debt Financing, which will mature within one year of the consummation of the Offering, providing the lender with certain remedies which may cause a loss of income and asset value to the Company;
- Risk of potential increases in leverage due to the absence of any provision in the organizational documents of the Company or the Operating Partnership that limits the amount of debt which may be incurred;
- Taxation of the Company as a regular corporation if it fails to qualify as a REIT;
- Risks associated with real estate, such as the effect of economic and other conditions on real estate operations and values, the difficulty of obtaining construction and permanent financing and exposure to increases in interest rates with respect to indebtedness subject to floating interest rates;
- Limitations on stockholders' ability to change control of the Company due to restrictions on ownership of more than 5.0% of the Company's capital stock, a classified Board of Directors and other provisions that may have the effect of impeding a change in control;
- Possible inability of the Company to pay its estimated annual dividend; and
- Dependence on certain key tenants.

THESE SECURITIES HAVE NOT BEEN APPROVED OR DISAPPROVED BY THE SECURITIES AND EXCHANGE COMMISSION OR ANY STATE SECURITIES COMMISSION NOR HAS THE SECURITIES AND EXCHANGE COMMISSION OR ANY STATE SECURITIES COMMISSION PASSED UPON THE ACCURACY OR ADEQUACY OF THIS PROSPECTUS. ANY REPRESENTATION TO THE CONTRARY IS A CRIMINAL OFFENSE.

	Price to Public	Underwriting Discount [1]	Proceeds to Company [2]
Per Share	$21.50	$1.45	$20.05
Total [3]	$217,150,000	$14,645,000	$202,505,000

(1) The Company has agreed to indemnify the Underwriters against certain liabilities, including liabilities under the Securities Act of 1933. See "Underwriting."

(2) Before deducting expenses payable by the Company estimated at $2,727,000.

(3) The Company has granted the Underwriters an option, exercisable within 30 days after the date of this Prospectus, to purchase up to an additional 1,010,000 shares of Common Stock on the same terms as set forth above, solely to cover over-allotments, if any. If such over-allotment option is exercised in full, the total Price to Public, Underwriting Discount and Proceeds to Company will be $238,865,000, $16,109,500 and $222,755,500, respectively. See "Underwriting."

The shares of Common Stock offered by this Prospectus are being offered by the Underwriters, subject to prior sale, when, as and if delivered to and accepted by the Underwriters, and subject to the approval of certain legal matters by Cahill Gordon & Reindel, counsel for the Underwriters. It is expected that delivery of the certificates representing the shares will be made against payment therefor on or about October 21, 1993 at the offices of J.P. Morgan Securities Inc., 60 Wall Street, New York, New York.

J.P. Morgan Securities Inc.

A.G. Edwards & Sons, Inc.

Dean Witter Reynolds Inc.

October 14, 1993

Exhibit 4 Selected Pages from Offering Prospectus (continued)

BUSINESS AND PROPERTIES

General

The Company has increased its total developed GLA from approximately 287,000 square feet at the end of 1988 to approximately 2.0 million square feet at the end of 1992. New centers and expansions opened to date in 1993 or currently under construction are expected to bring total GLA to approximately 2.9 million square feet by the end of 1993.

As of August 31, 1993, the Company's centers in operation were approximately 99% occupied. In 1992, tenants in the Company's centers generated average sales per square foot of approximately $250, compared to $160 per square foot for all retail centers in 1992, as published by *National Research Bureau*.

The Company believes that its centers provide its tenants with a distribution outlet that generates higher than average revenues for the tenants at lower than average costs (minimum rent plus total expense recoveries paid by tenants). The following table illustrates the cost to sales ratio for the Company's centers which were open during all of 1992 compared to the cost to sales ratio for "super regional" shopping centers (as reported in "Dollars and Cents of Shopping Centers: 1993," *The Urban Land Institute*) for the year ended December 31, 1992:

	Average Sales per Sq. Ft.	Average Operating Costs per Sq. Ft.	Average Cost to Sales Ratio
Super regional shopping centers	$205.90	$23.29	11.31%
Company shopping centers	$249.61	$17.60	7.05%

The Company believes that the manufacturer outlet shopping center business is not simply a real estate development business, but also an operating business in which a retail-oriented approach to the on-going management and leasing of the centers is essential. The Company believes it has differentiated itself from its competitors by adhering to a "pure outlet" strategy, leasing primarily to high-quality, nationally recognized manufacturers and generally excluding discount and off-price retailers. This strategy promotes consistent quality and price integrity and attracts value-conscious consumers with an average annual median household income of approximately $59,000 to the Company's centers.

Exhibit 4 Selected Pages from Offering Prospectus (continued)

The Company's Outlet Centers

The following table summarizes certain information as of September 2, 1993 with respect to (i) centers in operation, (ii) centers and expansions under construction and scheduled for opening during the remainder of 1993 and (iii) new centers and expansions which the Company currently plans to open in 1994 through 1997 and as to which the Company owns or has an option to acquire the site. The Company is pursuing the acquisition of additional sites for future development, but these sites are not reflected in the table. No assurance can be given that any particular center or expansion will open on the date projected in the table or at all.

Name and Location of Center[1]	Major Metro Area	Currently in Operation — Approx. GLA; Year of Opening/ Most Recent Expansion; No. of Phases	Under Construction — Approx. GLA; Scheduled Opening Date; Phase Under Const.	Planned Development — Approx. GLA; Anticipated Opening Date; Phase to be Developed	Total — Approx. GLA
Berkeley Commons Outlet Center Williamsburg, VA	Richmond, VA Norfolk, VA	167,160 sq. ft. 1988/1990 Phases I-III	— — —	— — —	167,160 sq. ft.
Lakeside Marketplace Outlet Center[2][3] Kenosha, WI	Chicago, IL Milwaukee, WI	269,581 sq. ft. 1988/1991 Phases I-IV	— — —	— — —	269,581 sq. ft.
Silverthorne Factory Stores[3] Silverthorne, CO	Denver, CO Aspen, CO Vail/Keystone, CO	155,434 sq. ft. 1988/1990 Phases I-II	87,647 sq. ft. 4th Qtr 1993 Phase III	80,000 sq. ft. 1994 Phase IV	323,081 sq. ft.
Pacific Edge Outlet Center Burlington, WA	Seattle, WA Vancouver, BC	174,105 sq. ft. 1989/1993 Phases I-III	— — —	— — —	174,105 sq. ft.
Chesapeake Village at Queenstown[4] Queenstown, MD	Annapolis, MD Washington, DC	217,147 sq. ft. 1989/1993 Phases I-V	— — —	— — —	217,147 sq. ft.
Village Shops at Birch Run Birch Run, MI	Detroit, MI Flint, MI Saginaw, MI	117,583 sq. ft. 1989 Phase I	— — —	— — —	117,583 sq. ft.
Southwest Outlet Center at Hillsboro Hillsboro, TX	Dallas/Fort Worth, TX	196,095 sq. ft. 1989/1991 Phases I-II	—	150,000 sq. ft. 1995/1996 Phases III-IV	346,095 sq. ft.
Chesapeake Village at Perryville Perryville, MD	Baltimore, MD Philadelphia, PA	148,134 sq. ft. 1990 Phase I	—	50,000 sq. ft. 1994 Phase II	198,134 sq. ft.
Medford Village[5] Outlet Center Medford, MN	Minneapolis/St. Paul, MN	121,660 sq. ft. 1991 Phase I	—	130,000 sq. ft. 1995 Phase II	251,660 sq. ft.

Exhibit 4   Selected Pages from Offering Prospectus   (continued)

Name and Location of Center[1]	Major Metro Area	Currently in Operation — Approx. GLA; Year of Opening/Most Recent Expansion; No. of Phases	Under Construction — Approx. GLA; Scheduled Opening Date; Phase Under Const.	Planned Development — Approx. GLA; Anticipated Opening Date; Phase to be Developed	Total Approx. GLA
Lake Elsinore Outlet Center[1][6] Lake Elsinore, CA	Los Angeles, CA San Diego, CA	209,460 sq. ft. 1991/1992 Phases I-II	82,930 sq. ft. 4th Qtr 1993 Phase III	60,000 sq. ft. 1995 Phase IV	352,390 sq. ft.
Dry Ridge Outlet Center Dry Ridge, KY	Louisville, KY Cincinnati, OH Lexington, KY	105,980 sq. ft. 1991 Phase I	— — —	110,000 sq. ft. 1994 Phase II	215,980 sq. ft.
Southwest Outlet Center at Conroe Conroe, TX	Houston, TX Galveston, TX	92,790 sq. ft. 1992 Phase I	— —	160,100 sq. ft. 1994 Phase II	252,890 sq. ft.
Bellport Outlet Center[7] Patchogue, NY	Long Island, NY New York, NY	94,940 sq. ft. 1992 Phase I	— — —	300,000 sq. ft. 1995/1997 Phases II-III	394,940 sq. ft.
Calhoun Outlet Center[8] Calhoun, GA	Atlanta, GA Chattanooga, TN	123,120 sq. ft. 1992 Phase I	— — —	165,000 sq. ft. 1994/1995 Phases II-III	288,120 sq. ft.
Jeffersonville Outlet Center[9] Jeffersonville, OH	Cincinnati, OH Dayton, OH Columbus, OH	248,820 sq. ft. 1993 Phases I-II	— — —	— — —	248,820 sq. ft.
New Mexico Outlet Center Algodones, NM	Santa Fe, NM Albuquerque, NM	— — —	155,145 sq. ft. 4th Qtr 1993 Phase I	105,000 sq. ft. 1994 Phase II	260,145 sq. ft.
Warrenton Outlet Center Warrenton, MO	St. Louis, MO Columbia, MO	— — —	119,175 sq. ft. 4th Qtr 1993 Phase I	120,000 sq. ft. 1995 Phase II	239,175 sq. ft.
Pismo Beach Outlet Center[10] Pismo Beach, CA	San Luis Obispo, CA Santa Barbara, CA	— — —	— — —	140,000 sq. ft. 1994 Phase I	140,000 sq. ft.
Tracy Outlet Center Tracy, CA	San Francisco, CA Sacramento, CA	— —	— —	250,000 sq. ft. 1994/1996 Phases I-II	250,000 sq. ft.
West Houston Outlet Center Sealy, TX	Houston, TX Galveston, TX	— — —	— — —	250,000 sq. ft. 1994/1996 Phases I-II	250,000 sq. ft.
Finger Lakes Outlet Center Finger Lakes, NY	Rochester, NY Syracuse, NY	— — —	— — —	275,000 sq. ft. 1995/1996 Phases I-II	275,000 sq. ft.

Exhibit 4   Selected Pages from Offering Prospectus   (continued)

Name and Location of Center[1]	Major Metro Area	Currently in Operation — Approx. GLA; Year of Opening/Most Recent Expansion; No. of Phases	Under Construction — Approx. GLA; Scheduled Opening Date; Phase Under Const.	Planned Development — Approx. GLA; Anticipated Opening Date; Phase to be Developed	Total — Approx. GLA
DeKalb Outlet Center DeKalb, IL	Chicago, IL Quad Cities[11]	— —	— —	250,000 sq. ft. 1995/1996 Phases I–II	250,000 sq. ft.
Quail Lake Outlet Center Gorman, CA	Los Angeles, CA Bakersfield, CA	— —	— —	325,000 sq. ft. 1995/1996 Phases I–II	325,000 sq. ft.
Totals (Approx. GLA)		2,442,009 sq. ft.	444,897 sq. ft.	2,920,100 sq. ft.	5,807,006 sq. ft.

(1) Except as set forth below, each of the centers currently in operation will be 100% owned by the Operating Partnership upon consummation of the Offering and the other Formation Transactions described below under "Formation of the Company."

(2) This center had a book value as of December 31, 1992 equal to 10% or more of the total assets of the Company. See "Business and Properties—Additional Information Concerning Lake Elsinore Outlet Center, Lakeside Marketplace Outlet Center and Silverthorne Factory Stores."

(3) Gross revenues from this center for the year ended December 31, 1992 represented 10% or more of the Company's total revenues for the same period. See "Business and Properties—Additional Information Concerning Lake Elsinore Outlet Center, Lakeside Marketplace Outlet Center and Silverthorne Factory Stores."

(4) The Operating Partnership will use a portion of the net proceeds of the Offering and the Debt Financing to acquire the land and improvements comprising Phases III, IV and V of this center. See "Use of Proceeds."

(5) Upon consummation of the Formation Transactions, the Operating Partnership will be a limited partner owning an aggregate of 99% of the economic interest in the Property Partnership which owns Phase I of this center and will own 100% of Phase II of this center.

(6) The Company currently owns the improvements at Lake Elsinore Outlet Center (Phases I through III) subject to a ground lease for the land on which the center is situated. The Operating Partnership will use a portion of the net proceeds of the Offering and the Debt Financing to purchase the ground lessor's interest in the underlying real property. See "Use of Proceeds."

(7) Upon consummation of the Formation Transactions, the Operating Partnership will be the general partner and a limited partner owning an aggregate of 49.99% of the partnership interests in the Property Partnership which owns Phase I of this center. The Company has entered into an agreement with the owner of the land which is the proposed site for Phase II of the center, pursuant to which such landowner will contribute the land to a partnership in which the Operating Partnership will own a 45% general and limited partnership interest. The Company has purchased the land on which it plans to develop Phase III of the center. The Operating Partnership will own a 95% general and limited partnership interest in the partnership that will develop and own this phase.

(8) Upon consummation of the Formation Transactions, the Operating Partnership will be a general and limited partner owning an aggregate of 50% of the economic interest in the Property Partnership which owns this center.

(9) The improvements at this center are currently owned by an unaffiliated third party and are subject to a ground lease for the land from the Company. The Operating Partnership will use a portion of the net proceeds of the Offering and the Debt Financing to purchase the improvements from the third party. See "Use of Proceeds."

(10) Certain members of the McArthur/Glen Group will contribute to the Company their 50% interest in a partnership to be formed to own this center.

(11) Moline, IL; Davenport, IA; Rock Island, IL; and Bettendorf, IA.

Exhibit 4   Selected Pages from Offering Prospectus   (continued)

Business and Operating Strategy

The Company's business strategy is comprised of four key elements:

- *Tenant Relationships*—maintaining long-term relationships with key tenants and continuously enhancing the tenant mix at its centers;
- *Promotion and Marketing*—employing market research, advertising and merchandising techniques to attract shoppers to each center;
- *Asset Management*—monitoring and enhancing performance through intensive tenant and property management and employing quality property maintenance standards; and
- *Conservative Development Strategy*—limiting exposure to development risk.

The Company's strategic approach is to provide an attractive environment in which tenants can showcase their brand names and to convey an image at its centers of consistency, high quality and pricing integrity designed to attract knowledgeable, value-conscious consumers and encourage repeat visits.

The Company believes that tenant mix is the single most critical factor in assuring a center's success, and that its ability to attract to its centers a mix of nationally recognized manufacturers of upscale designer and brand-name merchandise selling at a substantial discount from retail prices is its principal competitive advantage. The Company has established long-standing relationships throughout the apparel manufacturing industry and has developed a nucleus of key tenants and an expanded group of core tenants which operate stores at many of the Company's centers. Liz Claiborne and Nike, each of which has stores in 13 of the Company's 15 open centers, have committed to 15-year leases for all their stores. In almost every case, leases are signed by the tenant's parent corporation.

Key tenants are placed strategically in locations designed to draw customers into the center and to encourage them to shop at more than one store. The Company continually examines the placement of tenants within each center and, in collaboration with the tenants, adjusts the size and location of their space within the center to improve sales per square foot. Upon lease expirations, the Company has, in most cases, achieved base rent increases, longer lease terms and an enhanced tenant mix.

All aspects of the Company's development strategy are designed to maximize success and minimize risk. During the site selection process, the Company consults with certain of its anchor tenants to identify major markets which, based on such tenants' knowledge of those retail markets, provide attractive development opportunities. Combining the Company's real estate experience with the tenants' retail market knowledge, the Company seeks to locate optimal sites within an 80-mile trade area of the identified market, taking into account the tenants' sensitivities, competitive developments and site considerations. Frequently, representatives of certain of these anchor tenants travel with Company executives on site visits. The Company generally selects sites for its new centers based on a set of clearly defined demographic criteria that the Company has developed in cooperation with such tenants. These criteria currently include:

- A population of at least two million people within the 80-mile trade area;
- Average household income within the trade area of approximately $35,000 or more per year;
- Visibility and convenient access from a major highway, with average daily car traffic of at least 20,000;
- Minimum distance of approximately 35 miles from the nearest department store; and
- An affluent base of female professionals and young families within the trade area.

Exhibit 4   Selected Pages from Offering Prospectus   (continued)

Financing Strategy

The Company's financing strategy is to maintain for itself and the Operating Partnership, taken together as a single enterprise, a conservative ratio of debt to total market capitalization (defined as the aggregate market value of all outstanding shares of Common Stock, assuming the exchange of all Units for shares of Common Stock, plus total consolidated debt) which generally will not exceed 40%. The market capitalization of the Company (as opposed to the appraised value of the assets of the Company), will be based upon the current market value of the Common Stock and will fluctuate with changes in the market price of the Common Stock. Such market capitalization may not necessarily reflect the book or fair market value of the underlying assets of the Company. Although the use of market capitalization may result in greater fluctuations than would the use of appraised values, the Company has used market capitalization because it believes that the book value of its assets does not accurately reflect its ability to borrow and to meet debt service requirements, and the Company has not obtained appraisals of its assets. After giving effect to the Offering, the other Formation Transactions and the Debt Financing, the Company's ratio of debt to total market capitalization will be approximately 22.1%.

The Company intends to finance future developments and expansions with the most appropriate sources of capital, which include undistributed cash flow, the issuance of debt or additional equity securities and bank or other institutional borrowings. The Company presently is negotiating with certain of its existing construction lenders to obtain a $125 million line of credit (the "Construction Line") for funding new developments and expansions. The Company also is negotiating with an existing lender to obtain a $50 million line of credit secured by certain of its Properties (the "Secured Line"), which will be available for general corporate purposes, including funding future developments and expansions.

FORMATION OF THE COMPANY

The Properties and other assets (other than the net proceeds of the Offering) to be transferred to the Operating Partnership as described above constitute the business and assets that will be consolidated in the financial statements of the Company. See Note 1 of the Notes to the Combined Financial Statements of McArthur/Glen Entities. The net book value as of June 30, 1993 of the assets to be transferred by participants in the Formation Transactions was a deficit of approximately $10.1 million and the value of the shares of Common Stock and Units allocated to such participants is approximately $195.9 million (based upon the initial public offering price), which exceeds the net book value as of June 30, 1993 of the assets to be transferred by approximately $206.0 million. The aggregate value of the shares of Common Stock, Units and cash allocated to Cheryl McArthur, Alan Glen and the other members of the McArthur/Glen Group is approximately $154.3 million (based on the initial public offering price), which substantially exceeds the net book value of the assets that they will contribute in the Formation Transactions.

The Formation Transactions may have certain disadvantages to purchasers of shares of Common Stock in the Offering. These disadvantages, which are explained more fully under "Risk Factors" and "Formation of the Company," include:

- Conflicts of interest involving management of the Company and the Board of Directors in the Formation Transactions, including conflicts associated with the receipt by Cheryl McArthur, Alan Glen and certain other members of the McArthur/Glen Group of certain benefits not generally received by others participating in the Formation Transactions, which may conflict with the interest of others participating in the Formation Transactions and the interest of persons purchasing shares of Common Stock in the Offering;

Exhibit 4   Selected Pages from Offering Prospectus   (continued)

- Conflicts of interest involving management of the Company and the Board of Directors in business decisions regarding the Company, including conflicts associated with sales of Properties that may arise due to the more adverse tax consequences of such sales to Cheryl McArthur, Alan Glen and other members of the McArthur/Glen Group and conflicts arising as a result of the fiduciary duties that the Company may owe as the general partner of the Operating Partnership and fiduciary duties that the Operating Partnership may owe as a general partner of certain other partnerships, which may result in decisions that are not in the best interests of the stockholders of the Company;

- Lack of third party appraisals and the fact that the valuation of the Company and the allocation of equity interests therein among the participants in connection with the Formation Transactions were not determined as a result of arm's-length negotiations with purchasers in the Offering; accordingly, no assurance can be given that the value of equity interests received by participants in connection with the Formation Transactions will not exceed the fair market value of the assets transferred by such participants to the Company; and

- Immediate and substantial dilution in the net tangible book value of shares of Common Stock purchased in the Offering.

In response to the current economic and financial environment, including the diminished availability of conventional debt financing, the McArthur/Glen Group decided to explore the formation of an investment vehicle to provide access to the public capital markets. For a further discussion of the reasons for the formation of the Company and a discussion of the detriments and benefits of the Formation Transactions to the partners in the Property Partnerships, see "Formation of the Company—Reasons for Formation of the Company."

Exhibit 4   Selected Pages from Offering Prospectus   (continued)

The following chart depicts the beneficial ownership of the Company, the Operating Partnership, the Third Party Services Corporation and the 15 existing manufacturer outlet shopping centers upon consummation of the Offering and the other Formation Transactions:

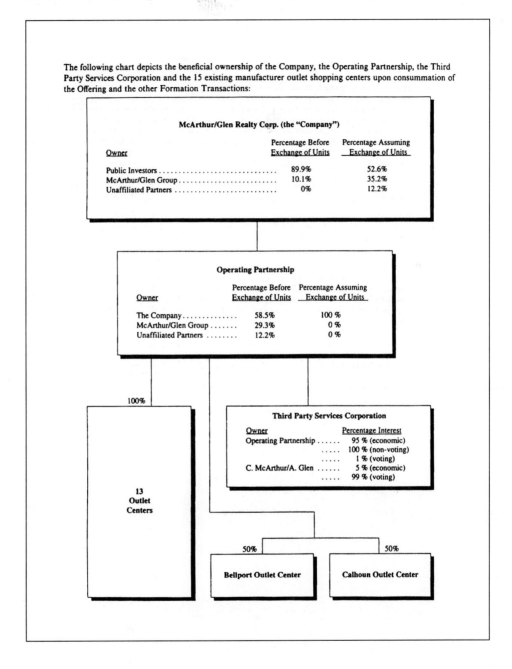

McArthur/Glen Realty Corp. (the "Company")

Owner	Percentage Before Exchange of Units	Percentage Assuming Exchange of Units
Public Investors	89.9%	52.6%
McArthur/Glen Group	10.1%	35.2%
Unaffiliated Partners	0%	12.2%

Operating Partnership

Owner	Percentage Before Exchange of Units	Percentage Assuming Exchange of Units
The Company	58.5%	100 %
McArthur/Glen Group	29.3%	0 %
Unaffiliated Partners	12.2%	0 %

100%

13 Outlet Centers

Third Party Services Corporation

Owner	Percentage Interest
Operating Partnership	95 % (economic)
	100 % (non-voting)
	1 % (voting)
C. McArthur/A. Glen	5 % (economic)
	99 % (voting)

50%   **Bellport Outlet Center**

50%   **Calhoun Outlet Center**

Exhibit 4   Selected Pages from Offering Prospectus   (continued)

SUMMARY SELECTED COMBINED FINANCIAL DATA

The following table sets forth selected financial and operating data on a pro forma basis for the Company and on a combined historical basis for the Property Partnerships and the Service Companies. The combined historical financial data of the Property Partnerships and the Service Companies at December 31, 1992 and 1991 and for the years ended December 31, 1992, 1991 and 1990 have been derived from the historical Combined Financial Statements audited by Deloitte & Touche, independent certified public accountants, whose report with respect to such audits is included elsewhere in this Prospectus. The historical financial data for the six months ended June 30, 1993 and 1992 and the years ended December 31, 1989 and 1988 have been derived from the unaudited combined financial statements of the Property Partnerships and the Service Companies. In the opinion of management, the historical financial data for the six months ended June 30, 1993 and 1992 and the years ended December 31, 1989 and 1988 include all adjustments (consisting only of normal recurring adjustments) necessary to present fairly the information set forth therein.

Historical operating results, including net income, may not be comparable to future operating results because of the historically greater leverage of the Property Partnerships. In addition, the Company believes that the book value of the Properties and the assets of the Service Companies, which reflects the historical costs of such assets less accumulated depreciation, is not indicative of the fair market value of the Properties or the assets of the Service Companies.

The selected pro forma financial and operating data is presented as if (i) the Offering, the other Formation Transactions and the Debt Financing had occurred on June 30, 1993 in the case of the consolidated balance sheet and January 1, 1992 in the case of the consolidated statements of operations, (ii) the Property Partnerships and the Service Companies were not subject to tax and thus incurred no income tax expense during the periods and (iii) the Company qualified as a REIT, distributed all of its taxable income and, therefore, incurred no income tax expense during the periods. The pro forma financial data is not necessarily indicative of what the actual financial position and results of operations of the Company would have been as of and for the periods indicated, nor does it purport to represent the Company's future financial position and results of operations.

Exhibit 4   Selected Pages from Offering Prospectus   (continued)

	Six Months Ended June 30,			Years Ended December 31,					
	Pro Forma	Historical		Pro Forma	Historical				
	1993	1993	1992	1992	1992	1991	1990	1989	1988
	(Dollars in thousands, except per share amounts)								
Statements of Operations									
Revenues:									
Minimum rents	$14,937	$14,521	$11,809	$25,672	$25,375	$17,193	$11,328	$5,117	$842
Percentage rents	829	756	669	1,702	1,702	937	934	573	11
Recoveries from tenants	4,350	4,241	3,187	7,063	6,994	4,570	2,891	1,253	345
Other	1,705	1,701	499	1,622	1,622	1,968	727	142	166
Total revenues	21,821	21,219	16,164	36,059	35,693	24,668	15,880	7,085	1,364
Expenses:									
Operating and maintenance	4,729	5,134	3,852	8,356	9,195	6,316	4,760	2,559	574
Real estate taxes	1,589	1,576	1,316	2,653	2,641	1,491	906	405	20
Interest	3,473	7,214	6,746	7,070	14,296	12,763	9,837	4,855	839
Depreciation and amortization	6,388	5,771	4,791	11,387	10,101	6,761	4,913	2,638	513
Total expenses	16,179	19,695	16,705	29,466	36,233	27,331	20,416	10,457	1,946
Income (loss) before minority interests	5,642	1,524	(541)	6,593	(540)	(2,663)	(4,536)	(3,372)	(582)
Minority interests in (income) loss[1]	(2,498)	(268)	54	(2,775)	(66)	101	—	—	—
Net income (loss)	$3,144	$1,256	$(487)	$3,818	$(606)	$(2,562)	$(4,536)	$(3,372)	$(582)
Net income per common share[2]	$.28			$.34					
Other Data									
Funds from operations before minority interests[3]	$12,030	$7,295	$4,250	$17,980	$9,561	$4,098	$377	$(734)	$(69)
Total GLA at end of period(000's)	2,254	2,099	1,845	2,078	2,049	1,657	1,145	757	287
Number of centers at end of period	15	14	13	14	14	11	8	7	3
Occupancy percentage at end of period	99%	99%	99%	99%	99%	92%	98%	93%	83%

	June 30,			December 31,				
	Pro Forma	Historical	Historical		Historical			
	1993	1993	1992	1992	1991	1990	1989	1988
	(Dollars in thousands)							
Balance Sheets Data								
Investment in rental property (before accumulated depreciation)	$235,345	$202,469	$171,726	$188,803	$154,211	$110,032	$74,722	$30,290
Net investment in rental property	212,532	179,656	157,375	170,364	143,419	104,324	72,617	29,967
Total assets	266,502	208,420	180,593	194,428	164,558	119,483	82,072	33,171
Total liabilities	124,009	218,717	192,186	212,184	177,101	127,598	86,230	33,944
Stockholders' and partners' equity (deficit)	83,446	(10,147)	(11,593)	(17,495)	(12,471)	(8,115)	(4,158)	(773)

(1) Historical minority interests represent the approximately 50% interests in the Property Partnerships which own the Calhoun Outlet Center and the Bellport Outlet Center which will not be owned by the Operating Partnership. Pro forma minority interests also represents the 41.5% minority interest in the Operating Partnership which will not be owned by the Company.

(2) Pro forma net income per common share is based upon 11,238,910 shares of Common Stock outstanding.

(3) Industry analysts generally consider funds from operations to be the most appropriate measure of the performance of an equity REIT. Funds from operations is generally defined as income (loss) before certain non-cash items, primarily depreciation and amortization. For all periods presented, depreciation and amortization were the only non-cash adjustments. Funds from operations should not be considered an alternative to net income as an indication of the Company's performance or to cash flows as a measure of liquidity. For the year ended December 31, 1992, pro forma funds from operations consists of $10.5 million for the stockholders and $7.5 million for the Unit holders. For the six months ended June 30, 1993, pro forma funds from operations consists of $7.0 million for the stockholders and $5.0 million for the Unit holders.

Exhibit 4   Selected Pages from Offering Prospectus   (continued)

THE COMPANY

The Company will operate as a self-administered and self-managed real estate investment trust that will continue and intends to significantly expand the manufacturer outlet shopping center business developed by the McArthur/Glen Group. The Company, as the general partner of the Operating Partnership, will succeed to ownership of interests in 15 manufacturer outlet shopping centers located in 13 states and containing a total of approximately 2.4 million square feet of GLA. As of August 31, 1993, the Company's centers were approximately 99% occupied. The centers contain an aggregate of approximately 650 stores, feature a diversified mix of nationally recognized manufacturers of upscale designer and brand-name merchandise, and each is anchored by one or more of Liz Claiborne, Nike, Mikasa, Carter's Childrenswear, Corning/Revere, Eddie Bauer, Guess?, Levi's, Phillips-Van Heusen and Sara Lee (L'eggs/Hanes/Bali), with which the Company has developed long-standing relationships. See "—The Company's Business and Operating Strategy—Tenant Relationships" below. The Company is a fully integrated real estate company, focusing exclusively on manufacturer outlet shopping centers throughout the United States and employing approximately 175 employees who provide a full range of development, leasing, marketing and management services to the Company's centers.

The McArthur/Glen Group was founded in 1986 by Cheryl McArthur and Alan Glen to develop, design and manage upscale manufacturer outlet shopping centers. Based on their knowledge of and contacts in the apparel and retail industries, the founders perceived a demand for outlet centers in which a complementary group of manufacturers could operate in an upscale environment and attract a large customer base.

Manufacturer outlet shopping centers have been among the fastest growing segments of the retailing industry with the number of such centers increasing at a compound annual growth rate of approximately 20% in the last five years. According to *Value Retail News*, a leading industry publication, the McArthur/Glen Group was one of the largest active developers of manufacturer outlet shopping centers in the United States in 1992, as measured by total square feet constructed. In 1992, the McArthur/Glen Group received the *Value Retail News* Award of Excellence and, in 1993, the Company received *Value Retail News* Market Savvy Awards for accomplishments in advertising, marketing and promotion. The McArthur/Glen Group was ranked the 28th fastest growing private company in 1992 by *Inc.* magazine.

To take advantage of the growth opportunities in the industry, the Company intends to continue to pursue an aggressive development strategy. The Company currently has under construction two new centers and expansions at two existing centers containing, in the aggregate, approximately 445,000 square feet of additional GLA, all of which is expected to open by the end of 1993. During 1994, the Company plans to build approximately one million square feet of additional GLA. The Company estimates that the total cost of these new centers and expansions will be approximately $137 million, of which it is expected that approximately $31 million will have been expended at September 30, 1993. The Company owns sites or has contractual rights to sites on which it intends to build approximately 1.9 million square feet of additional GLA after 1994.

The Company believes that it has achieved its historical success by assembling a senior management team consisting of ten individuals who have significant experience in their respective areas of operation and who will continue in those positions after the consummation of the Offering. The senior management team has employed a strategy of (i) working closely with certain of the Company's anchor tenants in selecting the sites for its centers and the location of stores therein, (ii) acquiring sites and commencing construction only upon receipt of signed leases from anchor tenants and other tenants covering a substantial portion of the center's GLA, (iii) maintaining tight control on the quality and timing of construction and (iv) actively managing each center's tenant mix to increase its overall sales per square foot. The Company's centers produced an average of approximately $250 per square foot in annual retail sales in 1992.

The Company believes it has differentiated itself from its competitors by adhering to a "pure outlet" strategy, leasing primarily to high-quality, nationally recognized manufacturers and generally excluding discount and off-price retailers. This strategy promotes consistent quality and price integrity and attracts value-conscious consumers with an average median household income of approximately $59,000 to the Company's centers.

Exhibit 4 Selected Pages from Offering Prospectus (continued)

Overview of the Value Retail Industry

The Company's centers are part of a retail industry sector known as value retail. In the value retail sector, merchandise is sold at a significant discount from prices charged by traditional retailers, such as department stores and specialty stores.

Value retail generally consists of three segments: discount retailers, off-price retailers and manufacturer outlet stores.

- *Discount retailers* offer inexpensive non-branded goods and some manufacturers' seconds at low to mid-level price points.
- *Off-price retailers* buy excess inventory and seconds from manufacturers, and as a result, offer a narrow selection in a number of assorted brand names, which can vary daily or weekly in every store.
- *Manufacturer outlet stores* are operated by manufacturers and sell directly to the consumer. Manufacturer outlet stores generally carry the same name as the designer or manufacturer and feature a full selection of brand-name goods discounted between 20% and 70% from full retail. The manufacturer outlet stores generally feature moderate to high price points and target a middle- and upper-income clientele.

Manufacturer outlet stores are distinguished from the other two value retail segments principally by the manner in which their goods are sourced: discount and off-price retailers buy their goods from manufacturers, whereas outlets are operated directly by manufacturers. Manufacturer outlets are further distinguished from discount retailers by generally higher price points and a generally more affluent target clientele, and from off-price retailers by a wider selection and a generally higher level of customer service.

Evolution of Value Retail

Value retail originated as a solution to manufacturers' excess inventory problems which resulted from production overruns and returns of unsold merchandise. These overruns and returns were historically sold to discount and off-price retailers. As vehicles for inventory management, discount and off-price retailers have certain disadvantages for manufacturers:

- Discount and off-price retailers frequently buy at distressed prices, with manufacturers often selling at a loss;
- Uneven presentation and merchandise mix tend to erode brand image; and
- Location of discount and off-price retailers often brings a manufacturer's discounted goods into competition with those same goods in nearby department stores.

In response to these shortcomings, manufacturers began to develop their own direct outlets, allowing them to:

- Avoid selling inventory at distressed prices and improve profit margins;
- Maintain brand image through attractive presentation of merchandise and association with other designer label goods;
- Gain some control over the distribution of products, reducing conflicts with full-priced goods in department stores; and
- Provide a showcase setting for their full product line.

While manufacturers have become aware of the benefits of selling excess inventory through outlets, consumer attitudes have also been changing. Consumers have increasingly been demanding quality merchandise and lower prices. In addition, declining real disposable income and the proliferation of promotions by department stores and specialty retailers have contributed to a "bargain-hunting" mentality and a renewed focus on value, which attracts shoppers to value retail.

Exhibit 4 Selected Pages from Offering Prospectus (continued)

Manufacturer Outlet Centers

Outlet stores are operated by manufacturers and sell primarily first-quality, brand-name goods. Manufacturer outlet centers are typically located near tourist destinations or on interstate highways outside of metropolitan areas, allowing access to major markets while avoiding direct competition with the manufacturers' traditional retail channels.

Outlet centers are mutually beneficial to consumers and manufacturers. Consumers benefit by having access to a full selection of brand-name designer goods at below-retail prices in an attractive environment with a high level of service. Manufacturers benefit by:

- Selling out-of-season, overstocked or discontinued merchandise without alienating department stores or eroding brand image;

- Optimizing the size of production runs to achieve economies of scale by selling any resulting excess through outlets; and

- Achieving significant contributions to profits by selling directly to consumers at above-wholesale prices and by reducing the practice of "dumping" excess inventory at a loss to off-price retailers.

While manufacturers originally entered the outlet business for these benefits, they have discovered that outlets offer a variety of additional benefits:

- A showcase for a manufacturer's full product line, which department stores generally cannot provide because of limited space;

- A vehicle for product testing and brand extension (for example, Van Heusen, a men's wear manufacturer, introduced a women's wear line through its outlet centers and Bass Shoe launched an apparel line available only in its outlet stores); and

- An opportunity to use trained sales professionals specializing in the manufacturer's line who can educate consumers about the products and provide a level of customer service that is uncommon in most retail stores.

As a result of these advantages, the number of manufacturers who regard outlets as an important element of their business has continued to grow. From 1988 to 1993, the number of manufacturers that operated outlet stores nearly doubled from 260 to 500, making outlet stores one of the fastest growing segments in the retail industry, and the number of outlet centers nationwide has increased at a compound annual rate of approximately 20% from 108 to 275. In 1992, total outlet sales reached a record of $8.3 billion, an increase of 12% from the previous year, as compared to an estimated 4.1% increase in total sales for all retail centers.

Exhibit 4   Selected Pages from Offering Prospectus   (continued)

Tenant Relations

The Company's core tenant group is presented in the following table:

Tenant	Number of Stores*	% of GLA*
Adolfo II	15	1.58%
American Tourister	10	.87
Anne Klein	8	.88
Brooks Brothers	3	.60
Brown Shoes/Naturalizer	13	1.31
Capezio/Banister Shoes	15	1.91
Carole Little	5	.38
Carter's Childrenswear	11	2.10
Corning/Revere	11	1.87
Donna Karan	1	.19
Eddie Bauer	2	.45
Etienne Aigner	11	.92
European Collections	7	1.22
Evan-Picone/Izod/Gant	9	1.91
Famous Brands/Lechter's	15	2.00
Guess?	9	1.99
harve benard	8	.97
I.B. Diffusion	9	.77
J. Crew/Clifford & Wills	6	.95
JH Collectibles	9	1.46
Jones New York	26	2.18
Jordache	11	2.56
Kitchen Collection	8	1.01
Leather Loft	14	1.42
Levi's	5	1.63
Liz Claiborne	16	6.06
Maidenform	17	1.83
Mikasa	14	3.94
Nike/I.E. Side/Cole Haan	18	5.29
9 West	12	1.21
Osh Kosh	10	1.61
Phillips-Van Heusen		
Bass Shoe	18	3.04
Cape Isle Knitters	14	1.05
Geoffrey Beene	15	1.81
Van Heusen	16	2.38
Windsor Shirt	5	.50
Polo	1	.24
Sara Lee		
Coach Leather	1	.09
Socks Galore	15	.76
L'eggs/Hanes/Bali	10	1.91
Champion Hanes	6	.63
Sara Lee Outlet Bakery	2	.15
The North Face	6	1.67
Toys Unlimited	8	1.58
Welcome Home	16	1.31
Totals	461	70.19%

*Includes stores currently open and stores scheduled to open in 1993.

Exhibit 4   Selected Pages from Offering Prospectus   (continued)

Promotion and Marketing

The Company's Marketing Department consists of six employees who use marketing techniques to attract shoppers to the Company's centers. While individual brand names cannot be advertised because of the potential conflict with department stores, the Marketing Department advertises the overall center through television, radio and print advertising, promotions and an extensive public relations program.

These programs are supported by quantitative and qualitative market research which utilizes such information gathering techniques as focus groups, detailed customer surveys and syndicated research. Focus groups are conducted regularly in the Company's markets around the country to provide insight into such topics as site selection, tenant mix variables and marketing effectiveness. Quantitative research is conducted at least three times per year at each center and generally consists of at least 300 surveys that provide a statistically reliable and projectable database. Syndicated research used by the Company includes *SMRB Profiles, Lifestyle Market Analysis, Scarborough Qualitative Analysis* and *Claritas.* As a result, the Company has a detailed and current customer profile for each center and for the portfolio as a whole. The Company-wide customer profile is currently as follows:

Median Age:	39.9 years
Gender:	75% are female
Marital Status:	62% are married
Education:	76% have college degree/48% have graduate degree
Average Median Household Income:	$59,000
Average Distance Traveled:	69 miles
Average Visits Per Year:	4.6
Average Time Spent at Center:	75% spend from one to four hours

Asset Management

The Company monitors each center through approximately 100 full-time, on-site employees. In addition, members of the Asset Management Team make frequent site visits and closely monitor the sales performance of each tenant. Monthly sales reports are prepared on a tenant-by-tenant basis for each center. The data is analyzed for trends and tenants are evaluated on their performance. The Asset Management Team holds both formal and informal communication sessions with tenants throughout the year and is involved in promotions and marketing.

Key tenants are placed strategically in locations designed to draw customers into the center and to encourage them to shop at more than one store. The Company continually examines the placement of tenants within each center and, in collaboration with its tenants, adjusts the size and location of their space within the center to improve sales per square foot. Upon lease expirations, the Company has, in most cases, achieved base rent increases, longer lease terms and an enhanced tenant mix.

Since every tenant's performance is closely monitored, the Company identifies potential problems at an early stage. To date, the Company has worked successfully either to improve the performance of its weaker tenants or to replace such tenants before any lease default occurs. The Company has not lost any material revenue related to tenant bankruptcy or other lease default.

The Company works continually to preserve and enhance its relationships with its tenants by providing a high level of tenant services at each center. The Company's portfolio-wide standards for rigorous property maintenance seek to ensure attractive landscaping, cleanliness and appropriate security measures. On-site property managers are hired from the local area and are trained by regional property managers to maintain uniform quality across the portfolio. Maintenance is important to tenants, who want their brand names to be associated with an attractive environment, and to upscale consumers, who prefer to shop in a pleasant setting. The Company believes that its consistent ability to provide well-managed centers is a central factor in the loyalty of its core tenant group.

Exhibit 4   Selected Pages from Offering Prospectus   (continued)

Conservative Development Strategy

Upon identifying an acceptable site, the Company obtains an option for the site which allows the Company to complete pre-development work, such as title searches, soil analyses, environmental studies and design, without risking significant capital. Each center is built in phases to mitigate vacancy risk and the Company typically will not begin construction of, or purchase the land for, any phase unless it has obtained lease commitments for at least 60% (including the anchor tenants) of the anticipated GLA of the phase. During construction, the Company has the ability to adjust the final size of the phase to reflect lease commitments so that each phase achieves close to full occupancy at opening. Typically, construction of each phase takes approximately six months from groundbreaking to the opening of the first tenant store. Each phase is generally fully occupied within 45 days of the opening.

The Company's Construction Department employs four full-time construction managers who contract for and supervise all new construction. The Company's centers are built using standardized techniques, making new outlets simple to design and construct. Local contractors are hired for each project, reducing construction costs, increasing efficiency and building relationships between the Company and the local community.

The centers developed by the Company are all open-air malls with the stores typically arranged in a "U" shape configuration with the parking lot in the center so that all stores are clearly visible. This configurations provides the shopper with good visibility of all of the stores.

Future Developments

The Company intends to increase its cash flow over time by developing new centers and expansions of existing centers and by continuing its intensive asset management and marketing practices to maximize the performance of its centers. The Company has developed a growth plan; many of the strategic markets that the Company plans to enter have been identified; and land is already owned or under option for the development of new centers and expansions of existing centers aggregating approximately 2.9 million square feet of additional GLA. For additional information regarding the Company's currently planned future development activities, see "Business and Properties."

DISTRIBUTIONS

The Company intends to pay regular quarterly dividends to its stockholders. The first dividend, for the period from the consummation of the Offering until December 31, 1993, is expected to be approximately $.28 per share, which is an amount equivalent to a quarterly dividend of $.3625 per share (which, if annualized, would equal $1.45, or an annual yield of 6.74% based on the initial public offering price).

The Company established its initial dividend based upon an estimate of the cash flow that will be available for dividends in the twelve-month period after the consummation of the Offering. This estimate is based upon pro forma consolidated funds from operations for the twelve months ended June 30, 1993, with adjustments for certain events and contractual commitments that are not reflected in the Company's historical or pro forma financial statements. The Company believes that its estimate of adjusted funds from operations for the twelve months ended June 30, 1993 constitutes a reasonable basis for setting the initial distribution amount and expects to maintain its initial distribution rate for the first twelve months following the consummation of the Offering, unless actual results of operations, economic conditions or other factors differ from the assumptions used in the estimate. No assurance can be given that this estimate will prove accurate and actual results may vary substantially from the estimate. See "Risk Factors—Partial Dependence on Projects under Construction in Estimating Initial Dividend Rate." The Company will enter into interest rate cap agreements that will protect the Company from increases in LIBOR above 4% and the prime rate above 6% during the twelve-month period after consummation of the Offering. The amount of dividends which would be distributed at the Company's expected payout ratio of 90% represents 92% of the funds which would be available for distribution in the event that the Company incurs the maximum interest rate expense possible giving effect to such interest rate cap agreements. The Company does not intend to reduce the expected distribution per share if the Underwriters' over-allotment option is exercised.

Exhibit 4   Selected Pages from Offering Prospectus   (continued)

The following table sets forth the Company's adjusted pro forma consolidated funds from operations (in thousands except per share information):

Pro forma consolidated funds from operations before minority interests for the year ended December 31, 1992	$17,980
Plus:	
Pro forma consolidated funds from operations before minority interests for the six months ended June 30, 1993	12,030
Less:	
Pro forma consolidated funds from operations before minority interests for the six months ended June 30, 1992	(8,401)
Pro forma consolidated funds from operations before minority interests for the twelve months ended June 30, 1993	21,609
Adjustment for minority interests in two Property Partnerships for the twelve months ended June 30, 1993	(724)
Pro forma consolidated funds from operations before minority interests in the Operating Partnership for the twelve months ended June 30, 1993	20,885
Adjustments:	
Plus:	
Additional net revenues from contractual minimum rent increases[1][2]	719
Additional net revenues from annualizing minimum rents for new centers and expansions opened during the twelve months ended June 30, 1993[1][3]	3,291
Additional net revenues from minimum rents for new centers and expansions open or under construction by October 1, 1993 based on executed leases[1][4]	6,055
Estimated adjusted consolidated funds from operations before minority interests in the Operating Partnership for the twelve months ending September 30, 1994	$30,950
Expected initial dividend[5]	$27,855
Expected initial dividend payable to the Company	$16,296
Expected initial dividend per share of Common Stock	$ 1.45
Expected payout ratio[6]	90%
Reserves for capital expenditures and working capital	$ 3,095

(1) The Company anticipates that all material increases in operating expenses will be reimbursed in the form of tenant recoveries. Additional net revenues reflect the deduction of all additional operating expenses, including real estate taxes, insurance costs, management and maintenance costs and interest expense.

(2) Reflects minimum rent increases specified in executed leases and an estimate of minimum rent increases which are contractually based on the Consumer Price Index (the "CPI") assuming a 3.4% increase in the CPI.

(3) Reflects the contractual minimum rents for the period based on executed leases for centers opened during the twelve months ended June 30, 1993, less the related actual contractual minimum rents included in pro forma funds from operations for the twelve months ended June 30, 1993.

(4) Reflects the contractual minimum rents for five expansions of existing centers and two new centers which will be open or under construction by October 1, 1993 that are expected to be realized during the twelve months ending September 30, 1994 based on existing executed leases for 597,000 square feet of GLA. Two of these expansions opened prior to the date of this Prospectus, two other expansions and the two new centers are scheduled to open by December 31, 1993, and the fifth expansion is scheduled to open during the second quarter of 1994.

(5) Based on the total number of shares of Common Stock and Units expected to be outstanding after the Offering assuming the Underwriters' over-allotment option is not exercised.

(6) Calculated as the expected initial dividend divided by the estimated adjusted consolidated funds from operations before minority interests for the twelve months ending September 30, 1994.

Exhibit 4   Selected Pages from Offering Prospectus   (continued)

The Company will have new shopping centers and expansions open or under construction as of October 1, 1993 aggregating approximately 895,000 square feet of GLA. The above table reflects approximately $6.5 million of minimum rent income calculated only with respect to the approximately 597,000 square feet of GLA of this space that is subject to executed leases and only for an average open period of 274 days of the twelve months ending September 30, 1994. The average minimum rental for this additional space, based on such executed leases, is $14.64 per square foot. There can be no assurance that such centers and expansions will open as scheduled.

CAPITALIZATION

The following table sets forth the consolidated capitalization of the Company (based on the combined financial statements of the Property Partnerships and the Service Companies whose financial results will be combined in the financial statements of the Company) as of June 30, 1993, and as adjusted to reflect the consummation of the Offering, the other Formation Transactions and the Debt Financing and the use of the net proceeds from the Offering and the Debt Financing as described under "Use of Proceeds."

	Historical	As Adjusted
	(In thousands)	
Note payable	$ —	$ 50,000
Mortgages, notes and loans payable	203,732	64,634
Minority interests	(150)	59,047
Stockholders' equity:		
Common stock, $.01 par value, 40,000,000 shares authorized, 11,238,910		
shares issued and outstanding[(1)]	4	112
Additional paid-in capital	—	140,480
Accumulated deficit	(10,151)	(57,146)
Total capitalization	$193,435	$257,127

(1) Does not include (i) 7,971,435 shares that may be issued upon the exchange of Units in the Operating Partnership for shares of Common Stock and (ii) 1,921,034 shares of Common Stock reserved for issuance under the Plan and the Performance Bonus Plan. See "Management—1993 Long-Term Incentive Plan" and "—Performance Bonus Plan."

Exhibit 4   Selected Pages from Offering Prospectus   (continued)

USE OF PROCEEDS

The Company will receive approximately $199,778,000 (approximately $219,973,000 if the Underwriters' over-allotment option is exercised in full) from the Offering after deduction of underwriting discounts and estimated expenses payable by the Company in connection with the Offering. The Company expects to use all of the net proceeds from the Offering, together with the assets of the leasing Service Company, to acquire its interest in the Operating Partnership. The Operating Partnership will receive approximately $48,750,000 from the Debt Financing after deduction of estimated commitment fees payable by the Operating Partnership in connection with the Debt Financing. The Operating Partnership will apply the net proceeds of the Offering and the Debt Financing as follows: (i) to repay approximately $145,538,000 of mortgage indebtedness encumbering the Properties (including approximately $6,440,000 expected to be incurred for development activities subsequent to June 30, 1993 and prior to the consummation of the Offering and $8,700,000 to be paid to the lender at the Calhoun Outlet Center to acquire the indebtedness secured by such center) and $1,771,000 in prepayment penalties relating thereto; (ii) to pay approximately $25,738,000 to certain of the Unaffiliated Partners or unaffiliated lenders (either directly or through the Property Partnerships) with respect to the transfer of certain Properties to the Operating Partnership; (iii) to pay approximately $14,641,000 to acquire the improvements at the Jeffersonville Outlet Center; (iv) to pay approximately $9,535,000 to acquire the land under the Lake Elsinore Outlet Center; (v) to pay approximately $9,000,000 to acquire certain expansions at Chesapeake Village at Queenstown; (vi) to pay an aggregate of approximately $4,700,000 to Cheryl McArthur and Alan Glen as partial consideration for the acquisition of the assets of the management Service Company (which will be used by them primarily to pay certain taxes and other expenses incurred by them in connection with the Formation Transactions); (vii) to pay approximately an aggregate of $4,122,000 to Cheryl McArthur and Alan Glen as partial consideration for the acquisition of the assets of the development Service Company (which will be used by them to repay certain indebtedness incurred by them and secured by their interests in certain of the Property Partnerships); (viii) to repay approximately $2,065,000 of indebtedness (including accrued interest at the Applicable Federal Rate) of the development Service Company owed to Cheryl McArthur and Alan Glen; (ix) to pay approximately $1,477,000 in cash to members of the McArthur/Glen Group relating to cash advanced (which amounts do not bear interest) to fund certain Properties in development; and (x) to pay accounting, legal, transfer taxes and other expenses of approximately $6,000,000 relating to the other Formation Transactions and the Debt Financing. The approximately $23,941,000 balance of the net proceeds of the Offering and the Debt Financing (together with any net proceeds from the exercise of the Underwriters' over-allotment option) will be used to provide funds for current and future development and to establish working capital reserves.

Pending such uses, the Company will invest the net proceeds of the Offering and the Debt Financing in short-term, income producing investments such as depository accounts, investment grade commercial paper, government securities or money market funds that invest in government securities.

Exhibit 4   Selected Pages from Offering Prospectus   (continued)

The indebtedness to be repaid or acquired, none of which is currently in default, consists of the following:

Secured Property	Principal Amount (In thousands)	Interest Rate Per Annum	Maturity Date
Calhoun Outlet Center—Phase I	$ 8,700	Prime + .75%	07/27/94
Chesapeake Village at Perryville—Phase I	14,390	Prime + 1.0%	04/30/94
Lake Elsinore Outlet Center—Phase I	15,700	Prime + 1.0%	08/31/94
Lake Elsinore Outlet Center—Phase II	9,032	Prime + 1.0%[1]	08/31/94
Lake Elsinore Outlet Center—Phase III	3,736	Prime + 1.0%[1]	08/31/94
Lakeside Marketplace—Phase II	5,734	Prime + 1.5%	04/30/94
Lakeside Marketplace—Phase III	7,125	Prime + 1.5%	02/21/94
Lakeside Marketplace—Phase IV	3,894	Prime + 1.5%	05/31/94
Pacific Edge Outlet Center—Phase I & II	14,500	Prime + 1.5%	09/30/96
Pacific Edge Outlet Center—Phase III	4,434	Prime + 1.0%[1]	09/11/95
Silverthorne Factory Stores—Phase II	8,375	Prime + 1.5%	10/30/94
Silverthorne Factory Stores—Phase III	3,259	Prime + 1.5%[1]	05/14/95
Southwest Outlet Center at Hillsboro—Phase I	8,700	Prime + 1.5%[1]	05/23/94
Southwest Outlet Center at Hillsboro—Phase II	6,938	Prime + 1.5%	06/24/94
Village Shops at Birch Run—Phase I	12,000	Prime + 1.5%	09/30/96
Total Variable Rate Loans	126,517		
Jeffersonville Outlet Center—Phase I & II	683	6.000%	09/01/96
Lakeside Marketplace—Phase I	8,151	10.375%	07/01/94
Quail Lake Outlet Center—Phase I	1,642	12.000%	12/31/93
Silverthorne Factory Stores—Phase I	8,243	9.625%	03/01/97
Southwest Outlet Center at Conroe—Phase II	302	12.000%	06/03/08
Total Fixed Rate Loans	19,021		
Total Loans to be Repaid or Acquired	$145,538		

(1) Interest on these loans is currently being paid pursuant to variable rate contracts, all based on **LIBOR** plus a spread. All of such contracts expire prior to October 15, 1993. Upon expiration, the interest paid will be calculated based upon the rate shown.

Exhibit 4 Selected Pages from Offering Prospectus (continued)

Corporate Headquarters

The Company leases approximately 19,000 square feet of office space in McLean, Virginia in which its corporate headquarters is located. The leases covering the Company's office space have a term of ten years, expiring on April 30, 2002 (subject to one five-year renewal option), and require monthly payments of approximately $17,500 subject to standard adjustments over the term of the leases. The leases also require the Company to pay its pro rata share of operating expenses for the building. The Company believes that its existing office space is suitable and adequate to meet its current and future needs.

Employees

As of July 31, 1993, the Company employed 74 persons at its corporate headquarters in McLean, Virginia and 101 persons at its on-site offices located at the various centers.

Legal Proceedings

Except for claims arising in the ordinary course of business and which are covered by the Company's liability insurance, the Company is not presently involved in any litigation involving claims against the Company nor, to its knowledge, is any litigation threatened against the Company or the Properties which in either case is likely to have a material adverse effect on the Company, the Properties or its operations.

MANAGEMENT

Directors and Executive Officers

The Board of Directors is currently comprised of Cheryl McArthur and Alan Glen. Upon consummation of the Offering, the Board of Directors will be expanded to seven members, five of whom will be unaffiliated with the McArthur/Glen Group (the "Independent Directors").

The persons who are directors or will be elected directors upon consummation of the Offering ("Proposed Directors") and executive officers of the Company and their positions are set forth below:

Name	Age	Position
Cheryl McArthur	44	Chief Executive Officer, President and Director
Alan Glen	67	Chairman of the Board of Directors
Nicholas McDonough	36	Executive Vice President—Finance and Secretary
James S. Harris	45	Chief Operating Officer
William Glen	36	Executive Vice President—Construction
Margaret M. Ernst	36	Executive Vice President—Development
Lee W. Campbell	52	Chief Financial Officer and Treasurer
James E. Button	43	Vice President—Property Management
Elizabeth E. Quier	35	Vice President—Marketing
Robert S. Marona	35	Vice President—Leasing
Kenneth N. Smith	33	Vice President—West Coast Operations
Stephen D. Harlan	59	Proposed Director*
Linda M. LoRe	39	Proposed Director*
Norman Perlmutter	59	Proposed Director*
M. Ronald Ruskin	62	Proposed Director*
Jean Head Sisco	68	Proposed Director*

*Mr. Harlan, Ms. LoRe, Mr. Perlmutter, Mr. Ruskin and Ms. Sisco have agreed to be nominated as directors and are expected to be elected directors immediately after the consummation of the Offering.

Exhibit 4   Selected Pages from Offering Prospectus   (continued)

The following is a biographical summary of the experience of the directors, Proposed Directors and executive officers of the Company:

Cheryl McArthur, Chief Executive Officer, President and Director—Along with Alan Glen, Ms. McArthur founded the McArthur/Glen Group in 1986. Ms. McArthur has served as the Company's President and a Director since its incorporation in 1988, as well as the Company's Treasurer from the Company's incorporation until February 1993. She became the Company's Chief Executive Officer in July 1993. Ms. McArthur oversees leasing, promotion and advertising management for all projects developed by the Company. Prior to founding the McArthur/Glen Group, Ms. McArthur founded and managed a knitwear manufacturing company in New York City which identified European designers, selected product lines and imported clothing for the U.S. market. Her career has also included positions in residential and commercial real estate sales and commercial leasing with Raskin & Associates, a shopping center development firm based in Phoenix, Arizona. Ms. McArthur is a member of the Value Retail News Advisory Council, the U.S. Chamber of Commerce and The Committee of 200 as well as the ICSC, the Urban Land Institute, the Young Presidents Organization and the Women's Forum. Ms. McArthur studied business and fine arts at Bowling Green University and the Chicago Art Institute, respectively.

Alan Glen, Chairman of the Board of Directors—Along with Cheryl McArthur, Mr. Glen founded the McArthur/Glen Group in 1986. Mr. Glen has been with the Company and has served as a Director since its incorporation in 1988. He also served as its Vice President and Secretary from its incorporation until May 1993 when he became the Company's Executive Vice President. He served as the Company's Executive Vice President until July 1993 when he became Chairman of the Company's Board of Directors. Mr. Glen oversees development of all projects developed by the Company. Mr. Glen has been in the real estate development and construction business as a principal since 1963, primarily in the Washington, D.C. area. During that time, he was involved in over $750 million of real estate projects not related to the McArthur/Glen Group. Prior to 1963, Mr. Glen was an executive in his family's women's apparel manufacturing business, the Glen Manufacturing Company, the third largest women's apparel manufacturer in the United States at that time. Mr. Glen graduated from the University of Wisconsin. Mr. Glen is the father of William Glen.

Nicholas McDonough, Executive Vice President—Finance and Secretary—Mr. McDonough has been with the McArthur/Glen Group for six years and has served as a Vice President of the Company since May 1993. In July 1993 he became the Company's Executive Vice President—Finance. Prior to becoming the Company's Executive Vice President—Finance and Secretary, Mr. McDonough served in a similar capacity for the McArthur/Glen Group. Mr. McDonough's responsibilities include oversight of all project and corporate finance transactions. Prior to joining the McArthur/Glen Group in 1987, Mr. McDonough spent six years at Beers & Cutler, a Washington, D.C. public accounting firm specializing in real estate, where he provided consulting services and structured both debt and equity transactions for property management firms and national and local developers of commercial and residential properties. He also assisted in corporate financing and organization restructuring for the firm's clients. Mr. McDonough graduated from the University of Maryland and is a Certified Public Accountant.

James S. Harris, Chief Operating Officer—Mr. Harris has been with the McArthur/Glen Group for five years and served as a Vice President of the Company from November 1990 to July 1993 when he became the Company's Chief Operating Officer. Prior to becoming the Company's Chief Operating Officer, Mr. Harris served in a similar capacity for the McArthur/Glen Group from November 1992 until July 1993 and was the Vice President—Director of Leasing from 1988 until November 1992. Mr. Harris's responsibilities include supervision of all leasing, marketing and property and asset management. Prior to joining the McArthur/Glen Group in 1988, Mr. Harris spent six years with the Taubman Company of Bloomfield Hills, Michigan, initially managing large regional shopping centers and subsequently leasing projects in the Northeast and Mid-Atlantic regions. Prior to his affiliation with Taubman, Mr. Harris worked in the I. Magnin Division of Federated Department Stores. Mr. Harris graduated from Seattle University.

12

THE JKJ PENSION FUND

In September 1994 Sarah Griffin, portfolio manager for real estate of the $3.5 billion JKJ Pension Fund, must assess the individual values for the 11 properties held by the fund and propose an overall portfolio strategy. After several years of a holding pattern of activity, the Trustees had indicated a willingness to increase the fund's investments in real estate from slightly over 5% to 10% of the total portfolio.

Discussion Questions:

1. Fill out the Portfolio Summary Sheet in Exhibit 1 evaluating the 11 individual properties owned by the fund.
2. Propose a portfolio strategy for the fund that incorporates recommendations for the existing properties and future investments as well as your approach to management of the fund.

INTRODUCTION

In September 1994, Sarah Griffin joined JKJ as the portfolio manager in charge of real estate investments for the JKJ Pension Fund. When she was hired, the Trustees had promised Sarah that JKJ was interested in again becoming an active participant in the real estate industry and that she would have the opportunity to reshape the existing portfolio and make new investments.

Now with the real estate markets beginning to recover, the Trustees have asked Sarah to create a business strategy for 1995. The strategy should begin with what to do with the existing portfolio, but also include guidelines for new investments. Specifically, the Trustees wanted Sarah to:
- Describe her strategy for the portfolio as a whole, including what the general guidelines should be for new investments.
- Place a market value on each of the properties.
- Indicate which properties should be sold and which should be held based on the property itself and the overall portfolio strategy.
- For those properties Sarah wanted to sell, recommend a reservation price (i.e. the lowest sales amount she would accept) and time frame for sale.

With almost $163 million currently invested in real estate, Sarah considered JKJ a significant player in the real estate industry. The Trustees had also indicated, however, that over the next few years, they were willing to increase their allocation to real estate to 10% of the entire Pension Fund Investment Portfolio which would mean another $170 million.

PENSION FUND INVESTMENT INTO REAL ESTATE

Pension funds are the fastest growing source of savings in the domestic economy, and one of the largest pools of private capital in the world. In 1950, U.S. private pension fund assets totalled $12 billion. Forty-four years later, in 1994, those same assets approached $3 trillion. Because pension funds do not pay taxes they have an advantage over private taxpayers, especially since 1986 when Congress took away many of the tax benefits accorded to ownership of real estate.

Lecturer John H. Vogel, Jr. prepared this case under the supervision of Adjunct Professor William J. Poorvu as the basis for class discussion rather than to illustrate either effective or ineffective handling of an administrative situation. It is based on materials originally developed by Charles Laven and Esther Sandrof.

($ in billions)

YEAR	CORPORATE AND GOVERNMENT ELEEMOSYNARY BENEFIT FUNDS	UNION MEMBER BENEFIT FUNDS	EMPLOYEE BENEFIT FUNDS	TOTALS
1971	$ 80	$ 5	$ 50	$ 135
1972	90	10	60	160
1973	105	10	60	175
1974	124	13	90	227
1975	125	15	97	237
1976	135	15	107	257
1977	155	15	115	285
1978	186	16	132	334
1979	224	22	147	393
1980	265	27	167	459
1981	318	34	186	538
1982	398	38	210	646
1983	439	55	233	727
1984	571	63	290	924
1985	616	72	325	1,013
1986	685	88	391	1,164
1987	912	121	486	1,519
1988	1,053	131	576	1,760
1989	1,050	146	618	1,814
1990	1,188	156	706	2,050
1991	1,319	192	806	2,317
1992	1,372	191	897	2,460
1993	1,529	216	1,055	2,800
1994 (est.)	1,620	227	1,163	3,010

Source: *Money Market Directory*

Prior to 1950, pension fund assets were invested primarily in fixed income products, government bonds, and other conservative investments. By the 1950s and 1960s, however, an increasing percentage of fund assets were invested in common stocks. Today, institutional trading of stock by pension funds represents a majority of all stock market transactions. By the early 1970s, pension funds were considering adding another major asset class to their investment portfolios—real estate equities.

In 1974, the enactment of ERISA (Employee Retirement Income Security Act) guidelines imposed fiduciary standards for managing the invested portfolios of pension funds, and encouraged the distribution of resources across a diversified range of asset categories. Within these guidelines, what became known as the "prudent man" definition of investment stressed that a fiduciary of trusteed funds should make portfolio decisions, acting with the "care, skill, prudence, and diligence under the circumstances then prevailing that a prudent man, acting in like capacity and familiar with such matters would use in the conduct of an enterprise of a like character and with like aims; by diversifying the investments of the plan so as to minimize the risk of large losses, unless under the circumstances its is clearly prudent not to do so."

This one legislative act had a significant effect on the investment strategies of funds looking for an optimal combination of assets, as for the first time real estate was targeted as a viable investment vehicle. Up until that time real estate had been perceived as largely illiquid, management intensive, and dominated by local market specific firms. It had performance that was difficult to measure, no reliable data base for evaluation, pricing which was non-standard, and transactional costs which were burdensome. Though national tax policy, development regulations, and other government intervention can affect real estate returns, the "real" pricing of unique properties was difficult to assess, unlike the more easily measurable shares of common stock or bonds whose value was set through numerous market transactions.

However, as high rates of inflation eroded the performance of stocks and bonds, institutional investors found that real estate offered favorable risk adjusted returns relative to other assets, offered a hedge against inflation, and provided diversification insofar as it was found that positive real estate returns did not seem to move in tandem with those of other asset classes.

Varying Risk/Return Characteristics of Five Asset Classes
Quarterly Returns 1979–1991

ASSET	MEAN RETURN	MEDIAN RETURN	STD. DEV.	MAX. RETURN	MIN. RETURN	RISK-ADJ. RETURN
Property	2.83	2.47	1.41	6.43	0.20	2.65
Stocks	4.22	5.73	7.99	21.31	−22.67	2.46
Bonds	2.70	2.09	6.09	22.38	−12.16	2.29
T-Bills	2.21	2.07	0.66	3.82	1.38	—
Inflation	1.49	1.25	1.05	4.31	−0.43	—

Though the mean quarterly return of property over a 12 year period appears to be significantly less than that of stocks (2.83% vs. 4.22%), the standard deviation (level of volatility, or risk) of common stocks is five times that of property.

Source: AEW Research

JKJ'S INVESTMENT APPROACH

JKJ Pension Fund (the "Trust") currently holds $3.3 billion in assets. In 1979, the Trust made its first real estate investment, a $10 million investment in Prudential Real Estate's open-ended, commingled separate account.[4] For the next three

[4]Separate accounts allow pension funds to receive the financial benefits of real estate ownership without the non-financial risks associated with direct ownership, like environmental liability. In an open-ended, commingled fund there are a number of pension plans whose funds are pooled. Each pension plan receives shares which are valued on a quarterly basis. New investors can be admitted and existing investors can redeem their shares on a quarterly basis, subject to certain rules related primarily to availability of funds.

years it continued to invest in Prudential's and then Equitable's real estate separate account and earned excellent returns.

In 1983, JKJ's real estate portfolio manager recommended that the Trust take more control over its real estate investments by opening a Separate Account with a leading pension fund advisory firm. Unlike their commingled accounts, because JKJ was the sole investor in this Separate Account, the advisor could customize the real estate portfolio and investment strategy.

For the JKJ Separate Account, the JKJ staff worked closely with the advisor to establish guidelines and annual investment targets. Each property selected by the advisor had to be approved first by the JKJ staff and then by the Trustees. Although the process was cumbersome at first, the advisor and fund manager soon developed a good working relationship that enabled them to act quickly and consider some unusual investments. As a result, the Trust's portfolio consistently outperformed most commingled accounts and the JKJ Trustees voted to sell their investments in Prudential and Equitable and concentrate the Trust's real estate investments in the Separate Account.

In 1988, the Trust's investment in real estate peaked at 18 properties. Because there had been substantial appreciation in the value of the portfolio, the Trustees requested that the advisor sell some of the properties. During the next two years, the Advisor sold seven properties, all at prices in excess of JKJ's investment and all at prices above the appraised value.

In 1990, however, the real estate market had collapsed to the point where it was difficult to make additional sales. From the end of the first quarter of 1990 to the end of the third quarter of 1994, office properties across the U.S.A. lost an average of 45% of their value and all institutional properties declined by 31%.[5] For the next three years, JKJ made no new investments or new sales, and simply redirected its efforts to managing the eleven existing properties.

In September 1994, however, with a softening in the market for equities, long term government securities yielding 7.68% and double AA bonds yielding 8.14%, the JKJ Trustees decided it was time to reconsider its overall portfolio strategy and consider new investments in real estate. They were particularly impressed by Griffin's numbers showing how well real estate had done coming out of the last recession from 1978–82 when it had averaged 15.2% (6.2% real return) and had outperformed both stocks and bonds:

---

[5]NCREIF combined index. NCREIF stands for National Council of Real Estate Investment Fiduciaries. The data in the NCREIF are contributed by some of the largest pension funds, and all of the large real estate pension fund investment managers.

Comparison of Stock, Bond, and Real Estate Investments
(Inflation Adjusted Real Returns for the Last 20 Years)

	1973–1977	1978–1982	1983–1987	1988–1993
Real Estate Return*	2.3%	6.2%	6.1%	−3.2%
S+P Real Returns	−5.4%	5.3%	14.6%	11.1%
Corp. Bond Real Return	−1.2%	−2.0%	10.9%	8.4%

*PRISA then NCREIF. This exhibit is based on research by Dr. Michael Miles, Fidelity Investments.

1995 PORTFOLIO PLAN

To prepare a strategy for the JKJ Trustees, Griffin decided that first she needed to analyze the existing portfolio. **Exhibit 1** provides a summary of the properties and a form on which to answer the key questions about value and whether to hold or sell. All eleven properties in the JKJ portfolio are 100% owned by the Trust through its Separate Account, and all are debt free except the Midtown Mall which has a mortgage with a current balance of $63.5 million.

Using a back of the envelope analysis, Griffin assumed the following capitalization rates for the major types of properties:

TYPE OF PROPERTY	CAPITALIZATION RATE
a) Office and Industrial Properties	8.5% − 10%
b) Residential and Retail Properties	7.5% − 9.5%
c) Hotels	9.5% − 12%
d) Garage	10.0% − 12%

Based on these capitalization rates, and making adjustments for the reliability of the cash flow, Griffin felt she could prepare a market value for each of the properties.[6]

Using these values and her overall strategy for the portfolio, Griffin would then make a recommendation of whether to hold or sell each property. If the decision was to sell, she would then establish a reservation price, or the lowest amount for which she would consider selling that property.

---

[6]Although she did not need to do an elaborate internal rate of return analysis at this point, Sarah knew that the pension fund expected an overall return from cash flow and appreciation of at least 11% on its real estate investments, 3% to cover expected inflation and 8% as a real return. Thus, if a property was valued at an 8% capitalization rate, it would need to have the potential for appreciation (based on increasing cash flow) in order for the portfolio to meet the pension fund's targeted return.

In her overall portfolio strategy, Griffin would also have to consider a range of issues such as diversification by property type, geographic location, size, potential for growth and ease of management. In constructing a model portfolio, she would have to consider what types of properties she would be able to acquire; and a time frame in which to get this done. She would also want to consider the advantages of continuing with one advisor, or hiring additional advisors who specialized in a particular geographic area, property type or investment strategy. Creating this business plan would not be easy, and valuing the properties could not be done with much precision. But she thought she might as well give it a try. After all, she asked for this job.

Exhibit 1 Portfolio Summary Form

PROPERTY/LOCATION	TYPE	DATE COMPLETED	AMOUNT INVESTED	MARKET VALUE	HOLD OR SELL	RESERVATION PRICE	COMMENTS
1. Undeveloped Land, Los Angeles, CA	Land	N.A.	$ 3,600,000				
2. Wilshire Plaza Garage, Los Angeles, CA	Parking	1969	21,400,000				
3. Wilshire Ground Leases, Los Angeles, CA	Ground Leases	N.A.	1,500,000				
4. Riverbank Center Hotel, Mobile, AL	Hotel	1985	18,750,000				
5. Riverbank Center Office Building, Mobile, AL	Office	1988	12,400,000				
6. Empire Hotel, Rochester, NY	Hotel	1969	14,320,000				
7. Maplewood Apartments, Las Colinas, TX	Multifamily	1977	12,160,000				
8. Midtown Mall, Foxboro, MA	Retail	1988	60,000,000				
9. Alpha Center, Westborough, MA	Office/R&D	1989	9,350,000				
10. Pathmark Supermarket, Fort Lee, NJ	Retail	1963	900,000				
11. Flamingo Village, Dade County, FL	Multifamily	1990	8,900,000				
Total			$163,280,000				

Exhibit 1 Portfolio Summary Form

Property 1 Investment: $3,600,000
Undeveloped Land, Los Angeles, CA

The portfolio contains three undeveloped sites in the Wilshire section of Los Angeles. The sites are labeled as Lots A, B, and C and are described as follows:

Lot A: A 120,000 SF parcel where 812,000 SF of space can be built according to current zoning. An adjacent hotel leases the parcel for use as outdoor tennis courts and picnic facilities. The monthly rent covers, maintenance real estate taxes and insurance for the property and generates a $35,500 annual return to the Fund. The hotel lease has 20 years to run.

Lot B: A 180,000 SF parcel where 900,000 SF of space can be built according to current zoning. There are no interim users for this site and carrying costs are currently running at $24,000 per year.

Lot C: A 60,000 SF parcel where 270,000 SF of space can be built according to current zoning. The parcel is rented regularly by civic organizations and community groups for outdoor festivals. After covering real estate taxes, maintenance and insurance, the Fund breaks even on this parcel.

All three lots are zoned to allow for a range of land uses including office, retail or residential. Development plans for these parcels would require approval by the City Council and the Planning Commission. An Environmental Impact Statement would have to be prepared, as well as traffic studies and public hearings. Land in the area zoned in similar ways has recently been selling for an average of $32.00 per square foot of land.

Exhibit 1 (continued)

Property 2 Investment: $21,400,000
Wilshire Plaza Garage, Los Angeles, CA

The Wilshire Plaza Garage in Wilshire contains 3,500 spaces on five levels, three of which are subterranean. The garage is located off Wilshire Plaza beside the Royale Plaza Hotel.

There are approximately 1,600 monthly cars parking on a random self-park basis. Currently the rate ranges between $50 and $60 per month for a total of $1,060,000. Another 1,000 spaces are transient spaces and are available on a daily and hourly basis. In 1994 these spaces are expected to generate income of $628,000.

Finally, approximately 900 spaces are committed to be used by an adjacent hotel and the ABC Entertainment Center on a cost reimbursement basis, meaning they pay $200,000 per year or approximately 28% of the current operating cost. This arrangement came about because the project required special city zoning covenants. This lease with ABC expires in 1997. In 1997, the hotel and ABC Entertainment have the option to lease these 900 spaces for a series of ten year periods at a rate based on the fair market value of monthly parking spaces.

The Wishire Plaza Garage has begun an intensive marketing program among neighboring office buildings to generate growth in monthly contract parking.

WILSHIRE PLAZA GARAGE: PROJECTED INCOME STATEMENT FOR 1994

Income

Monthly Parking	$1,060,000
Transient Parking/Validations	628,000
Hotel and ABC Reimbursement	200,000
Total Income	1,888,000

Operating Expenses

Salaries, Tips, Taxes	(285,400)
Uniforms	(10,500)
Repairs and Maintenance	(159,500)
Insurance	(90,000)
Data Processing and Postage	(11,500)
Accounting	(3,600)
Licenses and Permits	(1,000)
Management Fee	(31,200)
Consultants	(15,000)
Real Estate Taxes	(100,000)
Total Operating Expenses	(707,700)
Net Operating Income	$1,180,300

Exhibit 1 (continued)

Property 3 Investment: $1,500,000
Wilshire Ground Leases, Los Angeles, CA

The portfolio contains the following three ground leases:

	WILSHIRE EAST ASSOCIATES*	SID'S RESTAURANT	BANCO LOS ANGELES
Dated:	10/15/68	10/27/81	7/16/73
Lease Term	December 31, 2043	February 28, 2017	August 31, 2023
Renewal Options	N.A.	2 x 5 yrs @ FMV	N.A.
Fixed Rent (Net)	$58,000 annually	$74,996 annually	$85,000 annually

*Wilshire Power Plant for all Wilshire property east of Wilshire Park East

Property 4 Investment: $18,750,000
Riverbank Center Hotel, Mobile, AL

Property Description

The Riverbank Center Hotel is a 28-story structure containing 375 guest rooms. The hotel is connected to a 13-story 161,618 square foot Riverbank Center Office building by a walkway.

Opened in June 1985, the hotel is Mobile's most luxurious, and has earned Mobil's 4-star and AAA's 4-diamond ratings. Located in the center of downtown Mobile at the corner of Water Street and Government Street, the hotel enjoys easy access via interstate 10 and 65. It is three blocks from the Mobile Municipal Auditorium Complex and 20 minutes from Mobile Municipal Airport.

The hotel has the best convention and meeting facilities in the city of Mobile and outlying areas. Meeting and banquet space totals 17,000 square feet in 12 rooms; the largest banquet room is over 10,000 square feet and can accommodate 900 people.

The Riverview has three food and beverage outlets and recreational amenities including an outdoor swimming pool and lounge area with adjacent whirlpool, sauna and locker facilities. Parking is provided in an adjacent six-level, 1,500 space city-owned garage.

The hotel is managed by a reputable nationwide operator. Listed below is a 1993 cash flow analysis for the property. Occupancy in 1993 was in the low 50s. With a strengthened economy, management believes it can bring this occupancy to 58% in 1994 and 60% in 1995.

The Mobile Hotel Market

Located on the Gulf of Mexico, 165 miles east of New Orleans, Mobile is the seventh largest port in the United States based on tonnage per year. The Tennessee–Tombigbee Waterway reaches the Gulf of Mexico at Mobile, which has become a major link to the mid-American heartland. The area's economy is also influenced by pulp and paper production, petroleum refining and major chemical production, and the processing of food products.

In recent years Mobile has attracted an average of 161 conventions annually, attracting 55,000 delegates per year. The city's tourist attractions include the World War II battleship U.S.S. Alabama, Forts Morgan and Conde, the NCAA Senior Bowl and yearly Mardi Gras. Additionally, Mobile Greyhound Park, off Interstate 10 provides potential demand for hotel rooms.

The Mobile market demonstrated demand for approximately 330,000 room nights in 1994. Hotel room accommodation in this market are classified into three market segments: commercial demand, group and convention demand, and tourist demand.

Exhibit 1 (continued)

The Riverbank Center Hotel is geared primarily toward hosting group and convention demand and does not compete with the hotels offering budget rates which tend to attract highly price sensitive travelers. With its location in downtown Mobile it competes directly with the Radisson, a 170-room hotel also in the downtown area.

RIVERBANK CENTER HOTEL PROJECTED 1993 CASH FLOW

Rooms	375
Average Rate	$57.77
Occupancy	53.00%
Revenue:	
Rooms	$4,190,852
Food and Beverage	3,000,000
Other	349,000
Total Revenue	7,539,852
Department Expenses:	
Rooms	(1,089,621)
Food and Beverage	(2,460,000)
Other	(286,180)
Total Department Expenses	(3,835,801)
Net Revenue	3,704,051
House Expenses:	
Administrative and General	(548,000)
Base Management Fee	(228,000)
Advertising and Promotions	(720,000)
Repairs and Maintenance	(456,000)
Heat, Light and Power	(486,000)
Total House Expenses	(2,438,000)
Gross Operating Profit	1,266,051
Other Cash Expenditures:	
Real Estate Taxes	(197,000)
Insurance Premiums	(226,000)
Normal Capital Expenditures	(108,000)
Equipment Rental	(81,000)
Incentive Fees	0
Ground Lease	(55,000)
Total Cash Expenditures	(667,000)
Reserve for Replacement	(200,000)
Net Operating Income	$ 399,051

Exhibit 1   (continued)

Property 5: Investment: $12,400,000
Riverbank Center Office Building, Mobile, AL

Property Description

Riverbank Center is a 13-story, 161,618 (rentable) square foot office building. The office building is part of the Riverbank Center Complex in downtown Mobile. The office building is connected to the 28-story Riverbank Center Hotel by a walkway. The building is also connected to a 1,500-space city-owned garage. Opened in October 1988, the subject is the premier office building in downtown Mobile.

In December of 1993 a tenant occupying two full floors moved out when its lease expired. The building is currently 54% leased with the following major tenants:

TENANT	SQ. FT.	% OF BUILDING	GROSS RENT P.S.F.	EXPIRES
AmSouth	30,290	18.7%	$12.05	12/97
Ambrecht, Jackson	26,237	16.2%	13.00	12/97
Merrill Lynch	13,241	8.2%	15.50	1/99

The Mobile Office Market

The office market in Mobile is soft as is indicated by the table below. A small amount of this competitive space can be considered Class A. The closest competition to Riverbank Center in downtown comes from two recently rehabilitated small office buildings and the 20 year old First National Bank Building.

Local brokers believe that the greatest opportunity for leasing the remaining space in the building will come from tenants moving up and out of older downtown office buildings. Shown below is the projected cash flow from the property for 1994 at current occupancy.

Mobile Office Space Overview

	DOWNTOWN	MIDTOWN	OTHER	SHORE	TOTAL
Avg. of Quoted Price Per S.F.	$10.95	$ 10.00	$10.11	$ 8.73	$10.35
Available S.F.	252,998	93,655	121,090	20,320	488,065
Total S.F.	1,160,454	872,866	627,564	159,640	2,820,524
Occupancy	78.2%	89.3%	80.7%	87.3%	82.7%

Riverbank Center Office Building Projected Cash Flow 1994

Revenues:

Current Tenants (87,274 S.F. × $13.17)	$1,149,973
Expense Recoveries	0
Effective Gross Income	1,149,973
Operating Expenses ($5/S.F. for rented space, $2/S.F. for unrented)	(585,057)
Net Operating Income	564,916

Tenant Costs:

Tenant Improvements	(3,350)
Leasing Commissions	(553)
Net Cash Flow before Debt Service	$ 561,013

Exhibit 1   (continued)

Property 6   Investment: $14,320,000
Empire Hotel, Rochester, NY

Property Description

The Empire Hotel is a seven-story structure containing 364 guest rooms. Located in the heart of downtown Rochester at 70 State Street, the hotel is accessible from the city's major highway network via I–90, I–130, I–190, and I–590. Originally constructed in 1969, the hotel was substantially renovated in 1985 and is currently the leading hotel in its price range in the downtown market. The hotel is one block away from the recently completed Rochester Riverside Convention Center and 10 minutes from Monroe County Airport.

The hotel has two food and beverage outlets—a 170-seat restaurant, the Riverview Cafe, and a 150-seat lounge, the State Street Bar. Recreational amenities include a health club and enclosed pool located on the fourth floor. The property also contains 147 surface parking spaces. Overflow parking is accommodated in an adjacent city-owned garage.

The hotel has over 16,000 square feet available for banquets and meetings in up to 14 rooms. Meeting facilities at the hotel can accommodate up to 1,500 people with 16,000 square feet of available space. The grand ballroom can seat 800 people for banquets and is divisible into three smaller rooms. Eleven additional rooms provide meeting space for groups ranging in size from 5 to 60 people.

The hotel is managed by a reputable nationwide hotel operator. A 1994 projected cash flow is included on the next page.

The Rochester Hotel Market

The City of Rochester, located on the south shore of Lake Ontario, is the eighth largest exporter of goods in the nation. Five companies predominate in Rochester's employment base: Eastman Kodak Co., Xerox Corporation's Instrument System Group, General Motors Rochester Products Division and Delco Products Division and Sybron Corp. The manufacturing base of these large corporations is expected to stabilize after recent streamlining efforts.

In the 1980s, downtown Rochester underwent a major revitalization program. It was aimed at creating an environment that offers an efficient transportation system and promotes retail and consumer services. A keystone of the revitalization effort was the construction of Rochester's Riverside Convention Center, which opened in the fall of 1985. The 40 million dollar facility contains 100,000 square feet of event space, 50,000 square foot divisible exhibit hall with direct drive-on access, banquet hall for up to 5,000 diners and a 9,000 square foot galleria. Combined with the redevelopment of the downtown area and the new Hyatt Hotel, this new center has succeeded in attracting large conventions, trade shows and exhibitions.

The central location of Rochester to the entire Northeast and Eastern Seabord regions makes it an attractive location for conventions. Locally it is central to the Buffalo, Syracuse, Niagara Falls, and the Finger Lakes resort area. By air it is less than two hours from Montreal, Atlanta, Chicago, and St. Louis and 90 minutes from Albany, New York, Philadelphia, Boston, Pittsburgh, Washington, Baltimore, Cleveland, Detroit, and Toronto.

The Empire Hotel competes with eight hotels located in the downtown, airport and suburban areas of Rochester. The closest competitor is the Holiday Inn Genesee, the only other hotel with comparable prices and amenities downtown. The Holiday Inn has 467 room and charges between $61 and $80 per night. Occupancy in the market has recently begun to edge upwards and no new hotels are in the pipeline.

Exhibit 1 (continued)

EMPIRE HOTEL 1994 PROJECTED CASH FLOW

Rooms	364
Average Rate	$72.00
Occupancy	60%
Revenue:	
Rooms	$ 5,739,552
Food and Beverage	3,900,000
Other	361,000
Total Revenue	10,000,552
Department Expenses:	
Rooms	(1,386,676)
Food and Beverage	(2,925,000)
Other	(267,140)
Total Department Expenses	(4,578,816)
Net Revenue	5,421,736
House Expenses:	
Administrative and General	(790,000)
Base Management Fee	(301,000)
Advertising and Promotions	(690,000)
Repairs and Maintenance	(522,000)
Heat, Light and Power	(472,000)
Total House Expenses	(2,775,000)
Gross Operating Profit	2,646,736
Other Cash Expenditures:	
Real Estate Taxes	(569,000)
Insurance Premiums	(307,000)
Normal Capital Expenditures	(153,000)
Equipment Rental	(290,000)
Additional Workers Comp. Premiums	(16,000)
Total Cash Expenditures	(1,335,000)
Reserve for Capital Improvement	(200,000)
Net Cash Flow before Debt Service	$ 1,111,736

Exhibit 1 (continued)

Property 7 Investment $12,160,000
Maplewood Apartments, Las Colinas, TX

Property Description

Maplewood Apartments contains 304 rental units housed in 19 two-story buildings. The management office for the complex is based in a separate building that includes an additional apartment for the building superintendent. The complex was completed in 1977. Amenities include a swimming pool, two tennis courts, on-site laundry facilities, an exercise room and 350 outdoor parking spaces. The complex includes a mix of one bedroom–one bathroom apartments and two bedroom–two bathroom apartments. The average apartment unit contains 866 square feet.

The property is beginning to show its age. Some capital improvements are needed to update its image and remain competitive. Aspects of the property requiring repairs include leaking roofs, broken yard fences, rutting parking areas, and peeling paints on the exterior. Individual units have dated kitchen appliances, and most need new carpeting, drapes and paint. Roof leaks have necessitated taking some units off the market. The cost of the improvements is estimated at $950,000. When the repairs and improvements are completed it is hoped that vacancy will be more in line with the market.

The Location

Maplewood Apartments are located along in Las Colinas, a suburb to the north and west of Dallas. The project is less than two miles from a large regional shopping mall, several retail strip centers, the public library, post office, and service stations.

The Dallas/Fort Worth Residential Market

Housing starts in Dallas/Fort Worth peaked at about 110,000 units in 1983, then slowed and bottomed out in 1990 at just under 14,000 units. Now starts appear to be on a solid rebound. While some residential growth continues in nearly all parts of the region, the primary growth centers in 1993 were in the northern suburbs of Dallas.

Overall apartment occupancy in the Dallas area is stable at 92%. Rents are up about 2% this year, with the average per square foot rent creeping above 60 cents per square foot per month. Most of the new complexes being constructed are targeting renters who will spend 75 cents to $1.00 per square foot for a more finished apartment with a higher level of amenities.

Luxury apartments have been the hottest development sector in the Dallas area during the last two years. At mid-year building permits for almost 2,000 luxury apartment units had been filed in the area. Trammel Crow Residential has started two projects—one just north of downtown and another in the suburb of Irving—that will together contain 400 units and cost about $24 million to construct. In addition, a local developer is working on its third luxury rental complex in the McKinney Avenue district just north of downtown. The 160-unit complex will rent for about 85 cents per square foot.

Exhibit 1   (continued)

PROJECTED 1994 CASH FLOW FOR MAPLEWOOD APARTMENTS

Gross Potential Rental Income

(304 units × $459 per mo.)	$1,674,359
Other Income	30,240
Vacancy (15%)	(258,660)
Effective Gross Income	1,445,939

Operating Expenses:

Real Estate Taxes	(200,000)
Insurance	(40,000)
Utilities	(154,800)
Maintenance Staff	(74,000)
Administration	(3,500)
Pool Supplies	(600)
Garbage Collection	(2,000)
Landscaping	(4,000)
Total Operating Expenses	(478,900)
Replacement Reserve	(75,000)
Net Operating Income	$ 892,039

Property 8   Equity Investment: $60,000,0000, Current Debt: $63,500,000
Midtown Mall, Foxborough, MA

Property Description

The Midtown Mall is a regional shopping center with a gross leasable area of 920,000 square feet which includes three anchor stores and 150 shops. The anchor tenants are Macy's, Lord and Taylor, and Jordan Marsh. The mall is configured with three corridors radiating from a central court. The center opened in 1988.

The center is faced with dark brown iron stop brick, accented with horizontal brick and stone bands. The center's arched entrances are framed with indigenous stone. The roof is green and the tri-level parking deck is masked behind dense foliage borders.

Location

The center has excellent regional and local accessibility. The site has both north/south and east/west access. It is located in south suburban Boston at the intersection of route 128.

Freight and commuter passenger rail service are available in the region. Logan International Airport, located approximately 15 miles north in Boston, and Worcester Memorial Airport, located 30 miles west, offer commercial service. The central location of the site makes it attractive for a multitude of uses. A 1994 cash flow projection is included on the next page.

The Suburban Boston Retail Market

The Midtown Mall is located in the Boston SMSA, the seventh largest metropolitan area in the United States with a population of over 4.1 million persons. Average household income in the Boston SMSA is $47,000, according to the 1990 census, well above the national median household income of $29,420.

Boston is New England's economic hub and one of the nation's largest diversified financial centers. The area is known for its high technology industries, especially those related to computer applications and medical and defense instruments, which contributed to the strong economic growth Boston experienced in the 1980s. Boston is also an international center for medical research and a national center for higher education with 65 colleges and universities, including Harvard University and Massachusetts Institute of Technology (MIT).

Exhibit 1 (continued)

Currently, the metropolitan Boston area has 24 regional shopping centers with a total of 14.7 million square feet. Including specialized retail centers in Boston like Quincy Market, Lafayette Place, Copley Place, and Cambridge Side Galleria, the total is approximately 17.3 million square feet. The average age of the Boston area's existing regional malls is 19 years.

Developable land is extremely scarce in metropolitan Boston. Many potential sites are adjacent to environmentally sensitive wetland areas which are subject to long, costly, and uncertain approval processes. Anti-development sentiment is prevalent throughout the Boston area populace. Due to these development constraints, few regional shopping centers were developed in Boston since the mid-1980s. In addition, large sites with good access and suitable zoning are no longer available inside Route 495, further constraining new development.

Rental rates are usually double net plus a percentage of revenues (although some are triple net) and vary depending on the location of the regional center as well as on the location of the tenant within the center. Ten-year leases with periodic rent adjustments are customary. Retail rents were flat from 1992 to 1993, ranging from $18 to $35 per square foot in major malls.

MIDTOWN MALL PROJECTED 1994 CASH FLOW

Revenue:

Anchors (570,000 S.F.)[7]	$ 1,624,500
Mall Shops (300,000 S.F. × $31.00)	9,300,000
Cinema (20,000 S.F. × $16.00)	320,000
Restaurants (20,00 S.F. × $20.00)	400,000
Food Court (10,000 S.F. × $50.00)	500,000
Percentage Rent	278,500
Reimbursements: CAM	2,125,000
Taxes and Insurance	506,000
HVAC	842,000
Other	85,000
Gross Revenue	15,981,000
Vacancy	(650,000)
Net Income	15,381,000

Expenses:

Common Area Maintenance	(1,800,000)
HVAC	(700,000)
Management Fee	(400,000)
Real Estate Taxes	(588,000)
Other Expenses	(300,000)
Total Expenses	(3,800,000)
Net Operating Income	11,581,000
Debt Service[8]	(7,126,440)
Cash Flow After Financing	$ 4,454,560

[7]Two of the anchor tenants built and own their own store. Lord and Taylor has a 25-year lease for its 190,000 square foot store, and pays $8.55 per square foot. All three anchor stores pay their proportionate share of Common Area Maintenance (CAM) reimbursements, taxes, and insurance.

[8]When JKJ purchased this property in late 1988, they obtained a $70 million, 25 year mortgage at 9.00%. As of 12/31/94 the mortgage will have a balance of approximately $63.5 million.

Exhibit 1 (continued)

Property 9 Investment: $9,350,000
Alpha Center, Westborough, MA

Property Description

Alpha Center is a two-story building containing 92,738 square feet of gross area which includes 73,383 net rentable square feet of office/R&D space with 6,372 net rentable square feet of storage space in the basement. The building was completed in 1989. It is constructed of brick and glass with a marble atrium lobby with a mahogany finish. Parking is available for 300 cars. The building is a build-to-suit facility for a credit multinational corporation which uses the facility as a regional computer programming center.

In 1989, the tenant signed a 12-year lease for the facility at base rent of $12.65 per square foot for the office space and $7.00 per square foot for the storage space, on a triple net basis with a renewal option at 88% of the market rent at the time of renewal

The Westborough Office/R&D Market

The parcel is located in Westborough, MA in the immediate vicinity of the intersection of Routes 495 and the Massachusetts Pike, 22 miles from Boston. This facility is centrally located in an area which has established itself as a center for Class A corporate tenants over the past decades.

Historically, Westborough has been a residential community. However, due to its strategic location, the town saw significant growth in office and R&D uses during the 1980s. Westborough is extremely convenient as a place of employment, due to its proximity to a series of local and regional highways. Companies located in Westborough are able to draw on an excellent labor pool including both skilled and unskilled employees, from an extended area including the City of Boston.

The Westborough R&D market is one of the strongest R&D submarket in the Boston region. Of the 1,175,408 square feet of existing R&D space, 70,524 square feet, or 6% is currently vacant. This is down from 11.3% last year. This rate is substantially lower than the 24.8% vacancy rate for the suburban Boston R&D market as a whole. In the current market, rents for new R&D space with leases comparable to Alpha Center generally range from $6 to $9 per square foot depending on the level of finish and location. Typical leases included $10 per square foot for tenant improvements.

ALPHA CENTER PROJECTED 1994 CASH FLOW

Office Space Income	$ 928,295
Storage Space Income	44,604
Gross Projected Income	972,889
(Vacancy Loss)	(0)
Effective Gross Income	972,899
(Management)	(0)
(Reserves)	(7,338)
Net Operating Income	$ 965,561

Exhibit 1   (continued)

Property 10   Investment: $900,000
Pathmark Supermarket, Fort Lee, NJ

Property Description

The Fort Lee Pathmark Supermarket is located on Main Street, one of the primary commercial thoroughfares in Fort Lee, NJ. The property consists of a 2.3 acre site containing a 21,632 square foot supermarket. The supermarket was built in the early 1960s and is currently in fair condition. There is parking for 250 cars in the parking lot.

The Location

The property is located in a C–2 Neighborhood Business Zone. Permitted uses include retail/service, business/professional office, banks, movie theaters, and restaurants. Maximum building height is 3 stories. The supermarket is considered homogenous with its surroundings. Surrounding uses include garden apartments, a police station, a high rise residential project with ground level convenience retail space, a small retail strip center and other small retail tenants.

Fort Lee is located on the eastern border of Bergen County. Demographic data for the county indicate a very affluent population and home values in Fort Lee confirm the existence of substantial purchasing power. Average single-family home values are in the $300,000 range with condominiums in the $125,000 to $190,000 range. Population and households in Fort Lee have been relatively stable over the past decade and are projected to remain so.

The Competitive Market

The Borough of Fort Lee has five supermarkets including this property. There are no recent additions to the supply of supermarket space. None of the other supermarkets are located in the same neighborhood as this property. There are no new supermarkets planned in the Borough and little land is available for development, particularly in the vicinity of this supermarket.

Performance

This Pathmark has the highest per square foot sales of any store in its supermarket chain, with estimated gross sales at approximately $1,300 per square foot. More typical gross sales for newer, larger supermarkets in the region are in the $400 to $600 per square foot range. The property's extremely high per square foot sales are partially a result of the smaller size (22,000 compared with 50,000+ for the newer stores). However, another smaller supermarket in Fort Lee has estimated sales of $600 per square foot. Supermarkets can typically afford to pay about 2% of gross sales in rent. Thus, a supermarket with average sales per square foot of $600 could afford about $12.00 per square foot in rent, according to industry sources.

New supermarkets in Bergen County typically pay rents ranging from $10.40 to $17.50. This supermarket currently pays rents of $4.78 per square foot. Its lease extends until 2005 at the current rate. See the next page for a summary of the current lease and projected 1994 cash flow for the property.

Exhibit 1   (continued)

SUMMARY OF CURRENT FORT LEE PATHMARK LEASE

Tenant:	Pathmark of Fort Lee
Space:	21,632 square feet of building plus 250 parking spaces
Term:	March 1, 1965 to February 28, 1990
Option:	March 1, 1990 to February 28, 2005
Rent:	$103,400 per year ($4.78 per square foot—during the option period)
Additional Rent:	This is a triple net lease. Tenant pays all operating expenses, insurance, water and sewer, real estate taxes and assessments and is responsible for repairs and maintenance. Landlord's only cost is management and structural repairs.

FORT LEE PATHMARK PROJECTED 1994 CASH FLOW

Revenue	$ 103,400
Credit Loss	0
Effective Gross Income	103,400
Operating Expenses	
Management Fee (1.5%)	(1,551)
Net Operating Income	$ 101,849

Exhibit 1   (continued)

Property 11   Investment: $8,900,000
Flamingo Village, Miami, FL

Property Description

Flamingo Village is a multifamily rental project in North Miami, Florida. It was completed in January of 1990. The 220-unit complex reflects a contemporary stucco design with Spanish style roofs. Each unit comes equipped with frost-free refrigerators, dishwashers, microwaves, window treatments, alarms and a ceiling fan in the living room. The following is a breakdown of units in the complex:

NUMBER OF UNITS	TYPE OF UNIT	SIZE (SQ. FT.)	RENT/ UNIT	RENT/ SQ. FT.
48	1 Bed/1 Ba	750	$599	$0.80
156	2 Bed/2 Ba	1,000	$729	$0.73
16	2 Bed/2 Ba	1,100	$759	$0.69

Amenities include a swimming pool with a poolside Tiki Bar/restroom building, a Jacuzzi, a tennis court, a volleyball court, a car wash area, a clubhouse and an exercise building with a sauna.

The complex is surrounded by a wall and has an electronic card entry gate that is monitored by a video camera that tenants can view via closed circuit on their own television sets.

The Location

The 10-acre complex is located on N.W. 57th Avenue in an area of unincorporated Dade County. There are a mix of uses near the site including a 20-acre naval reserve center, a retirement village, an older low-rise condominium complex that is about 10 years old and an exclusive walled community built in the mid- to late-1980s.

There are three community retail centers within a one mile radius of the site as well as a Wal-Mart store and a Home Depot. The complex is about 10 miles from Miami International Airport and 4 miles from Joe Robbie Stadium, home of the Miami Dolphins and the Miami Marlins.

The Market

The State of Florida has just completed its largest decade of growth in its history. During the 1980s the population increased by 3.4 million residents. Florida added 1.9 million nonagricultural jobs during the 1980s, including 94,000 manufacturing jobs. During the same period, the United States as a whole lost 900,000 manufacturing jobs. Dade County is one of the most populous counties in Florida. Most of the population growth in Dade during the 1980 was due to births and the continued influx of Latin Americans to the area. Major contributors to Dade County's economy have traditionally been the tourism, high technology and banking industries.

However, after a decade of unprecedented growth, Florida's economy was stalled by the national recession of the early 1990s. Goods-producing industries that recorded jobs losses in Dade County included the construction industry, manufacturing and mining. All industries in the service sector recorded job losses, with substantial losses in transportation and public utilities and air transportation. When Eastern Airlines and Pan American World Airways shut down operations in 1991, approximately 18,500 local jobs were lost.

Exhibit 1 (continued)

The Rental Housing Market

Except for two high-rise buildings, the rental housing market in the vicinity of Flamingo Village is almost exclusively comprised of two- and three-story, garden-type buildings. Increased competition for tenants during the mid-1980s had forced developers to provide a greater quantity and variety of amenities in rental complexes.

The overall vacancy rate among stabilized rental apartment complexes in Dade County was 6.2% as of June 1994. This represents a slight decrease in vacancy since the last reporting period. The overall average monthly rent for stabilized apartment complexes in Dade County was $598 as of June 1994. This represented a $4 increase over the prior quarter and a .4% increase for the 12 months ended in June 1994.

FLAMINGO VILLAGE PROJECTED 1994 CASH FLOW

Revenue:

Gross Rental Income	
(220 units × $703 × 12 mos.)	$1,855,920
Furniture Rentals	31,920
Laundry Income	66,000
Miscellaneous	26,400
Gross Scheduled Income	1,980,240
Vacancy (11.4%)	(225,747)
Effective Gross Income	1,754,493

Operating Expenses:

Real Estate Taxes	(250,000)
Insurance	(22,000)
Property Management	(95,000)
Payroll	(105,000)
Trash Removal	(17,000)
Utilities	(90,000)
Contract Services	(55,000)
Advertising and Promotion	(25,000)
Repairs and Maintenance	(16,000)
Miscellaneous Expenses	(20,000)
Total Operating Expenses	(695,000)
Replacement Reserves	(22,000)
Net Operating Income	$1,037,493

13

JKJ/GELCO

In July 1995, Sarah Griffin, the Portfolio Manager for Real Estate Investments for JKJ Pension trust is considering an investment in a new fund developed by Gelco, a major New York investment bank. Gelco already active in real estate is trying to enter the pension fund market with a product with a short time horizon that combines direct property investments and listed securities.

Discussion Questions:

1. As Clint Bidwell, be prepared to make a presentation to JKJ. What features would you stress?
2. As Sarah Griffin, would you recommend that JKJ invest in the Gelco Limited Partnership? If so, how much should they invest?
3. Do you think that Gelco is well suited to complete in the pension fund market?

For Sarah Griffin, the Portfolio Manager for Real Estate Investments for the JKJ Pension Trust (the "Trust"), the last nine months had been frustrating. In November 1994, she had made a presentation to the Trustees of the JKJ Pension Fund describing the strategy she recommended for diversifying the real estate portfolio and increasing the Trust's overall investment in real estate. Her strategy included selling several of the Trust's existing properties and then taking advantage of the pension fund's size by publicly announcing a campaign with its advisor to acquire $200 million of new investments. She was sure that with that amount of money, she would get to look at the widest possible range of investment opportunities, and be able to put together a dynamic, diversified real estate portfolio.

The Trustees listened carefully and praised her for her hard work and insightful presentation. But rather than increase the Trust's allocation to real estate to 10%, as she had hoped, they asked for additional time and information. As Griffin patiently tried to educate the pension fund staff and Trustees about real estate, she became aware of the level of discomfort that the Trustees felt toward real estate. She also noted, that although Vernon Fitch, the Treasurer and her boss, was supportive, he was never willing to make investment in real estate his issue, and put his own credibility on the line. And the final problem for Griffin was that the Trust's stock investments continued to perform very well up over 20% in the first half of 1995, defusing the urgency to increase the amount allocated to real estate.

In January 1995, out of desperation, Griffin asked for permission to at least reposition the Trust's real estate portfolio. Over the last six months, she sold two properties and bought one. Each of these transactions required three levels of approval—Griffin and the Real Estate Advisor, The JKJ Pension Trust Investment Committee and the Trustees. This approval process was so time consuming and laborious, that Griffin often felt that she did more negotiating with insiders, than with the entity buying or selling the property.

Last week, as she was feeling particularly frustrated, she got a call from Clint Bidwell, whom she had known from meetings at the Urban Land Institute and the National Council of Real Estate Investment Fiduciaries. Bidwell recently joined Gelco from an insurance company where he had been an Executive Vice President. On the telephone, he told Griffin that Gelco had almost completed development of a new real estate product for institutional investors. The product

---

Lecturer John H. Vogel, Jr. and Adjunct Professor William J. Poorvu prepared this case as the basis for class discussion rather than to illustrate either effective or ineffective handling of an administrative situation.

was unique and substantially different from any real estate investment on the market. Bidwell said that he had sent her some materials about the Gelco Real Estate Limited Partnership and that he and Kelly Hayes, the Head of the Real Estate Group, would like to meet with her and discuss it. Griffin agreed to meet in a week and in the meantime had spent a couple of hours reviewing the material and getting Bidwell to send some additional information.

JKJ PENSION FUND

In June 1995, JKJ Pension Fund had assets of $3.7 billion. JKJ is what is called a defined benefit plan, which means that once a participant is fully vested, he or she is guaranteed a certain monthly payment from the retirement fund, starting as early as age 62 until death. The amount of the monthly payment is based on: years of service; the participant's average salary for his or her three highest paid years; the age at retirement and whether or not the retiree's spouse will continue to receive benefits after the retiree's death. An actuary performs a yearly financial analysis of the JKJ Pension Fund that factors in variables like: the age of the participants, salary levels, assets in the fund, the current payout to retirees and the Trust's investment returns. The actuary then calculates how much JKJ needs to invest that year to keep the fund healthy.

In recent years, many corporate pension funds have switched from defined benefit plans to defined contribution plans, where the company makes no promises about the ultimate payout, but instead makes an annual payment into the plan.[9] JKJ has considered switching to a defined contribution plan, but believes that its current defined benefit plan makes it more competitive in recruiting and retaining high quality employees.

The JKJ Pension Fund is administered by three Trustees (see **Exhibit 1** for organizational chart). The Trustees have a fiduciary responsibility to the beneficiaries of the Trust, which means that they have ultimate responsibility for the assets of the Trust and responsibility for ensuring that the activities of the Trust comply with all statutes and policies, especially the Employee Retirement Income Security Act (ERISA). Among other responsibilities, the Trustees perform three important administrative functions: monitor the inflow of payments into the Trust to be sure that it is adequately funded; oversee the payments to beneficiaries; and invest the Trust's assets.

[9]In 1994, according to the *Money Market Directory,* there were 20,425 Corporate Defined Benefit Plans with $918 billion in assets, and 18,662 Corporate Defined Contribution Plans with $169 billion in assets. The fastest growing corporate pension fund account is the 401K plan (which is also classified as a defined contribution plan) where employees make a contribution, and the company matches some percentage of the employee contribution. There are now 8,426 401K plans with assets of $350 billion. In the government sector, 93% of the $1.1 trillion of pension fund assets is concentrated in defined benefit plans. Thus, of the $3 trillion in U.S. pension fund assets, almost 85% are concentrated in these areas.

In setting the investment policy for the Trust, the Trustees "endeavor to make investments which yield an overall rate of return in accordance with the Trust's tolerance for risk, and at the same time accommodate the Trust's cash flow and liquidity needs." (Excerpt from the JKJ Pension Fund 1994 Annual Report.) The latest financial statements from the Trust show that the investments are currently allocated as follows:

TYPE OF INVESTMENT	%	COMMENT
Fixed Income	30%	Five outside managers are utilized specializing in: U.S. Government, Corporate, High Yield, International and Residential Mortgage Securities. 20% of the fixed income investments are handled internally.
Equities	58%	Seven outside managers are currently utilized specializing in: growth, international, small cap, value, and core diversified. 10% of the assets are invested by the internal staff in index funds.
Cash	5%	Handled internally by the staff.
Real Estate Equities	4.5%	Separate Account managed by a large, investment advisory company, in close coordination with JKJ's staff, (see the JKJ Pension Fund case study)
Venture Capital	1.5%	Invested in four venture funds
Other	1.0%	Oil and Gas, Leveraged Buyouts, etc.

The Trustees meet at least monthly, and the outside managers meet individually with the Trustees at least annually. The Trustees receive monthly reports from the outside managers and both monthly and quarterly reports from the JKJ Pension Fund staff. Because it is expensive to value real estate, the properties are carried at cost for the first year, and then 25% of the properties in the portfolio are valued each quarter.

GELCO

Gelco is a major "buy side" investment firm in New York that is active in the real estate field both as an advisor to defined benefit pension plans and endowments and in the management of retail investment funds.[10] The firm had only recently begun raising money for the Gelco Limited Partnership. It felt that putting together the talents of its existing staff with that of an expanded research and

---

[10]A buy side firm invests for its clients where a sell side firm creates invesments such as an IPO to sell to buy side firms. Some investment firms are both on the buy and sell sides.

acquisitions group would give it the organizational capabilities to manage such funds. Gelco had already invested substantial money from its clients' funds in REITs and CMBS successfully. The firm had participated for its retail funds in the purchase of several portfolios of property auctioned by the RTC.

The Gelco Real Estate Limited Partnership

1. **The Fund Will Invest in Both the Public and Private Market:** No other real estate fund includes both publicly traded and private investments. Gelco believes that there are significant advantages to having one fund invest in both markets. For example, the current market makes it more advantageous to invest in regional shopping centers by purchasing REIT shares than by acquiring whole centers directly. Purchasing REIT shares also will enable the fund to achieve broader and better diversification, and therefore reduce overall portfolio risk.

   In the Guidelines for the Fund, Gelco states that a minimum of 35% of the portfolio will be invested in public market investments and a minimum of 35% will be in private market investments. In the investment policies, (which can only be changed by an investor vote) it states that the Fund will maintain 20% liquidity to facilitate active portfolio management. (Liquid investments are defined as those that can be converted to cash in 30 days with a minimal loss in value.)

2. **Extensive, Multidimensional Research:** Gelco plans to invest substantial resources in developing research tools and techniques that provide timely and accurate information. Gelco's research will begin with macroeconomic forecasting which tracks and forecasts the supply and demand conditions by metropolitan area and by property type. Second, through its relationship with a major appraisal company (who will coordinate the work of local appraisal firms), Gelco will generate information about specific properties in 80 metropolitan areas on a real time basis and extensive information and analysis about all publicly traded real estate companies. All this research will then be compiled, verified and used by the five teams and the portfolio manager in making investment decisions.

   This process of gathering data and then turning it into investment knowledge for making individual investment decisions is depicted on the following page:

INFORMATION GENERATION

Data	Dodge—Supply DRI-Demand NCREIF-Returns Capital Market Factors Global Factors	Field Analyst Network Location Functionality Occupancy Tenant Satisfaction	Public Company Detail Operating Ratios Property Characteristics
Databases	*One* Macro, Long Term Space Market ———————— Econometric analysis Learning everything we can from the past	*Two* Micro, Real Time space Market ———————— Property-by-property real-time information	*Three* Capital Market ———————— Company-by-company management and property statistics
Subcontractors turn data into information			Comparative capital structure & returns
		Default Models	
	MSA/Property type rent growth forecasts		REIT geographic prospectus screen
		Private Market Due Diligence	
In-house research turns information into investment knowledge			Diversification Fit
		Sector weightings and individual buy/sell decisions	

3. **Active Portfolio Management:** Gelco will actively manage its portfolio in several ways. First, Clint Bidwell, the Portfolio Manager will be responsible for allocating and reallocating the fund's assets between market sectors. He will set specific targets for each of the five teams to insure the investments are in line with the recommendations from the research. He will also actively manage the portfolio to be sure it conforms to the latest in modern portfolio theory and to the diversification guidelines.[11] The second piece of the Gelco strategy of active portfolio management relates to the duration of the investments and of the fund. Gelco's marketing literature states: "We structure our private acquisitions to have a four year or less exit strategy. CMBS (Commercial Mortgage Backed Securities) and REIT interests usually have a shorter expected holding period, but there can still be significant costs to rapid sales which we try to avoid." The Offering Memorandum is even more definitive about the time horizon for the fund. It states: "The Fund will terminate five years from the closing date."

In describing specific investments in the private market, Gelco will seek local owners and investors who are capable of and interested in managing the property. The ideal local manager will make a modest equity investment in the property so that there is proper goal alignment. Gelco will control the investment; however, the local manager will have strong incentives to maximize the value of the investment, including selling the property in three to four years.

4. **A Unique, Benchmarked Fee Structure:** Gelco will charge a 1% management fee, based on invested capital, to cover its costs. Unlike some other real estate advisors, it will receive no upfront fees, acquisition fees or disposition fees. Likewise, there is no escalation or fee for reinvested capital or appreciation. If the Partnership outperforms the market, however, Gelco will receive a "Performance Fee" equal to 20% of the amount by which the fund outperforms its benchmarks.[12] The Performance Fee will be paid at the liquidation of the fund, once the investors have received 100% of their invested capital and a return equal to the Benchmark Rate of Return. The Benchmark Rate of Return is defined as "the simple average of the National Council of Real Estate Fiduciaries (NCREIF) Combined Index[13]

[11]The investment guidelines include the following points to insure adequate diversification: No more than 5% of the Fund may be invested in a single issuer; no more than 10% will be invested outside the United States, and no more than 50% leverage. There will also be specific ceilings with respect to metro area, economic location and property type.

[12]Internally, Gelco's goal was to beat the benchmark by 200 basis points.

[13]The NCREIF index is made up of institutional properties owned through open and closed-end commingled funds and similar, professionally managed investment vehicles. It currently has a market value (for the equity) in excess of $40 billion. The NAREIT Equity Index has a total value of over $35 billion and tracks the performance of all public REITs, except Health Care REITs, which own equity real estate.

and the National Association of Real Estate Investment Trusts (NAREIT) Equity (without Health Care) Index." Gelco believes that, in contrast with its competitors, this fee structure better aligns its interest with the interests of its investors. Most real estate commingled funds, according to Gelco, have an incentive to "buy and hold" property since most of their compensation comes from acquisition fees and management fees. Every property they sell reduces their management fee. The base management fee, for large pension advisors had been approximately 1%, but has recently dropped to about .6%. Many firms charge fees for acquisition, dispositions and refinancing which ranged from 1 to 2%.

A hot issue for pension plans was the trend to take investment discretion away from the investment managers, as JKJ had done, and keep that discretion in-house. While this practice has become the dominant trend in the industry, Gelco chose to buck the trend and keep full authority for deciding when and which properties or REIT stocks to purchase and sell. Gelco chose this approach for two reasons: (1) As a company policy, Gelco does not do anything which is non-discretionary; and (2) it takes up too much time for the fund and the investment manager when it is a non-discretionary account. Clint Bidwell had often heard pension funds complain, "real estate is 5% of our portfolio and takes 90% of our time."

THE COMPETITION

In a follow-up telephone call, Griffin asked Clint Bidwell to describe his competition. Bidwell defined his primary competition as the thirty real estate investment advisory firms and life insurance companies that each manage over $1 billion of tax exempt funds. These thirty companies currently manage a total of $102.3 billion or 83% of the tax exempt money invested in real estate. Of these thirty companies, Bidwell singled out fourteen whom he thought would be Gelco's strongest competitors. Griffin then collected views from several consultants about these fourteen advisors (see **Exhibit 3**).

In discussing the competition with Bidwell, Griffin learned that the last successful entrant into pension fund real estate investment management was AMB which began in 1986. In fact, in the last five years there had been considerable consolidation with a number of large advisors merging or going out of business. Bidwell believed, however, that there was an opportunity for someone like Gelco to break into the market because the real estate funds that the 30 major investment advisory companies manage have done so poorly the last ten years especially in the last three years. This weak track record created an opportunity for someone new, like Gelco, and meant that none of his competitors had its "reputation totally intact." Looking at the returns for four of the larger open end funds illustrates this point:

Total Annual Returns—Before Fees*

	1984–86	1987–90	1991–93	1984–93
Aetna—R.E. Separate Account	10%	4%	−4%	3.5%
Cigna—Separate Account R	12%	4%	−3%	4.2%
Equitable—Prime Account	11%	7%	−3%	4.9%
Prudential—PRISA	10%	8%	−7%	3.5%

*Based on information from Evaluation Associates.

In explaining this poor performance, Bidwell attributed it to a combination of seven factors, some of which were structural, others tied to the management of the funds and some to macro economic factors beyond the manager's control.

1. Asset accumulation formulated the investment strategy.

2. Capital market relationships were ignored.

3. Clients were oversold (higher returns, less volatility, good portfolio diversification, inflation hedge).

4. The wrong vehicles (from the client's perspective) were used. Open end funds lost their liquidity when there were a lot of withdrawal requests.

   Closed end funds were even more illiquid than normal real estate.

5. The wrong compensation schemes (from the client's perspective) were utilized.

6. Real estate execution was weak:
   Buy to hold strategy (missed selling opportunities).
   Over improvement—(spent too much on capital improvement).
   Passive management.

7. Macro factors made everything worse.
   Overbuilding—especially in office.
   Japanese/foreign investment—distorted the market.

INVESTMENT OPPORTUNITIES

Although the Gelco Real Estate Limited Partnership was not designed as a vulture fund or as a market timing fund, the draft Private Placement Memorandum makes Gelco's case for why it is now a good time to invest in real estate (see **Exhibit 4**, Real Estate Market Overview). In Gelco's view there is a "cyclical opportunity" based on the fact that construction is down, rents are starting to move up, and returns are usually attractive coming out of a real estate recession (at least based on the returns from 1978 to 1982).

Gelco also thought changes in the way real estate is financed and the resulting shortage of capital for real estate should improve returns. The introduction of "risk based capital" requirements for both commercial banks and life insurance companies reduces the amount of money they have available to finance real estate, particularly speculative development. Similarly, Gelco predicted that the Japanese which invested as much as $15 billion per year at the height of the 1980s boom, in high profile U.S. Real Estate would continue to be "net disinvestors" during the 1990s.

Third, Gelco believed that the rapid growth in the public markets would create some unusual opportunities that would not be available in a more stable, established market. For example, new issues of commercial mortgage backed securities (CMBS) had propelled the CMBS market from under $10 billion in 1991 to nearly $60 billion in 1994. With few companies adequately equipped to analyze these securities, take risk and move quickly, Gelco was convinced there would be some great opportunities to earn high equity returns purchasing the unrated pieces of these securities.[14]

THE MEETING

As Griffin prepared for her meeting with Bidwell and Hayes, she tried to think of questions that would help her decide if the Gelco Real Estate Limited Partnership made sense. Gelco's lack of a track record as a manager was both a plus and a minus. The people managing the fund did have a track record and reputations, however, which she would want to explore. The second big area of inquiry would be the strategy of the fund. Did the public market, private market mix make sense? Did Gelco add significant value in the way it managed the portfolio? Were there things Gelco could do that she and her staff could not do? Was the short holding period a good idea?

If the fund made sense, the next question would be how much to invest. The minimum investment was $5 million. Gelco Real Estate Limited Partnership would have a first closing once it reached $150 million in commitments and could go as high as $300 million. Griffin felt that if she was going to go through all the trouble of getting the Trustees to approve of Gelco's fund and the Gelco Real Estate Group, she would want to make a sizable investment. She also liked the

---

[14]In creating a CMBS, an investment banker begins by pooling individual mortgages to create at least $100 million of assets. The investment banker will then take the mortgages to a rating agency like Standard and Poors or Fitch where different tranches of the mortgage pool will get rated based on the type of property, its operating history and the collateral and debt coverage ratios. A CMBS that results from this mortgage pool may have three or four different tranches such as a double A piece, a B piece and an unrated piece. The unrated piece might, for example, have only a 1.1 debt coverage ratio where the double A piece might have a 1.4 debt coverage ratio.

fact that if this investment went well, she would be able to make additional investments into subsequent, similarly structured Gelco funds. Gelco hoped to bring out a new fund each year. Another opportunity Gelco was offering was that for an investment of at least $150 million, Gelco would create a separate account, utilizing the same basic approach, but customized for JKJ.

Finally, Griffin thought about her alternatives. She could continue to reposition the portfolio and hope that the Trustees might increase their allocation to real estate. She could look for a second real estate advisor whose approach would help her to gain the confidence of the Trustees. Or she might consider investing in a fund managed by one of the established real estate advisors, though she felt that was a step backwards, since JKJ had proven that it could generate better returns investing in its own separate account than through a commingled fund.

As Griffin prepared for the meeting with Bidwell and Hayes, she wanted to begin by making a list of the pros and cons of their partnership. Next she would create a list of questions to ask Gelco. And finally, she tried to think about how her bosses and the Trustees would view this investment. Vernon Fitch, her boss, had, in fact, asked her to stop at his office before her meeting with Gelco and let him know if this Gelco investment seemed like a good fit for JKJ.

Clint Bidwell had sent her a chart showing his view of the pension fund industry (**Exhibit 5**). For a medium sized corporate pension fund such as JKJ, he felt that the Gelco fund would be an excellent fit.

Exhibit 1

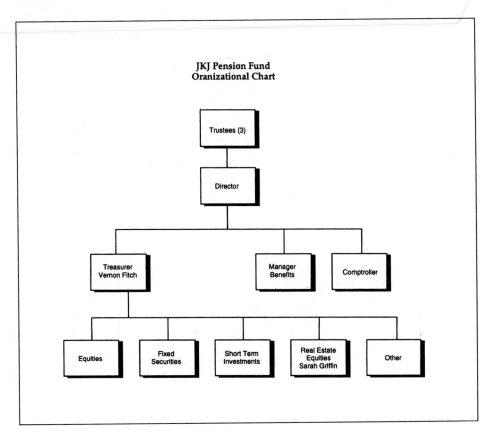

JKJ Pension Fund
Oranizational Chart

Exhibit 2

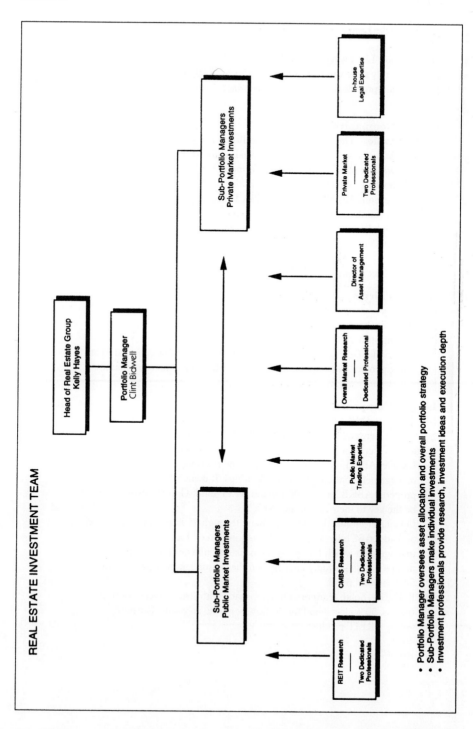

REAL ESTATE INVESTMENT TEAM

Head of Real Estate Group
Kelly Hayes

Portfolio Manager
Clint Bidwell

Sub-Portfolio Managers
Public Market Investments

Sub-Portfolio Managers
Private Market Investments

REIT Research
Two Dedicated Professionals

CMBS Research
Two Dedicated Professionals

Public Market
Trading Expertise

Overall Market Research
Dedicated Professional

Director of
Asset Management

Private Market
Two Dedicated Professionals

In-house
Legal Expertise

- Portfolio Manager oversees asset allocation and overall portfolio strategy
- Sub-Portfolio Managers make individual investments
- Investment professionals provide research, investment ideas and execution depth

Exhibit 3   The Competition (drawn from comments by several consultants)

1. **The Life Insurance Companies**
Basic Points
(a) They are Life Insurance Companies which has good and bad implications.
(b) Frequently structure investment vehicles as open end funds.
(c) The first providers of real estate investment management.

Largest Companies	Rank	Assets in Billion $
(a) **Equitable**—The largest fund is the Prime Property Fund with $3 billion in assets and 50% in regional malls. Multi product; core product plus a hotel fund and a mortgage fund.	1	$11.4
(b) **Prudential**—PRISA was the first major fund in the industry and currently has $2.5 billion. PRISA II has $600 million. PRISA ran into some appraisal problems.	4	6.7
(c) **Metropolitan**—Spinning small advisory group out as an "independent."	26	<u>1.1</u>
Sub-total		$19.2
Percent of Tax Exempt R.E. Market		15.6%

2. **Mega Firms**
Basic Points
(a) Generally boutiques that grew at the expense of others.
(b) Varying strategies; varying histories.
(c) To varying degrees trying to offer REITs, CMBS *and* private real estate. These people "move to the market" faster than insurance companies.

Largest Companies	Rank	Assets in Billion $
(a) Heitman–JMB—Resources to be a powerhouse. A new and untested merger between companies who, both have strong retail/syndication arms. Over 75% of their business is separate accounts.	2	$10.7
(b) LaSalle–ABKB—Recent merger. LaSalle is strong in property management and corporate relationships. It owns a lot of office property. ABKB has a $400 million REIT fund. Good management may be the key to their future success.	3	8.0
(c) O'Connor—Linked to Morgan Bank through $500 million Argo Fund and added $2 billion through the acquisition of Eastdil's asset management which has given them size. Significant relationships in Japan and Germany have helped them broaden their investment focus beyond retail.	5	5.8
(d) RREEF—Solid, team oriented approach with strong, recent overall success. 50% closed end funds, 50% separate accounts. Currently selling a REIT product.	9	<u>4.8</u>
Sub-total		$29.3
Percent of Tax Exempt R.E. Market		23.8%

Exhibit 3 (continued)

3. **Rising Stars**

Barriers to entry have increased materially since 1980. Even with a niche strategy, it's hard to be competitive with less than $1B of assets. Current market uncertainties, however, have given smaller players the opportunity to grow and a few firms have seized the opportunity. New boutiques will continue to be formed despite barriers to entry but most will probably fail.

Largest Companies	Rank	Assets in Billion $
(a) **Jones, Lang, Wooten (JLW)**—One of the few investment managers whose core business is brokerage and appraisal. JLW's wide scope, reputation and talent base give them a continuing presence in the market. They have a mix of U.S. and foreign clients.	12	$3.4
(b) **MacFarlane**—Minority owned firm that is growing. A mix of clients and assets. The firm is the result of a recent merger with McMahon and the Boston Company Real Estate Counsel.	16	2.0
(c) **AMB**—Conservative approach and on everyone's list to talk to. Started a new $400 million REIT.	22	1.3
Sub-total		$6.7
Percent of Tax Exempt R.E. Market		5.4%

4. **Former Stars**

The first three of these firms, in particular, played a major role in development of the industry in the 1980s. Due to a large number of client relationships, they may find a way to grow again.

Largest Companies	Rank	Assets in Billion $
(a) **Copley**—Has a unique investment strategy emphasizing land development and industrial properties that may or may not fit the pension market. Returns have been volatile.	6	$5.4
(b) **Aldrich, Eastman and Waltch (AEW)**—Known as one of the most creative firms. Lack of capital currently constrains its alternatives. AEW is 13% owned by United Asset Management which also bought Heitman–JMB. Most of its investments are large, separate accounts.	11	3.4
(c) **Trust Company of the West (TCW)**—Has been slow to respond to a changing market. All its investments are in closed-end funds.	13	3.0
(d) **TCC**—Trammell Crow has had its reputation seriously damaged during the real estate recession, which is hurting its ability to market to pension funds. The company has separated its service business from its property ownership side, which still has problems.	20	1.6
Sub-total		$13.4
Percent of Tax Exempt R.E. Market		10.9%
Total: 1–4		**$68.6**
Percent of Tax Exempt R.E. Market		55.7%

Exhibit 3 (continued)

5. **Non-Traditional Competitors**

Weakness in the "traditional providers" has brought in several different types of firms who have raised substantial capital in the last three years. These include:

(a) **Morgan Stanley & Goldman Sachs managed funds.**
Co-investment relationships.

(b) **Soros Realty, Tiger Realty, Hicks Muse**, etc.
Their overall strategy is unclear.

(c) **Zell/ML Realty.**
$1B in office properties. Reputation as a vulture fund.

(d) **Starwood Capital.**
Has used private capital effectively.

(e) **Colony Capital, Lennar, Amresco, other special servicers and related firms.**
Recycling of RTC debt has created some strong firms. Where will they put their energy?

Exhibit 4   Real Estate Market Overview
(Excerpted from the "Confidential Private Placement Memorandum")

The commercial real estate market today is still experiencing the effects of the construction boom of the 1980s. This overdevelopment was fostered by unprecedented access to both debt and equity financing and the inflated property values which ensued. From 1980 to 1989, approximately $1 trillion was used to buy, build and finance commercial real estate in the United States, doubling the inventory which existed in 1979. In 1986 alone, over one billion square feet of commercial space was added to a market already showing signs of oversupply. By the late 1980s, this oversupply manifested itself in high vacancy rates which, coupled with declining inflation rates and adverse changes in tax laws, resulted in declining real estate values.

More recently, however, the real estate market has experienced a substantial reduction in new construction. With the exception of retail and more recently apartment development, there has been very little commercial construction anywhere in the U.S. over the last few years. This lack of new development, combined with growth in demand and some obsolescence, has caused rents and occupancy rates to stabilize and begin to rise in most markets, in turn improving the value of the underlying properties.

In addition, several negative factors which impacted the overall real estate market and prolonged the downturn appear to have passed. First, the introduction of risk-based capital requirements for commercial banks and insurance companies restricted the ability of the largest capital providers of the 1980s to participate in the real estate market. This negative impact, which assisted in fundamentally restructuring the market, has largely been absorbed and in addition should help reduce the financing available for future speculative development. Second, foreign financial institutions, principally Japanese banks, whose large investments in high profile U.S. properties in the mid and late 1980s did much to inflate property values and exacerbate overdevelopment, are a much less serious factor. This should result in a more conservative approach to larger developments and a more rationally priced market. Lastly, certain compensation structures of the 1980s which rewarded speculative development have since been reformed. Today, fee driven development is practically obsolete as concern is greater with a property's underlying economic fundamentals.

Exhibit 4 (continued)

While prospective risk is considerable given significant vacancy rates and changing socioeconomic fundamentals, Gelco believes the commercial real estate market is an attractive and essential area for institutional investment. The Fund will seek to capitalize on the favorable conditions of commercial real estate by investing in both the public and private markets and continually comparing values across these sectors. In this regard, the Fund represents a new and unique "core" investment vehicle for institutions to participate in this $3 trillion market.

Public Real Estate Markets

The Fund will invest primarily in two sectors within the public commercial real estate market, real estate investment trust (REIT) beneficial shares, and commercial mortgage-backed securities (CMBS), primarily non-investment grade classes of CMBS.[15]

The REIT industry has undergone dramatic growth over the past few years, with market capitalization more than doubling to over $40 billion since the beginning of 1993. This tremendous growth reflects increasing demand for commercial real estate ownership combined with the enhanced liquidity afforded by the public markets. However, while the industry has been in existence since 1960, only a handful of REITs attracted institutional interest prior to 1992. The public offering boom of the last two years has since changed that, with the industry now composed of a larger number of true operating companies with sound, experienced real estate management.

The Investment Manager expects the securitization of real estate ownership through REITs to continue, thereby increasing market capitalization and facilitating expanded liquidity. In addition to initial public offerings, recovering property fundamentals and increased institutional demand should propel existing public REITs to return to the market to access external capital for growth. The increased number of secondary offerings by larger, high quality REITs should increase trading liquidity, thereby benefiting the entire market. Further, the very existence of the rapidly expanding public REIT market should add new discipline to the commercial real estate market.

The real estate debt market has also experienced rapid securitization over the last three years, as evidenced by the dramatic increase in CMBS market capitalization from under $10 billion in 1991 to nearly $60 billion in 1994. Several factors have led to and should contribute to continued growth, including: (i) risk-based capital regulations which have forced traditional portfolio lenders to dispose of existing and newly originated debt; (ii) the substantial amount of debt maturing over the next few years which requires refinancing; and (iii) debt needed to finance property acquisitions made with the significant amount of equity raised over the last three years.

The Investment Manager believes that within the broader CMBS market, the non-investment grade classes represent a timely opportunity to earn superior risk adjusted returns. While the investor base for senior real estate obligations has grown rapidly, the lack of expertise necessary to properly analyze subordinated classes of CMBS has restricted demand, allowing investors to command substantial yield premiums relative to comparably rated corporate bonds. In addition, as the entire CMBS market continues to expand and comfort with credit quality increases, below investment grade CMBS spreads should narrow over the next several years resulting in an opportunity for significant price appreciation.

---

[15]All investments of this type, whether or not publicly registered or freely tradable will be classified as public real estate market investments.

Exhibit 4   (continued)

Private Real Estate Markets

The private real estate market is benefiting from the same improving property fundamentals which are aiding the public real estate markets. While the pace of recovery is varying among sectors and regions, the relative lack of new development and gradual absorption of excess space has led to occupancy and rent stabilization, and the initiation of property value improvement.

Moderate but broad-based economic growth, combined with the passing and absorption of several negative factors which fundamentally restructured the overall commercial market, has helped to differentiate, and should help to sustain, the recovery currently underway. In addition, the rapidly growing public markets are playing an increasingly positive role by imposing discipline on the industry. These current conditions reflect constructive changes over the last few years and represent attractive opportunities for private ownership of commercial real estate.

However, many properties and companies remain unable to take part in the current recovery despite improving market fundamentals. Restrictions on traditional real estate participants have created opportunities for experienced and well capitalized investors to acquire assets at attractive values. In some cases, specific properties have positive fundamental attributes, but a poorly capitalized owner unable to improve and reposition the asset prevents it from competing effectively within its respective market. A growing number of opportunities to add value also exist within the corporate real estate realm. Certain operating companies such as private REITs, with attractive underlying assets but poor management and inflexible balance sheets, present opportunities to unlock significant value through potential restructuring.

The Fund will undertake both private and public market real estate investments to capitalize more efficiently on the attractive opportunities available in the commercial real estate market. This continuous exposure to both markets, combined with the experience of the Real Estate Team and the resources of Gelco, will enable the Investment Manager to compare relative values across sectors and periodically reallocate the Fund's assets in an effort to maximize returns. In addition, the inherent diversification of a combined pubic and private investment strategy should moderate overall portfolio risk. Gelco believes the Fund's unique approach offers an attractive opportunity for institutional investors to earn superior risk adjusted returns in commercial real estate.

Exhibit 5   Pension Fund Prospects

CATEGORY	DESCRIPTION	THE SALE
"The Big Corporates" $5B+	Many have separate real estate staff and multiple existing managers. Tend to like to retain discretionary authority (or at least *soft discretion*). Frequently look at managers as "core," "distressed," "niche," etc. We are "enhanced core," but that isn't the sale.	You need to know about what we're doing to be effective in managing your other managers—only need $10m to do so.
Medium Corporates $1B to $5B	Real estate will generally be a part time job for someone. May have multiple managers but does not want discretion. Simpler views on diversification.	We're your *new* core account.
Small Corporates	May not be in real estate. Real estate part of "alternatives."	We're the safest way to take a small step in real estate.
Big State Funds	Many of these will have the characteristics of large corporates [multiple managers, etc.] plus require lots of time to make decision. These funds tend to have staffs that want to get involved.	You need to know about what we're doing—only need $10m to do so. We will help you learn about the public/private trade off.
Medium and Smaller Government Funds	The key determinate will be how political and how flexible in choosing the prospect.	We're your *new* core account. Wide net, not too much effort on anyone due to "political risk."
Consultants Real Estate General	Most real estate specialists have lost clout. The general consultants need education.	This is new. By recommending something which is different, you can add more value.

PART III Development of Real Estate

14

503 CRICKET ROAD

In 1995, Mason Sexton, a young, inexperienced developer, was making plans to replace a rooming house he had inherited next to the University of Virginia campus in Charlottesville with a new 14 unit, 5 story apartment house. His attempts to assemble the information, approvals, and resources necessary to go ahead point out the steps and risks inherent in the development process. Using the example of a small scale residential project, the case illustrates development lessons applicable to projects of any scale.

DiscussionQuestions:

1. How well does Sexton carry out the conceptual, investigative, and planning stages of this development?
2. How and why does Sexton change his initial plan over time?
3. How does Sexton's return compare with his investment as the setup is revised over time?
4. Which problems that Sexton incurred were avoidable and which were beyond his control?

In September 1995, Mason Speed Sexton was evaluating how he should proceed with his property at 503 Cricket Road, Charlottesville, Virginia. He had inherited the stucco house in 1985. It was located on a 14,000 sq. ft. lot approximately one block from the main campus of the University of Virginia. Four years later he attended that institution as a first-year student and immediately took over management of the property. This was his first exposure to real estate management and to the benefits and problems of rental property.

Before Sexton took control of the house in 1989 it had been divided into individual rooms that were rented to students. There were 7 double bedrooms, 6 large single bedrooms, 2 kitchens, a large living room, and 5½ bathrooms. He spent two summers with a local handyman cleaning, painting, refurnishing and generally improving the long-neglected property. After remodeling, he was able to raise the rents by percentages varying from 25% to 40% and began to operate the property at a profit for the first time (see **Exhibit 1**). His experience taught him the importance of several factors crucial to real estate management. He learned that his property's location made it possible to demand rents in excess of those justified by the space and the facilities alone. He also learned that the age of the current structure and the resulting high maintenance costs were consuming the little profit there was. As the building continued to age and deteriorate, he concluded, the situation would only get worse.

During the period of his management, he filled the house with his undergraduate friends. As a precaution he required his tenants to sign a formal lease drawn by his lawyer and to get their parents' signatures if they were under twenty-one. Among these friends were two architectural students who came to him in the spring of 1994 proposing to build an apartment house at 503 Cricket Road. Their original concept was to design an "architectural commune" under the supervision of one of the professors in their graduate program. In fact, the professor asked if 503 Cricket Road could be used as a studio project for his second year architecture students. The idea seemed logical to Mr. Sexton and a way to get some free help.

Adjunct Professor William J. Poorvu and Donald A. Brown prepared this case as the basis for class discussion rather than to illustrate either effective or ineffective handling of an administrative situation. This case is derived from "503 Rugby Road" HBS case 9–373–146.

PLANNING A NEW BUILDING

After graduating from the University of Virginia in June 1993, Mason took a job with a small software company and moved to New York. In mid-1994, Sexton was admitted to Harvard Business School and planned to enroll in the fall. At that time he sought the advice of his mother on his idea to tear down the old house and erect an apartment building. In his opinion, her 20 years of real estate experience as a successful broker on Long Island—coupled with her interest in the property—made her a source of sound judgment and invaluable advice. After the first set of plans had been submitted by five different groups of architecture students, he and his mother were able to envision a feasible design that would fulfill the property's best use. They had learned that Charlottesville's "R–3" zoning laws for this location restricted building construction to one housing unit per thousand square feet of available land. This meant that they could build a maximum of 14 units, but these units were unrestricted as to the size or number of rooms in each unit as long as the structure adhered to required setbacks from the property line and the 5-story height limitation. Sexton decided that his objective was to maximize the value of the property with any project that might be built, since it was his only inheritance, and he wanted to make the most of it both in terms of current cash flow and cash to be realized at the time of sale.

After choosing the design and architect he liked best, Mr. Sexton spent many hours with his mother and the architect. He repeatedly revised the sketches and the floor plans until he was satisfied that he had met his maximum-use criteria and had an aesthetically pleasing and economically feasible set of plans. Among the decisions he made at this time were: (1) to make each unit, on average, 1,000 s.f. and to provide each of the 14 units with its own kitchen and bath; (2) to use concrete decking planks and brick bearing walls as the primary means of construction because of their cost advantages, long durability, and maintenance-free characteristics; (3) to build all bedrooms large enough and with enough closet space for at least two people; (4) to build all bathrooms, kitchens, and facilities to withstand maximum wear and tear while requiring the least possible amount of maintenance; and (5) within the constraints above, to attract affluent students by making the apartments as attractive, airy, convenient, and luxurious as possible. The overriding goal of this early planning phase was to decide upon a structure of lasting value that would require a minimum of time and expense to maintain.

During the design phase, Sexton became concerned about the property management. Since his mother was sixty-five, he decided to ask her if she wanted to move to Charlottesville, become a broker there and take over the management of the building. In order to make this proposal attractive to his mother, who was divorced, he promised her a "penthouse designed to her specifications." He did not know whether he could afford this offer, or, if he could, whether his mother would be amenable to the idea.

Concurrently, at the beginning of the summer of 1994, he surveyed the list of available contractors in Charlottesville who were willing and able to undertake this kind of job. To his great chagrin he discovered that since his project was to be one of the first mid-rise apartment buildings in several years in Charlottesville, most local contractors were not geared up even to bid on it. He explained his concept to the one general contractor with the most experience and showed him the plans and sketches. Sexton then asked for an estimate of what the contractor thought it would cost to build. Within a day the contractor produced a construction cost estimate of $630,000. Mr. Sexton estimated his total development costs from that base.

MARKET RESEARCH

Before making any major dollar commitment to the project, Sexton wanted to do a more in-depth survey of the local rental housing market and, if possible, get a verbal commitment for permanent financing on the basis of the plans and numbers he had at that time. On an overall basis he liked Charlottesville as a market (see Appendix A). He spent two full days in July 1994 talking to local real estate brokers to determine what the demand might be for his new luxury apartments and whether he could get rents of around $700 per unit. Reactions were mixed. Most of his contacts agreed that such rents were too high for young families, professionals, and nonstudents and that $700 was at the high end of the rental range for Charlottesville apartments (see **Exhibit 2**).

A visit to the Off-Grounds Housing Bureau was much more encouraging. There he learned that the off-grounds housing situation was critical. Students would pay almost anything for good, clean housing that was within walking distance of the university. The director informed him that in the last two years, available apartments had been given out by lottery. More recently, they had done away with the lottery system as it had proved unworkable. The current situation was described as a "free-for-all" with local landlords responding by increasing rents sharply. This was a change from the early 1990s when rents were flat with some vacancies.

During this same trip to Charlottesville, Sexton got a break in the form of a tip from his contractor that a "Special Report" from the Housing Guidance Council had recently been released and that he might get a copy from one of the largest builder–developers in central Virginia. He called the developer's office and a secretary told him that he could read the report while he was there, but that it couldn't leave the office. He therefore took a small tape recorder and recorded the parts he felt to be important to his project, while he was in an empty conference room.

In general the report indicated that there was a strong market for rental property within walking distance of the University and that demand would remain strong through 1998, even without further expansion by the University of Virginia. Since he planned to rent to students who were willing and able to live two to a bedroom, he had to make rent comparisons on a per-student basis. He was able to get information on the few comparables for rental units in mid-rise buildings (see **Exhibit 2**).

The large rooms in the existing 108-year-old, deteriorating structure had rented during the last three to five years for $125 per person per month with four or five people sharing the same bathroom and kitchenette. Occupancy levels had been virtually at the 100% level for the entire period of his ownership with long waiting lists for any available rooms. Many students seemed to be quite willing to pay this price for conveniently located housing despite its run-down condition and lack of amenities. Bedrooms in the new structure would rent for an average of $350 per month and could easily accommodate two persons, resulting in a per-person cost of $175 per month.

Next, based on his knowledge of the local rental market and some preliminary research he had conducted with the help of the general contractor, he estimated his operating expenses including vacancy and derived his expected cash flow (see **Exhibit 3**). On the basis of this rough analysis he decided that with cash flow of $90,034 and a total cost of $850,000 the project was economically feasible and that he should proceed to the next stage.

AVAILABILITY OF CREDIT

Armed with his new market data, the "Special Report" excerpts, and his pro forma income and expense statement, Sexton visited the local Crestar Bank where, after presenting his proposal, for an $850,000 project he got a verbal commitment for $45,000 per unit or a $630,000 first mortgage at an interest rate of 8.5% with an amortization period of 25 years and a mortgage constant of 9.67% based on 300 monthly mortgage payments. This was some $70,000 less than the loan he was hoping for. It would require an equity investment of $220,000: $150,000 through contributing the land and $70,000 in cash. He was told that the bank had never lent more than $40,000 per unit before and that they were stretching themselves to reach this higher level. Other visits to the Shenandoah Life Insurance Company, the local savings bank, and others produced similar results. The general feeling Sexton encountered seemed to be that this project was "too rich for our blood." In his opinion, this experience underscored the problem of dealing with small town, local financial institutions. First, since this was a pioneering effort in the sense that it was to be the first mid-rise in several years in the town aimed at students, most lenders approached it cautiously and, in his opinion, with undue conservatism. Secondly, he had received the impression that the size of the loan was "too heavy" for several institutions, who were still recovering from their real estate loan losses a few years earlier.

Although Sexton's available time in Charlottesville was drawing to a close he still had not received very encouraging results. Looking for additional sources, Sexton sought out the most reputable mortgage broker in town. The gentleman to whom he was referred turned out to be the executive vice president of the commercial bank where he kept a house account. He was very helpful in suggesting sources of mortgage money and assured Sexton that for 2% of the loan he could secure financing of $700,000 with a carrying cost of $67,690 quickly and easily. As a precondition, however, Sexton would have to get final bids on the project to determine the construction costs more exactly in order to finalize his commitment. This, in turn, required that Sexton procure a complete set of working drawings and specifications by an architect certified in Virginia. Unfortunately, the architect who had done all the work up to this point was with a New York firm and not licensed in Virginia. In addition, a local engineer had to take test borings on the land to determine what kind of foundation would be needed. To proceed further, Sexton had to commit almost $25,000 in architectural and engineering fees. These would have to be paid whether or not the building was built. But on the basis of Sexton's mother's credit, Sexton would be able to delay payment of these bills until they got financing or the project was shelved.

PROBLEMS WITH THE PLANNING COMMISSION

In late August 1994, a disturbing piece of news arrived which caused Sexton added expense and worry through the fall. All plans for multi-family housing, office, and industrial buildings had to be approved by The City Planning Commission. A new planning director was hired who stated that he was very concerned that each project meet the highest planning standard. Since Sexton's project was the first to seek approval under the new director, it was being treated as somewhat of a test case. The planning director was very "tough" in his meetings with Sexton and insisted that Sexton take pains not to disturb a single tree or bush in putting up the building. If Sexton did not comply with the rules, he would not receive his certificate of occupancy. In addition, Sexton had to present detailed landscaping plans and elevations of the building to get his project approved. He therefore hired a local landscape architect at a cost of $5,000 to do the plans and appear before the commission on his behalf. The outcome of the meeting was that the Planning Commission not only approved Sexton's plans, but "hailed" them as a model for future development in Charlottesville.

NEW COST ESTIMATES

Once the working drawings were completed, the general contractor sent out invitations to local subcontractors to bid on the property. By March 1995, when the bids were returned, the building market had taken a dramatic turn from its status a year earlier. The real estate downturn a few years earlier had caused the biggest developer in Charlottesville to go bankrupt, leaving debts of $17 million. Little new construction had gone on since. Many contractors, architects, and other subcontractors were out of jobs and hungry for work. By the spring of 1995, however, the economy was heating up and construction in Charlottesville, especially in single-family homes and townhouses on the outskirts of the city, was booming. The University was retrofitting a number of its existing buildings. These reasons, coupled with the fact that this was Sexton's first real estate venture, made it difficult to attract bids on the project. When he got bids, his worst fears were realized. The lowest bid came in at $120,000 over his estimates.

The multitude of factors behind this huge difference required a great deal of time and effort to discover and, in some cases, eliminate. A major reason for the high construction costs was the fact that the test borings showed the need for reinforced spread footings which had to go down 40 feet. This foundation work which included other related expenses, increased his costs by $50,000. To get around this problem, Sexton attempted to swap his piece of land for a similarly sized, but less attractively located piece owned by the University. Unfortunately, the Board of Overseers was not interested in his proposal and he was stuck with the extra cost.

During this period, his general contractor, architects, and his mother were of tremendous help in finding ways to save money and cut costs. Ultimately, the original bids were reduced by $40,000 a development absolutely critical to keeping the project economically viable. For instance, he quickly discovered that he could save $13,000 on the masonry (see **Exhibit 4**) by changing from the 8'4″ ceilings called for in the plans to 8 ft. ceilings and by using oversized instead of standard brick. This change also meant that precut, regulation 8 ft. wallboard could now be installed without the extra labor it would require to patch every piece and use extenders. It also meant saving 10% on the cost of cheaper bricks that required less mortar and labor. Some other ways in which he cut costs were to: (1) eliminate all the ceramic tile work; (2) take out all dishwashers and garbage disposal units making them optional on a rental basis; (3) replace the electric switches called for in the specifications with ones costing less and moving the position of the boxes in order to use less electrical cable; (4) make kitchens smaller by 1½ feet and switching to lower-grade cabinets. Unfortunately, he was not the only one in Charlottesville facing high building costs. A recent article in the local paper showed that Charlottesville's average building cost of $45 per square foot was among the highest in the nation. Despite these high cost levels, Sexton expected a reasonable return on his investment. The total development budget of $940,000, based on a 12-month construction period, is shown in **Exhibit 5**.

PRO FORMA INCOME STATEMENT

A major reservation voiced by potential lenders was centered around Sexton's pro forma income statements (see **Exhibit 3**). Specifically, bankers believed that his operating expenses of $21,686 were too low since they totalled only about 19% of the net rent of $111,720. The bankers wanted to see operating expenses, including real estate taxes, in the neighborhood of 25% of net rental income or $29,400 since their experience had indicated that this would be their probable cost to run the building should there be a default on the mortgage. In particular, the lender felt that real estate taxes would be $2,500 higher and management and administration, repairs and maintenance, and utility charges should all be increased. Making these adjustments, Sexton projected the return on investment of $82,320 on a cost of $940,000 (see **Exhibit 6**).

Requiring a coverage ratio of about 1.2 of net operating income to debt service, Sexton felt that he could still obtain a loan of $700,000 at an 8.5% interest rate (9.67% mortgage constant). This left a cash return of $14,630 on an equity investment of $240,000 or 6% (see **Exhibit 6**). As bad as this seemed, he thought there were some positives: the partial sheltering of income and the anticipated increase in value through appreciation. He felt rents would grow and in a few years he could justify a sale at an 8.25% capitalization rate.

TAX SHIELD AND DISCOUNTED CASH FLOW ANALYSIS OF RETURN

Sexton had decided to use the "discounted cash flow analysis of return" format in the pro forma, because he believed it was the only method clearly relating the estimated value of a project with its cash flow over time. He knew that real estate investors establish value and base their investment decisions on four sources of entrepreneurial reward: (1) appreciation, (2) loan amortization, (3) income tax savings, and (4) cash flow. He believed that the method used in his analysis integrated all four elements and told "The Cricket Road Story" effectively. Sexton felt confident that the after-tax projected return of close to 20% would awaken the interest of most investors (see **Exhibit 7**).

CURRENT SITUATION

By September 1995, when Sexton returned to the second-year MBA program, the project was in limbo. He had not been able to obtain permanent financing on acceptable terms. He had almost completely ceased to deal with his original mortgage broker because the broker had not lived up to his promise to secure a take-out loan. At this point his architects had become very helpful in arranging meetings with interested lenders and investors. On his own, he had spoken to a number of recently-formed public real estate investment trusts (REITs) to which he had sent proposals. Although these were still being evaluated and reviewed, Sexton had received the distinct impression that his project was too small to warrant viable consideration. He had not yet received any favorable responses. Moreover, as time passed, it became less and less likely that the building could be completed before the original target date of January 1, 1997. This meant that he would miss the change in semesters at the University when a new influx of students would be looking for housing. Consequently, he would have a difficult time renting the property until the following September and would incur large additional carrying costs. He was left wondering about his next steps.

Exhibit 1

INCOME AND EXPENSE STATEMENT FOR PRESENT USE

Income

Gross rental income (Note 1)	$30,000
Allowance for vacancies and bad debts	(900)
Net rental income	$29,100

Operating Expenses

Real estate taxes	($3,000)
Water and sewer	(1,000)
Heat and electricity	(2,800)
Insurance	(1,200)
Janitor	(1,600)
Repairs	(2,900)
Management fee	(1,600)
Total Operating Expenses	($14,100)
Income from Operations	$15,000

Note 1: 13 rooms with 20 students paying $125 per room, per person, per month.

Exhibit 2

Charlottesville Apartments

	600 BRANDON	CRICKET MCINTYRE	OXFORD HILL	WOODROW APARTMENTS	CAMBRIDGE SQUARE	ASH TREE
1 Bedroom Unit						
1 person	$500	685	540	690	590	675
2 people	500	685	540	690	590	675
2 Bedroom Unit						
3 people	530	685	570	690	620	725
4 people	560	685	600	690	650	775

Exhibit 3

PRELIMINARY PRO FORMA INCOME AND EXPENSE STATEMENT

Gross rental income

(14 units × 4 students × $175 × 12 mos.)	$117,600
Vacancy allowance (5% of gross rent)	(5,880)
Net rental income	$111,720

Operating Expenses

Real estate taxes	7,300
Water and sewer	1,000
Gas	1,000
Insurance	2,200
Janitor	2,000
Reserve for general repairs	1,400
Electricity	1,200
Management fee (5% of net rent)	5,586
Total operating expenses	$21,686
Income from operations (Note 1)	$90,034

Note: Total development cost estimated at $850,000 including land at $150,000, construction at $630,000, and soft costs (i.e. financing, architecture, legal, etc.) at $70,000.

Exhibit 4

Projected Construction Cost, Spring 1995

ITEM	MARCH BID	REVISED BID	DIFFERENCE
Demolition	$ 8,800	$ 8,800	$ 0
Reinforcing and steel	0	3,700	3,700
Concrete	43,500	43,000	(500)
Masonry	137,900	124,900	(13,000)
Structural steel	17,600	17,000	(600)
Steel stairs	11,000	11,000	0
Rough carpentry	21,100	21,100	0
Rough hardware	900	900	0
Finish carpentry	16,400	14,400	(2,000)
Finish hardware	2,000	2,000	0
Drainage	1,900	1,900	0
Roofing	12,000	12,000	0
Door A. Metal	3,000	3,000	0
Door Bi-Folding	1,800	1,800	0
Windows	18,000	16,000	(2,000)
Drywall	19,000	17,500	(1,500)
Tile work	400	0	(400)
Resilient tile	3,000	3,000	0
Painting	8,800	7,800	(1,000)
Special decoration	1,600	1,600	0
Kitchen cabinets	18,500	14,400	(4,100)
Appliances	14,100	12,000	(2,100)
Blinds & shades	1,500	1,500	0
Carpets	13,400	13,400	0
Metal shelving	1,300	1,300	0
Elevators	40,500	37,500	(3,000)
Plumbing	58,000	56,000	(2,000)
Tubs & showers, toilets, basins	6,000	6,000	0
Termite protection	300	300	0
Precast slabs	51,000	51,000	0
Heating, ventilating, air conditioning	29,000	29,000	0
Electric	39,500	37,000	(2,500)
Fireplaces	1,400	1,400	0
Caulking	900	900	0
Earth moving	6,000	6,000	0
Site work	2,600	2,600	0
Walks, etc.	10,700	9,600	(1,100)
Lawns	4,400	3,000	(1,400)
General requirements	53,000	50,000	(3,000)
Tools	2,000	2,000	0
Total	$682,800	$646,300	($ 36,500)
Taxes	19,400	18,400	(1,000)
Overhead & profit	47,800	45,300	(2,500)
Total	$750,000	$710,000	($40,000)

Exhibit 5

Total Development Cost Budget,(1) Spring 1995

Land at market value	$150,000
Construction costs(2)	710,000
Architectural and Engineering	30,000
Legal, builder's risk insurance, taxes	20,000
Interest on construction loan	30,000
Total development costs	$940,000
Less assumed loan	700,000
Equity investment required	240,000
Less land	150,000
Cash required	$ 90,000

Notes:
(1) Based on plans and specifications included in Proposal.
(2) See "Projected Construction Costs," **Exhibit 4,** for a detailed breakdown.

Exhibit 6

Cash Flow Analysis (Using 25% Expense Ratio)

INCOME AND CASH FLOW

Gross rents	$117,600
Less: 5% vacancy	5,880
Net rental income	111,720
Total expenses	29,400
Net cash flow if free and clear of debt	82,320
Annual debt service $700,000: 8½% interest, 25 yrs; 9.67% constant*	67,690
Net cash flow after debt servicing	$14,630

*Based on monthly mortgage payments.

Exhibit 7 Pro Forma Discounted Cash Flow Analysis ($000)

	0	1	2	3	4	5	6	7	8	9	10
Net Revenues (1)		$111.72	$117.31	$123.17	$129.33	$135.80	$142.59	$149.72	$157.20	$165.06	$173.31
−Operating Expenses (1)		(29.40)	(30.87)	(32.41)	(34.03)	(35.74)	(37.52)	(39.40)	(41.37)	(43.44)	(45.61)
Free and Clear Return		82.32	86.44	90.76	95.30	100.06	105.06	110.32	115.83	121.62	127.71
−Financing		(67.69)	(67.69)	(67.69)	(67.69)	(67.69)	(67.69)	(67.69)	(67.69)	(67.69)	(67.69)
Before Tax Cash Flow		14.63	18.75	23.07	27.61	32.37	37.37	42.63	48.14	53.93	60.02
+Amortization		8.52	9.27	10.09	10.98	11.95	13.01	14.16	15.41	16.77	18.25
−Depreciation (2)		(28.73)	(28.73)	(28.73)	(28.73)	(28.73)	(28.73)	(28.73)	(28.73)	(28.73)	(28.73)
Taxable Income		(5.58)	(0.71)	4.43	9.86	15.59	21.65	28.06	34.82	41.98	49.54
Tax Payable @ 39.6.% (3)		2.21	0.28	(1.75)	(3.90)	(6.18)	(8.57)	(11.11)	(13.79)	(16.62)	(19.62)
AFTER TAX CASH FLOW		16.84	19.03	21.31	23.70	26.20	28.80	31.52	34.35	37.31	40.40
−Equity in	(240.00)										
+Net Cash from Sale											$725.69
TOTAL RETURN	($240.00)	$16.84	$19.03	$21.31	$23.70	$26.20	$28.80	$31.52	$34.35	$37.31	$766.08

Sales price (4)	$1,547.94
Net Book Value (5)	($652.73)
Gain on Sale	($895.21)
Tax Liability at 28% (6)	($250.66)

Sale Price	$1,547.94
−Income Tax	($250.66)
−Mortgage Balance	($571.60)
Net Cash from Sale	$725.69

NET PRESENT VALUE AT 12%	$138.14
INTERNAL RATE OF RETURN	18.57%

Assumptions:
(1) Net operating income and operating expense increase at 5% per year.
(2) The depreciable base is assumed to be $790,000 and is divided by the 27.5 year cost recovery period for residential properties.
(3) Taxes are based on the 39.6% maximum federal tax rate. It is assumed the investor has passive income and can utilize any tax benefits.
(4) The sales price is based on capping the 10th year net operating income of $127,710 at an 8.25% capitalization rate.
(5) The book value assumes a total development cost of $940,000 less depreciation of $28,727 per year for ten years.
(6) The tax liability is based on a federal capital gains tax rate of 28%.

Appendix A

Charlottesville and Albemarle County are situated in central Virginia along the eastern slope of the Blue Ridge Mountains just 30 minutes away from the Skyline Drive. Charlottesville is 67 miles west of Richmond and 115 miles southwest of Washington, D.C. The 1990 census listed Albemarle County's population as 56,000 and Charlottesville's population as 40,000. Census projections indicate that the populations will continue to grow at an average rate of 3% per year, and that growth was expected to come in spurts rather than as a single smooth trend. The proportion of Charlottesville's employed population classified as professional is 45%; 52% work in managerial, sales, or clerical positions.

Manufacturers in many different industries provide a payroll in excess of $150 million. There are nine electronics firms in the immediate area including General Electric, Sperry Marine Systems, and Stromberg–Carlson. Morton's Frozen Foods employs 1,500 people in a plant 12 miles to the west of the city. Three printing plants—the Allen Press, the Michie Press and the Lindsey Printing Company—employ over 400 persons and are located in Albemarle County. Martin-Marietta operates a quarry to the north of the city. Two concrete manufacturers serve the growing needs of the construction industry. Two clothing and textile firms have plants within the county. An office equipment manufacturer, the Acme Visible Record Co., and a tire plant for Uniroyal complete the list of major industrial installations.

Although there are indications that General Electric may locate another plant in the Charlottesville–Albemarle area, the prospect of further industry growth is limited by the diminished pool of available labor and the opposition of many local groups to any activity which might damage the local environment.

Charlottesville has many government jobs. The city serves as a regional center for the state and as the county seat for Albemarle County. The federal government has a substantial payroll here on the staff of the Army Judge Advocate General's school and the Army Foreign Service Technological Center. Federal employment in the area is not considered likely to grow. It took substantial pressure from the local congressional delegation to bring in the Army Foreign Service Technological Center and even this did not replace all the jobs lost when HEW vacated the federal office building several months earlier.

Albemarle County remains an active agricultural area. There are extensive apple and peach orchards within the county. Many large firms still specialize in cattle breeding, dairy products or horse raising.

The single most important influence upon the future of the county and the city is the University of Virginia. This is a prominent educational institution with graduate schools of law, medicine and business which rank among the best American professional schools. The University has attracted a well-educated and affluent group of professionals and is also an important source of employment for unskilled workers in the county and city. Additionally, the University serves as the center for much of the cultural and social life in the area by sponsoring concerts, lectures and exhibits. Increases in enrollment will continue to foster growth in the area.

The city's rich historical background, its natural scenic beauty and the remarkable examples of Jeffersonian architecture have made it into an important tourist center, drawing over 400,000 people a year.

The city and county are relatively well served in terms of transportation. Interstate 64 runs east–west through the city and connects it with Richmond and Norfolk to the east, Roanoke and ultimately St. Louis to the west. Dual-lane Route 29 connects with Washington, D.C. Both the Chesapeake and Ohio and the Southern Railroads serve the city and use Charlottesville as an important switching point. Charlottesville has a regional airport with daily scheduled flights to points as distant as New York and Atlanta.

Appendix A   (continued)

Charlottesville and its surrounding area represent one of the small sustained growth areas in the South. While many communities are dependent for their growth on a single source like commerce, recreation, politics, professionals, or education, Charlottesville is fortunate enough to have a strong base in many of these areas. Its numerous advantages virtually guarantee a stable and prosperous economy.

15

CONCORD CENTER

In the spring of 1993, Jennifer White, a junior partner with Morgan Sachs, faced a complex problem in trying to put together the financing for a $133 million three story super-regional shopping center at the confluence of three major highways in Concord County, 45 minutes from Metropolis. The joint venture partners, the Sturgess Group, and Galactic Insurance Company had spent ten years and $28 million getting the project to this point. At issue is whether the retail market will support a project of this size and cost.

Discussion Questions:

1. Based on the location, the market, the product, and the people, do you think this project will be successful?
2. Given your analysis, how would you structure the financing and ownership? If additional capital is required, who should provide it and on what terms?

Jennifer White, a junior partner with Morgan Sachs, faced a complex problem in trying to put together the financing for a $133 million super-regional shopping center. Ten years ago in 1983, the Sturgess Group had won a competition and been awarded the rights to develop a three story super-regional shopping center at the confluence of three major highways in Concord County, 45 minutes from Metropolis. Morgan Sachs had then helped to put together a joint venture between the Sturgess Group and Galactic Insurance Company. Despite the delays that this project encountered, this partnership had worked well and Galactic and Sturgess had invested about $28 million in acquisition costs and off-site road improvements, with Galactic providing the bulk of the money.

In the spring of 1993, with all the regulatory hurdles behind them and leases signed with three anchor department stores, Sturgess and Galactic had approached Morgan Sachs again, to help them obtain the financing to begin construction. After reviewing the project budget, the projections and talking with several bankers, Ms. White concluded that the financing would not be simple. Based on current underwriting standards, she doubted that the project would be able to secure more than an $85 to $100 million construction loan, leaving a gap of $5 to $20 million.

Several weeks later, one of the general partners from the Sturgess Group and a senior executive from Galactic Insurance Company requested a meeting with Jennifer White and the senior partner in charge of real estate at Morgan Sachs. It was clear from the outset of the meeting, that strains had developed between the Sturgess Group and Galactic. In many ways both parties wanted to go back to square one and rethink the whole deal and the whole partnership. As they laid out the assignment to Morgan Sachs, they wanted Ms. White to help them restructure the investment based on the current value of the project and the need for additional financing.

THE SHOPPING CENTER

Concord Center is designed as a three story super-regional shopping center in the Township of Bismuth, in Concord County, 45 minutes from Metropolis. The term "super-regional shopping center" is a classification devised by the Urban Land Institute (ULI).

This case was prepared by Lecturer John H. Vogel, Jr. and Adjunct Professor William J. Poorvu as the basis for class discussion rather than to illustrate either effective or ineffective handling of an administrative situation. It is based on a case written by Esther Sandrof and Charles Laven from Hamilton, Rabinovitz and Alschuler.

ULI distinguishes among four types of shopping centers based on their size and use: neighborhood centers, community centers, regional centers, and super-regional centers (see **Exhibit 1**). According to ULI, a super-regional center "provides for extensive variety in general merchandise, apparel, furniture, and home furnishings. . . It is built around three or more full line department stores of generally not less than 100,000 square feet each. The typical size of a super-regional is about 800,000 square feet of gross leasable area."

The approved plan for Concord Center consists of 1,025,000 of gross area of which there is a gross leasable area (GLA) of 900,000 square feet which will include three anchor tenants and 160 shops. "Anchor" refers to the lead tenant in a shopping center. In regional and super-regional centers, the anchors are usually full-line department stores. In community centers, the anchors tend to be junior department stores, off-price chains, or home improvement centers. In neighborhood centers, the anchor is usually a grocery store. For Concord Center, the anchors will be: Abraham and Strauss, Steinbach, and Macy's.

Because of their integral role in making the deal fly, the anchors have a significant influence on the development of the center including considerable input into the mix of stores in the mall and the design and configuration of the center. When anchors lease their space, they tend to pay a lower per square foot rent than the smaller stores. In Concord Center, Abraham and Strauss negotiated a 30-year lease at $6 per square foot plus $150,000 per year for Common Area Maintenance (CAM) and other operating expenses. Steinbach and Macy's negotiated an arrangement where they will build and own their space and pay no rent. Together they will contribute $310,000 per year toward mall events and other operating expenses, which, after 1998, will rise proportionately as the center's operating costs increase. Although leases have not yet been signed, a great deal of interest has been expressed by smaller stores in leasing space at the mall.

Perhaps the most important consideration for shopping center developers is creating a flow of traffic through the mall that will result in a significant volume of sales in the mall stores. Mall stores typically pay base rent plus a percentage of their sales. The usual "rule of thumb" in the industry is that the total occupancy costs for mall stores including base rents, percentage rent and reimbursables should be no more than 14% of their sales. Thus, if a store sells $200 per square foot, its occupancy costs should be no more than $28 which might break down as $20 in base rent, $2 in percentage rent, and $6 in reimbursables for insurance, and other mall operating costs.

THE FLOOR PLAN

The plan for Concord Center shows three corridors radiating from a central court. This design is typical for most three anchor malls. In designing a shopping center, the developer tries to create the feeling of strolling down 5th Avenue. Stores must be well lit, visible to passing shoppers and easily accessible. Since it is the anchor stores that draw customers into the mall, and it is the smaller stores that pay higher per square foot rents, it is advantageous to design the mall so that customers pass as many shops as possible, while traversing from one anchor to another.

The design of Concord Center is unusual in that each of the three floors is designed to appeal to a different market segment. Based on its analysis of the trade area, the Sturgess Group determined that three distinct markets existed: affluent customers, middle-class families, and "fashion-forward" youth (see **Exhibit 3**). In order to appeal to all three groups, the developers decided to group their tenants by floor according to the clientele they serve and to design each floor to reflect the tastes of the target customers.

The first floor will feature stores that sell luxury apparel and accessories. The floor will be appointed in marble, granite and bronze with free-standing Corinthian columns and elaborate light fixtures to give it a sophisticated look.

The second floor will feature stores carrying moderate to better-priced clothing, linens, decorative accessories, and other goods for families. The middle floor will be finished in ceramic tile floors and wood paneled walls with a variety of painted murals which the developer believes will give it "an upscale, yet unpretentious appearance."

The third floor will be outfitted with neon lights, polished chrome, and brightly painted corridors. The stores will carry moderately-priced, fashionable apparel and other goods directed at teenagers. The top floor will also contain a multi-screen movie theater, a food court with 15 eateries, and three full line restaurants.

The exterior of the center is designed to blend with the local terrain. The exterior facade will be built out of dark brown, iron spot brick, accented with horizontal brick and stone bands. Each entrance will be framed with indigenous stone. The roof of the center will be green and the tri-level parking deck will be masked behind dense foliage borders.

HISTORY OF CONCORD CENTER

Concord Center has had a long and tangled history. The original plan for the mall was drawn up in 1983 when the Bismuth Redevelopment Authority issued a Request for Proposal to develop this 70 acre site. The Sturgess Group, a major national shopping center developer, was selected from a field of 37 competitors.

This would be the Sturgess Group's first project in the Metropolis metropolitan area. Sturgess proposed to build on this 70 acre site a mall with gross area of 1,300,000 square feet including gross leasable area of 1,125,000 square foot and 5,600 parking spaces.

The site sits at the confluence of three major highways, Route 49, 602, and Eastern Freeway (see **Exhibit 2**). Over 90,000 vehicles pass the site each day. In order to provide access to the center, it was necessary to widen Route 49 from a two- to three-lane road and to build connector ramps on all three roads. In 1985, after a year and a half of feasibility analysis and negotiations, the State and Federal government transportation departments backed away from commitments to fund the road improvements, forcing Galactic to commit $20 million of its own funds, on behalf of the Partnership, to construct the ramps and widen Route 49.

During the next seven years, the project was stalled by a host of problems. The first problem was securing anchor tenants. With the frenetic acquisition, merger and bankruptcy activity in the mid to late 1980s, several department stores cancelled their commitments to the project. There was also a great deal of community opposition to the shopping center. Several local environmental groups denounced the center as detrimental to the ecological balance of the area. They alleged that the appearance of the center would disrupt the natural beauty of the local terrain, that the run-off from the site would flood adjacent forests and neighborhoods, and that the traffic generated by the center would overburden the capacity of local streets. Additionally, local merchant groups attempted to obstruct the project based on fears that it would steal their customer base.

As a result of all the delays, the Redevelopment Authority was forced to grant a series of extensions on the original contract with Sturgess. In 1992, the Redevelopment Authority sued to terminate their development contract with Sturgess, claiming that the developer had defaulted on the agreement and should relinquish its rights to develop the property. Sturgess threatened to counter-sue.

By the fall of 1992, nine years after signing the original contract, the various conflicts appeared to be resolved. The Redevelopment Authority relented and renegotiated its contract with Sturgess after a successful lobbying effort in which Sturgess convinced the local government officials that the center would bolster the local economy, generate significant tax revenues, and create jobs (see **Exhibit 6**). As a concession to environmentalists, Sturgess reduced the size of the shopping center to 1,025,000 gross square feet with 900,000 square feet of leasable space and redesigned the exterior facade so that it would blend into the natural surroundings. They also agreed to create a raised berm along the perimeter of the property to correct the run-off problem and make the center less obtrusive. The $20 million of transportation improvements which had been started were scheduled to be completed by the summer of 1993.

With favorable interest rates and a recovering economy, Sturgess was able to secure commitments from the three anchor tenants. It then negotiated a final gross maximum price construction contract with a contractor and secured final design approval from all the relevant agencies. The last step was to obtain construction financing and begin the two year construction process.

THE MARKET

Jennifer White reviewed a copy of the market analysis that had been prepared and updated for Sturgess by the RRG Group, a real estate consulting company that specialized in retail market studies. RRG's report began by identifying the

Primary Trade Area for Concord Center. A trade area is the area from which a commercial development can expect to draw its customers. Once the trade area is delineated, RRG can model and analyze the size and spending power of the local population using U.S. census data.

The Urban Land Institute has identified some "rules of thumb" about driving times and distances for different types of shopping centers which help define the trade area (see **Exhibit 1**). For a center the size of Concord Center, customers will generally drive about twelve (12) miles or thirty (30) minutes. This kind of "rule of thumb" analysis needs to then be modified to take into account competition, natural barriers such as rivers and mountains, social barriers such as neighborhood divisions and traffic conditions.

A trade area analysis can be tricky in urban settings where there are a variety of competitors and a wider range of racial, ethnic, and economic groups. More densely populated areas also pose the problem of "leakage," which is defined as the percentage of local retail dollars spent in other trade areas. Conversely, in sparsely populated places and areas with little competition, a trade area can extend well beyond the "rules of thumb" set forth by ULI.

In the case of Concord Center, RRG defined the trade area as all of Concord County and all of Wadsworth County. The trade area extended west from the site approximately 25 miles along Route 49. This distance, well in excess of ULI standards, reflects the lack of competition to the west of the site and the lack of traffic on the road. The trade area also extended eight miles to the east, twelve miles to the north, and fifteen miles to the south. The shorter distances reflected increased traffic congestion and competition from existing malls (see **Exhibit 2**).

According to RRG's market study, there are no regional malls within the trade area and no plans for any have been announced other than Concord Center. The nearest shopping centers are all more than five (5) miles outside the boundaries of the trade area. **Exhibit 2** shows the location of the four regional shopping centers that effect the delineation of the trade area and describes the size, number of stores, and anchors at each of these competitors.

THE DEMOGRAPHICS

The RRG market study contains extensive information on the population and growth trends in Concord and Wadsworth Counties and compares them to the region as a whole. **Exhibit 3** also shows employment trends in the region.

In determining the household buying power in the Concord Center trade area, RRG referred to the *Sales and Marketing Management, 1993 Survey of Buying Power*. Their data shows that the Concord Center trade area has a median Effective Buying Income (EBI) that is higher than the median income for the Region (see **Exhibit 3**).

The *1993 Survey of Buying Power* estimates that the total EBI for Wadsworth County is $2.1 billion, and is $2.9 billion for Concord County. Of that $5 billion, the *1993 Survey of Buying Power* calculated that $1.99 billion had been spent on retail sales in 1992 and, of that, $1.3 billion had been spent on general merchandise.

RRG then calculated that of the $1.3 billion spent on apparel, home furnishings and other general merchandise, Concord Center could capture about $188 million of these sales. Finally, based on sales at other super-regional centers, RRG estimated that, if the center were in operation today, the anchors would capture about 56% of that $188 million in sales, and the rest of the mall including mall shops, cinema, and restaurants would capture about 44%.

THE SPONSORS

The owner of the center will be a joint venture in which The Sturgess Group and the Galactic Insurance Company will be the general partners. The Sturgess Group has been developing shopping centers since 1973. They are ranked as the twelfth largest shopping center developer in the United States. **Exhibit 8** is a list of the top ten shopping center developers in 1992 and the amount of square feet they have developed. Between 1990 and 1992, Sturgess developed over 3.2 million square feet and has 26.6 million square feet under ownership/management. In fiscal year 1992 the company had a net worth of $423 million based on the market value of its interests in its real estate holdings. Sturgess had annual operating revenues of $120 million. The company has the following operating philosophy.

1. Develop only two or three projects per year.
2. Minimize the amount of open-ended construction loans.
3. Secure commitments from the majority of anchors prior to commencement of construction.
4. Minimize interest rate exposure on floating debt through fixed rate loans or interest rate swaps.

The Galactic Life Insurance Company is one of the largest mutual life insurers in the United States. The company has an A+ (excellent) rating from Best's Insurance reports. As of 12/31/92 Galactic had a net worth of $3.3 billion and net gain for the last year of $219 million. Its equity real estate investments are handled through its subsidiary, Galactic Realty Group, which has an excellent track record. As part of the joint venture, Galactic promised to provide a take out loan[1] as the "lender of last resort" if they could not find someone else when the construction loan came due. On the other hand, if the loan turned out to be

---

[1]A "takeout loan" or "permanent financing" is a loan that is made when a project is completed and substantially leased. It is usually structured as a first mortgage and pays off the construction loan. Most construction lenders now require that a commitment for permanent financing be in place, before they will make a construction loan. The permanent lender usually specifies certain thresholds that must be met before they will fund such as: satisfactory completion of construction, a certain amount of occupancy, and achievement of a certain rent level. Unlike a construction loan which is often as short as one or three years, the permanent loan usually has a term of at least 10 years and an amortization schedule that is even longer.

attractive, the Partnership would look for the best deal in the marketplace, and Galactic would only get it if they could match the best offer.

The original deal struck between Sturgess and Galactic was that Sturgess would put up the original $5,000,000 to purchase the land. Galactic would provide the balance of the pre-development financing up to $18,000,000. The Partnership would pay a preference (like the dividend on preferred stock) on these capital contributions at the rate of 9% per year, as long as there was sufficient cash flow from the project. If the cash flow in any year was insufficient, the preference payment would accrue and be paid out of future cash flow. This accrual would begin when the center was completed. Once the project paid its operating expenses, debt service, reserves and preference, additional cash flow would be split 50–50 between the parties.[2]

Upon sale, after paying the outstanding debt, each partner would receive back its capital contribution plus any accrued preference payments and then the profits would be split 50–50. In 1985 when the Partnership was required to invest $20 million in roadwork and other off-site improvements, Galactic agreed to a one time increase in its commitment from $18 million to $23 million on the same terms, meaning that it would receive a 9% preference on the additional $5 million but not increase its 50% share of the profits. In the spring of 1993,

[2]To give a simple example of how this partnership accounting would work, let us assume that in a particular year the property generated net operating income of $13.5 million, and that it set aside $500,000 for reserves and capital expenditures. Then let us further assume that the annual mortgage payments are $9 million and that Galactic has invested $20 million and Sturgess has invested $5 million. Partnership distributions would be calculated as follows:

	($000)
Net Operating Income	$13,500
Reserves and Capital Improvements	(500)
Debt Service	(9,000)
SUB-TOTAL	$4,000
Preference to Galactic ($20,000 × 9%)	(1,800)
Preference to Sturgess ($5,000 × 9%)	(450)
Available for Distribution	$1,750
50% to Galactic	875
50% to Sturgess	875

It is important to note that these calculations and distributions are based on pre-tax, cash flows. The partnership would keep a second set of books in which they would calculate each partners' tax liability taking into account depreciation, amortization, reserves, and capital improvements. Each partner would then be responsible for paying its own taxes, based on its 50% share of the partnership's taxable income after first allocating the preference distribution to each party.

In this situation, both partners had complex, internal tax situations because of income and tax shelter, from other partnerships. Galactic's situation was further complicated by the unique way in which insurance companies are taxed. For this case, you can assume that both partners did their financial analysis based on pre-tax, cash flows, and considered the tax benefits of secondary importance.

between the land purchase, the amount committed and partly spent on road improvements, legal, architectural, and other consultant costs, the full $23 million from Galactic had been committed. No provisions had been made for any money beyond the $23 million from Galactic and the $5 million from the Sturgess Group.

THE DEVELOPMENT BUDGET

The general contractor for the construction of the project will be the Sturgess Construction Company, which was formerly part of the Sturgess Group but is now a separate entity. The Sturgess Construction Company has been general contractor on most Sturgess shopping centers.

The original development budget was estimated at $120,000,000. However, due to increases in various line items including the off-site work, the total budget for the project is now set at $133 million (see **Exhibit 4**). This budget was based on working drawings that were 85% complete. Sturgess indicated that the estimate had been reviewed by an independent cost estimator who wanted to see the cost breakdown between the different trades, but felt the construction costs were achievable.

THE BANKS

Jennifer White asked Sturgess to put together a ten year, cash flow projection that was conservative, but realistic. After several modifications and revisions, she felt she had a set of numbers based on reasonable assumptions that she could present to the bankers.

Having been badly burned in the 1980s, many bankers were reluctant to even look at a loan of this size, even with such strong sponsorship. Eventually, however, Jennifer White found two or three bankers willing to consider making the loan.

Based on her discussion, she believed she could secure a 5-year, interest-only loan which the bankers call a mini-perm. This kind of loan would enable the Partnership ample time to complete construction (2 years), lease up the center (1 year) and develop an operating track record. Bankers would base the amount of their loan, Ms. White surmised, on the stabilized 1997 income using the quantitative criteria shown in **Exhibit 7**. She hoped construction would start October 1, 1993 with completion in December 1995.

At this point, Ms. White felt she had gotten as far as she could get with the bankers without spending money. They all indicated that the most the sponsors could expect in a loan was in the range of $85–$100 million and the interest rate would be approximately 9%. Ms. White had also obtained a copy of the general guidelines that TNT bank (which had expressed interest in the project) used in evaluating loans on super-regional shopping centers (see **Exhibit 7**).

Once the project was complete, a possible takeout for the mini-perm loan would be a fixed rate, 10 year loan with a 30 year amortization schedule. She hoped that she could securitize this loan as part of an overall package of 10 year shopping center loans that Morgan Sachs would arrange. The loans would have a fixed rate that would result in a savings to the borrowers of at least 0.25% to 0.5% per year. There were, however, prepayment penalties that would make it difficult for the borrower to refinance or to change standard loan terms or conditions, either prior to or during the term of the loan. She was unsure whether the principals would regard it as worthwhile.

THE DECISION

As the meeting started, Bill Sturgess expressed his disappointment that Ms. White could not obtain the full $105,000,000 of construction financing. She replied that if Sturgess and Galactic were willing to provide corporate guarantees, she was sure that she could, but that her assignment had been to minimize the partners' exposure on the debt to guarantees of the completion of construction and cost overruns.

Bill Sturgess then went on to describe how much time and energy his company had put into this project over the last ten years. He was confident that this super-regional center would do even better now than it would have ten years ago when they purchased the land. Unfortunately, the Sturgess Group was not in a position where it could invest any more money in this project.

Anthony Stevens, from the Galactic Realty Group, then stated his position. He was aware of the amount of time and effort that had gone into this project, which is why Galactic had invested an additional $5 million beyond their initial commitment. Before he could go back to his finance committee again, he would need more information and a solid proposal. That is why, Stevens explained, he and Sturgess had agreed to commission Jennifer White to study the problem and make a recommendation. If she could come up with a reasonable set of recommendations, they would give her exclusive rights to arrange the construction and permanent financing for this project.

As Ms. White sat down at her computer, she tried to sort out the many different layers of this assignment. Her first job was simply to figure out if the project still made sense. Was there enough demand for a mall of this size? Did they have the right product for this market? Or, should they cut their losses and try to sell the land?

Then there were all the financial issues to consider. How large a construction loan could they realistically obtain? If they sold the property in ten years, what kind of a return could the partners expect on their investment?

Finally there was the Partnership Agreement. If they went forward with the investment, and Galactic invested another $5 to $20 million, how should they be compensated? Should they receive the same preferred return or should the whole partnership structure be adjusted? Ms. White needed to come up with something both partners would think was fair. By starting with an analysis of the whole investment, she hoped that it would lend credibility to her final recommendation.

Exhibit 1   ULI Shopping Center Classification

ULI SHOPPING CENTER CLASSIFICATION

TYPE	TYPICAL CONFIGURATION	ANCHOR TENANT	GENERAL RANGE GLA	MINIMUM POPULATION SUPPORT	RADIUS/ DRIVING TIME
Neighborhood Shopping Center		Supermarket	30,000 to 100,000 square feet	3,000 to 40,000	1.5 miles or a 5 to 10 minute drive
Community Shopping Center		Junior Department Store, Large Variety Store, Discount Department Store	100,000 to 300,000 square feet	40,000 to 150,000	3 to 5 miles or a 10 to 20 minute drive
Regional Shopping Center		One or Two Full-Line Department Stores	300,000 to 900,000 square feet	150,000 or more	8 miles or a 20 minute drive
Super Regional Shopping Center		Three or More Full-Line Department Stores	500,000 to 1.5 million square feet	250,000 or more	12 miles or a 30 minute drive

Exhibit 2   Map of Concord Center Trade Area

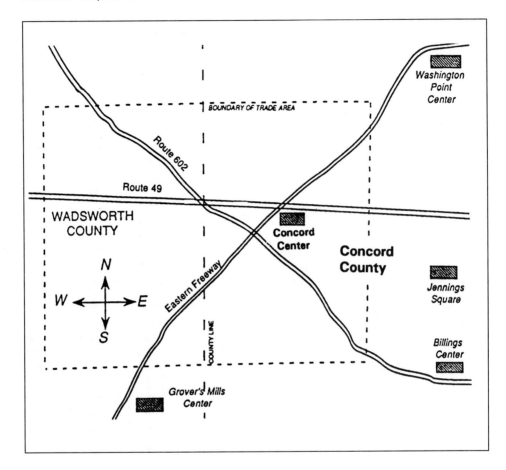

Exhibit 2   (continued)

Present Competitors to Concord Center

NAME	GLA	ANCHORS	SHOPS	NOTES:
Billings Center	1,000,000	Stern's JC Penney Orbach's Abraham and Strauss	235	Billings Center is approximately 17 miles southeast of Concord Center. It is a very successful and popular center. The area around this mall is very developed and traffic is very heavy. As a result of traffic congestion, people from the Billings area are not likely to go to Concord and people from west of Concord are not likely to go to Billings.
Jennings Park Mall	566,000	Alexander's Macy's	100	Jennings Park, which opened in 1970, is the oldest mall in the region. Because of its age and distance from Concord (15 miles), it will offer little or no competition.
Washington Point Centre	1,200,000	Stern's B. Altman Bloomingdales Bonwit Teller	165	Washington Point is approximately 17 miles northeast of Concord. It is a very upscale mall with high end anchors and many designer shops. This will prove to be a competitor to Concord in the northeast portion of the Concord trade area. However, given the lower prices offered in much of Concord (excluding the upscale first floor), Washington Point should not prove to be major competition.
Grover's Mill Center	1,121,000	Macy's JC Penney Steinbach's Sears	132	Grover's Mill serves the area south of Concord and may prove to be competition but should not severely impact sales for the new mall.

Exhibit 3

Demographic Information for Concord and Wadsworth Counties (1992 Estimates)

	WADSWORTH	CONCORD	THE STATE	THE REGION
Population (000)	90	111	7,827	38,038
Median Age	34.6	35.8	35.1	34.9
% Population by Age				
18–24	9.2	8.2	9.6	10.1
25–34	19.7	16.2	16.6	16.1
35–49	24.2	28.5	22.9	22.1
50+	24.9	23.1	27.4	27.9
Total EBI (000,000)(1)	$2,116	$2,914	$162,124	$662,349
Median Household EBI	$57,881	$64,788	$47,655	$37,541
% Households by EBI Group:				
10,000–19,999	5.1	5.5	10.4	14.2
20,000–34,999	13.2	10.9	17.0	21.2
35,000–49,999	18.0	13.7	17.6	18.4
50,000 +	60.0	66.6	47.3	35.0
Projections:				
Population:				
1992	90	111	7,827	38,038
1997	100	116	7,735	38,649
% Change	11.1%	4.5%	2.5%	1.6%
EBI (000,000):				
1992	$ 2,116	$ 2,914	$ 162,124	$ 662,349
1997	3,618	4,729	263,289	1,050,486
% Change	70.1%	62.3%	62.4%	58.6%
Median Household EBI:				
1993	$57,881	$64,788	$47,655	$37,541
1998	84,448	91,934	68,909	53,496
% Change	45.9%	41.9%	44.6%	42.5%

Excerpted by The RRG Group from : *Sales and Marketing Management, 1993 Survey of Buying Power.*
(1)EBI = Effective Buying Income.

Exhibit 3 (continued)

Employment Trends, Kenfield SMSA (1980–1990)

	1980		1990		1980–1990	
CATEGORY	#	%	#	%	#	%
Agricultural and Mining	1,200	0.14%	800	0.09%	(3.62%)	(4.96%)
Construction	35,600	4.17%	31,500	3.34%	(1.11%)	(1.98%)
Manufacturing	271,200	31.75%	244,700	25.95%	(0.93%)	(1.81%)
Transportation, Communication and Utilities	66,000	7.73%	73,800	7.83%	1.01%	0.12%
Wholesale and Retail Trade	166,000	19.43%	181,100	19.20%	0.79%	(0.10%)
F.I.R.E.	56,000	6.56%	65,000	6.89%	1.31%	0.42%
Services	144,000	16.86%	200,700	21.28%	3.04%	2.13%
Government	114,300	13.38%	145,400	15.42%	2.21%	1.31%
TOTAL/AVERAGE	854,300	100.00%	943,000	100.01%	0.89%	0.00%

Exhibit 4

Concord Center Development Budget

ITEM	AMOUNT
Land	$ 5,000,000
Construction Contracts*	79,364,000
Consultants	7,000,000
Legal	1,900,000
Insurance	100,000
Property Tax	3,000,000
Development Fee	2,000,000
Project Administration	2,000,000
Leasing Costs	5,896,000
Advertising and Promotion	540,000
Other Costs	2,900,000
Contingency	4,500,000
Financing @ 9%, plus 2 points	16,690,000**
Capitalized Operating Costs	2,110,000
TOTAL COSTS	$133,000,000

*Includes $20 million of off-site road work but does not include stores for Steinbach and Macy's.

**This includes interest payments on the construction loan during the period October 1, 1993–December 31, 1995, plus 75% of the annual interest payments during the initial year of leaseup, 1996.

Exhibit 5

Most Likely Scenario

	SQ. FT. (000)	RENT/SF
A&S	162	$ 6
Mall Shops	318	28
Cinema	31	16
Restaurant	15	20
Fast Food	6	70

($ in thousands)

	1996	1997	1998	1999	2000	2001	2002	2003	2004	2005
Income										
A&S	972	972	972	972	972	972	972	972	972	972
Mall Shops	6,233	8,904	9,260	9,631	10,016	10,416	10,833	11,266	11,717	12,186
Cinema	347	496	516	536	558	580	603	628	653	679
Restaurant	210	300	312	324	337	351	365	380	395	411
Fast Food	294	420	437	454	472	491	511	531	553	575
Percentage Rent	0	278	506	818	916	1,072	1,213	1,280	1,584	1,584
CAM Reimb.	2,001	3,558	3,808	4,149	4,404	4,675	4,964	5,269	5,594	5,939
Gross Income	10,057	14,928	15,811	16,885	17,676	18,558	19,462	20,326	21,467	22,345
(Vacancy)	0	(746)	791)	(844)	(884)	(928)	(973)	(1,016)	(1,073)	(1,117)
Net Income	10,057	14,182	15,020	16,041	16,792	17,630	18,488	19,310	20,394	21,228
Expenses										
(Common Area Maintenance)	(1,234)	(1,849)	(1,960)	(2,078)	(2,202)	(2,334)	(2,474)	(2,623)	(2,780)	(2,947)
(HVAC)	(849)	(733)	(777)	(824)	(873)	(925)	(981)	(1,040)	(1,102)	(1,168)
(Mgmt. Fee)	(252)	(436)	(462)	(490)	(519)	(550)	(583)	(618)	(656)	(695)
(RE Taxes)	(385)	(588)	(623)	(661)	(700)	(742)	(787)	(834)	(884)	(937)
(Other Expenses)	(191)	(282)	(293)	(305)	(317)	(330)	(323)	(357)	(371)	(386)
Total Expenses	(2,911)	(3,888)	(4,116)	(4,357)	(4,612)	(4,882)	(5,168)	(5,472)	(5,793)	(6,133)
NOI	7,146	10,294	10,905	11,683	12,180	12,748	13,320	13,838	14,601	15,094

Assumptions:

1. Minimum rents increase at 4% per year.

2. Percentage rents are tied to projected sales growth and lease structures.

3. CAM Reimbursements: Mall tenants contribute their pro rate share of total expenses. Those contributions are calculated based on 370,000 SF of mall GLA. In addition, Macy's and Steinbachs will contribute a total of approximately $310,000 per year toward expenses and A and S will contribute $150,000 per year through 1997. After that, their reimbursements will increase proportionally based on increases in operating expenses. CAM Reimbursements include taxes and insurance, common area maintenance, HVAC, real estate taxes and other operating expenses.

4. Operating expenses are projected to increase by 6% per year, beginning in 1997.

Exhibit 6 Excerpts from the Revised Redevelopment Agreement

I. Parties
The Parties to the Redevelopment Agreement are the Township of Bismuth Redevelopment Agency ("Agency") and the Sturgess Group ("Developer").

II. Land Purchase
The developer purchases approximately 70 acres of land comprising the Site from the Agency for a sum of $5,000,000 subject to: (i) sewer, drainage, water, and utility easements shown in the Township Redevelopment Plan, (ii) applicable building and zoning laws, (iii) this Agreement.

III. Improvements
The Developer shall construct substantial off-site improvements generally consisting of road widening, on ramps, off ramps, ramp connections, signals and other traffic improvements and access routes to the Project more specifically described in a separate agreement entitled "Off-Site Improvements Agreement."

The Developer shall also construct (i) a regional shopping center of up to 900,000 retail square feet with not more than three major department stores, and (ii) other on-site improvements. Subject to certain approved delays, the Developer must (i) commence construction of the shopping center and other improvements by September 1993 and (ii) substantially complete construction of all improvements by January 1996.

Parking
The Developer shall maintain a parking ratio of 4.5 to 5.0 spaces per 1,000 square feet of retail area for the shopping center. No less than 30% of such parking shall be in parking structures (including the ground floor).

IV. Letter of Credit
The Developer has delivered a Letter of Credit in the amount of $1,500,000 to the Agency to secure the Developer's performance under the Redevelopment Agreement. Upon the issuance of the certificate of completion, the Agency shall return the letter of credit.

V. Equity Maintenance
The Developer shall maintain at least $10 million in equity in the Project until it has received a certificate of completion.

VI. Evidence of Financing
Promptly after the Agency approves the final site and construction plans for the Improvements, the Developer must submit to the Agency reasonable evidence of financing commitments or internal funding sources necessary for the construction of such improvements.

VII. Limitation of Encumbrances
The Developer may not encumber the Site to secure financing for costs other than (i) hard and soft costs for off-site and on-site improvements, (ii) the Land Purchase and Additional Consideration.

VIII. Transfer
Prior to the issuance of the final certificate of completion, the Developer may not, without the Agency's consent, transfer the site to a Partnership or joint venture except for a partnership or joint venture which will include the Developer (as managing general partner) and the Galactic Insurance Company.

Exhibit 7   TNT Bank Guidelines for Evaluation

Construction Loans for Super-Regional Shopping Centers (Excerpts)

I. Observations

TNT will only finance regional shopping centers developed by Tier I developers. Tier I developers are defined by the following four variables:

Net Worth:	$100MM
Cash Flow:	$10MM per annum
Minimum Square Feet Developed:	10,000,000
Minimum Square Feet Owned:	5,000,000
Years in Business:	10

As the industry becomes more and more competitive, retail markets are, in effect, becoming "mature." It is necessary to focus on the importance of generating a mass of buyers to support the project.

II. Quantitative Criteria

- Sponsor must meet minimum requirements as outlined in Section I.
- Financial requirements of project must be in proportion to sponsor's net worth.
- Stabilized free and clear cash flow should be a minimum of 1.2 times the then-prevailing market constant on permanent debt (currently assumed to be 9%, 30-year amort., 9.73% constant).

III. Loan Structure

- Maximum Term: 5 years (interest only).
- Security: First Mortgage on project.
- 75% maximum loan to appraised value.[3]
- Anchor Tenants must be secured.
- Completion guarantee is required. Principal repayment guarantee is required as appropriate to the transaction and equity invested. Operating deficit and debt service guarantees are required until agreed upon stabilization.

[3]In 1993 high quality super-regional shopping centers were selling at cap rates ranging from 6–8%. For this case you can assume that Concord Center would be valued at 7.5%.

Exhibit 8

The Top Ten Shopping Center Developers in the United States: 1992

NAME	TOTAL GLA
1. The Edward J. Debartolo Corp.	71,279,755
2. Equitable Real Estate Investment Management	67,975,295
3. Melvin Simon and Associates	63,015,042
4. JMB Retail Properties	61,314,754
5. The Rouse Company	45,148,000
6. The Richard and David Jacobs Group	40,121,775
7. The Prudential Realty Group	38,040,000
8. The Hahn Company	34,926,000
9. The Cafaro Company	34,543,406
10. Crown American Corporation	30,887,645

Source: *Shopping Center World*, January 1993.

16

GROSVENOR PARK

In September 1988, Dick Dubin is attempting to gain final approval for a 189 unit single family home subdivision in Bethesda, Maryland targeted to young, upwardly mobile professionals working in the Washington, D.C. area. The case spans the project life cycle from predevelopment to sellout, and addresses issues ranging from land acquisition, construction phasing, finance, design, and marketing, to managing a critical relationship with a powerful local planning board.

Discussion Questions:

1. Evaluate Dubin's performance to date. What are the risks he faces in this project? How has he managed those risks to date? What should he do going forward?
2. Assess the demands of the Planning Department. Are they reasonable? What would you do if you were Dubin?
3. Would Grosvenor Park appeal to you as a place to live? As an investment vehicle?
4. How does the development of single family homes differ from development of multi-family homes?

Dick Dubin loosened his tie and sank exhausted onto the sofa. On this September night in 1988 he was frustrated by yet another negotiation with the Montgomery County Planning Department (PD) over his Grosvenor Park project, a 189 unit single family subdivision in Bethesda, Maryland. The latest demand on the long list of PD requirements was a cool $1 million worth of road improvements. This amount, added to PD demands totaling $2.6 million for developer contributions toward schools, sewers and mitigation of sound pollution made Dubin decide to reexamine some of the assumptions he had made about the best way to go forward with the project. These demands were on top of requirements in Montgomery County which mandated that fifteen percent of the project, 28 units, had to be included at affordable rates to median income families.

The developer had to make some choices soon because he was scheduled to make his financing commitments in one week. He had planned to open model units while construction was underway and offer all 189 units in the same phase, completing the entire project within three and a half years. Dubin's original strategy had been to price the units slightly below market at prices calculated to ensure a quick sellout. The expense of the PD demands, however, tempted him to consider increasing the price of the market rate units to cover fully the additional expenses, raising them slightly above market. Should he fight the PD and delay construction, or should he give in and fold the additional costs into his sales price? How would the bank view the increased uncertainty in the sell-out period caused by increasing sales prices?

THE DEVELOPER

Dick Dubin began his development career soon after graduating from Boston University. After a brief but memorable interlude as a croupier in Las Vegas, Dubin relocated to Maryland and successfully developed over 4,000 residential units, both sales and rental. Over the course of his 20-year career in the Maryland area, he built a variety of residential products ranging from subsidized housing for the elderly to moderate income housing to market rate luxury townhouses.

In 1985, Dubin completed Grosvenor Tower, a highly successful luxury high rise featuring 190 two bedroom units. Grosvenor Tower was located two blocks

---

Research Assistant Katherine Sweetman prepared this case under the supervision of Adjunct Professor William J. Poorvu as the basis for class discussion rather than to illustrate either effective or ineffective handling of an administrative situation.

from the Grosvenor Park site. The high rise tower rented rapidly and had enjoyed a 98 percent occupancy rate since opening. Dubin attributed the success of the project to its quality and its ability to meet the needs of its tenants. Seventy percent of its tenants were young professional couples who worked in downtown Washington and who took advantage of the building's location near the Metro, Washington's subway system. The remaining thirty percent were mostly single professionals, primarily working downtown, either living alone or sharing apartments. Shopping malls and entertainment were becoming increasingly available along the rapidly developing Route 270 corridor, a short drive away. The building had health club facilities which enabled the tenants to meet each other and encouraged a collegial atmosphere. Rents for the two-bedroom, 1,000 square foot apartments averaged $950 per month in 1988 and had increased at an average rate of 5 percent per year since the building opened. Dubin knew from the financial data that his tenants had supplied on their rental applications that many of the households grossed about $100,000 in pre-tax income per year. He also knew from chatting with them that they liked the area and would eventually like to own homes there. The general feeling was that they would like to buy but were in no rush because they felt that their "dream homes" were still out of reach financially. Many of them had in mind homes in sections of Montgomery County which sold for over $400,000.

Dubin felt that he could profitably apply his local experience to market Grosvenor Park to these young professionals as a bridge home priced between the apartment and the "dream house." While the Grosvenor Park site was in a pioneering location for this concept since the immediate neighborhood had been characterized by moderately priced garden apartments for decades, Dubin felt that the success of his rental building indicated that conditions were right for him to take the chance. Dubin would act as land speculator, zoning negotiator, land developer and builder.

SINGLE FAMILY HOUSING

By 1987, 40 percent of America from Maine to California lived in the suburbs. Post World War II economic and population booms rapidly increased the pace of development begun earlier in the century and encouraged wholesale development of large tracts of land in many parts of the country. Sometimes the houses were very similar; sometimes they simply adhered to building and design restrictions; sometimes the purchaser had total freedom over the design of his or her home. By 1987, fully ten percent of all Americans lived in planned suburban communities which were often the product of such large-scale development.

In the late 1980s, most young people were unable to afford a single family home due to rapidly escalating land prices. This economic reality led to a new suburban art of high density planning, where issues of topography (such as slope and drainage) were carefully married to market needs in terms of lot size, building size and landscaping. In the past, suburban planners fit 7 to 8 units per acre; however, with innovative cluster and parking plans, developers were now squeezing 10 to 12 units per acre.

THE OPPORTUNITY

The Grosvenor Park site was located in Bethesda, Maryland, a community of 80,000. Having served as a bedroom community to Washington, D.C. for most of its history, (see **Exhibit 1**). Bethesda was newly emerging as a city in its own right. The site was well-located in terms of transportation, with quick access to Interstate 270 and sited across the highway from the newest stop on the Washington, D.C. Metro. The stop was a 17 minute ride from DuPont Circle in the heart of Washington's business district. The surrounding neighborhood was characterized by middle class garden apartment complexes developed during the 1960's and 1970's (see **Exhibit 2**). The only exception to this was Dubin's own Grosvenor Tower development.

The 25 acre property in question had been on the market for years at the prevailing rate for garden apartments. Under its R–30 zoning, the site could legally support 426 garden apartments. When Dubin first investigated the site in mid-1987, the owner was asking about $12,700 per zoned unit, or $5,400,000. The property remained unsold because the number of garden apartment units legally permissible could not physically be accommodated on the site. Located at the bottom of a hill, parts of the property collected runoff from the land "upstream." Legally, the wetlands portion of the property could not be developed, though development rights could be transferred to the dry portions of the parcel. In the case of high density garden apartment development, this would have necessitated building underground rather than surface parking, an expensive proposition.

Dubin saw a better use for the land. His unscientific market survey within Grosvenor Towers fueled his hunch that the time was right for single family homes in that area. With 189 single family homes, the unit density would be greatly diminished, but the unit value greatly enhanced. While a 1,000 square foot two-bedroom garden apartment would rent for $950 per month, a new 2,300 square foot two-bedroom plus convertible study would sell for $250,000. With only 189 units, inexpensive surface parking could easily fit the grounds. The wetlands could be incorporated into the landscaping designs (see **Exhibit 3**).

Dubin also took into account that 15 percent of all new construction in Montgomery County must be available to moderate income groups in the form of MPDU's—Moderate Price Dwelling Units. In the case of Grosvenor Park, this translated to 28 units to be sold at an average price of $85,000 each. These units had to be comparable to the market rate units in size, configuration and quality.

With the single family plan in mind, Dubin paid the asking price for the site. A local S&L, the Bethesda Federal Savings and Loan, supplied $7,200,000 for the land portion of the project, based on an appraisal valuing the parcel at $8,600,000, or $45,500 per single family home. The $1.8 million differential between the purchase price and the loan based on the single family valuation would be advanced for related project costs and gave Dubin a comfortable sum to begin his planning. Dubin gave a personal guarantee for the portion of the loan above the land cost.

THE INITIAL PROCESS

Dubin planned to position Grosvenor Park as an opportunity for young couples to live in a compatible community, enjoy comfortable homes, and build equity toward their dream houses in a residential market currently appreciating at a rate of about ten percent annually. He would offer two designs, a Cape Cod and a brick colonial, each selling for an average price of $250,000 and each containing 2,300 square feet (see **Exhibit 4**). Owners could park their cars in the private road in front of their homes. While Dubin did not plan to provide any health club facilities or community amenities of that nature, such facilities were easily available along Route 270.

Dubin would market all the sites during the construction period through the use of models and floor plans. To lower his risk, he would have only six homes in inventory at a time. All other construction would start once a binding contract was signed with a 10% nonrefundable deposit. Dubin would contract to deliver the home six months from the signing of the contract. He figured that the development would take three and a half years to fully build out, and expected that he could have sales contracts for all units within that period. The buyer would select the model and site, and would choose among a variety of options including skylights, customized kitchens and lofts. Purchasers would pay premiums of up to $20,000 for locations with attractive views.

Dubin planned to design a Homeowners' Association similar to those in his other developments which would administer care of the common areas, including the grounds. The Association would be entirely the responsibility of the homeowners once 80% of the units had sold.

AFFORDABILITY

Dubin recognized that a key success factor for this development would be affordability to its target audience. Dubin ran some rough numbers to see if the young couples of Grosvenor Tower could afford new single family homes. In addition to the sales price, Dubin estimated that other costs of ownership including utilities, maintenance, homeowners' assessment and other fees would total about $4,400 annually and increase at about 5% per year. Property insurance would be about $1,500 per year and increase at 5% per year. In addition, property taxes would be 1.25% of the sales price. Closing costs upon purchase would be around $5,000.

Dubin also made assumptions based on his knowledge of the requirements banks would place upon purchasers. Most area banks originated their own loans, then sold them in the secondary mortgage markets in bundles. In order for a bank to sell a mortgage, the mortgage had to meet the following strict FNMA underwriting guidelines:

1. A buyer putting less than 20% down must buy mortgage insurance at an extra cost at closing.
2. Monthly principal, interest, real estate taxes and mortgage insurance payments (PITI) cannot exceed 28% of the purchaser's gross monthly pre-tax income.
3. Monthly payments for total long term indebtedness (greater than 10 months left to pay) cannot exceed 36% of the purchaser's gross monthly pre-tax income.

Although not part of the above calculation, payments of interest and real estate taxes were deductible by the buyer for income tax purposes.

HOME MORTGAGE INTEREST RATES

A major factor in affordability is the cost of funds to the purchaser. A favorable mortgage finance climate contributed greatly to Montgomery County's active residential real estate market in 1986. The fixed interest rate for conventional mortgages fell below nine percent by Christmas of 1986. Low mortgage rates began to creep up by the spring of 1987, due to a combination of factors. These factors included a weakening U.S. dollar overseas, balance of trade difficulties, soaring national debt, and increased need for federal borrowing. By September 1987, area home mortgage interest rates had risen to 11 percent and were expected to continue to climb. The Federal Reserve Bank's response to the stock market shock in October of 1987—to increase the money supply—led to a decrease in interest rates by November. By Christmas of 1987, conventional fixed rate mortgages had stabilized around 10.5 to 11.0 percent. Residential mortgage rates in August of 1988 hovered around 10.5 percent in the Washington, D.C. mortgage market. By September, there were as many predictions regarding the future of interest rates as there were experts.

THE MARKET

From 1970 to 1987, the suburban Maryland area of Washington experienced tremendous population growth. This growth was attributable to several factors, including the continued expansion of government facilities into Montgomery County, expanding job markets in the private sector, immigration of new residents attracted by new employment opportunities in Montgomery County, the exodus of former downtown city residents to the more spacious suburbs and the lower crime rate in the suburbs. In the 1970s, the County experienced an annual growth rate of 7,000 jobs. By contrast, annual job growth from March, 1984 to March, 1985 was 25,000; job growth from March, 1985 to March, 1986 was 23,000. Thirty-nine percent of the job growth was in the service sector.

The trends are expected to continue upward, as seen in the table below:

Montgomery County Long Range Forecasts "Most Probable" Scenario
As of March 1987

	1980	1987	1990	2000
Population	579,000	669,000	710,000	785,000
Households	206,793	256,400	278,000	333,000
Employment	304,600	405,000	455,000	575,000

Source: Montgomery County Planning Board, Research Division.

According to the 1984 Census, the latest Census available to Dubin at the time of his decision, the population was segmented as outlined below:

Montgomery County, Maryland 1984 Census Update

1984	HIGH RISE	GARDEN APT.	TOWNHOUSE	SINGLE FAMILY DETACHED	ALL TYPES
No. Households (HH)	26,223	43,959	25,246	133,008	228,436
HH Population	41,640	86,945	68,071	407,344	604,000
Average HH Size	1.59	1.98	2.70	3.06	2.64
Age 0–4 yrs.	1,256	5,832	7,763	23,813	38,664
Age 5–17 yrs.	2,366	10,097	12,014	83,106	107,583
Average Age HH Head	53	41	40	50	48
Average Yrs. in Same House	5.6	4.1	4.4	13.0	9.5
% with Grad. Degree	20.8	14.7	20.1	24.9	22.6
1983 Median HH Income	$24,705	$22,806	$37,772	$49,823	$39,154
Female Workforce Participation (%)	52.3	71.7	70.5	57.5	60.7
Work Location:					
Inside Belt	28.2	22.7	17.2	21.2	21.5
Outside Belt	20.6	40.4	50.4	38.6	39.1
to D.C.	37.9	22.6	18.2	25.2	24.8

Source: Montgomery County Planning Board, Research Division.

RESIDENTIAL ACTIVITY

Since the 1984 Census Update summarized above, the single family housing market continued to grow. Montgomery County experienced completion of 4,125 new single family units in 1985 and 5,175 new single family new housing units in 1986, the highest annual production since 1960. In 1988, the county was experiencing monthly sales of 1,200 units. Virtually all homes offered on the market sold in a reasonable period of time.

Homes also continued to increase in value. The average resale price for a market rate single family home in Montgomery County in 1988 was $214,500. The average price for newly built single family homes was $240,000. Single family housing prices had been rising at a rate of eight to ten percent each year. The Potomac section was the wealthiest section of the county with homes ranging from $400,000 to several million dollars.

Dubin used the following chart compiled by a local real estate research firm as another indicator that housing activity was healthy. No data was available which directly addressed the specific profile of his targeted purchasers.

Montgomery County Housing Market Profile
Sales of Market Rate Single Family Homes First Six Months 1988

PRICE RANGE	NUMBER OF UNITS SOLD	NUMBER OF MO. ON MKT.	ORIGIN OF PURCHASER		
			MONT. CO.	DC	OTHER
$159–$199,000	1,440	2.6	50%	10%	40%
$200–$249,000	2,376	2.5	48%	11%	41%
$250–$299,000	1,944	3.1	52%	12%	36%
$300–$349,000	576	7.1	46%	12%	42%
$350–$449,000	474	8.2	53%	14%	33%
$450–$599,000	360	8.3	47%	11%	42%
$600–$999,000	23	9.0	55%	15%	30%
$1,000,000 plus	7	9.0	15%	30%	55%

INFRASTRUCTURE

The extension and completion of new road systems including the Capital Beltway, Interstate 66 on the Virginia side, Interstate 95, the continuing development of research and development firms along the Route 270 corridor and the construction of a subway system servicing metropolitan D.C. and its suburbs have contributed to the continuing growth of Maryland counties near D.C. Montgomery County's two major residential growth areas are the I–270 and US 29 corridors. Combined, the two growth corridors have, in years preceding 1987, accounted for nearly two-thirds of total housing completions in Montgomery County. Dubin felt that the location of Grosvenor Park near Route 270 was prime.

MONTGOMERY COUNTY DEPARTMENT OF PARKS AND PLANNING

As Dubin moved forward with his plans, he encountered some difficulties with the planning department (PD) regarding his Subdivision Plan. The PD controlled all zoning issues, including the variances which Dubin would require to develop single-family homes on a parcel zoned for multifamily units. The PD was known to be a conservative body, dedicated to protecting the existing community and the environment. The Planning Commission of the PD consisted of six board members (three elected and three appointed), whose backgrounds ranged from architecture to law, business, and academics. The Commission had made several demands on Dubin:

1. The PD claimed that the location of the site next to the Beltway resulted in noise pollution which would impair the quality of life of future residents in the development. The PD insisted that noise barriers be erected at a cost of $600,000 to protect future residents.

2. The PD cited the Adequate Public Facilities Ordinance of Montgomery County to show that Grosvenor Townhouses would adversely affect the schools by bringing more children into the system. Dubin was convinced that the demographic profile of his targeted purchasers meant that they would add very few, if any, children to the school system. He felt that the purchasers would wait to have their children until they were more settled. How could he convince the PD that their concerns were unfounded? If he could not prove his case, he could be assessed $750,000 for the Montgomery County School Superfund or be refused a building permit.

3. The PD insisted that Grosvenor Park enlarge the storm water drainage system to accommodate the entire neighborhood. The PD feared that Grosvenor Park's upstream residential neighborhoods might not be handling their drainage well and that Grosvenor Park might find itself flooded by their drain water. The PD wanted Dubin to construct a sediment pond to collect any drainage, settle out the pollutants and, in effect, recycle the water portion of the drainage. Dubin would also be required to maintain the sediment pond ad infinitum. The cost to construct the system would be $1.2 million, and Dubin's soil engineers calculated that annual maintenance costs would approach $50,000. Dubin's soil engineers had also surveyed the upstream neighbors and were satisfied that the PD's fears were unfounded.

The most recent demand was traffic-related. Under a Road Adequacies Provision of the Montgomery County Growth Plan, the PD argued that Dubin should widen 3,500 feet of road providing access to the site, including installing new storm drains for the full two-thirds of a mile, at a cost of $1 million. Dubin's traffic consultants argued back that all that was needed to avoid traffic snarls was a 400 foot deceleration lane at a cost to the developer of $80,000. Dubin felt that this was a disagreement that he could probably win.

FINANCING

Dubin had based his finance negotiations on the numbers he had developed in **Exhibit 5** (the costs in **Exhibit 5** do not reflect the final $1 million demand of the PD). Dubin and the S&L had agreed upon a joint venture for financing Grosvenor Park: a non-recourse loan with no origination fee at prime plus one based on New York bank rates, with the S&L also receiving one quarter of the profit after the repayment of the loan. The bank would lend up to $9 million. If costs in any quarter exceeded $9 million, Dubin would have to make up the difference out of his own pocket.

As a marketing tool, Dubin negotiated to protect the ultimate purchaser from fluctuations in the mortgage market. Dubin locked in Bethesda S&L's promise to provide 30-year mortgages for qualified purchasers with the rate fixed at 10 percent for the first three years of the mortgage or 10.53% constant plus a fee of 1.5 points payable by the purchaser at closing. The maximum interest rate over the term would be adjusted up or down but not exceed 14 percent. Those purchasers who put less than 20% down would require mortgage insurance at a cost of 4% of the amount borrowed, payment of which would be spread out and payable monthly over the 30-year term of the loan. There would be an additional 1% fee at closing. This package would be available during the first year of the home sales.

THE DECISION

Dubin realized that he had better develop spread sheets for the project, extending the sell-out rate to four years to help figure out the consequences of a slower sales rate (see **Exhibit 6**). When should the affordable housing portion be built? Is his pricing appropriate for selling the units? Despite all the work and money that has gone into this project to date, if he cannot compromise with the PD, should he call off the whole project? In that regard, how should he approach the PD?

Exhibit 1 Area Map

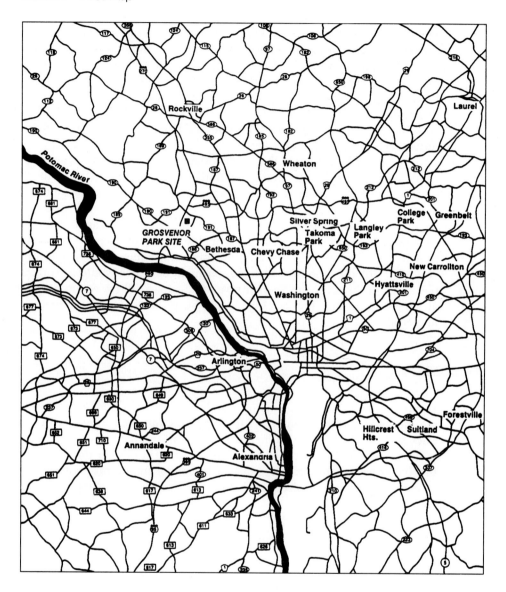

Exhibit 2   Neighborhood Map

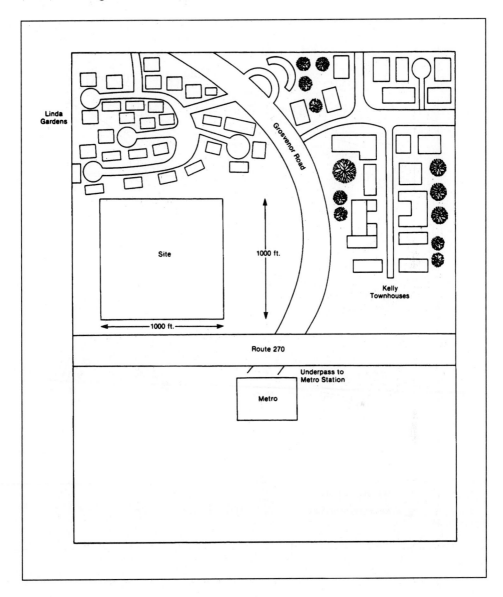

Exhibit 3   Site Plan (as proposed initially)

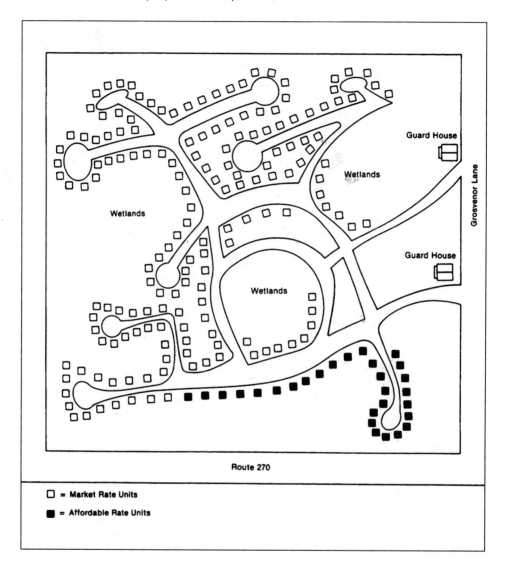

Exhibit 4 Devonshire

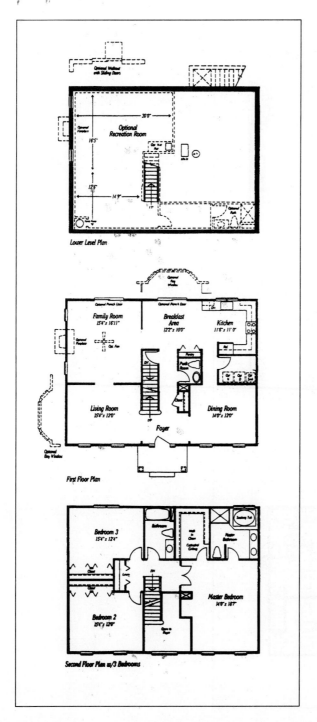

Exhibit 4 (continued) Andover

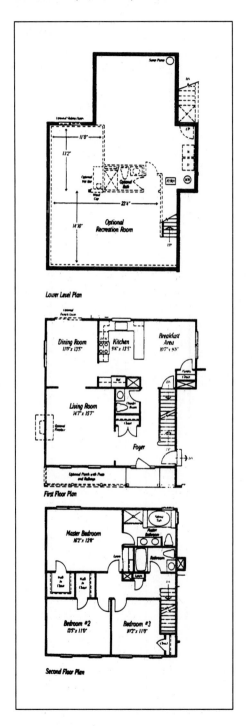

Exhibit 5

	Quarter 1	Quarter 2	Quarter 3	Quarter 4	Quarter 5	Quarter 6	Quarter 7	Quarter 8	Quarter 9	Quarter 10	Quarter 11	Quarter 12	Quarter 13	Total
Quarterly construction starts	0	15	15	15	15	15	15	15	15	15	15	11	0	161
Cumulative starts	0	15	30	45	60	75	90	105	120	135	150	161	161	161
Quarterly sales	0	15	15	15	15	15	15	15	15	15	15	11	0	161
Cumulative sales	0	15	30	45	60	75	90	105	120	135	150	161	161	161
Quarterly settlements	0	0	10	15	15	15	15	15	15	15	15	15	16	161
Cumulative settlements	0	0	10	25	40	55	70	85	100	115	130	145	161	161
NET RECEIPTS & REVENUES			2,500,000	3,750,000	3,750,000	3,750,000	3,750,000	3,750,000	3,750,000	3,750,000	3,750,000	3,750,000	4,000,000	40,250,000
PROJECT COSTS:														
Land acquisition	5,313,000													5,313,000
Land development/approvals		2,012,500				2,012,500								4,025,000
Direct construction		800,626	1,601,250	1,601,250	1,601,250	1,601,250	1,601,250	1,601,250	1,601,250	1,601,250	1,601,250	1,494,500	480,376	17,186,752
Onsite OH/indirect construction		75,000	75,000	75,000	75,000	75,000	75,000	75,000	75,000	75,000	75,000	55,000		805,000
Subtotal	5,313,000	2,888,126	1,676,250	1,676,250	1,676,250	3,688,750	1,676,250	1,676,250	1,676,250	1,676,250	1,676,250	1,549,500	480,376	27,329,752
Acquisition & Dev. loan interest		109,875	172,349	170,879	142,322	112,800	121,677	91,459	60,221	27,929				1,009,512
Construction loan interest		79,564	124,805	123,740	103,060	81,683	88,111	66,229	43,608	20,224				731,026
Subtotal		189,439	297,154	294,620	245,382	194,483	209,788	157,688	103,830	48,153				1,740,537
Marketing, media, and models		54,000	54,000	54,000	54,000	54,000	54,000	54,000	54,000	54,000	54,000	39,600		579,600
Commissions			50,000	75,000	75,000	75,000	75,000	75,000	75,000	75,000	75,000	75,000	80,000	805,000
Other closing costs			50,000	75,000	75,000	75,000	75,000	75,000	75,000	75,000	75,000	75,000	80,000	805,000
Subtotal		54,000	154,000	204,000	204,000	204,000	204,000	204,000	204,000	204,000	204,000	189,600	160,000	2,189,600
General Admin. / Offsite OH	300,000	60,000	60,000	60,000	60,000	60,000	60,000	60,000	60,000	60,000	60,000	60,000		960,000
Contingency			37,500	56,250	56,250	56,250	56,250	56,250	56,250	56,250	56,250	56,250	59,000	602,750
Subtotal	300,000	60,000	97,500	116,250	116,250	116,250	116,250	116,250	116,250	116,250	116,250	116,250	59,000	1,562,750
TOTAL PROJECT COSTS	5,613,000	3,191,565	2,224,904	2,291,120	2,241,882	4,203,483	2,206,288	2,154,188	2,100,330	2,044,653	1,996,500	1,855,350	699,376	32,822,639
NET CASH FROM OPERATIONS	(5,613,000)	(3,191,565)	275,096	1,458,880	1,508,118	(453,483)	1,543,712	1,595,812	1,649,670	1,705,347	1,753,500	1,894,650	3,300,624	7,427,361
Working capital reserves			(200,000)										200,000	0
Net loans received/(repaid)	5,613,000	3,191,565	(75,096)	(1,458,880)	(1,508,118)	453,483	(1,543,712)	(1,595,812)	(1,649,670)	(1,426,760)				0
NET DISTRIBUTABLE CASH	0	0	0	0	0	0	0	0	0	278,587	1,753,500	1,894,650	3,500,624	7,427,361
Developer's distribution										208,940	1,315,125	1,420,988	2,625,468	5,570,520
Lender's distribution										69,647	438,375	473,663	875,156	1,856,840
Cumulative loans outstanding	5,613,000	8,804,565	8,729,469	7,270,588	5,762,471	6,215,954	4,672,243	3,076,431	1,426,760	0	0	0	0	0

Note: In addition, 28 units of affordable housing had to be built. The fixed additional cost of each of these units was $150,000 resulting in a loss of $65,000 per unit or $1,720,000 in total. The impact of these units are not shown above.

Exhibit 6

	Quarter 1	Quarter 2	Quarter 3	Quarter 4	Quarter 5	Quarter 6	Quarter 7	Quarter 8	Quarter 9	Quarter 10	Quarter 11	Quarter 12	Quarter 13	Quarter 14	Quarter 15	Quarter 16	Total
Quarterly construction starts	0	12	12	12	12	12	12	12	12	12	12	12	12	12	5	0	161
Cumulative starts	0	12	24	36	48	60	72	84	96	108	120	132	144	156	161	161	161
Quarterly sales	0	8	12	12	12	12	12	12	12	12	12	12	12	12	9	0	161
Cumulative sales	0	8	20	32	44	56	68	80	92	104	116	128	140	152	161	161	161
Quarterly settlements	0	0	8	12	12	12	12	12	12	12	12	12	12	12	12	9	161
Cumulative settlements	0	0	8	20	32	44	56	68	80	92	104	116	128	140	152	161	161
NET RECEIPTS & REVENUES	0	0	2,000,000	3,000,000	3,000,000	3,000,000	3,000,000	3,000,000	3,000,000	3,000,000	3,000,000	3,000,000	3,000,000	3,000,000	3,000,000	2,250,000	40,250,000
PROJECT COSTS:																	
Land acquisition	5,313,000																5,313,000
Land development/approvals		2,012,500			2,012,500												4,025,000
Direct construction		640,500	1,281,000	1,281,000	1,281,000	1,281,000	1,281,000	1,281,000	1,281,000	1,281,000	1,281,000	1,281,000	1,281,000	1,281,000	1,281,000		17,186,752
Onsite OH/Ind/direct constr.		75,000	75,000	75,000	75,000	75,000	75,000	75,000	75,000	75,000	75,000	75,000	75,000	75,000	75,000		1,085,000
Subtotal	5,313,000	2,728,000	1,356,000	1,356,000	3,368,500	1,356,000	1,356,000	1,356,000	1,356,000	1,356,000	1,356,000	1,356,000	1,356,000	1,356,000	1,356,000		27,609,752
Acq. & Dev. loan interest		109,874	169,215	170,766	149,908	128,345	145,449	123,736	101,290	78,087	54,100	29,304	3,671				1,263,746
Construction loan interest		79,564	122,535	123,658	108,554	92,939	105,325	89,602	73,348	56,546	39,176	21,220	2,658				915,127
Subtotal		189,438	291,750	294,424	258,461	221,284	250,874	213,338	174,638	134,633	93,276	50,524	6,339				2,178,873
Marketing, media, & models		54,000	54,000	54,000	54,000	54,000	54,000	54,000	54,000	54,000	54,000	54,000	54,000	54,000	39,600		741,600
Commissions			40,000	60,000	60,000	60,000	60,000	60,000	60,000	60,000	60,000	60,000	60,000	60,000	60,000	45,000	805,000
Other closing costs			40,000	60,000	60,000	60,000	60,000	60,000	60,000	60,000	60,000	60,000	60,000	60,000	60,000	45,000	805,000
Subtotal		54,000	134,000	174,000	174,000	174,000	174,000	174,000	174,000	174,000	174,000	174,000	174,000	174,000	159,600	90,000	2,351,600
General Admin. /Offsite OH	300,000	60,000	60,000	60,000	60,000	60,000	60,000	60,000	60,000	60,000	60,000	60,000	60,000	60,000	60,000	6,000	1,146,000
Contingency	0	0	37,500	50,000	50,000	50,000	50,000	50,000	50,000	50,000	50,000	50,000	50,000	50,000	50,000	3,750	641,250
Subtotal	300,000	60,000	97,500	110,000	110,000	110,000	110,000	110,000	110,000	110,000	110,000	110,000	110,000	110,000	110,000	9,750	1,787,250
TOTAL PROJECT COSTS	5,613,000	3,031,439	1,879,250	1,934,424	3,873,784	1,890,775	1,853,338	1,853,338	1,814,638	1,774,632	1,733,276	1,690,524	1,646,330	1,640,000	1,003,920	649,682	33,927,475
NET CASH FROM OPERATIONS	(5,613,000)	(3,031,439)	120,750	1,065,576	(873,784)	1,109,225	1,146,662	1,146,662	1,185,362	1,225,368	1,266,724	1,309,476	1,353,670	1,360,000	1,996,080	1,600,318	6,322,525
Working capital reserves	0	(200,000)	0	0	0	0	0	0	0	0	0	0	0	0	0	200,000	0
Net loans received/(repaid)	5,613,000	3,031,439	(79,250)	(1,065,576)	873,784	(1,109,225)	(1,146,662)	(1,146,662)	(1,185,362)	(1,225,368)	(1,266,724)	(1,309,476)	(187,543)	0	0	0	0
NET DISTRIBUTABLE CASH	0	0	0	0	0	0	0	0	0	0	0	0	1,166,127	1,360,000	1,996,080	1,800,318	6,322,525
Developer's distribution	0	0	0	0	0	0	0	0	0	0	0	0	874,595	1,020,000	1,497,060	1,350,239	4,741,894
Lender's distribution	0	0	0	0	0	0	0	0	0	0	0	0	291,532	340,000	499,020	450,080	1,580,631
Cumulative loans outstanding	5,613,000	8,644,439	8,723,113	7,658,113	7,430,359	6,321,133	5,174,472	3,989,110	2,763,742	1,497,019	0	0	0	0	0	0	0

Note: In addition, 28 units of affordable housing had to be built. The fixed additional cost of each of these units was $65,000 per unit or $1,720,000 in total, resulting in a loss of $150,000. The impact of these units are not shown above.

17

PETERBOROUGH COURT

In May 1988, Sheridan Schechner reviewed his notes once more. He was scheduled to appear before the Management Committee with an update on the development of Goldman Sachs' proposed corporate headquarters in London. The decision to construct a new London facility would represent the largest single commitment of capital the firm had ever made. Both his career and the profitability of the firm would be dramatically affected by the success or failure of this project. In the context of the development practice in U.K., he had to recommend whether Goldman should be pro-active in managing the details of the process.

Discussion Questions:

1. Should Goldman develop Peterborough Court? Explain the reasons for your recommendation.
2. How would you answer the development issues raised in the case?
3. What are the implications of the various occupancy alternatives for the firm?
4. In what ways do development practices in England differ from those in the U.S.?

In May 1988, Sheridan Schechner reviewed his notes once more. He was scheduled to appear before the Management Committee with an update on the development of Goldman Sachs' proposed corporate headquarters in London. His team had made enormous progress since he began exploring the consolidation of the firm's disparate European offices under one roof in 1986. However, the decision to construct a new London facility would represent the largest single commitment of capital the firm had ever made. Both his career and the profitability of the firm could be dramatically affected by the success or failure of this project.

GOLDMAN SACHS—THE FIRM

Goldman Sachs is a leading, full-service international investment banking and securities firm serving corporations, institutions, governments and individuals worldwide. Founded in 1869, it is one of the oldest, largest and most strongly capitalized firms in the industry and the only private partnership among the major Wall Street organizations. The firm has approximately 7,000 employees located in offices throughout the U.S. and in Canada, London, Hong Kong, Madrid, Paris, Singapore, Sydney, Tokyo, Zurich and Frankfurt.

London serves as the Firm's European headquarters, where key operating units include the Investment Banking Division, the Fixed Income Division, the Equity Trading and Arbitrage Division, the Securities Sales Division, and the Currency and Commodity Division.

LONDON 1986

In early 1986, Schechner ("Shecky") had been asked to review the firm's space needs in the city of London, and to analyze whether it made sense for Goldman Sachs to consolidate its London and/or European operations into a single headquarters. In the early 1980s Goldman had built 85 Broad Street in the Wall Street area, and had consolidated its New York-based operations. The significant benefits had generally been well recognized throughout the firm. The building was

Research Associate Elizabeth H. McLoughlin prepared this case under the supervision of Adjunct Professor William J. Poorvu as the basis for class discussion rather than to illustrate either effective or ineffective handling of an administrative situation. Many of the numbers in this case have been disguised.

later sold for a considerable profit, which at the time was the single most profitable investment in Goldman's history.

In 1986, the pursuit of European business was an integral component of the firm's global strategy. It was evident that trade barriers in Europe were falling, and talk of a unified Europe seemed to be making significant progress with the signing of the Single European Act. The planned 1986 deregulation of the securities industry, the so-called "Big Bang" in London was expected to abolish fixed commissions, accelerate computerized trading, and open the market to international financial institutions. In addition, the mergers craze in the United States was just starting to find its way to Europe, and several transactions were driven by hidden real estate value.

In looking at the current/projected headcount of Goldman Sachs' European personnel it was apparent that forecasting personnel needs more than a few years out would be difficult.

Growth at Goldman Sachs was occurring at an unprecedented pace in the mid 1980s. Clearly, some provision for future expansion had to be planned for, but what would happen if that growth slowed? Shecky felt that the firm needed to retain some flexibility throughout the decision making process.

One point that all players seemed to agree on was that the current London office space occupied by Goldman Sachs was inadequate (both in terms of size and technology) to handle the firm's anticipated needs over the next ten years, even with major renovations. It barely handled the 1986 needs. However, one of the potential problems was that the lease at Old Bailey ran to 2009 (see **Table A**). At the time of lease negotiations, it had been felt that Old Bailey would accommodate all of Goldman Sachs' London needs for 15–20 years. One year after move in, it had already grown out of the space. Just before Shecky's arrival in London, the firm negotiated a five year sublease for 65,000 square feet in the Strand House and spent substantial sums to upgrade the space in order to accommodate the explosive growth of their business. (Fit-out costs averaged £50 per square foot, and were paid by the tenant). Knowing that even that space might be inadequate to handle the firm's needs beyond 1988, Goldman contemplated other, more long term alternatives.

Table A   Goldman Sachs European Offices

LOCATION	DIVISION	SQUARE FEET	TERM	1986 RENT	PERSONNEL 1986	1988 PROJECTED
London Old Bailey	Sales & Trading	57,000	2009	£17.90	375	450
Strand House	Investment Banking	65,000	1990	£23.00	150	225
Queen Victoria	Systems/Operations	28,000	1991	£35.00	75	90
Madrid	Sales	2,500	N/A	N/A	6	—
Paris	Sales	2,500	N/A	N/A	6	—
Zurich	Fixed Income Sales	10,000	N/A	N/A	40	—
Total		164,000			652	715

1992 Estimate (All European Personnel) 1,060
1993 Estimate (All European Personnel) 1,200

Source: Jones, Lang, Wooten

THE OCCUPANCY ALTERNATIVES

Shecky's mission was to study the various London alternatives for Goldman Sachs and dertermine the logical next step in finding space for headquarters. First, he conducted an in-depth analysis of the London office market and its various submarkets.

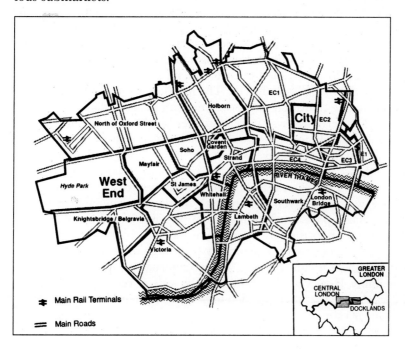

The experience was an instructive one. Real estate leases were completely different than those seen in the United States. Overall, the financial obligations of the tenant were almost equivalent to ownership. The lease terms were long (usually 25 years) and the tenant was responsible for all ownership costs including taxes, insurance, maintenance and security. Total non-rent occupancy costs approximated 50% of base rent. There were no long-term fixed rent leases, and every 5 years there were upward-only rent reviews based on prevailing market rents and inflation. When landlords and tenants could not agree on an appropriate rent, the case was turned over to third-party arbitration. As well, expansion space for tenants was handled differently in the London market. Instead of tenants having expansion options, they typically took more space than they needed and subleased the excess with short term leases. However, this technique really worked best in strong markets. If a firm, looking for a headquarters, were unable to use all the net square footage in a building, it typically would lease the entire usable space, (a "letting of the whole"), and sublet the remaining with short term leases, thereby providing itself with flexibility for expansion. Consequently, in calculating a building's value, capitalization rates were typically applied to gross rents, with no provision for vacancy.

The London City rental market had few large class "A" buildings, particularly for tenants with space needs greater than 150,000 square feet. One choice that Shecky felt might make sense for Goldman Sachs was the new development, Broadgate, near the Liverpool Street station. The first phase had been quickly leased, and subsequent phases were being actively marketed to tenants. Outside of the city there was some progress being made with the docklands project, Canary Wharf. Both First Boston and Morgan Stanley had committed to Canary Wharf, yet there was significant skepticism in the market about who the developer would be, the location, the infrastructure and the promised transportation system that would connect it to the city. The location was considered pioneering and had not been able to attract any non-American firms to date.

Another alternative was to rent smaller blocks of space in proximity to the current Goldman offices. This would reduce the sublease risk with Old Bailey.

A third major alternative was to develop its own building either as a joint venture with a developer, its own acquisition and development project, or as a sale/leaseback. The general feeling among many members of the Management Committee was that, given the strength of the market and the uncertainty of Goldman Sachs' space needs (a minimum of 150,000 s.f.), it made sense to look at development opportunities where there was sufficient expansion space and/or the opportunity to reduce occupancy costs through the benefit of third party leases. While a single tenant building was an alternative, it was clear that it would limit flexibility. However, if Goldman Sachs were to retain an ownership interest, Shecky was aware that there needed to be some strategy for the firm to realize the value of its investment.

There were a number of obstacles to development in London. First, most of the land available in the city was held under leasehold interests as opposed to freehold interests. Under a leasehold interest, the owner of the improvements leases the land under a long-term ground lease (in Britain usually in excess of 100 years). Leasehold interests create another layer of complication in terms of both the financing and eventual sale of the project. In addition, very few large footprints were available for development, impeding site assembly. The planning and zoning process was difficult, time consuming and uncertain. Finally, land was very expensive in London and represented a much higher percentage of total building costs than in the United States. Thus the capital needed to purchase a site and fund the associated carrying costs was significant.

However, by mid 1986, after a fiercely argumentative meeting regarding the benefits of the various occupancy alternatives, it was decided to pursue the purchase of a site. While the Management Committee hadn't ruled out leasing space at another development, Shecky was confident that they would endorse an economic development deal. Both the projections of Goldman's space needs, and the strong fundamentals of the London real estate market encouraged him to take an aggressive approach. If the London market was as strong as the papers claimed, he felt that a development could be extremely profitable.

THE ACQUISITION PLAN

His primary research of the various London submarkets led him to focus on a few areas where more sites seem to be available—primarily, the Holborn/Fleet Street district, just northwest of the City core. However, his first two acquisition attempts were not particularly successful.

By the time Shecky had exhausted most of his primary alternatives, he concluded that he would have to find a more complicated (or risky) situation with fewer interested bidders where Goldman could add value. Shecky decided to take another look at the Daily Telegraph Site in the Fleet Street area (located near the current Goldman offices) which was eliminated from his target list initially because of a number of problems. On a positive note, the site had a huge rectangular footprint, was owned in a freehold interest, and allowed for a very large office building by London standards. Shecky felt that the pricing of this site should be more reasonable given its complications. While the location was not in the heart of the City, he felt it would lie in what was considered new expanded City-related office core.

THE PLANNING PROCESS

In late 1986 the 69,000 square foot Daily Telegraph site in the EC4 district was acquired by Goldman for £50 million, and renamed the Peterborough Court development. While the site had planning consent approval for approximately 475,000 gross square feet, there were several design features in the existing development schemes that were not optimal for Goldman Sachs. The floorplate sizes were inadequate, the floor to floor heights did not allow for sufficient raised flooring and modern trading floors, and the tower was not sympathetic with the surrounding architecture. Shecky felt that it might be possible to achieve additional density on the site as well. However, he was concerned that the approval process required to secure a new planning consent would involve substantial risk.

Shecky knew that there were various zoning issues related to the Daily Telegraph site. "Rights of lights" is a British concept founded in English common law. In England, every landowner is entitled to light. When a new development is planned, landowners who have had the benefit of light on their property for at least twenty years can stop the development if it infringes on their common law right to light. Shecky discovered that there were four landowners who bordered Peterborough Court who had potential rights of lights claims. One was seeking an exorbitant sum, and two of the owners were willing to negotiate. As the fourth needed Goldman's approval to keep his fire escape, Shecky felt that he wouldn't be a problem.

Another planning consent issue was that two of the office buildings and a pub on the site were "listed" (historical) buildings. The pub was seeking permission to renovate. While this did not affect Goldman's ability to build the 475,000 as granted in the current planning consent, or perhaps more, there was widespread concern that this and the office buildings be preserved in a manner sympathetic to the surrounding architecture.

On October 19, 1987, while the planning consent application was being finalized, the stock market crashed. The effect on the investment banking industry was catastrophic. The optimistic growth scenarios were sorely pared, and many firms were reevaluating their strategy and personnel needs. Unfortunately for Shecky, the senior management at Goldman Sachs was no different. The firm wanted to reconsider the development of Peterborough Court, and to see a presentation on all of Goldman's London occupancy alternatives. Meanwhile Shecky was to continue the pursuit of a new planning consent, in hopes that were the firm to sell the undeveloped site, it could do so for a profit.

THE DEVELOPMENT PLAN

Plans for the development continued throughout the spring of 1988. **Exhibits 1–2** summarize the development program as requested in the planning consent application. Peterborough Court, the main office building, was designed to have 11 stories and 488,000 gross square feet (386,000 rentable square feet). In addition, Daniel House,[4] which encompassed the renovated Fleet Street buildings, would have 7-stories and 93,000 gross square feet (50,000 rentable square feet). There would be 32 parking spaces. (The London regulatory market allowed only 1 parking space per 12,000 rentable square feet). The construction process from start to finish was anticipated to take 36 months. With the considerable time and money spent to date, Shecky knew that the Goldman Sachs partners would want assurances that the project would be built on schedule, within budget, and up to specifications. While everything had gone well up to this point, he had heard horror stories about the quality of London office building construction. The first thing he discovered was that British construction companies absolutely would not agree to fixed price contracts (except at some exorbitant sum). How could he cap his costs? What other ways could he control construction costs? There were a number of Japanese construction companies actively involved in the London market; however, they typically preferred an ownership interest or joint venture arrangement. While it seemed as if he'd already won several battles to get to this stage, he realized that he was nowhere near the finish line.

Shecky also wondered what other members of the team should be assembled to carry the project through predevelopment and construction. With regard to architects, should a U.S. or British architect be chosen or some combination? Should a British developer be brought in on a fee basis at this point to spearhead the project? Would they be more familiar with the workings of the British real estate market and the planning process? What other members of the team would be important to the project's success?

Preliminary negotiations with prospective members of the development team had brought to light some fundamental differences in the management of U.S. versus U.K. development projects. While Shecky fully expected to hire a battery of British based consultants on a variety of special process items—building codes, noise containment, property laws, the adjudication of the rights of lights issue—he was uncomfortable with the typical British paradigm where all decision making was allocated to the project manager, and not to the owner.

However, some of his colleagues at J. P. Morgan who had recently completed a large development project in the City had warned him that the more "confrontational," hands-on approach of American owners was not likely to be well received by many British parties. He knew that the relationship between a British contractor and his subcontractor was predicated on the contractor having control over all negotiations. However, with his career on the line, and rumors of the "typical" London office building coming in at 30% over budget, Shecky was reluctant to hire a general contractor/construction manager and relinquish all decision making. Should he serve as the general contractor and handle all the details, he wondered?

While Goldman Sachs had a great deal of experience in real estate, very few people at Goldman had actually developed a building (let alone one in London). One possible solution might be to take the British approach of giving leeway to the consultants for zoning and planning where knowledge of the approvals process, the regulatory agencies, and the players who could expedite the project was paramount. For construction and cost negotiations, it might make more sense to "go American." Even if the final construction contract were signed on a cost plus basis, Shecky felt that direct negotiation with subcontractors would allow Goldman Sachs to more creatively manage the total construction budget.

This type of approach had seemed to work so far. Utilizing a concept called value engineering, Shecky had been able to increase the rentable square feet in the new building by 20,000 square feet (366,000 to 386,000). Working with a respected British surveyor, he was able to secure planning approval for the expansion. There were great tensions in the actual design of the space, however. The problem was that many members of Goldman's development team wanted to have the space designed with greater flexibility so that if they were to sell the building, it would be viewed as relatively easy to convert to other uses.

On the other hand, the Goldman Sachs London space planning committee, which was charged with determining the needs from the tenant's perspective, had different objectives. Among other things, they wanted additional trading space with high ceilings for future growth. Already, several Goldman traders had reminded Shecky of the grand trading floors Salomon Brothers had just completed in London. However, Shecky knew that high ceilings on several floors would reduce the amount of potential square footage in the building (because of height limitations), and in turn the potential sales price. For example, trading floors typically required floor to ceiling clearances of at least sixteen feet, compared to 10–12 feet for conventional office space. Four floors of offices could stack within the same vertical envelope as three trading floors. However, occupancy can vary significantly depending on space use. For example, trading applications provide more positions per unit of space than other applications.

Shecky based his proforma on the development of three trading floors, though one additional floor had sufficiently high ceilings to be adapted if need be. He based his proformas on Goldman Sachs' leasing the lower floors, which, with their large deep floorplates were more difficult to lease to third party tenants. While the trading operations liked these floors, investment banking despised them because they forced people to take interior offices with no outside light. How could he resolve these conflicts without losing building value and/or key employees?

THE LEASING PROGRAM

From the day the firm had closed on the site in late 1986, the leasing strategy of the project had become one of Shecky's most important assignments. He had an updated report on the London office market, which still appeared very strong (see **Exhibits 3–4**). Given the strength of the market in 1987, his objective during planning consent had been to get approval for the largest amount of square footage, knowing that even if he were successful, leasing the excess space to third parties would require significant effort. In addition, the firm would have the added burden of subleasing its existing space at Old Bailey, which had a lease through 2009. He expected, however, that the increase in rental rates in the area surrounding Old Bailey would be sufficient to pay all subleasing costs, and allow Goldman to break even on the arrangement.

Table A described the estimated London personnel count for Goldman Sachs as of 1986, with estimates for 1988. In late 1987 and early 1988, Shecky's associates had assured him that these projections were still an accurate reflection of their space needs. However, past experience had taught him that flexibility is an extremely important component of any long-term space decision. Given the cyclical nature of the investment banking industry, it was possible that Goldman could need the whole building or very little of it, if at all. His best guess was that the Goldman Sachs requirement would be approximately 150,000 net square feet in 1991–1992 assuming some efficiencies from consolidation.

Ideally, Goldman Sachs would want to have expansion options every five years. Shecky realized, however, that this would severely limit his ability to rent the space to third party tenants, as he would have to offer short terms with no renewal options. How could he retain some flexibility for Goldman Sachs without greatly restricting his ability to lease the space?

As well, he was not sure he could accommodate both the floor preferences of the various divisions—trading on the lower larger floors and investment banking on the higher shallower floors. Personally, he would rather have Goldman in contiguous space. Given the different size floorplates in the main building, and the additional space in Daniel House, how could he think about leasing this space?

With regard to third party tenants, the Management Committee had already warned him that they wanted only blue chip tenants in Peterborough Court. They felt it was critical to the image of the firm that they control the tenant selection, not only upon lease-up, but when spaces turned over. He wrote himself a note to remember this when he reviewed sale and financing alternatives. While he could appreciate their concern, it made his job more difficult. How should he go about finding tenants? Was it necessary to hire a local leasing broker to comb the market? At what point in the development process should he try and sign up tenants? What kinds of tenants would be compatible with Goldman Sachs? How should the leasing strategy be coordinated with his financing objectives? How could he keep his final options open?

THE DECISION

"Members of the Committee," he began. "It is now time to make a decision. I am fully confident that with a major push we will be able to get our planning consent as requested in the next four weeks. When we first entertained the thought of developing a flagship London headquarters, I prepared a series of analyses of the London office market, Goldman Sachs' space needs, and the various occupancy alternatives open to us. Our space requirements have continued to grow; current projections place the count of total personnel at approximately 1200 by 1992. We have space constraints in our current locations; new, more modern space in developments throughout the city is currently being preleased (see **Exhibits 5–6**). Two of the more likely choices for Goldman Sachs might be Broadgate, or Canary Wharf (see **Exhibits 6–7**). Broadgate is currently leasing blocks of space in excess of 100,000 square feet for rates ranging from £35–£47. Canary's rates are closer to the £25–£35 range. In my comparative calculations I have used £42 per square foot, and £31 per square foot, respectively. In each of these cases, Goldman Sachs would be responsible for a fit-up cost of £50 per rentable square foot.

"Were we to decide not to go ahead with development, I think that we could sell the 69,000 square foot Daily Telegraph property at a profit to the firm. As rental rates have appreciated, so have land costs. Two recent sales of parcels in the EC4 postal district where Peterborough Court is located have been in excess of £1300 per square foot. Our costs to date are approximately £58 million (£50 million acquisition cost, plus £8 million of interest, based on borrowing of £40 million.)

"However, I believe that there is the opportunity for us to create significant value should we decide to develop Peterborough Court, though not without some risk, both from a construction and a leasing standpoint. I have prepared a development proforma showing projected costs and revenues (see **Exhibit 8**), and have included a rendering of the proposed buildings (see **Exhibit 9**).

"Total development costs of £220 million include the settlement of the right of lights and historic issues, which were resolved this month for slightly less than £3 million. Ultimately, as it turned out, only two of the four claimants had injunctable rights of lights claims which required substantial negotiation. The lion's share of the settlement went for the purchase of one of the properties itself, in order to prevent a possible suit, whereby the claimant could have been entitled to all the imputed profits on the portion of our building which infringed on his right to light. The expertise of our planning consultants, property agents, and other British colleagues resulted in what we feel to be a very favorable settlement for Goldman Sachs. While we have not yet finalized a construction contract, we are confident that price will not exceed £118 million.

"Though the London market has remained strong, there is a large supply of new space coming on line in the early 1990s. Our development will not be without competition in the marketplace.

"To sum up, our occupancy alternatives are as follows:
1. Remain in our current locations
2. Move to a newer facility such as Broadgate or Canary Wharf
3. Develop Peterborough Court, and sell, or retain full (or partial) ownership.

"While there is some uncertainty as to our space needs in 1991, for comparison purposes I have calculated all occupancy costs on our current usage of 150,000 net square feet.

"I recommend that we all take the time to review the consequences of each of the various options, and make a decision as to what is best for Goldman Sachs today. I have prepared an analysis of the various alternatives, comparing each option in terms of risk, flexibility, capital outlay and control features, design elements, and ability to satisfy occupancy needs. I have also tried to lay out the economics of each alternative in terms of its potential to minimize occupancy costs and create value for Goldman Sachs.

"Should we decide to go forward with our own development, let me just touch on a few issues which we have not yet addressed in depth.

"A critical element in the process will be the decision as to how to finance the project—traditional bank financing, equity, a pre-sale of other more creative funding vehicles. In the London market today we can expect to be able to borrow up to 60% of the projected value of a completed, fully leased building. Peterborough Court is estimated to be worth approximately £300 million upon completion in 1991 (see **Exhibit 8**). In the current interest climate it is expected that our borrowing costs will not exceed 12% interest only for ten years.

"We need to think about the advantages and disadvantages of the various funding structures from a tenant/owner's perspective. What are the risk and control profiles of each alternative? It is important to understand that there is tremendous disparity between interest rates of 12 percent and "cap" rates of 7 percent. How can we create value from this spread? What are the implications of a sale versus ownership? I might point out that one of the many differences between U.K. and U.S. property ownership laws is that there is no analog for depreciation in Britain. Only by owning the property through a U.S. partnership will we be able to use the substantial depreciation benefits generated from the project. A U.S. ownership structure will allow us to deduct the value of taxes paid to the U.K. from those due in the U.S. Will that affect our ability to have a partner in the deal, or sell a partial interest? How will it affect our approach to financing? What are the implications of offshore ownership?

"If we do sell, what kind of lease should Goldman Sachs sign? Though there are no depreciation benefits for the owner, there is however, a 'capital allowance' whereby the costs of tenant fixtures—which has many interpretations in Britain—can be depreciated by the lessee. This might argue for a sale/lease-back arrangement. Even should Goldman contract for more space than it currently needs, by subletting to another firm, the value of that capital allowance can be retained by Goldman. How can we use this in our leasing strategy? Or should we give up the flexibility of expansion space in favor of negotiating long term (and likely more profitable) leases with "blue chip" tenants? How do market conditions and control objectives come into play? Are financial proceeds the major issue for us, or are there qualitative issues that are important as a tenant? What would be an appropriate resale price that would be acceptable to the firm should we decide not to retain ownership? What are the trade-offs between the cost of occupancy and value creation?

"A more difficult question is, what is Goldman Sachs' exit strategy with regard to the significant capital invested in our new European headquarters building? What are our expectations of British inflation rates? As a base case development analysis, I recommend using the following assumptions—a discount rate of 15% based on a ten year holding period, with a sale in year 11. While there are uncertainties in the London market, an average annual rental appreciation rate of 5% seems reasonable to me.

"Clearly the period between 1984 and 1988 has been one of huge volatility in currency rates. Assuming that our London operations are not generating significant sterling cash flow, and we must make our construction and land payments in sterling, how do we manage the currency risk? Do we hedge our costs or do we hedge our implied profit as well? What would it cost us to do so? With regards to financing, are we better off borrowing in sterling or dollars? In what currency should Goldman Sachs' rent payments be made? While there a number of tax implications to the various ownership structures, I have computed all of my calculations in pounds, pretax.

"As several members of the Management Committee have reminded us, the development of Peterborough Court is a highly visible transaction for the firm as well as one which can have a significant effect on Goldman Sachs' public reputation and image (as well as my career). This project has many moving parts. The London tenant market, the investor markets, the space needs of Goldman Sachs, construction costs and the political environment are only a few of the pieces to this puzzle.

"I leave it to you to decide. Should we go forward, and if so, how? Are we ready for the development business?"

Exhibit 1   The Development Program

The proposed development, Peterborough Court, is located at the site of the former Daily Telegraph printing presses. It will encompass approximately 581,000 square feet, including the existing structures on site and a new building. The new building will be entered through a semi-circular main lobby, with escalators to the upper ground level and elevators. Three levels of dealing floors will overlook the gallery and Peterborough Court. Above the third floor, the floors will be devoted to traditional office use. The flexibility of the sixth floor, however, would allow it to be easily converted to a dealing floor, if required.

Four existing buildings on the site, #130–131 Fleet Street, Mersey House, and the former Daily Telegraph building are aligned along Fleet Street itself. They will be connected to one another as a single entity, and will be renamed Daniel House. The facades and interiors of all buildings will be extensively renovated. The reinstatement of original design features will include stonework, moldings, and pillars, and the restoration of the Daily Telegraph clock, a dominant symbol on the street.

The new 11 story building maintains a prestigious address, 133 Fleet Street. It will be accessed through a grand entrance on Fleet Street, which will lead into an interior courtyard and the new building itself. In the corner of the site, the historic Cheshire Cheese Pub will remain.

The Development Plan

	PETERBOROUGH COURT (THE NEW BUILDING)		DANIEL HOUSE (THE FLEET STREET BUILDINGS)	
	NET SQUARE FEET	GROSS SQUARE FEET	NET SQUARE FEET	GROSS SQUARE FEET
11th Floor	6,000	11,000	7th Floor	3,000
10th Floor	15,000	21,000	6th Floor	6,000
9th Floor	28,500	33,600	5th Floor	6,000
8th Floor	28,400	33,500	4th Floor	7,000
7th Floor	28,400	33,400	3rd Floor	7,000
6th Floor	27,000	33,200	2nd Floor	7,000
5th Floor	30,000	34,000	1st Floor	6,000
4th Floor	39,000	44,000	Mezzanine	4,000
3rd Floor	40,000	46,000	Ground	4,000
2nd Floor	40,000	46,000		
1st Floor	40,000	46,000	Subtotal	50,000
	93,000			
Mezzanine	2,700	4,900		
Ground	36,000	50,700		
B–1 (1)	25,000	49,700		
Subtotal	386,000	488,000		

TOTAL GROSS SQUARE FOOTAGE   581,000
TOTAL NET SQUARE FOOTAGE   436,000

(1) Does not include 32 car parking spaces (10,300 square feet) located on level B–1

Exhibit 2   The Site Plan

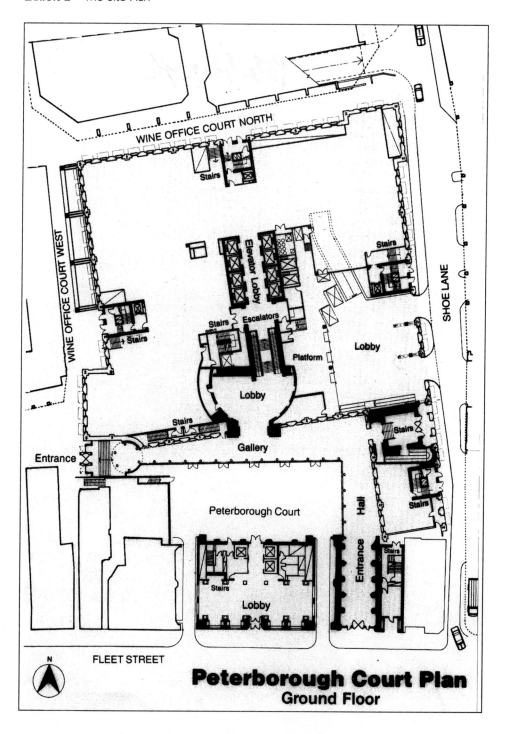

Exhibit 3   London Office Supply and Demand 1987–1988

Although the supply of available office space stood at over 9 million square feet in 1984, very little of this space could satisfy new users. As a result, property developers embarked upon a building surge not seen in London since the early 1970s. For example, in 1987 alone, an aggregate amount of 8.5 million square feet came onto the market for letting. Due to the shortage of supply and increased rental rates, developers undertook early marketing of their schemes. It was estimated that 72% of 1988 completions were pre-let and 17% of completions scheduled for 1989 and 1990 were already under offer or let. In the past five years, the volume of new lettings in central London has risen by over 70%, and rental rates have appreciated at approximately 10% annually.

It is important to recognize that the lion's share of these new projects will be built on the fringes of the central City. The Docklands, where the Canary Wharf project has received strong enthusiasm, is one such "fringe" area. The Broadgate complex is another enormous project that has attracted strong tenants. It too is situated just outside what is considered the City core. It must be highlighted, however, that the City's growth, coupled with the success of Broadgate, has led to its general acceptance into the City limits.

As the City's inability to provide large, up-to-date facilities continues to plague tenants with such needs, the "fringes" will continue to grow in volume and stature. Total office stock in the whole of Central London currently amounts to just over 120 million square feet in 1988. The City contains around 35–40 million square feet, while the West End is substantially larger with 50–55 million square feet. A further 20–30 million square feet is located on the border of these two areas. Demand for space in this area is generally a function of activity in the City or the West End. As the City continues to thrive in concordance with the financial, legal and service industries, and with the arrival of the European Community in 1992, demand for space in the "fringe" areas will remain strong, and rental growth will inevitably follow.

The creation of a single market in Europe by 1992 creates the opportunity for London to adopt the role of Europe's domestic financial capital to add to its current status as one of the three international finance centers of the world. Clearly, if this position is earned, it would have the greatest impact in the field of financial and professional services and will therefore tend to enhance the demand for space in the London area. London's position is protected and will thrive due to the following: its business climate, international status, language, quality of life, staff availability and time zone. In addition, the fact that the European Bank for Reconstruction and Development has chosen to locate here leads many to envisage 1992 as the time when the next major growth phase will take place in London.

Exhibit 4   Rental Growth

Both the City and its fringes have recently seen very substantial rental growth. Rental growth in the City has averaged approximately 12.5% per annum since 1965. Growth in fringe area rents has also been significant.

ICHP Rent Index

YEAR	CITY	% GROWTH	FRINGE	% GROWTH
1977	104.0	4.0	104.0	4.0
1978	120.0	15.4	119.0	14.4
1979	137.0	14.2	154.0	29.4
1980	155.0	13.1	184.0	19.5
1981	163.0	5.2	195.0	6.0
1982	198.0	21.5	203.0	4.1
1983	215.0	8.6	210.0	3.4
1984	232.0	7.9	232.1	10.5
1985	260.0	12 1	265.6	14.4
1986	303.2	16.6	349.7	31.7
1987	440.0	45.4	460.6	31.7
1988	482.0	9.3	576.0	25.1

First Quarter 1977 = 100.0
Source: Investors Chronicle Hillier Parker Rental Indices

Growth in Rental Values by Postal District
New Accommodation in £'s PSF

REGION	LOCATION	JUNE 85	JUNE 86	JUNE 87	JUNE 88
City					
Financial and adjacent boroughs	EC2	33.50	40.00	57.50	65.00
Insurance	EC3	28.50	32.50	45.00	60.00
Northern	EC3	25.00	27.00	40.00	47.50
Holborn	WC1	18.50	24.00	35.00	40.00
Fleet Street	EC4	17.50	23.50	35.00	40.00
Aldgate	EC3/E1	17.50	18.00	32.50	42.50
Southward	SE1	15.00	18.00	25.00	35.00
West End					
Mayfair	27.00	30.00	37.50	57.50	
St. James		27.00	30.00	40.00	50.00
Victoria		19.50	19.50	25.00	35.00
Knightsbridge		18.00	18.50	25.00	35.00
Strand		19.50	21.00	26.50	34.00
Euston		15.00	15.00	18.50	28.50

Source: Healey & Baker Research, *Annual Guide to Rental Values*

Exhibit 5

Districts EC1–EC4 Available Floorspace: Available and Absorption (000s omitted)

| YEAR | ALDGATE (EC1) | | FINANCIAL SECTOR (EC2) | | INSURANCE/ NORTHERN (EC3) | | FLEET STREET (EC4) | | TOTAL | TOTAL NET |
	AVAIL.	NET ABSORP.	AVAIL.	NET ABSORP.	AVAIL.	NET ABSORP.	AVAIL.	NET ABSORP.	AVAIL.	ABSORP.
1985	2245	724	2817	1990	2776	1183	1510	1447	6459	4650
1986	1397	1183	1786	2061	1566	1044	1258	1539	6007	5827
1987	1209	1052	2205	2823	827	957	703	877	4944	5709
1988 (Q1,Q2)	776	632	2131	865	1110	584	571	265	4580	2346
1988 (Q3,Q4)	975		2802		1843		625		6245	
1989	4162		7851		5411		1707		19131	

Available space is defined as space ready to occupy within the next six months. Quarters 3,4 of 1988, and 1989 are estimates. Net absorbed reflects the amount of available space let during the period.

Source: Debenham, Tewson, and Chinnocks; Goldman, Sachs & Co.

Note: As of 1988, the City had a total of 35–40 million square feet, the West End 50–55 million, with an additional 20–30 million bordering these two areas (per **Exhibit 4**).

Exhibit 6   Location of Representative Developments

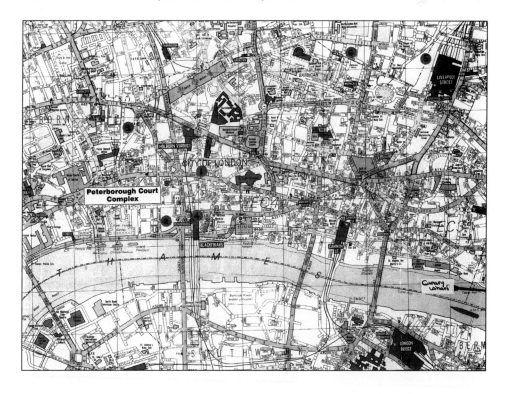

MAP KEY

Peterborough Court	Marked
5 Old Bailey	1
Boys School Site	2
Strand House	3
Queen Victoria	4
Broadgate	5
Ropemaker Place	6
Canary Wharf	Marked by Arrow

Exhibit 7

Broadgate Center

The Broadgate complex now partially completed, is expected to comprise over three million square feet of commercial floor space, and be one of London's top comprehensive commercial developments. The property is firmly established in the northeastern sector of the City's prime business district. It will be comprised of eleven separate office buildings that are integrated with, and complemented by, shops, restaurants, bars, a sports and leisure center, and an open air amphitheater. Unlike most of the traditional London office buildings, Broadgate is marketed as a modern alternative, which has been honored with several architectural and construction awards. The design ingenuities, coupled with the quality office space and the adjacent public spaces and amenities, give the complex its own identity and sense of ambience.

Rental values in the Finsbury/Liverpool Station sector of London, where Broadgate is located, have historically been at a 10–20% discount to those of the traditional City core, though the improving location and completion of the second phase of the Broadgate site in 1990 is expected to eliminate the difference in lease rates. (Phases are scheduled for completion from 1987 to 1993). Broadgate serves as home for several leading financial institutions and professional firms. It has evolved into the premier address for high specification offices in the City (with 98% occupancy in buildings so far completed) on the strength of its near central location, its scale, and the exceptional rail, underground, bus and taxi facilities available in the immediate vicinity.

Canary Wharf

The Canary Wharf development project in London's Docklands area was originally conceived in 1984 by an American developer, and later taken over by Olympia & York of Canada in 1987. Part of former Prime Minister Margaret Thatcher's ambitious plan to revive the wharf district, Canary Wharf is the largest real estate development project in Europe. Targeted for completion in 1997, the 71-acre site will include 26 buildings with 10 million s.f. of office space; up to 500,000 s.f. of stores, restaurants, a 400-bedroom hotel, and parking for 6,500 cars.

The first phase, including an 800-foot tower that will be the tallest building in Britain, will be largely completed by mid-1991. Canary Wharf is no further in mileage from the City to the East than Bond Street is to the West. However the project is risky not only because of its immense size in a London market that is losing some of its pre-1986 steam, but mainly due to its untested location which is difficult to reach by public transportation. The expansion of the new transportation program will not be completed until early 1993. Some do not expect to see London's subway system extend into Canary Wharf until early 1996. However, the complex offers a number of advantages including:

- Rents that will be about two-thirds the typical city rents.
- Large, flexible, modern space close to London and residential areas.
- An architecturally attractive site for businesses, shoppers and pedestrians.

Exhibit 8   Development Proforma

ASSUMPTIONS

Gross Square Feet	581,000
Net Square Feet	436,000
Office	406,000
Storage/systems	25,000
Retail	5,000
Parking	32 spaces
Rental Rate PSF (1988)	
Office	£ 42.50
Retail	100.00
Storage/systems	18.00
Parking	3,125/space
Annual Inflation	5%
Development and Marketing Period	36 months
Capitalization Rate	7%

DEVELOPMENT AND MARKETING COSTS (1988–1991)	TOTAL	PSF
Acquisition Cost	£ 50,000,000	£ 86
Construction Cost	118,000,000	203
Interest Expense (1)	39,000,000	67
Fees and miscellaneous	23,000,000	40
Contingency	12,000,000	21
Total Development Costs	£242,000,000	£417
Less Tenant Reimbursables (2)	22,000,000	
Adjusted Development Costs	£220,000,000	

RENTAL INCOME: (1988) (3)		
Office	£ 17,255,000	
Storage	450,000	
Retail	500,000	
Parking	100,000	
Total	18,305,000	
Projected Rental Income 1991	21,190,000	£49.00
(inflated at 5% annually)		
@ 7% cap	£ 302,718,400	

(1) Includes interest during holding period
(2) Tenant reimbursables represent fit-out of £50 per square foot which is expensed to the tenant
(3) It is assumed that all expenses are passed through to tenant

Exhibit 9 Peterborough Court
Rendering of Proposed Building

18

THE DOMIK PROJECT

In May 1994, Cameron Sawyer, after working in real estate in Moscow for several years, wants to build there a 1,200 square meter office building costing $2.3 million. He has found a site, prepared plans and pro formas, and negotiated a joint venture agreement with the land owner. He is searching for U.S. equity financing of $800,000. The case discusses the process as well as the risks and rewards of developing Russian real estate.

Discussion Questions:

1. As Cameron Sawyer, present the case for investing in this project to a U.S. investor. How would you evaluate and explain the risks?
2. As a potential investor, respond to the presentation and to the proposed deal structure. As Sawyer, do the returns to you warrant the work you have put in?
3. What are the key differences between developing in Russia and the U.S.?
4. If you were starting a career in real estate, would you be better off doing it in Moscow or Atlanta? What would it take for you to be successful in Moscow?

In May 1994, Cameron Sawyer, President and CEO of Sawyer and Company, boarded an airplane for his all too frequent flight from Moscow to Atlanta. Packed in his briefcase was a draft of a private placement memorandum that he had been working on since Christmas. In it he discussed all the details related to an office building Sawyer and Company proposed to develop on the campus of Moscow Aviation Technology Institute (MATI) in Moscow, Russia (see attached excerpts, **Exhibit 1**). On this long airplane flight, Cameron wanted to go over the memorandum one more time before presenting it to investors. In particular, he wanted to make sure that the proposed financial structure would adequately compensate him for his hard work and entrepreneurial successes over the last year. He also wanted to make sure that the investment was attractive enough that investors would seize the opportunity.

CAMERON SAWYER

Colleagues describe Cameron Sawyer as high energy, very intelligent and entre-preneurial. He has a particular talent for languages. In 1984–85, he received the German Academic Exchange Services Scholarship (in Gratitude for the Marshall Plan) which enabled him to spend a year in Munich, Germany. Within six months, he was speaking fluent German and lecturing at the law school. On the side, he started a business exporting luxury German automobiles to the United States where partners in various cities sold them. His partner in Atlanta was a Russian emigre.

In 1986, Cameron joined the real estate department of one of the largest and most prestigious law firms in Atlanta. During the next five years, as he helped his clients put together deals he observed that: (1) "they were having more fun," (2) "they were no smarter than he was," and (3) "they were making a lot more money." In July 1991, his former business partner, the Russian emigre, suggested that Cameron consider doing real estate development in Russia. With the collapse of Communism, Cameron's former partner had gotten heavily involved in trade with Russia. He claimed that there were unlimited real estate opportunities, espe-cially compared with the slumping U.S. real estate markets. He also had heard that Perestroika Joint Venture, the first successful developer of speculative office

Lecturer John H. Vogel, Jr. prepared this case under the supervision of Adjunct Professor William J. Poorvu as the basis for class discussion rather than to illustrate either effective or ineffective handling of an administrative situation. It is based on material gathered as part of a student report by Joseph M. Thompson.

buildings in Moscow, needed a Deputy General Director and suggested that Cameron seriously consider the position.

By September 1991, Cameron was the new Deputy General Director of Perestroika Joint Venture (Perestroika) and, with a three word Russian vocabulary, got on his first plane to Moscow. A year later, Cameron could converse and even negotiate deals in Russian. He could also read and draft legal documents.

As part of his job, Cameron was responsible for setting up relationships with most of the American companies who had offices in Moscow. One of his successes was in establishing a relationship with Mobil Oil which led to the development of an office building for Mobil Oil's Russian operations. Unfortunately, Perestroika was having significant internal problems, which made it impossible for him to continue to work there. So he left and set up Sawyer and Company and hired a couple of colleagues from Perestroika, including Vera Setskaya, his most talented leasing agent. Perestroika's turmoil continued and within a couple of months ceased all construction and development activities.

THE RUSSIAN MARKET

Most commentators on the Russian economy tend to focus on conventional indicators like the fact that since Yeltsin declared independence in December 1991, GDP fell by 19% in 1992, and by 9% in 1993. They also highlight skyrocketing inflation (20% per month in 1993) and large budget deficits (20% of GDP). Others, closer to the scene, note that in 1994 inflation has fallen dramatically to 4–5% per month. They also argue that the official statistics have always overstated production in the State sector and now understate the majority of private economic activity.

As prices continue to rise and the standard of living for many Russians worsens, some commentators have speculated about a reemergence of a centrally planned economy. In Cameron's view, these commentators miss the incredible changes that have transformed the Russian economy in just two and a half years. He cites a recent speech by former Senator Howard Baker who states "70,000 firms have been privatized and 70% of the Russian economy is now in private hands." As additional evidence that the change is permanent, one can look at the fact that when the Hungarian Communists were voted back into power, they kept their promise of continuing the transition to a market economy. A similar pledge is now contained in the new platform of the Russian Communist Party. While Cameron worries that Russia will erect trade barriers and become like "Brazil" (with a stagnant economy and high inflation), he is convinced that the fundamental change to a market economy is permanent.

From a real estate perspective, Cameron looks at Moscow as the largest city in Europe with a population of 15.5 million and "less quality office space than Columbia, Tennessee." There is a 0% vacancy rate in office buildings and many Western firms find themselves working out of hotel rooms. Russia also has a highly educated population, as Boeing Aircraft recently confirmed when it announced it was setting up a facility in Moscow to design the aircraft bodies for its next generation of planes.

As outlined in the attached private placement memorandum, Cameron saw his primary market for office space as American companies like Mobil and Chevron who are setting up offices in Russia to help develop its rich natural resources. In addition to American companies, however, some Russians are doing very well. Last year, Cameron pointed out, Moscow dealers sold more S–Class Mercedes (the most expensive class) than were sold in all of Western Europe put together, including Germany.

THE PROJECT

After leaving Perestroika, Cameron helped support Sawyer and Company by doing legal work while looking for a development site. As described in the attached memorandum, the rules and laws related to property rights are not well established which makes fee simple ownership difficult to obtain. Developers therefore end up with long term leases and joint ventures with firms and institutions who have controlled land since the days of communism and have strong ties to the current government. After months of searching, Cameron found such a partner, the Moscow Aviation Technology Institute (MATI) which owns an attractive piece of land on its campus. This site, Cameron believed, would provide an "office park" like setting with good security and plenty of parking.

The arrangement he and his Russian vice president, Vera Setskaya worked out with MATI was that Sawyer and Company would pay MATI $180,000 upfront, plus 6% of the gross revenues each year for the first ten years, as ground rent. After the tenth year, MATI's interest would be converted to a 45% equity ownership in the project.

As detailed in the attached memorandum, Cameron believed that securing a good, developable site was the most difficult development problem. Leasing, Cameron believed, would not be much of a problem, given the strength of the market. One peculiarity of leasing in Moscow, however, was that no one would sign a lease until the building was under construction. Too many people had been burned by signing a lease only to see the project get stalled for years or abandoned.

THE DECISION

Cameron was anxious to secure the financing and get the project under construction. He was confident that this would be the first of many buildings that Sawyer and Company would build in Moscow. He hoped that he could find an investor who would provide financing not just for this project, but for many more as well. Cameron also wanted to make sure that his company received adequate cash flow from this property, so that he could stop doing legal work and concentrate all his energy on developing buildings.

As he thought about the presentations he would soon be making to investors, he wondered first about the financial structure. Were investors getting a reasonable return for the risk they were taking? Conversely, were the returns higher than they needed to be and was he giving away too much? Who were the best prospects to make this kind of investment he wondered and was the Domik Project structured appropriately for them.

Cameron also thought about other risks. Investing in Russian office buildings would be viewed as a risky investment. In his presentation to investors, he wanted to carefully consider which of these risks should be highlighted and addressed.

As a former musician, Cameron loved his life in Moscow with all the opportunities to go to concerts and symphonies. He also felt that the opportunities to develop real estate there were as good or better than any place in the world. But before he could make his dream a reality, he would have to convince investors that it was worth making an investment in the Domik Project.

Exhibit 1   (Excerpts from a "private placement" memorandum)

Background

Sawyer & Co. was created to take advantage of the booming real estate opportunities that currently exist in Moscow and throughout Russia. The Company has three employees including: Cameron F. Sawyer (President), Vera Setskaya (Vice President), and Gennady Sivitsky (General Counsel). All of these employees are veterans of Perestroika Joint Venture, live in Moscow, and speak a combined total of eight languages. The Domik project is Sawyer & Co.'s first attempt to develop property in Moscow. The company currently earns enough cash to cover operating expenses by acting as a real estate consulting firm.

Project Overview

The site for the Domik building is on the campus of the Moscow Aviation Technology Institute (MATI), on the Yauza River (pronounced Yow–za) within the Garden Ring and within walking distance of the Kremlin. Located within the major business and government district, the property is in a particularly desirable area in Moscow. The MATI campus already contains one successful Western-standard office building, the Forum Business Center, which was recently completed by the Austrian firm Negrelli, and now houses the Moscow headquarters of Price Waterhouse Moscow and Credit Lyonnaise.

With 1,200m^2 of gross space and 1,000m^2 [5] of net rentable space, the proposed building will be finished to grade "A" Western standards including imported American carpeting, central heating and air-conditioning, and dropped ceilings with parabolic lighting. (All rare in Moscow.) The building exterior will be stucco with a distinctive, post modern Neoclassical design. There will be abundant on-site parking and a security fence with an iron gate surrounding the property. (Also rare in Moscow.)

Market Analysis: Demand[6]

A number of Western businesses have operated in Moscow for many years, and for many years had been in desperate need of reasonable-quality office space. Such space, until recently simply did not exist. This pent-up demand was the basis for Perestroika Joint Venture's pioneer development projects in the late 1980s. Buildings were built for companies such as BASF, Monsanto, Ciba–Geigy, DuPont, Bank Austria, Hoechst AG and other blue-chip companies.

This pent-up demand, among firms which have always been committed to Russia, is relatively insensitive to local economic conditions. However, in the last two years Russia has undertaken a total transformation of its political and economic system, involving the privatization of over half of Russia's industrial concerns and the opening of the Russian economy to foreign businesses. This added a virtual flood of Western businesses seeking opportunities in Russia to the base of companies which were already operating there, and the demand for office space in Moscow now totally overwhelms the modest supply.

Practically overnight, opportunities for Western companies were created in virtually all sectors of the Russian economy. In particular, Western companies are already very active in the areas of: (a) oil and gas (with nearly all major Western oil companies having established or seeking to establish permanent operations in Moscow); (b) timber; (c) metals (which are trading in huge quantities particularly through Marc Rich et Cie); (d) aerospace (the former Soviet space program has been put on acommercial basis and there are many Western companies in Moscow involved in launching satellites. Boeing has a substantial operation in Moscow that includes a full-scale research institute. Gulfstream

[5] 1 square meter equals approximately 10.76 square feet.

[6] Information from a market research report conducted by Sawyer & Co.

Exhibit 1   (continued)

has a major joint venture with Sukhoi for the production of business jets.); (e) arms trading; (f) consumer goods (Pepsi, Coca–Cola, Procter & Gamble); (g) financial services (Citibank, Bank Austria, Deutsche Bank, Bayerische Hypobank, Credit Lyonnaise, and Credit Suisse); (h) telecommunications (AT&T and GTE have major projects and planned expansions); (i) heavy manufacturing (Otis Elevator, and several other manufacturers of machine tools, trucks and diesel engines have full-scale factories and substantial export operations in Russia); (j) medical equipment and services (Hospital Corporation International); (k) transportation (Land–Sea); (l) retailing.

All of these opportunities have been created incredibly quickly—in December 1991, just over two years ago, the Soviet Union was still in existence, and Russia's economy was still organized as a centrally planned communist system that was entirely closed to the West.

Supply

This explosive growth in the private sector—from almost nothing to over 50% of the economy in just over two years—has overwhelmed all infrastructure for business, particularly real estate. The communist economic system was notoriously unable to produce adequate quantities of any goods, particularly buildings. The existing stock of office space in Moscow is inadequate in quantity, even for the non-commercial purposes for which it was built, and is in atrocious condition. Existing spaces are characterized by inefficient floor plans. Interiors are broken up by interior support columns and low ceilings. Wiring cannot handle the heavy electricity loads required by the modern automated office.

Renovation

Competition for tenants exists from both renovated spaces and newly constructed buildings. Renovation is a very complicated and time consuming process. Before renovation can occur a proper building must be located. This involves finding a building which is for sale or finding a Russian partner who wants to renovate. Problems are two fold. First it must be established that sellers or partners actually have title to the building. Because of the new system of property rights in Russia, this is complicated at best. Failure to establish property rights can result in the complete loss of the project. Second, all serviceable buildings in Moscow are rented. Renovation requires existing tenants to move out. With no place to move, even temporarily, many tenants are simply willing to increase their rent in order to make the opportunity cost of renovation unacceptably high.

Once a building is located a developer must obtain a series of permits from the government. These permits ensure that nothing of historical value is destroyed in the renovation.[7] The time required for approval varies tremendously depending on a variety of factors including: who the developer knows, the number of applications currently in process, whom else is "interested" in the property, and the general unpredictability of the government. Even when permission is given to begin construction, depending on the building, progress can be delayed as government officials periodically inspect to ensure that preservation standards are being met. In general the more attractive the location of the building (i.e. the closer to the Kremlin) the more historical value the building has, and therefore the more costly in terms of time and restoration expense the project becomes.

[7]The Russian concept of an "historic" building is more subjective than in the West and may be applied to buildings with little aesthetic or historic importance. Once a building is designated "historic" it falls under the jurisdiction of the Historic Building Commission. The developer is required to enter into a 25-year lease with the Historic Building Commission. The rental rate is set for the first five years and then is subject to renegotiation with no pre-set ceiling on what the Historic Building Commission can charge.

Exhibit 1 (continued)

Other than historical restoration costs, other renovation costs can also be high. Structural elements of many buildings were either not built safely and or have decayed due to the harsh climate and neglect. Interior spaces, as mentioned above, are broken up and have low ceilings. The result is that renovation can be more expensive than building a new building. Further a new building, because of its efficient use of space, will always have more net rentable space than an equally sized renovated space.

New Construction

Moscow became a major city in Eastern Europe in the 11th century and since that time has been the center of culture and trade for the vast stretches of land from the Ukraine and Byelorussia in the West through Central Asia and Transcaucasia in the South to the Sea of Japan and the Bering Strait in the East. The geographic reach of Moscow during the last 800 years is truly astounding.

As a result of its historic preeminence, most of the prime building locations within the city have existing structures. It is very rare to find a suitable site which has not been built on. Most available building sites are located well outside the center of the city, thereby making them less attractive. Demolition of buildings to make way for new construction is also complicated. The Russian people and government are very conscious of their national treasures and the value of their architecture. As a result, the government has established strict laws forbidding the destruction of historic sites. Obtaining permission to demolish most buildings is very difficult.

Conclusion

The unique opportunity with the Domik project is that a greenfield site has been located within the Garden Ring of the city. The Domik site originally housed a garage which burned down a number of years ago and was never rebuilt.

According to an extensive market survey conducted by Sawyer & Co. in the fall of 1993, there is less than 200,000m^2 of reasonable-quality office space in the entire city of Moscow, in 2 buildings consisting of 92,000m^2 inside or near the Garden Ring Road (which defines the city center), and about 73,000m^2 of space in 20 buildings outside of the Garden Ring Road.[8]

There are presently nine office projects under construction in Moscow (including greenfield and remodeling). This represents approximately 42,000m^2 of net rentable office space that will be ready for occupancy in 1994 and 1995. No project larger than 12,000m^2 is actually under construction.[9] The office vacancy rate in Moscow is presently 0%.[10]

Absorption

According to the major British brokerage house Ferguson–Hollis, absorption of office space in Warsaw and Budapest has averaged about 500,000m^2 per annum for the last two years. Only about 50,000m^2 of new or renovated office space was brought onto the Moscow market in 1993. Moscow is the largest city in Europe, and is the capital of the largest country in the world in terms of geographic area, and as such is potentially vastly more significant than Warsaw or Budapest, which have, at most, regional significance. It can be expected that the potential absorption of office space in Moscow is many times greater than in Warsaw or Budapest. Poland and Hungary began their reforms about two years before Russia did.

[8]Sawyer & Co. research report.

[9]Ferguson Hollis "Moscow Office Market Report," August 1993.

[10]Ferguson Hollis.

Exhibit 1 (continued)

Rents and Other Economic Terms[11]

Rents range up to $1,000m² per annum, triple net, with the average net annual rental rate being $800 per m² inside the Garden Ring Road and $700 per m² outside.[12] During the early stages of development of the office market in Moscow, tenants paid up to 6 years of rent in advance, prior to buildings even being brought under construction. That is no longer the case because a number of tenants got burned. Free rent, moving allowances, and other similar concessions do not exist. Rents are usually expressed in triple net terms.

Most office space is leased in prime shell form, with no allowance for tenant finish. Some office space in Moscow is offered finished or semi-finished. There is an acute shortage of new construction. Most good-quality office space is in renovated older buildings that have inefficient floor plates and floor plans fixed by extensive load-bearing walls. Such space is often leased semi-finished since the tenant would have so little choice in designing its buildout anyway.

Domik Design

The building is designed to be constructed quickly using the traditional European building technique of monolithic poured concrete and incorporating some prefabricated materials from the West. The design is under development by an internationally recognized Western architectural firm in coordination with Moscow architects associated with the Moscow Aviation Technology Institute. The architects are currently finalizing their designs.

Design is a major factor which will contribute to the success of this project. Located within the Garden Ring of the City of Moscow this building will be surrounded by other structures which date from the turn of the century. It is important that the Domik Project complement the surrounding architecture. Such a design is often an "unwritten" requirement in order to receive the proper authorization to begin building, though Cameron felt the authorities would not care that much in this case because the adjacent buildings were ugly.

Appendix 1 contains front, back and side elevations as well as a floor plan of the proposed design. What is notable is that the exterior surfaces maintain a Neoclassical design which, while clearly a modern construction, is of the style of the existing neighborhood. This traditional facade gives way to interior spaces marked by an open functional floor plan. Such a plan will easily accommodate the needs of the modern corporation.

This building is designed to attract high quality tenants. The exterior is strong, formal and traditionally Russian. The interior is decidedly modern. Such a combination is rare in the city of Moscow. This building will be desirable to a target market of prestigious blue-chip companies.

Construction

The primary construction will be carried out by a large Western-oriented contractor such as Hakka (Finnish), Mir (Turkish), Akpinar (Turkish), Codest (Italian), Morganti (American), McHugh (American), Bau (Austrian), or Swatstori (Canadian), any one of which is capable of providing a guaranteed-price, guaranteed-delivery time contract. The use of such a contractor greatly reduces the construction risks. Negotiations are currently under way with several firms to finalize the contractor. (Construction costs in **Appendix 2** represent average costs from preliminary bids.)

[11]Ferguson Hollis.

[12]It is standard to express rent in terms of $ per rentable square feet. This concept of rentable square feet is closer to American practices of taking useable square feet and adding a load factor. Most other European cities quote rents based on useable square feet.

Exhibit 1   (continued)

Construction contracting in Russia continues to be difficult. The most obvious problem is the harsh climate. Secondly, local construction workers are not familiar with modern building technology and Western management styles. Most of the foremen are still Western, because no Russians have more than three years experience with modern buildings. Building materials are also sometimes difficult to obtain, and the process of orchestrating the coordination of contractors, suppliers, and workers is a major logistical challenge.

The notion that Russian construction workers are lazy or hard to motivate has generally proved not to be true. As the wages of construction workers have increased (in some cases 20-fold in dollar terms) competition for jobs has increased, as have the pride, skill and diligence of the workers. Most contractors have learned to instantly spot and fire the workers with drinking problems, and then are quite happy with the quality and productivity of their crews. And even though wages have soared, labor is still significantly cheaper than in the West.

Another factor that defines the current market is the presence of significant competition. Construction companies are scrambling to gain experience in Moscow. Several companies have built one or two buildings, thereby gaining valuable experience. They are beginning to learn how to use local contractors, which building materials need to be imported from the West, and how to import those materials. These firms are working to become adept at building in this environment and have developed some expertise and at the same time are competing with one another for business and market share. They are therefore willing to enter into fixed price contracts.

It should be noted however that the fact that construction is promised to be completed on time does not mean that construction will be completed on time. While the developer is protected against having to pay the direct costs of construction delays, nothing protects against the indirect costs. In emerging markets such as Moscow, potential tenants place a lot of faith in their developer. Construction delays and poor craftsmanship serve to deteriorate the developer's reputation. Even in such a booming market, such problems can adversely affect the ability to lease or more importantly to pre-lease the project.

Lease Overview

The project will be leased under six year, bankable, triple net leases. The triple net leases will be controlled by western law, and the lease payments will be payable in the United States, in dollars. The state of the market in Moscow permits the obtaining of "bankable leases." The general terms state that the tenant is obligated to pay the rent in any event, even if, for example, the building burns down or is confiscated by the government. Much of the risk that is inherent in Russian real estate transactions is thus transferred to the tenant.

Summary and Analysis of "Form Single-User Domik Lease"

The lease to be used for the Domik Project is a fairly typical freestanding building lease on the American model. It is a fully net lease, drafted in a way to transfer the burden of all expenses relating to the building to the tenant. All rents are payable in the United States in dollars. The lease form requires that the tenants will contract directly with the appropriate utility providers for electricity, gas, hot water, cold water, sewage, and telephone service. The tenant is required to pay directly all taxes of any kind relating to the building. The tenant is required to reimburse the landlord for all costs of insurance relating to the building (including deductibles paid). The landlord is obligated to maintain the building after the expiration of the contractor's warranty, but the tenant is required to pay the landlord for any repairs which it carries out. All common area expenses such as snow removal and landscape maintenance are also to be paid by the tenant.

Exhibit 1   (continued)

A unique feature of the lease is that it is a "bankable lease." This type of lease has two main characteristics. The first is that there is no abatement of rent in the case of destruction of the property. The second is that the tenant has no right to offsets or deductions against rent, no right to terminate the lease for any reason, and the lease is fully mortgageable by the landlord such that the tenant's interests in the lease are subordinated to the mortgage on the building.

The lease will be governed by Georgia (U.S.) law, other than core property rights issues, such as title to the property, which must, under international law, be governed by the law of the nation where the property is located. Therefore, jurisdiction to settle disputes such as contractual obligation to pay rent would be settled by the State Courts of Georgia.

Although this lease appears to transfer much of the project risk from the investor to the tenant, it cannot always fully protect the investor. If a tenant were to renege on rent payments, Sawyer & Co. would be forced to sue in U.S. court. This action takes time and money and the outcomes can never be sure. If such a situation were to arise, it would undoubtedly decrease the value of the project.

Lease Agent

In order to further assure the success of the project, Sawyer & Co. intends to engage Hines Interests or Ferguson Hollis to lease the Domik Building. Sawyer & Co. has an in-house leasing capability (see "Analysis of Developer"), and due to the extreme shortage of space in Moscow, the leasing of a good quality office building which is actually under construction is not a difficult job. Nevertheless, in order to lease it as quickly as possible after the start of construction, Sawyer & Co. intends to engage someone like Hines Interest whose leasing staff is presently completing the leasing of a large, successful project in Moscow, and has an active list of potential tenants that it was unable to accommodate in its existing project.

Political Risks

A new constitution of the Russian Federation has recently been approved which settles many questions about the legitimacy of Boris Yeltsin's government, and establishes fairly clear procedures for deciding questions of policy and settling disputes between the branches of government. It is widely hoped and expected that this development will end the sort of confrontation which would result in an armed struggle.

Nevertheless, some power elements in the country do not favor Yeltsin's program of reform. Recent national parliamentary elections resulted in a strong showing by Vladimir Zhirinovsky's Liberal Democratic Party, which gained 25% of the vote. This Party advocates a belligerently nationalistic foreign policy. In the event Zhirinovsky is elected President of Russia in 1996, (an office which is very strong under the new constitution) it is possible that he might get Russia involved in military and economic confrontations both with other countries and within its own boundaries.

Zhirinovsky does not publicly advocate communism or the nationalization of property. In fact, both the Liberal Democratic Party and the Communist Party publicly favors a market economy and increased foreign investment. Risk does however exist in disruption of the financial structure of this transaction. Namely the government may force that rents be payable in Russia, subject to taxation and the vagaries of the Russian banking system. Project cash flows to investors could be adversely effected.

Russia is undergoing such a rapid political and economic change that it is difficult to predict the future with any confidence. Two characteristics of this project were designed to help defray some of this risk. First, Sawyer & Co.'s partner in this venture is a former government agency. MATI played an influential political role in the former Soviet Union. It would be expected that the institution would play a significant role if such a regime were to return. Second, some of the inherent political

Exhibit 1 (continued)

risk is mitigated by the bankable lease concept. It is however impossible to fully immunize an investment in Russia from political risks. The economic returns for this project are above normal market returns (see "Economic Assumptions and Returns"). Such returns are meant to compensate the investor(s) for this risk.

Organized Crime

Organized crime has grown quickly in Russia. So far organized criminal groups have not been extensively involved with real estate or services relating to real estate (such as trash removal, cleaning, etc.). Cameron Sawyer and his partners, through their experience in working and living in Moscow, have developed close ties and personal relationships with powerful governmental organizations. Further MATI has similar and even stronger ties. Such relations will help to defend against interference by organized criminal groups.

Nevertheless, it is difficult to be certain how powerful the criminal groups might become. Several knowledgeable sources have confirmed that organized crime is a problem especially in the retail and restaurant business. They claim that "protection" money is simply a cost of doing business in Moscow. Such expenses may increase projected yearly operating costs for the project and therefore decrease cash flow. This is clearly an inherent risk to the project.

Analysis of Developer

It is clear that, because of the constantly developing political and business climate in Russia, any investment which is made in this project is an investment made in Cameron Sawyer. Therefore, an evaluation of his background and qualifications is important.

Cameron F. Sawyer, is an attorney and real estate developer from Atlanta, Georgia, who has lived and worked in Moscow since the collapse of communism. During this time, he participated in the Moscow commercial real estate market as it developed from ground zero as the Deputy General Director of Perestroika Joint Venture (PJV). This company has been by far the most successful commercial real estate developer in Moscow.

During his association with PJV, Mr. Sawyer was involved in the successful development of five small office buildings in Moscow. Responsibilities included contracting with construction and architectural firms in order to ensure the timely completion of these projects. These buildings are presently 100% leased to Mobil Oil Co., Chevron, AT&T, KPMG/Peat Marwick, Toepfer, and DHL Worldwide Express. Mr. Sawyer was also involved in the development of the Syetun Townhouse Community, consisting of 86 units of housing.

Among his other responsibilities, Mr. Sawyer managed PJV's seven-person leasing and marketing staff, and was responsible for leasing all of PJV projects. Mr. Sawyer and his staff obtained bankable leases for the PJV projects ranging from $750 to $975 per square meter, triple net.

As Deputy Director of PJV and at Sawyer & Co., Mr. Sawyer and his staff have maintained an active role in the legal community in Moscow. Negotiations with the government and others on behalf of PJV as well as other clients has given him a unique insight into how business in Moscow is conducted. Personal relationships with government officials enable Mr. Sawyer to expedite the permit and approval process.

In addition to Mr. Sawyer, the other key principal and shareholder in the company is Ms. Vera Setskaya. Ms. Setskaya is a very talented businesswoman who worked closely with Mr. Sawyer at PJV and plays a very important role in working with MATI and other potential partners. Mrs. Setskaya's father was a former high government official. Her husband is a nuclear scientist.

Exhibit 1   (continued)

Analysis of Partner

Moscow Aviation Technology Institute, after the fall of Communism, was left in a difficult position. Dramatic reductions in funds from the government forced MATI and other former government institutions to look for alternative sources of funds. MATI established a corporation within its organization whose mission is to identify alternatives to raise capital. Mr. Sawyer got to know the director of this corporation and developed a personal relationship after leaving PJV. In exploring alternatives, Mr. Sawyer convinced MATI that the best way to maximize the value of its land holdings was through a joint venture, and that he would be able to bring in institutional capital for the development.

Dealing with such a partner has many opportunities as well as drawbacks. The opportunities are four fold. The first is that MATI is a motivated partner. Strapped for cash, it needs investments with positive cash flow in order to fund its current cash obligations. Second, MATI cannot complete this transaction on its own. Third, because MATI is a former government institution, it has strong ties to the existing government. A Russian partner with political ties can help to speed up the government approval process which is required when any new construction is started. Finally, the University possesses its own electrical substation and water, sewage and heating connections. This means that the developer does not have to apply to the City Authorities for utility capacity—a great advantage particularly in the area of electricity where there is an acute shortage in the center of the city.

In terms of property rights, some foreigners worry about the Eastern European problem of former property owners coming back and making a claim. In Russia, this seems less likely to happen. The first reason is because the period of land ownership in Russia was very short. Up until 1860 most Russians were not allowed to own land and, after 1917 all land was owned by the state. In addition, during the early years of the Communist Government, the land owners were systematically killed. In contrast, in Eastern Europe, the land was not confiscated until 1949, and far fewer people were executed.

Another important consideration is the way Russian property law works. In Moscow land is not generally given in fee simple, but rather on long-term leases, and such land leases are not generally freely alienable. Land leases are generally given only for the specific purpose of building a building, and the leases often stipulate that they will terminate if no building is built within some specified period of time.

Property transactions generally focus on buildings to the extent that they already exist, because buildings are subject to outright ownership (unless they are registered as historic), and if privatized are freely alienable. If a building already exists, land use rights are considered secondary and are often not even registered until after the building is bought. Building control, therefore, is the strongest form of property rights. This is the opposite of the situation in the U.S. where the land title is key, and overcomes any contrary claim to a building (which does not even have any separate kind of title, being considered part of the land under the U.S. system).

When dealing with Russian partners, including MATI, the basic capitalist concept of mutually beneficial or synergistic market transactions is difficult to convey. Russians often have trouble understanding that a deal can (and usually should) leave both parties better off than without each other, which makes them very suspicious and hard to negotiate with. They also rarely have any understanding of modern financial concepts like the time value of money, which makes negotiating a deal structure very difficult. Yet another problem is the awe in which they hold property rights—to own a building or control a piece of land is psychologically so awesome for them that it is hard for them to think rationally about selling or sharing those rights with a foreigner in order to develop the property, even when they are absolutely penniless and the building may be falling down around their ears. They have seen the market go through the roof in the last couple of years and assume that the trend

Exhibit 1 (continued)

will continue into infinity, so they typically will not let go of property, until they are simply forced, no matter how profitable the deal is for them and no matter how unable they are to do anything with the property at the present time. In the case of MATI, although they were willing to enter into this joint venture with Sawyer and Company, the MATI Rector was never comfortable that he was doing the right thing, and that he was not selling out MATI's future.

Second, and most importantly, is the issue of cash. There are several players in the Moscow real estate market who would love a chance to develop this land. As such, while Mr. Sawyer's personal relationship with MATI has enabled Sawyer & Co. to pursue this project, it is always possible that another player could come in with a higher bid and disrupt the development process. Further, if Sawyer & Co. is not able, fairly quickly to begin construction, MATI may become nervous and start looking for another partner.

Investment Opportunity

Completion of the Domik project is projected to require $2.3 million of capital (see **Appendix 2**). Thirty-five percent of this investment will come in the form of equity with the remaining 65% to be financed through loans from Western banks. MATI will contribute the land for a one-time cash payment of $180,000 plus a preferred rate of return equal to 6% of the annual rent roll during the first 10 years. Thereafter, MATI is to receive a 45% equity interest in the project. Sawyer & Co. will receive a development fee of $188,050 for the development of the project plus "sweat equity" of 40% of the equity of the project prior to conversion and 22% after conversion. Finally, investors will make a cash contribution of approximately $800,000 and receive a 60% share of the equity prior to conversion and 33% after conversion.

Construction financing is available from a European bank for an amount equal to the $800,000 equity investment. When the building is 50% leased, bank financing will be available up to $1.5 million. This is a two year bullet loan with an interest rate of 15.0% that can be prepaid at any time.

Permanent financing can be obtained for the project once "bankable leases" are obtained. A $1.5 million of permanent ten year fully amortizing debt has been arranged through a large United States based bank at an interest rate of 12.0%.

Project Timing

From the time project funding is opened, approximately 12 months will be required until the building is ready for move-in. Of that, approximately six weeks will be required for design and preliminary approvals. Upon completion of that work, excavation, foundation work, and utility work may begin, and marketing will also commence. It is estimated that approximately three months will be required to locate suitable tenants for the project and to negotiate leases with those tenants. Therefore, the time between opening project funding and obtaining leases is estimated to be approximately four and one-half months.

From the fall of Communism until recently, projects funded themselves. Developers were able to extract several years of rent in advance from future tenants and use these moneys to fund the construction of the building. This practice has stopped. Several developers who rented buildings in advance were unable to complete construction. Tenants lost all of their money. The current market environment requires that the developer demonstrate that the building will be completed, as specified, before tenants will agree to sign leases.

The majority of the risk in this project therefore exists between the time that funds are committed until the time that the building is completed. The equity investor is most exposed during construction, before leasing. The equity investment is used to begin the project. Once it becomes clear that the project will be completed, leases can be signed. And once 50% of the building is leased, con-

Exhibit 1   (continued)

struction debt financing becomes available. If at any point during the development process, the economic or political environment changes, the project is at risk. For example, civil war could erupt during the initial construction phase. Because completion of the building would then be in question, tenants would not sign leases. Construction financing would not be available and the project could not be completed.

Any investors in the project must understand that these risks exist during construction.

Economic Assumptions and Returns

Appendix 2 outlines the preliminary development budget. These costs are based on very conservative estimates which have been compiled through a combination of Mr. Sawyer's experience in developing property in Moscow, and estimates compiled from construction companies by the architects. In the budget, it is expected that the project will be financed in part by a construction loan. Construction period interest is calculated by assuming that the loan will be outstanding for half a year with an interest rate of 15% on an annual basis.

Appendix 3 gives a preliminary setup on a per square meter, and total basis.

- Because of the market environment the rent is triple net—operating, insurance, and tax expenses are paid by the tenant. Rent of $840 per net rentable square meter is shown for comparison to Western rents. When compared to other rents in Garden Ring, this is slightly below current market rates.

- Net vacancy expense is assumed to be 2%. This is justified by strong absorption in the current market place. It is expected that the building will be 100% leased with 6 year leases immediately upon completion. This expense is therefore conservative.

- Non-operating expenses are assumed to be 6% of the rent roll. Operating expenses are included in the triple net leases, however, there will be a certain amount of non-operating expenses such as managing the partnership accounting.

- MATI's preferred return is 6% of the rent roll.

- A structural reserve of $6.56 per square meter is included.

- Debt is assumed to be 65% of development costs, carries an interest rate of 12%, and is amortized over a 10 year period.

Appendix 4 shows the projected cash flows from the project and to the investors. It is assumed that cash flow remains flat for ten years, and that the investment is sold at a capitalization rate of 10% after the tenth year at which point the debt is completely paid down.

Equity returns are shown at the bottom of the page. The payback period to the investor is $2^3/_4$ years. This occurs during the initial lease term. Because it would be impossible to pick a discount rate in order to determine a present value for the project, it is more appropriate to look at an internal rate of return. For this project, the IRR is expected to be 38% (33% assuming that the terminal value is zero). With the current long term bond at 7.5% this represents a substantial return on invested capital.

Exhibit 1   (continued)

Conclusions

The real estate market in Moscow is booming. Moscow is the largest city in Europe (population 15.5 million including catchment area[13]), and if its development path follows those of other Eastern European capitals, its potential is great. Russia, however, is still at a cross roads in its development path. Political revolution, corruption, and organized crime pose serious obstacles to the development path. Any investment in Moscow is exposed to these potential problems.

From a project specific point of view, any investment in the Domik project, is an investment in Cameron Sawyer. While Mr. Sawyer has worked as a developer and a leasing agent in Moscow for a number of years, he has never attempted a project on his own. The challenges of developing a project in the context of Moscow's political and economic environment are substantial. This represents a serious risk.

Mitigating these risks are the location of the project, the MATI partnership, and the lease feature which the current leasing market in Moscow allows. Equity returns to investors are conservatively projected to be 38% and down side protection is provided by the fact that all invested capital is returned by the end of the third year of the investment and during the initial leases.

Any investor in the project must weigh these risks and benefits.

[13]Fergusen Hollis

Exhibit 1   (continued)

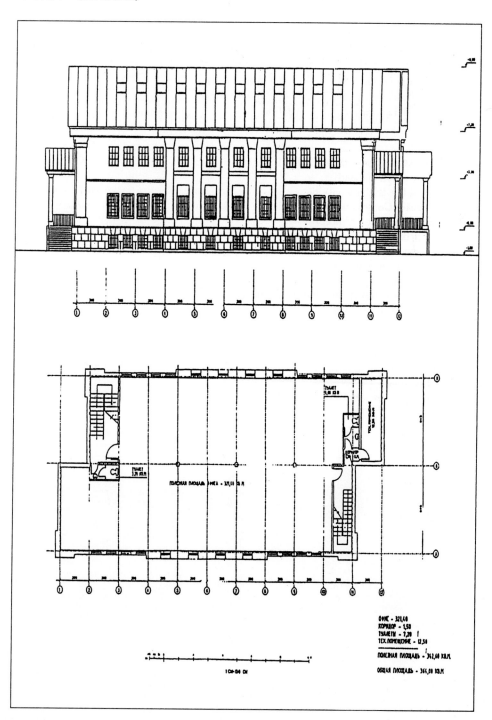

Exhibit 2

Preliminary Development Budget Based on Gross Buildable Area

Gross Buildable Area: 1,200 square meters
Net Buildable Area: 1,000 square meters
Overall Loss Factor: 16.6%

	PER METER^2	TOTAL
Land Cost (Prepayment to MATI)	$150.00	$180,000
Reservation of Land	0.71	847
Land Use Rights Consulting	4.17	5,000
Turnkey Construction Costs, Including Foundations	1,000.00	1,200,000
Site Preparation, Fence, Paving	83.33	100,000
Sketch Design (Russian)	25.42	30,508
American Architect (Design Development; Space Planning)	19.17	23,000
Working Drawings	30.37	36,441
Approvals	19.77	23,729
Geological Testing and Survey; Utilities Evaluation	2.50	3,000
Utilities Construction	75.00	90,000
Contingency	100.00	120,000
Construction Period Interest (1)	56.64	67,970
Development Fee	156.71	188,050
Leasing Commissions	150.00	180,000
Tax Advice	12.50	15,000
Total Preliminary Development Budget	$1,886.29	$2,263,545

Notes:
(1) Based on 6 months outstanding at 15% interest.

Exhibit 3   Preliminary Setup

	PER METER^2	TOTAL
Gross Rent (Net) (1) (2)	$ 840.00	$ 840,000
Vacancy @ 2%	(16.80)	(16,800)
Net Rent	823.20	823,200
Non-Operating Expenses (5%)	(42.00)	(42,000)
MATI preferred cash flow (6%)	(50.40)	(50,400)
Structural Reserve	(6.56)	(6,560)
Cash Flow before Financing	724.20	724,240
Debt Financing Costs (3)	(260.40)	(260,398)
Net Cash Flow	$ 463.84	$ 463,842

Notes:

(1) Net of taxes, insurance, and operating expenses.

(2) Rents in Russia are expressed as if the tenant were renting total gross space. For comparison with non-Russian projects, rent per meter is expressed by dividing rent by net rentable space.

(3) 65% budget, 12% interest, 10-year amortization schedule.

Exhibit 4 Projected Cash Flow and Equity Returns

YEAR	0	1	2	3	4	5	6	7	8	9	10
Cash Flows											
Net Rent	—	$823,200	$823,200	$823,200	$823,200	$823,200	$823,200	$823,200	$823,200	$823,200	$823,200
Non-Operating Expenses	—	42,000	42,000	42,000	42,000	42,000	42,000	42,000	42,000	42,000	42,000
MATI preferred cash flow	—	50,400	50,400	50,400	50,400	50,400	50,400	50,400	50,400	50,400	50,400
Structural Reserve	—	6,560	6,560	6,560	6,560	6,560	6,560	6,560	6,560	6,560	6,560
Cash Flow before Financing	—	724,240	724,240	724,240	724,240	724,240	724,240	724,240	724,240	724,240	724,240
Debt Financing Costs	—	260,398	260,398	260,398	260,398	260,398	260,398	260,398	260,398	260,398	260,398
Net Cash Flow	—	$463,842	$463,842	$463,842	$463,842	$463,842	$463,842	$463,842	$463,942	$463,842	$463,842
Mortgage Analysis											
Interest Rate	12%										
Level Payment	$260,398										
Mortgage Beginning of Period	—	$1,471,304	$1,387,463	$1,293,561	$1,188,391	$1,070,600	$938,675	$790,918	$625,431	$440,085	$232,498
Interest	—	176,557	166,496	155,227	142,607	128,472	112,641	94,910	75,052	52,810	27,900
Principal	—	83,841	93,902	105,170	117,791	131,926	147,757	165,487	185,346	207,587	232,498
Mortgage End of Period	$1,471,304	$1,387,463	$1,293,561	$1,188,391	$1,070,600	$938,675	$709,918	$625,431	$440,085	$232,498	$0

Investor's Equity Performance Analysis

Investor Contribution	$792,241	
Assumed Exit Cap Rate	10%	
Terminal Value	$7,242,400	
Investor % of Net Cash*	60%	
Investor % of Exit Value	33%	

YEAR	0	1	2	3	4	5	6	7	8	9	10
Investor's Net Share of Cash Flow	($792,241)	278,305	287,305	278,305	278,305	278,305	278,305	278,305	278,305	278,305	278,305
Investor's Share of Terminal Value	—	—	—	—	—	—	—	—	—	—	2,389,992
Total Investor's Cash Flow	($792,241)	278,305	278,305	278,305	278,305	278,305	278,305	278,305	278,305	278,305	2,673,337
Internal Rate of Return	38.28%										
Internal Rate of Return w/o Terminal Value	33.12%										

*During the first 10 years, MATI receives only a ground lease payment, and cash flow is split between the investor and developer based upon their respective interests. The investors' interest in the partnership is 60% before the MATI conversion and 33% afterwards. If the building is sold during the first ten (10) years, MATI will receive 45% of the net sales proceeds.

19

THE TEXTILE CORPORATION BUILDING

In March 1987, Martin Donwill hopes to submit the winning offer in a sealed bid auction for a 350,000 square foot Boston office complex. Although he feels his skills in management and rehabilitation, as demonstrated specifically in the case, give him an economic advantage over his competitors, he has to quantify the ways in which he can create value, and profitably outbid his competitors. The art of bidding, can be discussed within the greater context of theories of negotiation.

Discussion Questions:

1. How much should Donwill bid for the Textile Corporation Building and why? Be prepared to explain how you arrived at your price.
2. How has Donwill planned to increase the cash flow from operations for this property? What do you think of his approach?
3. What are the problems of improving or rehabilitating an existing building? How do they differ from the problems of new construction?
4. Has Textile Corporation picked the best method for selling the property?

In March 1987, Martin E. Donwill was trying to decide how much to offer for the properties owned and 50% occupied by the Textile Corporation. Textile had issued an invitation on February 21, 1987, for sealed bids for the four parcels comprising: a 12-story building with 300,000 total square feet of space; a 6-story office building, with 50,000 square feet of space; a 3-story garage with parking space for 355 vehicles; and an adjoining vacant parcel of approximately 8,400 square feet, used as a parking lot for approximately 40 additional vehicles.

The minimum acceptable bid price was announced by Textile to be $16,000,000, and because of the size and prominence of the properties and its location in a rapidly improving area only a few blocks from Boston's financial district, there was considerable interest in the bidding on the part of local and out-of-town realtors.

DESCRIPTION OF PROPERTY

The buildings were completed in the 1920s and were solidly constructed. A broad arched entrance in the main building led into a magnificent brick, high-ceilinged lobby and large arched entrances. From the upper floors, there were views of the harbor. The Textile Company had originally used the property for its offices and manufacturing facilities. Over the years, its manufacturing operations were moved out of the area, and approximately half of the 12-story building and all of the six-story building was converted for use by other firms, primarily distributors who liked the location, and were willing to accept class C minimally modernized space. The buildings had been well-maintained, serviced by eight recently installed passenger elevators that replaced the manually operated ones. Each floor was air-conditioned with individual package units.

Approximately 80% of the gross footage was usable. The remainder was for public space such as stairways, elevators, utility rooms, public corridors and bathrooms on multi-tenanted floors. Gross rents for tenants other than Textile averaged $15 per rentable square foot in the larger building and $12 in the smaller including electricity. Occupancy had traditionally been about 97%.

Adjunct Professor William J. Poorvu prepared this case as the basis for class discussion rather than to illustrate either effective or ineffective handling of an administrative situation.

COMPANY HISTORY

The Martin E. Donwill Company, a sole proprietorship real estate investment company, was one of the largest private property owners in the area. Since 1970, Mr. Donwill had accumulated approximately 10,000 apartment units and over 1,200,000 square feet of office space in the area. He specialized in modernizing older apartment houses and office buildings, and felt that he should invest exclusively in this area of real estate as opposed to constructing new buildings in which he had no experience. According to Mr. Donwill, each area of real estate required its own special talents and his talents were in this area.

He saw the risks of developing new properties as being considerable because of the uncertainties of predicting five to seven years ahead the costs of construction, financing charges, tenant rentals, and completion dates. He felt that he was making a positive contribution to society, and the preservation of urban values, by rehabilitating areas that were not yet fully recognized. He was able to do this without government subsidies or without destroying or demolishing neighborhoods. Also, the pricing of his rental or condominium units enabled middle-class residents to live and work in the city. One had to know what was worth rehabilitating, and how much one should spend to still make a profit.

He prided himself on his ability to control costs. A continuous and large volume of work was one factor that enabled him to achieve this efficiency. He was able to develop a full-time, year-round, experienced staff of construction and maintenance personnel. He attained economies through large-scale purchasing, often of manufacturer's closeouts. He closely supervised all phases of his operation, from maintenance to the negotiation of most office leases. His imagination was important in solving many difficult problems. Because of his attention to detail, he considered it desirable to concentrate his real estate investments in the Boston area.

Mr. Donwill managed his real estate operations from his office, consisting of four rooms and a small secretarial area in an older office building he had renovated. This office handled the bookkeeping for all of his properties and the rental and management for the office buildings. The apartments were managed from local offices and maintenance was handled by full-time maintenance personnel operating from company-owned, radio-controlled trucks dispatched from a central supply warehouse.

He had begun by acquiring apartment buildings in one area close to and accessible to public transportation. Rents for older one-bedroom apartments then ran from $300 to $400 per month. He looked for stable neighborhoods with middle class residents capable of paying higher rents if their apartments were renovated. The increase to $450 or $550 per month seemed substantial but still produced a market rental well below that of new construction.

As an example of the economies of his operation, Mr. Donwill would spend $9,000 to modernize the kitchen and bathroom and to redecorate a one-bedroom apartment. By increasing the rents by $150 a month or $1,800 per year, he could recapture his investment in five years. Immediately, his $9,000 investment was worth $18,000 since apartment buildings in the area were being valued at ten times their annual cash flow. The value of his investment was increased still further since the modernization program resulted in the reduction of maintenance costs and in the elimination of the substantial vacancies in the buildings he bought. Because most of the operating costs of a property do not relate to the level of occupancy, a difference of 5% in vacancies can have a major impact on the owner's return on investment.

Donwill next started to acquire warehouse buildings in neighborhoods close to downtown for conversion to commercial space. He felt that market conditions at that time were ideal. The high cost of new construction, the growth in service industries and the interest of many firms in attractively renovated older space provided him with an opportunity. He was imaginative in his approach. In one building, he added 9% to the building's rentable floor area by building an extra floor between the old first and second floors, exploiting a ceiling height of 20 feet on the first floor. At another, he enclosed an interior court and added 10% to the rentable floor area. The additional space was quickly rented since the modernization of the building made the interior space, now air-conditioned and properly lit, desirable.

PROPOSED SALE OF PROPERTY

Mr. Donwill first heard of the proposed sale of the Textile Corporation Building in February 1987. The thought of owning this building was very appealing to him. He had always regarded the building as one of the best and largest of the existing buildings near downtown. He doubted whether he would again have an opportunity to purchase this building. Textile Corporation owned and had been the major tenant of the building since its completion in 1926. It had fully depreciated the property on its balance sheet and as a result decided that its investment in the building could better be used in other areas of its business. An earlier purchase offer was almost accepted, but the company was uncertain about the optimum price available. As a result, the company decided to have a sealed-bid auction for the property with the prospective bidders prescreened as to their financial responsibility. Bids had to be received by March 30, 1987, and would be acted on by April 15. To insure that any bids submitted would be serious, a $1 million deposit was required with each submission. An offering circular was printed describing the terms and conditions of the proposed sale with the current income and expense figures. A floor plan was also shown (see **Exhibit 1**).

Textile decided to utilize the services of six local established real estate brokerage firms to offer the property. The broker of the successful bidder was to receive a commission, to be paid by the seller, of $250,000 plus 2% of the amount that the successful bid exceeded the minimum price of $16,000,000.

EVALUATION OF PROPERTY

Based upon the income and expense figures supplied to him by the seller (see **Exhibit 2**), Mr. Donwill attempted to evaluate the property. He saw that the gross income figure of $4,400,000 was based on a new lease for $1,650,000 entered into by the Textile Corporation for 12 years. Textile had also retained rights to extend the lease for two 5-year periods at an annual rent of $2,200,000 including electricity. The space covered by the lease was 139,000 gross square feet or 46% of the gross rentable area in the 12-story building. Although the rental averaging $11.87 per square foot at first seemed low to him, Mr. Donwill was satisfied when he saw that the area rented included a considerable amount of basement space, was calculated on a gross square footage basis and included public areas. This made the effective office rent on a net usable basis about $14 per square foot. Also, Textile was taking the space in its present condition. There also was a tax clause which specified that Textile would pay 46% of any property tax increase over the 1986 level, and an operations clause covering a similar portion of increased cleaning expenses and all utilities. The operating expenses for the building were based on the actual experience of the Textile Corporation with the building and totalled $2,950,000. This left a net before financing of $1,450,000. Mr. Donwill then took an allowance for vacancies of 3% of gross income and a management expense figure of 2% which reduced this net figure to $1,230,000.

Mr. Donwill estimated that he would probably be able to get an institutional first mortgage equal to 75% of the price paid for the property. The mortgage term would be for 26 years with interest at 10%, requiring a constant annual payment of 10.9%. He had recently placed another mortgage at this level. On this basis, if he made the minimum bid of $16,000,000 he could obtain a $12,000,000 first mortgage costing $1,308,000 per year. This left a negative cash flow of $78,000 based upon Textile's numbers with only minor adjustments.

Cash Flow from Operations (see **Exhibit 2**)	$1,450,000
Less: 3% Vacancy	132,000
2% Management	88,000
First mortgage: Interest & Principal	1,308,000
Net Cash Flow	($78,000)

There was a possibility of obtaining an interest-only first mortgage for the first three years with an annual cost of $1.2 million. This would put his cash flow in the black, yielding $30,000 per year.

Mr. Donwill, obviously, was not satisfied with such a low return on his investment. Yet, he felt that competitive bids would be in excess of the minimum as indicated by the high level of public interest.

INCOME

There was a considerable amount of new office space downtown under construction at rents in excess of $30 per square foot. Published figures showed a two to three year absorption period. It was difficult to calculate the size of the demand for Class C space or Class B space if he improved the Textile Building. How many professional firms would move from downtown to save money? Moreover, he was not sure how many of the present tenants would remain, first, because Textile Corporation was no longer the landlord and second, because he had a reputation for upgrading and raising rents.

He began to analyze those factors that affected the income of the property. He first considered the general market area. He next considered the amount of space available for rent. He knew from his past experience that although a building was fixed in size, there were several approaches to measuring rentable square footage. He saw that there were about 25,000 square feet of non-income-producing yet potential rentable space. Of the 25,000 feet on each floor of the 12-story building, approximately 2,200 square feet were used for elevators, the elevator lobby, and stairs and would always be public and unrentable. But some of the corridor space and the toilet and storage spaces might become rentable if used by a single tenant. By rearranging certain areas and by attempting to lease individual floors to only one or two tenants, he thought it was reasonable to expect that he could increase his rentable space by at least 15,000 square feet which, at $15 per square foot, could increase his income by $225,000. Another 5,000 square feet with income potential of $75,000 per year could be "created" by measuring space from the window or glass line of the building to the glass line of the entrance door. In the past, measurements were taken from the inside walls of the space. In an older building with 18-inch masonry walls, the 9 inches included in rentable area could add up. The periphery of many of the floors was as much as 750 feet.

Mr. Donwill also had an idea which he thought could add to the total fixed space of the property. Between the two buildups was an open area of approximately 600 square feet. By filling this area with a new structure, he could not only create 500 square feet of rentable space at each level but make it possible for the floors of the 6-story building to be entered off the elevator lobby of the building with the greater prestige and the higher rental levels. The 3,000 rentable square feet created could be rented at $15 per square foot or $45,000 per year. In addition, the 40,000 square feet now renting at a lower level could then be worth as much as $2.00 per square foot more or $80,000 per year, merely because of the change in entrance.

Another means of increasing income was to increase the quality of the space offered through modernization. He estimated that he could increase rentals by $325,000 by improving 110,000 square feet of space for both existing tenants and new tenants coming into the building.

He analyzed whether rental income could be increased by offering additional services to the tenants. Although Mr. Donwill intended to clean, operate and maintain the building in a first-rate manner, he knew that Textile had also done so. Therefore, he concluded that he would probably not be able to increase income in this manner. Mr. Donwill felt, though, that his active promotional efforts, his encouragement of local rental brokers, and his existing institutional advertising might give him a broader choice of tenants and since the building was not yet well known, he felt that this advantage might be substantial. The more property he owned, the more likely it was that tenants would come to him for space either in this property or other buildings he owned.

In summary, through renovation, the building of new space, and the remeasuring of old, Mr. Donwill expected to increase rents by $750,000. Mr. Donwill knew that this increase would not be achieved immediately but would probably take about three years. A reasonable estimate would be that the income would increase over the $4,400,000 by $100,000 in Year 1, $300,000 in Year 2, $500,000 in Year 3, and $750,000 in Year 4. In addition, parking and other miscellaneous income generated $470,000 annually.

CAPITAL EXPENSES

To remodel space and to build the new addition involved substantial capital expenses. Also, additional vacancy must be expected since a tenant could not occupy space until the work was complete. In addition to the 3% for vacancy already included in his expense statement, Mr. Donwill allowed for an additional $150,000 in vacancy the first year, $300,000 the second year and $150,000 the third year. Then the present over-all allowance of 3% should again be adequate. The major capital expense would come from the renovation of 110,000 space feet of presently leased space and approximately 15,000 square feet of public space to permit its inclusion as rentable area. Mr. Donwill felt that this renovation would cost the normal property owner $25 per square foot or $3,125,000 but that because of his expertise he could probably do the work for $20.00 per square foot or $2,500,000.

For this $20.00 per square foot, he could remodel a typical office to include carpeting, dropped acoustic ceilings, recessed fluorescent lighting, air-conditioning, the enclosure of all pipes and radiators, partitioning finished at the tenant's option with prefinished wood paneling, paint, or vinyl wall covering, overhead storage cabinets, shelving, new entrance doors, counters, closets. The layout was designed to the tenant's particular specifications, prepared by an architect selected and paid for by Mr. Donwill. Yet, Mr. Donwill chose materials that he expected would reduce the landlord's future maintenance responsibilities.

There were many reasons why Mr. Donwill's costs were lower than average, none of which he felt affected the quality of his finished product. First of all, because of the amount of work he was doing, he could effect large economies through mass purchasing. As an example, he bought his own lumber direct from Oregon with carload deliveries. Walnut paneling bought in quantity cost 25% less. The vinyl wall covering was bought direct from manufacturers' closeouts at 60% off. Rather than buy 8-foot long, four-tube lighting fixtures from a manufacturer, he bent and painted the metal troffers himself and then separately purchased and added the ballast, socket, tube and plastic cover. In renovating one major building, he had taken out the old-fashioned marble dividing partitions in the toilet areas and replaced them with new metal partitions. Then he had the marble repolished and reused to create an elegant marble entrance lobby. Imagination was an important factor in remodeling.

Besides savings on material, Mr. Donwill's labor costs were well below average. In an industry noted for its cyclical employment practices, Mr. Donwill had experienced, non-union work crews whom he employed on a year-round basis. He was able to take non-skilled workers at $8 per hour and teach them to do tasks that normally were done by employees receiving $12 per hour. Each individual was expected to do work in more than one trade. By subcontracting only ceiling, floor tile, and air-conditioning installation, he was able to reduce the number of outside trades involved, saving both time and money.

The six-story addition of 600 square feet per floor would cost $200,000 to complete. The cost of this was high because of the difficulty of installing steel and materials in such a small enclosed space. Few outside contractors would even attempt the job. Mr. Donwill expected to install two new boilers costing $100,000. Presently the heat was purchased from Edison Steam, a method Mr. Donwill, from his experience in other buildings, knew to be very expensive. Mr. Donwill also put in an allowance for $200,000 to cover contingencies for the whole project.

These capital costs totalling $3,000,000 would be spent equally over the three year period. The increased vacancies over the three-year period totalled $600,000. Mr. Donwill expected to finance this $3,600,000 partially through reinvesting any money received from operating the property over the three-year period and the remainder through a second mortgage from a private source. Until he knew his actual mortgage cost based on the amount of his bid to Textile, he could not estimate exactly how much would be available from operations. But by Year 4, the $30,000 profit should rise to $1,052,000.

OPERATING EXPENSES

Mr. Donwill then examined the various operating expense figures submitted to him by Textile to see whether or not through more efficient operation he could increase his return. He knew that in any building that had been owned by the same owner for a long period of time inefficiencies in operation would be bound to occur. This was especially apt to be true in a company such as Textile where the property was being operated not for its real estate return but for the service of the office and executive employees of the company. He expected to reduce the building payroll figure of $810,000 to $530,000 (not including payroll taxes). This reduction was accomplished in three ways. First, since the buildings had been recently converted to automatic elevators, 12 operators could be released immediately, saving $180,000. Second, another major cost of building payroll was office cleaning. His cost in other buildings was $.60 per square foot and he expected his cost to be the same here, resulting in another saving of $60,000. Third, the permanent maintenance staff would consist of an engineer and three helpers at a cost of $80,000 per year as compared with Textile's cost of $120,000. In addition to the direct wage cost savings, he expected to save an additional $40,000 for payroll and FICA taxes. He realized that his costs were below that of published national average figures. Yet, because of his efficiencies and because the building would be easier to maintain and clean as it was modernized, he felt the $320,000 figure of savings for payroll and related taxes was appropriate. Also, he knew that in the early years of owning a property, the owner normally pays more attention to details and is more efficient. Then it was natural even in his own properties for a certain degree of inefficiency to creep in.

Mr. Donwill knew that he was not expected to retain any of the present building employees or be responsible for their severance, vacation or unemployment pay when they were discharged. Textile was prepared to assume these costs. As payroll costs were reduced, there would be a corresponding percentage decrease in payroll taxes.

Heating costs could be expected to drop from $280,000 to $200,000 for two reasons. He was installing his own boiler system, probably in the summer of the third year when the present Edison contract expired. In addition, as the ceilings in the offices were dropped, less area was required to be heated.

He checked with his insurance agent who told him that because of a special package policy written by the Factory Mutual Insurance Company for all his properties, his insurance costs would be reduced by $10,000.

Electricity, which cost $500,000 per year, was a large expense and was a service included in the basic rent. In other buildings he owned, each tenant had a meter and paid the utility company directly. On a rent-inclusion basis, the landlord could make money since electricity was purchased on one meter at a bulk rate. A disadvantage was that a tenant, even though it was more expensive, might be inclined to rent space at $13.50 per foot without electricity rather than at $15.00 with electricity. In any case, Mr. Donwill knew that it would be a very expensive electrical job to change over the system to individual meters, and Textile had recently put in a new modern electric service to the building capable of handling all the foreseeable needs of the tenants based upon the rent inclusion principle. The electricity charge also included the usage for air conditioning. He would have to wait for more experience before deciding if there were any savings in electricity. Besides, he thought it would be safer to have the tenants share in increases and decreases in electricity costs rather than predict future energy prices.

Mr. Donwill next analyzed the repairs and decorating figure. Historically, this figure had been $260,000. This seemed high to him. He thought it might represent some unusual expenditures because of the impending sale of the property. Furthermore, as the building was modernized, repairs should decrease. He calculated that $200,000, approximately 4% of income, was reasonable especially since Mr. Donwill's staff was accustomed to doing most repair work themselves.

Real estate taxes were the largest operating expense item, and it was in this area that Mr. Donwill was especially sensitive. Mr. Donwill had a special problem with the local assessors since his business was modernizing and increasing the rent rolls of older buildings. The assessors kept careful watch of his operations and continually tried to raise his assessments. In this case, he anticipated an increase of $100,000. Over that initial rise, the tenants would pay their share of further increases. Still, Textile's tax clause would result in their paying 46% of any initial increase in the 12-story building or 40% of the bill for the whole project. Therefore, he adjusted his own cost by the net amount, $60,000.

A management figure of 2% seemed fair to him for this property even though this percentage was higher than his cost in other areas. He knew that this high-grade property would require special attention. The $103,000 figure would include the salary of a manager and secretary plus office expenses and professional fees.

In any case, he knew that a potential mortgagee always put a figure for management in an expense set-up to determine the net income of the property for appraisal purposes. The reason for this is that a potential mortgagee must consider the fact that if it comes into ownership of the property through foreclosure, it would have to hire an outside management firm.

Mr. Donwill now made a new income and expense statement which he expected to achieve by year 4 based upon his adjustments of the figures submitted to him (see **Exhibit 3**). His income after vacancy on a stabilized basis was increased to $4,996,000 and his expenses on an adjusted basis were reduced to $2,643,000. This left a figure of $2,353,000 before financing after deducting 3% for vacancy and 2% for management.

BIDDING STRATEGY

The question now became how much to bid for the property. He wanted to win the auction. The prestige of owning the property was worth $500,000 to $1,000,000 to him both in pride and in the fact that this building would upgrade his whole portfolio of properties. The more property he owned, the more flexibility he would have in satisfying space needs of new or existing tenants. Mr. Donwill, however, did not want to pay any more for the property than he had to. He knew that all the other bidders as well would use the income method for determining value. Replacement cost produced a value far higher than the actual market value of the property. The 67,771 square feet of land for all the parcels was worth at least $3 million as raw land. He would use that figure as a deduction from his purchase price to determine his depreciable base. To be conservative, he decided not to depreciate the improvements until Year 4. In accordance with the new 1986 Tax Act, depreciation would have to be taken on a straight line basis over a 31.5 year life. The income tax rate he estimated at 28% for ordinary income and capital gains.

Normally, Mr. Donwill expected a cash return after federal income taxes of 15% on his invested capital even though he knew other bidders might be satisfied with a 12% return. Yet, he doubted whether other bidders would see as many areas to increase net income as he did, especially with regard to the connection between the two buildings. The $200,000 expenditure increased income by $125,000. Another bidder might be willing to modernize 110,000 square feet to obtain the extra $325,000 income, but it might cost $625,000 more. Other bidders, if experienced in the area, would also plan on converting from steam and would know of the elimination of the elevator operators. They would also make an effort to reduce public areas and would try to use the revised measurement standard. Whether they could be as persuasive as Mr. Donwill in obtaining tenants, he did not know.

His prospective mortgage lender had informed him that as long as his purchase price was within reason, he could still expect a 75% mortgage at 10% interest. The term of the mortgage would be ten years and amortization would not start until the fourth year and then would be on a 26 year basis. Based upon his personal reputation and guaranty and the prestige of the property, he was able to secure the pledge of a three-year $3 million second mortgage at 12% annual interest with interest only payments during the three-year period. At that time, he felt he could increase his first mortgage by an amount adequate to repay the second, on the same terms as his present mortgage. In the meantime, he would have to put in any cash flow deficits personally. He also had enough passive income from other properties to offset any losses from this project.

The number of competitors he would have in this bidding was another question. He knew that virtually all the outstanding real estate firms in the area and a few from New York City were analyzing the property, but he expected only five or six to put up the $1,000,000 deposit and actually make a bid. Mr. Donwill sat down to weigh all these factors and prepare his bid.

Exhibit 1

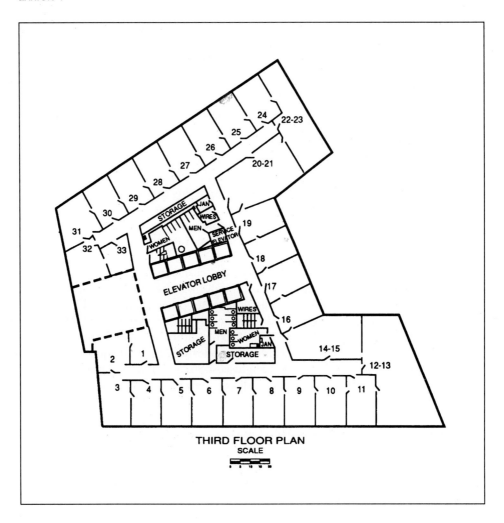

THIRD FLOOR PLAN
SCALE

Exhibit 2   1986 Operating Income and Expenses

Income

Textile Corporation	$1,650,000
Other Tenants: 12 Story Building	1,800,000
6 Story Building	480,000
Parking	320,000
Miscellaneous	<u>150,000</u>
Gross Revenues	4,400,000

Operating Expenses

Building Payroll	810,000
Payroll Taxes	140,000
Window Cleaning	20,000
Elevator Maintenance	30,000
Insurance	40,000
Water	20,000
Heat	280,000
Electricity	500,000
Decorating and Repairs	260,000
Miscellaneous	<u>50,000</u>
Building Operations	2,150,000
Real Estate Tax	<u>800,000</u>
Total Operating Expenses	2,950,000
Cash Flow from Operations	$1,450,000

Exhibit 3   The Textile Corporation Building

PROJECTED INCOME AND EXPENSES (AS OF YEAR 4)

Income

Textile Corporation	$1,650,000
Other Tenants	3,030,000
Parking	320,000
Miscellaneous	150,000
Gross Revenues	5,150,000
Vacancies	154,000
Net Revenues	4,996,000

Operating Expenses

Building Payroll	530,000
Payroll Tax	100,000
Window Cleaning	20,000
Elevator Maintenance	30,000
Insurance	30,000
Water	20,000
Heat	200,000
Electricity	500,000
Decorating and Repair	200,000
Miscellaneous	50,000
Management	103,000
Building Operations	1,783,000
Real Estate Taxes	860,000
Total Operating Expenses	2,643,000
Cash Flow from Operations	$2,353,000

Exhibit 4

Syndications/John Brown

Boston Business Journal/February 23, 1987

Looking at leases: It takes two to tango

When we're talking investment property, we're talking leases. Most appraisers will agree that the value of investment property is primarily determined by its income, and income is determined by the leases that are in place.

Leasing has to be looked at from two vantage points: that of the lessor (landlord or owner) and that of the lessee (tenant). The relationship is an adversarial one—but it needn't be unfriendly. After all, the tenant needs space, and the owner must have tenants in order to survive and prosper.

The relationship is shaped by the existing market and the type of property that's being leased. For the purposes of this discussion, let's focus upon office leasing, from the viewpoint of both the owner and the prospective tenant.

The discussion that follows is for non-professionals who occasionally get involved with the leasing process for their company or for other reasons. It may also be helpful for prospective investors in investment real estate or real estate limited partnerships, who have some understanding of leasing but could use further knowledge in order to evaluate potential investments or offerings.

If the office-space market (or retail or industrial markets) is soft, the tenant will have an advantage. The tenant will have more space to choose from and will be in a better position to get "concessions" or "incentives," whether they be lower rental charges, a period of free or reduced rent, higher quality buildout allowances (interior finishes) or even a possible equity position in the property. The latter would apply only to a long-term, large-space user.

Space measurement

The measurement of space is part of the adversarial relationship we mentioned above. The tenant thinks in terms of usable space, while the owner usually thinks in terms of gross area. Let's pause for a moment and sort out some terms, such as "gross," "gross rentable," "net rentable," "leasable" and "usable," among others.

The Institute of Real Estate Management (IREM) defines "gross rentable" as all area within outside walls minus stairs, elevator shafts, flues, pipe shafts, vertical ducts and balconies. It defines "net rentable" as the above minus utility rooms, restrooms, corridors and other areas not available to the tenants for their furnishings and personnel.

In years past, the Boston area largely rented on a "usable" basis, which was the actual space available to the tenant. Most areas of the country followed this pattern except for New York City. The so-called "New York system" was what we would now call "gross area" or "gross rentable" and included all area of the building (and sometimes part of the thickness of the walls), prorated to each tenant.

For example, you might lease 10,000 square feet but find that only 8200 square feet usable. The rest is scattered throughout the building in the form of restrooms, corridors, stairways, utility closets, etc. The lost space is called the "waste" or "efficiency" factor and is expressed as a percentage (in this case, 18 percent).

Boston started moving toward the New York system in the early '60s and has been pursuing it with a vengeance in the past eight to 10 years. Most buildings are now leased on what is called a "leasable space" basis (the terms net and gross are dropped entirely). Leasable space is usually the space actually occupied by the tenant plus a proportionate share of the waste factor (except stairways and elevator shafts). This can vary from building to building.

If you are contemplating leasing space, the important thing to have is a floor plan (to scale) of the space being offered. Actually measure it to determine how much space you will have to use. This is important for space-planning purposes, but it will also allow you to calculate the waste factor by comparing your usable space to the leasable space figure in your lease. Waste factors range from less than 5 percent to about 20 percent depending upon the type of building and tenancy, and the size of individual tenant spaces. Usually, the lower the waste factor, the better deal you will be getting, but you will have to do the calculations.

Tenant buildout

When you bought your first tract home, the builder probably had allowances for this and allowances for that, things such as electrical and plumbing fixtures or wall coverings. Any upgrades over the standard allowances were "extras." The same is usually true for the office developer. The standard tenant improvements (buildout) might include two coats of off-white paint, medium-grade carpeting, acoustical ceiling with fluorescent lighting and a specific length of interior ceiling-to-floor partitioning, depending upon the number of square feet being rented.

The longer the term of the lease, the longer the period for amortization of these costs, and the less impact on per-square-foot annual rent rates. If, for example, extras come to $60,000 on 10,000 square feet of space, the increase in the rental rate might be about $2 per square foot on a five-year lease. On a three-year lease the increased rate would be about $3 per square foot.

Some space is advertised with no buildout allowance included and obviously sounds like a bargain. Once buildout is added, the rate could increase by as much as $6-10 per square foot.

Tenant charges

The terms "gross" and "net" above refer to the way space is measured. Just to confuse things, the same terms apply to the way certain charges are made to the tenant: gross leases, net leases and triple net leases, to name a few.

All leases charge what is called "base rent." This is the rent that is due without regard to any backcharges for operating costs or real estate taxes. If only base rent is charged, it is termed a "gross lease." This means that the landlord provides services such as cleaning, utilities, security, maintenance and repair and pays all real estate taxes. In today's market, this is rare. The usual type of gross lease establishes a base year (usually the first year of occupancy) and then charges for any increases in operating costs or real estate taxes.

Such a gross lease, with operating cost and real estate tax "escalators," usually requires that electricity the tenant uses for lighting, air conditioning and other purposes be separately metered and paid for by the tenant. This is sometimes called a "single net" lease or a gross lease "net of electricity."

At one time, we had single, double and triple net leases. Today, if we say "net lease" we normally mean what once was called "triple net."

As you can see, it will pay to read the fine print in a lease proposal and have your calculator handy. You may also find it appropriate to be represented by a real estate consultant or broker who will both advise you on options available and help you negotiate the best deal.

John A. Brown is president of John Brown Associates of Cambridge, a city planning and real estate firm.

20

LAKESIDE CENTER

In November 1989, Maria Sanchez, the leasing agent for a 95,000 s.f. class A office building in Boca Raton, Florida, has to prepare and negotiate lease proposals with three prospective tenants. It is early November 1989 and the once hot Boca Raton market has cooled considerably. This case is designed to expose students to the strategy and tactics of lease negotiations in a deteriorating market, and the impact of such an environment on financial and partnership structures.

Discussion Questions:

1. How would you assess the current situation at Lakeside Center? What leasing strategy should Sanchez propose to Martin?
2. What lease rates and terms should Sanchez offer to the prospective tenants: SFS, A&G, and BCI? How should she structure her presentation? How should she handle the negotiations?
3. What are the financial implications of your lease proposals? How should Southern handle the deficit?
4. What options does the financial partner CREA have? How might CREA respond to your lease proposals and your solution to reducing the deficit?

Maria Sanchez, the leasing agent for Lakeside Center, stared intently at her computer monitor as she tried to prepare for a breakfast meeting with John Clark, the CFO of SouthEast Financial Services (SFS). SFS was actively seeking to lease 13,000 s.f. of office space. Clark had called the previous afternoon and told her that two competing projects, Financial Place and 700 Glades Road, had beaten her initial offer by almost $5 p.s.f. If she wanted her project to stay on his short list of potential sites, she would have to come up with a better proposal. She also had to update proposals for Anderson & Gray (A&G) and BCI Marketing, two other potential tenants for Lakeside Center.

It was early November in 1989, and the once hot Boca Raton market had cooled considerably. Potential tenants had become increasingly elusive. Even though Sanchez's building, Lakeside Center, had been ready for occupancy for almost a year, the building was only 38% filled and it had been almost three months since the last tenant had signed on. As a result, the project had fallen behind its lease up schedule and it was not meeting its pro forma projections. On a more personal level, Sanchez was working on a commission basis and she was struggling to pay off a mountain of student loans from her MBA education. She needed to sign a tenant.

MARIA SANCHEZ

Sanchez had quickly become one of Southern Tier Development's top leasing agents after she joined Southern in July of 1987. A year later, she had been given responsibility for the leasing of Lakeside Center, a 95,372 s.f. office building in Boca Raton, Florida. Sanchez had grown up in southern Florida, and she wanted to pursue a career in real estate development. Completing the leasing of Lakeside Center would be a tough, high profile job; it was the type of challenge that she had thrived on in the past.

The last year and a half had been filled with cold calls, presentations, and negotiations. At times it had been tough. Sanchez had encountered repeated rejections as she tried to fight her way into the close knit leasing community. The Southern name and organization had helped but she had found that she was being judged, both personally and professionally, as an individual. Leasing was a profession where the successful were highly compensated and the unsuccessful were quickly let go. She had to perform.

Research Assistant Richard E. Crum prepared this case under the supervision of Adjunct Professor William J. Poorvu as the basis for class discussion rather than to illustrate either effective or ineffective handling of an administrative situation.

Sanchez's job description was simple: find and sign strong tenants that were willing and able to pay market rents. Her first step was to locate and contact prospective tenants. This entailed making cold calls, working her list of contacts within the business and brokerage communities, and developing a marketing program to advertise the project. Her second step was to contact the prospective tenant and make a presentation to the executive in charge of real estate decisions. Her third step was to analyze that tenant's specific needs, determine the tenant's credit worthiness and overall attractiveness to her project, and then to formulate a detailed lease proposal. The fourth step was to negotiate with the tenant and close the deal. Finally, after the deal was closed and Sanchez's formal responsibilities were over, she would work informally with Southern's in-house property management team to follow the tenant fit up and move in process.

Southern had established a commission plan that was competitive with the commission plans of competing projects. Outside leasing agents would receive 3% of the value of the lease. In this case, the lease value was defined as the total gross rent that would be paid over the life of the lease. The commission would be paid as a lump sum when the tenant moved in. In addition, Sanchez would receive 25% of the amount that the outside broker was receiving as an "override." She would receive 1.5% of the lease value if she located a tenant directly and no outside leasing agent was involved.

She had found that she had to sell her abilities not only to prospective tenants but also to the other leasing agents in the area. Contacts and market information were critical ingredients for success as a leasing agent. Access to both had only become available after she had established herself with the other leasing agents. In return, they expected her to generate business, contacts, and market information for them.

Sanchez had found herself working from early morning breakfast meetings through late night receptions and parties. What kept her going was the brief, euphoric high of closing a deal and the substantial commission check that followed. Experienced leasing agents in a strong market could easily make upwards of $100,000 per year if they had a good reputation, a strong project, and the tenacity to chase every potential tenant that they encountered. Of course, she had also had quite a few doors slammed in her face.

LAKESIDE CENTER

Lakeside Center was a six story, 95,372 s.f. office building (see **Exhibit 1** for the Southern marketing material that describes the project). The building was part of a larger "business community" that Southern had developed on a 25 acre site. In addition to the office building, there was a 202 room hotel, a 34,000 s.f. retail structure, a fitness club, a bank, and four restaurants. There were 500 parking spots dedicated to the office building. The entire complex was centered on a small lake which served as a focal point for the development. The project was heavily landscaped and it had a pleasant, campus like atmosphere.

The building was 38.4% occupied. The tenants and their lease terms are summarized below in **Table A**. The building had a gross area of 95,372 s.f. and an efficiency ratio of 86% which translated into a rentable area of 82,020 s.f. The rentable area listed below would be applied to the lease rate quoted below in order to calculate the lease payment for each tenant. In this case, the lease rate is the gross rental rate including operating expenses. Free rent was the length of time during which the tenant could occupy the space for free before it was required to pay rent. It was customary in the area for parking to be offered at no extra charge.

TI was the tenant improvement allowance that Southern was giving to the tenant in order to offset the costs of customizing the space to the tenant's needs. Generally, in new office construction, the office space was not finished and the TI allowance was used for such items as carpeting, ceiling tiles, lighting, wall coverings, and interior partitions. Typically, the budgeted TI allowance would be held back by the lender and only disbursed when a tenant had signed a lease and was ready to begin the finish work. Often, a tenant spent more than the TI allowance to finish its space in which case the tenant was responsible for the additional cost. $18 per s.f. had been budgeted for TI allowances at Lakeside Center.

Table A   Lakeside Center Lease Terms

TENANT	S.F.	RATE	TERM	TI	FREE RENT	SIGN DATE	OCCUPANCY DATE
Southern	13,700	24.00	12	18.00	—	8/88	1/89
Workman & Rhine	2,910	23.00	5	18.00	—	8/88	1/89
Verten	4,094	23.00	10	18.00	6 months	9/88	1/89
Sache, Halsey & Witt	4,856	23.00	8	18.00	6 months	12/88	4/89
Centex Marketing	3,130	23.00	5	19.00	6 months	7/89	9/89
Sullivan & O'Brien	2,790	23.00	5	21.00	6 months	8/89	11/89
Totals/Average	31,480	23.44	10	18.37	3 months		

Construction on Lakeside Center had started in December of 1987. The certificate of occupancy was received twelve months later on January 2, 1989. Total development costs had initially been estimated at $14,500,000 or $152 per s.f. (see **Exhibit 2**). As the market had begun to soften in early 1988, the project manager had worked with the project's architect to "value engineer" the design. The resulting $550,000 in savings had come almost exclusively from downgrading the heating, ventilating, and air conditioning (HVAC) systems and simplifying the entry lobby. The $550,000 in savings had been added to the $450,000 allowance for operating losses that was already incorporated in the development budget.

Original gross income projections for 1990 were $1,968,000 (82,020 × $24.00 p.s.f.). Operating expenses for the building at 100% occupancy were budgeted to be $410,000 per year (see **Exhibit 3**). This budget amount provided a base stop of $5 per s.f. for operating expenses as part of the initial rental rate quoted above. The tenant would be required, however, to pay its pro rata share of any future increases in operating expenses. This additional charge would be calculated by multiplying the increase in operating costs by the tenant's rentable area and then dividing by the building's rentable area. In this case, the net rent that the owner would receive was the gross rate quoted in **Table A** minus the operating stop of $5 per s.f. The $5 per s.f. in operating expenses was considered to be in line with expenses at competing buildings.

Southern had formed Lakeside Associates, a limited partnership, to own and develop the complex. Southern, as the managing general partner, would make all day to day operating decisions for the project as well as be responsible for lease up. In addition, in the event of cost overruns or unbudgeted operating deficits, Southern would be required to fund these deficits in the form of a 10% interest only, subordinated loan to Lakeside Associates.

If the operating deficit exceeded the $1 million that had been budgeted, Southern had guaranteed that it would fund the next $1.2 million in unbudgeted operating deficits. If the total deficit exceeded $2.2 million and Southern decided not to fund the excess, Cambridge Real Estate Advisors (CREA) had the option to purchase Southern's position for $1. Southern was well capitalized and it had access to significant amounts of additional capital. Raising the cash to cover an operating deficit would not be difficult for the company. Any requests for additional funds, however, would have to be approved by Southern's Executive Committee.

CREA, which was the real estate subsidiary of a large insurance firm, had provided a $14,500,000, seven-year, 10% interest only, non-recourse, first mortgage loan to Lakeside Associates in return for the right to convert the loan into a limited partnership interest at any time. After conversion, CREA would receive an 8% cumulative, preferred return, and then any remaining cash flow would be split 50/50 with Southern. If CREA did not convert, the loan would come due in full in January of 1995.

In practice, this meant that CREA would receive either $1,450,000 per year as interest on its loan or, after conversion, $1,160,000 per year as its preferred return plus a 50% share in any excess cash flow. Upon the sale or refinancing of the project, CREA would first receive either its outstanding loan balance or its invested capital. Southern would then receive the outstanding balance of any loans that it had made. Finally, any remaining proceeds would be split 50/50. CREA had the right to approve all leases, asset sales, and refinancings.

THE COMPETITION

700 Glades Road was a 240,000 s.f., four story office building located at the corner of Glades and Powerline roads. The building had a serpentine floor plan, an interior atrium, and structured parking for 850 cars (see **Exhibit 4**). There were 180,000 s.f. of rentable space in the building. This corner site was considered by many brokers to be the prime location in Boca Raton. Across the street was Boca Center, a super regional shopping mall with over 200 shops. Gary Stamfel, the local entrepreneur who owned 700 Glades Road, had been extremely aggressive in matching his asking rents to the current market conditions.

Still, occupancy at 700 Glades Road was only 29%. The first tenants had moved into 700 Glades Road during May of 1989. A listing of the tenants and a summary of what Sanchez had been able to learn about their rents and lease terms are listed below in **Table B**.

Table B 700 Glades Road Lease Terms

TENANT	S.F.	RATE	TERM	TI	FREE RENT	SIGN DATE	OCCUPANCY DATE
The BTF Corporation	14,000	22.00	5	18.00	6 months	10/88	5/89
Simpson & Post	3,000	21.50	5	18.00	6 months	10/88	5/89
Greyrock Financial	6,000	21.50	10	18.00	6 months	10/88	5/89
The Matte Group	12,000	21.00	10	18.00	6 months	10/88	5/89
Boca Medical Group	4,000	21.00	5	18.00	6 months	1/89	6/89
Mizner Securities	4,000	21.50	5	18.00	6 months	3/89	8/89
Morton Diskin Inc.	3,000	20.50	10	18.00	6 months	4/89	8/89
Winniker Investments	2,000	20.00	5	18.00	6 months	6/89	10/89
Tobias Enterprises	4,200	20.00	5	18.00	6 months	8/89	1/90
Totals/Averages	52,200	21.25	7	18.00	6 months		

Financial Place was a 66,000 s.f., six story, office building located at the corner of Glades Road and I–95 (see **Exhibit 5** for a typical floor plan). The building had 52,800 s.f. of rentable space. Access was complicated, however by the fact that Glades Road was divided and elevated at this point. As a result, even though the building enjoyed visibility from I–95, tenants would have to exit I–95 at Glades Road, loop onto Military Trail, and finally enter the project from the northeastern corner. The building was five years old and there was parking for 350 cars.

Occupancy at Financial Place was 62%. Eight tenants had left Financial Place during 1989 after their initial leases had expired. The institutional owner of Financial Place had been aggressive in offering free rent and generous tenant improvements in an effort to lease the vacant space. The project was plagued, however, by a reputation for having poor maintenance and difficult management. The tenants and their lease terms are summarized below in **Table C**.

Table C Financial Place Lease Terms

TENANT	S.F.	RATE	TERM	TI	FREE RENT	SIGN DATE	OCCUPANCY DATE
MLR	4,200	16.00	10	15.00	—	3/83	2/84
Laflor	1,680	16.00	7	15.00	—	3/83	2/84
ManTech	1,680	15.50	10	16.00	—	3/83	2/84
Cannif Industries	2,520	17.00	7	16.00	—	6/83	5/84
Carlstrom Metals	5,040	16.50	10	16.00	—	9/83	7/84
Olympis Services	3,360	16.50	7	16.00	—	12/83	11/84
CDL Associates	4,200	17.50	5	16.00	—	4/84	12/84
AFC Corp.	2,520	23.00	5	20.00	1 year	11/88	2/89
Boca Index Fund	2,520	23.00	10	22.00	1 year	1/89	4/89
Fiske & Mel	1,680	23.00	5	23.00	1 year	4/89	8/89
Clunan & Cocco	1,680	23.00	5	23.00	1 year	7/89	11/89
Belden Insurance	1,680	23.00	5	23.00	1 year	9/89	1/90
Totals/Averages	32,760	18.53	8	17.06	4 months		

THE MARKETING PROGRAM

Sanchez had a marketing budget of $350,000. She used that money to create and fund a marketing program that targeted prospective tenants at three levels: national, state, and local. At the national level, she made a contribution of $50,000 to the Southern Commercial Industrial Division's national advertising campaign. At the state level, she had allocated $80,000 for print advertisements in the Miami and Fort Lauderdale newspapers as well as listings in the *Southeast Real Estate Journal* and an office leasing guide. At the local level, she had invested $75,000 in a new brochure and mailing packet. $50,000 had been allocated for promotional events. Signage was also placed at the front of the site in order to generate interest.

Sanchez had positioned the project in the marketing campaign to exploit the project's high quality standards, its Boca Raton address, the convenience of a mixed use development, the pleasant ambiance of a master planned community, and the Southern name and reputation.

THE WEST BOCA MARKET

During the late sixties, Southern had responded to an anti-growth movement within the city of Boca Raton by moving the focus of its activities to the unincorporated area due west of the city. In this area, which later came to be called West Boca, Southern had started by creating the 850 acre Southern Corporate Park and the 1000 acre Glades West residential community. When first IBM, and then Siemens, Mitel, Microtel, Allstate Insurance, Burroughs, AT&T, Castle &

Cooke and a host of other companies built facilities in the area, the white collar, high tech, Fortune 500 nature of the real estate market was established.

The growth which transformed West Boca from an unpopulated tract of scrub pines, sand, and rattlesnakes to a densely populated suburban center of corporate headquarters, golf courses, and luxury homes, was dramatic. Growth in West Boca had been centered on the area surrounding Glades Road but by 1988 almost all of the land in this area had been developed and many developers had started to develop on secondary sites along I–95.

During the eighties, both supply and demand for office space had been strong. The figures for all of Boca Raton, including both the city of Boca Raton and West Boca, are listed below in **Table D**. The figures for 1989 and 1990 are estimates for the full year.

Table D Greater Boca Raton Supply and Absorption Figures

YEAR	OFFICE SPACE	NEW SUPPLY	ABSORPTION	OCCUPANCY
1980	647,000	130,000	140,000	98.9%
1981	980,000	333,000	220,000	87.8
1982	1,200,000	220,000	180,000	86.7
1983	1,625,000	425,000	250,000	79.4
1984	2,150,000	525,000	380,000	77.7
1985	3,000,000	850,000	560,000	74.3
1986	4,350,000	1,350,000	625,000	65.6
1987	4,600,000	250,000	290,000	68.4
1988	5,200,000	600,000	260,000	65.6
1989E	5,500,000	300,000	310,000	67.5
1990E	5,550,000	50,000	450,000	75.0

THE PROSPECTIVE TENANTS

Sanchez had three prospective tenants who were currently considering lease proposals that she had prepared. All three were also considering both 700 Glades Road and Financial Place. A summary of Sanchez's previous contact with each firm along with the lease terms are detailed below.

SouthEast Financial Services Sanchez had arranged to meet John Clark, the CFO of SouthEast Financial Services, at the Boca Raton Chamber of Commerce monthly luncheon series. She had heard from a friend that SFS's lease was expiring. They currently occupied 10,000 s.f. in an older building in downtown Boca Raton. Clark had brushed off Sanchez's initial attempts to talk about their space needs and had suggested instead that they talk over drinks or dinner. Sanchez had followed up by arranging for dinner at one of Boca Raton's better restaurants.

At the dinner, Sanchez had presented her proposal. Southern would lease the entire sixth floor of Lakeside Center, over 13,000 s.f. of space, to SFS at $24 per s.f. Southern would also provide $18 per s.f. for tenant improvements plus six months of free rent. By taking an entire floor, SFS would not only have a prestigious space but it would gain by having a more efficient floor layout. Clark had been pleasant but noncommittal. "These items," he had said, "were all negotiable anyway." He would be, however, interested in an "equity kicker" with the lease if that could be worked out. This would be an equity position in the project that would allow SFS to participate in any future appreciation in value of the project. Clark had toured the project later in the week and had been impressed by the building.

SFS was a regional discount brokerage house for financial securities. The firm had aggressively expanded throughout the bull markets of the 1980s. Its current lease was due to expire on March 31, 1990 so Sanchez was confident that it would sign a deal within the next thirty days. SFS wanted a five year lease with an option to renew for an additional five years at its discretion. Clark had insisted that the space had to be ready by March 15, 1990. Sanchez had checked with Southern's construction division and had been told that they would be hard pressed to complete the tenant improvements in less than 10 weeks. Work could only start after the design drawings had been completed and these drawings would take between two weeks and two months to complete depending on the tenant and the architect.

Anderson & Gray Sanchez had been contacted by Paul Nolan, a local broker, who had been hired by Anderson & Gray, a local law firm, to represent it in its lease negotiations. In October, Nolan had asked Sanchez to submit a proposal for Anderson & Gray to take 8,000 s.f. for 10 years. He had explained that a number of projects were also submitting proposals and that Anderson & Gray would, after evaluating the leases, enter into negotiations with the top three projects.

Nolan had also explained the basic criteria by which the leases would be evaluated:
- Net effective rent. This was defined as all charges minus all concessions divided by the term of the lease.
- Location
- Layout and design of the building
- Amenities
- Parking
- Reputation of the owner and quality of the management team.
- Tenant Improvement Allowance of $20 per s.f.

Anderson & Gray would also need to have 500 s.f. of the space reinforced to support the high loads associated with their law library. The cost of this work was assumed to be $20,000 and this amount could be either included as a higher base rent or charged directly to Anderson & Gray.

Sanchez had submitted a proposal of $24 per s.f. for ten years. She had also offered $18 per s.f. in tenant improvements, six months in free rent, and no charge for the reinforcement of the library floor slab. Nolan had called later that week to tell her that her offer had been on the high side but that the partners wanted to include Lakeside Center in the final group. Nolan had asked her to prepare a second proposal for Anderson & Gray for the following week.

BCI Marketing Sanchez had cold called Gail Mahoney, the CEO of BCI Marketing, late in October. BCI was a small firm which sold low priced gifts and other marketing materials to financial institutions to give to their customers. Another leasing agent at Southern had heard that BCI's lease was expiring and Sanchez had simply walked in through the front door early one morning and caught Mahoney alone at her desk. The two had hit it off almost immediately and Sanchez felt that she had the inside track in signing BCI. She had considered asking for $26 per s.f. but had ultimately decided to offer $24 per s.f., $18 per s.f. in TI, and six months free rent. BCI was looking for 3,000 s.f. and a four year lease. BCI was currently in an older building located in a secondary location. The current asking rate in this building was $18 per s.f. Mahoney had called recently and asked Sanchez why she should pay more than $18 per s.f. in rent. Could Southern improve its offer?

Unfortunately, these were Sanchez's only prospects at the moment. This did not mean, however, that additional prospects weren't just around the corner.

LEASING STRATEGY AND NEGOTIATING TACTICS

In preparing for her meeting with Clark, Sanchez had to make a number of decisions. First, she had to decide what type of leasing strategy she would pursue. Second, she had to decide what combination of lease rate per s.f., TI per s.f., and amount of free rent to offer. Third, she had to prepare a presentation and decide on her negotiating tactics.

Her decisions would rest, at least in part, on her assessment of the market and on how important signing SFS was for the project. How aggressive should she be in cutting her rental rate? Was SFS willing to pay a premium for space at Lakeside Center? What would the competition offer? What was the current market rate? How should she structure her presentation? How should she handle Clark?

In order to estimate the current market rental rate, Sanchez decided to calculate the net present value for the last lease that had been signed at each of the three competing projects. As an example, for the Sullivan & O'Brien lease at Lakeside Center, a five year lease with no unusual expenses, a net rent of $18 ($23 gross rent less a $5 expense stop), six months free rent, and $21 in TI allowance, the cash flows for Lakeside Associates would be as follows:

Cash Flow to Lakeside Associates

	1	2	3	4	5
Net rent	$18	$18	$18	$18	$18
−Free rent	(11.5)	—	—	—	—
−Extra TI	(3)	—	—	—	—
Cash flow	$3.5	$18	$18	$18	$18

For simplicity, Sanchez had assumed that all cash flows occurred at the beginning of the year and that $18 had been budgeted for TI at all three properties.

Using this method and a 12% discount rate, Sanchez calculated NPVs of $58.17, $50.56, and $44.67 for Lakeside Center, 700 Glades Road, and Financial Place.

From an owner's standpoint, these calculations were often valuable in evaluating alternative lease proposals. Sometimes an owner would compare the cash flows or net present value of a lease proposal with a building standard. In some cases, an owner might not take free rent allowances into account if he or she felt that the space would remain vacant anyway.

It was also appropriate in some situations to do an analysis from the tenant's standpoint. In this case, the cash flows from the tenant's perspective for the Sullivan & O'Brien lease at Lakeside Center would be as follows:

Cash Flow from Sullivan & O'Brien

	1	2	3	4	5
Gross rent	$23	$23	$23	$23	$23
−Free rent	(11.5)	—	—	—	—
−Extra TI	(3)	—	—	—	—
Cash flow	8.5	$23	$23	$23	$23

From the tenant's perspective, Sanchez calculated NPVs of $78.36, $70.75, and $64.86 for Lakeside Center, 700 Glades Road, and Financial Place.

Finally, Sanchez decided to calculate the rent in a simpler way for the three leases. She added the cash flows and divided by the number of years of the lease to arrive at an average rent.[1]

From these cash flows, she calculated average rents of $20.10, $18.00, and $17.40 for Lakeside Center, 700 Glades Road, and Financial Place. Sanchez knew that many real estate professionals and many tenants did not bother with discounted cash flow analyses of leases. The simplified rent calculation neglected the time value of money but it was easy to do and the final number was easy to understand.

It was not that the numbers alone would dictate a tenant's decision, but it was certainly the first ingredient. Sanchez had to decide on what basis she was going to make her lease recommendations.

After deciding on her base offer, Sanchez still had to prepare a presentation and decide on her negotiating tactics. What should she stress in her presentation? Where should she make it? What other information should she include?

Sanchez believed that Clark would still want to negotiate, even after she had made her second offer. She knew that there was no way to predict exactly how the meeting would go but she knew that she had to be prepared for a variety of contingencies. She felt that momentum was important in some deals and that she might have to make a series of quick decisions in order to keep the deal alive. What should her final position be?

[1]In this case, Sanchez only took into account those tenant improvement and leasing costs above or below the amount included in the development budget. After the initial development period, to calculate the net effective rent over the lease period, she would deduct the total costs.

Sanchez was not sure what to make of Clark. He seemed to enjoy pushing her. She had heard from a personal friend at SFS that 700 Glades Road and Financial Place had offered lease terms that were only two to three dollars lower than her offer and yet Clark had told her that her offer was five dollars too high. She knew that Clark had been on elaborate fishing and golfing trips with the other two leasing agents. She wasn't sure how or if she should use her information about the other offers in her negotiations. This was an important deal. She didn't want to hurt the project, but she also didn't want to compromise her principles.

Sanchez also had to prepare responses for both Anderson & Gray and BCI Marketing as well as performing her ordinary marketing and leasing duties. As always, she was short on time and had to set some priorities for the coming week.

SOUTHERN TIER DEVELOPMENT

Her boss, Bill Martin, had asked her to meet with him that afternoon in order to update him on the status of the leasing program and to help him prepare for the partnership meeting with CREA the following week. The leasing program would be, as always, the initial item on the agenda.

The problem, however, was more than the lease proposals themselves. At the current 38% occupancy level, the project had already exhausted the initial $450,000 carried for operating losses and it would consume by the end of 1989 the additional $550,000 that had been saved during construction. Southern had guaranteed that it would fund the next $1.2 million in operating losses. Martin was considering three strategies for dealing with the impending cash flow deficit: (1) fund the deficit from Southern's other resources; (2) attempt to bring in a second financial partner; or (3) begin negotiations with CREA to get CREA to loan additional funds to the partnership on the same basis. In order to assess these strategies, he knew that he would have to come up with a revised income and expense projection for the project as well as an estimate of the carrying costs. Sanchez knew that Martin would rely heavily on her in making his decision.

Sanchez also knew that senior management at Southern was currently reviewing the company's strategy, organization, and human resources at the annual management conference. She was concerned about a number of the issues that would be raised. How important was it for Southern to have in-house leasing versus hiring an outside leasing company? Should it compensate the leasing agents with commissions or salaries or a mixture of both? Why was Lakeside Center not performing as projected? What should the company do to improve returns?

Sanchez would not attend the management conference but she knew that both her performance in leasing Lakeside Center and her assessment of the current situation would go a long way towards making or breaking her career at Southern.

Exhibit 1

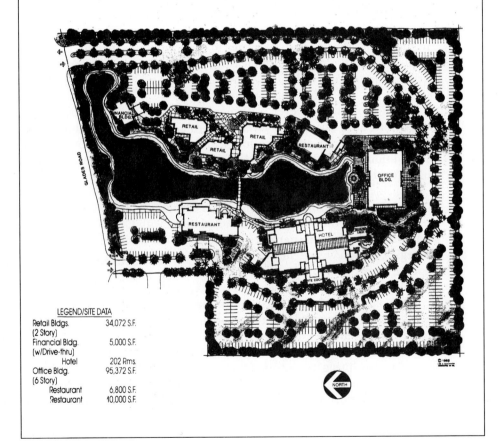

Site Plan

Not only are a shady park setting and shimmering lake part of your working environment, nestled amid all the beauty are a variety of retail shops, professional services, fitness center and lakeside restaurants. And, with a Radisson Suite Hotel, you and your clients may enjoy a jogging/exercise trail, conference rooms and 202 beautifully appointed suites. Plans for banking facilities will round out the myriad of conveniences.

LEGEND/SITE DATA

Retail Bldgs. (2 Story)	34,072 S.F.
Financial Bldg. (w/Drive-thru)	5,000 S.F.
Hotel	202 Rms.
Office Bldg. (6 Story)	95,372 S.F.
Restaurant	6,800 S.F.
Restaurant	10,000 S.F.

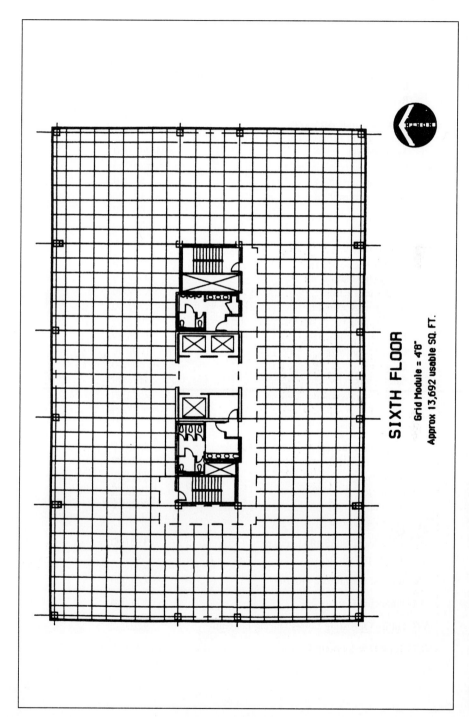

SIXTH FLOOR

Grid Module = 4'8"

Approx 13,692 usable SQ. FT.

Exhibit 1 (continued)   Lakeside Center Floor Plan

Exhibit 2 Pro Forma Development Cost Analysis, January 14, 1988

Project Description

Acreage	5.1
F.A.R.	0.43
Building Area	95,372
Efficiency	86%
Rentable Area	82,020

Development Cost Analysis

I. Planning and Professional

Architectural		$ 295,000
Engineering		120,000
Landscape architect		50,000
Graphics consultant		40,000
Legal		80,000
Subtotal		585,000

II. Development

Site work		0
Hardscape feature		250,000
Shell construction	$59 per sq. ft.	5,627,000
Tenant improvements	$18 per sq. ft.	1,476,000
Landscaping	$40,000 per acre	204,000
Fees, bonds, and taxes		189,000
General conditions		100,000
Graphics		60,000
Contingency		387,000
Project management		262,000
Subtotal		8,555,000

III. Marketing

Leasing commissions	350,000
Brochures and displays	50,000
Advertising	200,000
Promotion	100,000
Subtotal	700,000

IV. Land

5.1 acres @ $653,400 per acre	3,332,000
$15.00 per sq. ft.	

V. Interest 10% for 12 months	725,000
VI. Financing Cost	153,000
VII. Future Operating Losses During Leaseup	450,000
VIII. Total Development Cost	$14,500,000

Exhibit 3

Pro Forma Income Statement 1990

Projected gross income	$1,968,480
Less 5% vacancy	98,424
Effective gross income	$1,870,056
Less operating expense	410,000
Net operating income	$1,460,056

Pro Forma Full-Year Operating Budget

	ANNUAL BUDGET	VARIABLE PORTION
Repairs and Maintenance		
General	$15,000	
Structural	5,000	
HVAC	5,000	
Elevator	8,000	
Janitorial		
Janitorial service	45,000	$30,000
Pest control	4,000	
Window washing	5,000	
Utilities		
Electric	100,000	79,000
Water/sewer	10,000	8,000
Trash	7,000	5,000
Security	18,000	
Insurance	14,000	
Landscape and Parking Lot Maintenance		
Landscape and irrigation maintenance	23,000	
Parking lot sweeping	6,000	
Real estate taxes	90,000	
Contribution for roads and maintenance	15,000	
Management fee	40,000	40,000
Total operating budget	$410,000	$164,000

Exhibit 4

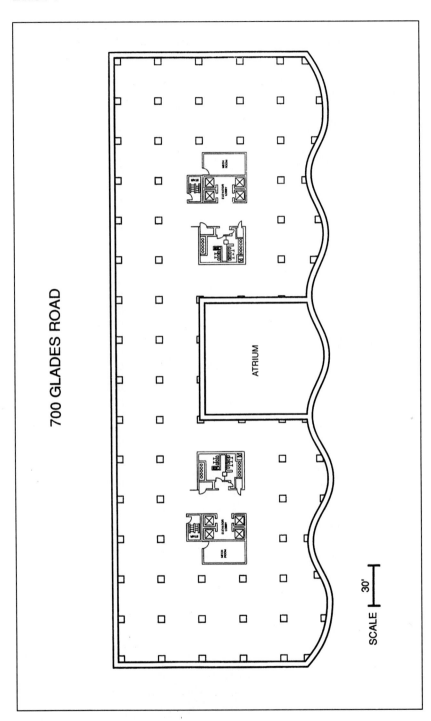

Exhibit 5 Financial Plaza

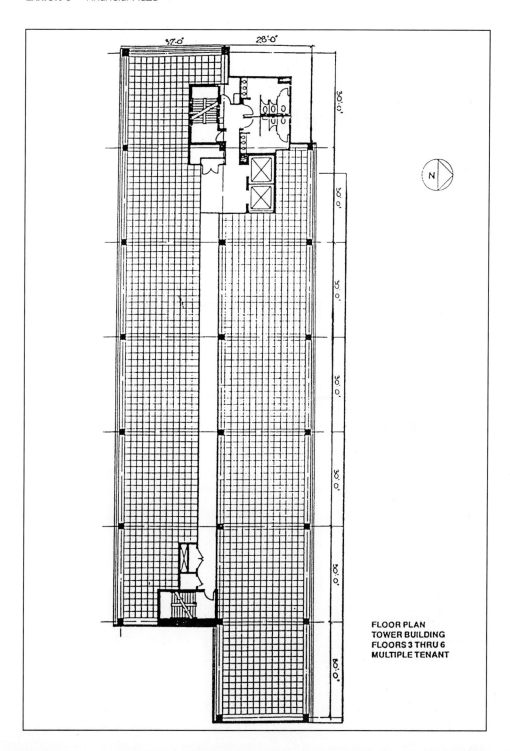

FLOOR PLAN
TOWER BUILDING
FLOORS 3 THRU 6
MULTIPLE TENANT

21

TYSONS CORNER

In July 1989, the partnership owning the Tysons Corner Marriott in Virginia is facing a cash flow deficit. The opening of a number of new hotels in the area, and the increased trend to product segmentation have resulted in lower occupancy rates and reduced cash flow. This case provides an overview of the hotel industry, the history of this particular hotel, and the dilemma of the general partners as they deal with changes in the market environment.

Discussion Questions:

1. Why is the partnership losing money? What will the cash flows look like in 1992? What are your assumptions?
2. What options and obligations does Green have? What should he do?
3. What can be done to improve operations at the hotel?
4. How is hotel development different from commercial or residential development?

John Green, the managing general partner of Hollinswood Associates, casually inspected the lobby of the Tysons Corner Marriott. Green had been intimately involved in the development and operation of the hotel for the past eight years. Whenever he entered the hotel he felt a deep sense of pride. It was a Friday afternoon in July of 1989, and the hotel was busy with families and tour groups checking in and business men and women checking out. Green was pleased by what he saw but he also knew that the hotel faced a projected cash flow deficit of almost $700,000 for the year. The partnership meeting was set for the following Thursday, and Green knew that as the managing general partner he would be expected not only to explain the problems that the hotel faced but also to provide solutions.

THE HOTEL

The Tysons Corner Marriott was a 392-room, full-service hotel. The hotel complex consisted of a modern, 14-story concrete tower, and a two-story parking structure (see **Exhibits 1** and **2** for a rendering and floor plan for the project). Amenities at the hotel included the 200 seat Rumsford's Restaurant and Tavern, a state-of-the-art disco called Raffles, a 5,000 square foot grand ballroom, 10 meeting rooms, an indoor atrium swimming pool, an exercise room, and a gift shop. Overall the site covered approximately five acres. Surface and structured parking was available for up to 600 cars.

The site was located at the intersection of Route 7 and I–495 in Tysons Corner, Fairfax County, Virginia. The Northern Virginia area was experiencing rapid growth due to its geography, access to major highways, and proximity to a number of major markets including the Federal Government. As of 1989, there existed 16.6 million square feet of office space in the Tysons Corner area. Corporate residents of the market area included NEC, AT&T, Honeywell, McDonnell Douglas, Ford Aerospace, AAA, and TRW. Over 400,000 persons were employed in the area.

Adjacent to the hotel was Tysons Corner Center, a recently renovated major shopping mall offering 250 stores with Nordstrom's, Bloomingdale's, Woodward & Lothrop, and Hecht's as anchors, as well as restaurants and 12 movie theaters.

Research Assistant Richard E. Crum prepared this case under the supervision of Adjunct Professor William J. Poorvu and Senior Lecturer Donald A. Brown as the basis for class discussion rather than to illustrate either effective or ineffective handling of an administrative situation.

Directly across the street from this mall was the Tysons II Galleria featuring Macy's, Saks Fifth Avenue, Neiman Marcus, and approximately 100 other specialty stores.

Washington, D.C. was approximately 10 miles from the hotel. Washington Dulles International was approximately 20 minutes away and Washington National Airport was 35 minutes away.

THE CONCEPTUAL STAGE

In the spring of 1979, Green and George Kettle, a local broker and developer, had formed Hollinswood Associates to build and own a proposed Marriott hotel in the Tysons Corner area. Kettle had been actively involved in the local real estate market as the Century 21 regional franchise holder, and he knew that Tysons Corner had been undergoing explosive demographic and commercial growth. Kettle had originally proposed that they build a 40,000 s.f. office building on a small piece of land that he controlled in Tysons Corner. The parcel was on a small knoll overlooking the rest of the Tysons Corner area and, although the area was zoned for commercial use, it was currently being used for Kettle's Century 21 office and single family housing.

Kettle had estimated that a 40,000 square foot class A office building could be built for an all in cost of $100 per square foot, and that it would yield triple net rents of $11 per square foot. The local area had an occupancy level of 99% and Kettle was confident that most of the space would prelease. He was also fairly sure that he could get an interest only, 30 year loan at 10% interest for 80% of the development costs. Since Kettle owned the land free and clear, no additional equity would be required.

Green had agreed with Kettle's assessment of the Tysons Corner area but he felt that they should acquire the rest of the block and build a 200 room hotel. He pointed to the limited competition in the area, the high occupancy levels and the rising average room rates in the area to support his position (see **Exhibit 3** for a summary of the original market study).

Green knew that hotels, as compared to residential, retail, and office projects were perhaps the riskiest and most complex form of real estate development and ownership. Hotels were generally characterized by large capital building costs, complicated design and construction, high fixed costs of operation, management intensity, and high levels of uncertainty relating to occupancy levels. Hotels, in effect, had to re-lease their entire facilities every night, a constraint which significantly increased operating risks, and which imposed a need for specialized management expertise and an ongoing refinement of market positioning.

The proposed hotel would be subject to not only internal management issues, but also to exogenous factors such as imbalances of supply and demand in the market, fluctuations in interest rates and building costs, and the availability of permanent financing, all of which would significantly affect the hotel's profitability.

Lenders typically required premium rates for hotel development loans because they were lending on a business, not a real estate venture. In fact, both Green and Kettle had seen surveys showing that lenders' hurdle rates for free standing hotels averaged two to three percentage points above office, retail, and industrial real estate projects. Most lenders also had strict selection criteria requiring affiliation with an established national chain.

Room rates were often used as a benchmark to determine the feasibility of new hotel construction or acquisition. One industry rule of thumb for full service hotels was that for every $1000 of project cost on a per room basis, a hotel must achieve $1.00 of average daily room rate. If, for example, total development costs of the hotel amounted to $100,000/room, an average daily rate of $100/room must be achieved.

THE HOTEL DEVELOPMENT PROCESS

After a brief discussion, Kettle and Green decided to form a joint venture partnership to develop a hotel on the site. Together they assembled the land, talked to lenders, and decided to pursue a Marriott management agreement. Green and Kettle had briefly considered other hotel operating companies but had quickly settled on Marriott due to their superior track record, national brand name, and high quality standards. Marriott would not come cheaply but Green believed that Marriott would be able to more than compensate for their high fees by increasing net operating income.

Green knew that expenses, commitments, and risk would all escalate rapidly as the development process progressed. In an attempt to disperse risk and gain professional experience for the project, Green invited a number of professionals that he had worked with in the past to join Hollinswood Associates as partners. The new partners included Jim Clark, a general contractor, Jim Beers, an accountant, Alex Jeffries, an architect, and Manuel Fernandez, a hotel owner. Each contributed cash except for Kettle who contributed cash and land. Green considered asking each to contribute their professional services in return for an interest in the project but then discarded the idea. The total amount raised was $2.5 million, which was expected to provide sufficient equity to fund a 200-room hotel.

During their initial talks, Marriott had urged the partnership to build a 400 room hotel in order to maximize the use of the site and to gain operating efficiencies. Marriott had recently identified Tysons Corner as the number one market that they wanted to enter and they were eager to strike a deal. Green was concerned, however, about the amount of risk Hollinswood Associates would be assuming. He briefly considered a two phase design in which a smaller hotel would be initially built and then expanded later. A proposed development budget and a stabilized pro forma operating budget were prepared for a full service, 400 room hotel (see **Exhibit 4** for a summary of both).

After a brief negotiation with Marriott, the partnership decided to build a 392 room full service hotel. The increase in size from the original plan, however, meant that the partnership now had to raise an additional $2.5 million in equity.

The partners decided to raise the additional equity by forming Tyman Associates, a limited partnership, which would receive a 50% share in Hollinswood Associates in return for $2.5 million. Clark, Kettle, and Green became general partners in Tyman Associates and they took a 20% subordinated interest in Tyman Associates in return for raising the money. The limited partners would get a 9% preferred return from Tyman Associates before the general partners received their distribution (see **Table A** below for a breakdown of each partnership). Green, as the managing general partner, had the option to "call" for an additional $500,000, allocated on a prorata basis amongst the Hollinswood Associates partners, in the event of cost overruns.

Table A   The Partnerships

HOLLINSWOOD ASSOCIATES			TYMAN ASSOCIATES		
John Green	18%	$900,000	Limited Partners	80%	$2,500,000
George Kettle	14%	700,000	John Green	11%	10
Jim Clark	10%	500,000	George Kettle	5%	10
Manuel Fernandez	6%	300,000	Jim Clark	4%	10
Jim Beers	1%	50,000			
Alex Jeffries	1%	50,000			
Tyman Associates	50%	2,500,030			
Total	100%	$5,000,030	Total	100%	$2,500,030

The management contract gave Marriott 3% of gross revenues and 20% of cash flow before debt service. Marriott's 20% fee would be subordinated, however, to the initial mortgage on the property. Marriott gave the partnership a noncompete clause for a three mile radius around the hotel.

Alex Jeffries, the partnership's architect, and Marriott quickly began design work on the proposed hotel. Site planning was somewhat complicated. The partnership had been unable to convince Marriott to sell their Roy Rodgers restaurant located on the front corner of the site. In addition, the County had established a height restriction of 145 feet and the hotel had to be set back behind a plane that started at the property line and rose at 28 degrees.

Inside, the hotel would represent Marriott's latest design and furnishing plans. The lobby would feature a two story atrium finished in red oak and quarry tile. A state of the art disco would be located to the right and immediately adjacent to the lobby. An all purpose restaurant would serve breakfast, lunch, and dinner to hotel guests. A grand ballroom and ten meeting rooms would be included so that the hotel could compete for banquet and meeting business. Behind the lobby, a 25-yard indoor pool would be located under another 40-foot atrium. Three floors of rooms would have walkways looking out over the pool. The rooms would be decorated in the traditional Marriott colors of orange, brown and yellow. The furnishings would be early colonial reproductions.

Based on the Marriott agreement and the construction drawings, the partnership obtained permanent financing in the form of a $20 million loan with a term of 20 years and an interest rate of 10.5%. The loan was non-recourse. A two year construction loan at the same interest rate but with a one point placement fee had previously been obtained from the National Bank of Washington.

The hotel was completed on time and on budget. On February 5, 1981, the partners invited all of their potential clients and many of their friends to the grand opening of the brand new Tysons Corner Marriott. The atmosphere was festive and everyone seemed pleased with the new hotel.

OPERATING THE HOTEL

The hotel almost immediately began to make money. Occupancy levels and average room rates were high; by 1985, the average daily room rate had climbed to $85.42 and the occupancy level was 75.9%. The Marriott name and high level of service, a good location, and an excellent design provided the strong results. During this time, regular quarterly cash disbursements were made to the partners.

Marriott considered average daily rates (ADR) and occupancy levels to be the key measures of the general strength of a hotel. While occupancy levels often reflected industry wide patterns, they were also a significant measure of a hotel's position within its local competitive market. As of 1985, the Tysons Corner Marriott was a leader in both market share and in ADR.

As the operating results continued to improve, Green began to consider refinancing the project. Connecticut General Life Insurance Company, the original lender on the project, agreed to provide a $10 million second mortgage in 1985. The loan was interest only at a rate of 12% and it had a term of 7 years with an option to extend for 3 additional years. The loan closed on October 4, 1985. The cash, once obtained, was distributed to the partners. Because this was a refinancing the partners incurred no tax liability.

In 1985, Marriott recommended that the partnership authorize a major renovation plan for the hotel rooms and public spaces. A capital expenditure budget and schedule was prepared and approved. Some of the guest rooms were completely renovated in 1986 at a cost of $1.8 million. Subsequently, the Raffles lounge, the lobby, the ballroom, the gift shop, and the mezzanine level were all renovated. The total cost of all renovations and capital expenditures was approximately $2.5 million. Some of the funds had come from a capital budget escrow account that was required by the Marriott management contract and funded from operations, and the rest had come from funds that would otherwise have been used for partnership distributions.

MARRIOTT

The Marriott Corporation was a diversified company involved in lodging, food service, and entertainment. Founded in 1927 by J. Willard Marriott, the company began as a small root beer stand in Washington, D.C. As of 1988, the company had revenues of almost $7.4 billion and net income of approximately $232 million. Marriott owned or managed 121,000 rooms and it ran nearly 1,100 restaurants. The company had consistently finished first in customer surveys conducted by Business Travel News. The company's occupancy level was proclaimed to be ten points higher than the industry average of 63%. Between 1978 and 1988, Marriott averaged an ROE of 21.7%.

In 1988, Marriott developed over $1 billion in hotel properties. During the mid eighties, the company began to pursue a strategy of concentrating on hotel management and development, and as a result almost all of the new hotels were sold off or syndicated, subject to a management contract to Marriott, as they were developed. At the same time, Marriott began a program of rapid product expansion as the company pushed into the extended stay, budget, economy, suites, and elderly care markets through its Courtyard, Fairfield Inn, Residence Inn, and Brighton Gardens chains. Marriott's position as a market leader allowed the company to command profit sharing of 20% of operating cash flow versus an estimated industry average of 20–30% of cash flow after debt service.

THE CURRENT SITUATION

By 1989, the operating results had begun to deteriorate for the Tysons Corner Marriott. Average room rates had leveled off and occupancy levels had fallen slightly. Intense competition in the area had developed; four new hotels had been built in the area since 1985 and six more were planned for the next two years. Food and beverage profits had also fallen precipitously. Expenses had risen slowly but with the flattening of revenues even modest increases had had a negative impact on the operating profits (see **Exhibit 5** for a summary of operating results). During 1987 and 1988, the general partners had personally guaranteed $900,000 of third mortgage loans to cover the cash flow deficit.

At the national level, hotel operating performance had also begun to decline. A sharp downturn in hotel construction in the mid-seventies had been followed by strong industry operating performance in the early eighties. This led to increased interest on the part of developers and investors in building new hotels, and, combined with an influx of funds, caused a tremendous oversupply of hotel rooms.

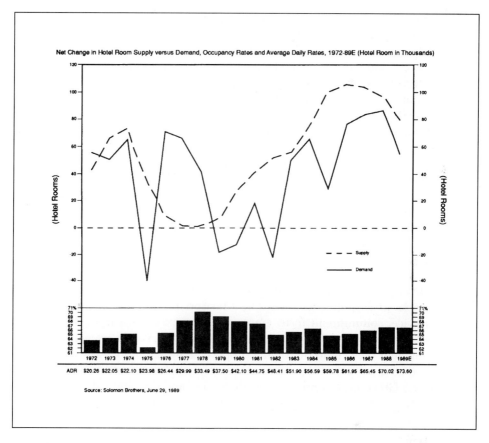

Net Change in Hotel Room Supply versus Demand, Occupancy Rates and Average Daily Rates, 1972-89E (Hotel Room in Thousands)

	1972	1973	1974	1975	1976	1977	1978	1979	1980	1981	1982	1983	1984	1985	1986	1987	1988	1989E
ADR	$20.26	$22.05	$22.10	$23.98	$26.44	$29.99	$33.49	$37.50	$42.10	$44.75	$48.41	$51.90	$56.59	$59.78	$61.95	$65.45	$70.02	$73.60

Source: Solomon Brothers, June 29, 1989

At the industry level, profitability had been declining since the early eighties. Overbuilding, declining occupancy, increased competition, an inflationary cost spiral, soaring labor costs, and huge increases in insurance premiums had all had a negative impact on the bottom line. The 1986 tax reform bill further increased pressure on the industry by eliminating accelerated depreciation, reducing the value of interest deductions, and limiting allowable passive investment losses.

Within the Tysons Corner area, competing hotels had begun to use sophisticated marketing programs to segment the market and selectively attack for market share. This trend was particularly troubling to Green since many of the new hotels were using newer designs and additional amenities to selectively target the most profitable segments (see **Exhibit 6** for a summary of the competitive situation). Was the Tysons Corner Marriott correctly positioned for the 1990s?

Green believed that it would cost $140,000 per room to build a hotel comparable to the Tysons Corner Marriott. This seemed to imply that the Tysons Corner Marriott, with a debt level of only $75,000 per room, should be able to compete based on its low cost position, and yet as new hotels continued to enter the market room rates remained flat. Budget hotels, such as Rodeway Inns, which could be built for as little as $25,000 per room, were also entering the market, albeit in less desirable locations. Conversely, Green knew that his net operating income could not support the debt level of $75,000 per room. How could the new hotels be making money, he wondered? He knew that comparable hotels were selling with cap rates of 10% but this also did not seem to make sense. How should the Marriott rooms be valued? Was this the right time to sell the hotel? What would the tax consequences be? Should they hang on until operating results improved?

Immediately behind the hotel, the JTL Tyson Towers I office building had recently opened with almost 500,000 square feet of office space. Two additional towers, each with 500,000 square feet of space, were planned for 1991 and 1993. Overall, experts were estimating that almost a million square feet of office space would be delivered to the Tysons Corner market in 1990 and that an additional eight million square feet would be completed by 1999.

Marriott had assigned five managers to the property over the eight years that the property had been in operation. The managers had all seemed to be extremely professional, and the hotel and staff had received consistently strong marks in customer surveys. The Marriott reputation for attention to customer service, commitment to its employees, and excellence in operations appeared to be warranted. And yet, Green still wondered if they were getting all of the cash flow that they could out of the property. How should he assess Marriott's performance in keeping costs down and rates up? How should he manage them?

Green also wondered how the design and the physical condition of the hotel were affecting the hotel's performance. The newer hotels "felt" different and many of them offered additional amenities and services. Which amenities and services should the hotel offer? How much would it cost to offer them? Should additional funds be committed to the seemingly endless rounds of renovation?

However, Green was sure of two things: he would have to come up with a way to fund the deficit and he would also have to come up with a solution to the underlying problem. Green knew that the raising of any new, outside equity would require a vote of the partners. Local lenders had offered to lend against the property but only if the general partners guaranteed the loan. Green wondered if the other general partners would be willing to give a personal guarantee. What about the limited partners? Where else could he raise some cash?

In addition, the second mortgage would initially come due in three years. Green could extend the loan for 3 years but this would only delay the problem. Would operating results improve enough in the next six years to allow the partnership to roll over the loan or should they cut their losses and sell now? How much would operating results have to improve in order to breakeven? Would it be a mistake to commit more capital since they had no personal liability? What were his other options?

Over the past eight years, Green had acted as the managing partner of Hollinswood Associates, and he had often acted alone to make day to day operating decisions for the partnership. He wondered now what his obligations were to his friends, investors, partners, and employees? How should he weigh their different interests and rights? How should he go about implementing a solution?

Many things had changed since his first meeting with Kettle back in 1979. Green was proud of the hotel and proud of what the partnership had accomplished. The complex development process had been successfully completed. The hotel, with close to 400 employees, was a major employer in the local community and the existence of the hotel had helped to spur local development. His partners had all earned handsome profits. Now however, the hotel was struggling, and Green wondered how the various partners would react to the changes which threatened the project. What should he recommend to them?

Exhibit 1 Project Analysis—Rendering of Tysons Corner Marriott

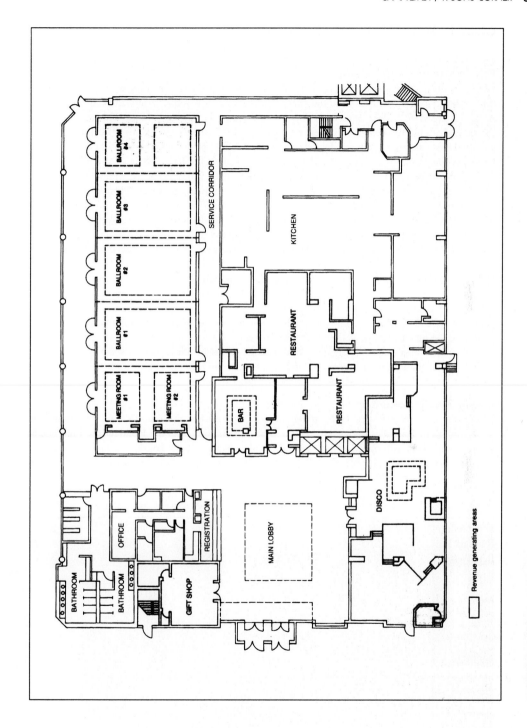

Exhibit 2   First Floor Plan

Exhibit 3   Summary of Market Analysis—June 1979

Fairfax County and Tysons Corner Data

Fairfax County, a 406 square mile area, is located in Northern Virginia. It lies at the confluence of three major interstate highways and the region's primary circumferential artery, the Capital Beltway. As of January 1978, there were 578,300 persons residing in Fairfax County. This represents an increase of 11,300 persons or 2% over the estimated 1977 population of 567,000. The County's population is expected to increase by approximately 47,700 persons by January 1980. The average family income after taxes is more than $22,300, the highest in the United States.

In June 1978, there were 221,304 persons employed in Fairfax County. Major categories of employment include industrial (16%), Federal, State and Local Government (23%), Retail (19.2%), Finance and Real Estate (5.8%), Services (19.7%), and Other (15.5%).

Tysons Corner is the center of the most active transportation corridor in Fairfax County. According to County figures, the daily traffic count through this area is 48,570 cars on Route 7, 46,400 cars on Route 123, and 74,830 cars on I–495. The new Tysons II regional mall is expected to attract an additional 30,000 cars.

Tysons Corner is presently the largest and fastest growing office concentration in suburban Metropolitan Washington. Almost half of the 7.5 million square feet of office space in the County is located here. Demand for office space has been strong and developers currently report an occupancy rate of 99% for the area's nearly 4 million square feet. Developers currently have plans for an additional 2.4 million square feet of new office space.

Two major office parks, Westgate and Westpark, represent almost 60% of the existing office space. The corporate group and transient business generated by the corporate base in these two parks will be the dominant midweek market at the proposed hotel.

Competitive Information

The Tysons Corner area is presently served only by a Holiday Inn on Route 123 and a Ramada Inn on Route 7. The Ramada Inn is newer and is in better condition than the Holiday Inn. Both hotels will be competitive with the Marriott; however, neither facility can be considered first class. A proposed 300 room Best Western Hotel at Route 7 and Westpark drive should open in 1979. Its level of quality will be close to that of the Ramada.

FACILITY	ROOMS	AVERAGE RATE	OCCUPANCY	TRANSIENT	GROUP
Holiday Inn	240	$33.00	80%	75%	25%
Ramada Inn	209	$35.00	80%	85%	15%
Best Western	301	N/A	N/A	N/A	N/A

Exhibit 3   (continued)

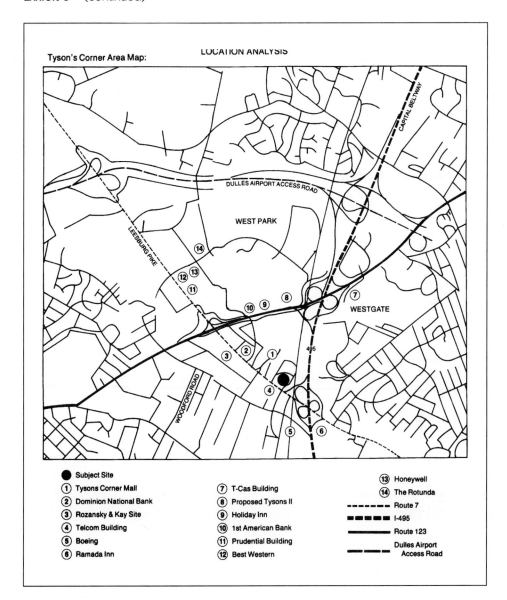

Tyson's Corner Area Map:

LOCATION ANALYSIS

CAPITAL BELTWAY

DULLES AIRPORT ACCESS ROAD

LEESBURG PIKE

WEST PARK

WESTGATE

WOODFORD ROAD

495

● Subject Site
① Tysons Corner Mall
② Dominion National Bank
③ Rozansky & Kay Site
④ Telcom Building
⑤ Boeing
⑥ Ramada Inn
⑦ T-Cas Building
⑧ Proposed Tysons II
⑨ Holiday Inn
⑩ 1st American Bank
⑪ Prudential Building
⑫ Best Western
⑬ Honeywell
⑭ The Rotunda
- - - - - - Route 7
▬ ▬ ▬ ▬ I-495
━━━━━ Route 123
━ ━ ━ ━ Dulles Airport
          Access Road

Exhibit 4   Stabilized Pro Forma Operating Statement—June 1979 ($000s)

	KEY BRIDGE MARRIOTT 1977		1978		TYSONS CORNER MARRIOTT 1980	
Sales						
Rooms	$ 4,671	46.8%	$ 5,311	48.8%	$ 6,658	51.2%
Food and beverage	4,027	40.3	4,158	37.2	4,000	30.8
Banquet	694	6.9	852	7.8	1,600	12.3
Other	599	7.0	558	6.2	748	5.7
Total sales	9,991	100.0	10,879	100.0	13,006	100.0
Department Profit						
Rooms	3,718	37.2	4,331	39.8	5,193	39.9
Food and Beverage	1,032	10.3	1,037	9.5	984	7.6
Banquet	312	3.1	384	3.5	928	7.1
Other	64	0.1	65	0.1	250	1.9
Total dept. profit	5,126	51.3	5,817	53.5	7,355	56.6
Expenses						
On-site management	694	6.9	483	4.4	715	5.5
Heat, light and power	324	3.2	317	2.9	468	3.6
Repairs and main.	292	2.9	320	2.9	507	3.9
Corporate overhead	300	3.0	310	2.8	390	3.0
Advertising and sales	313	3.1	336	3.1	429	3.3
Capital reserve	300	3.0	327	3.0	390	3.0
Taxes	234	2.3	275	2.5	325	2.5
Other	323	3.2	379	3.5	390	3.0
Total expenses	2,845	28.5	2,812	25.8	3,614	27.8
Profit for Dist.	**2,281**	**22.8**	**3,005**	**27.6**	**3,741**	**28.8**
MARRIOTT FEE	**456**	**4.6**	**601**	**5.5**	**748**	**5.8**
NOI	**1,825**	**18.3**	**2,404**	**22.1**	**2,993**	**23.0**
Number of rooms	372		372		400	
Average occupancy	85%		85%		80%	
Average room rate	$40.60		$46.75		$57.00	

Exhibit 4 (continued)   Proposed Development Budget—June 1979

Land		$ 1,400,000
Real Estate Taxes and Insurance		35,000
Architect and Engineering		820,000
Civil Engineering	37,000	
Architectural	430,000	
Marriott Design and Review Fees	257,000	
Miscellaneous Consultants	6,000	
Construction Inspection	90,000	
General Overhead		690,000
Office and On-Site Personnel	110,000	
Preliminary and Feasibility	11,000	
Marriott Purchasing Fee	150,000	
Developer Fee	420,000	
Legal Fees		100,000
Zoning	30,000	
Syndication	30,000	
Loan Closing	30,000	
Reimbursables	10,000	
Hotel Pre-opening		800,000
Wages—Sales, Marketing, and Management	95,000	
Hourly Wages and Benefits	160,000	
Moving	150,000	
Media	150,000	
Sales Non-Wages	70,000	
Miscellaneous	150,000	
Opening Party and Other PR	25,000	
General Contract		14,000,000
Hotel Furniture and Fixtures		3,000,000
Other		693,000
Caissons	100,000	
Sound and Audio–Visual Equipment	45,000	
Telephone System	270,000	
Wall Vinyl	150,000	
Miscellaneous	128,000	
Contingencies		492,000
Interest Expense		2,720,000
Operating Deficit Allowance		250,000
Total Development Budget		25,000,000

Exhibit 5   Summary of Operating Results, 1981–1988 ($000s)

	1981	1982	1983	1984	1985	1986	1987	1988
Sales								
Rooms	$5,437	$6,688	$7,740	$9,052	$9,455	$9,747	$9,453	$9,754
Food and beverage	2,052	2,559	2,925	2,860	2,806	2,778	2,554	2,148
Banquet	1,254	1,543	1,912	2,030	1,850	1,963	2,112	2,531
Other	506	629	673	770	732	769	786	739
Total	9,249	11,419	13,250	14,712	14,843	15,257	14,905	15,172
Department Profit								
Rooms	4,631	5,708	6,651	7,813	7,989	8,261	8,021	8,165
Food and beverage	696	892	1,051	958	848	718	587	340
Banquet	594	721	851	971	863	927	865	809
Other	80	106	95	181	198	186	181	209
Total	6,001	7,427	8,648	9,923	9,898	10,092	9,654	9,523
Expenses								
On-site management	890	934	985	1,111	1,221	1,255	1,317	1,383
Heat, light, and power	420	432	535	523	509	439	434	515
Repairs and maintenance	360	383	445	458	501	542	608	665
General and administrative	335	334	388	430	435	450	475	482
Advertising and sales	517	453	495	611	757	751	768	794
Capital renovation allowance	90	167	291	430	435	490	508	515
Taxes	239	317	313	346	314	470	482	506
Other	118	129	142	150	152	206	277	317
Total expenses	2,969	3,149	3,594	4,059	4,324	4,063	4,869	5,177
Cash Flow from Operations	**3,032**	**4,278**	**5,054**	**5,864**	**5,574**	**5,489**	**4,785**	**4,346**
First mortgage @ 10.5% interest	2,430	2,430	2,430	2,430	2,430	2,430	2,430	2,420
Marriott fee								
(3% of gross + 20% CFO)	884	1,198	1,408	1,614	1,560	1,556	1,404	1,325
Second mortgage	0	0	0	0	0	1,200	1,200	1,200
Third mortgage	0	0	0	0	0	0	12	55
Capital expenditures								
in excess of allowance	0	0	0	0	1,584	0	0	0
Free cash flow	**(282)**	**650**	**1,216**	**1,820**	**0**	**303**	**(261)**	**(663)**
Depreciation	(1,447)	(1,888)	(1,917)	(1,971)	(2,027)	(1,659)	(1,320)	(1,486)
Add back: Amortization	300	362	400	442	488	549	597	659
Capital expenses	213	0	107	210	1,423	357	930	197
Taxable income	(1,216)	(876)	(194)	501	(116)	(450)	(54)	(1,292)
Occupancy	**75.8**	**79.6**	**80.3**	**80.1**	**75.9**	**77.5**	**74.3**	**74.7**
Average daily rate	**$50.13**	**$58.67**	**$67.34**	**$79.00**	**$85.42**	**$87.87**	**$88.93**	**$91.48**

Exhibit 6 Property Positioning and Planning, February 9, 1989

I. TCM Property Definition

We are a suburban corporate transient hotel in a highly competitive market. We are a well established, full service facility. In addition, we are accessible to Dulles and National Airports, Washington, D.C., Tysons Corner Mall and many local defense, commercial, and high tech companies in the Tysons Corner area.

II. Marketplace Considerations

A. Market Segments

1. Mid-Week Transient—This segment makes up 78% of our Sunday–Thursday business. The largest segment within this segment is corporate. We continue to experience a decline in corporate to special corporate and mid-week super saver. This segment is the most profitable at a rate of $104.24.

2. Mid-Week Group—This segment makes up 18% of our Sunday–Thursday business. The average rate is around $84.52. Most of this business is made up of short term, corporate business of (30) rooms or less, which we have two executive meeting managers covering. We have contracted one large producer (ICS) which produces 5,000 Sunday–Thursday room nights. This is the second most profitable segment.

3. Weekend Transient—Weekend transient (Friday and Saturday) makes up 67% of the weekend business. We continue to book between 80–100 two for breakfast (TFB) per Friday and Saturday. This average rate is around $69.00. Our proximity to the Tysons Corner Mall is a big advantage. This is the third most profitable segment.

4. Weekend Group—This segment makes up 29% of our weekend business. Most of this business is in conjunction with an in house catering event, i.e., weddings, bar/bat mitzvah, reunions, etc. Also we host (4) large soccer tournaments per year in addition to many bus tours in April, May, and June. The average rate is around $61.74.

5. Contract—We presently enjoy the pleasure of Saudi Arabian Airways (15) rooms on Thursdays and Sundays with a rate of $64.00. We are presently negotiating an agreement with British Airways and have concluded a deal with Mobil Oil for (6) rooms at $75.00 each for approximately (4) months.

B. Competition

1. Hilton—The Hilton has 456 rooms and is considered a suburban, luxury hotel with over 30,000 square feet of convention meeting space. They are relatively new in the market place (approx. one year) and they compete in all segments, in addition to large local catering events. We feel that their accessibility is a disadvantage.

2. Marriott Fairview—The Marriott Fairview is a 400 room suburban, luxury hotel located within a major office park complex. Although they will not be completed until late 1989, we feel that because they are a Marriott and only 5.1 miles from Tysons Corner, they will be a major competitor. Their business will primarily be corporate, although they feature over 13,000 square feet of meeting space for conventions. They are accessible to Mobil Oil's headquarters in addition to Dulles and National Airports.

3. Sheraton—They are a 455 room suburban, full service, luxury hotel with over 27,000 square feet of meeting space. They compete in all segments especially corporate. Most of the growth is heading west and we feel in the coming years that their location will improve.

Exhibit 6   (continued)

4. Ramada—The Ramada is a 404 room full service hotel with over 10,000 square feet of meeting space. They appeal to the government sector on weekdays and tour groups and travel on weekends. They have had a recent upgrade. However, the service continues to suffer.

5. Embassy Suites—The Embassy Suites is a 232 all suite limited service hotel with very limited meeting space. It is accessible to many of the local businesses and restaurants. In addition to a 2 room suite, you receive a buffet breakfast for up to five along with two hours of complimentary cocktails. They compete in the business transient segment and weekend pleasure segment.

6. Hyatt Dulles—Opens May 1989—We may feel the impact with AT&T (headquarters located next to Dulles), catering, and social business. They have approximately 8,000 square feet of meeting space and 317 suites.

C. Relative Position within Customer Segments—Although it is difficult to determine who the leader is in market share within each segment, the following was determined from our data:

1. Weekday Transient—Our honored guest award (HGA) program continues to make TCM the market share leader in this segment. This program is represented by 53% of our weekday transient business. We continue to see our competitors improve in this segment in that we are fighting for the same customer. The Embassy Suites is probably second in this segment because of their superb price/value. This segment continues to decline by over 8.2% compared to 1987. The shift continues to fall into special corporate which has increased by over 10% compared to 1987. The remainder is shifting into the government segment.

2. Weekday Group—Because of meeting space capacity, the Hilton and Sheraton are the leaders within this market. The Embassy Suites presents no threat because they have no meeting space. However, we believe that because of Marriott's high standards and executive meeting manager (EMM) that we are the first hotel called.

3. Weekend Transient—The Embassy Suites is the market share leader in this segment because of their excellent price value. Our two for breakfast program continues to make us the second choice. In addition, our location is the best in the Tysons Corner area. The Hilton and Sheraton are third and fourth choice and the fifth is the Ramada.

4. Weekend Group—We believe that TCM is the leader in this segment. We do host kids groups which the Hilton and Sheraton do not. In addition, our social segment is very strong because of our reputation and name recognition. However, the Sheraton and Hilton feature a distinct advantage with large conventions because of meeting space size and capacity.

5. Contract—We presently have Saudi Arabian Airlines as contract rooms. They chose us because of reputation, location, competitive pricing, and excellent past experience. The Embassy Suites does not pursue this business and because of the location and size of the Hilton and Sheraton, it is difficult for them to book contract business. We continue to be the leader in this segment.

Exhibit 6 (continued)

D. Competitive Information

HOTEL	YEAR BUILT	INITIAL COST	# ROOMS	1988 OCCUPANCY	WEEKDAY RATE	WEEKEND RATE
Tysons Marriott	1981	$25MM	392	74.7	$126	$82
Embassy Suites	1985	30MM	232	79.6	124	87
Hilton	1987	67MM	456	67.1	130	81
Sheraton	1986	70MM	455	65.7	132	81
Holiday Inn	1974	13MM	314	67.6	92	81
Ramada Inn[a]	1975	10MM	404	62.1	85	81
Residence Inn[b]	1988	12MM	96	N/A	113	59

[a]The Holiday Inn was renovated and expanded to 314 rooms in 1986 at a total cost of $6 million.
[b]The Ramada Inn was renovated and expanded to 404 rooms in 1987 at a total cost of $20 million.

III. Future Projections

A. Aggregate Share and Demand—In 1989 we see that the demand for the TCM and the marketplace is relatively flat. In 1989/90 with the opening of the Marriott Fairview, we expect demand to decrease. Office buildings continue to be built yet occupancies for them are down. 1988 office building occupancies compared to 1987 are down by 3%. Office building occupancies are projected to be flat for 1990.

B. Occupancies—In 1988 year to date (YTD) occupancy is better than last year and close to budget '88. However, overall average rate is down. We expect occupancies to remain flat. 1988 YTD 74.7%—ACT budget 74.5%—LYTD 74.3%.

C. Market Shares—We see that TCM is maintaining itself as the leader in the market. However, with continued hotel openings our overall market share will decrease, particularly in the weekday segments.

D. Targets—We must continue to focus in on our major advantages over the competition, i.e., service, location, and HGA. The continued use of yield management will help us maximize our revenue in relation to price and mix. Finally, we must target in on the shortage of labor and enhance our overall service.

E. New Competition

April 1989	Hyatt Dulles	350 rooms
June 1989	Hyatt Fair Lakes	350 rooms
September 1989	Marriott Fairview	420 rooms
November 1989	Marriott All Suite	250 rooms
November 1990	Ritz Carlton Tysons	380 rooms
June 1991	Hyatt Reston	550 rooms

The above projected hotel openings are going to impact the supply of rooms in the marketplace in that they are all within a 5–8 mile radius of the Tysons Corner Marriott.

22

THE SCHNEIDER BUILDING

In May 1995, Jonathan Schneider, the President of the Schneider Company is faced with two related problems. First he needs to find a new facility that can accommodate his expanding business. Second, he needs to decide whether to lease or purchase this new facility. And third, he needs to decide what to do about the existing facility which he leases from his father.

Discussion Questions:

1. Using the numbers in Exhibit 5 and the facts in the case, where should Jonathan move his company? Should be buy or lease?
2. How should Jonathan manage the disposition of the existing building? How should he compensate his father if he moves out?
3. In what way does the fact that Jonathan is an owner-user affect his decision-making? Which property would he pick if he were strictly an investor?

In May 1995, Jonathan Schneider had every reason to feel pleased that all his hard work was beginning to pay off. One year ago, in a leveraged buyout, he purchased ownership of the Schneider Group, the Schneider's family business. To the surprise of some members of his family, he was able to put together the bank financing to accomplish the acquisition. Some doubted that he could succeed. But through hard work and aggressive management he had grown revenues from $30 million to $38 million. He had also generated enough cash flow to pay off 55% of the debt from the leveraged buyout. With a little bit of luck, he expected to be totally out of this debt before his thirtieth birthday in 1996. His brother-in-law who had worked for the company for over 15 years left in 1994. His father continued to be part of the company and kept an office in the building, but served in a much more limited role. His other siblings were employed elsewhere.

The only cloud on Jonathan's horizon was the company's 46,949 s.f. building on Elm Street in West Dalton which serves as the company's headquarters and factory. In 1983 the Schneider Group had purchased the building at an auction for $355,000. When it purchased this building, Schneider moved out of 15,000 square feet of leased space and wondered what they would do with all the extra space in the Elm Street building.

Over the next twelve years as sales continued to increase, the Schneider Group found themselves constantly shoring up the floors to support new equipment and jerry rigging the ventilation systems. By 1995 they had completely run out of space, and the inefficiencies and inadequacy of the building were a constant drain on the business. In fact, Jonathan had to lease an additional 8,000 square feet of storage space in a warehouse in Carlton. Jonathan knew that if he wanted to continue to grow the business (to say nothing of maintaining the morale of his workforce), he needed to move out, and he needed to move out soon.

The problem was that the Schneider Group had entered into a five year lease on the Elm Street building that ended in 1999. That lease required the Schneider Group to pay Sheldon Schneider, Jonathan's father and the company's founder, $196,000 per year or $4.17 per square foot. The building had been transferred to him as part of the buyout in 1994. Sheldon was counting on these rental payments to repay the $400,000 mortgage balance on the property by the end of the lease term, and later to provide a nice annuity for his retirement. If

Adjunct Professor William J. Poorvu and Lecturer John H. Vogel, Jr. prepared this case as the basis for class discussion rather than to illustrate either effective or ineffective handling of an administrative situation.

the Schneider Group moved out of the building, Jonathan felt that he had a tenant's obligation to deal honorably with the lease until its end and perhaps even after. He also needed to think like a real estate investor about how to maximize the value of the building so that his father would not get hurt.

If he did move, he faced the problem as to whether to buy or lease his next facility. As of now he was leaning toward two options. The first was a 60,000 square foot building in nearby Preston that he could lease at $4.50 per square foot triple net or buy for $2,400,000. The second was a 120,000 square foot building further out in Grandon where he could rent 80,000 square feet at approximately $3.50 square feet. If both of these fell through, he knew there was land available in Preston for a build-to-suit structure.

THE SCHNEIDER FAMILY

Jonathan Schneider's grandfather founded a textile company in 1920 at a time when the textile business was a major industry in the area. In 1958, Sheldon left the business and started the Schneider Company which sold premium items for companies to give away to their customers. In 1964, Sheldon landed an oil company account which required that he go to Asia to buy the premium items. While in Asia, he purchased some other items, which he thought would make good, corporate gifts.

With the oil shocks in the early 1970s, oil companies cut way back on their promotions and Sheldon decided to concentrate on the tee-shirt and sweatshirt businesses. Today, these items are the largest part of Schneider's business. The line has been broadened to include other items. Many of these items are shipped from Asia to West Dalton where Schneider designs and silk screens a logo or other customized designs onto the product.

In Jonathan's experience the multi-billion dollar premium products industry has been undergoing a significant change. What used to be a commodity business where pricing was the overriding (and often only) issue has become a more segmented business. As Schneider has taken on higher profile clients, quality and delivery have become almost as important as price.

Jonathan joined Schneider on a full time basis in 1988. After working in West Dalton for two years, he moved to Asia to run Schneider's Asian operation. Jonathan enjoyed living in Hong Kong and the freedom to operate his business as an independent company. In 1992, when Sheldon asked Jonathan to come back to West Dalton his first response was "No, I do not want to leave Asia." Ultimately, his father convinced him that the company needed him in West Dalton and so he returned.

THE PROPERTY

The Schneider building is really three connected buildings. The main structure is a three story, wood and concrete block, mill style, industrial building that was originally constructed in about 1850 and for most of its history served as a shoe factory. Attached on one side is a one story concrete structure. Attached and connected on the other side is a two story (with basement) concrete building which the owner constructed in 1957 (see **Exhibit 1**, Site Plan). The overall result is a structure that contains 46,949 square feet as follows:

Basement	12,155
First Floor	13,596
Second Floor	12,996
Third Floor	8,202

The building sits on an irregular, 29,214 square foot parcel of land with 193 linear feet of frontage on Elm Street. About 15 parking spaces are available along the front of the building on Elm Street, and another 40 spaces are available on a 14,000 square foot parcel of land that Schneider owns on the other side of Elm Street, across from the building. (See **Exhibit 2** which shows pictures of the building and its surroundings.)

According to an appraiser, the condition of the two story section is excellent. It has a new rubber membrane roof that was installed less than two years ago. The three story building is in "average to good" condition. There is plenty of electric service including a 440v/220v three phase service and a new oil burning furnace. The office area consists of four offices, two conference rooms and large open areas with moveable partitions and cubicles (see **Exhibit 3** for the first floor layout). The office finish is typical of an older industrial building with a combination of carpet and tile floors, a suspended ceiling with fluorescent lighting and drywall. Most of the floors throughout the mill are wooden and are supported by brick, metal and wood columns. The building is fully sprinklered and the site is considered environmentally "clean."[14] The office space is air conditioned with older mechanical units, while the production and storage space are not.

THE NEIGHBORHOOD

The Schneider Building is located on Elm Street near the intersection of Elm and Marble Street. To the north, west, and east of the property are single family houses, with a few multi-family properties. Adjacent and to the south of the property is a four-story, 16,000 square foot fire station with arched windows and a hose tower.

---

[14]In order to get the mortgage at 20 Elm Street refinanced, the bank insisted on a phase I environmental study to determine if the site is clean. A phase I study includes an historical (paper) search on the past uses of the site, a visual inspection and a few soil samples. If anything had turned up in this phase I study, a phase II study would have been required which includes extensive, deep borings, and sampling of the underground water. In this case, the only potential problem that was discovered was the fact that an underground oil tank at the fire station next door may have leaked years ago and some of the oil may have migrated over to the Elm Street site. The responsibility for the cleanup was assumed by the Fire Department.

For trucks to get to the loading docks of the Schneider Building, they have to turn off Marble Street and use a gravel lot behind the fire station. This gravel lot is owned by the fire station. Over the years, an informal right of passage has been established between the Schneider Building and the fire station. Construction of a new fire station is almost complete and the Elm Street fire station will be decommissioned by the end of 1995.

The City has not made firm plans about what to do with the older fire station on Elm Street. Being a handsome structure built in 1852 that has long been the focal point for West Dalton Square, there will be strong popular sentiment to try to find a new use rather than tear it down. The costs to renovate this kind of structure, however, are likely to be very high. The fire department's first plan, in fact, was to renovate and expand this building, but they soon discovered that it was cheaper to build a new fire station. The West Dalton building inspector indicated that the most likely scenario for dealing with this building would be to have the fire station put up for public auction. He had no idea how soon that would happen or what kind of restrictions and conditions the City of West Dalton would put on bidders when, and if, the building were put up for sale. From Jonathan's perspective, the passage through the fire station lot was crucial for truck delivery to his site. What leverage he had was unclear.

Stevens Street, which is about 100 feet south of the Schneider Building, is the main commercial street in West Dalton. Stevens Street is lined with small retail shops and one new retail complex that also has second floor office space.

West Dalton itself is situated on the Runny River, twenty four miles north of Urbanville. It has a population of approximately 29,000 people which has remained at about the same level the last fifteen years. West Dalton is primarily a residential community and benefits from excellent highway access both in an east west direction along highway 118 and 82 and in the north south direction along Interstate 95. There are two major regional malls within 20 minutes of West Dalton and recently a number of discount warehouse stores have moved into the area such as Costco, HQ, Home Depot, and Circuit City. Unlike many towns, this retail competition has not devastated the local retailers, and there is high occupancy rate in the downtown West Dalton area for retail although the new office building has considerable vacancy.

THE PROCESS

In 1994, as part of the leveraged buyout, the Schneider family had an appraisal done of the property. Using conventional appraisal techniques, the appraiser determined that the building had a value of $675,000 (see **Exhibit 4**). The appraiser believed that the "highest and best use" for the property was its current use as industrial and office space. If the Schneider Company moved out, the appraiser believed the building could be rented to one or more tenants at an average rate of $2.60, per square foot which, after vacancy and expenses, would yield about $70,657 per year (see **Exhibit 5**).

In 1995, as the Schneider business continued to grow rapidly, Jonathan became convinced that the building was becoming unworkable. For example, he purchased a state of the art silk screening machine to keep up with his orders, but found that the only open space without columns that was large enough and strong enough to support it was near the loading area. So in January 1995, he hired Terrie Budd, a real estate consultant, to help him think about his building options He also hired some industrial engineers to help him calculate how much space he would need, and how he might configure his machinery in new space to improve his operations. If he moved the business, Jonathan was aware, the cost of moving the machinery, leveling it, hooking it up (with electricity and compressed air) and buying new equipment would be very expensive.

Terrie started by helping Jonathan think about where he might want to locate. After considerable thinking and some driving around, Jonathan decided that an important consideration was holding on to Schneider Group's "semi-skilled" labor force who did the silk screening in a high quality way. He felt that if he moved outside of the West Dalton–Preston–Carlton area, this workforce might not follow. He also liked the pro-business climate he found in Preston. Grandon which was 30 minutes further away was acceptable but not ideal.

In working with Terrie, Jonathan discovered that there were many fewer suitable buildings than he had originally thought. For example, he had heard about people who had bought warehouse buildings for under $20 per square foot, but after looking at a couple of these buildings, he concluded that the location, condition and configuration would never work for his business. Similarly, he found there was a lot more choice for someone who only needed 5,000 or 10,000 sq. ft., than someone who wanted 60–100,000 sq. ft.

After considerable investigation, Terrie presented Jonathan with the following list of available options, and their relative costs. She assumed Jonathan needed at least a 60,000 square foot, one story building with forty foot high warehouse space. To get current information she spoke to a variety of contractors, real estate brokers, and developers, and then did some analysis and interpretation of their information to make an apples–to–apples comparison. Based on her research she presented Jonathan with the following market analysis:

1. **Build a New Building**: To get exactly the building that Jonathan wanted there is no substitute to buying a piece of land and creating customized plans. Terrie knew there was some industrial land available in a couple of industrial parks and made the following estimates:

Land ($100,000 per acre × 8 acres)	$ 800,000
Warehouse space (40' high; 20,000 s.f. × $35/s.f.)	700,000
Production space (25,000 s.f. × $25)	625,000
Office space (mostly open, 15,000 s.f. × $50)	750,000
Total 60,000 s.f.	$2,875,000*

   *To these numbers should be added a 20% factor to cover soft costs like legal, architecture and engineering, and financing costs. Once all approvals were obtained, construction would take from six to nine months. The costs of an 80,000 square foot building would be proportionately higher.

2. **An Existing Building in Preston:** There was an industrial building in Preston that was in an established industrial park. The tenant was in the process of moving to a larger facility. Although this building was not perfect, it was more than adequate, and even had some additional land which might enable Schneider to build an addition if business continued to expand. The owner of this property might be willing to either lease at $4.50 per square foot triple net[15] or sell the building for $2,400,000. In the case of a lease, the owner indicated he would spend up to $150,000 in a work letter to customize the space to Jonathan's needs if Jonathan signed a 10 year lease. The owner further indicated that the lease would contain a cost of living increase after 5 years.

At this Preston site, there was adequate land to expand the building by 40,000 square feet, but that would require approval from the city and from the state environmental agency since the land was adjacent to some wetlands. It would also require a land swap the seller said he could arrange. Jonathan's advisers told him that they were not sure that the expansion would be easy to get approved.

3. **An Existing Building in Grandon:** A third option was a 120,000 square foot building in Grandon, an additional 30 minutes further away. Jonathan could buy this property for $3.2 million,[16] but it needed a new roof costing $400,000. There appeared to be no environmental problems. Terrie also thought he could negotiate a 10 year lease with 2 5-year options for 80,000

[15]Leases are generally categorized as gross leases, modified gross leases (with an expense stop) or a net leases (sometimes referred to as triple net leases), depending on how the expenses are allocated. Under a gross lease, which is now very rare, the tenant pays a fixed amount and the landlord is responsible for all capital and operating expenses. In a modified gross lease, which is the norm in most office buildings, the landlord is responsible for a fixed amount of expenses (say $5 per square foot or the actual first year expenses) and the tenant is responsible if the total of all operating expenses exceeds the expense stop during any lease year. Expenses include: real estate taxes, utilities, insurance, cleaning, repairs, and management. Finally, under a net lease or triple net lease, which is a common lease in industrial buildings, the tenant pays a lower base rent, but is responsible for all the operating expenses except, for example, the repair and replacement of the building structure and the roof. In actuality, these three lease categories are only the starting point in a lease negotiation. The lease document may run over 100 pages, and much of the legalese and negotiation is about which services and expenses are the responsibility of which party.

[16]Although Jonathan believed there were tax advantages to owning real estate, he felt that in deciding between buying and leasing, he would do his analysis based on pre-tax, cash flow. His accountant indicated that, in fact, the tax benefits would not be substantial. The lease payments would be 100% deductible if he leased but the interest payments on the mortgage would be deductible if he bought the building. The principal payments on the mortgage would not be deductible for tax purposes, but as the owner, he could depreciate the property over 39 years.

square feet at $3.75 per square foot with a further option to take the remaining 40,000 square feet at the start of each option period. If the Schneider Group leased the building, Terrie believed that the landlord would be willing to fix the roof and the office space. If Jonathan purchased the building, it would be delivered to him "as is," i.e., in its current condition. The manufacturing and warehouse space were in good condition but the 15,000 square feet of office space would require a complete rehab for $20 per square foot. The seller was a Swiss company who had moved its operations to North Carolina. For comparison purposes Jonathan assumed he could rent the 40,000 s.f. of additional space at $2.50 per square foot.

One thing that Jonathan discovered in his investigation was the availability of State Agency or Federal Small Business Agency financing. One of his friends mentioned this tax exempt financing, so he immediately called his investment banker, whom, it turned out, knew very little about it. But when Jonathan asked his accountant about low cost financing, he found that the accountant was very knowledgeable, and together they discovered that there were many programs whose purpose was to provide low cost financing to businesses as an inducement to locate its factory and jobs in a particular town. This financing could be used for 90% of the cost of purchasing or renovating plant and equipment, and had aggressive terms like a 6.5% interest rate and a 20-year term (an 8.95% constant). The Schneider Group would still have to put up the 10% cash equity, on which Jonathan expected to earn at least a 15% cash on cash return. A private investor would probably only get a 70% mortgage at about a 10% constant and would still want a 15% cash return on the remaining 30%.

ELM STREET

As Jonathan grew more confident that he would be able to move to a larger facility in Preston or Grandon he asked Terrie to advise him about what to do with the 20 Elm Street building. Terrie began by spending some time walking through the building and taking careful notes. She also asked for any blueprints of the building. She walked around the neighborhood carefully observing all the stores and houses.

Next, Terrie visited the West Dalton Building Department where she checked on the zoning restrictions. 20 Elm Street is situated in an Industrial I district. Uses permitted in an Industrial I district include: retail and wholesale sales; hotels and motels; bowling alleys, indoor theaters and ice skating rinks; shopping centers; restaurants; general office buildings; warehouses; light manufacturing assembly and processing; printing and publishing.

At the building department she also found the following zoning restrictions:

Dimensional requirements are:

Minimum Lot Area	None
Minimum Lot Frontage	50 feet
Minimum Setbacks	
Front	50 feet
Side	25 feet
Rear	25 feet
Setback from Residential District	50 feet
Maximum Lot Coverage	50%
Maximum Height	55 feet (four stories)

The current use of the site for light manufacturing and office, Terrie confirmed, is a legal use. The buildings, however, do not meet several of the dimensional requirements such as the front setback and the setback from the residential district. It is therefore considered a legal nonconforming use because it was built before the current zoning by-laws in 1946 and "grandfathered." If it were torn down, the new building would have to conform.

In talking with the building inspector, Terrie learned that it was quite possible to obtain a building variance and put the building to another use. For example, getting the property rezoned for residential purpose would probably not be difficult since so many neighboring properties were residential. The only hurdle would be ensuring that there was sufficient parking. On the other hand, it might be very difficult to get the property rezoned for a gasoline station or car dealership, since the abutting property owners would probably oppose it.

Terrie then went to speak with some brokers in town. Most of the brokers in West Dalton specialize in residential properties. They told her that the rental market for 1,000 sq. ft., two bedroom apartments currently averaged $800–$1,000 and the vacancy was relatively low. Condominiums were very rare. Houses in the area sold from a range of $90,000 to $140,000. The site could accommodate five house lots, or if approved by the city, 15 apartments.

Terrie talked with one broker who leased commercial space. He indicated that retail space currently rented for $12 per square foot, but he cautioned Terrie that the fact that the Schneider Building was not directly on Stevens Street might make it difficult to rent. He indicated that he thought he might be able to find some smaller, industrial tenants at $5 per square foot, especially for the first floor, if Terrie were willing to subdivide the building. He thought, however, that it would be difficult to market the space until Schneider moved out.

Terrie then invited an Urbanville developer whom she knew well to come to West Dalton and look at the building. He had experience renovating smaller, commercial properties, and so, as a favor, he drove up to West Dalton and walked through the 46,949 square foot building. He concluded that Sheldon Schneider would be lucky to sell the building for $400,000 and pay off the existing mortgage.

The developer's reasoning was first that the building was in a poor location for an industrial use. Trucks had to drive through West Dalton and had difficulty turning into the loading docks. Second, it would be difficult and expensive to subdivide the building. For example, every tenant would need access to the loading dock, the bathrooms, the freight elevator and two means of egress which would mean reducing the rentable space and building hallways and common areas. Third, the cost to retrofit the building and meet all the requirements of the American Disability Act including elevators, handicapped bathrooms, new hardware etc. would be prohibitively expensive. For example, it might cost $30 per square foot to modernize the building space and no one would pay enough even for office rent to justify that kind of expense. The parking was another limiting factor with only 55 spaces, in essence a 1.2 ratio of cars per thousand square feet.

THE DECISIONS

Jonathan's father knew that Jonathan was looking for new space and, in fact, suggested one or two buildings that Jonathan should look at. Sheldon was anxious, however, to see how his son dealt with him regarding the existing building. If Jonathan moved out of Elm Street, how would he compensate Sheldon for the lease, and the retirement income Sheldon was counting on? What action should he take on this building and how should he handle the City in regard to the fire station?

Second, Jonathan needed to decide whether to buy, build or lease. The 60,000 square foot building that Terrie had helped him find and analyze was probably about as good as anything he was likely to find in his target geographic area. But how important was the ability for further expansion to his business. Did Grandon make more sense? Or should he build what he needed now and not worry about the cost differential? Terrie had suggested that he fill out a chart that compared the cost of the three options (see **Exhibit 5**). He should look at the cost for each property both on an aggregate and a square foot basis. He would assume in Grandon for the purchase option his total carrying cost net of the $100,000 per year he might receive from subletting the extra 40,000 square feet.

Finally, Jonathan needed to think about his business. Finding a new building, he realized, was a strong incentive for a person to think about where his business would be in five or ten years. All the signs pointed toward continued growth, and Jonathan's personal goal was to grow revenues to $100 million in the next ten years. But as his customers grew, and became more demanding, he wondered how that would affect his space needs. He also wondered if he could outsource more of his business and ship apparel directly to his customers without having them pass through his factory. He wished that he had more time to decide, but every day that went by without a decision was one more day his 150 employees had to work in cramped, inferior space. Just recently he had to cut back on a purchase for inventory because of space limitations.

Exhibit 1 Site Plan 20 Elm Street

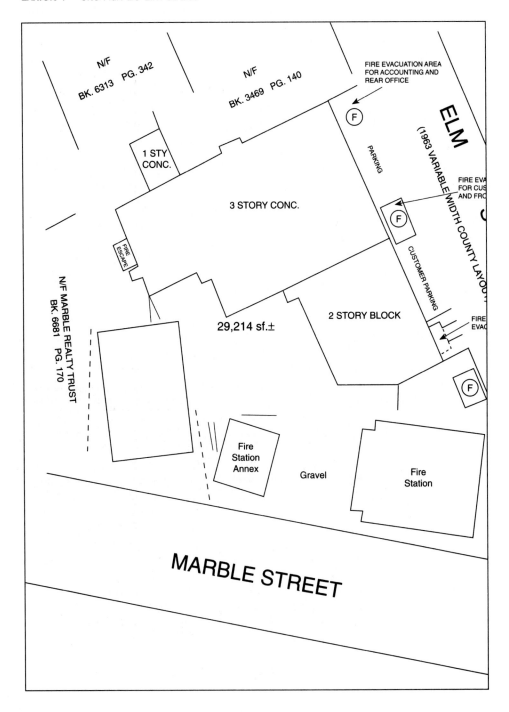

Exhibit 2

VIEW SOUTHWEST OF SUBJECT PROPERTY
from Across Elm Street of 20 Elm Street,
West Dalton, Massachusetts. The arched window of
the fire station is in the background and a
residential neighboring house is in the foreground

VIEW NORTH OF SOUTH SIDE OF SUBJECT PROPERTY
SHOWING MANUFACTURING LOADING DOCKS

Exhibit 3 Building Sketch
FIRST FLOOR

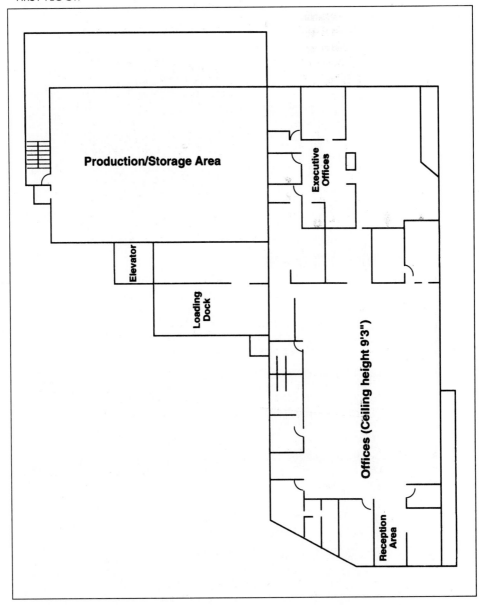

Exhibit 4   (Excerpts from the 1994 Appraisal)

Appraisal Process

The purpose of this report is to arrive at an estimate of the probable fair market value of the subject property. This is achieved by a systematic gathering, classification and analysis of data which is required in the development and consideration of the three approaches to value: the Cost Approach, the Sales Comparison Approach, and the Income Approach.

The Cost Approach consists of estimating the reproduction cost new of all improvements, deducting accrued depreciation from all sources, and adding the value of the land which is estimated by comparison to recent sales of similar land.

The Sales Comparison Approach involves a comparison of the subject to similar properties that have actually sold in arm's length transactions or are offered for sale. Sale and asking prices are adjusted to reflect the significant differences, if any, that exist between the sale property and the subject and the adjusted prices correlated into a final indicated subject value.

The Income Approach involves an analysis of the income producing capabilities of the property under review by estimating the market or economic rental value and deducting the operating expenses necessary to support the estimated rent. The net income remaining after expenses is then capitalized into an indication of market value.

For the purpose of estimating the market value of the subject property the appraisers have considered the relevance of al three approaches outlined above. Only the Sales Comparison Approach and the Income Approach will be utilized in this report.

Valuation Conclusions:
The Cost Approach

The appraisers did not apply the Cost Approach as a method of valuation in this appraisal due to the age of the subject improvements and the lack of comparable commercial land sales in the subject area.

The Sales Comparison Approach

The appraisers have utilized the Sales Comparison Approach as there was an adequate supply of comparable sales in the local market. Numerous sales of industrial building properties were researched as an aid in estimating the market value of the subject property in its present "as-is" condition. No sales truly similar to the subject in feature to feature characteristics were found. Four sales were discovered which are considered somewhat comparable to the subject.

The comparable sales indicate an estimated fee simple, market value range of $10.18 to $35.90 per square foot of gross building area. The adjusted per square foot values range from a low of $16.29 to a high of $25.13. After considering all of the factors influencing market value, the appraisers are of the opinion that the subject property has a unit value of $20.00 per square foot.

Then: 34,794[17](+/−) sq. ft. @ $20 = $695,880 rounded to $695,000.

The Income Capitalization Approach

The Income Capitalization Approach to value consists of methods, techniques, and mathematical procedures that an appraiser uses to analyses a property's capacity to generate benefits (i.e., usually the monetary benefits of income and reversion) and convert these benefits into an indication of present value.

Two capitalization methods, Direct Capitalization and Yield Capitalization, are most commonly used to estimate the market value of properties such as the subject.

---

[17]The appraiser did not include the basement space in this comparison with other buildings.

Exhibit 4 (continued)

Direct Capitalization is a method used to convert an estimate of a single year's net income expectancy, or an annual average of several years' net income expectancies, into an indication of value in one direct step, by dividing the net income estimate by an appropriate income rate.[18]

Yield Capitalization[19] is a method used to convert future benefits to present value by discounting each future benefit at an appropriate yield rate.[20]

Rental Analysis

In considering the rental of space in the subject property, the appraisers have concluded that space would be available on a floor by floor basis; i.e., the first, second, third floors and basement would be available for rental on a unit basis. It s unlikely that a single tenant could be found for the entire space; a likely scenario is that the first floor would be rented in combination with the basement space and the second and third floors would be rented separately.

Rentals #1–4 are typical current rentals for one story, first level space in the general subject area. The newest rent, and the one providing the most comparability to the subject first floor, in Rental #4. This renovated space would be similar to the subject first floor and would have better on-site parking than the subject, a factor which is reflected in the Expense Analysis. Based on these rentals, a market rate of $4.00/sf is defined for the subject first floor space.

Comparable rentals for upper level office/mill type space are not predominant in the locus. The appraisers are aware that similar space is available and rented in the area but these properties are not considered comparable in either location, condition or amenities to the subject. Rental #5 is an offering in the subject locus recently rented for $4.00/sf including heat. With adjustment for this expense and with consideration that the available space is smaller than the subject therefore need to be adjusted downward in comparison top the subject, a rental rate of $3.00/sf is derived for the second floor. Rental #6, which spans second and third floor space and would be considered similar to the subject's third floor space, is utilized to derive a rental rate of $2.00/sf for the third floor. The basement space, which would provide storage/warehousing for either a building tenant or for a third party, is typical of lower level space. Based on the appraisers' knowledge and contacts with knowledgeable people who broker this type of space, a rental rate of $1.00/sf is deemed appropriate.

The potential gross income for the subject property can now be calculated as follows:

First floor	13,884 sf	×	$4.00/sf	=	$55,536
Second floor	13,260 sf	×	$3.00/sf	=	$39,780
Third floor	7,650 sf	×	$2.00/sf	=	$15,300
Basement	12,155 sf	×	$1.00/sf	=	$12,155
Total	46,949 sf		$2.60/sf (avg.)		$122,771

[18]The income rate (or denominator in this mathematical equation) is usually referred to as a capitalization rate or cap rate.

[19]In this appraisal because the appraiser did not believe there would be an appreciation during the period in which a potential investor would hold this property, he did not utilize this approach in his appraisal.

[20]The yield rate is more commonly called the discount rate in this net present value analysis and is usually different than the cap rate, unless the appraiser assumes there will be no appreciation or depreciation in the income stream over the holding period. The discount rate is the yield or hurdle rate that the investor expects to receive over time from cash flow, tax benefits and residual proceeds.

Exhibit 4   (continued)

Expense Analysis

In order to calculate the estimated pre-tax net operating income for the subject property, it is necessary to deduct estimated annual operating expenses from the estimated annual, potential gross rental income. In general, the appraisers have observed that expenses of local area properties are absorbed by the property owners on a triple net basis, where tenants are responsible for their own utilities (i.e., heat, hot water, and electricity), and in some cases, a pro-rata share of expenses pertinent to the property such as real estate taxes and insurance. In the case of the subject property, it is the opinion of the appraisers that the "triple net" basis is applicable. Thus, the appraisers have estimated a vacancy and uncollectible loss reserve, legal and audit, management, real estate taxes, insurance and structural reserves based upon the local market for operating costs of other properties of similar use.

Income and Expense Statement

Potential Gross Annual Income		$122,771
Less Vacancy & Collection Loss—20%		24,178
Effective Gross Income		$98,593 = $2.10/sf
Expenses:		
Management at 6%	$5,916	
Legal & Audit	1,000	
Reserves for Replacement	4,930	
Real Estate Taxes*	15,995	
Total Expenses:		$27,841
Net Operating Income (NOI)		$70,752 = $1.50/sf

*Real Estate Taxes are based on a current value for land and building of $1,062,800 and a tax rate of $15.05/$1000 of valuation.

Capitalization Rate Calculation

In order to develop an overall capitalization rate, the appraisers have discussed the property, in general terms, with several area mortgage brokers and lenders as well as real estate investors. Based upon these discussions, the value estimate can be calculated as follows:

Value =	**Net Operating Income**
	Capitalization Rate
Value =	$70,657
	.105
Value by Income Approach	$672,924
Rounded	$675,000
Indicated "as-is" Value by	
the Income Approach	$675,000

Reconciliation and Final Value Conclusion

Cost Approach	Not Utilized
Sales Comparison Approach	$696,000.00
Income Capitalization Approach	$675,000.00

Exhibit 4 (continued)

The Sales Comparison Approach has been utilized in this appraisal. A minimal amount of reliable sales data was available from the market and analyzed relative to the attributes of the subject property. However, since the comparable sales data is considered marginal at best, in the opinion of the appraisers, the Sales Comparison Approach was not considered to be the most applicable approach to value.

The Income Capitalization Approach was also utilized in this appraisal. This approach was applied using a Direct Capitalization method which considered the motivations of a prospective investor. It is our opinion that the estimated gross rental income and operating expense estimates were very reliable and that the interest rate, loan to value ratio, equity yield rate and investor survey data employed in the derivation of the overall capitalization rate were reasonable and consistent with the expectations of buyers and investors in the present market.

The Cost Approach was not utilized for reasons previously discussed in the text of this appraisal.

In summary, it is our opinion that, as developed in this appraisal, the most reliable approach is the Income Capitalization Approach which indicates a fee simple, market value of $675,000.

Exhibit 5

The Schneider Building ($000 except per sq. ft. categories)

	TOTAL CAPITAL INVESTMENT	INVESTMENT SQ. FT.	UPFRONT EQUITY	ANNUAL MORTGAGE PAYMENT (4) OR LEASE PAYMENT	15% ANNUAL PAYMENT ON EQUITY	TOTAL ANNUAL COST	TOTAL ANNUAL COST/SQ. FT.
New Building							
Preston Purchase (1)							
Preston Lease	N/A	N/A	N/A		N/A		
Grandon Purchase (2)				(3)			
Grandon Lease	N/A	N/A	N/A		N/A		

(1) Total capital investment for Preston includes acquisition and fit out work to customize the space.
(2) Assumes buyer pays for new roof and tenant improvements.
(3) Assumes that Schneider occupies 80,000 square feet and sublets the other 40,000 s.f. at $2.50/sq. ft.
(4) Assume that financing equals 90% of the total capital investment and has a 6.5% interest rate and an 8.95% constant payment.

23

MANAGEMENT OF REAL ESTATE PROCESS

The Projects:	The Players:	The Panorama	The Process:

PRODUCT
Locational Characteristics
Business Definition/
Time Frame
Design/Physical Conditions
Capital/Operating Costs

STAKEHOLDERS
Principals: Investors
Developers
Asset Managers
Users: Tenants
Services: Legal/Accounting
Architects/Engineers
Contractors/Subs
Managers
Suppliers
Brokers:leasing/
sales/mortgage
Appraisers
Market analysts
Capital: Equity
Debt
Neighbors
Regulators
Competitors

INDUSTRY
Fragmented
Capital Intensive
Cyclical
Project Oriented

CONCEPTUAL STATE
Idea
Strategy Formulation
Preliminary Investigation
Market Analysis Projections

MARKET
Target Use
Absorption/Demand
Competition/Supply/Comparables
Timing of Entry

ECONOMIC
Capital Formation/Job Growth
Taxation/Incentives
General Regional Characteristics

PRE-COMMITMENT STAGE
Detailed Analysis/Design
Approvals/Environmental
Resource Assembly
Organizational Planning

SOCIOLOGICAL
Demographics
Lifestyles
Geography
Education

ACTION STAGE
Resource Acquisition
Financial Commitments
Construction
Leasing

FINANCIAL
Operating Projections
Sources/Uses of Funds
Financial Benefits/Returns:
Cash Flow Operations
Taxes
Appreciation
Risk/Reward Allocation

CHARACTERISTICS:	
Goals	Commitment
Experience	Time Frame
Competence	Compensation
Resources	Risk Profile
Interrelationships	Integrity

TECHNOLOGICAL
Communications
Infrastructure
Workplace
Building Materials, Techniques

CUSTODIAL STAGE
Asset Management
Operations
Rehabilitation
Re-use
Financial Management/
Tax Planning
Harvesting:
Sale
Refinancing

LEGAL
Site Control
Regulations
Ownership Structure
Agreements

SKILLS	
Analysis	Communication
Decision Making	Management
Negotiation	Leadership

POLITICAL
Land Use Patterns
Regulatory Environment
Power/Process

24

FINANCIAL ANALYSIS OF REAL PROPERTY INVESTMENTS

This note examines some of the methods by which real property investments are analyzed, including those most commonly used and others that will serve for purposes of comparison or illustration. It also offers suggestions about analytical techniques and provides sources of useful information.

The reader should be aware throughout that a successful analysis of a real property investment must consider many critical characteristics that are not easily reflected in the mathematics of a financial analysis. Among these are (a) the extremely long time horizon involved, (b) the lack of liquidity, and (c) the effects of an ever-changing environment. In short, the investor must temper financial analysis with an understanding of the risks involved before proceeding.

The task of analyzing a real estate investment may be divided into three components:

1. *Cash flow*   The amount of cash annually received by the investor, including revenues generated, minus all cash expenses incurred, with the exception of income taxes;

2. *Tax effect*   The amount by which the investment affects the taxes payable in the current year by the investor;

3. *Future benefits*   The amount by which the capital position of the investor is affected by the sale or refinancing of the property or entity owning the property on an after-tax basis. It takes into account prior mortgage amortization and the change in value of the asset.

This note examines each of these elements of return and their use in establishing an overall rate of return and valuation of the property as well as the effects the passage of time may have on all of the above.

THE SETUP

The term *setup* is real estate jargon for a combination of the income statement and cash flow statement. The purpose is to get a better measure of value than either of these statements alone could provide. For the purchaser of real property, the setup provides the basis for a measure of the value of the acquisition. By adjusting the setup, a purchaser can trace the effect on market value of any changes that might be made. Preparing a setup is also useful to the owner of property not currently producing income. It provides a measure of opportunity cost by showing the amount of carrying costs over time and the amount of money at risk in holding the property.

Preparing a setup for a specific piece of real property is a two-step process. The first step focuses on the pretax cash flow. The second measures the effect of taxes. By following the procedure outlined in **Table A**, the pretax cash flow may be determined.

Table A   Determining Pretax Cash Flow

Gross revenues:	Base rentals
	Rent escalators
	Expense reimbursements
	Other income
− Vacancies, bad debts	
= Net revenues	
− Operating expenses:	Real estate taxes
	Administrative
	Insurance
	Utilities
	Maintenance, supplies, and trash removal
	Repairs
	Replacement and other reserves
	Other expenses
= Cash flow from operations (also known as free-and-clear cash flow or operating cash flow)	
− Financial payments:	Mortgage interest
	Mortgage amortization
	Land-lease payments
− Capital expenditures	
= Cash flow after financing or cash flow before taxes	

Professor William J. Poorvu prepared this note as the basis for class discussion. Revised 1995.

A setup can be prepared using either actual or estimated expense figures. It is critical that a prospective buyer know what kind of information is being shown by the seller because: (1) historical and estimated cash flow may have a direct bearing on one's financial analysis, and (2) lenders use operating cash flow to determine the value of property offered as security for a loan. Lenders examine every expense item very critically.

The portion of the gross rental that goes to each of the expense items varies significantly according to type of property, age of property, its location, and whatever agreements might exist between the lessor and lessee concerning the apportionment of expenses. These factors are subject to careful research besides simple estimation. The allowances for replacement and repair deserve careful consideration; these are especially critical in older properties that may be subject to deterioration or stylistic obsolescence. In certain types of properties such as office buildings, reserves should be taken for tenant improvements and rental expenses at such times as leases expire.

ELEMENTS OF THE SETUP

This section looks at each of the elements of the setup, and it discusses the changes in emphasis within the elements themselves caused by dealing with different kinds of property (i.e., apartments, office buildings, industrial space, retail space, and, in some categories, raw land and mobile home parks).[1]

Gross Revenues

The analysis of an income property should start with *base rentals*. As a first step in the analysis of rentals, the investor should attempt to determine *comparables*. Comparables are rents or revenues generated by properties with similar features (e.g., size, age, quality of construction) and in similar locations. The gathering of baseline data on comparables is generally the first step in the collection of local knowledge required before investing. For apartments, mobile home parks, and some smaller commercial rentals, the daily or Sunday newspaper offers a first source of comparable data. The rental prices generally are quoted in a $-per-month rate and are apt to be at or above market. The primary function of such advertising is to generate demand; some discount may, however, be expected. Once a specific area is selected, the investor should check more localized sources to make certain of the range and distribution of the potential competition for the contemplated investment. The investor should consult the local realtor's listing book and regional weekly newspapers and should make a tour of the area, noting vacancies and other existing buildings.

[1]Fundamental data about the elements can be found in the Building Owners and Managers Association's *Experience Exchange Report*, the Institute of Real Estate Management Experience Committee's *Statistical Compilation and Analysis of Actual Income and Expenses Experienced in Apartment Building Operation*, and *The Dollars and Cents of Shopping Centers*, compiled by the Urban Land Institute.

Rental rates for office, commercial, and industrial space are generally quoted in dollars per square foot. The amount of the space may be the usable space or more commonly the rentable space which includes a pro rata allowance for certain common areas. Because of the difference in the way common area is allocated, comparability is difficult. The primary sources of information about current market conditions come from specialized journals and surveys by brokers and consultants. In addition, most of the major real estate brokers print listings of available office, industrial, and retail space. Industrial space may also be listed with the state government bureau responsible for commercial development. It is important to remember that the rents and terms noted in these listings are often only suggestive ones. Almost all of the terms will be negotiable, depending upon factors such as the market strength, the financial creditworthiness of the prospective tenant, the length of the lease and the tenant's requirements for improvements.

Two fundamental skills are required to develop significant comparables: (1) the ability to ferret out the greatest amount of useful data, and (2) the ability to put these data together into a meaningful picture of the whole. In dealing with all kinds of properties, the investor must understand the characteristics that make properties comparable: internal features such as layout, ease of maintenance, adequacy of utilities, decor and amenities are all critical items of comparability. Exterior considerations are also important. Properties that have very similar inside features but that have different: locations, access to transportation, parking and views, can command very different rentals. These differences can be determined by actually shopping the market.

The prospective investor or developer must determine what the competition is, what it is likely to be, and how effectively a particular property can compete. Once this task is accomplished, a realistic standard can be set for the income to be obtained from the property.

After baseline data are developed for gross revenue potential, the next step is to project the observable trends, such as government policy and inflation. Is rent control a reality or a possibility? Are there public incentives for particular groups of people, locations, or types of property? The impact of trends varies widely according to the type of property involved. In residential and smaller commercial properties, trends are very important. Generally the leases, if any, are of short duration. This provides an opportunity to adjust rents if price levels are rising or, conversely, to decrease rents if the neighborhood is declining.

For commercial and industrial properties under long-term leases, the impact of trend analysis is less important over the short term. The gross revenue figures will be those provided in the lease during the term of the lease. The investor should, however, carefully consider the impact of the observable trends on the willingness of present tenants to renew or, with commercial properties, the impact of the changes in the local market on average rents.

Beyond trend analysis, some of the key profit opportunities occur through the projection of discontinuities in the observable trends. Similarly, major losses may arise through failure to observe unfavorable discontinuities before they occur and to adjust the investment strategy accordingly. Some discontinuities that are of greatest importance are urban renewal activities, new-highway location, entry of national firms into the market, entry or exit of a major industry, and the changing socio-economic characteristics of a neighborhood.

The critical element in projecting discontinuities is timing. When predicting a favorable change, decisions taken too early tend to be risky. Decisions taken too late, although involving the investor in little risk, usually result in missed opportunities for profit. In predicting unfavorable changes, it is often better to be too early. The opportunities to bail out of a property get worse as the likelihood of the unfavorable event increases. "Holding out for the best price" may be simply an exercise in following the market down.

Analysis of trends and potential discontinuities is possible insofar as the general economic and political data are adequate. Such data are available through local newspapers and also through national journals such as *National Real Estate Investor* and *Real Estate Appraiser and Analyst*. These two publications provide facts useful in making specific projections relative to the properties that an investor holds or contemplates buying.

For commercial properties, the base rental in the lease is only part of the story. There may be built-in *rent escalators*. These may be fixed (such as defined step-ups in rent) or conditional (such as increases tied to changes in the cost of living). In retail leases, percentage-rent clauses tie the rent level to tenants' sales performance. The longer the lease term, the more likely there will be adjustments.

Expense reimbursements have also become common, especially in leases for nonresidential property (for such items as real estate taxes, heat, electricity, water, insurance, normal maintenance including cleaning and management). Typically, the tenant will agree to reimburse the landlord either for all such expenses or for changes from a predefined base which may be established as a specific dollar amount per square foot or as the actual expenses during the first or base year. Leases with these kinds of provisions are usually described as having an "expense stop," and lenders often insist on this provision to protect their mortgage. In a multitenant building, each tenant's share of these common charges is often expressed as a percentage based on total space rentable. In acquiring a property it is crucial to analyze the terms of each individual lease and to have a reporting system that takes such complexities into account.

Other income is an item that should be examined carefully in contemplating any form of real property investment. Sources such as laundry rental, furniture rental, parking charges, utility fees, and recreational club dues are often very important profit contributors in housing investments. The investor is cautioned to examine carefully the assumptions underlying such income projections. Similarly, agreements and leases should be examined, and the investor should be aware of local practice regarding the inclusion of certain items when making a forecast. For example, if amenities such as air conditioning are not included in the base rent where such inclusion is common practice in the locality, the occupancy of the property may suffer. Other income may, in fact, be an opportunity for the investor: to charge separately for the rental of major appliances or covered parking. It can yield a very high return on the marginal investment.

Commercial and industrial buildings also offer some opportunities for other income. Among the possibilities are special janitorial service, parking, and communication equipment on the roof. Again, the two factors to consider are the leases or agreements underlying such charges and the local practice. In commercial, industrial, and residential properties, the "other income" category, once established, should be reasonably stable—subject primarily to changes in vacancy. It is important, however, to be aware of the profit opportunities and, in initial analysis, to be certain that those opportunities that are projected, really exist. On the positive side, it is often wise to look for some of the unrealized potential that may come from the other income category when contemplating a future purchase or development.

Vacancies

The second item in the setup that the investor needs to analyze is vacancies. The prospective purchaser is often presented with a setup that makes no allowance for vacancies or collection problems. This is especially common with commercial properties. Nevertheless, some reasonable vacancy allowance is almost always necessary for all properties; the art lies in determining what is reasonable. The reader is reminded, however, that even for a property 100% rented to one tenant, a four-month vacancy period between tenants at the end of the lease term equals 33% or 3.3% per year for 10 years. With a special-purpose or an office building even this 3.3% vacancy may not be adequate. Failure to incorporate such an allowance into the overall scheme may materially distort the potential future return. In buildings with longer lease terms, special allowances may be taken to correspond with the expiration of the leases and the likelihood of renewal. Rent escalators, expense reimbursements, and other income that will not continue if the space is vacant should not be forgotten.

Bad debts and concessions are sometimes included in the vacancy allowance. The investor or developer is also cautioned to be wary of the difference between "allowance" and "actual". In many setups shown to the prospective purchaser, vacancies are shown as an allowance. Such allowance may or may not be related to the actual experience of the building under consideration. The investor should be certain about what is being shown as a basis for further investigation.

Comparable data for vacancies are often difficult to assess. Gross area vacancy statistics are readily available for the Standard Metropolitan Statistical Areas (SMSAs). HUD compiles statistics which are often reported in the *Real Estate Analyst*. Rental boards and surveys by brokers may also be helpful. In analyzing vacancies on apartment houses, the Census Bureau provides decennial counts. These are not particularly useful, however, in making an investment decision. For housing units, it is often necessary for the prospective investor or developer to cruise the neighborhood looking for empty nameplates on mailboxes and counting "For Sale" signs. Such counts are not statistically reliable, but they may simulate the purchasing behavior of the target consumer.

Commercial, office, and industrial vacancies are harder to pin down. The specialized regional journals cited previously and the *National Real Estate Investor* provide frequent reviews that give a view of the changing market scene. The *Real Estate Analyst* and the *Urban Land Institute* provide historical data for most markets, updated at least annually. Major local realty firms often conduct useful market studies and issue quarterly vacancy reports.

The developer or investor contemplating a project must always be aware of the trends in vacancy rates and prospective new developments, which might adversely affect the properties being studied. Although such trends are never totally reliable, some basis for judgment can be gained from building-permit data, from trade and local business publications, and from direct systematic observation of the local surrounding neighborhood. In examining the possible trends in vacancies, attention should be paid to consumer tastes in habitation, and the expansion or contraction of consumer spending patterns. National economic trends such as growth in service industries or cutbacks in defense spending are also important.

The prospective purchaser of an existing property should always examine leases and even interview tenants whenever possible to determine that the projected income is, in fact, in line with that required by the lease. The prospective purchaser should also be wary of concessions given to the tenants that might inflate the occupancy statistics or rental payments. Purchasers should also be concerned with leases in which property managers provide special services to the tenant for a higher rent. The type, size, and location of the property often indicate the likelihood of such side deals. For the new development, the prospective developer or investor should be concerned with the normal leasing terms in the area and with current practices regarding concessions and management absorption of costs.

Operating Expenses

The control of operating expenses is obviously one of the key elements in any real estate investment's profitability. This is also an area in which the buyer is subject to the highest degree of deception and an area in which good, current information is difficult to find. Reliable projections of the future are almost impossible. The best sources of data on operating expenses for all kinds of properties are the "experience exchange" type of publications such as those mentioned earlier. Using data obtained from these sources, the prospective developer or investor can begin to question intelligently the projections being made and search out sources of difference. Remember that averages for an area do not imply that most properties are at the average.

One of the key mistakes made in the analysis of operating expenses is that of leaving out a category of expense, such as the cost of exterior window washing. This section will review each category of expense and give indications of some of the factors to be considered. Consideration should be given to the underlying variables to which the expenses are related. Expenses vary in relation to: (1) the gross rent, (2) the square feet or cubic feet involved, (3) the number of units, (4) the services provided, and (5) the age, condition, and cost of the property. In preparing forecasts for future profitability it is critical to understand the different natures of the expenses.

The primary categories of expenses to be considered are the following.

- real estate taxes
- administrative
- maintenance, supplies, and trash removal
- repairs
- replacement
- utilities
- insurance

Within each of the above categories there are obviously subcategories. For further information one can consult sources such as the *Building Operators and Management Association* or *National Association of Apartment House Owners* publications, which set up accounting systems for property owners.

Real estate taxes   Real estate taxes are perhaps the single greatest source of uncertainty in property investment. History shows that they are almost always increased. In recent times, voters in California, Massachusetts, and elsewhere have passed referendum limiting the increases that can be imposed without voter approval. There is danger of a major increase if property is sold because a new market price is established against which the assessor can make a valuation. In many income properties an agreement with city officials can be reached in which taxes are assessed as a percentage of gross rent. These arrangements are not always legally enforceable.

Before any investment is made, the investor should examine the tax records for the property in question and make an analysis of comparable properties. Tax records are public documents. Histories of the assessments for the town or city in question are available. Changes that may occur in a city or town in the future can have major impact on tax rates and should offer warning signs. Among these are: (1) large population expansion, (2) new-school needs, (3) major public facilities projects, and (4) expansion of municipal services. On the positive side, one would expect stable tax rates if there is: a healthy mixture in the industrial base, a community with limited space for additional population, and/or growing voter resistance to tax increases.

Always the prospective purchaser or developer should consider the strength of the tax escalation clause in the leases being used and the willingness of any rent control agency to allow such clauses to be effective. Real estate taxes are a major variable in the profitability of any real property investment. All three forms of analysis—baseline, trends, and discontinuity potential—must be employed. The investor should also be aware that it is possible to successfully contest the amount of the real estate tax and therefore should understand the basis on which the local government calculates the property tax.

Administrative expenses   Rental, advertising, and management expenses are often interconnected. A residential property owner may choose to sign a rental brokerage agreement and a management agreement with a local firm that specializes in handling the particular kind of property. These property management companies will usually manage the property for a percentage of the collected rentals. Although the fee may be standard for the region or local market, it is often negotiable. If the property is sufficiently large, most investors would do well to consider having both management and rentals taken care of by direct employees of the property. The two primary trade-offs are cost and degree of owner involvement. Unfortunately, common practice in the sale of many properties excludes from the setup both management expense and rental expense. Such an omission materially distorts the return since, for small properties, these may be significant when related to the gross rentals. Even if the intention is for the owner to perform the services, some cost or value should be imputed to the owner's time. If sold, the potential buyer will make an allowance that will reduce the amount offered. Lenders will always input an allowance for management in considering the building's value.

For commercial and industrial properties, the same caveats apply. It is, however, more critical to examine exactly how the rental function is to be performed, by whom, and at what price. The more specialized the building, the more critical a good marketing-rental program is to the economic success of the development or investment. Where overage rents or percentage leases are involved, there is a further need for management.

Professional fees cannot be ignored. Legal help may be needed in many circumstances including: leasing, refinancing, collections, partnership matters, and regulatory issues. The project entity will have to file a tax return normally prepared by an outside auditor. Since real estate ownership has special tax implications, good advice is important. There are other consultants who may be called upon for design, engineering or public relations help. The more complicated the entity and project, the higher the allowance should be. As our society has become more litigious and income tax laws have become increasingly complex, the need for outside help continues to grow.

Maintenance, supplies, and trash removal   The total expenses in this category can vary greatly from year to year and from building to building. Several factors are, however, predictable. The age of a building is one of the prime determinants of the maintenance required. Even if a building's history is known, simple projection of that history into the future will understate maintenance substantially. The design of a building (including the materials used, the number and sizes of public spaces, and the quality of the original equipment installed) is another critical factor. Whether windows are accessible or must be reached from scaffolding makes a difference. The type of heating and air conditioning equipment and flooring are key determinants. Finally, the previous maintenance history is important since undermaintained assets may require exceptional future outlays.

Contracts for maintenance of major building elements, such as boilers, elevators, air conditioning units, or cleaning, are often available and provide for a program of systematic upkeep. Prices on such contracts often indicate the level of service required, although they are generally profitable for companies offering them and may not cover everything.

The amount of supplies needed are related to the services provided, such as office, rest room, or common area cleaning. The replacement of light bulbs can be a significant item. With increased environmental awareness resulting in the closing of many disposal sites, trash removal prices have risen considerably in recent years.

Repairs Repairs differ from maintenance predominantly in scope. In this category for residential units are such items as painting of apartments; replacement of broken doors and windows; repair of stoves, refrigerators, dishwashers, and disposals; and fixing leaky faucets. Obviously, the age of the building and equipment is going to be a major factor in the amount of money that must be allocated to this area. It should be possible to obtain comparables as outlined earlier, but considerable annual variations are likely. One should take into consideration the expected level of maintenance by the particular tenants occupying the space.

These items may seem minor to the investor, but are of major importance to the tenants. The ability of responsible management people to learn of and respond to these problems may be a major factor influencing the vacancy rate.

Replacement reserves and tenant improvements Replacement reserves are part of the setup closely related to the maintenance element but are rarely considered as expenses that are reimbursed by tenants under the operating cost escalator. Not all depreciation is simply a tax-oriented fiction. In any property, there are items that are subject to physical deterioration and, therefore, require periodic replacement. Carpets, roofs, paint, and mechanical equipment will not last the economic life of the building. It is critical, therefore, in calculating the cash flow to be derived from an investment, to consider the impact of such required replacement. This is especially true in the purchase of used residential property. Often such property has been purchased on the assumption of operation for five to seven years with sale contemplated as soon as the rental income has been increased. With such an investment strategy, items of major maintenance or replacement are often deferred. Unless such investment is made quickly, the new owner may be required to spend a substantial amount on repairs and maintenance or watch the attractiveness of the property decline. Unfortunately, too often, the newer the equipment, the shorter its life cycle.

Replacement reserves are not generally tax deductible. Some items, such as mechanical items or painting, may appear as expenses, but the investor should recognize that capital expenses generally have to be capitalized and then depreciated, as mandated by the tax code.

The replacement reserve for commercial and industrial properties are of two types. First, money needs to be set aside for major exterior items like the roof and parking lot and major common area expenses like refurbishing the lobby and replacing the elevators. Second, at the time of lease turnover, substantial money may be required to renovate the space and/or pay a brokerage commission. There is no way to predict future needs or market conditions. An allowance is generally taken, based on average length of tenant leases, expected rate of tenant turnover, and the amount of work to be done. Such costs point up the desirability of retaining existing tenants when leases expire.

Definitions of how the space is measured and allocated should be clarified. For example, leases written based on a "gross rentable" basis usually consider the entire gross square footage of a building and prorate it to each tenant. "Net usable" leases measure the actual space allocated to a tenant with no allowance for a proportional share of the hallways and other common areas. "Net rentable" includes some but not all of the common area.

Utilities and insurance Both of these items are generally verifiable when purchasing existing properties and are easily estimated by competent professionals for future developments. The key considerations for investors are whether the utilities are adequate and how steep the increases are likely to be in the future. Considerable expense may be incurred if the present utilities, such as electrical service, is inadequate. It is important to know the expected hours of use and the type of equipment that will be running as each tenant's needs may be different. Electricity costs are normally metered to each tenant directly but costs of common areas and central air conditioning may be apportioned. Major risk is assumed if insurance coverage is inadequate. A high purchase price may trigger the need for additional insurance. Both insurance coverage and utility services should be reviewed carefully before purchase or additional construction. Moreover, operating cost escalators in the leases should also be investigated.

Other expenses Items such as fire protection, security expenses, and "other expenses" items must be specifically related to the property under consideration. All elements of this category are somewhat extraordinary. The requirements in these areas are becoming stiffer; consequently, they are not subject to the same rules of thumb and should be treated as individual elements for analysis when seeking good baseline and trend data. They must be examined carefully for future discontinuities.

Indirect Expenses

There are also those items which under the lease are the responsibility of the tenant such as collection or environmental cleanup costs. The careful drafting of these clauses is most important to ensure that the tenant's responsibilities are carefully spelled out. If not, the landlord may have direct responsibility. The financial capabilities of the tenant are especially important in the environmental area since the exposure can be large and long term. Without receiving a bill of environmental good health, properties will be difficult to sell or refinance.

Tax Effects

Once the setup and the before-tax cash flow have been established, the second step is to propose a set of measures to find the effect of income taxes. Of prime importance to the real estate investor is the cash flow after taxes (CFAT). (See *Note on Taxation* HBS No. 379-192 for a detailed discussion of tax issues and trends.) This is in contrast to net income, which is the benchmark for stock market investors. CFAT is determined by first calculating the net taxable income and then multiplying by the appropriate tax rate. The tax is then subtracted from the cash flow after financing. Two approaches to calculate the cash flow after tax are shown in **Table B**.

Table B   Determining Cash Flow after Taxes: Two Approaches

I. Cash flow from operations	or	II. Cash flow after financing
+ Replacement reserve		+ Replacement reserve
− Mortgage interest		+ Mortgage amortization
− Depreciation		− Depreciation
= Net taxable income		= Net taxable income
× Tax rate		× Tax rate
= Tax		= Tax
Cash flow from operations		Cash flow after financing
− Mortgage interest		− Tax
− Mortgage amortization		= Cash flow after taxes
= Cash flow after financing		
− Tax		
= Cash flow after taxes		

Mortgage interest   The buyer is cautioned to examine tax effects over time as well as during the initial period. In general, the net taxable income from a real property investment will increase over time even if the operating cash flow remains stable. This is because many real property loans require a constant annual or monthly payment, but the components of that payment change.

The most common mortgage payment schedule is a level payment or direct reduction mortgage that most people obtain when they buy a house. The great advantage of this type of mortgage is that the payment that the borrower makes each month remains exactly the same for the entire term of the loan. Under a variable rate mortgage it usually is adjusted annually. With a level payment or direct reduction mortgage, the starting principal of the loan (pv) is the present value of an "ordinary annuity," or series of level loan payments. The borrower (or mortgagor) gives to the lender (or mortgagee) a prior claim upon the value of the property as security for the borrowed funds. Equal periodic installments "amortize" the loan, providing the lender with a desired return (i) on outstanding invested funds (pv). Each payment consists of interest on the outstanding principal and amortization or return of principal. As principal is repaid, therefore, the interest component will decline. The remaining principal on a mortgage at any time is simply the present value of remaining payments, discounted at the face interest rate of the note. The level or constant payment varies, depending upon whether payments are made monthly, quarterly, or annually. Most mortgages are written with monthly payments. Tables are easily available and most calculators and computer spread sheet programs allow one to calculate the constant payment percentages and the breakdown of the payments between interest and principal.

Note that in the first year of a 25-year loan at a 9% interest rate, approximately 89% of the financial payment is a deductible interest charge. In the fifteenth year of the same loan only 60% is interest. Since the financial payment may represent 50% of the gross rental income, this would indicate a change in taxability of 15% of gross rental income, a significant impact that may be 30%

to 50% of the cash flow after financing. **Figure A** graphically depicts this change in the percentage of each payment that goes for principal and interest over time.

Figure A   Deductible Interest Expense as a Function of Time; Constant Annual Payment

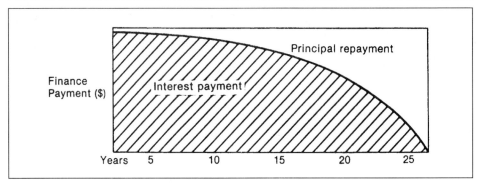

Depreciation   Under the 1993 tax law, residential property is depreciated over 27.5 years, and commercial property over 39 years. This depreciation is treated as a noncash deduction and expensed each year from the income statement. Depreciation is computed as a constant annual amount over the depreciable life (i.e., $100,000/27.5 years = $3,636 annual depreciation). When the depreciation deduction exceeds amortization, tax shelter dollars are created. During the early 1980s, most real estate property could be depreciated over a 15- to 20-year life for tax purposes. In earlier years accelerated methods of depreciation were permitted greatly increasing the deduction during early years of ownership. Because bank mortgages amortized over a longer period (usually 25 to 30 years), the tax shelters in the initial years of property ownership could be substantial. With the new tax laws this is no longer the case. (For a more complete discussion of depreciation, see the "Note on Taxation," HBS No. 379-192.)

Net taxable income   Calculation of the tax effect for a real estate investment involves simply a multiplication of the stream of taxable income by the appropriate tax rates of the investor concerned. Starting in 1993, the maximum marginal tax rate is assumed to be 39.6% for ordinary income. On this basis, every dollar of losses will reduce taxes paid by 39.6%. The capital gains tax rate remains at 28%, as set in 1987. This tax savings can then be added back to increase the total return, assuming that the investor has "passive" income to match against the "passive" loss.

Other tax considerations should include: (1) the impact of state and local income taxes, (2) the investor's probability of continuing to have high income, (3) the investor's continuing capacity to use such losses, and (4) the possibility of changes in the tax laws, which might adversely affect the tax benefits. Historically, however, the IRS policy has been to allow "grandfather clauses" on existing depreciation schedules, even though the tax rates themselves may change.

The investor should always identify the source of the tax benefits. In general there are three kinds of benefits: tax postponement, tax bracket switching, and tax avoidance. A typical real property transaction includes elements of all three. The use of depreciation tends to postpone the payment of taxes. Tax-free exchanges of real property have the same effect. Second, many types of real estate transactions are attempts to switch tax brackets, from ordinary income to capital gains. Such transactions include (1) the expensing of heavy maintenance charges to upgrade a property in hopes of a subsequently higher sales price and (2) use of depreciation to reduce income taxable at ordinary rates with subsequent sale at capital gains rates. Refinancing a property yields tax-free cash until the property is sold since the borrower is obligated to repay the principal of the loan with non-deductible dollars. This is a form of tax postponement or deferral. Tax avoidance occurs through holding of property until death, at which time the entire estate is taxed. One avoids the capital gains tax that would be imposed if the property were sold prior to death.

Cash flow after taxes   The calculation of CFAT is completed by deducting the taxes paid or adding the tax benefit received to the before-tax cash flow. This is equivalent to applying the tax effect to the operating cash flow reduced by financial payments. For many investors, CFAT is the appropriate *annual* cash flow for the evaluation of an equity investment. For analysis purposes, remember that CFAT is composed of two of the three components of a potential return on a real estate investment: cash flow before taxes and the tax effect. The third component, futures, must be estimated to calculate an overall return. This procedure is discussed later in this note.

IMPACT OF FINANCIAL STRUCTURING

With an understanding of the elements that make up a cash flow and the effects of these elements on taxes, the investor is able to begin an analysis of the impact of leverage on real property investments.

Leverage Concept

A fundamental characteristic of financial leverage (and often not recognized) is that there are two kinds: positive and negative. Positive leverage increases the return on the equity invested; negative leverage decreases the return on such investment. Positive leverage occurs when the cost of the debt payment, expressed as a percentage, is lower than the annual return on total assets. For negative leverage the reverse is true. The cost of debt is the total of interest and principal payments as a percentage of the initial principal balance. Negative leverage is not necessarily bad since it may reflect a more rapid pay-off of a mortgage. The percent return on total assets (ROA) is calculated by dividing the operating or free-and-clear cash flow by the total cost of the asset. Comparing the cost of debt with the return on assets is a good first-step calculation in determining the most appropriate financial structure for a property.

The size of the mortgage, the time period over which it will be paid off, and the interest rate, all affect the cost of debt and subsequently the return on equity. These items, to the extent allowed by the marketplace, can be controlled by the investors and adjusted to their needs. **Tables C, D, and E** indicate the effects of each on the cost of debt and the impact on the returns.

Table C   Relationship of Free-and-Clear Cash Flow to Cost of Asset Assuming no Debt

Total cost of asset:		$1,250,000
Setup:	Gross revenues	$270,000
	Vacancies	27,000
	Net revenues	$243,000
	Operating expenses	118,000
	Free-and-clear cash flow	$125,000
	Return on cost of asset	10%

As the table above shows, the return on the cost of the asset in the absence of debt is 10%.

Table D demonstrates the benefits of arranging a mortgage that is a large percentage of the total asset cost when the financial leverage is positive.

Table D   Effect of Mortgage Size on Pretax Return
(Variable: Mortgage size; 25 years, 7.5% interest, monthly payments)

MORTGAGE AS % OF TOTAL ASSET COST OF $1,250,000	EQUITY	DEBT SERVICE	BEFORE-TAX CASH FLOW	MORTGAGE CONSTANT	PRETAX RETURN ON EQUITY INVESTMENT
90%	$125,000	$99,787	$25,213	8.87%	20.17%
80	250,000	88,700	36,300	8.87	14.52
70	375,000	77,613	47,387	8.87	12.64
60	500,000	66,525	58,475	8.87	11.70

Since leverage is positive because the ROA is 10% and the cost of debt is only 8.7%, the more leverage the higher the return. As can be seen, an increase from 80% to 90% leverage increase the return or equity by 38.9%.

In **Table E** we see once again that leverage or using other people's money greatly impacts the return on one's equity investment. Obviously, there are benefits in having a long-term mortgage. In this case, a 15-year mortgage illustrates negative leverage. The same analysis as used in **Table D** indicates what happens:

Table E   Effect of Negative Leverage on Annual Returns

MORTGAGE AS % OF TOTAL ASSET COST OF $1,250,000	EQUITY	DEBT SERVICE	BEFORE-TAX CASH FLOW	MORTGAGE CONSTANT	PRETAX RETURN ON EQUITY INVESTMENT
90%	$125,000	$125,213	$(213)	11.13%	(0.2%)
80	250,000	111,300	13,700	11.13	5.48
70	375,000	97,388	27,612	11.13	7.36

As one would expect, in a negative leverage situation where the property generates a 10% return on assets and the cost of debt is 11.13%, the lower the leverage the higher the annual return on equity. It is important to realize, however, that in this situation, the debt is amortizing quickly and the overall return on the equity investment, including the sale and repayment of the mortgage might be higher with more leverage, even though the annual cash return will be lower.

Financial leverage offers benefits to the investor who is seeking to maximize return on investment as long as the property's income and appreciation results in positive leverage. The heavy use of leverage is normal in real estate. For the investor, leverage allows control of a greater asset base than would be possible simply through the use of equity. Through the use of nonrecourse clauses in the mortgage, the risk to the equity holder can be limited to the equity invested in the particular property with the creditor having no claim to other assets that the investor owns. A deed of trust can be structured with the same effect. Since the repayment of the debt is a fixed sum, the rate of return on the equity is increased disproportionately in the event of appreciation and similarly decreased or eliminated if price of the asset should fall (see **Figure B**).

Figure B   Effects of Leverage on Value of Equity

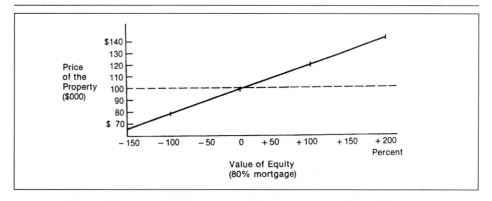

Value of Equity
(80% mortgage)

It is important to note that the above numbers are all calculated on a pre-tax basis. Since interest is a deductible expense, its effect is mitigated by the tax rate of the borrower, another factor which encourages the use of leverage and the use of long repayment terms.

Among the problems that need to be considered in choosing how much leverage is appropriate are some operational and tax considerations. The use of heavy leverage increases the risk to the equity owner which may force him or her to sell at an inopportune time. The heavy cash drain upon operations that results from the use of a relatively large amount of first-mortgage debt can force a property into a negative cash flow position precisely when sale prices for such properties are low.

The extensive use of second mortgages or mortgages with large balloon payments can frequently produce similar results. Many buyers of syndications have discovered that the financing that includes second-mortgage debt to the seller absorbs all of the cash flow. Secondary financing increases leverage, but often comes at high interest rates and short maturities, which make for a high total annual payment.

Should problems of cash flow arise, the investor may face another problem created by his or her tax position. As shown in **Figure C** below, there may be substantial period of time during which the book value of a property for tax purposes is less than the unamortized mortgage amount. This is particularly true in situations where a property has been refinanced to a level higher than the depreciated book value. In the event of foreclosure, the sale price would be deemed to be the unamortized amount of the mortgage; a capital gain would be reported even though the investor has lost his or her equity. Thus, the investor could face a tax liability without cash proceeds from the property to meet such liability.

Figure C   Book Value of Property vs. Mortgage Balance

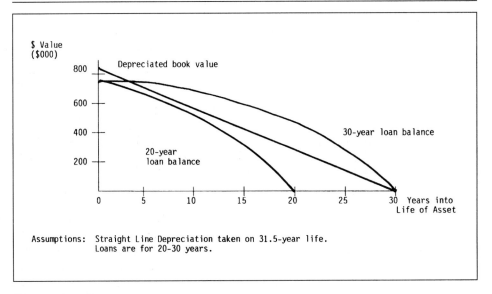

Assumptions: Straight Line Depreciation taken on 31.5-year life.
Loans are for 20-30 years.

Operating Leverage

In **Figure C** above, the analysis of leverage is based on the economic factors existing at one point in time. But with an ever-changing environment, the key factor in investment success is to anticipate correctly changes over time. Fundamental analysis of changes in a real property investment can be divided into three basic steps: (1) development of comparable data, (2) projection of trends, and (3) prediction of discontinuity. Each of these steps is critical to the informed investment decision.

Once the property has been developed and financed, operations become the area most affected by changing economic forces. The investor must be aware that there is such a thing as operating leverage which occurs when the income from operations changes while the financing payments remain fixed and that such changes can drastically affect: the yearly return, the ability to refinance at an appropriate time, and the future value of the investment.

Real estate investments are often made utilizing the maximum amount of financial leverage. Experienced investors, however, are often more concerned in a mortgaged property about the operating leverage available to them. Real property assets are unique in allowing the investor to obtain a high degree of financial leverage while benefiting from major operating leverage as well. Operating leverage arises because a major component of expense (normally the financing payment) in a real property investment is fixed, regardless of the revenue. A small change in revenue which might simply reflect inflation produces a large effect upon the rate of return to the equity investor. The example outlined in **Table F** for a garden apartment shows the impact of favorable operating leverage.

Table F   Example of Favorable Operating Leverage ($ in thousands)
(Cost of building: $1,100,000; mortgage $900,000; 25 years at 9% interest; constant payment 10.08%)

	YEAR 1	YEAR 2	YEAR 3	YEAR 4	YEAR 5	YEAR 6
Revenues	$200.0	$206.0	$212.2	$218.5	$225.1	$231.9
Operating expenses	90.0	94.5	99.2	104.2	109.4	114.9
Financial payment	90.7	90.7	90.7	90.7	90.7	90.7
Before-tax cash flow	19.3	20.8	22.3	23.6	25.0	26.3
Return on investment	9.65%	10.4%	11.15%	11.8%	12.5%	13.15%

The table above was prepared on the assumption that operating revenues inflated by 3% annually and that expenses inflated by 5%. Even in this example, where the operating expenses increase at a higher rate than revenues, the return on equity still rises each year. Operating leverage can be negative as well. Since a major portion of costs associated with owning a property is fixed, only a slight decrease in revenues can have a drastic impact on the return to the equity holder.

This negative outcome from operating leverage can be seen by using the example from the section on financial leverage and changing the amount of vacancy (**Tables G and H**):

Table G   Basic Setup

Cost of asset	$1,250,000	
Gross revenues	270,000	
Vacancies (10%)	(27,000)	
Net revenue		$243,000
Expenses		
Building operations	$69,400	
Property taxes	48,600	118,000
Free-and-clear cash flow		$125,000
Debt service (7.5% interest, 25 years on $1 million)		88,700
Net cash flow		$36,300

If we hold all other costs (except vacancies) constant, we observe the operating leverage shown in **Table H**. A change of 5% in occupancy levels makes a corresponding change in the return on equity, sometimes to levels that may not be tolerable to the investor. Also note that at 85% occupancy, the cost of debt is more than the return on asset, thus putting the investment into a negative leverage position. It is important in financial analysis to separate the impact of the additional return that arises from financial leverage from the impact of projected operating leverage. Such separation helps in making critical assumptions clear and open for specific attention.

Table H   Operating Leverage with Varying Occupancy Levels

OCCUPANCY	FREE-AND-CLEAR CASH	% RETURN ON ASSET	NET CASH FLOW	RETURN ON EQUITY INVESTMENT
100%	$152,000	12.16%	$63,300	25.32%
95	138,500	11.08	49,800	19.92
90	125,000	10.00	36,300	14.52
85	111,500	8.92	22,800	9.12
80	98,000	7.84	9,300	3.72

A major lesson that can be learned from this section on leverage is the importance of projections. One usually projects the future on the basis of the recent past. Yet in a cyclical industry like real estate, change is the norm, and when it occurs, highly leveraged properties can run into trouble. Over time, rents tend to rise but the ability to ride through down cycles can be crucial.

If the U.S. economy continues to be inflationary, the possibilities to increase returns through financial and operating leverage seem great. To this point, we have assumed that the original financing of an investment is fixed. In fact one of the great opportunities that is available in real estate is to refinance a mortgage when interest rates drop, unless the lender's agreement prohibits repayment or imposes a penalty that may equal the interest rate savings. This penalty is more common in commercial than residential mortgages.

MEASUREMENT OF RETURN

Valuation

The primary method of valuing income-producing properties is known as the *capitalization of income* or *capitalization rate* technique. For appraisal purposes, this technique is supplemented by an analysis of comparable sales and by an analysis of replacement cost. Even in the area of raw land, appraisals often rely on the value of the prospective income stream to be generated in the future through development.

Capitalization techniques are based upon the following formula:

$$\frac{\text{Annual cash stream}}{\text{Capitalization rate}} = \text{Value}$$

Determining the appropriate cash stream and the appropriate capitalization rate is never easy or precise. The uniqueness of each property and lack of clear, consistent information makes this calculation an art as much as a science. Still, it does give a rough approximation of how investors currently are valuing properties.

The two primary cash flows considered to be relevant are the *free-and-clear cash flow* and the *cash flow after financing.* (Cash flow after taxes will be discussed later in this note.) The former is used in determining the value of a property for lending purposes. The latter is most often used in considering the equity value of the property. In most instances, the cash flow is determined by the setup and is a static measure of the value at the particular moment in time with no adjustment for inflation, physical depreciation, operating leverage, tax benefits, or mortgage amortization.

For the purposes of a lender, the free-and-clear cash flow is the most relevant number since it represents the total funds that would be available to service the debt on the property in the event of foreclosure. The normal practice is to apply a capitalization rate somewhat in excess of the lending rate and then to loan a percentage of the value derived. The following example illustrates the principle:

Cash Flow	=	$1,000,000
Capitalization rate	=	11%
Loan to value ratio	=	.75

$$\frac{\$1,000,000}{.11} = 9,090,909 \text{ value} \times .75 = \$6,818,181$$

Note the sensitivity of the loan amount to the capitalization rate. For example, in the preceding example a change in the capitalization rate from 11% to 10% would yield an increase in valuation from $9.09 million to $10 million. Much has been written on capitalization rates. In general, however, these rates are chosen as measures of perceived risk at a point in time for the particular type of property, its rental and operating projections, its physical condition, current and projected interest rates and investors' expectations of returns in the light of alternative investment opportunities.

Lenders normally expect cash flow from operations to cover debt service by 110% to 130% or even more depending upon risk. Lenders also restrict loans to a specific percentage of value, often 75%.

Determining the value of the equity follows the same general approach. The cash flow after financing is capitalized at some rate to reflect equity value.

Future Values

Future benefits arising from sale or refinancing are the final component of return available to the real estate investor. Because of assumed appreciation, almost all real property transactions anticipate benefits from holding a property. The value calculated depends upon estimates of many future conditions. These include, but are not limited to: (1) the physical condition of the asset, (2) existing lease structure, (3) economic and interest rate environment, (4) change in the physical neighborhood, (5) consumer and investor preference for the kind of property involved, (6) expected inflation rates, (7) rate of return on alternative investments, (8) tax position of the seller, and (9) contemplated holding period.

The longer the time horizon, the more difficult it is to calculate future benefits. Probabilities increase for major changes, which may be either for the better or for the worse. In a financial analysis it becomes necessary to make judgments about such changes. These can be categorized as follows: operating, physical, financial, market

Operating changes can be brought about in two ways. First, in the analysis of the setup, projections can be made by assuming changes in operating income over time while financial payments stay constant. Second, change can come from operating policy decisions, such as: more efficient operation, limited maintenance; or upgrading to serve a different clientele. All of these changes should be reflected in the projected setup that the buyer and seller use to determine value.

Physical changes are of two primary sorts: those affecting the property itself and those affecting its environment. In both instances, however, the primary impact is made upon the expected revenues to be realized. If the property is physically upgraded, it should be in anticipation of higher revenues. If the property is allowed to run down, lower future revenues would naturally be expected. If that occurs, it can affect the value of surrounding properties, spiraling the downturn for all. Physical change of both the property and of surrounding properties have an impact on "highest and best use" of the property. Such change is the greatest source of discontinuity in real property analysis.

The prospective developer or investor should be aware of opportunities to use the purchase as a holding action anticipating future uses. Often duplexes or small commercial buildings are purchased in anticipation of the opportunity to develop them later either for higher-density dwellings or for more intense commercial uses. The purchase of a mobile home park is often a high-yield way of holding land for future high-density commercial or residential development. In these situations, however, it is probably wise to make alternative analyses showing the impact on return of both the change and no-change options. What is permissible zoning now may change with the political environment.

Financial changes affecting future value are projections relating to the future financial market conditions and the simple calculation of the changed financial structure of the deal as loans are repaid or refinanced. A projected financial change that assumes more favorable financial market conditions at the time of sale than are currently prevalent is generally a trap set for the unwary. If the major source of return comes from refinancing a property with a long-term mortgage at below present market rates, the investor might have a long wait.

Market changes derive from the assumption that at the time of sale someone will be willing to pay more using a lower cap rate for the same cash flow and associated benefits of ownership than the present owner is. Unless there is a compelling reason like an upgrading of the tenants in the building, it is risky to base one's investment on this kind of assumption. On the other hand, cap rates investors pay do change based on factors such as: the effect of physical or functional obsolescence, changes in tenant mix or use, changes in government tax policy, and/or the owner simply doing a better selling job. Probably though, the major factor that affects cap rates is investors' general perception of the real estate market at the time of sale. There is a herd instinct to valuation in real estate as well as in other forms of investments.

In conclusion, the reader should be aware throughout that a successful analysis of a real property investment must consider many critical characteristics of the investment. Among these are (a) the extremely long time horizon of most investments, (b) poor liquidity, and (c) uncertainty concerning the valuation of the property. Valuation of property is subject to vagaries caused by competition, changes in financial market conditions, physical depreciation, government action, and changes in the microenvironment. Any of these may seriously revalue the property. In addition, historical information on a particular property may be unavailable or, if available, either irrelevant or intentionally misleading.

Despite the uncertainties, future benefits should be estimated when evaluating a real estate investment. Sources of future benefits are mortgage amortization, return of initial equity, and sales price appreciation. As always, benefits should be evaluated net of taxes.

Table I below illustrates the benefits available to the investor who can refinance opportunely.

Table I   Setup Showing Benefits from Refinancing
(Cost of asset: $1,250,000; mortgage: $1,000,000)

	PRESENT	RATE OF INFLATION PER YEAR	YEAR 10
Gross revenues	$270,000	4.14%	$405,000
Vacancies	27,000		40,500
Net revenues	$243,000		$364,500
Operating expenses	118,000	4.14%	177,000
Free-and-clear cash	$125,000		$187,500
Debt service (7.5% interest, 25 years)	88,700		88,700
Cash flow after financing	$ 36,300		$ 98,800

At the end of 10 years, if the free-and-clear cash flow of $187,500 were capitalized at 9%, the property might be worth $2,085,000. An 80% mortgage on this value is $1,668,000.

New mortgage	$1,668,000
Less: Balance of old mortgage	792,000
Cash proceeds	$ 876,000
Less: Prior mortgage amortization	208,000
Original equity	250,000
Net new cash	$ 418,000

In the example shown in **Table I**, the investor will have (without immediate tax consequences) all his or her original equity returned, plus prior mortgage amortization payments, plus an additional $418,000 from refinancing. The investor will have obtained some of the potential future benefits without sale of the property, will have no cash invested, but will retain ownership. Because the new cash flow after financing will be $37,862, the investor will be receiving more income in year 11 than in year 1, and will be building equity once again. But as said before, although no income tax is due on refinancing, the tax is only deferred and becomes due after a sale or foreclosure.

To calculate the future benefits of sale, one again must face the added complication of computing the net cash to seller *after* taxes. To predict the future sales price of an income-producing property, the capitalization-of-income method previously discussed is generally used. Note that assumptions of future operating results are required and provide an area of much discretion. Alternatively, a simple growth assumption may be applied to the original purchase price though this can be very misleading. Once sales price and holding period assumptions have been made, the net cash to seller can be calculated:

Table J   Calculation of Net Cash from Sale

1. Calculation of book value
    Purchase price
    + Capital improvements
    − Accumulated depreciation
    = Book value
 	
2. Calculation of gain on sale
    Net selling price
    − Net book value
    = Gain on sale
	3. Calculation of tax
	    Gain on sale
	    × Tax rate
	    = Tax liability
	
	4. Calculation of net cash to seller
	    Net selling price
	    − Mortgage balance
	    − Income tax
	    = Net cash from sale

The net cash from sale is the appropriate cash flow in the year of sale to use when evaluating an equity investment. Note that the net cash from sale is composed of the three potential elements of future benefits, adjusted by taxes:

   Return of initial cash equity
+ Return of mortgage amortization
+ Increase in sales price
− Income taxes
= Net cash from sale

METHODS OF CALCULATING RETURN

The preceding sections have focused upon development of basic data for analyzing the profitability of a real property investment and upon elements that lead to change in such investments. This section shows how these data may be used to measure return on investment in such a property. There is extensive literature on valuation and return, but space does not permit an in-depth review of it here. This section simply reviews the various methods of valuation as they apply to real property assets. A cardinal rule of financial analysis—that the investment decision be made apart from the financing decision—does not hold for many real estate decisions especially for high income taxpayers. Although the operating cash flow may be used to determine the project value for mortgage purposes, the after-tax cash flows will determine the return on equity to the investor. Since the cash-flow-after-tax calculation requires financing assumptions, and since mortgages by definition are property specific, it is necessary to consider financing effects when comparing alternative investments in real estate.

The measurement of return on investment in real estate is a subject of great dispute and sales expertise. The careful builder or investor must be aware of the measures being used since one person's 28% return is another's 6%. The major differences occur in the elements of return that are included in the measurement and in the time horizon over which the measurement is made. The measures will be examined on the basis of the time horizon and with the inclusion of the three elements of return.

Return on asset   Basically, this measure of return may be defined as follows:

$$\frac{\text{Free-and-clear return}}{\text{Property cost}}$$

This measure of return is static in that it assumes the same cash flow throughout time. It ignores the risk or tax consequences of the investment and ignores the capital change brought about by disposing of the investment. However, it is most important for a lender who wants to insure that from the first year there is adequate income to cover mortgage payments.

Cash flow after financing return on equity or cash on cash return This measure of return may be stated thus:

$$\frac{\text{Cash flow after financing}}{\text{Equity}}$$

In this case, the equity is defined as the initial cash investment. This measure is also known as "cash on cash" return and is frequently applied by seasoned investors in the real estate field. The measure looks at return statically and omits both tax effect and capital change from sale or refinancing. The argument made by investors using this measure is "if a deal will stand up under this, everything else is a plus." It is perhaps the most rigid measure applied because it ignores all elements of return that are not reflected in the end-of-the-month checking account balance. The preceding two measures are commonly used by professionals, as a first cut or in a "back of the envelope" form of analysis.

The following measures are often shown to induce purchase. In general, they have major flaws that limit their usefulness. Either the simple measures or a full internal-rate-of-return calculation should be used.

Before-tax cash flow + first year's amortization return on equity
This measure is defined in the following way:

$$\frac{\text{Before-tax cash flow + Mortgage principal payment (year 1)}}{\text{Equity}}$$

This measure is the same as the previous one except for the addition of the amount repaid on the mortgage as an element of return. This return measure and the one that follows are often used by aggressive real estate salespeople. For example, if you assume the property has an 80% mortgage at $8^3/_4$% interest and a 20-year amortization schedule, the first-year reduction in loan balance amounts to 1.9% of the original balance. Thus this amortization by itself represents a 7.6% return on the equity investment. That 7.6% return is not available without either refinancing or selling the property. These events are considered only as future possibilities rather than as certainties, so some portion of that return should be discounted. This measure of return considers neither the tax effect nor the bulk of the change in capital position, positive or negative, that will arise through change in value of the property.

Cash flow after financing + tax effect as return on equity   This measure is defined as follows:

$$\frac{\text{Cash flow after financing + Tax effect (year 1)}}{\text{Equity}}$$

This measure gives the cash value of the investment to the investor in the first year of ownership. It ignores the change of after-tax cash flow over time and the impact of sale on the capital position of the investor.

Average returns   All of the last three measures are sometimes shown as averages based upon an estimated holding period. It is wise to look carefully at the components of these averages rather than to accept the average figure. It is also often the case that the largest portion of the return comes in the final year when the property is sold. Then, for example, in the tenth year alone of an $8^3/_4$% 20-year loan, approximately 4.2% of the original loan balance is paid off. For a property purchased with 80% debt, the loan amortization alone accounts for a 16.8% annual return on the original equity. Unless there are plans for the realization of the equity built up through loan amortization, the inclusion of such a large annual figure may materially distort the average and mislead the potential investor. This is especially critical given the long time before that portion of the return is to be realized. It also ignores the time value of money.

Payback period   This simple benchmark return measures the number of years required for the investor to recoup the cash equity invested. Discounted payback applies the investor hurdle rate to the future stream of after-tax cash flows. These measures are of limited value because they ignore benefits or the tax consequences beyond the payback period. This measure is useful, however, in a high risk investment environment where return of capital may be more important than a huge projected future payoff.

Net present value (NPV)   The net present value for a real estate investment may be found by applying the following formula:

N   =   holding period

$$NPV = \sum_{n=1}^{N} \frac{1}{(1 + i)n} [\text{CFAT year}n] - \text{Equity}$$

Where: *i*   =   investor hurdle rate.
CFAT   =   cash flow after taxes in year N
                    (= the sum of: before-tax cash flow in year *n* + tax effect in year *n* + futures in year *n*).

In other words, a stream of cash flows is discounted back at a predetermined discount rate, totaled, and then subtracted from the initial investment.

The NPV calculation considers all of the components of return available to the real estate investor. The relative sizes of initial investment are not explicitly accounted for by the NPV method; therefore, projects cannot be directly compared unless they are of the same size. This failing may be accounted for by the use of a profitability index, which is simply the ratio of the NPV to the amount of equity invested.[3]

Internal rate of return (IRR)   The internal rate of return for a real estate investment may be found by solving the following equation for *i*:

N   =   holding period

$$\sum_{n=1}^{N} \frac{1}{(1 + i)n} - \text{Equity}$$

[Before-tax cash flow (year *n*) + Tax effect (year *n*) + Future benefits (year *n*)] − Equity = 0

Thus *i* is the rate of return that will set the discounted present value of all cash flows less equity equal to zero. All of the standard caveats regarding discounted values apply. Arduous trial-and-error algorithms solve for the IRR and are best left to calculators or computers. Care must be taken in remembering the critical assumptions underlying the calculation of the IRR. The primary critical assumption is that the cash thrown off by the investment can and will be reinvested at the calculated internal rate of return. This assumption is often not true in practice. For a project with a pattern of large initial tax losses and then considerable taxable income, the tax savings must be reinvested or the investor may end up with a very poor investment. For example, the following cash flow stream has approximately a 12% internal rate of return, but the cash outlay is actually greater than the cash inflows.

---

[3]The NPV calculation is useful when the investor's cost of capital is known, when projections are made that involve many changes from positive to negative cash flows and might therefore produce multiple IRR solutions, and when investments with widely varying lives are compared.

–	$1,000	Year 1
+	500	Year 2
+	500	Year 3
+	500	Year 4
+	500	Year 5
	0	Years 6 through 11
–	$2,000	Year 12

The unwary investor who dealt with the $500 as though it were real return and did not reinvest it in some asset earning 12% (as is often done in tax-shelter investments) is in for a shock in Year 12.

SUMMARY

Analysis of real property investments is complicated. It is not, however, impossible. Since it most often involves projection of future events, it is well to err on the conservative side. Projections of compound growth over the periods involved in real estate must always be considered to contain a risk. The key tasks that need to be performed for all investments are the following:

1. develop baseline data
2. project trends, and
3. search out sources of discontinuity.

These tasks, adequately performed, will yield opportunities. One must understand what assumptions have been made. The number calculations themselves are not very complicated. Net present value and internal rate of return analyses can be done quite easily on calculators and computers. Basing the future on projections of the past may be the most logical way to start, but as any investor knows, events rarely work out that way. Fortunately, over time real estate has been one of the most profitable forms of investment. However, it is crucial to realize that the ability to sustain and take advantage of short-term downturns and to hold property for the long term has generally been the key to success.

25

NOTE ON TAXATION

INTRODUCTION

Every real estate transaction is affected by the tax consequences which result from its form and substance. Structuring a transaction without a thorough understanding of its tax considerations is likely to reduce the transaction's potential value. The failure to utilize the available tax benefits eliminates one of the major reasons for making a real estate investment.

This note provides a broad overview of the income tax factors most relevant to real estate ownership and operation. It is not intended as a definitive guide to the area, but to help the student better understand the basic factors and their interrelationships.

It cannot be overemphasized that all transactions should receive competent professional review. The field is highly technical with many interacting considerations which must be related to the personal circumstances of the participants. Most rules have variations and exceptions, and many exceptions have their own exceptions. The governing tax law changes frequently.

Some of the more recent acts were the Tax Equity and Fiscal Responsibility Act of 1982 (TEFRA), the Tax Reduction Act of 1984, the Tax Reform Act of 1986, the Revenue Reconciliation Act of 1990 and the 1993 Omnibus Budget Reconciliation Act. Whereas the 1982 Act expanded the tax benefits of real estate ownership, the 1986 Act substantially curtailed such benefits. The 1990 Act altered the tax rates imposed on individuals, with special treatment for long term capital gains. The 1993 Omnibus Budget Reconciliation Act increased income tax rates and lengthened the useful life of non-residential properties for purposes of depreciation.

This note deals with taxation at the federal level. In most cases states have income tax laws affecting real estate that are significant factors. However, because of local variations, the state laws will not be considered in this note but will be left to the individual investor to investigate. State taxes are deductible from federal income for tax purposes. Investors should be aware that state taxes are not deductible for taxpayers in the alternative minimum tax position (AMT). AMT is a complicated area and will not be discussed in much detail in this note.

The major distinction between real estate and other fields relates to the differences between cash flow accounting and income or accrual accounting. Real estate operations may generate a positive cash flow while also showing a loss for income tax purposes. Under current tax laws, all real estate income is considered passive. Losses may only be deducted from non-passive income if the taxpayer devotes 50% of his or her time to real estate, spends 750 hours and materially participates in real estate activities. Losses are limited to the taxpayer's basis in the property plus any personal liability such as guarantee of a loan.

As shown in the statement below, federal income tax law permits the deduction of depreciation, a noncash allowance as an expense in calculating taxable income. When the *noncash* depreciation allowance exceeds cash expenditures for principal amortization and replacement reserves, taxable income is less than the pretax cash flow for the period.

The relationship can be seen in the following diagram. In effect, the income tax due must be calculated first to determine the cash flow. The starting point is the before-tax cash flow *or* the cash flow from operations. The taxes due or saved depends on the individual or entity's actual tax rate.

Cash Flow from Operations

INCOME EFFECT			CASH EFFECT
	− Interest	− Interest	
	− Depreciation Allowance	− Principal	
		− Replacement reserves	
	= Net income before taxes	= Cash flow after financing	
	× Effective Tax Rate		
	= Income taxes →	− Income taxes	
		= Cash flow after taxes	

This note was prepared as the basis for class discussion and revised in 1995.

In a capital transaction, to determine gain or loss on sale, the original purchase price plus subsequent capital expenditures less the depreciation previously taken by the seller must be considered to derive the book value. Calculations for the sale of a property are done as follows.

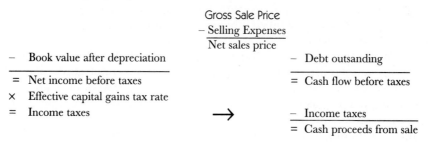

The owner–investor can judge the economic merits of a transaction only by reference to the sum of the total after-tax cash flows during ownership and the after-tax cash proceeds from sale. Both provide the input for calculating the after tax internal rate of return on investment.

Tax planning critically affects both the timing and the amount of income recognized. As the 1995 tax tables below indicate, the federal government can be up to a 39.6% partner in real estate operations. The alternative minimum tax rate was increased in 1993 to 24% for incomes up to $175,000 and to 28% for income above that level. The maximum tax rate imposed on long term capital gains remains at 28%.

The chart below summarizes the rates established by the new law. Each year the brackets are indexed for inflation although the rates remain the same.

1995 Tax Rates and Brackets

	SINGLE TAXPAYERS	MARRIED TAXPAYERS FILING JOINTLY	HEADS OF HOUSEHOLD	MARRIED FILING SEPARATELY
15%	$0–23,350	$0–39,000	$0–31,250	$0–19,500
28%	$23,350–56,550	$39,000–94,250	$31,250–80,750	$19,500–47,125
31%	$56,550–117,950	$94,250–143,600	$80,750–130,800	$47,125–71,800
36%	$117,950–256,500	$143,600–256,500	$130,800–256,500	$71,800–128,250
39.6%	over $256,500	over $256,500	over $256,500	over $128,250

This note assumes the perspective of the individual taxpayer, or the recipient of "passed through" partnership income. The decision as to the form of real estate ownership is discussed in the *Note on Forms of Real Estate Ownership* (9-373-148). Factors which contribute to the general preference for the partnership form of ownership are: the statutory complexity of corporations, the "double taxation" of corporate income and dividends, and the treatment of losses in excess of annual corporate income.[4]

Increasingly, in structuring a limited partnership, a Subchapter S Corporation can be established to hold the general partner's interest. An individual can be both a general and limited partner assigning virtually all of his or her interest to the limited partnership interest. The purpose of this corporation is to limit the personal liability of the general partner especially with respect to environmental matters, even though a separate tax filing is required for the new corporation. The tax effect is substantially the same for the general partner as if held individually.

This note is organized into four principal sections. Each section focuses on the major concerns affecting the taxation of the property investment—both the factual determinations required and the special problem areas encountered.

Section I: Theory of Income Taxation and Accounting

This section introduces the income tax concept of matching the timing and recognition of costs and revenues. It emphasizes the importance of clear and accurate records and discusses the difference between "cash" and "accrual" methods of tax accounting.

Section II: Tax Considerations in the Acquisition and Development of Real Property

This section focuses on the determination of the taxpayer's tax basis in a property; the allocation of that basis to the property's various components; the determination of the taxpayer's holding period of a property; the role of prepaid interest; the alternatives of capitalizing and expensing costs during property development; and the application of the investment tax credit to real property.

Section III: Tax Factors in Real Property Operation

This section discusses the nature of income, and the types of and eligibility for deductions in computing the tax liability from real estate operations. Particular attention is given to the concept and the calculation of the depreciation deduction.

Section IV: Tax Factors in the Disposition and Sale of Real Property

This section discusses the calculation of the gain on the sale or other disposition of property, the factors which determine ordinary income and long-term capital gains treatment, and the methods by which to defer the recognition of that income.

---

[4]The corporate tax rates are as follows: $0–$50,000 at 15%, $50,001–$75,000 at 25%, $75,001–$100,000 at 34%, $100,000–$335,000 at 39%, $335,001–$10,00,000 at 34% and over $10,000,000 at 35%. Corporations are taxed at ordinary rates on long-term capital gains.

I. Theory of Income Taxation and Accounting

A. Theory of Taxation

The federal income tax treatment of real estate has two basic, but sometimes conflicting, goals: the generation of revenue to support government, and the encouragement of private real estate investment relative to other investments. The incentive aspects have caused much investment in real estate. For example, hundreds of thousands of subsidized housing units have been built to take advantage of favorable tax incentives. Heated debate continues, however, over the costs of providing these incentives in terms of the loss or deferral of federal revenue.

The basic principles of tax law and accounting aim at taxing income as it is generated while granting offsetting deductions for valid expenses incurred in producing that income. The Internal Revenue Code (Code) requires that the taxable income be determined, in general, in the same manner used by the taxpayer in computing income for financial reporting purposes and that differences be reported on the tax return. It requires consistency in the manner in which the taxpayer reports from year to year. In all cases, the Internal Revenue Service (IRS) requires the taxpayer to maintain clear, written records to justify the deductions claimed. The taxpayer has the burden of documenting the logic underlying transactions so as to show both the business purpose of each expense and that the accounting procedures have not "materially distorted income."

B. Methods of Accounting for Income

A real estate business must select one of two basic methods of accounting. The most commonly used is the "cash receipts and disbursements method," often called the "cash method." The other is the "accrual method."

Under the cash method, income is recognized in the taxable year in which payment is received. Expenses are recognized in the year in which paid. The cash method offers much flexibility in timing billings, and accelerating expense payments; income can be increased by delaying payment of bills and by encouraging prepayment of rents or accounts receivable.

This control of reportable income has led many private individuals to choose the cash method. In addition, it limits the practical ability of the IRS to challenge the taxpayer's position. The major contestable issue is whether the taxpayer is in constructive receipt of income where funds have not changed hands. The doctrine of constructive receipt holds that a cash basis taxpayer who possesses an unqualified right to property, and the power to exercise that right, is to be treated as if he or she is in actual receipt of that cash.

The "accrual method" aims at matching income and expense. Income is recognized in the year in which all conditions are met which determine the taxpayer's right to receive it. The items recognized must be determinable with reasonable accuracy; unsubstantiated estimates usually are inadequate to trigger recognition. Most public companies use accrual accounting in order to reflect more accurately the financial condition of the company and to provide greater comparability among corporations.

It should be noted for income tax purposes, rental income is taxable when received without regard to the taxpayer's method of accounting. In other words, an accrual basis taxpayer who receives rental income prior to the time that income has been earned, i.e., prepaid rents, must still recognize that amount as income in the year received.

The decision to use the cash or accrual method of accounting is made by each taxpaying entity, whether that entity is an individual taxpayer or an intermediary business vehicle such as a partnership. Once adopted, the method must be consistently applied and cannot be changed without the consent of the Internal Revenue Service. The long term consequences of this decision make it important that the taxpayer get competent advice before selecting an accounting method and that the search for simplicity or tax gimmickry not be allowed to impede the development of a sound accounting and management information system. The 1986 Tax Act eliminated the decision making for certain entities by requiring all tax shelters and many C corporations, partnerships having a C corporation as a partner and tax exempt trusts having unrelated business income to use the accrual method of accounting for years beginning after 1986. There is an exception to this rule for entities other than tax shelters so that the cash method can be used if the entity has less than $5,000,000 in gross receipts.

II. Tax Considerations in the Acquisition and Development Stage

A long-term tax plan should be formulated during the acquisition and development of a project. Despite the fact that acts of purchasing or developing a property do not usually give rise to taxable income, because they involve merely the creation of a capital asset rather than income or loss generation, many decisions made at that time affect the seller in the short run and the buyer throughout the period of ownership.[5]

A. Determinations Which are Primarily Factual

The primary factual determinations involve the amount of the taxpayer's tax basis in the property, its allocation to the components of the land and buildings, and the length of ownership. Other important factors include the allocation of future payments between principal and interest, and the expensing or capitalization of items, such as real estate taxes, interest, loan fees, etc.

1. Determination of Basis

A. *The Cost of the Property:* The first factual determination to be made is that of the tax basis of the property. The fundamental rule is that a property's tax basis is its cost. For tax purposes, cost is not limited to the

---

[5]Considerable real property is being purchased today as investments by pension funds and other entities that do not pay income tax. Although the tax factors discussed in this note are not applicable to them directly, indirectly the lack of tax consequences could be more or less advantageous to them in competing for individual real property investments depending upon whether the taxpaying entity's income is positive or negative.

cash paid by the purchaser but includes any mortgages or notes assumed. Other costs to be included are those for: Attorney's fees; land survey; title examination; title insurance; tax stamps; appraisal costs; option payments; brokerage commissions; delinquent *advalorem* taxes.

The tax basis may change during the period of ownership. For example, capital improvements made by an owner increase his or her basis, and the depreciation deductions reduce it.[6] Capital improvements include the soft costs such as construction interest and marketing costs associated with the construction.

Basis allocations among the land, building and personal property reflect the fair market values of the separate elements. For new construction, actual cost serves as the basis for these allocations. In contrast, the price of an existing property is usually arrived at on an overall basis, and any separation into parts is done after the fact.

The most commonly used method to appropriately allocate between land and buildings is by using the ratio of assessed valuations placed upon those components by the local tax assessor. Sometimes an appraiser is hired to evaluate the components if the assessed valuation method does not give a satisfactory result.

The IRS may accept an allocation which the parties make in the purchase and sales contract. Acceptance occurs most often when arm's-

---

[6]*Other Forms of Acquisition:* The basis of properties acquired other than by purchase deserves special consideration. Common transactions include inheritance, gift, the satisfaction of a debt, payment for services and the exchange of other properties.

a. *Inheritance:* An owner's property becomes part of one's estate upon death. It is valued for the estate tax purposes at its fair market value on the date of death (or, at the option of the estate's representative, six months later). The recipient of the property takes that fair market value as a new basis in the property.

b. *Gift:* Property acquired by gift receives a basis equal to the lesser of the donor's basis or the fair market value of the property on the date of the gift. The donee's basis is increased by the federal gift tax paid on the gift; but the total cannot exceed the fair market value. Note that there is now a combined transfer tax system for gifts and estates.

c. *Debt:* The basis in property acquired in satisfaction of a debt or other claim is the lesser of the amount of the debt or the fair market value.

d. *Services:* The basis in property acquired for services is the fair market value of the property at the date of transfer. A person paid in property services includes that value as earned income.

e. *Exchange:* The basis in property acquired in exchange is dependent upon the tax treatment of exchange. If the exchange is tax deferred, the basis of the property transferred carries over to the property received. Adjustments are made when the exchange is partially taxable. These are discussed later under the heading Sales Transactions.

In a fully taxable exchange, the basis is the fair market value of the property acquired at the date of transfer. The taxpayer's gain or loss on the transfer is taken into account. The transaction is like a purchase at fair market value.

length negotiations have been conducted between parties with adverse interests. For example, when certain items sold, such as personal property, give rise to ordinary income to the seller, but permit rapid or high tax write-offs for the purchaser then the parties have adverse interests. Even the most reasonable approach may be affected by hindsight. Artificial allocations which produce unrealistic tax results are always subject to challenge.

2. Holding Period

The concept of holding period is an important consideration because of the differential between short-term and long-term rates. Prior to the 1986 Tax Act, capital gains received special tax treatment resulting in an effective tax rate of no more than 20% of the gain. The rate for capital gains since 1987 has been a maximum of 28% based on a holding period of more than one year. Short-term capital gains (and ordinary income) are taxed at a maximum rate of 39.6%.

The starting date of the holding period of property varies depending on the means used to acquire the property. The holding period of property acquired by purchase commences usually with the day following that on which the sale is closed and title transferred.

For property acquired by gift, the holding rules follow the basis rules for gifts. If the donor's basis is carried over, the recipient's holding period includes that of the donor. If the basis is the fair market value on the date of the gift because a loss is realized, the date of the gift governs.

The holding period of the property acquired in a tax-free exchange includes the taxpayer's holding period in the property transferred. Both basis and holding period are carried over from the original asset.

Property acquired by bequest, devise or inheritance usually acquires a holding period dating from the date of death. The holding period for improvements made by an owner begins with the date of construction of each item. Thus, a single sale can include both short- and long-term assets.

B. Areas for Management Decision-Making: Tax Treatment of Certain Expense Items at Time of Acquisition

The discussion to this point has been concerned with relevant factual determinations. Although some of the "facts" are subject to judgment, established rules usually determine their validity. Nonetheless, there are also managerial decisions which must be made during the acquisition and development period which also have major tax implications. Not all are under the control of a single decision maker. Good decisions may result in long-run payoffs. This section of the note will consider several important areas for managerial decision-making.

Buyer and seller often reach agreement largely as a result of structuring a transaction so as to create a more beneficial total tax picture for both parties. Negotiating upon, and sharing in, the tax trade-offs from allocating the total purchase consideration can allow both sides to come closer to objectives which otherwise would conflict.

The partnership as a form of ownership probably offers the greatest amount of flexibility, but this flexibility has been reduced in recent years as a result of perceived abuse. Two major areas where flexibility has been curtailed include special allocations and retroactive allocations. Current law requires items of income, loss, gain, deduction or credit to be allocated according to the partners' interest in the partnership. It discourages special allocations.

The second area of reduced flexibility comes through prohibition of retroactive allocation of income and loss. A partner who acquires a partnership interest during the year must be allocated income or loss for that portion of the year during which the interest was held. This allocation can be made either by determining actual income or loss for the period or by prorating the year's income or loss to the period the interest is held.

A major change in the 1986 tax law is the passive activity loss rule, which prohibits claiming most real estate losses against income not derived from real estate or other specified passive activities. Individuals, estates and trusts, S Corporations and personal service corporations will not be able to use losses from real estate to offset active or earned income, or portfolio income such as interest, dividends or gains from the sale of securities. Payments earned by partners for providing management or other services are considered earned income for the recipient and a passive deduction for the payer. Interest or guaranteed payments paid on capital accounts is also deemed portfolio income. The operation of nursing homes, hotels or other transient lodging facilities where substantial services are rendered is active, not rental income for the owner who materially participates in the activity. It should be noted that a limited partner cannot, by law, materially participate.

There are two exceptions to the passive activity rule. The first helps investors who, for example, own rental property and "materially participate" in the management of the property. These investors may deduct up to $25,000 of losses against their ordinary income, but this deduction is phased out for individuals with adjusted gross income between $100,000 and $150,000. The second exception applies to people who essentially make a living in real property trades or businesses. Beginning after 1993, eligible taxpayers who meet certain tests (like more than half of their work time being spent on real estate and more than 750 hours each year spent on real estate business) are allowed to offset non-passive income with passive losses from their real estate investments.

1. Prepaid Interest, "Points" and Contract Interest
Interest is deductible only in the year to which it relates, irrespective of when paid. Similarly "points" paid on a loan must be deducted ratably over the loan period. An exception is made for points paid on a secured loan for the purchase or improvement of a taxpayer's principal residence if the charge is typical for one geographical area.

Care must always be taken that some interest rate is stated in a contract. Contracts which specify no interest rate or annual simple interest rates of less than the market are subject to restatement under tax regulations which impute a market rate compounded semi-annually. The change made by the Tax Reform Act of 1984 extends original issue discount (OID) rules to obligations issued for nontraded property and require the interest rate be compared to 110% of the "federal rate" effective for taxable years beginning in 1985. Most leveraged real estate purchases will be subject to the OID rules in cases where adequate interest is not provided for or cases where adequate interest is charged but not payable annually. The IRS commissioner has the right and does, in fact, change these rates for tax calculations from time to time. The applicable federal rate is published monthly. There are special rules about interest rates for transactions involving related parties.

2. Election to Capitalize Normally Expensed Items

The investor may elect, subject to certain detailed rules, whether to capitalize or expense separately for each kind of expense. An owner of many projects may make different elections for the various kinds of expenses of the different projects.

After 1986, individuals, partnerships, trusts, and corporations are no longer allowed to deduct interest and property taxes or related administrative expenses on real property during construction. Those costs must be capitalized and amortized over the life of the property. Prior to 1986, interest and property taxes incurred during the construction period could be amortized over a ten year period.

A tax credit is used to offset income tax payable on a dollar-for-dollar basis.[7] An owner is eligible for a tax credit of 10% of qualified rehabilitation costs for work done on a nonresidential building built prior to 1936. An owner of a certified historic structure, which can be either residential or nonresidential, can take a tax credit equal to 20% of the rehabilitation costs. These tax credits can be carried back 3 years and forward 15. A lessee may also be eligible for these tax credits if the remaining lease is at least 15 years.

In both of the situations described above, to qualify for a tax credit the renovation must be substantial, basically defined as at least equal to the purchase price of the property. The renovation, especially for historical structures, must also meet certain technical requirements. The rehabilitation tax credit reduces the basis of the property eligible for depreciation. Thus, if $1,000,000 is spent renovating an historic structure, the owner receives a tax credit of $200,000 when the work is complete, but for depreciation purposes the basis of the building only goes up by $800,000. If the building is sold within five years of the rehabili-

---

[7]Actually, the tax law provides a dollar-for-dollar offset only for the first $25,000 of tax liabilities. Liabilities in excess of $25,000 are offset at a 75% rate.

tation work, a portion of the tax credit will be recaptured according to the following schedule: within one full year after placed in service 100%, declining 20% per subsequent year.

If an owner receives one of these investment tax credits, the rehabilitation expenditure must thereafter be depreciated on a straight line basis. In addition, the rehabilitation work associated with the investment tax credit is not eligible for other tax credits.

For low income housing, the special depreciation schedules and other benefits have been eliminated for projects placed in service after 1986, and replaced by low income housing tax credits (LIHTC). The LIHTC is claimed annually for ten years. The new credits are 4% for acquisitions and 9% for new construction and rehabilitation, unless financed with tax-exempt bonds or certain other Federal subsidies, in which case the credit is 4%. The credits are phased out for individuals with adjusted gross incomes of $200,000 to $250,000, and only $7,000 per individual investor can be used against "non-passive activity income." Corporations do not have these restrictions. The project must serve a substantial percentage of low and/or very low income people, defined as people having incomes less than 60% of median income for their area.

III. Tax Factors in the Operation of Real Property Investments

It is critical that the potential investor understand the tax factors which are relevant to the operating phase of a building's life. The primary activity of most people who are active in the real estate field is in its operation. This section considers three principal areas: eligibility for tax deductions; recognition and characterization of income; and determination of deductions.

A. Eligibility for Deductions

The federal income tax deductions which arise from real estate ownership fall into two classes: those available to all owners, even for property held for personal use; and additional ones available only to owners of property "used in a trade or business" or held for the "production of income."

1. Deductions Generally Available

Owners of a principal residence or a single second home may deduct interest on debt secured by a security interest and real estate or property taxes. However, for loans incurred after August 16, 1986, interest deductions are limited based on the lesser of the purchase price of the property plus the cost of improvements or the fair market value of the home at the time the debt is incurred (with maximum limitation amounts of $1 million for original acquisition indebtedness and $100,000 for home equity indebtedness). There is an exception for loans used to pay certain medical and educational expenses. For second homes and subject to a number of technical rules, to be able to deduct mortgage interest against ordinary income, rental use must not exceed 14 days. After taking into account lost income from the downpayment on a house, there is sometimes an after tax cash flow advantage to ownership versus rental of one's home, but the key variable in how a house performs as an investment is usually whether and how much the house appreciates in value.

All owners of real property are allowed itemized deductions for real estate taxes and interest expenses. However, holding mere legal title is insufficient to render an expense deductible to the taxpayer. The taxpayer must "bear the burdens and risks of ownership." Deals can be structured to take advantage of differing tax brackets or the need for some buyers and sellers to report earnings.

It is important to note that whereas interest payments are deductible for tax purposes, principal payments are not since the payer is reducing a liability and theoretically increasing net worth. Therefore, the term of the mortgage (which along with the interest rate determines the allocation of mortgage payments between principal and interest) has important tax implications.

2. Deductions Available with Respect to Property used in Trade or Business or Held for the Production of Income[8]

Income or business properties generate not only deductions for interest and property taxes but also additional deductions. Among these are deductions for operating expenses, repairs and maintenance, and depreciation. All will be considered in this section of this note.

There are two primary requirements for taking deductions for these items. First, the taxpayer must have a legitimate business purpose for incurring the expense, in contrast to mere personal benefit. Second, the taxpayer must have the benefits, burdens and risks of ownership. Allocation of deductions among partners and other joint owners of a property is subject to complex limitations which are based on the view that the benefits and burdens of ownership must be spread reasonably among the owners by reference to their economic interests in the property. Certain limitations on these deductions are footnoted below.

B. Recognition and Character of Income

The owner or lessor may receive compensation for the use of a property during its operating phase. This compensation is called *rent* and results in ordinary income to the lessor. In determining the owner's taxable income, the ordinary income is reduced by the operating expenses incurred in connection with the property. The rent payments are deductible by the lessee if the property is used in connection with a trade or business or for production of income.

Although defining reportable income is generally straightforward, issues are often raised as to advance rents, security deposits, lessee improvements, payments made under leases with options to purchase and payments

---

[8]Interest on debt used to purchase or carry investment real estate may be subject to investment interest limitations. This is a complicated area and will not be discussed in this note.

made to cancel, extend, or modify a lease. The primary determinants are the intent of the parties, the economic substance of the transaction, and any written agreement.

Advance rents protect a lessor against default by the lessee during the lease term. These payments are usually applied to the first or last periods of the obligations, but may be applied in any fashion which is agreed to in the lease. They become taxable income to the landlord upon receipt of cash or a marketable promissory note. The lessee does not receive a deduction for advance rent payments until the period for which the rent is actually due or the payment is applied as rent. Thus, the deduction may be separated from the recognition of income by many years.

Security deposits may be used in place of advance rentals. These differ from advance rentals in that the lessor is obligated to hold and account to the tenant for the monies advanced. There is no recognition of income until the deposit can be used without a duty to account for or repay it. Many states require that the security deposits on residential rental properties be placed in interest-bearing escrow accounts for the benefit of the tenants. The tenant is not allowed a deduction for a security deposit unless and until the deposit becomes rent under the lease terms.

Lessee improvements are a complicated area of income recognition. There are three basic categories of improvements: those made by a tenant which reduce the rental cost; those made to property owned by an unrelated party; and those made to property owned by a related party.

The fair market value of improvements made by a lessee in consideration of a rent reduction results in income for the lessor. The fair market value may differ from the cost of the improvements because the lessor does not receive the right to immediate use. The mere enhancement of the ultimate value of the property of the lessor does not automatically generate taxable income.

In a more usual case, the cost is treated as a capital expenditure for the tenant, and does not constitute additional rent or add to the lessor's basis. The tenant must recover the cost through either depreciation over the recovery period of the improvements or amortization over the term of the lease, including option periods, whichever is shorter. Leases between related parties are more likely to be scrutinized by the IRS since transactions by them are more likely to be entered into primarily to minimize the total tax due: the improvements must be depreciated over the recovery period of the improvements rather than the shorter period of the lease term.

Leases with options to purchase are especially complicated. The combination is usually made with the intention that during the lease all payments will be ordinary income to the landlord and deductible to the tenant. Upon exercise of the option, the payments become capital if the economic reality appears to be that some of the "rental" payments are in reality payments for the purchase of the buildings, and that the sale in fact occurs before the option is exercised. Inflated rents, below-market options and uneven payments over the lease indicate a nonstandard transaction.

Revenue received by the landlord as payment for *extending, canceling or modifying a lease* is ordinary income in the year of receipt. The landlord may deduct related expenses against the income generated. These costs include the unamortized portion of any lease acquisition expense. The payments are deductible by the tenant in the year in which paid, except that payments made to extend or modify a lease are amortized over the lease term.

C. Determination of Deductions

Although the general rule is that expenses incurred in the generation of income in an operating business are usually deductible, an awareness of the specific nature of deductible expenses can result in a major difference in the after-tax return available from a project. This section discusses the following kinds of expenses: cash operating expenses; depreciation and amortization expenses; and financial expenses.

1. *Cash operating expenses* affect the cash flow from operations. Several areas are of primary concern: vacancies, real estate taxes, repairs and maintenance, and rental expenses.

An allowance for vacancy is not a deductible expense. Only actual vacancies or unpaid rent, which results in a reduction of income, lessen taxable income, and vacancies must be accounted for in the year in which they occur. No provision is made for estimates.

Real estate taxes are deductible in the year in which payment is made or the assessment comes due, whichever is later. In the years in which the property is purchased or sold, however, there is mandatory allocation between the purchaser and seller of the real estate taxes attributable to the year. Payments on overdue assessments, due from the seller, are capitalized by a purchaser.

The deductibility of repair and maintenance costs is often a gray area. Deductibility is generally allowed for expenses like repainting and minor repairs which maintain the operating efficiency of an asset over its useful life. There is a narrow line, however, between expenditures which maintain a property and those which add to its value, extend its useful life or adapt it to a different use. This distinction has been the subject of much tax litigation, with the taxpayer usually seeking to deduct as many such items as possible and the IRS seeking to capitalize borderline expenditures. Although nondeductibility does not preclude an item from being expensed or depreciated over the benefit's recovery period, it does defer the tax benefit over a longer period. The fundamental categories of expenditures and their tax treatment are shown in the following table.

EXPENDITURE TYPE	ORDINARY EXPENSE	CAPITALIZED ITEM
Carpentry	Repair of minor damage	Replacement of major structure
Plumbing	Minor part replacement and regular maintenance	Major replacement or addition
Roofing	Repairs, patching	Significant replacement
Cement, Plaster and Paving	Repair of cracks, holes and minor damage	Renovation, remodeling or complete resurfacing
Electrical	Minor replacements and repair	New addition or general replacement of serviceable but obsolete equipment

It is especially important to keep records in order to apportion the costs properly where repairs are combined with replacement or modernization.

Expenses which are incurred incident to obtaining a lease are deductible ratably over the life of a lease. These include the expense of obtaining a specific tenant, such as attorney's fees and broker's commissions. More general items, such as advertising, can be deducted in the year incurred. When a lease terminates prior to the complete amortization of related capitalized expenses, unamortized amounts can be deducted in the year of termination.

2. *Depreciable allowances* form much of the foundation of tax shelter in the real estate industry. The concept of depreciation grew out of the recognition that property, other than land, has a limited physical and economic useful life. It has been the primary vehicle through which businesses recover the cost of a capital investment. The Internal Revenue Service allows an owner to recover the capital costs of an investment in a depreciable asset through periodic deductions of a portion of the costs.

This section addresses several critical areas with respect to depreciation: To whom is depreciation available? What property is depreciable? What methods of depreciation are allowed?

Depreciation deductions are available only on buildings and other depreciable property held or used either in a trade or business or for the production of income. This precludes depreciation deductions for personal residences or other property used solely for the personal benefit of the owner.

A tenant may take depreciation on improvements which are made to a leasehold interest, where the improvements are subject to declining value. The improvements are deductible over 27.5 years for residential properties and 39 years for non-residential. Upon the tenant's termination of the lease and vacating the premises, any remaining balance may be written off.

Property is depreciable if it has a limited useful economic life. Improvements to land are depreciable since they wear out, but the land itself is not depreciable since it either has or is deemed to have continuing economic utility.

The depreciation or cost recovery allowance is computed so that the total amount set aside through depreciation charges over a certain number of years plus the cost of the land equal the initial cost of the real estate. As an incentive to spur investment in tangible assets, the 1981 Economic Recovery Tax Act shortened the time period over which real estate could be depreciated to 15 years. Subsequent acts lengthened the cost recovery period to 18 and later 19 years and then 27.5 years and now 39 years for non-residential property. Generally, real property will be depreciated using the straight line method. A 40 year period is required for assets used abroad, by tax exempt entities, or if financed with tax exempt bonds. Most personal property connected with real estate is depreciated over seven years, using the 200% declining balance method.

Improvements to a tenant's space paid for by the landlord are depreciable over 27.5 years for residential or 39 years for non-residential buildings, not over the period of the tenant's lease term. If the tenant's lease expires and the improvements are removed, any balance can be written off at that time. If the tenant pays for the improvements through higher rents over the lease term, there is an unbalanced situation since the cash is received over the term of the lease and the expense is deducted over a 27.5 or 39 year period. Thus, there is a disincentive from a tax perspective for this kind of arrangement.

An important point to remember is that generally no distinction is made for depreciation purposes between new and used real property. Prior to 1982, there was such a distinction in order to stimulate new construction in the form of shorter depreciable lives and the use of more accelerated methods to calculate depreciation. Accelerated depreciation permits larger deduction in earlier years of ownership.

Now the building and all its systems must be depreciated as a whole. In doing rehabilitation work, if the addition is not substantial the cost can be added to the basis of the building and depreciated over the cost recovery period appropriate for that type of addition. If the addition is substantial, it must be depreciated separately. If the addition to the building is a stand-alone piece of equipment, that equipment can be depreciated separately using the appropriate cost recovery rate for that kind of equipment.

D. Summary of Tax Factors in Operating Real Property

The major tax factors in the operating stage of a property's life cycle relate to the determination of income and of deductions. The timing of income recognition may vary depending on whether the taxpayer is on a cash or accrual basis. The availability of the depreciation deduction is the principal factor which makes real estate more attractive than other investments. It allows the owner of real property to deduct a non-cash charge, which reduces taxable income but not cash flow. The taxable income often can be negative, while the cash flow is positive. This is most frequently the case with highly leveraged properties. It produces a tax shelter for the taxpayer's other income although there are limits as to the deductibility of such losses except against other "passive activity income" as discussed.

IV. Tax Factors in the Sale and Disposition of Real Property

When the taxpayer sells or otherwise disposes of real estate, there is an accounting of certain tax benefits received during the earlier operating stage. Factors, such as good records, proper form of ownership, and sound economic judgment come together to affect after-tax profit maximization. The most relevant tax considerations fall into three categories: calculation of gain or loss; income tax treatments of the gain or loss; and deferring taxation of any gain realized on the transaction.

A. Calculation of the Taxable Gain or Loss

Two factors determine the amount of taxable gain or loss: the selling price and the tax basis of the property. The gross selling price is the sum of the following:

- Cash received by the seller;
- Determinable amounts receivable from the purchaser;
- Liabilities against the property owned by the seller (such as the mortgage) where the buyer assumes the obligation or takes the property subject to the pre-existing liability;
- The fair market value of other property received by the seller.

From this amount, the seller is allowed to deduct the expenses of sale, such as the following:

- Selling Commission
- Legal Fees
- Recording Fees
- Tax Stamps
- Capital expenses incurred within 90 days of sale which have not yet been capitalized.

The taxpayer's basis in the property sold is the original basis established upon its acquisition adjusted by the following: (a) increased by any capital expenditures made during the period of ownership; and (b) reduced by the depreciation and other capital charges which have been deducted.

The calculation determines the amount of gain or loss realized. As the discussion which follows indicates, additional information is required in order to determine each taxpayer's tax liability.

B. The Importance of the Character and the Tax Treatment of Gain and Loss

1. The Different Characters of Income

The 1990 Act reintroduced a difference in tax rates between capital gains and ordinary income.

Capital gain or loss arises from the sale or other disposition of a capital asset, which is defined to include property held for investment purposes for at least one year.

Ordinary gain or loss arises from the sale or other disposition of property held for sale in the ordinary course of business, so-called dealer property.

The application of these definitions generates uncertainty and controversy for investors, who on occasion may inadvertently assume dealer status.

The importance of this distinction relates to the beneficial treatment accorded long-term gains on capital assets and certain long-term gains on Section 1231 assets. Where these assets have been held for more than one year, the gain or loss on them is treated as long-term. The effective tax rate applied to capital transactions provided an important incentive for investment in capital assets. It has ranged from 35% in 1978 to 20% in 1982–86, and is now back to 28%.

C. Deferring the Tax Consequences of Sale

The code also includes a category called Section 1231 income.

It is often desirable to seek ways of deferring the tax consequences of a sale by spreading the recognition of income over a period of years. For example, the sale of real estate often generates a large liability which must be paid in cash, but the seller may not receive payment of the sales proceeds until a subsequent year. Moreover, a large gain can cause an individual to pay taxes in a higher marginal tax bracket than would otherwise be applicable to that taxpayer.

Deferral of tax on a sale may be achieved by five general methods: the first involves delaying receipt of the total proceeds by an installment sale; the second involves the qualified reinvestment of the proceeds in a tax free exchange; the third arises out of an involuntary conversion; the fourth involves the sale of low and moderate income housing serving as a primary residence; the fifth involves sale of a personal residence. In all five cases, the seller benefits by deferring payments of tax monies. Tax deferred transactions must be carefully structured to meet all the requirements. When they are met, the benefits can be substantial. Each method of deferral and the associated requirements will now be considered in greater detail.

1. *Under the installment sales method,* the seller may report a pro rata share of the profits from a transaction over time as the cash proceeds are received. In order to qualify for the installment sales treatment, the sales price must be payable to the seller over two or more years. This reporting method has two primary advantages. First, the seller's tax liability can be timed to correspond better with cash receipts, thereby eliminating the need to borrow funds to pay taxes. Second, the seller does not recognize the full amount of the income in a single tax year; thus, the marginal tax bracket applied to the income is likely to be less.

The following example illustrates calculations made for an installment sale:

In 1987, an investor sells a plot of land for $150,000, subject to a pre-existing mortgage of $30,000 and a purchase money second mortgage of $90,000 with a down payment of $30,000 or 20% of the purchase price. The expenses of sale are $8,000. The seller's basis in the property is $30,000. The computations are as follows:

Sales price	$150,000
Selling expense	− 8,000
Net selling price	$142,000
Seller's basis	−30,000
Gain on sale	$112,000

Sales price	$150,000
Mortgage assumed	−30,000
Contract price	$120,000

Ratio of gain to contract price $112,000/$120,000 = .933%
Payments received in year of sale = $30,000
Gain taxable in year of sale .933% x $30,000 = $28,000

Selling the installment contract triggers recognition of the entire gain deferred. Pledging the contract can have similar results. Installment sales among related parties are subject to particular scrutiny. The 1986 Act also has developed a complex formula to deal with taxation of certain installment sales, requiring recognition of some or all of the gain based on the taxpayer's outstanding debt. This is true even if no payments have been received on the installment note.

2. *Tax-deferred exchanges* provide a technique for transferring real estate investments and reinvesting the proceeds in other investment assets without incurring a tax liability on the transfer. By deferring the tax, up to 28% or more dollars can be kept at work. This method is often used where there may have been major appreciation in value and where the original owner wants to continue to be an investor in real estate.

For an exchange to qualify fully for tax-deferred treatment, it must meet several requirements:

(1) The property must be held for use in a trade or business or for investment purposes. Fully passive investments such as corporate stocks and bonds do not qualify. If the property is sold too soon after the sale or held for sale or resale, it may be found that no investment intent was present.

(2) There must be an exchange of property for property rather than a sale, repurchase or reinvestment.

(3) The property exchanged must be of like kind.

If these conditions are met, deferral is mandatory for both gains and losses. Thus, a loss cannot be recognized even if it would be to the taxpayer's advantage to recognize it.

A qualifying exchange need not be limited to two-party transactions. Multi-party exchanges are allowable, so long as each transaction provides an exchange of properties. The "like kind" requirement has historically applied to real property so liberally that it covers almost every property. Office buildings, apartments, city lots, undeveloped land, warehouses, and many other kinds of real estate have been held to be "like kind" with other real estate interests. Recent tax court cases have significantly broadened this interpretation of "like kind." A taxpayer contemplating an exchange must seek competent counsel for both the mechanics of the transaction and the most recent ruling.

An exchange can be partially tax deferred where assets of a different character are included. Assets which do not qualify for a tax- free exchange are called "boot." These include cash, notes, personal property, and the assumption or transfer of liabilities. In a partially tax-deferred exchange, the amount of realized gain which is recognized is limited to the sum of the money and the fair market value of other nonqualifying property received.

3. *Involuntary conversions* generally arise out of the compulsory or involuntary loss of property through condemnation proceedings, theft, seizure or destruction. In contrast to "like-kind" exchanges, losses as well as gains must be recognized immediately and cannot be deferred unless reinvested according to specific rules.

Not all forced dispositions fall within the involuntary conversion rubric. Among those excluded are sales in foreclosure or in satisfaction of governmental assessments or liens. The exclusions can prove costly. If a property was purchased for $1 million, was depreciated to $800,000, and then was foreclosed with a mortgage balance outstanding of $900,000, the owner would realize a $100,000 capital gain, subject to possible depreciation recapture at ordinary income tax rates.

In a qualifying involuntary conversion, the entire gain is deferred if the full amount of proceeds is reinvested so as to satisfy the rules for replacement. If only partial reinvestment is made, the treatment of the part which is not reinvested is similar to that accorded to "boot" in a tax-free exchange, i.e., it is taxable.

Replacement must take place within two years after the taxable year in which any part of the gain on conversion is realized. For condemnation awards, the period begins with the earlier of the date of the award or that on which condemnation first becomes imminent. The IRS has the discretion to grant extension periods.

Qualification of property as replacement property depends upon the cause of the conversion. For condemnations, the test has been the liberal "like-kind" rule which also governs tax-free exchanges. For other causes, stricter tests apply which look to whether there is the same end use (such as warehouse or factory) or the same business purpose (such as investment or rental of land).

4. *Sales of low and moderate income housing* built under certain financing programs can have their tax consequences deferred. Generally, the sale must be made either to a qualified not-for-profit corporation, cooperative organization or tenant group. The proceeds must be reinvested within one year in another subsidized housing project.

5. *The sale of a principal personal residence* can also yield wholly or partially deferred gains if either the proceeds are reinvested or if the seller is over 55 years old. Taxpayers may elect to defer the full gain on such a sale when the entire proceeds are reinvested in another higher priced principal residence purchased within a prescribed time period (generally two years). Multiple deferrals in a succession of qualified purchases and sales are possible.

There are three basic requirements of this general provision. First, the property must satisfy the sometimes ambiguous definition of the taxpayer's "principal" personal residence. Units in cooperatives and condominiums can be included in this category, as well as single family homes. Second, the new residence must be purchased within 24 months before or after the disposition of the old residence. The taxpayer is allowed more than one rollover, or deferral, during the 24 months if the taxpayer is required to relocate by an employer. When replacement is through construction, the construction must be started within 24 months. Third, for the full amount of the gain to be deferred, the amount reinvested (or expended on construction within the replacement period) must be at least equal to the "adjusted sales price" of the old residence. This adjusted amount is the gross sales price reduced by selling expense including fix up expenses. The cost of the new residence includes its purchase price, construction costs, capital improvements, and various expenses, such as nondeductible finance charges, legal fees, survey costs, and the taxpayer's liabilities on the property. To the extent the proceeds are not thus reinvested, any gain realized is recognized. For married taxpayers, the exemption applies if the requirements are satisfied by either spouse as long as the property is held jointly or as community property and a joint return is filed for the year of sale.

Taxpayers, age 55 and older, are allowed a one-time elective exclusion of up to $125,000 of gain from the sale of a principal residence. The taxpayer must have owned and occupied the principal residence for three of the last five years immediately prior to the sale. Gains above $125,000 may also be rolled over by the purchase of a new principal residence at a higher price.

V.   General Precepts

This note has attempted to establish some attitudes and major themes regarding the taxation of real estate: careful planning, professional advice and thorough records. The economic importance of taxes cannot be overstated. The federal government is always a major partner in every real estate transaction. The tax collector participates at every stage: during acquisition, during the operations and at sale. The area is dynamic. Assume that Congress will periodically revise the tax treatment of real estate. Even if an existing owner's method of depreciation is grandfathered, subsequent purchasers from that owner will adjust their valuation based upon the tax rules in place at that time.

Good planning in tax matters means knowing the taxpayer's whole tax and cash flow picture and that of any intermediary entity involved in the transaction. It means detailed analysis of the effective average and marginal tax brackets on both current and projected future incomes. It means understanding the sources of the income and its stability. It further means understanding the objectives and tax structure of the other parties involved. Deal structures which optimize the overall tax situation can emerge only from this type of planning.

Good professional advice is also critical. It seeks out the unique and protects the unwary. The consequences of bad decisions can come back many years later to haunt the investor. It takes preparation, however, to be able to use good advice effectively. The principals must prepare themselves well enough to ask the right kinds of questions. Good advisors can answer good questions, but it is up to the individual to ask those questions, and to translate the answers in a way that maximizes profits.

Good records are crucial in all tax situations, and are essential. These records include not only documentation of the numerical data which support claims, but also the deal structure itself, the economic reality, and the intent of the parties. Unambiguous written documentation of the terms of any agreement can significantly reduce future problems and provide unforeseen economic benefits. Good records imply good planning, and a pattern of activity that has been consciously thought through in order to achieve a specified result. Much tax litigation occurs many years after the operative transaction, when key parties are often unavailable and the interests, memories and view of others are in conflict. Timely and complete documentation enables better resolution of any dispute, whether it be between the taxpayer and the IRS or between direct parties to the transaction. The presumption must be that a later review will occur in an adversarial proceeding.

The following ten guidelines should prove useful in practice if only for their simplicity:

1. Taxes are only one of many elements which contribute to the return on an investment—be certain to consider all of them and their interrelationships.
2. Cash, financial accounting, and taxable income are not the same—understand the difference.
3. Tax laws are designed to show reasonable relationships between reported income and the expense incurred in generating it.
4. An expense is currently deductible when it relates to current usage.
5. The person who pays the cost gets the deduction, unless it is a gift.
6. Unless otherwise provided, an expense must be capitalized.
7. Tax basis is the cost of an asset adjusted by all taxable transactions relating to the asset.
8. If a transaction is not at arm's length, expect fair market value to govern; but fair market value does not mean the same thing to all people.
9. Depending upon the tax code at the time, long-term capital gains usually are more beneficial than ordinary income, but long-term capital losses are less beneficial than ordinary losses.
10. A foreclosed property does not result in tax benefits—remember the underlying property value.

The real estate professional must adjust the form and substance of all business activities to the recognition that the tax treatment is an important element in managerial decisions. Beyond a general knowledge, the mechanics of a transaction are critical to its tax success. These aphorisms provide merely a basis for understanding the tax game. Be careful to consult your tax advisor before making your decision. Remember also that tax laws change. The assumptions as to taxation you make upon acquisition of a property may alter not only the after-tax return you achieve while holding the property, but the price that a new buyer will pay you if you want to sell that property.

26

NOTE ON FORMS
OF REAL ESTATE OWNERSHIP

I.   Introduction

This note addresses the question of the advantages and the disadvantages of various legal forms of organization used in owning and operating real estate properties.

Each of these forms should be approached from two different directions: from the general business management point of view and from the tax point of view. General business management is concerned with questions about formality of organization, continuity of existence, degree of liability and ease of transferability. Tax questions deal with the issues of taxation during the operation of income-producing property and during the sale or liquidation of real property assets.

For someone active in real estate, this note is especially important in that each real property investment is normally held in a separate legal entity as opposed to that of other businesses where it is customary to expand through existing corporations. The prime reasons for this difference are that most real estate financings both at the debt and equity levels are property specific; that it is common to have different lenders and investors in different projects; and that separation of ownership makes it easier to limit risk. Also, by having a separate entity it is possible to tailor the nature of the relationships among the parties to their specific needs and contributions. For income tax purposes, most investment properties are held in a partnership format to avoid double taxation.

It should be emphasized that this discussion is general and introductory in nature. It is therefore essential to consult with competent legal and tax advisors before deciding upon the vehicle through which property is to be purchased and managed.

II. The Single Proprietorship

A. General Description

The legal concept known as "single proprietorship" is exemplified by the individual who opens up a store front and begins to do business without further formality. The single proprietorship is literally a form of business organization where there is **no separate** form of organization: the business and the individual are one and the same. All proprietorship property is owned directly by the proprietor. All management decisions are the responsibility of the single owner. All the debts of the business are owed directly by the individual.

The creation and operation of a single proprietorship require, by and large, no form of official approval except for the filing of a certificate if the individual wishes to do business under another name.

B. Tax Situation

A single proprietorship does not pay taxes as a separate entity, nor does it file a return. If an individual buys, holds, operates and sells property as a single proprietorship, the results of the transactions are reported on the individual's tax return.

C. Advantages and Disadvantages

In general, the proprietorship form of organization is well adapted to the purposes of the individual property owner. It is an inexpensive way to do business. It also offers flexibility and sensitivity, since the legal power and the responsibility are vested in a single person.

The disadvantages of a single proprietorship, like many of its advantages, stem from the unity between the business and the individual. The owner/operator is subject to unlimited liability on account of the debts of the organization. This exposure to risk for the owner can be reduced through the use of "exculpatory clauses" in leases, loans or other contracts which means that recourse is taken solely against specified assets of the business. Negotiating such an agreement depends upon the respective bargaining-powers of the parties.

The proprietorship form of organization suffers from a lack of continuity of existence, since the proprietorship ends with the death, bankruptcy or incapacity of the owner. In some ways tax laws do not favor single proprietorships since the cost of pension plans, health and life insurance and other benefits for its owners are not deductible.

This note was prepared as the basis for class discussion and revised in 1995.

III. The General Partnership

A. General Description

A partnership is "a voluntary association of two or more persons to carry on as co-owners a business for profit." There are two categories of partnerships: (1) general and (2) limited. In a general partnership, all the partners have a voice in the management and are subject to unlimited liability.

A general partnership can also be created without any legal formalities; however, this approach is neither the typical one, nor is it the most sound. A preferred procedure is to hire an attorney to prepare a partnership agreement specifying: (1) the name and the nature of the business, (2) the term of the agreement, (3) capital contributions, (4) the allocation of profits and losses and cash distributions, (5) the salaries and drawings, (6) the sharing in initial expenses, (7) management duties and restrictions, (8) the banking arrangements, (9) the accounting books, (10) the consequences of the retirement, disability or death of a partner, and (11) the means of sale of an interest or dissolution and liquidation of the partnership. In effect the agreement establishes what provisions shall apply among the partners. The expense of organizing a partnership is usually not a controlling factor in selecting this form of ownership.

B. Tax Situation

For tax purposes a partnership is not considered to be a separate entity but a conduit. Although the income is earned or the losses incurred by the partnership as a whole, the partnership itself does not pay taxes. Rather, the profits and losses flow through the partnership to the partners, who compute and pay the taxes as separate individuals. The apportionment of tax profits and losses generally follows whatever the partnership agreement specifies. There must, however, be an economic or business purpose to the allocation of tax profits and losses.

In order to make this scheme operable, the partnership keeps records analogous to those of an individual or corporation and files an annual tax return.

This tax situation makes the partnership form of ownership an attractive business form. This is especially true in comparison with the corporate tax situation where the taxation of corporate profits and the taxation of distributed dividends combine to produce the effective tax. The single tax levied upon members of a partnership is, in all instances, substantially less. The ability to utilize taxable losses from real estate to offset other types of non-real estate income has been limited by recent legislation. It is limited as to the amount that can be applied and by the income bracket and business interests of the partner.

A general partnership is allowed to hire one or more general partners as employees and pay them fixed compensations which are tax deductible. However, like a proprietorship, a general partnership is not allowed to deduct the expense of fringe benefits such as pension plans, health and life insurance for the owners.

C. Advantages and Disadvantages

The main attraction of the partnership arrangement is that although it is based on a formal legal structure, it is an informal, flexible one.

A crucial weakness of the general partnership arrangement is that the general partners are exposed to unlimited liability for partnership debts. Given the substantial power of any general partner to make financial commitments in behalf of the partnership within that partner's actual or apparent authority, the feature of unlimited liability creates a real risk for all of the general partners.

A general partner is free to assign shares of the profits to a third person at any time. However, unless the unanimous consent of the other partners is obtained, this third person assignee will enjoy none of the other privileges of partnership. Like a sole proprietorship the partnership is extinguished by the death or insanity of any of the general partners. However, this defect can easily be corrected by the formation of a successor partnership or by providing in the original partnership agreement that, upon the termination of the original partnership, a new partnership is immediately reformed by the remaining partners to carry on the business.

IV. The Limited Partnership

A. General Description

A limited partnership is a partnership which contains one or more general partners and one or more limited partners. The status of the two groups is radically different. The general partners in a limited partnership have essentially the same relationship towards their fellow partners and towards the partnership as do the partners in a general partnership. By contrast, the limited partners are passive investors and are legally precluded from participating in day-to-day decisions of the partnership. A person may have both a general and limited partnership interest.

A limited partnership may only be created in accordance with certain statutory formalities. The limited partnership agreement governs the relationship between the partners. Sound practice recommends that an expert attorney be employed to draw up this agreement.

B. Tax Situation

For the purposes of taxation a limited partnership is treated the same as a general partnership and therefore is protected from the double taxation of a corporation.

C. Advantages and Disadvantages

The advantages of the limited partnership are a function of its hybrid status somewhere between a corporation and a general partnership. It shares with the corporation the appeal of centralized management and limited liability for some of the investors. At the same time, it offers the opportunity for tax savings which are available through the conduit treatment granted to all partnerships.

Exculpatory clauses can serve to reduce the risk borne by the general partners. Continuity of existence can be written into the partnership agreement by providing that the remaining general partners may elect a replacement for any among their number who might retire or be disqualified. A limited partnership interest will often have some restrictions on transfer but is more easily transferred than a general partner's interest.

As noted earlier the partnership agreement will spell out the allocation of profits for tax purposes as well as the priorities for cash distributions from operations, refinancing or sale of assets. The ordering is not always the same, but generally, the apportionment should correspond closely to the contributions made by different partners to the partnership. The I.R.S. will reject an apportionment of profits and losses in a partnership agreement when it concludes that the formula used is designed solely for tax avoidance and does not have a valid business purpose.

A corporation can be used to serve as the General Partner of a Partnership to reduce the liability of the General Partner. Many contractual liabilities such as for loans or leases can be made non-recourse to the General Partner by written agreement of the parties. Some risks can be substantially covered by general liability or fire insurance. However, as environmental laws now make the general partner legally responsible for cleanup, it is common for a corporate general partner to be formed for each entity.

V. The Corporation

A. General Description

A corporation is an artificial legal entity created for the purpose of carrying on a business. As a creature of statutory law, a corporation can be established only by careful adherence to statutory requirements and may not commence operation without first receiving state permission.

B. Tax Situation

For tax purposes, a corporation is considered a separate taxable entity and is taxed at both state and federal levels. In addition, shareholders pay income taxes on dividends paid to them by the corporation. Tax deductible fringe benefits such as deferred compensation schemes, health and life insurance and pension plans may change the timing of employees' income.

Subchapter S of the Internal Revenue Code permits some corporations to elect to be treated like partnerships for federal tax purposes. To qualify to Subchapter S status, a corporation must have a limited number of stockholders; all stockholders must be individuals; all stockholders must agree to pay personal income taxes on their share of partnership income, regardless of whether the corporation pays dividends; and the corporation must submit timely annual filings with the IRS.

C. Advantages and Disadvantages

The most important reasons for selecting the corporate form of organization are: (1) limited liability, (2) perpetual existence, (3) ease of transferability of shares, and (4) control of the timing and nature of income. The value of these different features will depend, of course, upon the situation. The use of multiple corporations to own separate properties may be appealing from a general management point of view. The disadvantages in the corporate form of organization are related to double taxation, the expense involved and the formality required.

VI. The Limited Liability Company

A. General Description

The limited liability company is an entity with hybrid characteristics organized according to formalities prescribed by State law. The limited liability company form is intended to have the flexibility of internal management of a general partnership, the limited liability of a corporation and the tax treatment of a partnership.

As a business entity, the limited liability company is a new concept. Very few states had limited liability company legislation as recently as three years ago. The nomenclature, powers and organizational documents vary from state to state. This business form may not be available in every jurisdiction.

"Limited liability partnerships" exist in some jurisdictions. They are much the same as limited liability companies, but are organized under separate statues.

B. Tax Situation

Given the novelty of the limited liability company structure, the tax treatment of limited liability companies is not as fully developed as the tax treatment of limited partnerships and other entities. In 1995, the Internal Revenue Service issued guidelines that, if followed, should assume that a limited liability company will be treated as a partnership for federal income tax purposes. State laws authorizing the limited liability companies generally provide that they will be treated as partnerships for state tax purposes.

C. Advantages and Disadvantages

Limited liability company statutes have been enacted with the intention of combining the beneficial features of corporations (namely, limited liability) and partnerships (namely, flexible management structure and favorable taxation).

In comparison to a limited partnership, a limited liability company does not require any member to have unlimited personal liability and does permit all members to participate in management in accordance with the organizational documents.

The chief disadvantage of the limited liability company form at this time is its novelty. Not all attorneys, accountants and lenders have experience with this form of entity, thereby increasing the cost of creating the entity and closing loans. If the limited liability company form gains acceptance in the real estate industry, these disadvantages will dissipate quickly.

VII. The Joint Venture

A. General Description

A joint venture is an association of two or more individuals, corporations or partnerships for the purpose of participating in a specific and limited business enterprise. A joint venture is a general partnership for a single special purpose. Operationally an agreement will generally cover the same points as in a partnership agreement.

B. Tax Situation

The tax code provides specifically that a joint venture is taxed to the participants in proportion to the respective interests. The tax affect is substantially the same as a general partnership.

C. Advantages and Disadvantages

The reasons for accepting or rejecting the joint venture format are the same that apply to partnerships. A joint venture has particular appeal because it is designed specifically for one-shot propositions. This explains its common occurrence in the field of real estate development and acquisition.

VIII. The Business Trust/Real Estate Investment Trust

A. General Description

A business trust is an unincorporated association established for the purpose of carrying on a business by declaration or deed of trust. Business trusts were first developed in Massachusetts in order to circumvent restrictions on the power of a corporation to acquire and develop real estate. For this reason they are often referred to as "Massachusetts trusts."

A business trust is created when capital is conveyed to a group of trustees who then execute a deed of trust to the effect that they hold this property, and any subsequent trust property, for the purposes stated and for the benefit of the shareholders of the trust. The contributors to the trust then receive shares, represented by certificates, in numbers proportionate to their respective contributions to the capital.

An important difference between corporations and trusts is that the latter may not have perpetual existence. The maximum life span of a trust is the length of a designated life in being, plus twenty-one years. Although trustees have a fiduciary responsibility, the trustees can be indemnified by the beneficiaries.

As a hybrid creation of both corporate and trust law, Massachusetts trusts have always occupied a slightly ambiguous position, particularly in geographic areas where they are infrequently used as a form of business organization. In different states and in different circumstances, business trusts have been variously treated by the courts as general partnerships, limited partnerships, and corporations. This leaves the question of the beneficiary's protection against unlimited liability a little uncertain. Even in those jurisdictions where limited liability has been accepted, it is unclear at what point excessive involvement in the affairs of management will strip the beneficiary of protective privileges.

B. Tax Situation

For tax purposes, a business trust is considered as a corporation. By virtue of certain revisions in the Internal Revenue Code made in 1960, business trusts are entitled to elect tax treatment as a modified conduit, similar to the treatment given to the different forms of partnership. This election will be discussed in detail under the topic of the Real Estate Investment Trust.

C. Advantages and Disadvantages

In those states where business trusts were initially developed or where they have become a familiar form of business organization, their advantages are virtually those of the corporations they were designed to resemble. In those states where business trusts are still unfamiliar, there is a certain risk involved in choosing this form, and it is more prudent to seek the clear-cut status of a corporation or some form of partnership. Because business trusts are relatively uncommon, the use of a specialist in planning and creating one is particularly appropriate.

Real Estate Investment Trusts

In the 1960 amendment to the Internal Revenue Code, Congress created a new category of business trust, the Real Estate Investment Trust (hereafter **REIT**). This is a business trust which is organized to invest in real estate and which pays out virtually all its income in the year earned. Congress wanted to create a vehicle analogous to a mutual fund which would allow a small investor with little money and experience to participate in a large, diversified and professionally-managed portfolio of real estate assets. At the same time, Congress wanted to avoid the penalty which comes from double taxation of corporations. To all qualified REITs, as defined in the statute, Congress gave conduit treatment with regard to income distributed in the year earned. With regard to income which is retained, the trust is treated like an ordinary corporation.

In order to be treated as a REIT a trust must meet specific requirements regarding its income, assets and business conduct. These requirements are described in Appendix A.

IX. Points to Remember in Selecting a Form of Real Estate Ownership

In an actual situation the process of selecting the most appropriate form of ownership for real property assets should include consideration of: (1) the formalities of organization and operation, (2) the capital and credit requirements, (3) management and control, (4) profits and losses from tax and cash standpoints, (5) extent of liability, (6) transferability of interest, (7) continuity of existence, and (8) income tax considerations, primarily federal but also state.

This note has made a rapid survey of the more salient features of the various legal forms of ownership as they can be used to organize real estate ventures. The reader is warned that the picture painted here is no more than a brief rough outline made with broad brush strokes. Under actual conditions, the assistance of an experienced attorney, especially a tax expert, and/or an accountant is essential to any successful planning for the ownership of real property assets. The attached checklist may be an oversimplification, but may provide a general road map in helping you in making your decision as to which form of ownership is most appropriate for your venture.

Checklist for Forms of Ownership

	LIABILITY	TRANSFERABILITY	FORMALITY	TAXABILITY
The Proprietorship	unlimited	easy	informal	conduit
General Partnership	unlimited	limited	informal	conduit
Limited Partnership	limited	limited	formal	conduit
The Corporation	limited	easy	formal	double
Joint Venture	unlimited	limited	formal	conduit
Business Trust	limited	easy	formal	conduit

Apendix A   Requirements for Qualification as a REIT

The **income qualifications** restrict the acceptable sources of income:

1. At least 75% of gross income must be derived from property rents, interest on obligations secured by a mortgage on real property, property tax refunds and abatements, gain from the sale or other disposition of real property interests, and gain from the sale of shares in other qualified REITs;

2. An additional 15% must come from these sources plus dividends and interest or gain from the sale or other disposition of stock or securities;

3. Less than 30% of the gross income must be in the form of short-term capital gains which are defined here as including gain on the sale or other disposition of stock held for less than six months and real property held for less than four years.

The effect of these restrictions is that 10% of the gross income can come from sources which are tainted. Many REITs use this allowance to cover income which comes from commitment fees, discounts paid out of loan proceeds and technically usurious interest where present.

There are **investment qualifications** which restrict the form and amount of acceptable investments. Likewise, there are conduct and cash distribution requirements in order to remain qualified as a REIT.

At least 75% of an REIT's assets must be invested in real estate interests, government securities, cash or cash items, and of the remainder not more than 5% of the trust assets can be invested in the securities of any one issuer. A REIT may not hold more than 10% of the outstanding voting stock of any one issuer.

A third set of restrictions applies to the **conduct of a REIT**. A REIT must pay out at least 95% of its taxable income exclusive of capital gains in the year earned (recent legislation permits certain exceptions to this rule for trusts that have experienced financial difficulties), must issue certificates of beneficial interest and have at least one hundred beneficiaries. No more than 50% of the shares may be held directly or indirectly by five or fewer individuals. A REIT should remain "passive," which means that it should not act as a property manager and that it should not acquire property as a broker/dealer. Normally, an advisory company is hired to perform these functions.

The REIT itself must be managed by a Board of Trustees or Directors, the majority of whom must be unaffiliated with the company's management. The REIT shares must also be freely transferable.